The Journal of Infectious Diseases

Published by the John McCormick Institute for Infectious Diseases

EDITED BY

LUDVIG HEKTOEN AND EDWIN O. JORDAN

IN CONJUNCTION WITH

FRANK BILLINGS F. G. NOVY

H. GIDEON WELLS KARL F. MEYER

Volume 37

1925

Chicago, 1925

Composed and Printed by
American Medical Association Press
Chicago, Illinois, U. S. A.

THE GREEN COLORATION BY CERTAIN STREPTOCOCCI ON BLOOD AGAR

ONE PLATE

William A. Hagan

From the Department of Pathology and Bacteriology, New York State Veterinary College at Cornell University, Ithaca, N. Y.

McLeod, Gordon and Pyrah [1] showed that certain peroxide-forming bacteria produced a greenish discoloration when they were grown in a cooked blood (chocolate) medium. This suggested the idea that in peroxide formation probably lay the explanation for the formation of the green coloration which appears about colonies of pneumococci and certain streptococci when they are growing on blood-agar plates. Since no satisfactory explanation of the mechanism of this phenomenon, which has long been used as an important criterion in the identification of organisms of these groups, had ever been offered, some experiments toward this end were undertaken.

Ruediger [2] was led to believe that the formation of a green discoloration around colonies of certain cocci growing on blood agar was due to acid formation. Certain streptococci which laked blood cells suspended in plain agar produced green when they were grown in the presence of blood on dextrose agar. On the other hand, pneumococci which produced a deep green color when grown in plain infusion or dextrose agar, produced only a faint trace of green when they were grown in a blood medium with a peptone water base. Ruediger's explanation does not take into account the zone of hemolysis which regularly occurs at the periphery of the zone of discolored cells.

Mandelbaum [3] assumed that Streptococcus mitior produced two substances which acted on the blood cells: One, his "hemoglobin-toxin," acted on the blood cells, changing the color of the hemoglobin and rendering the cells insusceptible to the second substance, his "hematoxin," which hemolyzed normal corpuscles. The first substance was supposed to be closely bound up with the living bacterial cells; hence it affected only those blood cells which lay in immediate contact with the colony. This explanation accounted very well for the presence of a

Received for publication, Jan. 12, 1925.

[1] Jour. Path. & Bacteriol., 1923, 26, p. 127.
[2] Jour. Infect. Dis., 1906, 3, p. 663.
[3] Ztschr. f. Hyg. u. Infektionskrankh., 1907-08, p. 26.

group of discolored cells lying immediately around the colony when cells farther away were hemolyzed, but it cannot explain the phenomenon described by Brown[4] who found that by changing the temperature while the colony was growing, multiple zones of discolored cells separated by zones of hemolysis could be produced.

Brown suggested an explanation which fitted in well with all observed facts, and with the new facts given in this paper. His explanation is given in his own words:

> It may be assumed that there are elaborated by the Streptococcus mitior colony two substances, one of which (*a*) produces hemolysis and the other of which (*b*) produces changes in the corpuscles visible as a greenish or a brownish green discoloration of the intact corpuscles, rendering them resistant to hemolysis by the first substance. It must be assumed that in the development of the colony the second substance (*b*) is elaborated first, or at any rate reaches a concentration sufficient to produce fixation of the corpuscles next to the colony before the hemolytic substance (*a*) is present in sufficient concentration to produce hemolysis. The hemolytic substance acts well at refrigerator temperature, but at temperatures much below that of the incubator the fixing substance (*b*) either is not produced or is inactive.

Butterfield and Peabody[5] showed that the oxygen capacity of blood cells which had been incubated with pneumococcus cultures was markedly reduced, and by means of the spectroscope demonstrated that the reason for this was that much of the hemoglobin had been changed to the form of methemoglobin. Cole[6] confirmed and extended the observations of these workers. He concluded that the formation of methemoglobin by the pneumococcus was an oxidative process, or possibly a mixture of oxidizing and reducing processes. Blake[7] concluded that the green color produced by streptococci of the viridans group was due to the formation of methemoglobin, but states that "the exact chemical change is unknown."

EXPERIMENTS

All of the cultural work reported in this paper was done with a single strain of a green-producing streptococcus which had been isolated from a normal throat. It was a typical alpha type (Smith and Brown[8]) or viridans type (Schottmüller[9]). It grew rapidly in infusion broth, producing marked turbidity in 12 hours or less at 37 C. Growth occurred, but less rapidly, at room temperature.

[4] Monograph No. 9, Rockefeller Inst. for Med. Res., 1919.
[5] Jour. Exper. Med., 1913, 17, p. 587.
[6] Ibid., 1914, 20, p. 363.
[7] Ibid., 1916, 24, p. 315.
[8] Jour. Med. Res., 1915, 31, p. 455.
[9] München. med. Wchnschr., 1903, 1, p. 849.

In blood-agar plates (10 to 12 c c. infusion agar, P_H 7.4 plus 0.6 c c. defibrinated horse blood), strong green pigmentation of colonies was evident after 24 hours' incubation at body temperature. When plates were incubated for 48 hours or longer at this temperature, an indefinite halo appeared around the colonies at the periphery of the zone of discolored cells (fig. 1). This was due to hemolysis of a portion of the blood cells which lay in this region. When the suggestion of Brown [4] was followed, that the plates be placed in the refrigerator for 24 hours after being incubated for 1 or 2 days, a sharply demarcated zone at the periphery of the discolored area always appeared. The cells in this zone were completely, or nearly completely, hemolyzed (fig. 2). It was noted that the peripheral hemolysis always appeared earlier and was more conspicuous in incubated plates when large numbers of colonies were present on the plate (previously noted by Smith and Brown), and in parts where the agar layer was thin. Hemolysis was also noted more frequently when the proportion of blood to agar was lower (previously noted by Rieke [10]). In the plates in which the colonies were numerous, the entire mass of blood medium was altered in a greater or lesser degree, the normal blood color being changed to brownish and greenish-brown tones.

When infusion agar plates were incubated at 20-25 C. instead of at body temperature, the effect on the blood medium was quite different. The colonies, instead of being surrounded by masses of deeply green tinged cells, showed only traces of green, and hemolysis was more marked. When the colonies had reached their maximum development after 4 or 5 days' incubation, they frequently presented an appearance very much like that of hemolytic streptococci (beta type, Smith and Brown). Microscopic examination always showed, however, that there were a few pale green tinged, intact corpuscles in the immediate vicinity of the colony, and the hemolyzed zone itself usually showed a few intact cells, so that it was not so clear as that of the true hemolytic streptococcus. The appearance was very much like that described by Brown foı streptococci of his alpha prime group (fig. 4).

When 1% dextrose was added to infusion agar as a basis for blood-agar plates, the appearance of the colonies was changed greatly. The most heavily seeded plates became opaque, grayish brown after 24 hours' incubation. In the less crowded plates, the colonies developed exceedingly rapidly. At first, green discoloration of the cells around the

[10] Centralbl. f. Bakteriol., I. O., 1904, 36, p. 321.

colonies could be seen, but by the time the colonies were 24 hours old, much of the green color had been replaced by a brownish black (fig. 3). Practically all of the corpuscles lying in the medium between the colonies were hemolyzed. The medium became perfectly clear but light brown.

On an extract agar base, the colonies always were small and green production slight. Hemolysis was always a prominent feature. The appearance was much like that of colonies of the same organism growing on infusion blood-agar plates but at room temperature.

When infusion blood-agar plates were incubated in a Brown anaerobic jar, or in a sealed jar with alkaline pyrogallol, growth always was tardy and the colonies small. Green production was always slight but perceptible when the jars were incubated immediately after they had been sealed. When they were held in the refrigerator for 24 hours before incubation so that growth of the organism was restrained until anaerobic conditions had been fairly established and the color of the blood had turned to the "burgundy red" of reduced hemoglobin, green formation never occurred. When the jars were opened after incubation and access of the air was allowed, green formation became evident around the colonies after a few minutes.

PRODUCTION OF PEROXIDE BY STREPTOCOCCUS VIRIDANS

The streptococcus used in this work was tested for its ability to produce peroxide by the method suggested by Avery and Morgan.[11] It proved to be a vigorous producer of peroxide when conditions were favorable for active growth in the presence of abundant free oxygen. Cultures grown in very shallow layers of infusion broth at 37 C. gave positive tests for the presence of peroxide in a few hours—after 8 or 10 hours' incubation, very strongly positive tests generally were obtained. When cultures were grown in tall columns of fluid with comparatively little surface, or if the surface was covered with petrolatum, tests for peroxide were always negative after 12 to 24 hours' incubation, but when the cultures were then poured into flasks so as to make a shallow layer of fluid freely exposed to the air, positive tests for peroxide could always be obtained in 1 or 2 hours at body temperature.

EFFECT OF AGE OF CULTURE ON ITS ABILITY TO PRODUCE PEROXIDE

When cultures were grown under a petrolatum seal in fluid mediums and subsequently exposed to the air by pouring them into large flasks,

[11] Jour. Exper. Med., 1924, 39, p. 289.

it was soon noted that the rapidity of peroxide accumulation, if it accumulated at all, depended on the stage of growth of the culture at the time it was exposed. Infusion broth cultures seemed to be in best condition for accumulating peroxide quickly when they were from 12 to 24 hours old. Dextrose broth cultures at 24 hours frequently failed to produce peroxide when exposed—the optimum time for this medium appeared to be less than 12 hours. Extract broth supported growth poorly, and peroxide formation was always slight in this medium, and rather slow to develop. Cultures in plain infusion, dextrose infusion, and extract broths which had been incubated under petrolatum seal for one week failed to accumulate sufficient peroxide when they were exposed to the air to give a positive reaction to the test reagents.

EFFECT OF TEMPERATURE ON THE RATE OF PEROXIDE ACCUMULATION BY STREPTOCOCCUS VIRIDANS

The rapidity of peroxide accumulation by cultures exposed to the air is markedly influenced by the temperature at which they are exposed. This is illustrated by the following experiment:

The strain was grown in plain infusion broth, P_H 7.4 for 24 hours at 37 C. under a petrolatum seal. The culture was then divided into 3 equal portions, 1 part being placed in each of three 250 c c. flasks, the fluid forming a shallow layer in the bottoms of the flasks. One flask was held at incubator temperature, the 2d at room temperature, and the 3rd was refrigerated. As a result of periodic tests, peroxide was detected in the first flask after 2 hours, and in the 2d after 6 hours. Repeated tests up to the 96th hour failed to demonstrate peroxide in the 3rd flask. At this time, the flask was placed in the incubator. A faintly positive test for peroxide was obtained after 3 hours, and after 6 hours a strongly positive test was obtained.

EFFECT OF COMPOSITION OF THE MEDIUM ON PEROXIDE FORMATION BY STREPTOCOCCUS VIRIDANS

A 10-hour culture of the organism in dextrose infusion broth grown under a petrolatum seal was thoroughly centrifuged to throw down the bacteria. The sedimented bacteria were suspended in a small amount of sterile physiologic salt solution. One c c. portions of this suspension were then placed in 10 c c. lots of culture fluids of varying composition and reaction. The amount of culture added was sufficient to make a very heavy suspension. The various mediums were then poured into large flasks so as to expose the fluids freely to the air. The flasks were incubated at 37 C. Tests for peroxide formation were made at intervals. The details are given in the table.

Inspection of the table brings out the fact that peroxide is produced most rapidly and in greatest abundance in those fluids in which the composition and reaction favored the growth of the organisms which were suspended in them. Although the quantity of bacterial cells added to each of the fluids was greater than would have developed in the mediums under optimum conditions, no detectable peroxide was formed in those fluids which were not favorable for the vital activities of the bacterial cells which were added.

The conclusions drawn from the experimental evidence relating to the production of peroxide by the strain of streptococcus studied are:

1. Peroxide formation occurs in cultures when they are held under suitable conditions. The necessary conditions are:

(*a*) Free oxygen must be present in sufficient amount. This requirement may be met by cultivating or exposing the cultures in shallow

EFFECT OF COMPOSITION AND REACTION OF MEDIUM ON THE RATE OF PEROXIDE ACCUMULATION BY STREPTOCOCCUS VIRIDANS

THE SYMBOLS REPRESENT THE COMPARATIVE INTENSITIES OF THE TESTS OBTAINED FOR THE PRESENCE OF PEROXIDE

	Immediately	Hours				
		1	2	4	9	24
Extract broth P_H 5	—	—	—	—	—	—
Extract broth P_H 6	—	—	—	—	—	2+
Extract broth P_H 7	—	+	+	2+	4+	3+
Extract broth P_H 8	—	—	+	2+	4+	3+
Infusion broth P_H 5	—	±	2+	2+	—	—
Infusion broth P_H 6	—	+	3+	6+	10+	5+
Infusion broth P_H 7	—	3+	5+	7+	10+	8+
Infusion broth P_H 8	—	2+	4+	6+	8+	5+
Dextrose infusion broth P_H 5	—	—	+	3+	4+	+
Dextrose infusion broth P_H 6	—	±	3+	4+	10+	4+
Dextrose infusion broth P_H 7	—	+	3+	4+	6+	3+
Dextrose infusion broth P_H 8	—	—	±	2+	5+	±
Infusion broth P_H 7 plus 0.1% formalin	—	—	—	—	—	—
Infusion broth P_H 7 plus 0.5% phenol	—	—	—	—	—	—
Infusion broth P_H 7 plus 0.1% phenol	—	±	2+	6+	8+	4+
Infusion broth P_H 7 heated for 20 minutes at 60 C. after the addition of the culture	—	—	—	—	—	—
Physiologic salt solution	—	—	—	—	—	—

layers of fluid mediums in free contact with air. Peroxide is not produced, at least not in a quantity sufficient to be detected by the methods used, in cultures grown in the absence of air.

(*b*) The organisms must be living and under conditions which permit active exercise of their metabolic processes. Organisms killed with heat and chemicals do not form peroxide. Living organisms held under conditions which do not permit active multiplication—that is, when they are suspended in physiological salt solution, when they are suspended in fluids saturated with their own products of growth (old cultures), when they are suspended in media of unsuitable composition, and when they are suspended in mediums of suitable composition but at a temperature too low for active multiplication—do not produce peroxide.

These conclusions are somewhat at variance with those of Avery and Neill,[12] who found that whole cultures of pneumococcus held under conditions not permitting active growth and even sterile extracts of pneumococcus cultures were capable of producing peroxide when they were exposed to air.

2. Peroxide is produced most rapidly and, consequently, accumulates in greatest amount in those mediums which allow the most rapid growth. In extract medium, a rather unfavorable substrate for this organism, peroxide always accumulates slowly and in low concentration.

3. Peroxide is produced in greatest amount during the period of logarithmic increase. Cultures incubated anaerobically until this period has passed show little or no tendency to accumulate peroxide, and in cultures which have been allowed to form peroxide during the logarithmic phase of growth, the concentration rapidly decreases after this period has passed.

ACTION OF PEROXIDE AND OF ACIDS ON BLOOD AGAR

It seemed that if the green coloration which appeared around the colonies of certain micro-organisms when they were growing in blood medium was due to the action on the blood of peroxide produced by the organisms, it should be possible to produce this color artificially. With this idea in mind, solutions of peroxide of varying strength were dropped on the surfaces of blood plates. The stronger solutions showed strong effervescence, and the agar frequently was fractured by the violence of the gas liberated; but in no case was there any discoloration of the corpuscles.

Interesting results were obtained when small drops of acid solutions were placed on the surfaces of sterile blood plates. Sulphuric, hydrochloric, acetic, butyric and lactic acids gave identical results; hence it appears that the phenomena are due to the activities of the hydrogen ions alone.

When the acid was in concentrated solution, the medium immediately beneath the drop promptly became grayish brown and somewhat translucent. Within a few minutes, the translucency gave way to opacity, and the color changed to a greenish gray. Around the periphery of the opaque area, a somewhat translucent zone began to become apparent after a few minutes, and after some hours this region was perfectly transparent because of complete hemolysis of the corpuscles (figs. 5

[12] Ibid., 1924, 39, p. 347 and p. 357.

and 7). The width of this zone varied according to the nature of the medium in which the blood cells were suspended, being widest in extract agar (low buffer content) and narrowest in infusion agar which had been buffered highly with a phosphate mixture. When a very small amount of acid solution was introduced into the agar layer by stabbing it with a very fine pointed pipet, the small group of discolored cells surrounded by a completely hemolyzed zone which resulted, simulated so closely the appearance of a colony of a green-producing streptococcus which had been refrigerated after incubation that it would easily deceive a casual observer examining the "colony" without magnification (fig. 6). The green color was lacking, however, the discolored cells in this case being greenish gray instead of the characteristic bottle green of the true colony.

When more dilute acids were used, the area beneath the drop became transparent more slowly, and the final opacity was less, but the character of the hemolyzed zone about the central opacity remained about the same. When still weaker solutions were used, a concentration could be found which gave a completely hemolyzed area beneath the drop without the development of a central opacity (2%-3% lactic acid on infusion medium; less than 1% lactic acid on extract medium). In this case, there was little immediate change in the medium beneath the drop, but gradually transparency developed as the hemolysis progressed. Usually 6 to 8 hours were required for hemolysis to become complete.

Acid solutions which were slightly too weak to produce hemolysis caused the red color of the blood to change to a reddish brown. This color was also seen frequently around the periphery of the zone of hemolyzed cells when stronger acids were used. The color is the same as that seen in plate cultures of Streptococcus viridans which are crowded.

It was decided to ascertain the combined effect of acid and peroxide on blood agar. Accordingly, a series of dilutions of lactic acid were made up, and after a drop of each dilution had been placed on the surface of a blood-agar plate, approximately 1 part in 5,000 of commercial hydrogen peroxide was added to each of the solutions, and a 2d series of drops was made on the same plate. The effect produced by the acids containing a trace of peroxide was strikingly different than when acid alone was used. The differences were: (1) strong acids plus peroxide produced opaque deep green zones instead of the greenish gray of acid alone, and (2) the peroxide exerted a distinct protective action on the corpuscles when in hemolyzing concentrations of acid. This action was evidenced when the stronger acid solutions were used by the absence of the initial stage of translucency, but it was most strikingly seen in concentrations of acid which were just capable of completely hemolyzing the corpuscles. Hemolysis in this case was always completely inhibited, and instead the blood cells were given a light green tinge (figs. 8 and 9).

THE MECHANISM OF GREEN PRODUCTION BY STREPTOCOCCUS VIRIDANS WHEN GROWING IN BLOOD AGAR

The experimental evidence given in this paper leads to the conclusion that the green pigmentation produced by certain streptococci in blood-agar plate cultures is due to the action of peroxide on the blood corpuscles, probably hydrogen peroxide, in the presence of acid. Both of these substances are produced simultaneously by the organism and diffuse outward from the colonies, thus bringing about changes of the blood in the immediate vicinity of the colony. The evidence for this hypothesis is as follows:

1. Acid alone does not account for the phenomenon, as was argued by Ruediger. Strong acids alone produce a greenish-gray discoloration, but not the bottle green which is characteristic of Streptococcus viridans colony.

2. Green-producing organisms are peroxide producers, but peroxide, or hydrogen peroxide at least, does not cause discoloration of blood corpuscles.

3. Hydrogen peroxide, in the presence of a suitable acid concentration, has been shown to produce the characteristic bottle green color in blood corpuscles. A low concentration of hydrogen peroxide in sterile broth of a reaction of P_H 7 will not discolor a small amount of blood corpuscles added to it, but the same concentration in broth of a reaction of P_H 4.5 will cause brownish-green discoloration.

4. When precautions are taken to prevent the formation of peroxide by organisms growing on blood-agar plates by incubating them under strictly anaerobic conditions, green formation does not occur. When access to air is allowed to these plates, the green discoloration rapidly appears around the colonies.

5. Green production is slight when the organism is cultivated on blood plates made with an extract-agar base, and strong when made with infusion agar. It has been shown experimentally that little peroxide is formed when the organism is growing in the first medium, while the latter is favorable for its production.

6. Green production is slight when the organism is cultivated on infusion-agar blood plates at room temperature. It has been shown that peroxide formation proceeds very slowly when organisms are cultivated at this temperature.

THE MECHANISM OF HEMOLYSIS BY STREPTOCOCCUS VIRIDANS

The hemolysis produced by streptococci of the green-producing group after long incubation or, better, by refrigerating the plate cultures after a period of incubation, seems capable of adequate explanation on the basis of acid production alone. This fact is suggested by the behavior of acid solutions on blood agar, but other evidence is at hand.

1. Hemolysis is always most marked in plates made with basic medium of low buffer content (extract agar).

2. It has been shown that acid hemolysis is restrained by the presence of peroxide. Whenever peroxide formation is inhibited by placing the organisms under conditions where growth is less rapid (lower temperature of incubation, composition of medium less suited for growth), hemolysis becomes a prominent feature of the colony characteristics.

3. Hemolysis in cultures growing at body temperature is always a belated phenomenon. It has been shown that peroxide formation, which goes on rapidly during the early hours of growth, soon ceases or diminishes; hence it would be expected that its restraining influence on hemolysis would be removed after the period of rapid growth had ceased. Complete suppression of peroxide production in young cultures by refrigeration thus leaving the acid free to cause hemolysis would also adequately explain the facts observed. Peroxide quickly disappears when it ceases to be produced, but acid continues to diffuse.

4. Hemolysis is always more marked in crowded plate cultures where it is evident that the colonies exert a mutual effect on each other. The general alteration of the color of the hemoglobin to a brownish cast is evidence of the general diffusion of acid throughout the medium. In this case, conditions are favorable for the more rapid accumulation of a hemolyzing concentration of acid around the colonies, and the inhibiting effect of crowding causes peroxide formation to be curtailed early. Less opportunity for the diffusion of the acids is found on plates on which the agar layer is thin; and when fewer blood cells are present in the medium, the smaller number of cells engaged in absorbing the acid produced allows for a greater accumulation of acid per cell. Under these conditions, it has been noted that hemolysis is always marked.

THE RÔLE OF PEROXIDE AND ACID FORMATION ON THE COLONY CHARACTERISTICS OF STREPTOCOCCUS VIRIDANS IN BLOOD AGAR

The application of the data at hand results in the following explanation for the appearance of colonies of Streptococcus mitior or viridans when growing in blood-agar plate cultures.

When growing in a medium which allows vigorous growth in the presence of an abundance of free oxygen, peroxide and acid are formed simultaneously; and these substances, diffusing outward from the colonies, cause the green discoloration of the blood corpuscles lying in the immediate vicinity. The cells here are not hemolyzed by the acid because of the protective action of the peroxide on them. When the period of active growth of the organism nears its end, or when the growth processes are checked earlier by refrigeration, peroxide formation is diminished or checked altogether, with the consequence that its protective influence on the blood corpuscles lying beyond the greenish zone is lost, and they fall prey to the hemolyzing concentration of acid, which continues to diffuse. The multiple zones of green but intact and hemolyzed corpuscles described by Brown are easily explained on the basis of continuous acid diffusion and intermittent peroxide production, green cells being produced when peroxide is being formed (during incubation) and hemolysis resulting when it is not being formed (during refrigeration).

No attempt has been made to study the chemical changes by which the green color is produced and the cells are protected from hemolysis, but as others (Butterfield and Peabody,[5] Cole,[6] Blake [7]) have shown that methemoglobin is formed by an oxidative process by organisms now known as peroxide producers, it seems highly probable that methemoglobin formation is part of the process at least. Methemoglobin, however, is of a brownish cast instead of greenish, hence it appears that the process is not a simple one.

CONCLUSIONS

The formation of a green discoloration about the colonies of certain streptococci, and presumably of other green-forming bacteria when growing on blood agar, is due to the action on the blood corpuscles of peroxide and acid, substances which are produced simultaneously by these organisms when in the period of active multiplication.

The hemolysis which occurs about the periphery of the green zone when the period of incubation is prolonged, or when the plate culture is refrigerated while yet in an actively growing condition, is probably due to diffusing acid. Peroxide and acid have an antagonistic action on blood corpuscles, peroxide tending to discolor and protect them from hemolysis by the acid. Hemolysis results, therefore, only when peroxide production diminishes or ceases.

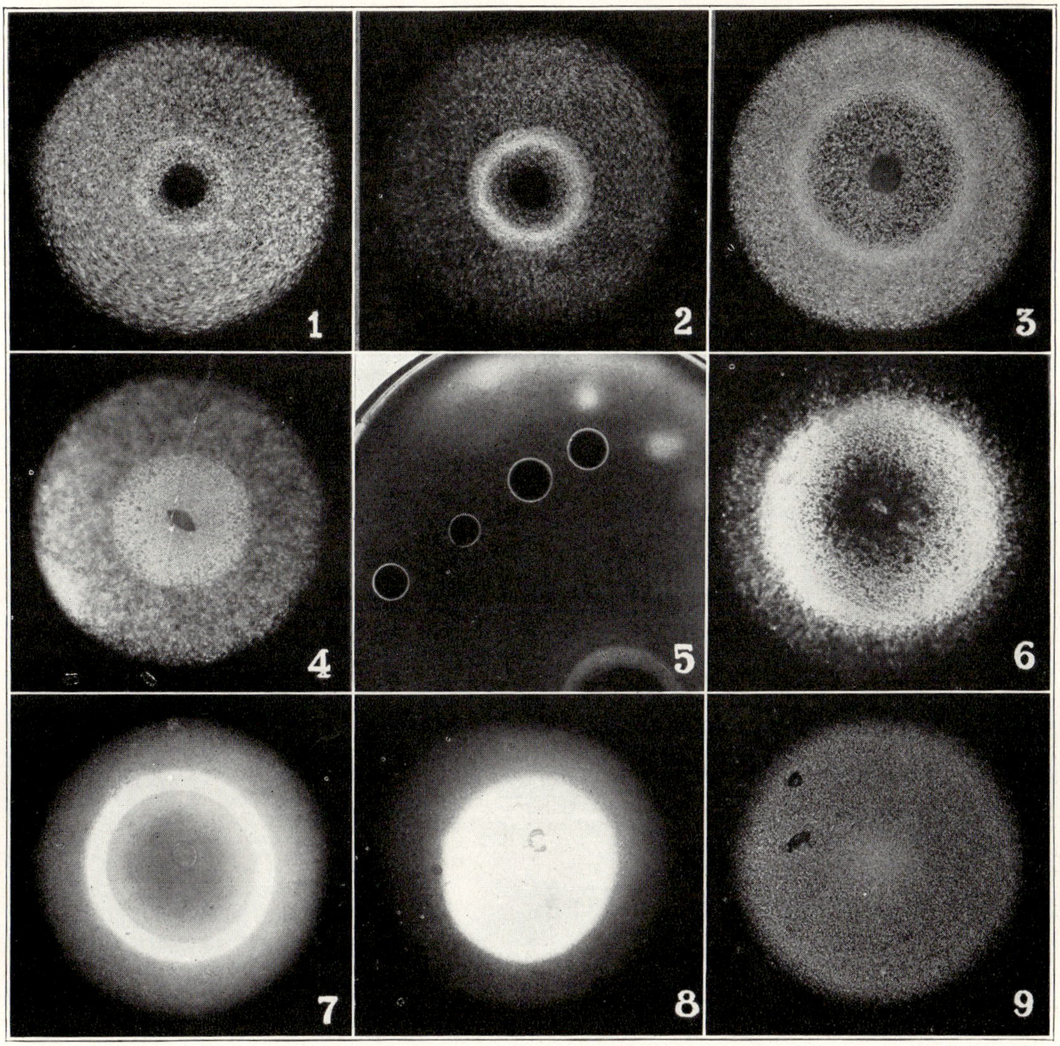

Fig. 1.—Streptococcus viridans. Deep colony in blood-infusion agar plate which has been incubated for 48 hours at 37 C. The corpuscles lying immediately in contact with the colony are intact, but of a greenish color. At the periphery of the zone of green corpuscles, some of the blood cells are hemolyzed, hence the lighter color; × 20.

Fig. 2.—The same colony of Streptococcus viridans as in fig. 1 which has been refrigerated for 24 hours, following the 48-hour period of incubation. The zone of hemolysis now is very much more distinct; × 20.

Fig. 3.—Ibid. Deep colony in dextrose-infusion-blood agar after 48 hours' incubation. Growth occurred more rapidly, a greater amount of peroxide was produced, and hence the zone of fixed (green) cells is wider than in fig. 1; × 20.

Fig. 4.—Ibid. Deep colony in plain infusion blood-agar after 5 days' incubation at 20 C. At this temperature of incubation, peroxide production is slight; hence the fixed cells are scarce and hemolysis is prominent; × 20.

Fig. 5.—Effect of drops of concentrated lactic acid on a blood plate. Photograph taken 24 hours after the application of the acid. The peripheral hemolysis began to appear after several hours and was not complete until the following morning. Reduced about one fifth.

Fig. 6.—Artificial "colony." Effect of a minute amount of concentrated acid introduced into the layer of medium by a very fine tipped pipet. When not magnified, the effect very closely resembled a true colony. (Cf. fig. 2.) × 20.

Fig. 7.—Effect produced by a small drop of 5% lactic acid placed on the surface of a blood-agar plate. Photograph taken 24 hours after the application of the acid; × 20.

Fig. 8.—Acid hemolysis produced by placing a very small drop of 3% lactic acid on the surface of an infusion blood-agar plate. Hemolysis is complete. Photograph 24 hours after application of the acid; × 20.

Fig. 9.—Same acid solution used for producing effect shown in fig. 8, after the addition of 1 part of hydrogen peroxide to 5,000 of acid, was dropped on the same blood plate at the point shown in this figure. Acid hemolysis has been entirely prevented by the peroxide; × 20.

RELATIONSHIP OF HARD WATER TO HEALTH

II. EFFECT OF HARD WATER ON GROWTH, APPEARANCE AND GENERAL WELL-BEING

JOHN T. MYERS

From the Department of Hygiene and Bacteriology, University of Chicago, and the Department of Pathology and Bacteriology, University of Nebraska, College of Medicine, Omaha

There is a popular idea that hard water has a bad effect on animals in some general indefinite way. It is thought that the coat of horses and cattle is made rougher, and that the animals do not "do as well" if forced continually to drink hard water. This belief is particularly prevalent among poultry raisers. Veterinary literature contains numerous allusions to the deleterious effect of hard water, some of which have been quoted in connection with previous papers on concretions.

McCoy,[1] discussing the water of North Dakota, says that the natural waters of the state are reasonably good for drinking, but the well waters are too highly mineralized.

Hulbert[2] of North Dakota says, "It may be stated with some assurance that with a hardness up to three hundred parts per million water may be considered suitable for drinking. It is difficult to say whether greater hardness has any effect on health. The possibility of its causing certain non-specific diseases is mentioned by several authorities. Among these are constipation, dyspepsia, diarrhoea, goiter and concretions."

Rideal[3] states that constipation and dyspepsia are known to be caused sometimes by very hard water.

Distilled water has been used in the navy for long periods of time. This has been cited as proof of its desirability as compared with hard water. But as has been often pointed out, the navy contains a selected group of healthy young men, and other hygienic conditions are good. Hence these data have little significance.

Wedekind[4] maintains that distilled water dissolves any excess of salts in the body, thus tending to prevent high blood pressure and arteriosclerosis. However, no real proof is advanced.

Many sanitarians think that hard water has no effect either good or bad. Thresh[5] remarks that hard water has no bad effects on health. He bases his conclusions on a comparison of the death rate from typhoid fever and similar diseases in hard water regions and in soft water regions. One would not expect hardness materially to affect bacterial diseases.

Sherman[6] says, "Since inorganic forms of calcium are utilized in nutrition the lime of drinking water may be added to that of the food in calculating the

Received for publication, Jan. 14, 1925.

1 Jour. Am. Watersworks Assn., 1924, 11, p. 408.
2 N. D. Agric. Exper. Station Rep., 1918, 8, p. 21.
3 Water Supplies, 1914, p. 138.
4 Med. Rec., 1915, 37, p. 59.
5 Lancet, 1913, 2, p. 1057.
6 Chemistry of Foods, 1919, p. 267.

amount consumed, and to this extent the nutritive supply may be greater than the dietary studies show, but unless a very hard water is used for drinking, it is unlikely that the lime from this source will cover more than a small part of the calcium requirement."

Rosenau[7] dismisses the question thus: "Hardness in water is more of an economic question than one of sanitary interest, except perhaps as the encouragement of the use of soap is of fundamental importance in hygiene and sanitation."

Others consider that hard water is better than soft or distilled water. Rector[8] remarks: "The weight of evidence is in favor of the use of a natural hard water containing a moderate amount of mineral."

In the annual report of the War Department for 1910, we find this statement: "The long continued use of boiled or distilled water is not conducive to health."

Van Saceghem[9] says: "Osteoporesis is very common in Belgian Congo in districts where the soil and water is low in calcium, but never where the calcium is high."

Lewis[10] concludes that while among the diseases alleged to be due to calcareous drinking water are gout, rheumatism, calculus, constipation, biliousness, eczema, goiter and arteriosclerosis, there is no evidence for the view. The evidence is in fact all the other way.

Berg[11] compiled data from the examination of school children in different regions.

He is convinced that the harder the water, the better are the teeth.

Opitz[12] compiled a large amount of statistical data, from which he draws the following conclusions:

"Communities with a very hard water are better as regards frequency of dental trouble in registrants for military service, among disability claimants, and in school children. Also there was a better body weight and degree of robustness among registrants for military service. The vitality of the new-born was better. There were fewer signs of nervous hyperexcitability in infants, school children, and those insured for disability. There was a slight advantage as regards size of infants and school children and with reference to mortality from tuberculosis."

Soft water had the advantage as regards calcification of arteries in recipients of invalidity allowances.

Hardness had no perceptible effect on size of registrants, stillbirths, birth and death rates, or frequency of tuberculosis among invalidity insurees.

Meyer[13] gathered similar statistical data. He interprets it to indicate a smaller incidence of diseased teeth among persons from hard water regions. He even ventures the opinion that the percentage of young men fit for military service in the armies was larger in the calcareous regions than in those in which other formations prevail. He cites specific instances of a deterioration in the quality of recruits at Gotha after the population was compelled to change its supply of drinking water from one of hard quality to softened water.

These data are suggestive, but have little real weight as evidence.

[7] Prev. Med. & Hyg., 1921, p. 1061.
[8] N. Y. Med. Jour., 1916, 104, p. 1142.
[9] Bull. soc. path. ecol., 1919, 12, p. 238.
[10] Brit. Med. Jour., 1911, 2, p. 158.
[11] Biochem. Ztschr., 1910, 24, p. 281.
[12] Deutsch. med. Wchnschr., 1920, 46, p. 1391.
[13] Jour. Am. Med. Assn., 1921, 77, p. 656.

An editorial[14] comments thus on Meyer's findings. "The suggestions should not be passed without some attention to their possible wider significance. The teeth are only a small part of the body structures that may suffer from an inadequate supply of calcium, although defects may be more conspicuous in the mouth. Experience has shown that it is not easy to enrich the body suddenly by therapeutically prescribed lime compounds. We must therefore learn the 'natural' ways in which the calcium equilibrium is ordinarily prevented from showing a negative balance."

Luce[15] reports work which has an indirect bearing on the hard water problem. She found that rats on a low calcium diet did not grow as fast as those on a normal calcium diet. Also they developed an enlargement of the parathyroids, which was due to hyperplasia not to hypertrophy of cells.

Almost no direct experimental work has been found on the relationship between natural hard water and the growth of animals. Hence experiments have been undertaken with white mice, white rats, rabbits, dogs, calves, pigeons and chicks.

EXPERIMENTS WITH MICE

Sixteen adult white mice were divided into 2 groups. Group 1 was given the same natural hard water used in the concretion experiments.[16] Group 2 received distilled water.

Roentgen-ray pictures were made in order to exclude the possibility of beginning with animals which had spontaneous concretions so that concretion formation as well as growth could be observed.

The mice were kept in identical cages and interchanged at intervals. The cages were cleaned each week and sterilized by live steam. The cages were of galvanized wire. A small wooden box containing paper strips or cotton was placed in each cage. Food was given twice daily and consisted of crackers, dog cakes and oats. Water was given at the same time on clean absorbent cotton.

Pregnant mice were removed to separate cages to prevent the young from being killed. The young from the hard and from the distilled water groups were kept separate, and therefore received only hard or distilled water, respectively, from birth.

The mice were weighed twice per week. At the conclusion of the experiment, the animals were grouped by sex for purposes of comparison.

A comparison of the weights and averages of the mice which were adult at the beginning of the experiment seems to yield no information of value. The mice under observation from birth obviously furnish more important data.

No differences were observed between the two groups at necropsy either in the case of those which died or those which were killed at the end of the experiment. No general differences in appearance or behavior were noted between the two groups during life.

The only apparent conclusion is that the hard water used in this experiment had no bad effects.

[14] Jour. Am. Med. Assn., 1921, 77, p. 655.
[15] Jour. Path. & Bacteriol., 1923, 26, p. 200.
[16] Jour. Infect. Dis., 1925, 36, p. 566.

EXPERIMENTS WITH ALBINO RATS

Although the results with mice showed little difference between hard and distilled water, it seemed advisable to work with white rats. Donaldson [17] has published a large body of data showing the normal rate of growth of the albino rat, which might serve as a basis of comparison.

A number of pregnant rats were obtained. Six of them raised families. One was put on each of the following waters: distilled, natural hard, distilled plus 10 parts per million of calcium carbonate, distilled plus 100 parts per million of calcium carbonate distilled plus 2,000 parts per million of calcium chloride. Several families were put on distilled water plus 100 parts per million of calcium chloride, and some on distilled water plus 200 parts per million of magnesium chloride, but none of them reached maturity.

Each family was removed from the mother at the age of 4 weeks, and the mother again mated. Only 2 males were used, and they were brothers. The same male was used in most instances, hence the 2d and 3rd generations were related. Each mother that had been used for a distilled water family was put on one of the calcium waters when a 2d family was born, and vice versa. The manner of breeding was an attempt to rule out hereditary factors.

Clean water was kept constantly before the rats in bottles with a stopper and a bent glass tube. The bottles were wired to the outside of the cages, the tubes extending through the meshes. This proved very satisfactory when the bore of the tube was at least 5 mm. and the angle properly adjusted.

The diet was the same as that used by Donaldson. It consisted of white bread moistened with whole milk, with a supply of yellow corn meal constantly before the animals.

Table 1 includes those animals which reached the age of 112 days. Those which died before this age were omitted.

As in the case of white mice, there was no marked difference between those which received hard or distilled water or those which received distilled water containing calcium salts. This diet is of course high in calcium and rich in vitamines, which might overbalance the lack of calcium in distilled water. At any rate, no bad effect of hard water is demonstrated.

RAT EXPERIMENTS WITH SYNTHETIC DIETS

The next step was to compare a diet low in calcium with one high in calcium to determine whether hard water would compensate for a low calcium diet. The concretion work was going on at the same time, hence the synthetic diets and salt mixture used there were chosen.[16]

Rats were secured from the Wistar Institute of Anatomy of Philadelphia in order to work with pedigreed animals.

The diet in preliminary experiments was that Luce,[15] with 5% of autolysed yeast (1.25% dry weight) substituted for 5% of "marmite." Marmite is a commercial yeast extract much used by British workers. The pregnant rats gave

[17] The Rat. 1915.

birth to apparently normal offspring. But with the original diet, family after family died. They usually became weak, "pot bellied," and somewhat rachitic in appearance. Many of them developed diarrhea, although it was uncommon among the rats on a milk, bread and corn meal diet. The autolysed yeast was increased from 1.25% to 5% dry weight. Several families are now under observation. They are developing better than formerly, but no data worth tabulating are yet available.

EXPERIMENTS WITH RABBITS

Series 1.—Two litters of rabbits were discovered, one only 3 days older than the other. One litter consisted of 6 rabbits and the other of 7. Three from each litter were interchanged on the day that the youngest was born. One group

TABLE 1

RESULTS OF EXPERIMENTS ON RATS

Age in Days	Distilled Water	Natural Hard Water	Distilled Water 10 Parts per Million of $CaCO_3$	Distilled Water 100 Parts per Million of $CaCl_2$	Distilled Water 2,000 Parts per Million of $CaCl_2$	Distilled Water 200 Parts per Million of Na_2HPO_4
Males						
	12 Rats, Average Weight, Gm.	10 Rats, Average Weight, Gm.	19 Rats, Average Weight, Gm.	3 Rats, Average Weight, Gm.	6 Rats, Average Weight, Gm.	7 Rats, Average Weight, Gm.
0	5.4	5.0	5.4	4.6	5.0	5.0
21	23.4	23.0	20.6	18.2	19.0	24.5
42	47.0	44.5	41.2	34.6	38.3	42.1
63	76.0	66.7	63.2	54.8	60.0	67.6
84	107.0	99.2	91.3	84.0	84.9	101.9
98	121.0	115.4	111.3	103.3	100.9	132.1
112	129.0	128.7	125.1	125.7	115.4	Dead
Females						
	9 Rats	9 Rats	13 Rats	5 Rats	7 Rats	5 Rats
0	4.9	5.0	5.4	4.9	5.4	4.9
21	22.0	21.6	21.2	21.8	20.2	22.1
42	46.1	40.1	42.2	38.8	38.3	43.6
63	70.0	58.0	63.4	58.4	59.9	60.2
84	94.5	84.3	85.1	77.4	82.9	78.8
98	101.5	95.0	97.1	92.4	99.6	94.8
112	106.5	115.6	112.2	99.8	106.0	105.6

received the same hard water used in the previous experiments, and the other received glass-distilled water. Conditions were the same, and the quarters were interchanged each time the animals were weighed.

The group receiving hard water developed a decided superiority over the distilled water group. At the end of 32 days, they were on the average 31.49% heavier. The general appearance of the rabbits was much better on hard than on distilled water.

At this time the water was interchanged, to determine whether the hard water group would lose the advantage which it had gained, and vice versa. The hard water group began to lose its excess weight very soon, but the approach of the

2 groups to a similar weight was slow. The hard water group had attained its excess weight in about 32 days. When the distilled water group was changed to hard water, it did not catch up with the other for about 118 days, and so long as the animals were under observation, did not surpass it.

It remains a question whether the apex of the advantage of the hard water had not been reached when the water was interchanged. It is possible that the 2 groups would have begun to approach a common

TABLE 2

SUMMARY OF AVERAGE AND EXCESS WEIGHTS AND AVERAGE EXCESS PERCENTAGE WEIGHTS IN RABBIT SERIES 1

Length of Exper. in Days	Hard Water Group (7 Rabbits)			Distilled Water Group (8 Rabbits)		
	Average Weight, Gm.	Average Excess Weight, Gm.	Percentage Excess Average Weight	Average Weight, Gm.	Average Excess Weight, Gm.	Percentage Excess Average Weight
1	162	0	0	190	28	17.28
6	280	7	2.50	273	0	0
19	502	65	10.95	437	0	0
32	851	268	31.49	583	0	0
Water Inter-changed						
46	1,150	345	29.84	801	0	0
60	1,306	300	22.89	1,006	0	0
74	1,432	285	19.90	1,147	0	0
88	1,648	275	16.68	1,373	0	0
104	1,824	413	22.64	1,411	0	0
120	1,746	170	9.77	1,576	0	0
135	1,982	191	9.63	1,791	0	0
150	1,971	63	3.19	1,908	0	0

TABLE 3

RESULTS OF EXPERIMENTS IN RABBIT SERIES 2

Length of Exper. in Days	Hard Water Group (11 Rabbits)			Distilled Water Group (11 Rabbits)		
	Average Weight, Gm.	Average Excess Weight, Gm.	Percentage Average Excess Weight	Average Weight, Gm.	Average Excess Weight, Gm.	Percentage Average Excess Weight
1	108	0	0	121	13	12.12
7	169	0	0	173	4	2.36
14	262	57	21.28	206	0	0
21	255	101	28.45	254	0	0
28	454	139	30.83	315	0	0
35	527	185	35.10	342	0	0
42	581	177	30.46	414	0	0

weight in any case as they neared maturity. Nevertheless, the results suggest the superiority of hard water. Table 2 summarizes the data.

Series 2.—One litter of 6 and one of 5 rabbits were placed on hard water, and 2 similar litters on distilled water from birth. Conditions were the same as for series 1 except that litter mates could not be interchanged. Table 3 summarizes the findings. The group which was given hard water was again superior in weight and general appearance.

EXPERIMENTS WITH DOGS

Eight puppies were divided into 2 groups. Five were just weaned and 3, while somewhat older, were young dogs. The animals were kept indoors in identical cages with an occasional interchange of quarters until the weather became sufficiently warm to permit them to remain outdoors. They were then kept in similar pens. Each morning they were given all the distilled or hard water, respectively, that they would drink. Next they were placed in the same pen and fed, care being taken to make sure that each animal received all that it cared for. They were allowed to remain together all day. In the evening, they were separated and given all the water and food that they would consume. The food consisted of meat, cornmeal mush, and an occasional meal of Spratts dog cakes.

The dogs were weighed twice per week for 27 weeks. Table 4 summarizes the changes in weight of each dog at the beginning and end of the experiment.

TABLE 4

RESULTS OF EXPERIMENTS ON DOGS

Weight at Beginning of Exper., Gm.	Weight After 27 Weeks, Gm.	Gain in Weight, Gm.	Loss in Weight, Gm.	Percentage Gain in Weight	Percentage Loss in Weight
Hard Water					
4,800	12,050	7,250	—	151.0	—
3,880	7,700	3,820	—	98.4	—
2,415	4,200	1,785	—	73.9	—
4,520	4,700	500	—	11.0	—
Distilled Water					
3,720	8,400	4,680	—	125.8	—
3,720	5,300	1,580	—	42.4	—
7,200	6,620	—	580	—	8.1
5,200	4,700	—	500	—	9.6

As the experiment progressed, the appearance of the dogs receiving hard water became noticeably better than that of those receiving distilled water. They were livelier, more active, and more playful. They ate and drank better, and their coats were smoother.

At necropsy the dogs were all normal except no. 1 of the hard water group. This animal had some enlarged tuberculous lymph glands and a small tuberculous area near the apex of the right lung. During the course of the experiment, the dogs had escaped from their quarters and had eaten some dead tuberculous guinea-pigs which had been left exposed by a laboratory helper. The urinary organs and passages of all of the dogs were normal. There was no evidence of concretions.

All of the dogs receiving hard water were better developed muscularly than the others. The deposits of fat about the kidneys and in the subcutaneous tissues were greater in these dogs.

The number of dogs is much too small for the results to be conclusive. However, the evidence as far as it goes is favorable for the use of hard water and corroborates the findings in rabbits.

WORK WITH CALVES

Six pure bred Holstein male calves were obtained when about a week old. Two died too soon to be of any value. All were given a normal, identical diet of whole milk, oats, corn, and alfalfa. Two were given distilled water, and 2, Omaha tap water, which averages about 200 parts per million of calcium carbonate.

As can be calculated from table 5, the total gain of the calves on hard water was 20.6% greater after a period of 240 days than that of the calves on distilled water. The former had smoother coats and a better general appearance.

TABLE 5

RESULTS OF EXPERIMENTS WITH CALVES

Length of Exper. in Days	Distilled Water				Omaha Tap Water			
	Calf No. 1		Calf No. 2		Calf No. 3		Calf No. 4	
	Weight in Lbs.	Total Gain	Weight in Lbs.	Total Gain	Weight in Lbs.	Total Gain	Weight in Lbs.	Total Gain
0	107	0	81	0	95	0	108	0
30	135	28	100	19	122	27	138	30
60	150	43	115	34	132	37	159	51
120	190	83	162	47	184	89	197	89
150	230	123	210	129	232	137	239	131
240	260	153	230	149	300	205	320	202

Again, the number is too small to be conclusive, but the evidence favors hard water and corroborates the results obtained with rabbits and dogs.

EXPERIMENTS WITH PIGEONS

A little work was done with squabs. They were unsatisfactory because difficult to feed when removed from the mothers. They are accustomed to having food dropped into their mouths. It required a considerable period of hand feeding and watering before they would learn to eat and drink voluntarily.

One group was given distilled water and the other, water containing 100 parts per million of calcium carbonate. Little was learned. Six members of each group lived 4 weeks. All suffered a loss in weight for a few days which was a little greater for the group receiving calcium water. However, they quickly caught up with and surpassed those which received distilled water.

WORK WITH CHICKS

Series 1. Natural Hard Water Compared with Distilled Water Series.— One hundred and four 1-day old White Wyandotte chicks were divided into 2 groups. For 2 weeks they were kept in cages side by side in a warm room. After this they were placed outdoors in pens of the same size during a part of each day, with a wooden coop for shelter. Later in the summer, they were allowed to remain in the pens all of the time, until a number were killed by rats. After that they were placed in cages each night. Throughout the experiment the quarters of the 2 groups were regularly interchanged.

The food of each group was identical and consisted of oatmeal and cornmeal. The chicks were given all that they would consume twice per day. Water was kept constantly before them in clean vessels. Group 1 received distilled water coming directly from a copper still lined with tin. Group 2 received the same kind of hard water used before.

All chicks that died were weighed and necropsies performed. The older hard water chicks were heavier than the distilled water ones which died near the same age. No other differences were noted.

TABLE 6

RESULTS OF EXPERIMENTS ON CHICK SERIES 1

Age in Days	Distilled Water		Hard Water		Average Excess Weight, Gm.	Average Percentage Excess Weight
	No. of Chicks	Average Weight, Gm.	No. of Chicks	Average Weight, Gm.		
3	50	33.4	50	34.0	—	—
37	24	78.9	25	101.4	22.5	28.6
58	20	120.9	24	152.0	31.1	20.4
72	18	150.3	20	174.6	24.3	16.1
91	14	167.3	16	251.2	83.9	45.3

All living chicks were weighed at intervals. A marked difference between the 2 groups soon became apparent. The chicks on hard water forged ahead of the others and remained ahead. Table 6 illustrates this.

The general observations favored the chicks which received the hard water. When several weeks old they ate more, drank more, and were more active. The feathers developed sooner and more uniformly. They retained these advantages throughout the experiment.

The necropsy findings at the end of the experiment corresponded with the general observations and the weights. In the hard water group, the breast bones were more completely ossified, the muscles were larger, and deposits of fat in various parts of the body were markedly more extensive, than in the case of the distilled water group.

Figure 1 is a photograph of all the tibias available. Figure 2 is the six largest and six smallest bones from each group. The difference in size and weight was not limited to soft tissues but included the bones.

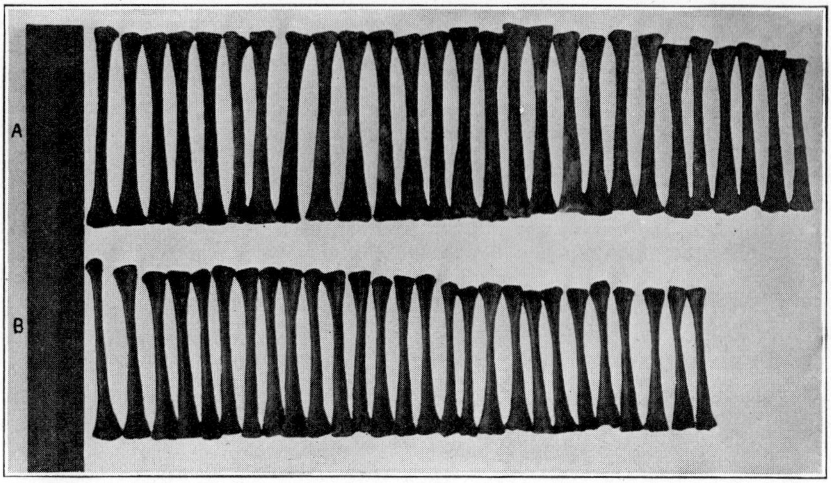

Fig. 1.—All available tibias from chick series 1. *a,* tibias from the chicks which received hard water; *b,* tibias from the chicks which received distilled water.

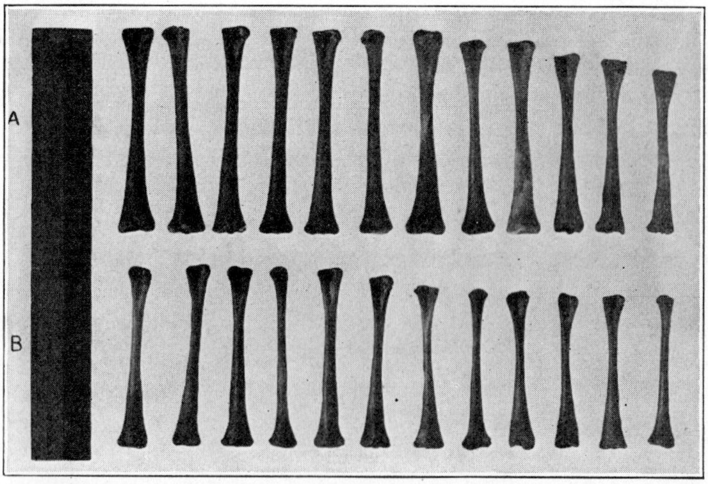

Fig. 2.—The six largest and the six smallest tibias from chick series 1. *a,* tibias from the chicks which received hard water; *b,* tibias from the chicks which received distilled water.

Chick Series 2.—The question arose whether water coming from the metal still might contain sufficient traces of copper or tin to exert a deleterious effect on young chicks. A second series of day old White Wyandottes were treated in exactly the same manner as the first series, except that the water was redistilled from resistance glass.

The weights and ages were tabulated for the chicks whose death occurred spontaneously, but yielded no more information than did series 1.

As in the first series, the weights, ages and postmortem condition of the dead chicks seem to have little significance except that in the later part of the experiment the chicks in the hard water group were heavier. As in series 1, the general observations were greatly in favor of the hard water group. A great many of the chicks died, perhaps because they were received during the extreme hot weather of the summer. At times some of the chicks showed slight diarrhea, which might possibly have accidentally affected one group more than the other. The necropsies at the end of the experiment showed the same differences as did those in series 1, but to a lesser degree since the chicks were younger. This series was less satisfactory but markedly favored hard water, and indicated that there were no toxic metals from the still in the distilled water.

TABLE 7

RESULTS OF EXPERIMENTS IN CHICK SERIES 2

Age in Days	Hard Water		Distilled Water		Average Excess Weight, Gm.	Average Percentage Excess Weight
	No. of Chicks	Average Weight, Gm.	No. of Chicks	Average Weight, Gm.		
1	50	33.9	50	33.3	—	—
19	25	44.5	29	50.1	5.6	12.3
37	11	49.9	17	80.2	30.2	60.9

Chick Series 3. Experiments Using Distilled Water Containing Various Salts.—A 3rd series of experiments with chick was undertaken in an effort to determine which of the salts present in the natural hard water were responsible for the increased vigor and rate of growth of the animals. Four groups of day old White Wyandotte chicks were procured, each consisting of about 40 members. Group 1 received distilled water, group 2 hard water from the same well as that previously used, group 3 a synthetic hard water made as nearly like the natural hard water as was practicable by adding the salts to distilled water, and group 4 distilled water to which was added as nearly as possible the same amount of calcium carbonate found in the hard water. To dissolve the calcium carbonate in the synthetic hard water and in the water for group 4, it was necessary to bubble carbon dioxide through it for several hours. This is the reverse of removing temporary hardness by boiling. The insoluble calcium carbonate was changed to soluble calcium bicarbonate. Only about 400 parts per million could be dissolved in this way. Analysis revealed only the ions. From them the following hypothetical salts were calculated. This was difficult as it is impossible to tell how the ions in the water were originally combined. According to the laws of ionization in dilute solutions, it should make little difference. In these concentrations the salts should be almost completely ionized.

	Parts Per Million
$Ca(HCO_3)_2$, calcium bicarbonate	602.7
or $CaCO_3$, calcium carbonate	519.8
$CaSO_4$, calcium sulphate (Hemihydrate)	72.7
$MgCl_2$, magnesium chloride	11.0
Na_2CO_3, sodium carbonate	23.0
NaCl, sodium chloride	23.0
Na_2SO_4, sodium sulphate	489.4
$NaNO_3$, sodium nitrate	1.0
$Al_2(SO_4)_3$, aluminum sulphate	1.8
$Fe_2(SO_4)_3$, ferric sulphate	1.0
SiO_2, silica	8.0

TABLE 8

EFFECT OF THE VARIOUS SALTS IN THE WATER IN CHICK SERIES 3

Length of Exper. in Days	Distilled		Natural Hard		Synthetic Hard		Distilled, 400 Parts per Million $CaCO_3$	
	No. of Chicks	Average Weight, Gm.	No. of Chicks	Average Weight, Gm.	No. of Chicks	Average Weight, Gm.	No. of Chicks	Average Weight, Gm.
1	41	34.7	42	35.8	41	37.0	41	36.0
18	23	60.3	16	64.3	19	61.6	14	54.6
33	17	71.0	14	86.5	18	76.6	9	67.1
50	12	91.6	11	140.6	7	84.8	5	91.6
65	10	97.2	11	169.9	0	0	5	117.0

There was a considerable loss of chicks by death. The synthetic hard water group all died from an epidemic of diarrhea when about 40 days old. Up to this time, they had been doing almost as well as the chicks on natural hard water. The number in the 3 other groups was small at the end of the experiment, but may be worth recording. The distilled water group soon began to fall behind the other groups. The calcium carbonate group did not do so well for a time, but there was some sickness among them. Toward the conclusion of the work they surpassed the distilled water group.

This series strengthens the probability that hard water is more favorable to the development of young animals than is distilled water.

Chick Series 4.—A 4th series of chicks was made up of 5 groups, each group consisting of about 40 individuals. Four of the groups were given the same kinds of water as in the case of series 3. The 5th group received natural hard water which had been boiled and filtered to remove temporary hardness.

There was again a considerable loss of chicks. The work was carried on during hot weather, which may have been one cause of trouble. There was more diarrhea among the chicks receiving hard water than among any of the other groups. Also the proportion of males in the distilled water group was higher than in the others, which would tend to raise the average weight. Yet the average weight of the distilled water group as well as the general appearance of the fowls lagged behind all the others.

In general, the chicks which received water containing calcium seemed to be superior to the fowls receiving distilled water. It is interesting to note that the group receiving boiled water grew very well, suggesting that removal of the temporary hardness leaves sufficient calcium.

TABLE 9

EFFECT ON CHICK SERIES 4 OF VARIOUS SALTS IN THE WATER

Length of Exper. in Days	Distilled		Natural Hard		Synthetic Hard		Natural Hard, Boiled		Distilled Water Plus 400 Parts $CaCO_3$	
	No. of Chicks	Average Weight, Gm.	No. of Chicks	Average Weight, Gm	No. of Chicks	Average Weight, Gm.	No. of Chicks	Average Weight, Gm.	No. of Chicks	Average Weight, Gm.
1	39	37.4	40	34.8	40	36.4	38	35.8	38	35.0
15	24	49.3	22	50.9	21	51.4	28	50.7	19	49.6
34	17	70.8	18	82.0	13	79.4	13	80.3	16	80.9
71	8	169.0	12	171.1	11	177.9	13	172.9	12	174.4
91	6	210.0	11	236.8	7	215.5	10	242.3	10	234.5

Chick Series 5.—Chick series 5 was divided into 6 groups of about 40 each. Group 1 received distilled water; group 2, the same synthetic hard water as that used before; group 3, distilled water plus 400 parts per million of calcium carbonate; group 4, distilled water plus 100 parts per million of calcium carbonate; group 5, distilled water plus 200 parts per million of dibasic sodium hydrogen phosphate, Na_2HPO_4; and group 6, distilled water plus 200 parts per million of sodium sulphate.

Four hundred parts per million of $CaCO_3$ was chosen for group 3, the chicks receiving a large amount of calcium, because it is as close as practicable to the amount contained in the hard water of the previous experiments, being all that can be dissolved under ordinary conditions.

Another factor was introduced into the diet here. In order to determine whether vitamines might be causing the differences noted, green alfalfa and raw beef liver were added to the diet, which otherwise remained the same.

So many animals died, apparently from inanition, that the series is of little value. Yet table 10 is included because it tends to corroborate other work.

Chick Series 6.—Chick series 6 was begun in the same manner as series 5, using the same diet. Rather curiously, only 2 groups, those receiving distilled water and those receiving synthetic hard water, survived in sufficient numbers to be of value. The nine remaining in the other groups at 14 days were divided between these groups.

Table 11 shows that the fowls receiving distilled water lagged definitely behind the synthetic hard water group. The general appearance of the fowls corresponded with the weight curves. This would indicate that salts in the water and not vitamines were the essential factors.

TABLE 10

RESULTS OF EXPERIMENTS WITH CHICK SERIES 5

Length of Exper. in Days	Distilled Water		Synthetic Hard Water		Dist. Water Plus $CaCO_3$ 400 Parts per Million		Dist. Water Plus $CaCO_3$ 100 Parts per Million		Dist. Water Plus Na_2HPO_4 200 Parts per Million		Dist. Water Plus Na_2SO_4 200 Parts per Million	
	No. of Chicks	Aver. Wt., Gm.	No. of Chicks	Aver. Wt., Gm.	No. of Chicks	Aver. Wt., Gm.	No. of Chicks	Aver. Wt., Gm.	No. of Chicks	Aver. Wt., Gm.	No. of Chicks	Aver. Wt., Gm.
0	42	32.0	42	32.7	42	31.1	42	31.3	41	31.6	41	30.4
7	14	43.8	26	47.2	18	43.2	15	48.0	19	42.6	13	46.3
14	12	50.6	18	56.2	14	51.5	12	52.7	16	51.3	11	49.5
21	7	58.0	14	63.4	10	52.1	8	56.7	15	60.3	7	51.3
28	7	70.2	11	80.6	4	58.2	4	59.0	8	65.0	2	64.0
35	5	80.0	4	93.7	0	0	0	0	4	75.7	0	0

TABLE 11

RESULTS OF EXPERIMENTS WITH CHICK SERIES 6

Length of Exper. in Days	Distilled Water		Synthetic Hard Water		Excess Weight of Hard over Distilled Water	Percentage Excess Weight of Hard over Distilled Water
	No. of Chicks	Average Weight, Gm.	No. of Chicks	Average Weight, Gm.		
0	44	33.3	44	33.0	—0.3	—0.9
7	18	37.8	18	36.8	—1.0	—3.0
14	15	44.3	14	45.3	1.0	2.2
21	20	61.0	18	64.3	3.3	5.0
28	20	66.3	18	66.3	0.0	0.0
35	20	92.5	17	96.0	3.5	4.0
42	17	103.6	17	102.7	—0.9	—0.8
49	17	101.2	17	113.2	12.0	10.8
56	17	133.9	16	155.0	22.0	16.4
63	17	139.8	14	163.3	23.5	16.8
70	17	161.2	12	198.8	37.6	23.3
77	17	175.3	12	227.1	51.9	29.5
84	16	213.5	12	279.4	65.9	30.8
91	15	277.1	12	343.7	66.6	24.0
98	13	315.4	12	353.0	37.6	11.9
105	13	326.8	12	420.8	94.0	25.7
130	13	778.1	11	888.6	110.5	14.2
177	13	976.5	11	1097.5	121.0	12.3
1 year	7	1064.0	8	1148.2	84.2	7.9

These fowls were kept for a year to determine whether the ones receiving distilled water would catch up with the others. They failed to do so.

Chick Series 7.—This series was started with the same groups, the same diet, and under the same conditions as series 6. The sodium sulphate group was lost.

The results are interesting. As tables 12 and 13 indicate, the distilled water group lagged behind all of the others. The synthetic hard water, the high calcium, and the low calcium groups were nearly alike. The phosphate group was best, as might be expected as phosphates are

TABLE 12

RESULTS OF EXPERIMENTS WITH CHICK SERIES 7

Length of Exper. in Days	Distilled Water		Synthetic Hard Water		Distilled Water Plus $CaCO_3$, 400 Parts per Million		Distilled Water Plus $CaCO_3$, 100 Parts per Million		Distilled Water Plus Na_2HPO_4, 200 Parts per Million	
	No. of Chicks	Average Weight, Gm.	No. of Chicks	Average Weight, Gm.	No. of Chicks	Average Weight, Gm.	No. of Chicks	Average Weight, Gm.	No. of Chicks	Average Weight, Gm.
0	32	34.6	33	33.5	31	33.3	32	34.8	32	34.8
7	27	39.3	31	41.4	26	41.9	31	40.0	30	40.5
14	23	44.0	28	49.6	25	47.0	27	45.1	25	45.0
21	22	56.2	27	63.3	22	60.4	22	58.6	22	59.7
28	22	67.3	26	73.2	22	67.2	22	66.9	22	69.7
35	18	68.0	26	80.4	17	73.2	21	73.2	18	77.1
42	15	81.3	22	102.6	14	99.1	17	91.5	18	95.5
49	14	84.4	20	105.1	12	103.1	15	98.1	16	104.6
56	12	103.0	19	128.0	12	123.5	12	115.6	11	129.7
63	11	111.1	18	141.2	12	134.5	10	132.2	11	149.2
70	11	135.7	18	173.9	12	167.0	10	169.8	11	184.0
77	11	177.8	18	223.5	14	212.0	9	229.3	11	244.5
84	11	186.8	18	243.2	11	224.2	9	251.7	11	268.2
91	7	202.8	18	264.2	11	266.0	8	264.3	11	301.4
98	7	271.9	16	302.1	11	304.2	8	335.5	11	364.1

TABLE 13

PERCENTAGE EXCESS WEIGHT OF THE AVERAGE OF EACH OVER DISTILLED WATER IN CHICK SERIES 7

Age in Days	Synthetic Hard Water	Distilled Water Plus 400 Parts per Million $CaCO_3$	Distilled Water Plus 100 Parts per Million $CaCO_3$	Distilled Water Plus 200 Parts per Mililon Na_2HPO_4
0	—3.2	—3.8	—0.5	—0.5
7	5.3	6.6	1.8	3.0
14	13.5	6.8	2.5	2.2
21	10.8	7.4	4.2	6.2
28	8.7	0.0	0.0	3.5
35	23.5	7.6	7.6	13.3
42	26.0	20.6	12.5	16.8
49	24.5	22.1	16.2	23.9
56	24.2	19.9	12.2	25.9
63	37.5	20.9	18.1	34.2
70	28.1	23.0	25.1	35.3
77	25.7	19.2	28.9	37.8
84	30.1	20.0	34.6	43.0
91	23.2	31.1	25.3	48.6
98	11.1	11.8	24.1	33.9

supposed to stimulate metabolism. But this has little bearing on the effects of natural hard water, since phosphates are not often present in appreciable amounts.

Weights and Dimensions of Tibias from Chick Series 7.—The tibias from chick series 7 were dried to constant weight at 110 C. in an oven. The weights were recorded and measurements made of the length, the diameter of the proximal end, the diameter of the distal end, and the diameter of the smallest point of the shaft.

Tables 14 and 15 show that the differences in live weight were not due to soft tissues only, but included the bony structure.

Figures 2 and 3 further illustrate the fact that the differences in weight did not depend on soft tissues alone. The epiphysial lines were apparently normal in all cases, indicating that ossification had not been

TABLE 14

WEIGHTS OF BONE (TIBIAS) FROM CHICK SERIES 7

Type of Water	No. of Bones	Average Weight, Gm.	Excess Weight Gm. over Distilled Water	Percentage Excess Weight over Distilled Water
Distilled	14	0.500	—	—
Synthetic Hard	29	0.730	0.230	46.0
Distilled water plus 400 parts per million $CaCO_3$	17	0.633	0.133	26.6
Distilled water plus 100 parts per million $CaCO_3$	18	0.633	0.133	26.6
Distilled water plus 200 parts per million Na_2HPO_4	20	0.723	0.223	44.4

TABLE 15

MEASUREMENTS OF TIBIAS FROM CHICK SERIES 7 IN MILLIMETERS

Type of Water	No. of Bones	Length	Diameter of Proximal End	Diameter of Distal End	Diameter of Shaft
Distilled	14	63.0	11.1	8.4	2.8
Synthetic hard	29	69.3	12.0	8.9	3.1
Distilled water plus 400 parts per million $CaCO_3$	17	68.0	12.3	9.1	3.0
Distilled water plus 100 parts per million $CaCO_3$	18	69.3	11.9	9.1	3.1
Distilled water plus 200 parts per million Na_2HPO_4	20	70.7	12.5	9.6	3.2

disturbed. However, the bones from the chicks which had received distilled water were smaller in every dimension and weighed less than the others.

Chick Series 8.—Chick series 8 was intended to answer several questions. First, the effect of a larger amount of calcium; second, the effect of magnesium; third, possible inherent toxicity of distilled water. Group 1 received distilled water; group 2, distilled water plus sufficient $CaCl_2$ to be equivalent to 1,000 parts per million of $CaCO_3$; group 3, distilled water plus sufficient $CaCl_2$ to be the equivalent to 2,000 parts per million of $CaCO_3$; group 4, distilled water plus 200 parts per million of $MgCl_2$; and group 5, distilled water plus 200 parts per million of NaCl.

The diet and general conditions were the same as employed in series 7.

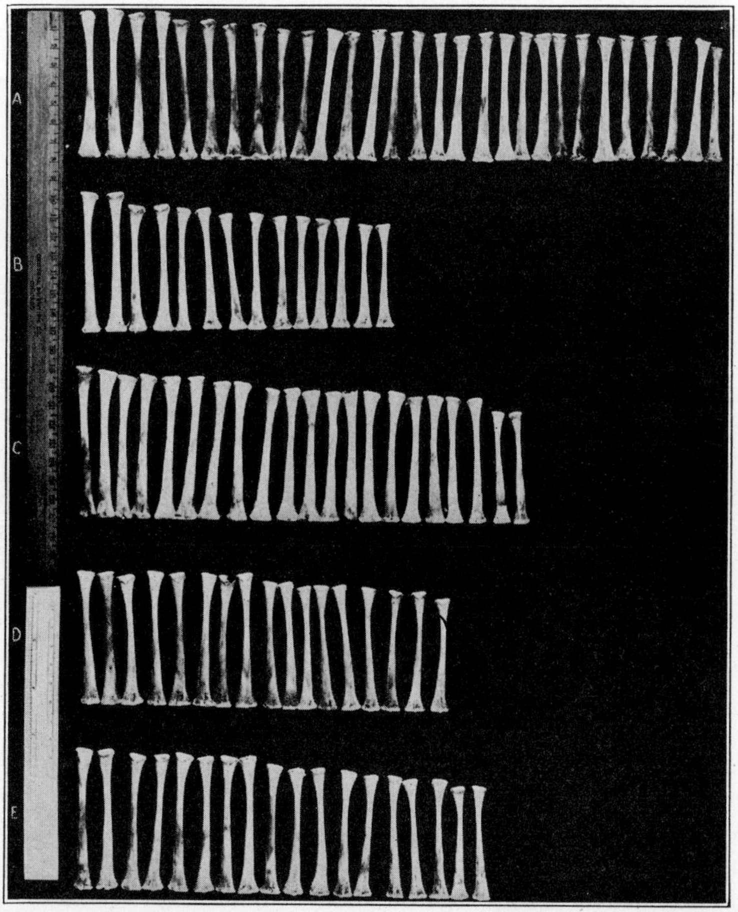

Fig. 3.—All available tibias from chick series 7. *a,* tibias from the chicks which received synthetic hard water; *b,* tibias from the chicks which received distilled water; *c,* tibias from the chicks which received distilled water containing Na_2HPO_4; *d,* tibias from the chicks which received distilled water containing 400 parts per million of calcium carbonate; *e,* tibias from the chicks which received distilled water containing 100 parts per million of calcium carbonate.

As table 16 indicates, the groups all developed at about the same rate. This would seem to suggest that 1,000 parts per million was higher than the optimum amount of calcium. But one cannot be sure, since these groups were all as heavy as the chicks receiving hard water in previous series. It seems probable, however, that the rate of growth of this series must have been higher because of other factors. This work should be repeated with a hard water in the series.

One rather interesting observation was made which may be mere coincidence. The magnesium group showed an earlier sex development than the others. The roosters began to crow and to display sex activities earlier.

CHICK WORK WITH HIGH AND LOW CALCIUM, SYNTHETIC DIETS

Since calcium waters gave definitely better results than distilled water with chicks on a grain diet, it was decided to compare high and

TABLE 16

RESULTS OF EXPERIMENTS WITH CHICK SERIES 8

Length of Exper. in Days	Distilled Water		$CaCl_2$, 1,000 Parts per Million		Distilled Water Plus $CaCl_2$, 2,000 Parts per Million		Distilled Water Plus $MgCl_2$, 200 Parts per Million		Distilled Water Plus $NaCl_2$, 200 Parts per Million	
	No. of Chicks	Average Weight, Gm.	No. of Chicks	Average Weight, Gm.	No. of Chicks	Average Weight, Gm.	No. of Chicks	Average Weight, Gm.	No. of Chicks	Average Weight, Gm.
7	34	35.2	28	34.2	30	32.6	37	34.7	25	35.7
15	23	45.3	25	43.5	23	39.5	25	41.3	25	44.0
22	20	55.3	22	54.0	21	50.4	22	50.4	23	55.2
29	20	71.1	19	69.7	20	61.1	18	65.0	21	67.2
36	19	81.3	19	83.2	16	75.6	15	75.2	20	75.6
43	14	96.6	17	93.8	15	90.0	14	100.6	14	88.9
50	14	110.5	17	113.7	15	113.6	13	107.3	12	108.6
57	14	158.3	17	153.6	15	150.3	13	149.8	12	147.5
64	14	177.4	16	173.3	15	182.0	12	190.0	12	175.8
71	14	218.1	14	206.2	15	200.0	12	205.5	12	203.0
78	14	270.2	14	227.4	15	227.3	12	232.0	12	257.3
92	13	280.5	13	265.0	13	273.0	12	297.0	12	285.2

low calcium diets to determine whether hard water would compensate for a low calcium diet. The diet employed in the concretion work was chosen.[16] In preliminary experiments, 1.25% dry weight of autolyzed yeast was used. In about a week, the chicks began to die. There was no diarrhea, they simply wilted, with rather indefinite symptoms. When between 2 and 3 weeks of age, they showed symptoms resembling those of polyneuritis, which suggested the addition of more yeast. Recovery was rapid. Some of those which were very ill revived in a day or two when a large dose of yeast was given. One group which was continued on the original formula died quickly. Evidently 1.25% of autolyzed yeast (dry weight) was insufficient.

Fifty white Leghorn baby chicks were put on the diet with 5% of yeast. Cod liver oil was used to determine whether it would compensate for the absence of light. It is ordinarily difficult to raise chicks indoors and in restricted quarters. They were observed for 6 weeks. Sixty per cent. survived, indicating that the vitamine B was adequate.

Eight groups of about 37 each were procured. Four groups were given a high, and 4 a low calcium diet. Four waters were used: distilled, natural hard,

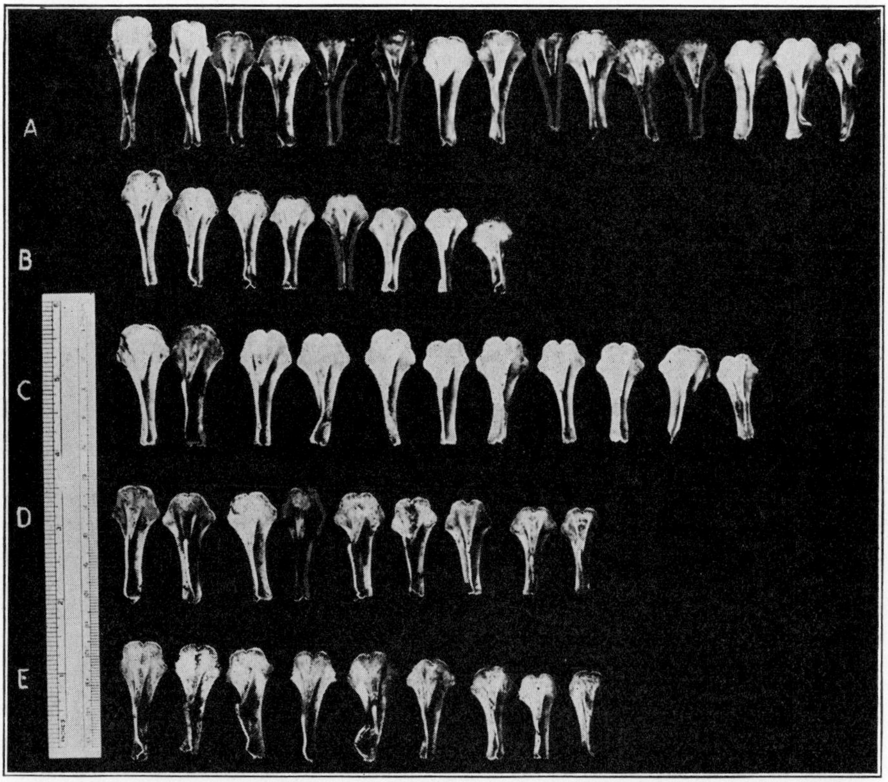

Fig. 4.—All available sternums from chick series 7. *a,* sternums from the chicks which received synthetic hard water; *b,* sternums from the chicks which received distilled water; *c,* sternums from the chicks which received distilled water containing Na_2HPO_4; *d,* sternums from the chicks which received distilled water containing 400 parts per million of calcium carbonate; *e,* sternums from the chicks which recovered distilled water containing 100 parts per miiiion of calcium carbonate.

distilled plus 100 parts per million of calcium carbonate and distilled water plus 100 parts per million of calcium chloride. Calcium chloride was used to determine whether calcium in the form of bicarbonate as found in natural hard water was preferable to other calcium salts.

They were kept indoors all of the time. Two brooders of 300 chick capacity each were divided into 4 compartments. A chicken wire pen 2 feet by 4 feet was connected with each brooder compartment. Food was placed in baby chick feeders, and water in inverted Mason jar chicken waterers. The chicks were changed from pen to pen at frequent intervals to equalize light and other conditions. A layer of clean sand was kept in the pens.

The experiment was continued for 60 days. Tables 17 and 18 summarize the average weights at weekly intervals for each water and diet.

There was little difference among the groups on either diet or on any of the waters. The chicks receiving distilled water were about the same

TABLE 17

RESULTS OF LOW CALCIUM DIET IN CHICK SERIES 8

Age in Days	Distilled Water		Natural Hard Water		Distilled Water + 100 Parts per Million $CaCO_3$		Distilled Water + 100 Parts per Million $CaCl_2$	
	No.	Average Weight, Gm.	No.	Average Weight, Gm.	No.	Average Weight, Gm.	No.	Average Weight, Gm.
4	38	35.7	38	35.3	37	36.4	38	35.6
11	28	48.9	33	47.4	30	48.9	30	48.6
18	26	67.2	26	54.1	27	56.5	30	57.0
25	26	72.0	26	68.6	27	75.3	23	73.8
32	25	88.8	25	83.9	27	85.2	23	84.4
39	25	101.8	21	95.0	23	101.7	22	94.3
46	22	121.5	18	125.2	21	124.5	18	125.8
53	21	157.0	18	158.2	19	157.3	14	155.0
60	22	167.4	17	160.3	19	162.0	14	165.7

TABLE 18

RESULTS OF HIGH CALCIUM DIET IN CHICK SERIES 8

Age in Days	Distilled Water		Natural Hard Water		Distilled Water + 100 Parts per Million $CaCO_3$		Distilled Water + 100 Parts per Million $CaCl_2$	
	No.	Average Weight, Gm.	No.	Average Weight, Gm.	No.	Average Weight, Gm.	No.	Average Weight, Gm.
4	38	37.0	38	36.5	38	37.1	38	36.0
11	31	47.2	31	48.9	30	48.3	30	47.6
18	30	57.6	29	59.3	27	61.7	29	57.7
25	29	71.2	25	71.5	24	72.7	22	78.7
32	28	85.4	25	86.9	23	93.2	21	92.2
39	27	94.0	22	93.0	23	99.0	19	98.0
46	24	116.0	21	119.5	20	124.5	14	145.3
53	19	141.9	22	138.2	18	142.6	12	183.0
60	18	155.7	21	153.7	15	157.1	12	190.5

as the chicks receiving calcium water. The group which had been on a high calcium diet and calcium chloride water was heavier than the others, but the smaller fowls had died in larger numbers.

Steenbock and others think that cod liver oil may increase calcium assimilation and permit a positive balance on a very low calcium intake. Hence its value in rickets. This may explain the good growth made by the distilled water chicks on this diet.

A STUDY OF THE EFFECT OF DISTILLED WATER ON THE URINARY OUTPUT OF CALCIUM AND PHOSPHORUS IN RABBITS

Twelve rabbits were divided into 4 groups. The diets were the same as those described for the concretion work, Part I, page 16.

Group 1 received distilled water and a low calcium diet; group 2, natural hard water and a low calcium diet; group 3, distilled water and a high calcium diet; group 4, hard water and a high calcium diet.

A composite sample of urine was collected from each group at least twice a day for 10 days on the customary laboratory diet of oats and carrots without water. Ten day composite samples were collected for 6 consecutive periods.

Table 19 is a comparison of the calcium and phosphorus content of the composite samples of urine while the animals were on the laboratory diet with that after they had been on the special diets and waters for 60 days.

TABLE 19

URINARY OUTPUT OF CALCIUM AND PHOSPHORUS IN RABBITS

Group	Diet	Water	Mg. $CaCO_3$ per 100 C c. of Urine		Mg. P per 100 C c. of Urine	
			Before Test	After 60 Days' Test	Before Test	After 60 Days' Test
1	Low Ca	Distilled	7.4	6.7	13.3	52.8
2	Low Ca	Natural hard	20.8	14.7	13.3	55.2
3	High Ca	Distilled	29.2	11.7	12.8	55.6
4	High Ca	Natural hard	8.8	14.3	9.6	56.0

The water apparently made no difference. The calcium content did not change appreciably. The phosphorus had gone up markedly and uniformly in all of the groups. Hence the change must have been due to the diet and not to the water.

SUMMARY

White mice on a diet of grains and a natural very hard water (520 parts per million of $CaCO_3$) showed no striking differences in growth or appearance from those on a similar diet receiving distilled water.

White rats on a diet of bread, milk and yellow corn meal exhibited no marked differences.

Young rabbits on a diet of oats, carrots and alfalfa and the natural hard water were about 30% heavier at the age of 42 days than similar rabbits on distilled water.

A few dogs on a mixed diet and the natural hard water grew faster and had a better general appearance than similar dogs with distilled water.

Two calves on a diet of milk, oats, corn and alfalfa and a moderately hard water (200 parts per million of $CaCO_3$) were 20% heavier at the age of 8 months than a similar pair which had received only distilled water.

Several groups of chicks on a grain diet and the natural hard water gained from 20 to 40% more during the first few months of life than did similar groups on a distilled water intake. In one instance, the experiment was continued for a year, and the chicks receiving distilled water did not catch up.

Distilled water to which had been added as nearly as possible the same salts as were in the natural hard water gave practically the same results with chicks, as did natural hard water.

Distilled water containing either 400 or 100 parts per million of calcium carbonate yielded almost the same results with chicks as the natural hard water.

Distilled water containing 2,000 parts per million of calcium chloride gave no better growth of chicks than did distilled water.

Distilled water containing 200 parts per million of Na_2HPO_4 increased the rate of growth of chicks as much as did calcium.

Two hundred parts per million of NaCl had no effect on growth of chicks.

On a synthetic diet containing the essential foods and including cod liver oil, chicks receiving distilled water grew at the same rate as those receiving the natural hard water, or distilled water containing $CaCO_3$ or $CaCl_2$.

The urinary output of calcium and phosphorus in rabbits was apparently not affected by the salts in hard water.

In no instance did animals on distilled water develop better than those on hard water, but the reverse was true under several conditions.

PROLIFERATIVE REACTION TO STIMULI BY THE LYTIC PRINCIPLE (BACTERIOPHAGE) AND ITS SIGNIFICANCE

ONE PLATE

PHILIP HADLEY

From the Department of Bacteriology of the University of Michigan, Ann Arbor

In connection with the mode of attack of the filtrable viruses on the cells and tissues of plants and animals, there is increasing recognition of the circumstance that one of the first reactions to the virus is one which manifests itself by increased growth energy, thereby resulting in proliferations. Sometimes these proliferations are concerned with the cells directly attacked, sometimes with related or surrounding cells. Regarding this point, d'Herelle[1] has stated it as a general law that "when a cell is attacked by an ultravirus, its primary reaction is always a proliferative process." Of this phenomenon several examples are noted:

1. The malignant tumors of plants as studied particularly by Erwin Smith.
2. The transmissible chicken sarcoma of Rous.
3. The proliferative processes in vaccinia, variola and sheep pox (mitotic cell division increased).
4. Cutaneous neoplasms as observed by Sanarelli in myxoma of the rabbit.
5. Molluscum contagiosum in man.
6. In rabies the accumulation of newly formed cells about the nerve cells of the medulla and bulb, or proliferation in the endothelial capsule as shown by Babes.
7. In canine plague the proliferation of the perivascular and periependymal neuroglia.

If the lytic principle is to be regarded as an ultravirus parasitizing the bacterial cells, it would seem probable that its growth in its proper substratum (living bacterial culture) would be accompanied by analogous proliferative changes; furthermore, that these would be manifested by some sort of excessive growth of the organism on solid or in liquid culture mediums. That something of this sort happens in liquid cultures of B. coli when submitted to the influence of its homologous bacteriophage was first remarked by Bordet and Ciuca.[2] They state in one of their

Received for publication, Jan. 14, 1925.

[1] Immunity in Natural Infectious Disease, 1924.

[2] Compt. rend. Soc. de biol., 1921, 86, p. 1095.

early studies: "Indeed we have been of the opinion that the phenomenon of lysis, appearing in a broth tube containing the lytic agent and inoculated with organisms, is always preceded by a multiplication of the organisms." Nothing in this statement would lead us to believe that this observed "multiplication" partook of the nature of a proliferation, which connotes something more than mere growth. This was, however, an important observation and was directed against the view, more or less current at the time, that when a lytic filtrate was added to a bacterial culture, the bacteria were killed "at once." This observation was, moreover, a necessary prop for the Bordet-Ciuca theory of lytic action.

Although this point of "multiplication before lysis" received but slight emphasis in d'Herelle's [3] earlier work, the conception is more strongly developed in his later book.[1] Even here, however, the amount of direct evidence of bacterial proliferation under the stimulus of the lytic agent is noticeably deficient in proportion to the marked significance which d'Herelle attaches to this point as contributing support to his ultravirus theory of the bacteriophage. Indeed, he merely states that a degree of multiplication which he seems to believe justifies the use of the term "proliferation" can be observed in liquid bacterial cultures submitted to the action of the lytic agent. His method of demonstrating this in bacterial suspensions is presented as follows:

> Take two identical bacterial suspensions and inoculate one with a bacteriophage of maximum activity. After two or three hours it will be seen that the parasitized suspension is more turbid than the control suspension. . . . The ultravirus, therefore, attacking the young bacteria, causes these bacteria to react immediately and to accelerate their process of division before they are definitely overcome and undergo lysis.

It is possible that this reaction can sometimes be observed in bacterial suspensions, but it is also obvious that slight proliferations of growth in a liquid culture of bacteria are likely to be difficult to detect or to measure; their grades of difference can only be guessed at. Proliferative growth in the form of a surface growth on solid culture medium would remove these objections and demonstrate more clearly what is taking place in a mass of bacterial cells under the stimulus of a lytic agent. Such proliferative growths were not mentioned by d'Herelle, nor by Bordet and Ciuca; and I am not aware that they have been reported in the literature since that time. It is therefore my aim in the first portion of this paper to call attention to three instances in

[3] The Bacteriophage and Its Rôle in Immunity, 1922.

which a noteworthy proliferation of cells takes place in bacterial cultures experiencing the influence of a lytic agent, presumably identical with that represented by the bacteriophage of d'Herelle. In these cases, however, the proliferation occurs in such a manner as to resemble more closely than can be seen in liquid cultures the circumstances attending the process of continuous proliferation in growing plant and animal tissue under the influence of diverse types of ultravirus.

OBSERVATIONS

The first case to which I wish to refer has been mentioned in my former article [4] dealing with transmissible bacterial autolysis of B. pyocyaneus, although the point in question did not receive special consideration at that time. The essential facts are as follows:

When a culture of the lysogenic strain (L-type) of B. pyocyaneus is plated on agar, two sorts of colonies arise: (1) large, green, spreading (L-type); and (2) small, yellow, compact (R-type). These are shown in figs. 3 and 7. Plating (1) will give again both sorts of colonies. Plating (2) will give the R-type colonies only. Both types of colony carry the lytic agent. But while the L-type shows the lytic manifestations, the R-type never shows them. It is resistant to lysis. Natural colonies of the L-type grow rapidly and usually come to possess a diameter 2 or 3 times as great as the diameter of the R-type colonies. The same is true of "artificial" colonies of the L-type. A colony of this sort is pictured in fig. 3. In the large colonies, growth and lysis proceed hand in hand. Sometimes lysis is eventually overcome by growth; sometimes, however, lysis overcomes growth, and the colony, as a unit thing, perishes. In all cases, however, there is at some time an extremely active cell proliferation, as is demonstrated in the photographs.

Since recording these observations on cultures of B. pyocyaneus, 2 other instances of proliferative bacterial growth accompanying colony lysis have come to my attention. The 1st of these concerns a white coccus from sewage-contaminated river water. The normal, sensitive colonies (S-type) are small, round, entire, convex, moist and whitish, having a diameter from 6 to 8 mm. when 48 hours old, and seldom attaining a size greater than this. The lytic (L-type) colonies are of the same general nature, but their size increases rapidly to attain a diameter of 12 to 18 mm. Lysis starts as a lytic arc, a lytic, wedge-shaped invagination, or sometimes as a complete circumferential ring. In all of these cases, the lytic area or zone develops inward. In rarer cases it starts in the center and develops outward. Wherever lysis occurs, the culture mass loses its whitish opacity and becomes transparent. The

[4] Jour. Infect. Dis., 1924, 34, p. 260.

same phenomenon occurs on slant agar cultures. Of these cultures, I have no photographs, but the subject will be considered in greater detail in a subsequent paper. The feature of present interest lies in the rapid, expansive growth accompanying the lytic action. It may also be added that the R-type of culture of this coccus has not yet been obtained. It was therefore necessary to make comparisons between the lysogenic type and the sensitive (normal) type of colony.

The third and last instance of proliferative growth in colony form under the stimulus of a lytic agent is the case of a coccus obtained from the air of the laboratory as a result of exposing sterile, agar plates for a few minutes. Here much the same results were obtained as in the lytic water coccus, except that in the case of the air coccus the degree of proliferation was much greater both relatively and actually. After a period of 2 weeks on infusion agar, the diameter of the lytic colonies was commonly about 25 mm. In these colonies, lysis usually started as a marginal fleck extending rapidly into a wedge-shaped invagination. Sometimes several such wedge-shaped areas of lysis were present. Sometimes the colony was entirely destroyed by the lytic action, or a large portion rendered transparent as shown in fig. 2. More commonly, however, certain areas of irregular shape remained intact, normal in form and in consistency as shown in fig. 6. Succesive stages in the growth and lysis of one of these colonies are presented in figs. 1, 2 and 6. When subcultures to agar were made from the unlysed growth, normal growth usually resulted. Subculturing from the clear areas, on the other hand, yielded a culture which showed the same progressive lysis. No resistant strain was obtained from these cultures.

In this coccus from air another point involving the proliferative growth was of special interest. Now and then, on a certain border of the colony, the proliferative growth would come to a halt; apparently the organisms had been killed by the lytic action. But a later observation of this area showed the presence of minute colonies of bacteria. These colonies would increase in size, and from their free margins (i. e., approximating the medium) a renewed and proliferating, but still lytic, growth would take place. Some of these subcolonies are shown in fig. 6.

Regarding these 3 cultures as a whole, there was of course much variation in the colony appearance, although all presented the outstanding characteristic of active proliferation. In all cases, however, there were some colonies which failed to manifest this characteristic. These negative cases were usually either colonies which "lysed out" quickly and completely or colonies which showed, at an early stage, a small patch of lysis which was immediately walled in by apparently normal cell growth. In some instances, masses of normal culture were cut off and segregated by the confluence of several lytic advances. In other cases, particularly in pyocyaneus, the bacterial mass was eroded, constricted, thrown into contours, or quite melted away by the forces operating. But during any or all these changes, the margin of the colony always extended, creeping forward as a thin, glassy film in which the constructive and the destructive forces were closely balanced. When, however, active proliferation finally ceased, it was apparently never because the growth energy had become entirely expended; for, in such cases, it seems probable that proliferation will continue just as long as the conditions in the medium favorable for growth are maintained. In the case of B. pyocyaneus, colonies more than 3 inches in diameter are often seen. Usually, however, before such a size has been attained, the drying of the medium, or its impregnation with antagonistic, metabolic products, brings growth to an end.

In concluding this series of observations, I shall merely add that in all of these cases it requires but little imagination to see in them the epitome of the infection of a specific tissue with an ultravirus, the appearance of the colony registering from day to day the inequalities of the struggle between the two opposing forces, and finally terminating in a manner at the beginning unpredictable, so far as the eventual integrity or annihilation of the colony mass is concerned. But, whatever the final outcome and whatever the explanation of the phenomena may be, the outstanding feature is active colony proliferation.

DISCUSSION

In discussing these observations, I should like to mention first that one reason for my wish to present these cases of colony proliferation under the influence of the lytic agent is that, as I have suggested earlier, these phenomena are in strict accord with the demands of d'Herelle's view of the lytic principle as a living, propagating ultravirus. Indeed, they present the only unequivocal evidence that has been furnished up to the present time in favor of the view that one effect of the lytic agent on its substratum of bacteria is to cause proliferation of the bacterial mass. We have here, therefore, a somewhat curious situation in which d'Herelle himself is not in a position to present such evidence from cases which are the most convincing, merely because he is not inclined to accept either the Twort phenomenon [5] or the phenomenon of transmissible lysis in B. pyocyaneus [6] as I have described it, as representing the action of a true bacteriophage. And, since d'Herelle does not accept these instances, we can scarcely expect that he would accept those cases dealing with the air coccus and the water coccus as outlined above. Whatever our view of the actual nature of the causative agent may be, all of these cases are manifestly of the same order; and, although they differ in many respects from the classical lysis of the Shiga dysentery bacillus, a careful study of them shows that, at the bottom, the same sort of causative agent is at work in all.

It is naturally true that cases of this sort, which show many aberrant features, should be analyzed with great care, for it can scarcely be doubted that instances of fairly rapid lysis of bacteria not due to a specific, transmissible lytic agent exist. But the essential similarities and differences must be kept clear. I believe it will be conceded that there are only 3 outstanding characteristics which served to mark bacteriophage action as it has been defined and delimited by d'Herelle. These are: (1) inhibition of growth; (2) lysis in series; (3) formation of lytic areas on a background of culture. These constitute the essential criteria for the recognition of the lytic agent as at present commonly understood. If a culture filtrate possesses these characteristics, it is a lytic filtrate in the d'Herelle sense; and minor variations in the speed of the reaction, the degree of reaction or in the size, number or shape of the lytic areas, cannot change the conclusion. This, it may be observed, is not the equivalent of saying that a lytic agent may not exist without manifesting all of these patent characteristics. To this point we shall return.

In the 3 examples of transmissible bacterial autolysis mentioned in the foregoing pages, these 3 criteria are satisfied, though in varying degrees. It is true that the mode of action differs considerably from the classical Shiga lysis of d'Herelle. Yet in so newly a developed field of biology, why should one insist that all lytic phenomena should give the same manifestations? Must all have the speed and lethal efficiency of the Shiga lytic agent? Must all give the clear-cut pictures in enumeration observed in members of the colon-typhoid-dysentery group, or manifest the therapeutic effectiveness of barbone? d'Herelle has repeatedly emphasized the attributes of variability and adaptability

[5] Lancet, London, 1915, Dec. 4, p. 1241.
[6] Personal communication to the writer.

for the lytic agent; but, even so, it may be that his limitations are still drawn too close. These same attributes, and particularly the former, must also be permitted to operate in the explanation of diversities in the mode of behavior of the lytic agent with different bacterial species, such for example as observed in the phenomenon of Twort, in the transmissible lysis of B. pyocyaneus, in the lysis of the air and the water cocci and in many other isolated instances. Indeed, if the phenomenon of the lytic agent actually represents an infection of bacteria with an ultravirus, as maintained by d'Herelle, the phenomenon should be one of the commonest in the bacterial world; and as such it should be permitted evidences of wide variation in its mode of expression.

Having opened the general field of our discussion, we may now attempt, in a more detailed manner, to extract some meaning from the occurrence of these peculiar proliferative growths, and to ascertain to what extent they may be explained on the theory of lytic action as outlined by d'Herelle, or by some modification of his view.

The most interesting and immediate question that arises concerns what is actually happening under cover of what we call "proliferation." In attempting to understand this, one may first study the effects on the bacterial mass experiencing the reaction. If we examine microscopically in stained preparations a little of the growth from the free, expanding margin of the proliferating colony, we find it to be made up of well-formed and intact bacteria, with little débris. If, on the other hand, we examine in a similar manner some of the apparently homogenous, transparent material, taken from a point a little interior to the growing edge of the colony, we find it made up of 4 intergrading categories of matter: (1) masses of faintly staining, amorphous or finely granular material; (2) faintly staining fragments of bacteria; (3) faintly staining intact bacteria, and (4) normally staining intact bacteria. The last are in small numbers. Thus, in any proliferating area of a colony manifesting this lysing characteristic, bacteria in large numbers are generating, dying and disintegrating. This, one may say, is normal enough; it happens in all cultures in the course of time. The circumstance that makes it abnormal, however, is the rapidity with which the cycle is completed. The growing edge of the colony contains normal bacteria. Back of this only a millimeter or two, and representing a difference in age of not more than 6 to 12 hours, the organisms are dead and have disintegrated. When this material is seeded to agar, only a few colonies appear; and these continue the lytic process.

This brings us to the second point, and naturally the more difficult one. What is the mechanism of reaction underlying these changes? Of this we really know nothing. One thing, however, is clear: That proliferation in the bacterial mass is not purely a matter of excess growth. Wherever it occurs it is growth plus lysis, appearing together in an equilibrium which is closely balanced, but in which growth keeps a pace ahead. In any attempt to gain insight into the interrelation of these constructive and destructive forces, one needs the aid of some definite hypothesis; and it may be of interest to ascertain to what extent, if at all, they might receive an explanation on the basis of d'Herelle's theory of lytic action. If we make use of his hypothesis regarding the micellar and virus-like nature of the lytic agent, the relation between the destructive agent and the bacterium naturally becomes a form of parasitism, an association bordering (in the cases mentioned above) on metabiosis, as this term is commonly understood: Only one member of the associated pair profits, while the other member remains uninfluenced or may eventually suffer harm.

But if we were to regard this sort of an association as a metabiosis, how should we explain those other instances of transmissible lysis from the classical example of d'Herelle where lysis is so-to-speak acute, to the situation which exists in the so-called resistant strains of bacteria which, as is well known, "carry" the lytic agent without undergoing lysis? In an attempt to answer this question, we may first pause to consider the relation which we might suppose to exist between the function of lysis and other possible manifestations of an assumedly living and propagating lytic corpuscle.

In such an hypothesis as d'Herelle's, it may be something of a disadvantage to unprejudiced observation (although naturally an unavoidable one) that the phenomenon which we are considering has become so widely known as "the lytic phenomenon," "the phenomenon of the lytic principle" and the phenomenon of "transmissible autolysis"; and that the causative agent has become known as "the lytic agent" or "the lytic principle." These terms have arisen naturally enough in an effort to fix what has thus far been observed as the chief phenomenon of the reaction; and they have persisted, on the part of many writers at least, not only because of their obvious appropriateness, but also because of a conscious attempt to avoid some of the biologic implications connoted by d'Herelle's original appelation, Bacteriophagum intestinale, or bacteriophage. But they have served the cause poorly, I believe, because they have not permitted the imagination to wander far from the lytic aspects of the phenomenon. It has often happened in the history of biology that undue emphasis on an obvious but incidental or subordinate characteristic (usually one of those first observed) has served effectually to conceal a major issue. It seems possible that this circumstance holds in the case of the lytic agent.

It is perhaps legitimate, therefore, to inquire on what grounds we should necessarily conclude that the phenomenon of lysis, on which all investigators have focused their attention, should be regarded as the most important characteristic and condicio sine qua non of the bacteriophage phenomenon. If we should come to regard the bacteriophage as an autonomous being, a living micella, we might conclude that its chief business in life is, not to produce lysis, but to live and to propagate itself. Even superficial reflection on the subject does not convince one that sudden lysis and destruction of the cell would be indispensable to the performance of either of these functions. Indeed, if we draw on analogy with other biologic phenomena, the production of lysis might appear more than likely to be of secondary significance in the daily routine of an assumedly living corpuscle, such as d'Herelle believes the lytic agent to be. Years ago, the observation of blue-green pus in wounds led to the later discovery of pyocyaneus. But we no longer regard the biologic significance of this organism as restricted to the "phenomenon of blue-green pus." Indeed we know that pyocyaneus may live and grow in the tissues, as well as in tubes, without giving the slightest evidence of this phenomenon (production of pyocyaninin); and, furthermore, to this organism we now attribute many other qualities, originally unrecognized. If we should come to regard the lytic agent as possessing a virus-like nature, might we not anticipate that, in a somewhat similar manner, it also could exist and go about its work without the production of lysis—at least in the classical sense alluded to by d'Herelle?

We have seen that if the lytic agent were regarded as a living micella, its inclusion within the bacterium would constitute an act of parasitism. But in parasitism there are all possible degrees from the most perfect to the most rudimentary. Could we deny such degrees of parasitism to the "ultravirus"? The perfect parasite has means of safeguarding its escape to the outside world. The sudden lysis of a bacterial cell and immediate escape of the lytic corpuscles would be interpreted, according to d'Herelle's view, as an instance of perfect parasitism on the part of the bacteriophage. But, if we accept this, we should not deny that there may also exist for the bacteriophage a type of parasitism so rudimentary that the agent is liberated only after the lapse of considerable time; or, it might be, after the death of the host cell. Under these conditions, the manifestations of sudden and vigorous lysis would be absent.

If we seek for some point of application for these views to the experimental data and observations presented in this paper and elsewhere, the first point that should be emphasized is that the assumed parasitism of the lytic corpuscles within the bodies of the bacteria does not cause the immediate destruction of the latter. Indeed, their death is not determined for a considerable time after the "invasion" has been accomplished. Multiplication of the bacteria—and a multiplication much faster than normal—occurs, and many generations of bacterial cells have time to develop before the majority succumb. We could therefore perhaps picture to ourselves a partition of the lytic corpuscles at the time when the division of the bacterial cell occurs, so that the daughter cells start their life possessing an "initial infection." It might furthermore be possible that this original infection is added to, through fresh, successive invasions; so that the assumed infective process would be, in a sense, cumulative in successive generations of bacterial cells. But we might assume equally that the intial infection does not menace the life of the cell, at least for some time; and perhaps, in some instances, not until the period of active growth has ceased. In such an assumed association of parasite and host amounting actually to a state of metabiosis, the mode of expression would, however, be expected to vary within wide limits, depending in part on the degree of adaptation of the host to its parasite and of the parasite to its host. Under such an assumption it would seem probable that more importance would need to be attached to the former; it would be the bacterium which, if it were to be saved, would be required to make the sacrifice of adaptation. This reaction, if successfully accomplished, would lead to greater tolerance, or even to complete resistance, next to be mentioned.

It is a common occurrence that a culture (such as the R-type of pyocyaneus) becomes "refractory"; it becomes resistant to lysis. The same phenomenon has been observed in the case of many other bacterial species under the lytic stimulus. Such resistant cultures must arise from the multiplication of resistant cells. In some species of bacteria (Shiga dysentery), such cells are comparatively rare, while in other cases (pyocyaneus) they are extremely common. In such instances, what might we assume has happened to the relation between the lytic corpuscles and the bacterial cells? One might at first be tempted to say that this "resistance" means that the bacterium has, in some unknown manner, prevented a threatened invasion by the lytic agent. But such a view would be readily contradicted by the observation that in such cultures the lytic agent is always present; and present in such amounts as compare favorably with sensitive cultures in the height of lysis. It therefore could not be said that resistant cultures owe their characteristic behavior to the circumstance that the bacterial cells comprising them are not invaded. The only logical alternative to this view would be that these cells, though infected, have undergone some change in the constitution of their cytoplasm by virtue of which they do not undergo lysis. It is certain that they do not dissolve, and there is ample evidence pointing to the fact that they are "modified" in several important respects, both morphologically and physiologically. What is also of interest in this connection is that such cultures never manifest the proliferative growth as a result of the inclusion of the lytic agent.

Still adhering to d'Herelle's point of view, these results might be interpreted best in the following manner: There has occurred in the cells of the resistant culture a degree of adaptation to the parasitic inclusions which amounts to a perfect metabiosis between the lytic agent and the bacterial cell. Each successive cell division, therefore, serves to perpetuate not only the bacterial strain, but also the bacteriophage infection. In many instances, and particularly in the R-type of pyocyaneus, this state of metabiosis would appear to be maintained over long periods of time, quite secure from disturbance on the part of the environment. In other cases, the association can be quite easily ruptured, and the previously resistant culture returns to the original condition of sensitivity.

Examining further the problem of susceptibility and resistance to lytic action from this point of view, there might be postulated at least three well marked states of association or relationship between the bacteriophage and the bacterial cell: [7]

1. Complete lack of adaptation on the part of the bacterium to the lytic agent. Here we would have a case of absolute susceptibility, as exemplified by the rapid lysis of the Shiga bacillus by the bacteriophage of the classical type. After a brief proliferative reaction (almost too slight to be regarded as

[7] It will be obvious that the formulation of these groups favors the ultravirus theory of the lytic agent no more than a chemical explanation.

significant) the mass of cells quickly succumbs to the attack. From the point of view of the ultravirus theory, there is established no metabiosis, but rather an antibiosis occurs. Resistant cultures are comparatively rare.

2. Partial adaptation on the part of the bacterium to the lytic agent. Here there would exist a partial susceptibility, as illustrated by the case of B. pyocyaneus, by the lysing air coccus and water coccus mentioned in this paper, and presumably by Twort's lysing coccus from vaccinia. In this type of association, many of the bacteria are destroyed, but the culture as a whole maintains itself, growing in the proliferative, lysogenic state. In the d'Herelle sense, this would be regarded as constituting a metabiosis, enduring for many bacterial generations, but leaning toward antibiosis in the final outcome. Resistant strains are, in most cases, easily formed.

3. Complete adaptation of the bacterium to the lytic agent. This would be shown by the resistant strains which "carry" the lytic agent but which manifest no susceptibility to lysis, as exemplified by the R-type of pyocyaneus and other species. In this case, there would be no injury to the cell, although it contains the lytic corpuscles. Although the bacteria are modified in many ways, there is no sign of proliferative growth. Employing the ultravirus theory, this instance would represent a perfect metabiosis, and would probably be found only in bacteria of the resistant type.

To the foregoing outline it should be added that, in addition to these 3 cases, regardless of their explanation, there appear to exist other intermediate states of lytic action. I have already studied briefly 2 other lysing cultures which might easily be regarded as standing between 1 and 2 above, and one culture as standing between 2 and 3. The 2 former were typical "suicide" cultures, one coming from the gastric mucosa of a rabbit, the other from a "spontaneous" rabbit abscess. The last type was also observed by Collins. These cultures, although attaining a luxuriant growth on slant agar during the 18 hours or so of the "proliferation stage," from that time on melted away again so that, at the end of about 30 hours, all that remained was a thin, glassy residue from which no, or few, living organisms could be cultivated. Both of these cultures were successfully cultivated for many generations on agar, and then were lost in a sudden burst of lysis. I was unable to obtain from them, or from the original source, the homologous, sensitive strain. The R-type of these cultures was, on the other hand, easily maintained.

I believe that it will be apparent from the considerations advanced in the preceding paragraphs that it is possible to make out as good a case for the transmissible lysis of pyocyaneus and the lysing air and water cocci mentioned in this paper as for the transmissible lysis of the Shiga dysentery bacillus, when it comes to the application of the d'Herelle ultravirus theory. This is not, however, the equivalent of saying that we must, at the present time, commit ourselves in either instance to a belief in the agency of an ultravirus. It simply means that we must extend the borders of the territory of transmissible autolysis to include these aberrant phenomena, and that they all must serve equally as legitimate subject matter for further inquiry. Although d'Herelle's explanation is the easiest one and the most obvious, it cannot yet be said that all other avenues are closed to the study of this complex phenomenon.

CONCLUSION

Although colony proliferation, as observed in cultures in the lysogenic state, is in harmony with d'Herelle's conception of the lytic agent as an ultravirus, certain well recognized instances should not be overlooked in which cell proliferations appear to arise under the influence of other stimuli, both mechanical and chemical. Among the latter might be especially mentioned incomplete combustion products—soot, creosote and tar—as cause of cancer of the testicle; also the cancer of guano workers, lead workers, arsenic workers, workers with distillation products, such as naphthol and anilin. All of these substances are believed to determine marked proliferations. In addition, one might mention the very old observation of Raulin on the peculiarly stimulating influence of zinc on Aspergillus. We cannot, therefore, safely regard the stimulus to excess growth as related exclusively to the influence of the ultraviruses, and must conclude that while proliferation in bacterial colonies under the lytic stimulus is in harmony with the ultravirus theory, it is by no means to be regarded even as a partial proof of this hypothesis. Indeed it may furnish equal support to the view of causation by a chemical agent.

Aside from the presentation of the data on proliferative growth of bacterial colonies, I regard what else I have said only in the light of an attempt to frame a more satisfactory working hypothesis for the broader study of the lytic phenomenon. Leaving aside the matter of the explanation of the lytic action, I believe there is ample evidence to convince us that transmissible bacterial autolysis is a phenomenon far less restricted in its manifestations and much more complex in its mechanism than d'Herelle, through the presentation of his few, well-chosen and clean-cut cases, would have us believe. It is obvious that the sort of cases which he admits to the sanctum of the bacteriophage are only those which have been brought into high relief through the compelling example of clear-cut lysis and inhibition. If, however, the phenomenon of transmissible lysis, due to an ultravirus, exists at all, it must be a thing of wide occurrence in the bacterial world and not limited in its manifestations to the narrow circle which, up to the present moment, d'Herelle has prescribed. And it is not, I believe, until this conception is more widely recognized and the "aberrant" and excluded instances of bacterial autolysis studied as vigorously as the formal examples (which, at the present time, tend to comprise the exclusive subject matter of research) that we shall arrive at a full understanding of the bacteriophage and the actual mechanism of the lytic phenomenon.

SUMMARY

This paper points out that abnormally rapid growth (proliferation) is frequently observed in bacterial colonies under the influence of the lytic agent. Moreover, although such proliferations may be regarded as analogous to those seen in the tissues of plants and animals experiencing an infection with an ultravirus, similar proliferation may also result from mechanical and chemical stimuli. The observations reported, therefore, while in harmony with d'Herelle's conception of the bacteriophage as an ultravirus, cannot serve as proof of this view.

The observations reported are also used as the point of departure for formulating certain modifications in d'Herelle's view which would make possible a correlation between his cases and a class of instances at present excluded by him from what he regards as the legitimate field of lytic action.

It is concluded that the phenomenon of transmissible bacterial autolysis is widespread in the bacterial world; and that, although d'Herelle's hypothesis offers the easiest and most obvious explanation of the problem, we should not yet close our eyes to other possible avenues of approach.

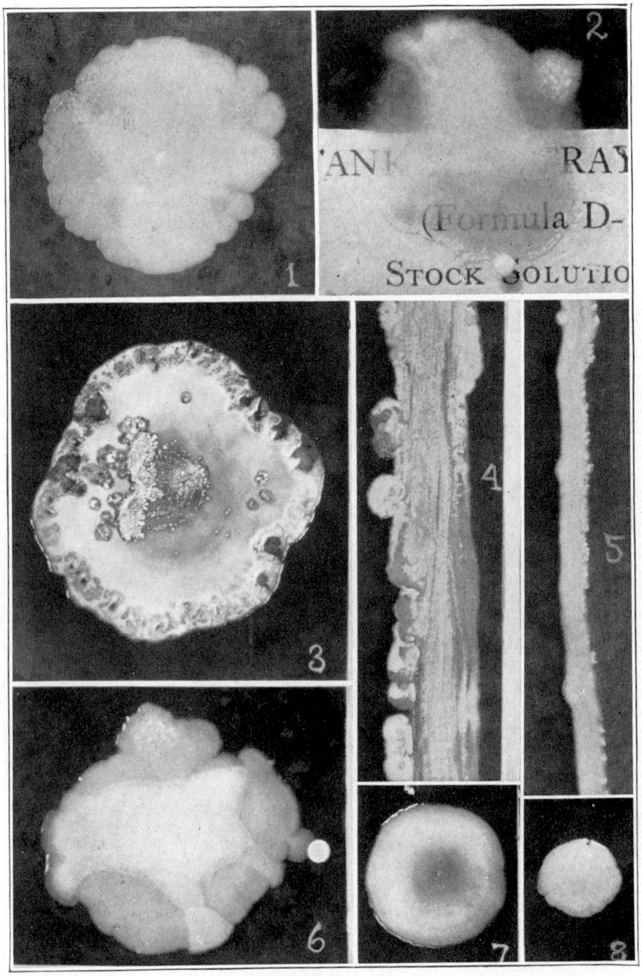

DESCRIPTION OF PLATE 1

Fig. 1.—Showing a plate colony of the lysing coccus from air in the early stage of lysis. Actual size, about 18 mm.

Fig. 2.—Showing the same colony in an advanced stage of lysis. Size, about 26 mm. The print on a strip of paper placed under the Petri dish can be seen through the margin of the body of the colony and the agar substratum.

Fig. 3.—Lysing and proliferating colony of B. pyocyaneus showing lytic areas and erosions. Actual size, about 55 mm.

Fig. 4.—Section of streak of lytic culture of B. pyocyaneus, showing proliferation and areas of lysis. Actual breadth at widest point, about 15 mm.

Fig. 5.—Section of streak of resistant culture of B. pyocyaneus, showing non-proliferative growth. Actual breadth of streak, about 4 mm.

Fig. 6.—Same colony as in figures 1 and 2, showing proliferative growth and intermediate stage in lysis. Small colonies appear on upper right margin. Actual size, about 22 mm.

Fig. 7.—Showing resistant colony of B. pyocyaneus. Actual size, about 22 mm.

Fig. 8.—Showing normal colony of the lysing air coccus with non-proliferative growth. Actual size, about 8 mm.

THE ANTIGENIC PROPERTIES OF TISSUE FIBRINOGEN

Cornelia M. Downs

From the Department of Bacteriology, University of Kansas, Lawrence.

In a series of papers Mills and his co-workers [1] described the physiological action and chemical nature of tissue fibrinogen. This substance seemed to be identical with the protein phospholipin compound described by Wooldridge. It is an active coagulant, widely distributed in the tissues. The lung appears to be most richly supplied with it, then the kidneys, testes, brain, heart and skin in the order named, with skeletal muscle, the pancreas and the liver possessing only small amounts. The active material appears to be a protein phospholipin compound which can be precipitated at the iso-electric point without loss of its coagulating activity.

As far as we can determine, no studies have been made of the antigenic properties of this coagulant, and accordingly this study was undertaken.

Swine and beef lungs were freed as nearly as possible from bronchi and blood vessels. They were then ground and soaked in two changes of water for 48 hours to remove as much blood as possible. This material was then dried rapidly and extracted with salt solution in the proportion of 4 c c. of solution to 1 gm. of lung. This proportion gives a saturated extract, according to Mills. This extract was then made N/500 acid by adding N/50 sulphuric acid. A light flocculent precipitate came down rapidly. This was allowed to settle in the icebox over night, and the supernatant fluid was siphoned off. The precipitate was then washed twice in N/500 H_2SO_4, each time being allowed to settle in the icebox. The precipitate could be easily dissolved by adding 2% salt solution to make a 1% solution and alkalinizing to P_H 8. This precipitation was repeated twice, and the final solution was used for tests and for the injections.

Ground kidney and liver were precipitated in the same way. Mills has shown that liver extracts have much slighter coagulating power than kidney extracts but that the protein fractions from both organs seem to be identical. The liver coagulants appear to differ from the kidney and lung coagulants in their phospholipin content.

Received for publication, Jan. 20, 1925.

[1] J. Biol. Chem., 1919, 40, p. 425; 1921, 46, pp. 135 and 167; Am. J. Physiol., 1921, 57, p. 395; 1923, 64, p. 160.

These purified liver and kidney extracts were found to be active coagulants before being used.

Since these coagulants cause intravascular clotting, it was necessary to inject rabbits intraperitoneally, and 10 c c. were injected every 2 or 3 days until 60 c c. had been given. The rabbit was then tested 4 days after the last injection. Frequently, it was necessary to give a second series of injections. It was found difficult to prepare an antiserum reaching higher than 1 : 250 or 1 : 500, but finally several were obtained reacting at 1 : 5,000. The material seemed to be toxic, as a number of the animals died, and all became much emaciated.

Several antiserums were prepared from swine and beef lungs, and in addition an antiserum was prepared by injecting beef serum into a rabbit.

TABLE 1

Precipitin Reactions with Serum Against Tissue Fibrinogen of Beef Lung

Antigens	Antiserum	
	Untreated	After Absorption with Same Quantity of Beef Serum 1:200
Beef lung	5,000	5,000
Beef kidney	2,000	1,000
Beef liver	2,000	500
Beef serum	3,000	No precipitation
Swine lung	50	
Swine serum	No precipitation	

The figures give the highest dilution of antigen with which definite precipitate resulted.

The precipitin reaction was made in the usual way by layering the serial dilutions of antigen over the antiserum in small vials. A positive reaction consisted of a definite cloudy ring after standing at room temperature one hour and a flocculent precipitate after shaking and standing over night (table 1).

Presumably the reaction with beef serum was due to traces of serum proteins precipitated with the coagulant. After absorption of the antiserum with equal parts of beef serum 1 : 200, the precipitins for beef serum were removed completely (table 1).

These results seem to show that beef lung contains a protein distinct from serum proteins and that beef liver and beef kidney contain proteins immunologically identical with the lung proteins.

The reactions of antiswine lung serum with swine lung, swine kidney, swine liver, swine serum and beef lung extracts were similar to those obtained with the beef preparations. After absorption with swine serum, reactions still occurred with swine lung, liver and kidney extracts. No reactions were obtained using antiswine or antibeef serum against human or dog extracts and serum. Antibeef serum, however, reacted with sheep antigens in the same titer as the beef antigens. This result bears out the close relationship between these animals. No explanation of the slight reaction obtained with antibeef lung serum and swine lung is ventured at this time.

An antiserum prepared by the injection of beef serum into a rabbit reacted at 1 : 10,000 with beef serum and at 1 : 100 only with beef lung preparation. We interpret this as due to serum proteins present in the lung extracts.

It might be reasonable to expect that a serum containing antibodies against the active tissue coagulant might lengthen the normal clotting time of blood. In two of the injected rabbits, a slight lengthening of the clotting time was observed. However, when the immune rabbit serum was added to normal recalcified beef plasma or to normal rabbit plasma, no lengthening of clotting time could be noted. The antibodies present apparently did not interfere with the normal clotting process.

Wells [2] has given a comprehensive review of the evidence which shows that specificity resides in the chemical structure of the protein molecule. Hektoen and his coworkers,[3] Wells and Osborne,[4] Bayne-Jones and Wilson,[5] Menne [6] and others have demonstrated the existence of a number of proteins which are antigenically distinct from serum proteins. The work now reported apparently adds to the list another protein which is chemically and antigenically distinct from serum protein. It is interesting that it exhibits practically no species specificity in its physiologic reaction in blood clotting but that antigenically it is highly species specific. Mills [1] considers that the activity of this coagulant is due chiefly to the ability of its phospholipin fraction to unite through calcium with blood fibrinogen. If the antigenic property resides in the protein fraction, this lack of correlation between the physiologic and antigenic properties is quite understandable. Hektoen in his work on hemoglobin has shown that this substance although similar in its physiologic activity in the different species, nevertheless exhibits species specificity to a high degree in its antigenic properties.

[2] Jour. Immunol., 1924, 9, p. 291.

[3] Jour. Am. Med. Assn., 1923, 80, pp. 81 and 386; 1924, 83, p. 300; Jour. Infect. Dis., 1922, 31, p. 72; 1923, 32, p. 167, and 33, p. 224.

[4] Jour. Infect. Dis., 1921, 29, p. 200.

[5] Bull. Johns Hopkins Hosp., 1922, 23, pp. 119 and 385.

[6] Jour. Infect. Dis., 1922, 31, p. 455.

We have noted that tissue fibrinogen is not highly antigenic. Mills found it impossible to sensitize guinea-pigs with his preparation. Two of our rabbits, however, showed the Arthus phenomenon.

CONCLUSIONS

A protein which is an active blood coagulant and which has antigenic properties distinct from the serum antigens can be precipitated from lung extracts.

Proteins that are chemically and antigenically identical with the lung protein can be isolated from liver and kidney extracts.

These proteins show species specificity in their antigenic properties but not in their action in blood clotting.

STUDY OF YEASTS FROM HUMAN SOURCES

Jane F. Peckham

From Laboratory of Pathology and Bacteriology, Rhode Island State Board of Health, Providence

The frequency with which yeasts appear in diagnostic cultures led to their isolation and study with the view of identifying them and determining their significance.

Beer wort agar, serum water containing Andrade indicator, gelatin, and litmus milk were used for the study of cultures of yeast. All mediums were titrated to P_H 7.4. Guinea-pigs were injected because they were found susceptible to yeast infection. Cultures were grown for 24 hours on blood serum slants; each slant was washed with 10 c c. of salt solution, and injection made into the groin with 0.5 c c. of this emulsion. When the yeast was pathogenic, an abscess appeared in the groin in from 3 to 5 days. From such abscesses, the yeasts were recovered in pure cultures. In animals with abscesses in the groin, abscesses were found after death in the pancreas, liver, spleen and omentum.

The results are briefly:

1. Fifty-one cultures were isolated, 41 of which were pathogenic and 10 not.

2. Twenty-five were from the throat, 23 of which were pathogenic and 2 not; 19 from infants' mouths, 14 pathogenic and 5 not; 6 from sputum, 4 pathogenic and 2 not; and 1, nonpathogenic, from the vagina.

3. Forty-five were monilia, 38 of which were pathogenic and 7 not; 5 oidia, 3 pathogenic and 2 not; and 1 nonpathogenic saccharomyces.

4. Among the 51 cultures were 10 different strains of monilia, 3 of oidia, and 1 of saccharomyces; 25 of the cultures belong to one strain of monilia.

YEAST 45

Yeast 45 was chosen as a typical pathogenic yeast for experimental work. Two pure cultures were isolated from a severe sore throat infection within an interval of 3 days.

It grows best at body temperature and most luxuriantly after being recovered from an inoculated animal. After 2 weeks' growth, it forms no membrane on beer wort slants, produces acid and gas in dextrose,

Received for publication, Jan. 25, 1925.

levulose and maltose, acid in saccharose and galactose, and no acid or gas in lactose, dextrin or inulin. After repeated transplanting, it no longer gives acid in saccharose and galactose. It does not liquefy gelatin, and causes no change in litmus milk. The size and shape of the cell varies depending on the medium and the tissue of the animal body. It is 5-6 microns in diameter and perfectly round, with a distinct capsule in sections from the kidney. In the gall-bladder, it is a large elliptical cell, 4-5 by 8-12 microns. The elliptical forms give rise to a few septate mycelia on solid medium and to many in liquid. The yeast cells are gram-positive in young cultures, gram-negative in old cultures and all shapes and sizes from 3 to 12 microns in diameter. On solid medium in young cultures, multiplication takes place by budding; in liquid medium and old cultures, by budding and by lateral and terminal chyamydospores.

According to Castellani's classification of yeast, this organism most resembles Monilia pinoys (Castellani 1910) which was isolated from sputum, but differs from the latter in producing acid in galactose and saccharose. No yeast that has been fully described has been found at the present time which is identical with yeast 45.

Changes in the Blood.—An emulsion of a 24-hour culture of yeast 45 grown on blood serum slants was injected intravenously into rabbits in various quantities. Leukocyte counts and cultures were made of blood taken from the ear vein at points distal to that of injection. There were 24 days between the 1st and 2d injections of rabbit 3 and 33 between the 2d and 3rd. Rabbit 5 received 4 intraperitoneal injections with increasing doses of dead yeast and 3 with live, followed by 2 intravenous injections with live at an interval of 21 days.

From the study of blood smears made hourly during the first 24 hours after injection, it was found that the lowest percentage of lymphocytes and the highest of amphophils came within this period, the more immune the animal, the earlier this point was reached. The leukocyte count was found to be as low as 3,000, and the increase in the percentage of amphophils to be due to a disappearance of lymphocytes. This lymphopenia sometimes persisted for 48 hours. When the count rose between 12 and 24 hours after injection into rabbits which showed only a moderate reaction, the rise was due to a real increase in the number of amphophils. In all the rabbits after the 3rd day, the amphophils were increased appreciably more than the lymphocytes unless the new mononuclears, which will be described, appeared. The count never rose as high as one would have expected it to from the number of abscesses found at necropsy.

A constant feature of the blood smears was an increase in endothelial cells. Protoplasmic processes extended out from some of them and to others platelets were attached by barely visible threads as if they were just breaking loose. In the blood of rabbits which showed a severe reaction or died, a large atypical mononuclear appeared. The nucleus with Wright's stain was reddish purple, and the cytoplasm, in the majority of cells, the deep blue of a lymphocyte.

but in a few it was the pale purple of an amphophil. Vacuoles were often found in the cytoplasm. As the percentage of such cells rose, the nuclei grew indistinct and stained poorly. The cytoplasm became packed with eosinophilic and basophilic granules, large and small. In smears stained with Goodpasture's

TABLE 1

TYPICAL DIFFERENTIAL BLOOD COUNTS

Rabbits	Amount Injected C c.	Days after Injection	Lymphocytes	Endothelial Cells	Basophils	Nucleated Red Cells	Amphophils‡	New Cells
Normal*	...	...	45-55%	2-8%	4-8%	..	40-50%	
2	0.5	Start	47	5	5	—	42	
		1	8	9	2	—	81	
		2	18	17	8	—	57	
		3	29	14	3	—	54	
		4	36	10	3	9	40	
		6	37	11	2	3	47	
		7	28	12	1	4	32	23%
		8 Died						
3	0.2	Start	71	5	6	—	18	
		1	18	2	2	1	77	
		2	37	1	4	2	55	
		4	47	9	4	—	36	
		5	53	7	5	—	34	
		6	47	13	5	2	33	
		7	52	5	5	—	36	
		8	51	10	6	—	32	
		11	40	10	8	—	42	
2	0.5	Start	61	—	7	—	32	
		1	15	10	5	—	70	
		2	28	16	2	—	54	
		3	50	9	4	2	35	
		4	37	16	2	2	43	
		5	47	10	2	1	40	
		7	32	12	4	—	49	
		9	57	4	3	—	36	
		10	57	4	2	—	37	
3	0.5	Start	66	5	6	—	23	
		1	10	4	—	—	80	6%
		2 Died						
5	0.3#	Start	34	7	10	—	49	
		1	15	2	6	—	77	
		2	16	22	2	—	18	42
		3	15	26	3	—	2	49
		4	17	12	5	—	16	50
		5	9	10	5	—	4	72
		6 Died						

* Taken from paper by Walter R. Brinckerhoff and E. E. Tyzzer, Jour. Med. Res., 1902, 2, p. 173.

‡ An amphophil in the blood of a rabbit corresponds to the polymorphonuclear cell in human blood.

Second intravenous injection; see page 8 for record of previous injections.

oxidase stain, these cells failed to show any granules, indicating that they were of lymphatic origin. It was found, however, that they took up yeast cells, and it was concluded to regard them as atypical endothelial cells.

The basophils remained the same in number after injection as in normal blood, but the decrease in the number of lymphocytes made the percentage of basophils appear higher. When the lymphocytes or amphophils had been increased, the basophils, remaining normal in number, were decreased in percentage.

There was a marked increase in the platelets appearing 2 hours after injection and lasting for at least 10 days. A secondary anemia, in which the red cells show a marked poikilocytosis, achromia and polychromatophilia, developed soon after injection. The spleen or bone marrow appeared to be stimulated to throw into the blood stream immature nucleated red cells of the normoblast type. Sections of the bone marrow showed foci of necrosis containing encapsulated yeast cells.

Many "basket" cells were found. The presence of these cells, the appearance in such numbers of large mononuclear cells resembling endothelial cells, the number of basophils, the increase in platelets and in basophilic and eosinophilic granules in all cells except the lymphocytes, gave the smears the appearance of acute leukemia. This was particularly true of blood smears from two animals in which the leukocyte count rose to over 40,000. The whole vascular system seemed to be stimulated by the yeast cells and their metabolic products.

Yeast Cells in Blood and Tissues.—The method of watching the effect of blood on yeast cells was as follows: Large loops of a 24-hour culture of yeast were emulsified in 2 c c. of salt solution with 2% sodium citrate. Rabbit 3, which was being immunized, was bled from the ear vein. To the blood an equal amount of the yeast emulsion was added immediately and the 2 thoroughly mixed. About 0.1 c c. of this mixture was drawn into each of several sterile capillary tubes, which were then sealed off and incubated. One tube was broken each hour for 12 hours, the blood forced out on a clean glass slide, a smear made and stained with Wright's stain.

From the study of the smears, it was found that the amphophil ingested one yeast cell after another until it contained from 2 to 3 distinct cells. The endothelial cell did likewise but more slowly. Even red blood cells were found which contained this organism, although they were rare. Finally, conditions became favorable for growth, and the yeast cell began to bud and send out mycelium. The leukocyte became indistinct in outline, lost its staining properties, and finally only a red hazy reticulum was left. The nucleus of the leukocyte, which at the ingestion of the yeast cell, was crowded out to one side, appeared to have been absorbed by the yeast. The yeast cell, which at first had a distinct wall enclosing it, was round, and stained a clear homogeneous blue, had taken on again its variations of shape, showed buds and mycelia and stained a bluish purple containing many fine granules.

In all the blood smears examined, no yeast cells were found, but from the same blood pure cultures of them were obtained. An inch of the marginal vein in a rabbit's ear was clamped off with paper clips and 0.5 c c. of yeast emulsion was injected into this part of the vein. Every 2 minutes for 16 minutes the ear vein was pricked and a smear made. From the smears it was found that the yeast cell, free in the blood stream for 4 minutes, stained an even indigo blue and took on a round form with a distinct cell wall. Platelets congregated around the yeast cells, and in 6 minutes completely surrounded the latter, which had become granular and took a purple stain the same as the platelets, except the nucleus, which was still indigo blue. The endothelial cells had begun to take up yeast cells, and in 12 minutes were so broken down as to be hardly recognizable, and together with ingested yeast cells had so changed in H-ion concentration that parts of both took the eosin of Wright's stain. Masses of platelets, the centers of which were cells shaped like yeasts but stained like platelets, were packed around the degenerating endothelial cells.

From this picture it appeared that the platelets either had collectively the same function of phagocytosis that the amphophils and endothelial cells exhibited individually, or they were the offsprings of the disintegrating endothelial cells. They increased as the endothelial cells decreased. In the animals that had received injections, the atypical endothelial cell that appeared may have been the result of an attempt of the body to produce enough endothelial cells to overcome the yeast infection, because the greater the immunity the higher the percentage of these cells.

In citrated blood, the yeast cells were ingested chiefly by the amphophils; in the blood stream, by the endothelial cells.

In the examination of the tissues from rabbits, the same difficulty was found in identfying yeast cells as in the blood. If the body of a rabbit lay 12 hours before it was examined, the yeast cells could be demonstrated in the smears from the organs. In the living animal, they had a form which made it impossible to recognize them by ordinary methods of staining; but in an animal dead a certain length of time, they again assumed the shape they have in cultures.

Immunization.—Rabbit 3 received 3 intravenous injections of live yeast emulsion, one of 0.2 c c. and two of 0.5 c c. at intervals of 3 and 4 weeks, respectively.

Rabbit 5, at intervals of 3 or 4 days, received 5 intraperitoneal injections of dead yeasts followed by 3 of live in quantities increasing from 0.5 c c. to 1.5 c c. These injections were followed by 2 intravenous injections with 0.2 c c. and 0.5 c c., respectively, of live yeasts at an interval of 21 days.

Guinea-pig 457 received at intervals of 3 or 4 days, 5 injections into the peritoneal cavity and groin with dead yeasts, 3 with live yeasts and 2 more with dead yeasts in quantities varying from 0.5 c c. to 1.0 c c., depending on the physical condition of the pig.

Guinea-pig 458 received injections in the same manner as guinea-pig 457; both were bled from the heart on the same day and guinea-pig 457 died; guinea-pig 458 then received 3 more injections with dead yeasts and 2 with live yeasts as previously.

Guinea-pigs 3 and 6 received 2 injections of live yeasts into the right and left groins, respectively, and 2 of dead yeasts into the peritoneal cavity, each at intervals of 5 days.

The rabbits were bled from the ear vein or heart and the guinea-pigs from the heart. The opsonic, agglutination and fixation tests were made. The highest titer of immune serum was obtained in rabbits by giving, first, intraperitoneal injections of increasing doses of dead yeasts with an interval of 3 days between the successive injections; then, by repeating with live yeasts; and finally, by giving small intravenous injections of dead and live yeasts, determining the periods between injections by the disappearance of albumin from the urine.

Opsonic Index.—Wright's method of determining an opsonic index was followed, except that 2% sodium citrate in salt solution was used instead of 1%, and the incubation period was increased to 1 hour because it was found that it took leukocytes longer to take up yeast cells than bacteria. The percentage of leukocytes that ingested yeast cells and the number of yeast cells that a leukocyte engulfed were both increased. In the blood of a rabbit being immunized, the phagocytic behavior of the endothelial cells described earlier in this paper was markedly increased. One cell was found that contained 9 distinct yeast cells, no one of which could be identified as a bud of any other. The opsonic index showed an increase before agglutination or fixation could be obtained.

Agglutination.—For agglutination, an emulsion of yeasts containing approximately 1 million cells per c c. was used. No difference was found in results whether live or killed yeasts were used, and the killed (0.5% phenol) were chosen for routine work. The tubes containing decreasing quantities of serum were kept 4 hours in the water bath and over night in the icebox. Tests of the blood of rabbit 3 after its 1st and 2d inoculation, and of 3 guinea-pigs after 1 inoculation of live yeasts into the groin gave no results. The first positive test was obtained with rabbit 3 after its 3rd intravenous injection.

Fixation.—The antigen was an emulsion of yeasts containing 1 million cells per c c. killed with 0.5% phenol. The period of the 1st incubation, before sheep cells were added, was changed from 35 minutes to 1 hour, because a longer one was found to be necessary with the yeast antigen than in the Wassermann test.

Metabolic Changes.—In the necropsies of animals that had received injections of yeasts the pancreas was found to be changed, and animals being immunized were put into metabolism cages, and the urine examined every morning. Blood counts and differential smears were made in the rabbits.

From the results, it appeared that the guinea-pigs had developed diabetes. The urine reduced Fehling's, Benedict's and Nylander's solutions. It was found by use of the polariscope, by fermentation tests with yeast, and the phenol hydrazine reaction that this reduction was due to sugar. On a diet containing 30 gm. of glucose or its equivalent a day, sugar appeared 3 days after injection in the slightest possible traces in the urine of most of the animals and increased to 10-12% in 2 weeks. In some cases, it did not appear until after a 2d or 3rd injection. The quantitative blood sugar of the same animals showed an increase of about 100% over the normal, 0.07-0.14% being the normal. On a sugar-free diet, the sugar in the urine disappeared; replacing it in the diet, it reappeared in the urine. When the guinea-pigs had no sugar in the urine or only a slight amount, the blood sugar was decreased. The tests for acetone and diacetic acid were positive, indicating acidosis. There appeared to be no correlation between the development of immunity and the appearance of glycosuria.

Intraperitoneal injections with live and dead yeasts in the rabbits caused no change in the sugar and albumin content of the urine but a rise in the percentage of amphophils. Intravenous injections lowered the leukocyte count and increased the percentage of amphophils by decreasing the percentage of lymphocytes. At the same time, a marked albuminuria appeared.

Changes Found After Death.—In rabbits in the acute stage of infection with yeasts, the surface of the liver and cross sections were mottled with granular, yellowish areas, 1-2 mm. in diameter. The tissue, stained with methylene blue and eosin, showed a widespread central and focal necrosis, confined chiefly to the portal areas. The kidneys were 4 times normal size and the cortex contained many miliary abscesses. In sections, a tubular and infectious nephritis was found. Some of the lungs contained areas of congestion, 0.5-1 mm. in diameter. The suprarenals, heart, and spleen were enlarged. Small microscopic foci of necrosis, well walled off by proliferating fibroblasts, were located in the bone, marrow, myocardium, pancreas, and spleen. Pure cultures of yeasts were isolated from all the tissues.

In the chronic stage in rabbits, the liver, the smoothness of the surface of which was broken by hard white nodules, 0.4-1 cm. in diameter, showed a marked scirrhosis; the kidneys, which were twice normal size, areas of sclerosis replacing the acute lesions; the lungs, congestion; and the spleen, fibrosis. No yeasts were recovered.

In guinea-pigs in the acute stage of infection abscesses, 0.3-1 mm. in diameter, were found; in the groin, always one; in the pancreas and liver, usually one or more; in the mesentery, when peritonitis developed, multiple abscesses with adhesions between the liver, the stomach, the pancreas, the right suprarenal and the kidney, and between the pancreas to the stomach and the spleen. Any one of these abscesses consisted of a center of necrosis surrounded successively by zones of polymorphonuclear cells, of infiltrating endothelial cells and foreign body giant cells, and of rapidly proliferating fibroblasts and congested capillaries. Yeasts were recovered from every abscess.

TABLE 2

RESULTS OF IMMUNE REACTIONS

	Opsonic Index	Agglutinin Titer	Fixation
Rabbit 3	3.4	1:20	4+
Rabbit 5	5.9	1:320	4+
Guinea-pig 457	...	1:160	4+
Guinea-pig 458	...	1:20	±
Guinea-pig 3	...	1:40	1+
Guinea-pig 6	...	1:10	Negative

In the chronic stage in guinea-pigs, changes occurred along the margin of the liver. In place of the pancreas, a hard nodular mass was found. Sections showed that the proliferation of fibroblasts in the abscesses had led to an atrophy of the acini and islands of Langerhans and a consequent hypertrophy and hyperplasia of the remaining tissue. The spleen in both acute and chronic stages contained a proliferation of endothelial cells. No yeasts were recovered.

DISCUSSION

The literature on pathogenic yeasts is so scattered and fragmentary that it is hard to identify the cultures isolated from infectious sources. The best classification of the yeasts existing at the present time is Castellani's and Chalmer's [1] which is based on carbohydrate fermentation. This is not entirely satisfactory, because experience in growing yeasts has taught that the results of fermentation tests with the same

[1] Manual Trop. Med., 1919, p. 1081.

culture will not agree, if the H-ion concentration of the medium, the length or the temperature of incubation is varied. Hines [2] attempted a classification based on agglutination, but found that there was no absolute degree of specificity between sprue yeasts, wild yeasts, and blastomycetes. A satisfactory complement-fixation test for yeast can be made, and it is being tried as the basis of a new classification of pathogenic yeasts.

Busse [3] showed experimentally that Saccharomycosis hominis, which he isolated from an infected tibia of a woman, was the cause of that lesion and had led to metastatic nodules in the lungs, spleen and kidneys. Thrush, sprue, blastomycosis of the lungs simulating tuberculosis, and blastomycetic dermatitis are recognized as being caused by pathogenic yeasts. Castellani and Chalmers, working in the tropics, have isolated 21 kinds of Monilia from cases of bronchomycosis, 5 from sprue, 5 from thrush and allied infections, and 6 from vaginal discharge.

The lesions produced in animals by different kinds of pathogenic fungi do not seem to vary as much as the morphologic and biochemical characteristics of these organisms. Busse found metastatic growths resembling sarcoma in the animals he inoculated with Saccharomycosis hominis. Hektoen [4] described the lesion in experimental animals caused by a yeast isolated from a case of blastomycosis dermatitis as "necrotic and leucotactic, associated with or followed by a growth of inflammatory granulation tissue." Wolbach [5] wrote about the lesions of Sporotrichum councilmani, "At the periphery of the lesions fibroblast proliferation becomes active. Early lesions therefore consist of a central mass of polymorphonuclear leucocytes, endothelial cells and giant cells surrounded by a zone of fibroblasts." The tumor-like growths in the pancreas, the peritonitis accompanied by foci of necrosis in the liver, and the abscesses in the groins of guinea-pigs injected with yeast 45, each resemble the lesions described, respectively, by Busse, Hektoen, and Wolbach.

SUMMARY AND CONCLUSION

Fifty-one cultures of yeasts from throat infections, bronchitis, stomatitis, and vaginitis were identified.

Forty-one of the cultures were pathogenic, producing abscesses in guinea-pigs; ten, nonpathogenic.

[2] Jour. Infect. Dis., 1924, 34, p. 529.
[3] Kolle and Wassermann: Handb. d. path. Mikroorganismen, 1903, 1, p. 661.
[4] Jour. of Exper. Med., 1899, 4, p. 261.
[5] Jour. Med. Res., 1917, 36, p. 337.

One of the pathogenic yeasts, isolated from a throat culture and injected into animals, causes a lymphopenia; induces the formation of antibodies; is toxic in systemic effect; produces localized lesions that are characterized by necrosis, by an infiltration of endothelial cells which fuse to form giant cells, and by a proliferation of fibroblastic tissue so marked in the pancreas that the islands of Langerhans may be obliterated and a consequent glycosuria developed.

From the effect of yeasts on the blood and tissues of animals, it seems possible that they may become additional etiologic factors in infections caused primarily by other organisms. Yeast infections in guinea-pigs may be of service in the study of experimental diabetes.

THE USE OF RABBITS IN THE STUDY OF INFECTIOUS ABORTION

B. L. WARWICK, E. M. GILDOW AND F. B. HADLEY
From the Department of Veterinary Science, University of Wisconsin, Madison

The experimental study of infectious abortion of cattle and swine is beset with many difficulties. Unexposed susceptible animals of these species are difficult to obtain. When such animals are obtained, experience has shown that it is difficult to keep the experimental and control groups under comparable environmental conditions without the infection spreading to the control group.[1] The long gestation periods of these animals limit the accumulation of data to the extent that it often requires several years to complete one project. The cost of the animals, their feed and care, and the cost of the equipment over this long period of time makes such experimental work very expensive.

To obviate these difficulties, small animals have been used extensively in the study of infectious abortion. Probably guinea-pigs have been used more widely for this purpose than any other species. The reasons for their selection are that they are susceptible to infection with Bact. abortus and developed specific lesions,[2] so they are of the greatest value for diagnostic purposes.[3]

We have found rabbits more resistant to Bact. abortus than guinea-pigs. They rarely pick up the organisms to a sufficient degree by cohabitation to cause an agglutination reaction even in 1 : 50 dilution of serum to antigen. When they are given intraperitoneal inoculations with different strains of the organism they usually develop a wider range of lesions than do guinea-pigs.

A few investigators have reported successful attempts to produce abortion in pregnant guinea-pigs and rabbits.[4] Rabbits would seem better adapted to this use than guinea-pigs, because they are not so susceptible to naturally acquired infection, and because they show more

Received for publication, Feb. 12, 1925.

[1] Birch, R. R., and Gilman, H. L.: N. Y. State Vet. College Rep., Cornell University, 1922-3.

[2] Smillie, E. W.: Jour. Exper. Med., 1918, 28, p. 585. Hagan, W. A.: Ibid., 1922, 36, p. 697. Surface, F. M.: Ibid., 1912, 11, p. 464.

[4] Bang, B.: Ztschr. f. Thiermed., 1897, 1, p. 241. Nowak, J.: Ann. de l'Inst. Pasteur, 1908, 22, p. 541.

[3] Schroeder, E. C., and Cotton, W. E.: Jour. Am. Vet. Assn., 1924, 64, p. 479.

differences in susceptibility to individual strains of the organism. Also, the short gestation period of 30 days makes it possible to secure results in a much shorter time. Consequently, we have concluded that if rabbits can be used successfully, the main difficulties encountered in using large animals will be in a large measure overcome.

It is in an attempt to answer the following questions that the work herein described has been carried out:

1. Will an apparently virulent strain of Bact. abortus produce abortion in rabbits?
2. If so, can the organism be recovered from the aborted fetuses?
3. What is the incubation period of Bact. abortus in rabbits?
4. How early in pregnancy can abortion be produced?
5. How late in pregnancy can abortion be produced?
6. Can a routine procedure be developed to secure this information?

METHODS

The intraperitoneal method of inoculation was chosen as most suitable. The dose in the earlier experiments was 0.25 c c. of the same density as that of standard agglutination test fluid. The disappearing loop method was used to standardize the inoculum. One apparently virulent porcine strain of Bact. abortus (Wis. 93) was used in this study. Later 0.5 c c. doses were used.

It was found that pregnancy could not be diagnosed by trying back the females after breeding, since many does would take the buck even when pregnant. Therefore, the following schemes were tried. The doe was bred for a normal litter, allowed to litter and then immediately bred again. However, the nursing litter interfered with the desirability of making the experimental inoculation. Then killing the normal litter at birth was tried, but little advantage was found over letting them nurse and rebreeding at or near weaning time.

No breeding test or procedure has been found by which pregnancy in the doe can be diagnosed earlier than about the 14th day. With experience, we have been able to diagnose pregnancy by palpation of the abdomen with a high degree of accuracy at 14 days and beyond. The nodules of the uterus can be distinguished from other parts of the adbominal viscera by palpation.

Some does were inoculated in the early stages and no aborted fetuses, or any normal litters, at the end of the gestation period, were observed. That some does aborted and ate the aborted fetuses seem certain. To avoid this difficulty, false bottoms of wire netting of 1 inch mesh were built, which could be placed in the cages. The does were placed on these false bottoms after being inoculated, and kept there until they aborted or approached within a day of the end of the gestation period. The value of this contrivance is that when abortion occurs the fetuses drop through the wire netting, which prevents their being molested by the doe.

The frame of the false bottom is so built that there is a space of 4 inches between the floor of the cage and the false bottom. A hayrack in the back of the cage, placed high enough to prevent the doe getting into it, is necessary to keep the hay off the wire. Water and grain are supplied in crocks not more than 5 inches in diameter. This precaution is necessary to keep the doe from littering in the containers.

We have found that abortion takes place occasionally in rabbits which are not infected. To determine the breeding capacity of the doe, we believe it desirable that she has had at least one normal litter before the inoculation.

Ten does were inoculated before these precautions had been worked out. Only one can be recorded positively as having aborted and in this case, since the doe had been bred more than once, the day of conception cannot be stated definitely.

After the importance of the false bottom was realized, the following routine, with few exceptions, was followed with each rabbit:

1. The doe was bred, and, if necessary, rebred until one or more live normal litters were produced. At least one of these normal young was preserved in formalin solution for purposes of comparison.
2. The doe was rebred at or after weaning of the litter.
3. The doe was palpated on the 14th day after breeding and a diagnosis of pregnancy established before inoculated. In case she was not pregnant at this time, she was rebred and the procedure repeated.
4. Before inoculation the doe was bled and the serum tested for agglutination. In every instance, the test was negative.
5. The doe was then inoculated intraperitoneally with 0.5 c c. standard suspension of a 24-hour pork agar slant culure of Bact. abortus, strain Wis. 93. The day of pregnancy in each case is noted in table 1.
6. That portion of the inoculum not used for inoculation was saved and tested against known positive and negative serum by agglutination, to determine the purity of the culture used.
7. Immediately after inoculation the doe was placed on a false bottom of 1 inch mesh wire and kept there until she either aborted or reached the 29th day of pregnancy. In the latter case, she was removed to an ordinary cage for parturition.
8. One or more young from each doe, whether she aborted or littered normally, were cultured for B. abortus in an attempt to demonstrate infection. One or more of the abdominal organs and the placenta were selected for this purpose.
9. Guinea-pig inoculation was also used with a saline suspension of the material mentioned in no. 8. This was to increase the chances of recovery of the organism.

   Each inoculated guinea-pig was bled and tested for agglutinins 10 days or more after inoculation.

   Six weeks after inoculation, each guinea-pig, was killed for examination and culturing.
10. The doe was bled 10 days or more after parturition, and the blood serum tested for specific agglutinins.
11. One or more fetuses (littered after inoculation) from each doe were preserved in formalin solution for comparison with normal fetuses carried to term by the same animal before put on experiment.

DISCUSSION OF RESULTS

Table 1 shows that, with one exception, every doe inoculated on the 14th to 20th day, inclusive, produced dead, undeveloped fetuses, most of which were expelled before the end of the normal gestation period. The appearance of the two litters which were carried to the end of the gestation period clearly indicates that development had been stopped before parturition.

Doe 226, inoculated on the 22nd day of pregnancy, produced dead, undeveloped fetuses before term. Doe 195, inoculated at this stage, produced a litter, part of which were normal and part undeveloped. The 3 inoculated on the 24th and 26th days of pregnancy, respectively, produced living litters. This indicates that the line of demarcation toward the end of the gestation period is about 22 days.

TABLE 1

RECORDS OF RABBITS INOCULATED WITH BACT. ABORTUS WIS. 93 AT 14 TO 26 DAYS OF PREGNANCY

Day of Pregnancy when Inoculated	Parturition Days after Inoculation	Fetuses Dead or Alive	Appearance of Fetuses	Parturition Days after Breeding	Cultures from Fetuses	Agglutination	
						Before Inoculation	After Inoculation
14	17	Dead	Undeveloped	31	Positive	0	0.002
14	14	Dead	Undeveloped	28	Positive	0	0.002
16	9	Dead	Undeveloped	25	Positive	0	0.001
16	14	Alive	Normal	30	Positive	0	0.0005
18	11	Dead	Undeveloped	29	Positive	0	0.002
18	7	Dead	Undeveloped	25	Positive	0	0.0001
20	10	Dead	Undeveloped	30	Positive	0	0.01
20	9	Dead	Undeveloped	29	Positive	0	0.002
20	9	Dead	Undeveloped	29	Positive	0	0.002
22	6	Dead	Undeveloped	28	Positive	0	No test made
22	9	{2 alive 7 dead}	{Partly normal, partly undeveloped}	31	Positive	0	0.002
24	8	Alive	Normal	32	Positive	0	0.005
26	5	Alive	Normal	31	Negative	0	0.005
26	5	{6 alive 3 dead}	{8 normal 1 undeveloped}	31	Positive	0	0.002

The incubation period in the cases of undeveloped fetuses is found to vary from 6 to 17 days, with the majority falling between 7 and 11 days. Thus we see that in most cases the interval between the 14th or 16th day of pregnancy and the end of the gestation period would be ample for the manifestation of the disease.

Bacterium abortus cultures were obtained from the fetuses of every litter of does inoculated between the 14th and the 24th day, inclusive. This indicates that the organism invaded the fetuses whenever the remaining portion of the gestation period equaled that of the incubation period of the organism.

The one exception to this summary is doe 172, inoculated on the 16th day, which produced a normal, live litter at term. Cultures from one of these, as well as cultures from a guinea-pig inoculated with its stomach contents, were positive for Bact. abortus in each case. This doe showed unusually strong resistance to the disease.

Two does not shown in the table which were inoculated with apparently avirulent strains of Bact. abortus were placed on the false bottoms, where they remained until the 29th day of pregnancy. They were then removed to ordinary cages, where they littered normal living young. The young were raised to weaning time. This indicates that the routine manipulation does not cause abortion.

On the strength of the experimental work described above, the questions asked at the beginning of this paper may be answered as follows:

1. A virulent strain of Bact. abortus was found to produce abortion in rabbits in most cases when inoculated on the 14th to the 20th day of pregnancy.

2. The organism has been recovered in each case from the aborted fetuses, and its identity proved by testing against known positive and negative serum.

3. The incubation period of Bact. abortus strain Wis. 93 varies in rabbits from 6 to 17 days, with the majority of cases falling between the 7th and 11th days.

4. Owing to the difficulty of determining whether pregnancy exists in earlier stages, 14 days is as early in pregnancy as inoculation can be practically used to produce abortion.

5. The 20th day seems to be the latest limit of inoculation definitely to produce abortion.

6. The routine procedure which has been worked out has proved to be satisfactory.

CONCLUSIONS

Inoculation of rabbits is adaptable to the study of the abortion disease from several angles. It should prove of value in the study of immunity production. The typing of Bact. abortus might be based on the results of inoculation of rabbits. The virulence of the organism under consideration can be quickly, definitely, and economically determined. The virulence so determined should be more accurate and of more value than that determined by lesions produced as a result of guinea-pig inoculation. Other organisms have been incriminated as the cause of abortion in cattle and horses.[5] It would be interesting to test these organisms by this method. The variations in resistance to Bact. abortus as shown by individual females of the same species suggests the probability of genetic differences in the germ plasm. Using this method of testing the females, it should be possible to determine whether strains of animals can be produced which are resistant to Bact. abortus.

[5] Good, E. S., and Smith, W. V.: Kentucky Agric. Exp. Station, Bull. 204, 1916. Smith, T.; Little, R. B., and Taylor, M. S.: Jour. Exper. Med., 1920, 32, p. 683.

MIXED INFECTION IN GUINEA-PIGS WITH BACTERIUM ABORTUM AND MYCOBACTERIUM TUBERCULOSIS

ADALYN F. SCHOENFELD AND CHARLES M. CARPENTER

From the Diagnostic Laboratory, Department of Pathology and Bacteriology New York State Veterinary College at Cornell University, Ithaca

Ever since Smith and Fabyan [1] observed that Bacterium abortum produces a disease in guinea-pigs, the lesions of which are similar to tuberculosis, these animals have been used extensively in studies on the disease due to the Bang organism. In examining the tissues of cattle for the presence of infection with Bacterium abortum, it was found necessary to inject extracts of lymph glands into guinea-pigs. Although there were no gross lesions of tuberculosis in the tissues which were injected, it was observed that some of the guinea-pigs became infected with this disease. The question arose whether guinea-pigs suffering from tuberculosis would show the presence of Bacterium abortum should the tissues with which the guinea-pigs were injected be infected with both organisms.

The presence of Bacterium abortum in guinea-pigs is determined as follows: (1) by the occurrence of typical macroscopic lesions, such as abscessed epididymes, enlarged nodular spleen, and pin-point lesions in the liver; (2) by the occurrence of specific agglutinins, and (3) by the isolation of the organism from the tissues. The presence of tuberculosis in the guinea-pig, which affects practically the same tissues as Bacterium abortum, makes it difficult to detect by gross examination the presence of the latter. Microscopically, the nodules produced by both organisms are not easily differentiated. Fabyan [2] calls attention to the fact that in the tissues involved and in the histologic changes produced, the disease closely resembles tuberculosis. Seyfarth [3] states that "the structure of the nodules is similar to, if not identical with, the tuberculous nodules, namely—a central portion of epithelioid cells surrounded by lymphoid cells."

Because of the resemblance between the lesions of these two infections in guinea-pigs, it seemed expedient to study the development of specific agglutinins for Bacterium abortum when there was a mixed infection. It appeared desirable also to determine whether Bacterium

[1] Centralbl. f. Bakteriol., I, O., 1912, 61, p. 549.
[2] Jour. Med. Res., 1912, 21, p. 441.
[3] Jour. Infect. Dis., 1924, 35, p. 495.

abortum could be recovered in culture in the presence of tuberculosis. Therefore the following work was done.

DESCRIPTION OF WORK

Thirty-two guinea-pigs were divided into 7 groups as follows: Group 1 contained 2 guinea-pigs receiving injections simultaneously with separate suspensions of Bacterium abortum and Mycobacterium tuberculosis. Group 2 was comprised of 5 guinea-pigs receiving injections with a mixed extract of tissues infected with Bacterium abortum and Mycobacterium tuberculosis. Five guinea-pigs in group 3 received injections with mixed suspensions of Bacterium abortum and Mycobacterium tuberculosis. Group 4 contained 4 guinea-pigs receiving injections with a suspension of Bacterium abortum prior to a suspension of Mycobacterium tuberculosis; while group 5 was composed of 4 guinea-pigs receiving injections with a suspension of Mycobacterium tuberculosis prior to a suspension of Bacterium abortum. Group 6 included 6 guinea-pigs having generalized tuberculosis receiving injections with a suspension of Bacterium abortum. Group 7 contained 6 guinea-pigs used as controls for the foregoing groups.

Cultures of Bacterium abortum, strain 80, were grown on infusion agar to which 1% glucose had been added and were washed off and suspended in a physiologic salt solution. This culture, originally obtained from Professor K. F. Meyer, has been used extensively as an agglutinating antigen and at present is extremely pathogenic for guinea-pigs. The suspension injected was very dilute, there being approximately 100,000,000 cells per c c. A practically water-clear suspension of a young culture of Mycobacterium tuberculosis of the bovine type was used in the work. The mixed suspension was made by placing 5 c c. of the two foregoing suspensions together and thoroughly agitating. In making the mixed tissue extracts, the spleen of a guinea-pig having generalized tuberculosis was ground with 10 c c. of a physiologic salt solution in a sterile mortar and combined with an equal amount of an extract of the spleen of a guinea-pig showing typical infection with Bacterium abortum. All guinea-pigs were injected intraperitoneally. The guinea-pigs were bled once in 2 weeks.

One-tenth c c. of blood was drawn from the heart of each guinea-pig into a graduated sterile hypodermic syringe and placed in tubes containing 0.9 c c. physiologic salt solution. This plasmal dilution was then set up with a Bacterium abortum antigen, and further dilutions were made, the highest being 1:960. Some of the guinea-pigs did not withstand the mixed infection as well as did the controls which received only one infection, several of the former dying in a comparatively short time after receiving injections. Others were killed 7 to 12 weeks after receiving the injections.

At necropsy, cultures of the heart blood, spleen, liver and testes were made on infusion agar to which 1% glucose had been added, and these were incubated at 37 C. The organisms recovered from the tissues were checked with a serum containing agglutinins specific for

Bacterium abortum. Smears from the spleen, liver, and some of the lymph glands were made on glass slides and stained for acid-fast bacilli by the Ziehl-Neelson method. The results are given in the various tables.

Results of Injections with Bacterium abortum and Mycobacterium tuberculosis

Number of Guinea-Pig	Date of Injection with Bacterium Abortum or with Mixture Indicated	Amount Injected, C c.	Date of Injection with Mycobacterium Tuberculosis	Amount Injected, C c.	No. of Days Between Respective Injections	Presence of Agglutinins for Bact. Abortum	Date of Necropsy	Bacterium Abortum Isolated at Necropsy	Presence of Acid-Fast Bacilli at Necropsy
Group 1. Simultaneous Injections with Individual Suspensions of Bacterum abortum and of Mycobacterium tuberculosis									
2698a	4/ 1/24	0.1	4/ 1/24	0.1	0	+	6/21/24	+	+
2703a	4/ 1/24	0.1	4/ 1/24	0.1	0	—	5/ 7/24	—	+
Group 2. Injections with Mixed Extract of Tissues Infected with Bacterium abortum and Mycobacterium tuberculosis									
2948a	10/16/24	0.25	....	...	..	—	11/18/24	—	+
2992b	10/16/24	0.50	....	...	..	—	10/29/24	—	+
3003a	10/16/24	1	....	...	..	+	11/25/24	+	+
3004b	10/16/24	1	....	...	..	—	10/18/24	*	+
3018	10/16/24	2	....	...	..	+	10/30/24	—	+
Group 3. Injections with Mixed Suspensions of Bacterium abortum and Mycobacterium tuberculosis									
3149	10/16/24	0.25	....	...	0	+	12/ 2/24	+	+
3150	10/16/24	0.50	....	...	0	+	12/12/24	+	+
3151	10/16/24	1	....	...	0	+	12/ 2/24	+	—
3152	10/16/24	1	....	...	0	+	12/ 2/24	—	+
3153	10/16/24	2	....	...	0	+	12/12/24	—	+
Group 4. Injections with a Suspension of Bacterium abortum Prior to a Suspension of Mycobacterium tuberculosis									
2699	3/20/24	0.25	3/25/24	0.1	5	+	5/12/24	+	+
2700	3/20/24	0.50	4/ 1/24	0.25	12	+	5/12/24	+	+
2701a	4/ 1/24	1	4/11/24	0.50	10	+	6/26/24	—	+
2702	3/20/24	2	4/17/24	1	27	+	5/ 5/24	+	+
Group 5. Injections with a Suspension of Mycobacterium tuberculosis Prior to a Suspension of Bacterium abortum									
2712	3/25/24	0.1	3/20/24	0.25	5	+	5/12/24	+	+
2713	4/ 1/24	0.25	3/20/24	0.50	12	+	5/12/24	+	+
2714a	4/ 4/24	0.50	4/ 1/24	1	10	+	5/ 1/24	*	
2876	6/ 7/24	0.25	5/22/24	0.50	16	+	10/ 6/24	+	+

Tumber of Guinea-Pig	Date of Injection with Bacterium Abortum or with Mixture Indicated	Amount Injected, C c.	Date of Injection with Mycobacterium Tuberculosis	Amount Injected, C c.	No. of Days Between Respective Injections	Presence of Agglutinins for Bact. Abortum	Date of Necropsy	Bacterium Abortum Isolated at Necropsy	Presence of Acid-Fast Bacilli at Necropsy
GROUP 6. GUINEA-PIGS HAVING GENERALIZED TUBERCULOSIS RECEIVING INJECTIONS OF A SUSPENSION OF BACTERIUM ABORTUM									
2829	5/ 8/24	0.50	....	...	0	+	6/26/24	+	—
3144	10/16/24	1	....	...	0	+	12/ 2/24	+	+
3145	10/16/24	2	....	...	0	+	12/ 2/24	+	+
3146	10/16/24	1	....	...	0	+	11/13/24	—	+
3147	10/16/24	0.50	....	...	0	+	12/13/24	+	+
3148	10/16/24	0.25	....	...	0	—	11/20/24	+	+
GROUP 7. CONTROLS									
2716	3/20/24	0.1 c c. suspension	....	...	..	+	5/12/24	+	..
2717a	3/20/24	0.50 c c. suspension	....	...	..	+	4/17/24	+	..
2849	....	....	5/10/24	1 c c. suspension	..	..	5/28/24	..	+
3154	....	....	10/16/24	1 c c. extract spleen	..	..	12/12/24	..	+
3155	10/16/24	1 c c. suspension	....	....	..	+	12/ 8/24	+	..
3156	10/16/24	1 c c. suspension	....	....	..	+	12/12/24	+	..

* No cultures made.

DISCUSSION

It will be noted from the table that the presence of the tubercle bacillus and the disease produced by it did not markedly alter the development of agglutinins for Bacterium abortum or the course of the disease, as shown by their presence. The guinea-pigs did not withstand the mixed infection as well as the control guinea-pigs that received injections of only one of the organisms. Soon after the injections they lost weight steadily and rapidly, dying in 5 or 6 weeks. Kolmer[4] states that "in an infection with one micro-organism a specific agglutinin will be formed for that micro-organism, and group agglutinins for other more or less allied micro-organisms, and consequently the specificity of the agglutinating reaction depends upon the principle of dilution, the

[4] Infection, Immunity and Biologic Therapy, p. 261.

specific agglutinin being present in largest amount and operative in dilutions above the range of the group agglutinins." It has been shown that even different strains of the same organism will develop agglutinins specific for each.

In Hektoen's[5] discussion on "multiple immunization," he states that "Several writers conclude that in multiple infections and immunization the production at the same time of different agglutinins takes place without any change in the onset, intensity, and duration of the production of any single agglutinin which is claimed to proceed as an infection or immunization with the single bacterium." On the other hand, he states that from his own work and from that of others it is seen that the normal development of agglutinins in secondary infection is altered. Evidently the formation of agglutinins in mixed infections depends on the type of antigens associated with each other.

Some observers contend that the lymphoid tissue especially is concerned in the development of agglutinins, although others hold that their formation is general and due to a widespread cellular activity. Of course it cannot be assumed that all of the lymphoid tissue in the cases of the guinea-pigs infected with Bacterium abortum and Mycobacterium tuberculosis had been destroyed, but, owing to the presence of the two infections, it was grossly diseased. Notwithstanding these pathologic changes, specific agglutinins for Bacterium abortum were produced. In the further discussion of Hektoen[6] on the formation and fate of antibodies, he states that "In guinea-pigs Deutsch found that splenectomy, soon after the injection of typhoid bacilli, reduced the production of antibodies and that if spleens so removed were placed in the abdomens of normal animals antibodies soon appeared in their blood. Ludke appears to have obtained similar results. On the other hand, splenectomy some days before the injection seemed to be without any effect, and Pfeiffer and Marx failed to find that splenectomy exercised any effect on the production of cholera antibodies in guinea-pigs."

It is interesting to note that 3 of the guinea-pigs, group 6, injected with a suspension of Bacterium abortum after they had developed generalized tuberculosis, did not show agglutinins for the former, although one of these, 3004B, died too soon after the injection for them to be present. Guinea-pigs 2992B and 3018 died on the 13th and 14th days, respectively, after the injection of Bacterium abortum. With

[5] Harvey Lectures, 1909-1910, pp. 163.
[6] Ibid., p. 173.

the exception of the 3 pigs mentioned above in group 6, and of guinea-pigs 2703A in group 1 and 3148 in group 3, the remainder developed specific agglutinins for Bacterium abortum. Lewis [7] showed that a guinea-pig infected with virulent tubercle bacilli develops much more antisheep ambocepter than do normal guinea-pigs when given like amounts of sheep red blood corpuscles. In several instances in our work, there seemed to be a delay in the development of agglutinins, although with the suspension we used they ordinarily appeared during the 2d or 3rd week after having been injected.

As a rule, as heavy a growth of Bacterium abortum was obtained in cultures of the tissues suffering from the mixed infection as from a guinea-pig infected with the abortion disease alone. In a few instances, Bacterium abortum was not recovered from the tissues cultured. In one case, guinea-pig 2701A was not posted until the 87th day after the injection, and it may be that the infection had been overcome. Guinea-pig 2703A which had received 0.1 c c. of each suspension simultaneously and was necropsied 5 weeks after injection failed to show any growth in culture, and no agglutinins for the organism were developed. This may be due to a high resistance to the infection. Tuberculous lesions were present in the liver, spleen and lymph glands, and acid-fast bacilli were demonstrated. Three other guinea-pigs, 3146, 3152 and 3153, failed to show a culture of Bacterium abortum, although specific agglutinins were present in the serum. Only one of the guinea-pigs, 3003A, in group 6, showed a growth of Bacterium abortum when cultures were made from the various tissues upon glucose-agar. In the case of guinea-pig 3004B, which died two days after the injection, no cultures were made.

The effect of Bacterium abortum on the tuberculosis infection was not apparent so far as the lesions and presence of the organism were concerned. In most cases it was, as is usual, difficult to find acid-fast bacilli in smears made from the spleen, liver and lymph glands, although the smears made from the nodules in the lung showed them to be more abundant. In a few cases, acid-fast bacilli were not demonstrated as shown in the table, but tuberculous lesions were always present in the mixed infection.

Schroeder and Cotton,[8] in their first studies on Bacterium abortum in milk, state that a cow affected with a tuberculous disease of the

[7] Lewis, P. A., and Loomis, D.: J. Exper. Med., 1924, 40, p. 503.
[8] Annual Report, Bureau Animal Industry, U. S. Dept. Agricult., 1911, p. 139.

udder was also eliminating the Bang organism in her milk. "Her milk caused both tuberculosis and the other disease [9] in the guinea-pigs injected with it, showing that the two diseases can live in harmony in one animal body; in fact, each seemed to increase the pernicious potency of the other. Guinea-pigs with the double infection formed interesting subjects, because the tubercle bacillus in the lesions could easily be demonstrated in stained preparations, while the other bacillus, which was microscopically invisible to us, could be cultivated on media that is unsuitable for the tubercle bacillus." This statement of their observation on the guinea-pigs receiving injections with a sample of milk containing Bacterium abortum and Mycobacterium tuberculosis corresponds with our results.

CONCLUSIONS

Agglutinins specific for Bacterium abortum were developed in guinea-pigs when the latter received simultaneously injections with cultures of Bacterium abortum and Mycobacterium tuberculosis. When either organism was injected several days prior to the other, or when an extract of tissues affected with tuberculosis and abortion disease respectively was injected into guinea-pigs, specific agglutinins for Bacterium abortum were also developed.

Bacterium abortum was recovered in pure culture from the livers, spleens and epididymes of guinea-pigs when a mixed infection with the Bang organism and tubercle bacillus had been produced as mentioned above. Bacterium abortum grew on a 1% glucose-agar which was unsuitable for the development of Mycobacterium tuberculosis.

The presence of the two infections did not change the gross appearance of the tissues from that observed in guinea-pigs suffering from generalized tuberculosis. The mixed infection results in a shorter disease course and is more fatal than tuberculosis alone.

[9] By "the other disease" is meant that due to infection with Bacterium abortum.

A STATISTICAL STUDY OF THE FORM AND GROWTH OF THE CHOLERA VIBRIO

THREE PLATES

ARTHUR T. HENRICI

From the Department of Bacteriology and Immunology, University of Minnesota, Minneapolis

It is well known that the cells of the cholera vibrio are subject to pronounced variations in form, and this organism has therefore been a favorite one for the study of pleomorphism. It is not necessary here to review the rather extensive literature which has accumulated. In plate 1, are presented photomicrographs collected from various papers, which illustrate well the extreme variations in form which may be manifested by this organism. It is apparent from the literature that not only may a single strain assume different forms in different mediums, but that different strains which are culturally and serologically identical will exhibit different morphologic characters in the same medium. These observations have been made so frequently that the question of purity of culture can no longer enter into the discussion. The variants from the typical vibrio form have been looked on by some authors as involution forms, that is, cells which have suffered an injury or are dead; by others, as unusual reproductive types; by still others simply as the result of the action of physical or chemical forces, particularly osmotic pressure, on the cells, implying neither necessarily an injury nor a change in the mode of reproduction. References to the various papers dealing with these views may be found in the article by Kolle and Schurmann in Kolle-Wassermann's Handbuch [1] and in Löhnis' monograph on "Life Cycles in Bacteria." [2]

A criticism which may be applied to almost all of the work on the pleomorphism of bacteria is that the various workers have not made continuous observation of the transformations from one type to another. Until this is done, it seems futile to speak of life cycles. It is not necessary to apply the eye to the microscope from the moment a culture starts growing until it is dead. Samples removed at regular intervals from a growing culture furnish material from which a picture of the entire cycle may be reconstructed. If this is done, however, it is almost essential to use quantitative methods; otherwise we may be led into

Received for publication, Feb. 16, 1925.

[1] Handb. der path. Mikrorg., 1912.

[2] Studies on the Life Cycles of Bacteria, Mem. Nat. Ac. Sc., 1921, 16.

error, particularly because the unusual forms always make a great impression, even though they may be numerically so few as to be insignificant. The work here reported has to do with such continuous observation of morphologic changes in the cholera vibrio.

A 5-day old culture on standard beef extract agar was emulsified in sterile broth and transferred to a series of agar slants. These were especially prepared with the idea of obtaining uniformly equal surfaces; measured tubes were selected, and each was filled with 5 c c. of agar, and the tubes were slanted as nearly as possible at the same angle. One loopful of the suspension was distributed as uniformly as possible over the surface of each slant. The tubes were incubated at 37 C., and at regular intervals tubes were removed for sampling.

The rate of growth was determined from direct microscopic counts according to a technic which has been previously described.[3] The growth from each slant was emulsified in varying quantities of water according to the heaviness of growth; the figures given represent the number of cells per cubic millimeter if the entire growth were suspended in 2 c c. of water. Morphologic observations were made from slides negatively stained by the method of Benians.[4] In previous quantitative studies of morphologic variations in bacteria,[5] measurement of the length of the cells has proved satisfactory because the principal variations encountered were changes in size rather than form, and because it was found that such variations in form as occurred were definitely correlated with changes in size.[6] A glance at the photomicrographs in plate 2 will show that in this culture on plain agar there were encountered almost all of the types that have been previously described in widely different mediums; rods, spheres and spirals, "budding" and branching forms are all to be found in some stage of growth of the culture. To handle such varying types quantitatively it was necessary to use some measure of the form of the cells and for this purpose I have adopted the area of the image divided by the length squared as a measure comparable with the weight-length index which has been used to deal with variations in form in larger organisms. These dimensions were determined as follows: A number of photomicrographs were made from the stained slides at a magnification of 3,000 diameters. The photographic negatives were then projected with a further magnification

[3] Henrici: Proc. Soc. Exper. Biol. & Med., 1923, 20, p. 293.
[4] Benians: Brit. Med. Jour. 1917, 2, p. 722.
[5] Henrici: Proc. Soc. for Exper. Biol. & Med. 1921, 19, p. 132; 1922, 20, p. 179.
[6] Ibid., 1923, 21, p. 215.

of 7 diameters, and the projected images were traced on index cards in such a way that the center of the cell coincided with the center of the card and that the major curvature was always on the same side. Of course, with such a high magnification the edges of the images are far from being sharp; but by tracing as nearly as possible through the middle of the zone of haziness, and by using a sufficiently large number of cells, the error from this lack of definition becomes a compensating one which may safely be ignored. Two hundred cells were chosen at random from each sample, 2,800 in all. From these cards the area was determined by a planimeter, the length by means of dividers. The composite photographs shown in plate 3 were made from these cards. This area-length index does not, however, take care of all of the variations encountered; it is only applicable so long as the cells are symmetrical about their axis, a condition which does not obtain in the so-called "budding cells." Since, however, most of the cells are symmetrical this measure does, at least roughly, classify the cells according to their form. The lower figure in plate 2 shows 200 cells from the culture after 5 days' growth, arranged in the order of their area-length indexes. It will be seen that these are arranged in regular order from long twisted cells at one extreme to almost perfectly spherical ones at the other, with a graded series of shorter oval cells between. Since asymmetrical cells are not classified, we find lateral projections almost anywhere in this series. The lower figure in plate 3 shows composite photographs of these same cells grouped in classes.

This measure of form also does not take care of another type of variation prominent in the cholera group, namely, the tendency to curvature or twisting of the cells. To deal with this character, I have used another measure referred to as the index of curvature. This is determined by measuring the length of each cell along its major axis and the shortest distance between the tips of the cells. The quotient of the difference between these two quantities divided by the first length serves as a measure of the degree of curvature in the cells. It is apparent from the illustrations that there is a degree of correlation between the amount of curvature and the form of the cells, the more slender long types showing the most marked curvature; this correlation, however, has not been worked out quantitatively.

As will be seen from the photomicrographs in plate 2, the organism went through a regular metamorphosis. The material used for seeding, being an old culture, contained a variety of forms: some typical vibrios, some spherical types, some showing lateral or terminal "buds." After growth was initiated, these were largely replaced by rather thick, straight bacillary forms which then became more slender and curved, assuming the "textbook" form of the coma bacillus. These forms persisted only up to 36 hours, after which the culture slowly returned to the original condition, developing more and more of the unusual types, occasional long, spiral cells, more and more irregular forms and a steadily increasing number of spherical types. The latter varied greatly in size, some being of the type which has been referred to as "giant coccoids" by several authors.

In plate 3, I have tried to present in graphic form the quantitative expressions of these morphologic variations. Smoothed frequency curves showing the distribution of the cells at each time interval according to their area-length index have been erected behind each other in isometric perspective. On the upper surface of the parallelopiped, the average area-length index is plotted. On the right hand surface, the rate of growth is indicated by plotting the logarithms of the number of cells; the index of curvature is also shown on this surface.

The cells in the inoculum consisted of 2 groups as will be seen from the 1st frequency curve, a major group of elongated cells and a minor group of oval or spherical cells; there are 2 distinct modes to the frequency curve. During the lag phase there was not much change; a slightly larger number of oval types appeared, with a corresponding increase in the average area-length index. During the accelerating growth phase the minor mode disappears, the distribution becomes more restricted, indicating a greater uniformity, and the average area-length index becomes distinctly smaller. During the latter stages of active growth, the cells become still more slender and elongated, so that the area-length index becomes still lower, and the distribution is further limited; but during this phase, the cells which were previously relatively straight now become more curved as indicated by the steady increase in the index of curvature. After the culture has reached its maximum growth at about 36 hours, the frequency curve gradually assumes the form of that for the original seeding. The distribution is more extended, there slowly develops a new mode for the oval and spherical types with an increase in the area-length index and a decrease in the index of curvature. These changes become progressively greater up to the 7th day. The frequency curve for the 10th day seems somewhat out of place, since it shows a decrease in the spherical types with an increase in the short oval forms; unfortunately, the experiment was terminated at this point. I rather suspect that there is an error in this last observation, for qualitative observations show that in older cultures there developed more and more of the coccoid types which are practically the only form seen in cultures a month old.

The degree of variation in form also underwent a regular change, the coefficient of variation decreasing steadily as long as growth continued, increasing again when growth came to a standstill. These values have not been plotted, but are available in table 1.

The actual size of the cells has not been treated by statistical methods in this work. It is apparent from the illustrations, however, that this

TABLE 1

VARIATIONS IN CHOLERA VIBRIO

Hour	Area-Length Index				Index of Curvature, Mean
	Mean	Median	Mode	Coefficient of Variability	
0	35.70	28.67	22.5	55.30	5.87
3	40.40	36.58	22.5	51.78	3.84
6	31.45	29.85	27.5	64.09	5.82
9	33.46	31.51	32.5	27.79	8.22
12	28.50	29.20	27.5	33.31	8.96
18	21.20	21.06	22.5	28.25	8.88
24	24.96	22.40	22.5	44.43	7.82
36	24.20	19.25	17.5	66.98	5.58
48	37.70	27.99	17.5	52.36	6.77
72	36.60	31.40	17.5	56.34	6.46
96	34.16	34.88	30.0	61.86	6.58
120	39.20	33.93	27.5	52.27	6.87
168	34.31	35.39	27.5	46.72	6.46
240	34.84	30.48	22.5	54.23	4.10

organism changes in size much as do B. megatherium and Bact. coli; the cells become much larger during the phase of accelerating growth.

It will be noted that the increase in curvature of the cells becomes marked at the point where the growth curve shows a change from positive acceleration to negative acceleration; and that the development of oval and spherical types forming the minor mode in the bimodal frequency curves occurs at the beginning of the death phase. It would appear from an inspection of this graph that the morphologic changes are correlated with the rate of growth. In the lag phase, such slight changes as occur are of the same nature as those which occur during the late stages of the culture in the death phase; that is, the organisms change in the same way that they would have, had they remained in the old medium. The elongated straight forms appear and persist as long as the rate of growth becomes increasingly more rapid. With the slowing up of growth, the curved vibrio forms develop and persist until growth comes to a standstill. With the initiation of the death phase, the organisms returned to the type originally introduced into the medium. It is clear then that the cholera vibrio may appear in 3 distinct forms; that the bacillary form characteristic of the period of active growth may be looked on as the embryonic type, the vibrio form characteristic of the resting phase as the mature form, and the irregular and coccoid forms which develop in the death phase as the senescent forms.

In this experiment, there were encountered developing in regular order practically all of the forms which have been described in the various published works on the pleomorphism of the cholera organism. It is probable therefore that the variations in form, both those exhibited

TABLE 2

Variation in Number of Cells per Cubic Millimeter

Hour	Cells per Cubic Mm.
0	2,506
3	2,780
5	3,230
7	21,560
9	194,320
11	725,120
14	2,402,900
18	3,333,200
24	3,465,600
36	4,428,800
48	6,480,800
72	5,964,800
120	5,510,400
168	2,757,200
240	585,000

by different strains in the same medium, and by the same strain in different mediums, are due rather to variations in the rate of growth than to actual changes in the organization of the cells. Simultaneous observation of cultures which are in the accelerating phase and the resting phase will show bacillary and vibrio forms, respectively; and similarly cultures which are in the resting phase and the death phase will show vibrio forms and coccoid forms, respectively.

It is apparent from the data here presented that the irregular and coccoid forms are not reproductive cells, for the growth curve shows that reproduction is not occurring, or if it is, that it cannot keep pace with the ever increasing death rate. Nevertheless, the fact that the frequency curves are bimodal would rather indicate that these forms are produced by budding instead of by a gradual transformation of the elongated cells. A large proportion, however, of these cells which show

Plate 1

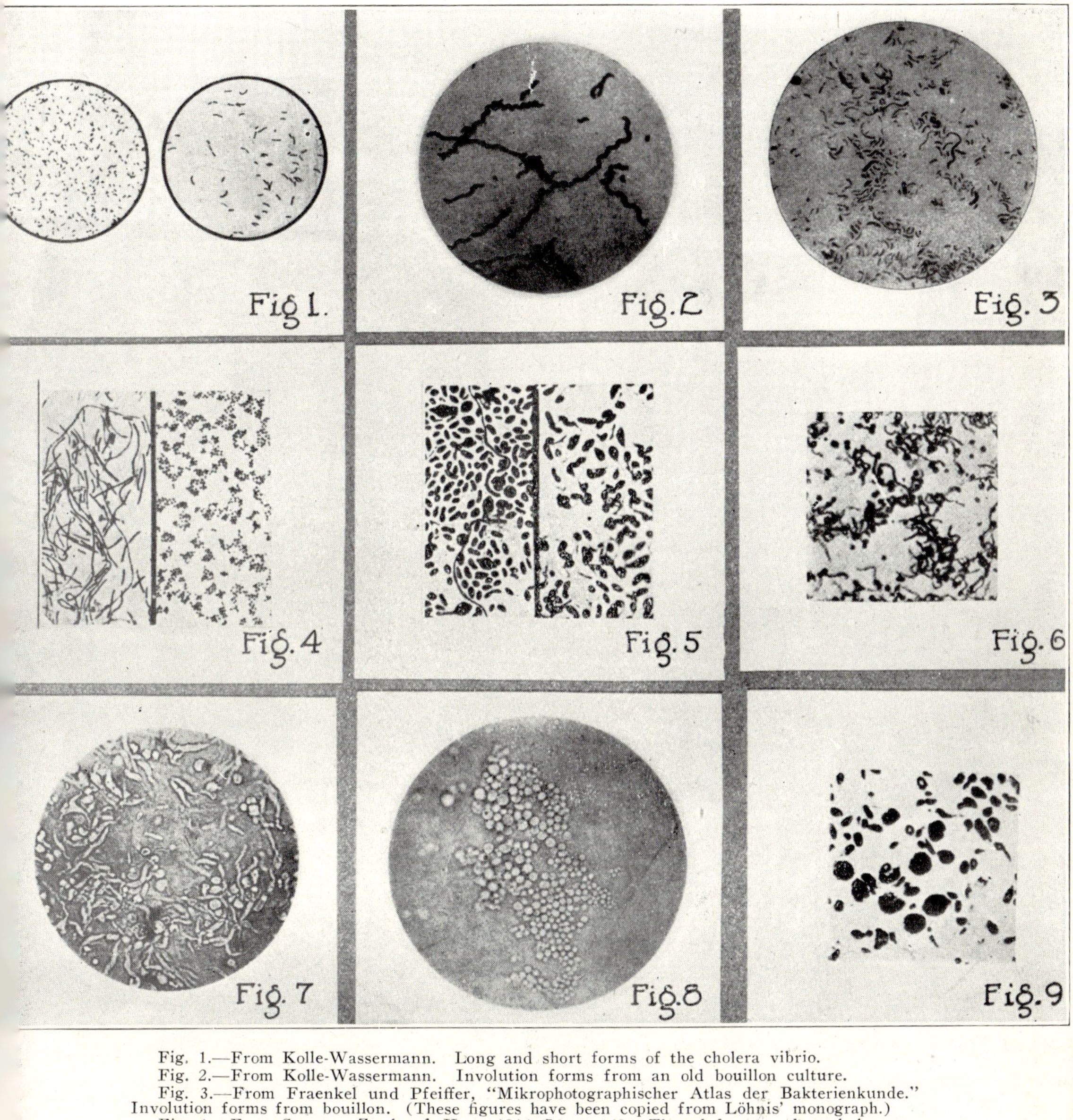

Fig. 1.—From Kolle-Wassermann. Long and short forms of the cholera vibrio.

Fig. 2.—From Kolle-Wassermann. Involution forms from an old bouillon culture.

Fig. 3.—From Fraenkel und Pfeiffer, "Mikrophotographischer Atlas der Bakterienkunde." Involution forms from bouillon. (These figures have been copied from Löhnis' monograph.)

Fig. 4.—From Stamm: Ztschr. f. Hyg., 1914, 76, p. 469. Thread forms and staphylococcus forms developing in water. (These figures have been copied from Löhnis' monograph.)

Fig. 5.—From Stamm. Hypertrophic forms in water. (These figures have been copied from Löhnis' monograph.)

Fig. 6.—From Almquist. Svenska Läkersällsk Handl. 1917, 43, p. 543. Development of "conidia." (These figures have been copied from Löhnis' monograph.)

Fig. 7.—From Hammerl: Centralbl. f. Bakteriol., O., 1906, Abt. I, 41 and 42. Forms from agar with lithium chloride.

Fig. 8.—From Hammerl. Forms in potassium nitrate peptone solution.

Fig. 9.—From Maassen: Arb. a. d. k. Gsndhtsemte, 1904, 24, p. 385. Forms from agar with lithium chloride. (These figures have been copied from Löhnis' monograph.)

Plate 2

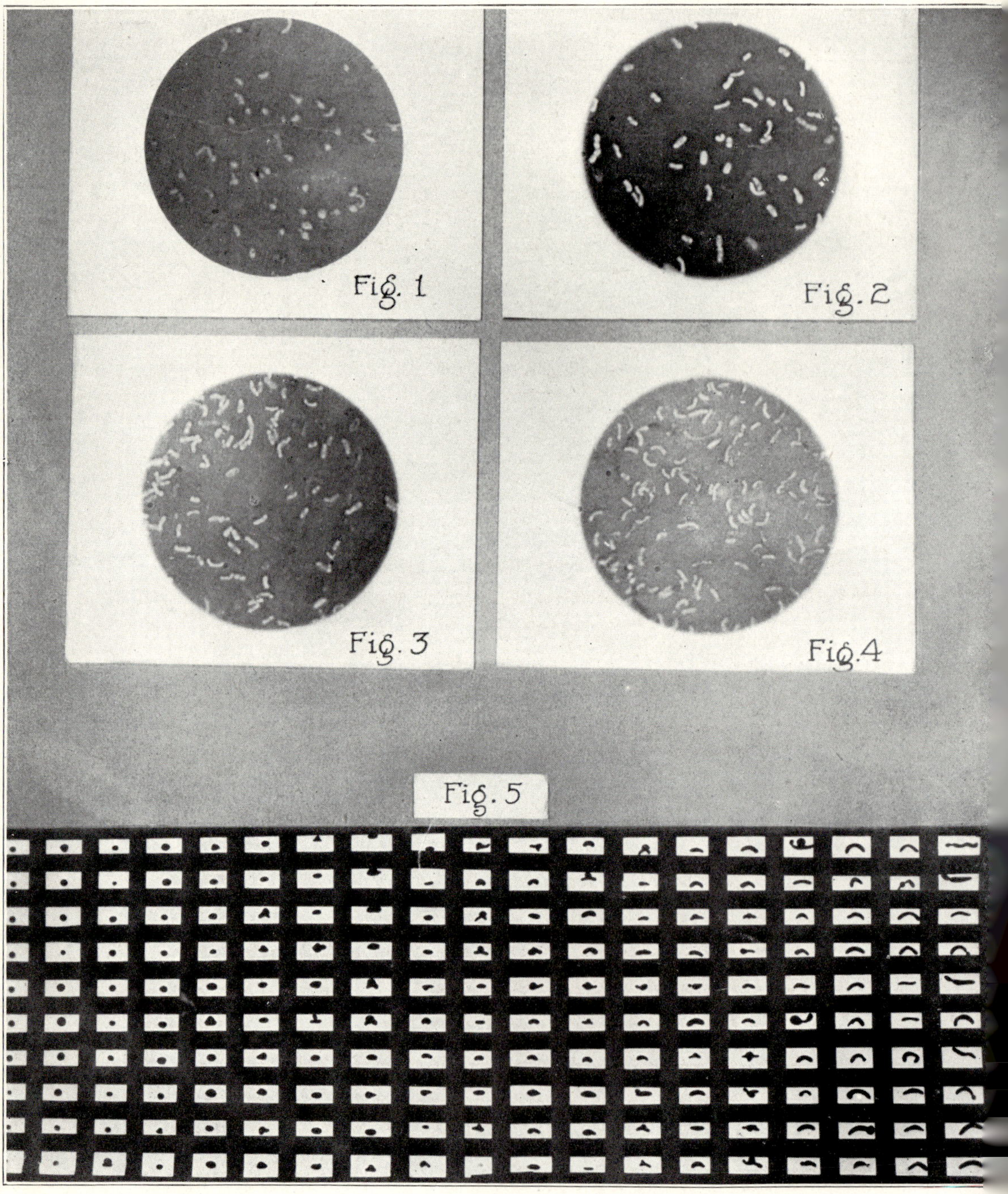

Fig. 1.—Photomicrograph from culture used for inoculation; Benians' stain.
Fig. 2.—Photomicrograph after 9 hours' incubation.
Fig. 3.—After 18 hours.
Fig. 4.—After 36 hours. After this time, the cells gradually returned to the form shown in fig. 1.
Fig. 5.—Two hundred cells from the culture after 5 days, arranged in the order of their area-length indexes, the lowest being at the upper right hand corner, the highest at the lower left.

PLATE 3

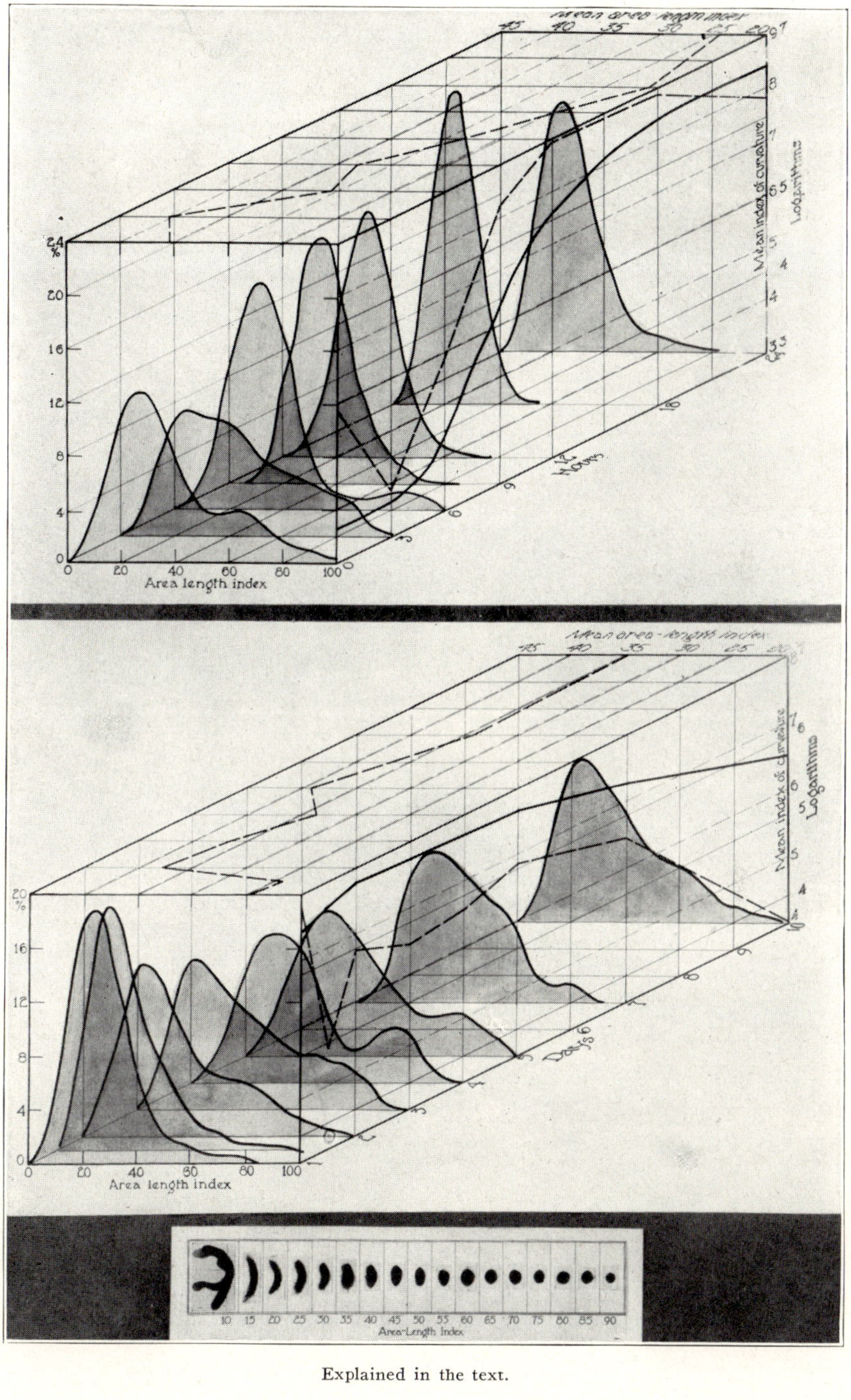

Explained in the text.

lateral or terminal "buds" are permeated by Congo red, which is an indication that they are dead. It is hard to understand just what is the significance of these irregular forms, but because they develop only in the death phase, I believe that they indicate a type of injury to the organism rather than the development of a new reproductive cycle. It is probable that changes in the rigidity or permeability of the cell wall render them more susceptible to the forces of surface tension and osmotic pressure which before were inactive.

SUMMARY

Almost all of the various cell forms of the cholera vibrio which have been described were observed developing in regular sequence in a normal culture on plain agar. It is probable therefore that many of the apparent morphologic changes of this organism reported in the literature are but variations in the rate of growth on different mediums or of different strains in the same medium.

A technic is presented by which morphologic variations in bacteria may be followed quantitatively. Such quantitative observations of changes in cell form of the cholera organism are presented in graphic form. It is shown that the cell changes are correlated with the rate of growth, and that 3 distinct phases can be recognized: an embryonic stage, characteristic of the period of accelerating growth, in which the cells are large and bacillary in form; an adult stage, characteristic of the period of decreasing growth rate, in which the cells assume the typical vibrio form; and a senescent stage, characteristic of the death phase, in which the cells divide into a group of irregular spiral forms and a group of short oval or coccoid forms.

THE FORMATION OF ANTIBODIES TO SHEEP BLOOD IN EXPERIMENTAL TUBERCULOSIS OF RABBITS

Ludvig Hektoen and H. J. Corper

From the John McCormick Memorial Institute for Infectious Diseases, Chicago, and The National Jewish Hospital for Consumptives, Denver, Colo.

There seems to be no report of any study of the effect of various types of tuberculosis in the rabbit on the formation of antibodies. Lewis and Loomis,[1] in a report that appeared after this work was in progress, state that the guinea-pig infected with virulent bovine tubercle bacilli develops much more antisheep amboceptor than controls given only the like amounts of sheep corpuscles. They suggest that tuberculosis may stimulate a normal mechanism or that the cellular basis of such a mechanism is increased rather than that a wholly new factor has been introduced by the disease. In the experiments now reported briefly, the rabbit was used because it is resistant to human tubercle bacilli and susceptible to bovine bacilli, is suitable for various modes of inoculation, and because its manner of forming antibodies to sheep blood is known fairly well. The technic for estimating the antibody content of the serum is the same as in the earlier work of the same general nature.[2]

In the first experiment, a rapidly progressive and fatal general tuberculosis was produced by the intravenous injection of 0.5 mg. of virulent bovine tubercle bacilli suspended in salt solution. This series included 15 rabbits; 3 controls receiving intraperitoneally only 10 c c. of citrated sheep blood per kilo of weight, 4 rabbits receiving the tubercle bacilli intravenously 7 days prior to the intraperitoneal injection of the same amount of sheep blood, 4 rabbits receiving the bacilli at the same time as the sheep blood, and 4 rabbits receiving the bacilli 7 days after the sheep blood. The serum was examined for agglutinins, lysins and precipitins before and at regular intervals after the injection of the sheep blood. All of the infected animals died within one month after the injection of the tubercle bacilli. Although there was a slight variation in the agglutinin and lysin titers of the individual animals, there were noted no significant differences in the formation of agglutinins and lysins for sheep blood in the infected animals as compared to the controls receiving

Received for publication, Feb. 16, 1925.

[1] Jour. Exper. Med., 1924, 40, p. 503.

[2] Hektoen: J. Infect. Dis., 1916, 19, p. 69; 1915, 17, p. 415; 1918, 22, p. 28. Hektoen and Corper: Ibid., 1920, 26, p. 330; 1922, 31, p. 305.

sheep blood alone, regardless of whether infection occurred at the same time as the injection of sheep blood or 7 days before or 7 days after. The rapidly fatal outcome of the tuberculosis in these animals was without appreciable effect on the blood content of agglutinins and lysins to within a few days of death. Precipitin formation, however, seemed to be retarded in most of the infected animals.

In view of the lack of striking effect on the formation of antibodies in the rabbit by a rapidly fatal general tuberculosis, it was decided to study the effect of a more chronic local disease produced by subcutaneous injection of a large amount of human tubercle bacilli and to follow the antibody formation early in the infection, when the infection was well under way and after retrogression had set in. In this experiment, 21 rabbits were used, 3 of which served as controls. The infected animals were given subcutaneous injections of 5 and of 100 mg. of avirulent human tubercle bacilli; citrated sheep blood, 10 c c. per kilo body weight, was injected intraperitoneally into 6 rabbits 10 days, in 6 others 26 days, and in the 6 remaining 43 days, after the infection. The rabbits receiving 5 mg. of tubercle bacilli in many cases developed only a slight or no appreciable local subcutaneous lesion, while the rabbits receiving 100 mg. all developed local subcutaneous tuberculous abscesses 3 to 6 cm. in size, many of which ruptured and formed tuberculous ulcers which gradually and slowly healed. Of the rabbits receiving 100 mg., those that lived longer than 6 to 18 months usually developed a secondary pulmonary tuberculosis of variable extent. Mild glandular involvement was also noted. The blood of these rabbits was examined for lysins and precipitins for sheep blood before and at definite intervals after its injection to note what effect if any the tuberculosis exercised on antibody formation. In comparing the lysin titers of the rabbits given the sheep blood 10 days after infection with the controls, there was noted no appreciable difference. In those given the sheep blood 26 days after infection, there appeared to be a slightly lower titer in 4 of the 6 animals. This was noted also in 2 of 4 of the rabbits that received sheep blood 43 days after infection. The precipitin titers seemed to parallel the lysin titers. In 2 of the 3 rabbits given intraperitoneal injections of sheep blood 43 days after subcutaneous injection with 100 mg. of human tubercle bacilli, high lysin and precipitin titers persisted in one more than 445 days and in the other more than 200 days. The figures at various intervals after the injection of the sheep blood are recorded in table 1.

Rabbit 16 was killed 254 days after the injection of sheep blood. Careful gross and microscopic examination of all the important organs of the body revealed a well nourished animal with a large healed subcutaneous tubercle at the site of injection of the tubercle bacilli; the abdominal organs, including the omentum, were normal; the lymph glands throughout the body were not enlarged and not tuberculous; in the upper part of the lower lobe and in the middle lobe of the right lung were about a dozen small transparent gray tubercles, and in the upper

TABLE 1

LYSIN AND PRECIPITIN FORMATION IN RABBITS RECEIVING SUBCUTANEOUS INJECTIONS WITH AVIRULENT HUMAN TUBERCLE BACILLI 43 DAYS PRIOR TO THE INTRAPERITONEAL INJECTION OF CITRATED SHEEP BLOOD

Intervals in Days after Injection of Sheep Blood	Nontuberculous Control Rabbit		Tuberculous Rabbits			
			Rabbit 16		Rabbit 17	
	Lysin	Precipitin	Lysin	Precipitin	Lysin	Precipitin
3	192	0	0	0	48	0
7	24,000	100	12,288	1,600	12,288	—
9	24,000	1,000	24,576	3,200	24,516	1,600
11	24,000	1,000	24,576	6,400	1,288	3,200
15	12,288	3,000	12,288	6,400	6,144	6,400
19	6,144	4,000	6,144	6,400	6,144	6,400
23	6,144	3,000	6,144	6,400	6,144	6,400
27	3,072	2,000	6,144	6,400	6,144	—
35	3,072	500	3,072	3,200	3,072	3,200
43	1,536	200	3,072	3,200	3,072	3,200
55	192	100	768	6,400	1,536	6,400
63	192	0	3,072	12,800	3,072	12,800
75	0	0	768	12,800	1,536	8,000
95	......	......	768	6,400	768	6,400
115	......	......	192	6,400	384	6,400
155	......	......	192	6,400	384	6,400
205	......	......	480	4,000	480	6,400
235	......	......	0	0	480	4,000
335	......	......	......	......	480	8,000
405	......	......	......	......	768	32,000
445	......	......	......	......	768	4,800

portion of the lower lobe of the left lung were found 3 small tubercles. The bone marrow appeared normal, also the eyes and head.

Rabbit 17 died 511 days after the injection of sheep blood. Gross and microscopic examination revealed an emaciated animal with no visible subcutaneous lesion at the site of inoculation, but with marked tuberculous involvement of the mesentery and mesenteric lymph nodes (injection intraperitoneal instead of subcutaneous?); there were a few miliary tubercles in both kidneys; the spleen, liver, stomach and intestines, suprarenals, uterus, ovaries and other abdominal organs including the omentum were normal; both lungs were massively involved in a caseopneumonic type of tuberculosis; the bone marrow was normal.

In view of the recent work of Portis [3] on the rôle of the omentum of the rabbit in the development of antibodies in response to the intraperitoneal injection of antigen, especial attention was paid to the microscopic examination of the omentums in our rabbits, but no changes of significance were found. Total leukocyte counts, differential and Arneth, in rabbits 16 and 17 on the 189th, 192d, 194th, 196th, 204th and 210th days after the injection of sheep blood revealed no significant changes as compared with counts in normal animals. Precipitin tests with the serum of rabbit 17 on the 385th, 395th and 405th days, included cat, rat, human, horse, dog and beef blood, but no reactions developed except with beef blood, the highest reacting dilution of which was 400% lower than the highest reacting dilution of sheep blood. Tests of the serum on the 395th day with sheep, human, dog and rat corpuscles showed the presence of agglutinins and opsonins for sheep corpuscles only.

The variations of the effect of tuberculosis on antibody formation were demonstrated well in a duplicate series of rabbits infected subcutaneously with 100 mg. of avirulent human tubercle bacilli and given 10 c c. of citrated sheep blood per kilo of body weight 2 months and 3½ months later. In comparison with control rabbits there was a slight stimulation of antibody formation, especially of precipitin for sheep blood, in a few of the 2 months rabbits, while the 3½ months rabbits showed no appreciable effect.

In a further series of 21 rabbits, the antigen was injected intravenously (1 c c. per kilo body weight) 1 and 2 months after the animals had received subcutaneous injections with 100 mg. of avirulent human tubercle bacilli or intraperitoneal injections with 30 mg. The results were, however, essentially the same as those in the other experiments, the tuberculous animals giving less pronounced response than when the sheep blood was given intraperitoneally.

SUMMARY

A rapidly fatal general tuberculosis in the rabbit from the intravenous injection of virulent bovine tubercle bacilli was without definite effect on the agglutinin and lysin content of the serum even to within a few days of death, while precipitin formation seemed to be slightly retarded.

Local subcutaneous tuberculosis in rabbits produced by the injection of avirulent human tubercle bacilli 10 and 26 days before the intraperito-

[3] J. Infect. Dis., 1924, 34, p. 159.

neal injection of sheep blood had no appreciable effect on lysin or precipitin formation, but 2 of the rabbits given sheep blood 43 days after infection maintained high specific lysin and precipitin titers for 200 and 445 days.

Whether the tuberculosis was the cause of the unusual reaction of these 2 rabbits has not been determined, but the results are similar to those that Lewis and Loomis [1] obtained in tuberculous guinea-pigs.

Rabbits infected subcutaneously with avirulent human tubercle bacilli and given sheep blood intravenously at different intervals after infection revealed slight variations in antibody formation from the usual course.

Tuberculosis in the rabbit, either general or local, apparently has no marked influence on the antibodies that develop from the injection of sheep blood. In exceptional cases, it may result in a prolongation of antibody accumulation in the blood.

BACTERIAL FACTORS IN PYORRHEA ALVEOLARIS

III. THE ISOLATION OF B. TETANI, B. WELCHII AND OTHER SPORULATING ANAEROBES FROM HUMAN SALIVA

IVAN C. HALL

From Cornell University, Ithaca, N. Y.

Although the bacteria of the mouth were among the first to be seen, our knowledge of the oral fauna and flora is still incomplete, and especially so as regards the obligately anaerobic micro-organisms.

Among the early investigators, Miller [1] detected a trace of butyric acid in fermenting saliva, suggesting B. butyricus, but was unable to secure direct proof of its formation in the mouth or of the presence of sporulating anaerobes, and considered the conditions of aeration in the mouth unfavorable to their development there. Goadby [2] also suspected the presence of gas forming obligately anaerobic bacteria in dento-alveolar abscesses, but was unable to isolate them.

The first serious investigation of the sporulating anaerobes of the mouth was made by Rodella,[3] who recorded the isolation of B. putrificus and of the nonmotile butyric acid bacillus (Granulobacillus saccharobutyricus immobilis liquefaciens of Grassberger and Schattenfroh). Baumgartner,[4] on the contrary, was unable to demonstrate sporulating anaerobes in carious teeth, although Kligler [5] recovered 15 strains which he regarded as B. putrificus, in apparent confirmation of Rodella's findings. But a critical examination of Rodella's description does not permit any conclusions as to either the purity or the identity of his cultures; in fact, he himself regarded "Bacillus putrificus-Bienstock, heutzutage nicht mehr eine einzige Art, sondern eine ganze Familie mit vielen Varietäten (darunter auch einige pathogene)." And the fact that Kligler's so-called B. putrificus strains all fermented glucose and lactose and some of them saccharose certainly invalidates his identification of this species.

Received for publication, Jan. 27, 1925.

[1] Mikro-organismen der Mundhöhle, 1892.
[2] Mycology of the Mouth, 1903.
[3] Arch. f. Hyg., 1905, 53, p. 329.
[4] Wien. klin. Wchnschr., 1913, 26, p. 178.
[5] Jour. Allied Dental Societies, 1915, 10, pp. 141, 282 and 314.

In 1917, I found B. bifermentans (no. 70) associated with a streptococcus in the dental packing of a carious tooth from which foamy pus flowed when it was first opened.[6] Since no other references to the isolation and identification of sporulating anaerobes from the mouth were available, and the existing data seemed so unsatisfactory, I recently undertook to determine whether these organisms are prevalent in saliva, and if so, to what extent.

The results have shown, first, that sporulating anaerobes are not commonly found as spores in the saliva; and second, that when they are found, it is usually impossible to detect the same species in subsequent samples from the same mouth. Their significance in saliva is therefore generally nil; but this conclusion should cause no prejudice as to their possible rôle in carious teeth, in which an active bacterial flora including sporulating anaerobes may perhaps exist without greatly contaminating the saliva.

EXPERIMENTS

Fifty-five samples of saliva were collected at various times from 43 persons, 39 of whom were male prisoners at San Quentin; four were members of my family. The subjects varied in age from 10 to 54 years. The collections were made by sucking on the teeth and gums and expectorating the saliva into sterile test tubes. Samples from the children were secured immediately on rising, before they had brushed their teeth or eaten breakfast. Those from the prisoners were secured after breakfast, between 9 and 11 o'clock. Most of them brushed their teeth before breakfast but none afterward. The samples varied in amount from 8 to 55 c c.

Immediately following the collection of saliva, a dental examination of each subject was made, for which I am indebted to Dr. Clayton Westbay of San Francisco. The details of these examinations have no significance here, but are summarized in tables 1 and 2 to indicate the variety of defects present.

The salivary samples were transported at once to the laboratory, which required about 1½ hours, when initial cultures were made by deep inoculation of freshly boiled and cooled brain medium[7] with 1 c c. of saliva per tube. The inoculated tubes were at once heated in a water bath at 80 C. for 20 minutes, to destroy all organisms except

[6] Jour. Infect. Dis., 1922, 30, p. 445.
[7] Ibid., 1920, 27, p. 576.

those present as spores.[8] They were then incubated at 37 C. for 48 hours or longer, and finally analyzed for their bacterial content by the usual methods.[7]

Heating at 80 C. for 20 minutes frequently did not suffice to destroy the nonsporulating forms, particularly streptococci, protected as they were in a rather dense mass of brain tissue; in these cases, heating at 80 C. for 30 minutes was found effective, and in the later portion of the work the initial heating after inoculation was continued for this length of time. As a criterion of obligate anaerobes in the cultures, gas production was found to be only suggestive and not conclusive evidence; some

TABLE 1

DENTAL DEFECTS IN PERSONS PROVIDING SALIVARY SAMPLES

	None	Slight	Moderate	Marked
Recession of gums	22	14	0	7
Detachment of gums	16	15	5	7
Pockets	17	16	6	4
Pus	23	13	1	6
Loose teeth	37	3	1	2
Inflammation of gums	19	14	3	7
Hypertrophy of gums	27	10	3	3
Serumal calculus	15	15	7	6
Salivary calculus	18	15	2	8
Food detritus	6	23	7	7
Caries	24	14	5	0

The figures indicate the number of persons showing each grade of defect out of a total of 43.

TABLE 2

NUMBER OF FILLINGS AND OF TEETH LOST IN PERSONS PROVIDING SALIVARY SAMPLES

Fillings	0	1	2	3	4	5	6	7	8	9	10	11	12	13	14	15	No Record
Persons	23	2	3	4	0	2	0	0	2	1	0	0	1	0	0	1	4

Teeth lost	0	1	2	3	4	5	6	7	8	9	10	11	12	13	14	No Record
Persons	16	4	4	3	3	3	1	1	1	1	0	2	1	0	1	2

sporulating aerobes produce gas and some anaerobes fail to produce it. More reliance can be placed in deep meat infusion agar shake cultures, in which, if the dilution is sufficient, the maximum oxygen tolerance of an obligately anaerobic micro-organism will clearly distinguish it from any facultative anaerobes that may be present. This criterion was used, with full appreciation of its limitation to cultivable forms.

Aerobic spores were recovered from 16 samples. An attempt was made to identify them, but the taxonomy of this group is at present so confused that this effort had to be abandoned temporarily. The aerobic

[8] A duplicate tube of brain medium similarly inoculated but not heated after inoculation was studied for nonsporulating anaerobic bacteria, with important results which will be reported separately under joint authorship with Miss Beatrice Howitt.

spore bearers are perhaps mainly significant in the mouth as scavengers, but incidentally participate in the reaction changes characteristic of fermenting or putrifying saliva; [9] they should be studied in more detail.

Only 6 specimens of saliva yielded sporulating anaerobes. B. welchii was recovered 3 times in pure culture, and identified as usual by its morphology, nonmotility, and stormy fermentation of milk. The first culture (374) came from the saliva of a man 54 years of age with remarkably well-kept teeth. His only dental defects were slight recession and detachment of the gums, but he had 8 good gold fillings. A second attempt made 3 weeks later to recover B. welchii from his saliva failed.

The next culture of B. welchii (408) came from the saliva of a man 25 years old who had moderate detachment of hyphertrophied inflammatory gums with pus pockets and both serumal and salivary calculus. Three teeth had been extracted. A slight amount of food detritus was present. In addition to B. welchii, another obligate anaerobe was isolated, namely, B. bifermentans (408 C.), which was identified by its morphology, nonmotility, putrefactive action in milk and fermentation of monosaccharides but not di-saccharides. This was the only time in this series that B. bifermentans was encountered. An attempt to repeat the findings with a second sample 7 weeks later failed to demonstrate any sporulating bacteria.

The third culture of B. welchii (440) came from the saliva of a man showing only slight recessions and slight hypertrophy of the gums but no detachment, pus pockets, or active inflammation. There was slight serumal, but no salivary calculus. There were also one small unfilled cavity, one filling, and 5 extracted teeth. B. welchii was evidently present only in the vegetative form, being recovered by Miss Howitt from the unheated brain culture; the heated culture showed only aerobic spores. Another trial 2 weeks later showed neither aerobic spores nor B. welchii in either sporulating or vegetative form.

B. tetanomorphus (446) was recovered from the saliva of a man 43 years old whose mouth was well-kept, there being no gingival lesions and only a slight amount of serumal calculus. He had, however, lost 3 teeth by caries, had one large unfilled cavity, and carried 5 gold fillings. An attempt to repeat the finding 2 weeks later failed, though another nonpathogenic obligate anaerobe (458), so far unidentifiable

[9] Jour. Am. Med. Assn., 1923, 81, p. 1676. Hall and Westbay: Dental Cosmos, 1925, 67, p. 115.

with any of our well-known species, was recovered. Its actual identity is of little consequence here, so that detailed description is omitted.

The most astounding result of all was that of finding B. tetani (420) in the saliva of my own little girl, a healthy child 10 years old, with no traces of gingival disease but with some predisposition to molar caries, which had not been repaired when the salivary examination was made. The deep brain culture inoculated with 1 c c. of saliva and heated to 80 C. for 20 minutes showed macroscopically after 24 hours' incubation at 37 C. a small amount of gas, and microscopically slender motile gram-positive rods without spores. A subculture on plain agar slant gave no growth; the original culture was therefore considered free from aerobes, and the similarity of the several small fluffy colonies in a deep agar shake indicated a pure strain of some obligate anaerobe. Notwithstanding, one of these colonies was transferred to a partly boiled and cooled tube of brain medium; microscopic study of this gave the same results as in the initial tubes, and again no spores were seen. A glucose broth culture was made; it became turbid, with slight gas production, and was alkaline to brom-thymol blue after 48 hours. One might have suspected B. tetani if the spores had been seen, but none was visible as yet. The first indication of a pathogenic organism appeared when a 500 gm. guinea-pig, that had received subcutaneous injections with 2 c c. of the 48-hour glucose broth culture was found dead the next morning. There was no opportunity to observe symptoms, but the restriction of local lesions to a slight subcutaneous hyperemia and edema, and congestion of the lungs coupled with the failure of a heart blood culture in brain medium suggested a toxin former. And this was confirmed as B. tetani by the characteristic symptoms in other guinea-pigs inoculated with doses of 0.01 c c., 0.001 c c., and 0.0001 c c., all of which proved fatal except the last, in which severe tetanus occurred but recovery followed. A guinea-pig inoculated with a mixture of 1 c c. of the culture with 1 c c. (potency undetermined) of tetanus antitoxin failed to show any symptoms whatever. Subsequent examination of the brain and glucose broth cultures showed the presence of the typical, terminal, round spores.

There is no available record to indicate that B. tetani has been recovered from the mouth before. One is tempted to speculate on the possibility of tetanus following faulty extraction, but the literature reveals only a few instances of tetanus referable to mouth infection. Thus A. J. N.[10] recorded a fatal case in 1875 due to a faulty root

[10] Dental Cosmos, 1875, 17, p. 167.

canal filling. And Conrad [11] thought he had a case in 1886 following double extraction but the details leave considerable room for doubt, even of the clinical aspects. He even said, "There is no need of anything very elaborate as the books contain all there is upon the subject, no new discoveries having been made recently." Yet Nicolaier [12] had described the tetanus bacillus only two years previously! Finally Miller [1] referred to another case ascribed by Delevie [13] to caries but the original is unavailable. And a search of the modern literature fails to show a single case.

The attempt to re-isolate B. tetani from the little girl's saliva was not made until after 3 months had elapsed, but the result was negative.

There was one other specimen of saliva in which a motile sporulating anaerobe was present. It came from a man 48 years old with marked recession and detachment of the gums, pus pockets, inflammation, serumal and salivary calculus, and accumulated food detritus. This man had lost 9 teeth through pyorrhea, for which he had been under treatment for some time. The culture was unfortunately lost through accident before it could be identified, and a subsequent attempt failed to reveal any sporulating bacteria.

SUMMARY

Sporulating anaerobic bacteria are only occasionally demonstrable in the saliva as spores.

B. welchii, B. tetani, B. bifermentans, and B. tetanomorphus have been recovered from saliva.

These organisms are evidently transient saprophytes in the mouth.

There is no evidence that the sporulating anaerobes have any direct pathologic significance in relation to pyorrhea, but certain species may participate in the deposition of salivary calculus and so indirectly contribute to irritations which in many cases predispose to pyorrhea. Opinion is reserved as to their possible rôle in the decay of dental pulp in caries.

[11] Archives of Dentistry, 1886, 3, p. 485.
[12] Deutsch. med. Wchnschr., 1884, 10, p. 842.
[13] Dissertation, 1891.

PRECIPITIN PRODUCTION THROUGH LENS INJURY

M. F. Guyer

From the Zoological Laboratory, Univerity of Wisconsin, Madison

The earlier experiments by Guyer and Smith [1] in which inheritable eye defects were produced in fetal young by the injection of lens antibodies or of pulped lens into pregnant rabbits, led to the present series of experiments to determine whether or not a tissue injured and left in situ would cause the formation of antibodies. If so, such changes might afford a means by which an injured or misplaced tissue could influence germ cells.

Because of the results already obtained with it in the earlier experiments, and also because of its distinctive nature as a tissue, the crystalline lens was chosen as the experimental tissue. In the operation, the eye, after treatment with a local anesthetic, was pierced with a needle by means of which the lens was more or less broken up. The procedure was much the same as that commonly followed by ophthalmologists in cases of children with congenital cataract.

The serums of the rabbits used were first tested for lens precipitins; without exception they were found negative in all dilutions commonly employed in making precipitin tests. In from 7 to 10 days after the needling operation, the serum of each rabbit was again tested for lens precipitins. The results are shown in table 1. It was found that in more than 50% of cases, when its lens is injured, a normal rabbit will develop lens antibodies in its own blood serum. The lowest positive titer was 1 : 40; the highest, 1 : 1280. Of 23 rabbits thus treated, 10 gave negative, 2 questionable, and 11 positive results. However, rabbit 11, although negative after the first needling, gave a positive reaction when reneedled. All tests were made in duplicate, and where there was any doubt as to the result, a second observer was called in to give an independent judgment without knowing what the first observer had recorded.

For purposes of comparison, 4 rats were similarly experimented on. Because the blood serum of the rats in question was more opaque than that of rabbits, the results were more difficult to see, and they are not

Received for publication, March 19, 1925.

[1] Jour. Exper. Zool., 1918, 26, p. 65; 1920, 31, p. 171; 1924, 38, p. 449.

regarded, therefore, as wholly satisfactory. All 4 were negative before the operation, and each showed a positive reaction after it. The results are shown in table 2.

The blood serum of each of 6 rabbits with hereditary eye defect was tested for lens antibody. Of these, 2 gave positive precipitin reactions with titers of 80 and 160, respectively; the other 4 were negative. The

TABLE 1

RESULTS IN LENS PRECIPITIN EXPERIMENTS PERFORMED WITH RABBITS

Rabbits	Titer Before	Titer After	Remarks
1	0	80	
2	0	1280	
3	0	160	
4	0	80	
5	0	160	
6	0	160	
7	0	0	
8	0	640	
9	0	?	
10	0	0	
11	0	160	Reneedled
12	0	0	
13	0	0	
14	0	640	
15	0	?	
16	0	0	
17	0	0	
18	0	0	
19	0	0	
20	0	80	
21	0	160	
22	0	0	
23	0	40	
24	0	160	

TABLE 2

RESULTS IN LENS PRECIPITIN EXPERIMENTS PERFORMED WITH RATS

Rats	Titer Before Needling	Titer After Needling
1	0	640
2	0	320
3	0	1280
4	0	640

2 which were positive had cataractous lenses, as did at least 1 of the 4 which responded negatively. Likewise, 6 rabbits with similarly defective eyes were tested by the precipitin reaction to determine whether lens antigen were present in their blood serum. For this purpose, goat serum which had been immunized to pig lens was employed. With one doubtful exception, all were negative.

SUMMARY

The blood serum of rabbits that have previously given negative precipitin reactions to lens often show lens precipitins within from 7 to 10 days after needling the lens in situ. In rabbits with hereditary cataract, lens antibody in the form of precipitin is present in some cases, at least, in the blood serum; lens antigen probably is not.

DIPHTHERIA IMMUNITY

EFFECT OF REPEATED INJECTIONS OF AVIRULENT DIPHTHERIA BACILLI, B. HOFMANNI AND B. XEROSIS, IN GUINEA-PIGS . . . .

M. J. Rosenau and G. Howard Bailey

From the Department of Preventive Medicine and Hygiene, Harvard Medical School, Boston

The object of this work is to throw light on the question as to why it is that about 85% of persons acquire immunity to diphtheria as they approach maturity. Two answers to this question suggest themselves: 1. Antitoxin is produced autogenously as a physiologic function with development and with increasing years. 2. Antitoxin production is stimulated by repeated association with diphtheria bacilli. D'Herelle [1] states that "the proportion of refractory persons is increased little by little with age, so that at 25 years the susceptible person is the exception. How is this natural antitoxic immunity acquired? It is not yet known."

Acquired immunity to diphtheria correlates with crowding and with association with the infection. Therefore, it is assumed on epidemiologic grounds that immunity to this, as to other infections, is favored by repeated carrier states. In other words, diphtheria bacilli may be present on the mucous membranes of the nose and throat, or even in the tissues, but be too few in numbers or lacking in virulence to produce effects reaching the threshold of clinical manifestations; nevertheless, they may produce small amounts of toxin that have the same effect in stimulating antitoxin production as repeated injections of toxin, now an accepted routine in the prevention of diphtheria. The assumption that acquired immunity is due to the carrier state is strengthened by the observation that persons living in an environment of sanitary isolation in small communities or under favorable situations in cities are likely to remain susceptible to diphtheria.

It is known, however, that the carrier state with true virulent diphtheria bacilli is not as common as formerly supposed, but that an appreciable percentage of the population at large carries avirulent diphtheria bacilli. The question then arises: Can long association with these avirulent bacilli stimulate antitoxin production? The question has interest as an academic study in immunity as well as for its practical

Received for publication, Feb. 16, 1925.

[1] Immunity in Natural Infectious Disease, 1924, p. 240.

bearings; and we therefore tried it out on guinea-pigs, into which were injected a number of avirulent strains of diphtheria bacilli and related organisms, such as B. hofmanni and B. xerosis.

PLAN OF IMMUNIZATION

Albino guinea-pigs with an initial weight of 350 to 500 gm. were treated in varying ways with the different cultures, as shown in table 1. Most of them were given repeated subcutaneous injections of fresh, young, live broth cultures. The amount at each injection was 2.5 to 5 c c., and the interval was one week throughout the experimental period except for occasional periods of rest. A series was started with filtrates, but these were soon abandoned when it was found that the cultures themselves were producing no evident effects. A limited number of guinea-pigs received intravenous injections, and others intraperitoneal injections. In view of recent developments in immunology, some of our guinea-pigs were treated with daily instillations of live cultures on the mucous membranes of the nose and throat. Another series was fed with the live bacilli, the cultures being placed in the food. Controls consisted of young guinea-pigs from each lot carried along without treatment. Another control series received injections with plain broth, and still another group with subminimal lethal doses of diphtheria toxin.

The results of this work, as given in table 1, show that of 179 guinea-pigs treated, none developed immunity, except the 5 controls which had received injections with diphtheria toxin.

CULTURES USED

Nonvirulent diphtheria bacilli and also cultures of B. hofmanni and B. xerosis were obtained from various laboratories. The authors received transplants from Dr. C. G. Bull, Baltimore; Dr. A. B. Wadsworth, Albany, N. Y.; Dr. W. H. Park, New York City; Dr. Philip Castleman, Boston, and Dr. F. P. Gorham, Providence, R. I. The source, reaction to carbohydrates and virulence tests are shown in table 2.

Three of the 23 cultures turned out to be somewhat toxic, and as our object was to work only with avirulent strains, these were discarded early in the experiments. The sugar reactions of the cultures were determined on plain unfermented broth using brom-thymol blue as indicator, and 0.1% disodium phosphate as a buffer. Control tubes without carbohydrates were inoculated and tested with the rest. More or less complete decolorization of the indicator was considered as positive, and the amount of decolorization of the controls when present was considered in recording the final readings.

TABLE 1

EFFECT OF REPEATED INJECTIONS OF AVIRULENT DIPHTHERIA BACILLI, B. HOFMANNI AND B. XEROSIS ON IMMUNITY AS DETERMINED BY SCHICK TEST IN GUINEA-PIGS

Guinea-Pigs	Weight in Grams Initial-Final	Cultures	Total Amount Injected in C c.	Experimental Period in Months	Schick Tests											Time of Death in Hours After Injection of Lethal Dose of Toxin (6/19/24)	Remarks
					Dec. 16, 1922	Jan. 20, 1923	Feb. 24, 1923	March 20, 1923	April 13, 1923	May 2, 1923	July 23, 1923	Sept. 19, 1923	Oct. 18, 1923	Feb. 12, 1924	June 18, 1924		
93	640-1060	1549	114	16	..	..	+	+	..	+	+	+	+	+	+	42	
94	360	1549	39	3.5	..	..	..	..	..	..	..	+	..	+	..		
95	325- 875	1549	64	8	..	..	..	..	..	..	..	+	..	+	+	60	
96	595-1010	1549	95	16	..	..	+	..	..	+	+	..	..	+	+	69	
6	400	1549	87	6	..	+	+	+	..	..	..	..	..	..	..	..	Filtrate subcut.
13	455- 900	1549	Weekly	12	..	..	+	+	..	+	+	+	..	+	+	62	Culture instillation
1	370- 900	1875	119	17	+	..	+	±	..	+	+	+	+	..	+	49	
33	780- 925	1875	111	14	..	+	+	+	..	+	+	+	+	+	+	68	Culture subcut. and intrav.
68	720- 910	1875	100	15	..	..	..	+	..	+	+	+	..	+	+	65	
69	570- 900	1875	91	14	..	..	..	+	..	—	±	±	±	+	+	67	
70	570- 945	1875	85	13	..	..	..	.	..	+	+	±	±	+	+	66	
71	510	1875	21	4	..	..	..	..	..	+	+	—	+	..	..		
72	550	1875	63	9.5	..	..	..	..	..	+	+	—	±	+	..		
188	550	1875	6	1.5	..	..	..	..	..	+	+	..	..	..	..		
109	400- 810	1875	45	8	..	..	..	..	..	..	..	..	+	+	+	50	
110	350- 850	1875	70	8	..	..	..	..	..	..	..	..	+	+	+	47	
111	330- 385	1875	70	8	..	..	..	..	..	..	..	..	+	+	+	45	
112	345- 610	1875	70	8	..	..	..	..	..	..	..	..	+	±	+	49	
113	420- 950	1875	70	8	..	..	..	..	..	..	..	..	+	+	+	52	
114	390- 835	1875	70	8	..	..	..	..	..	..	..	..	+	+	+	51	
115	325- 550	1875	70	8	..	..	..	..	..	..	..	..	+	+	+	42	
116	400- 900	1875	70	8	..	..	..	..	..	..	..	..	+	+	+	52	
117	380- 755	1875	70	8	..	..	..	..	..	..	..	..	+	+	+	42	
118	390- 790	1875	45	3.5	..	..	..	..	..	..	..	..	+	+	..		
2	495	1875	82	8	..	+	+	+	..	±	+	+	..	..	..	..	Filtrate subcut.
7	490-1020	1875	107	17	..	+	+	+	..	+	+	±	+	±	+	70	Filtrate subcut.
14	455- 840	1875	Weekly	12.5	..	+	+	+	..	+	+	+	..	+	+	45	Culture inst.
171	400	2098	23	3	+	..	+	—	..	..	..	..	..	..	..		
32	585- 900	2098	110	15	..	+	+	+	..	+	+	..	..	+	+	63	Culture subcut. and intrav.
59	385- 855	2098	97	14	..	..	..	..	+	..	+	+	+	+	+	54	
60	480-1060	2098	97	14	..	..	..	..	+	..	+	+	..	+	+	48	
61	385- 820	2098	64	7	..	..	..	..	..	..	+	+	..	+	+	60	
5	605	2098	85	6	..	+	+	+	..	±	±	..	..	..	..	..	Filtrate subcut.
174	500	2098	Weekly	1	..	+	±	±	..	..	..	..	..	..	..	..	Culture inst.
30	395	387-2	106	12.5	+	..	+	+	..	0	+	+	..	+	..		
73	550- 940	387-2	91	14	..	..	..	..	..	+	+	0	+	+	+	96	
74	340- 780	387-2	91	14	..	..	..	..	..	+	+	+	+	+	+	60	
75	425	387-2	17	5	..	..	+	+	..	+	..	..	..	..	..	..	Culture intrav.
177	650	387-2	21	2	..	..	+	+	..	+	..	..	..	..	..	..	Culture intrav.
99	345- 820	387-2	69	8	..	..	..	..	..	..	..	..	+	+	+	53	
100	550- 860	387-2	69	8	..	..	..	..	..	..	..	..	+	+	+	40	
101	330- 750	387-2	69	8	..	..	..	..	..	..	..	..	+	+	+	66	
102	370- 635	387-2	69	8	..	..	..	..	..	..	..	..	+	+	+	43	
103	345- 935	387-2	69	8	..	..	..	..	..	..	..	..	+	+	+	65	
104	340- 920	387-2	69	8	..	..	..	..	..	..	..	..	+	+	+	64	
105	375-1015	387-2	69	8	..	..	..	..	..	..	..	..	+	+	+	70	
106	350- 680	387-2	69	8	..	..	..	..	..	..	..	..	+	+	+	57	
107	410	387-2	44	3.5	..	..	..	..	..	..	..	..	..	+	+		
108	520- 885	387-2	69	8	..	..	..	..	..	..	..	..	+	+	+	65	
8	540- 700	387-2	110	17	..	+	+	+	..	+	+	+	+	+	+	48	Filtrate subcut.
16	500-1033	387-2	Weekly	12	..	+	+	+	..	+	+	+	..	+	+	67	Culture inst.

The amount at each injection was 2.5 to 5 c c. and the interval was one week throughout the experimental period except for occasional periods of rest; unless otherwise stated under remarks, whole culture was injected subcutaneously.

TABLE 1—*Continued*

EFFECT OF REPEATED INJECTIONS OF AVIRULENT DIPHTHERIA BACILLI, B. HOFMANNI AND B. XEROSIS ON IMMUNITY AS DETERMINED BY SCHICK TEST IN GUINEA-PIGS

Guinea-Pigs	Weight in Grams Initial-Final	Cultures	Total Amount Injected in C c.	Experimental Period in Months	Schick Tests											Time of Death in Hours After Injection of Lethal Dose of Toxin (6/19/24)	Remarks
					Dec. 16, 1922	Jan. 20, 1923	Feb. 24, 1923	March 20, 1923	April 13, 1923	May 2, 1923	July 23, 1923	Sept. 19, 1923	Oct. 18, 1923	Feb. 12, 1924	June 18, 1924		
35	400- 820	393-1	112	15	..	..	+	+	..	+	+	+	..	+	+	63	Culture subcut. and intrav.
84	440- 935	393-1	65	7	..	..	..	..	..	..	..	+	..	+	+	65	
85	-1025	393-1	79	13.5	..	..	..	..	..	+	+	+	..	+	+	96	
173	325	393-1	47	6	+	..	+	+	..	±	..	..	..	..	..		
182	395	393-1	27	3	..	..	..	..	+	..	+	..	..	..	..		
3	545- 930	393-1	15	17	..	+	+	+	..	+	+	+	..	+	+	55	Filtrate subcut.
18	510-1010	393-1	Weekly	12	..	+	+	+	..	+	+	+	..	+	+	70	Culture inst.
29	450-1075	790	125	8	+	..	+	+	..	+	+	+	..	+	+	70	
31	515- 900	790	107	7	.	..	±	+	..	+	+	+	+	+	+	67	Culture intrav. and subcut.
36	420	790	85	6	..	..	+	+	..	+	+	+	..	+	..	..	Culture intrav. and subcut.
64	560-1000	790	88	5	..	..	..	..	..	+	+	+	..	+	+	70	
4	470	790	76	3	..	+	+	+	..	+	+	+	..	+	+	..	Filtrate subcut.
17	540-1145	790	Weekly	8	..	+	+	+	..	+	+	+	.	+	+	9 days	Filtrate subcut., culture inst.
34	420	B-196-1	77	9.5	..	..	..	..	+	..	+	+	..	±	..		
38	500-1070	B-196-1	102	14	..	..	..	..	+	..	±	—	±	+	+	68	
39	550-1085	B-196-1	43	6.5	..	..	..	..	..	..	..	..	+	+	+	84	
129	410- 710	B-196-1	77	8	..	..	..	..	..	..	..	..	+	+	+	60	
130	510- 680	B-196-1	77	8	..	..	..	..	..	..	..	..	+	+	+	52	
131	560- 740	B-196-1	77	8	..	..	..	..	..	..	..	..	+	+	+	70	
132	425- 695	B-196-1	77	8	..	..	..	..	..	..	..	..	+	+	+	45	
133	500- 780	B-196-1	77	8	..	..	..	..	..	..	..	..	+	±	+	110	
134	460- 920	B-196-1	77	8	..	..	..	..	..	..	..	..	+	+	+	63	
135	455- 700	B-196-1	77	8	..	..	..	..	..	..	..	..	+	±	+	55	
136	440	B-196-[illegible]	52	3.5	..	..	..	..	..	..	..	..	+	+	..		
137	580- 740	B-196-1	77	8	..	..	..	..	..	..	..	..	+	+	+	62	
138	390- 635	B-196-1	77	8	..	..	..	..	..	..	..	..	+	+	+	43	
15	525	B-196-1	Weekly	6	..	+	+	+	..	+	..	..	..	..	..	..	Culture inst.
28	410- 800	B-370-1	1321	9.5	..	+	+	±	+	±	+	±	+	+	+	55	
41	605- 920	B-370-1	104	14	..	..	+	+	..	+	+	+	..	+	+	17	Culture intrap. and subcut.
42	539- 780	B-370-1	91	6.5	..	..	..	..	..	+	+	+	..	+	+	68	
43	500- 885	B-370-1	94	8	..	..	..	..	..	+	+	—	..	+	+	70	
44	485	B-370-1	71	8	..	..	..	..	+	..	+	±	0	+	..		
119	380- 640	B-370-1	70	8	..	..	..	..	..	..	..	..	+	+	+	42	
120	400	B-370-1	45	8	..	..	..	..	..	..	..	..	+	+	..		
121	350- 940	B-370-1	70	8	..	..	..	..	..	..	..	..	+	+	+	42	
123	330- 730	B-370-1	70	8	..	..	..	..	..	..	..	..	+	+	+	52	
124	385	B-370-1	45	8	..	..	..	..	..	..	..	..	+	+	..		
125	370	B-370-1	45	3.5	..	..	..	..	..	..	..	..	+	±	..		
126	360	B-370-1	45	8	..	..	..	..	..	..	..	..	+	+	..		
127	400- 790	B-370-1	70	8	..	..	..	..	..	..	..	..	+	+	+	60	
128	330- 575	B-370-1	70	6	..	..	..	..	..	..	..	..	+	+	+	40	
26	475	B-1746	46	4	..	+	+	±	..	0	..	..	..	..	..		
34	520- 890	B-1746	109	15.5	..	..	+	+	..	+	+	+	..	+	+	60	Culture intrap and subcut.
97	865- 790	B-1746	91	14.5	..	..	+	..	..	±	+	+	+	±	+	60	
98	325- 720	B-1746	91	13.5	..	..	..	..	..	+	+	±	±	±	+	55	
181	775	B-1746	17	1	..	..	..	+	..	+	..	..	..	..	..		
187	400	B-1746	12	1.5	..	..	..	..	..	±	±	..	..	..	..		
152	500	B-1746	45	3.5	..	..	..	..	..	..	..	..	+	+	..		
153	390- 725	B-1746	70	8	..	..	..	..	..	..	..	+	..	±	+	41	
154	345- 880	B-1746	70	8	..	..	..	..	..	..	..	+	..	+	+	52	
155	440- 775	B-1746	70	8	..	..	..	..	..	..	..	+	..	+	+	52	
156	460- 830	B-1746	70	8	..	..	..	..	..	..	..	+	..	+	+	70	
157	385- 920	B-1746	70	8	..	..	..	..	..	..	..	+	..	+	+	65	
158	500	B-1746	45	8	..	..	..	..	..	..	..	—	+	±	..		

TABLE 1—*Continued*

EFFECT OF REPEATED INJECTIONS OF AVIRULENT DIPHTHERIA BACILLI, B. HOFMANNI AND B. XEROSIS ON IMMUNITY AS DETERMINED BY SCHICK TEST IN GUINEA-PIGS

Guinea-Pigs	Weight in Grams Initial-Final	Cultures	Total Amount Injected in C c.	Experimental Period in Months	Schick Tests: Dec. 16, 1922	Jan. 20, 1923	Feb. 24, 1923	March 20, 1923	April 13, 19..3	May 2, 1923	July 23, 1923	Sept. 19, 19..3	Oct. 18, 1923	Feb. 12, 1924	June 18, 1924	Time of Death in Hours After Injection of Lethal Dose of Toxin (6/19/24)	Remarks
21	445- 910	6391	29	17	..	+	+	0	..	±	+	+	+	+	+	65	
56	515	6491	77	10	..	..	+	..	..	+	+	+	..	+	..	..	Culture intrap. and subcut.
51	560	6391	72	10	..	..	..	+	..	±	±	+	..	+	..		
52	460	6391	66	8.5	..	..	+	+	..	+	+	+	..	+	..		
178	410	6391	15	1	..	..	+	..	..	+	..	..	..	..	..		
186	550	6391	20	2.5	..	..	..	..	..	+	±	..	..	..	..		
146	400- 900	6391	70	8	..	..	..	..	..	..	..	..	+	+	+	60	
147	340- 965	6391	70	8	..	..	..	..	..	..	..	..	+	+	+	52	
148	440- 850	6391	70	8	..	..	..	..	..	..	..	+	..	+	+	52	
139	440- 945	6391	70	8	..	..	..	..	..	..	..	..	+	+	+	62	
141	400-1040	6391	70	8	..	..	..	..	..	..	..	..	+	+	+	72	
142	520	6391	45	3.5	..	..	..	..	..	..	..	..	+	+	..		
143	500- 915	6391	70	8	..	..	..	..	..	..	..	..	+	+	+	53	
144	410	6391	45	3.5	..	..	..	..	..	..	..	+	..	+	..		
45	500	6439	67	10	..	..	..	+	..	±	±	±	0	+	+	..	Culture intrap and subcut.
46	582-1050	6439	79	13.5	..	..	..	..	..	+	±	+	+	+	+	90	
47	560	6439	57	13.5	..	..	..	..	..	+	+	±	+	+	..		
48	575-1035	6439	93	14.5	..	..	..	+	..	+	+	+	..	+	+	7½ days	
49	700-1050	6439	97	14.5	..	..	..	+	..	+	+	+	..	+	+	68	
175	635	6439	39	3	..	+	±	0	..	+	..	..	..	..	..		
185	540	6439	15	1.5	..	..	..	..	..	+	+	..	..	..	..		
165	430- 560	6439	67	8	..	..	..	..	..	..	..	+	..	+	+	49	
161	310- 825	6439	67	8	..	..	..	..	..	..	..	+	..	+	+	40	
162	430- 600	6439	67	8	..	..	..	..	..	..	..	+	..	+	+	55	
163	390- 740	6439	67	8	..	..	..	..	..	..	..	+	..	+	+	60	
164	420- 810	6439	67	8	..	..	..	..	..	..	..	+	..	+	+	57	
166	440-1010	6439	67	8	..	..	..	..	..	..	..	+	..	+	+	67	
167	430- 900	6439	67	8	..	..	..	..	..	..	..	+	..	+	+	51	
168	390- 800	6439	67	8	..	..	..	..	..	..	..	+	..	+	+	63	
170	410- 950	6439	67	8	..	..	..	..	..	..	..	+	..	+	+	73	
27	400-1280	6466	131	17	..	+	+	+	..	+	+	+	..	+	+	70	
57	430- 870	6466	67	8	..	..	..	..	..	..	..	+	..	+	+	63	
58	425- 775	6466	100	14	..	..	..	..	+	..	±	±	±	+	+	60	
20	425	Gracia (B. Hof.)	56	3	..	+	+	±	..	+	..	..	..	..	..		
183	395	Gracia (B. Hof.)	20	4.5	..	..	..	..	+	..	+	±	±	..	..		
22	425- 675	Denberg	129	17	..	+	+	+	..	+	+	+	..	+	+	24	
62	600-1175	Denberg	97	14	..	..	..	..	+	..	+	+	+	+	+	72	
63	405- 930	Denberg	88	14	..	..	..	..	+	..	+	+	..	+	+	71	
53	440- 740	Abramowitz	67	8	..	..	..	..	..	..	..	+	..	+	+	58	
56	480- 625	Abramowitz	67	8	..	..	..	..	..	..	..	+	..	+	+	50	
54	455- 925	Abramowitz	97	14	..	..	..	..	+	..	+	+	..	+	+	42	
176	520	Abramowitz	33	3	..	+	+	+	..	+	..	..	..	..	..		
55	540- 875	Abramowitz	97	14	..	..	..	..	+	..	+	+	..	..	..	66	
25	425	Farise	76	10	..	+	+	+	..	±	+	+	..	..	..		
91	610- 955	Farise	91	14	..	..	..	..	+	..	+	+	..	..	..	63	
92	450- 835	Farise	67	8	..	..	..	..	..	..	..	+	..	+	+	58	
184	435	Farise	..	8	..	..	..	..	+	..	+	±	+	..	..		
24	420- 820	Pizano I	111	17	..	+	+	+	..	+	+	+	..	+	+	45	
86	390	Pizano I	..	..	..	..	..	..	..	..	+	+	..	..	..		
87	485- 985	Pizano I	91	14	..	..	+	..	..	..	+	±	..	+	+	65	

TABLE 1—*Continued*

EFFECT OF REPEATED INJECTIONS OF AVIRULENT DIPHTHERIA BACILLI, B. HOFMANNI AND B. XEROSIS ON IMMUNITY AS DETERMINED BY SCHICK TEST IN GUINEA-PIGS

Guinea-Pigs	Weight in Grams Initial-Final	Cultures	Total Amount Injected in C c.	Experimental Period in Months	Schick Tests: Dec. 16, 1922	Jan. 20, 1923	Feb. 24, 1923	March 20, 1923	April 13, 1923	May 2, 1923	July 23, 1923	Sept. 19, 1923	Oct. 18, 1923	Feb. 12, 1924	June 18, 1924	Time of Death in Hours After Injection of Lethal Dose of Toxin (6/19/24)	Remarks
65	390	Bruce (B. xer.)	48	4.5	..	..	..	..	..	..	+	+	..	0	..		
66	420	Bruce (B. xer.)	73	9	..	..	..	..	..	..	+	+	..	+	+	70	
57	475	Bruce (B. xer.)	60	8.5	..	..	..	..	..	+	+	+	..	+	..		
200	565	Sin (B. xer.)	60	..	..	..	..	..	..	+	+	+	..	+	..		
201	570- 945	Sin (B. xer.)	61	..	..	..	..	..	..	+	+	+	±	+	..		
202	540- 870	Sin (B. xer.)	48	..	..	..	..	..	..	..	+	+	..	0	+	60	
88	785-1035	Car	48	4.5	..	..	..	..	..	..	..	..	+	±	+	93	
89	640-1080	Car	73	9	..	..	..	..	..	..	..	..	+	+	+	68	
90	590	Car	60	8.5	..	..	..	..	..	+	+	..	..	..	..		
9	500- 690	Mixed cults	Weekly	10	..	..	+	+	..	+	+	+	..	+	+	30 days	Culture fed
10	660- 975	Mixed cults	Weekly	10	..	..	+	+	..	±	+	+	..	+	+	67	Culture fed
11	575- 885	Mixed cults	Weekly	10	..	..	+	+	..	±	+	+	..	+	+	65	Culture fed
12	570- 875	Mixed cults	Weekly	10	..	..	+	+	..	±	+	+	..	+	+	7 days	Culture fed
23	500	Sterile broth	81	3	..	+	±	0	..	+	..	..	..	..	..	..	Subcutaneously
80	600- 900	Sterile broth	82	14.5	..	..	+	+	..	+	±	±	..	+	+	53	Subcutaneously
81	570-1030	Sterile broth	82	14.5	..	..	+	+	..	+	+	+	..	+	+	69	Subcutaneously
82	610	Sterile broth	52	2.5	..	..	..	..	..	+	+	+	..	..	..		
83	565-1045	Sterile broth	73	14	..	..	..	..	..	+	+	+	..	+	+	66	Subcutaneously
179	830-1175	Sterile broth	88	14	..	..	+	+	..	+	+	+	..	+	+	70	Subcutaneously
180	350	Sterile broth	13	0.5	..	..	+	+	..	..	..	..	..	..	..	..	Subcutaneously
76	695-1065	Diphth. toxin	Weekly	15	..	..	+	+	+	..	+	+	+	+	+	51	Filtrate MLD +S. S. 1.944
77	580	Diphth. toxin	Weekly	13½	..	..	+	+	±	..	0	0	0	0	0	..	+S. S. 1.694
78	590	Diphth. toxin	Weekly	12½	..	..	+	+	±	..	+	+	+	+	..	..	+S. S. 1.364
79	560-1020	Diphth. toxin	Weekly	15	..	..	+	+	+	..	0	0	0	0	0	Lived	+S. S. 1.944
172	395	Diphth. toxin	Weekly	4	+	..	+	±	±	..	..	..	..	..	..	..	+S. S. 0.127

MATERIALS INJECTED

The medium used for the growth of cultures was beef infusion broth prepared according to the method of Dean, placed in 300 c c. quantities in 1-liter Erlenmeyer flasks and sterilized in the Arnold sterilizer, the final reaction being P_H 7.6. All the cultures grew well with marked turbidity on this medium. The broth cultures used for the routine weekly injections were grown in large slanted tubes and incubated at 37 C. for 48, 72, 96 and 144 hours during the course of the work. The filtrates were prepared from the respective cultures after growth on the medium mentioned for 9 days at 37 C. Cultures 1549, "Hogan," 393-1, 790, 1875, 2098, B-370-1, "Gracia," and "Denberg" showed a tendency to pellicle formation in the order named. Culture "Hogan" proved to be virulent for guinea-pigs, and its filtrate caused death with typical lesions of diphtheria toxin. Culture 1549 grew in all respects like the Park 8 culture as to pellicle formation and clumping, but neither culture nor filtrate was toxic.

TABLE 2

Guinea-Pigs	Source	Sugar Reactions						Virulence
		Dextrose	Saccharose	Dextrin	Lactose	Maltose	Mannite	
1549	Case contact	+	±	+	±	+	0	0
1875	Case contact	+	±	+	±	+	0	0
2098	Case contact	+	0	+	±	+	0	0
387-2	Carrier at large	+	+	+	±	+	0	0
393-1	Carrier at large	+	±	+	±	+	0	0
790	Carrier at large	+	±	+	±	+	0	0
B-196-1	Carrier at large	+	±	+	±	+	0	0
B-370-1	Carrier at large	+	±	+	+	±	0	0
B-1746	Carrier at large	+	±	+	±	+	0	0
6391	Carrier at large	+	+	+	+	+	0	0
6439	Carrier at large	+	0	+	±	+	0	0
6466	Case contact	+	+	+	+	±	0	0
Gracia (B. hof.)	Unknown	0	0	0	0	0	0	0
Denberg	Unknown	+	0	+	±	+	0	0
Abramowitz	Unknown	+	0	+	±	+	0	0
Hogan	Unknown	+	±	+	±	+	0	+
Farise	Case contact	+	0	+	±	+	0	0
Pizano I	Case contact	+	±	+	±	+	0	0
Bruce (B. xerosis)	Throat culture	+	+	0	0	+	0	0
Car	Surgical drainage	+	±	+	+	+	±	0
Sin (B. xerosis)	Chronic carrier	+	+	0	0	+	0	0
Izzy	Throat culture (scarlet fever)	+	±	+	0	+	0	±
"C"	Sore throat	+	±	+	0	+	±	±

No relation could be noted in any of the cultures between characteristics of growth and varying degrees of toxicity. No change in virulence was noted in any of the cultures during 18 months' cultivation on Loeffler's blood serum medium.

PATHOLOGIC LESIONS PRODUCED BY SOME AVIRULENT CULTURES

The fact that 20 cultures used in an attempt to immunize guinea-pigs were really avirulent is indicated by the fact that even massive doses injected subcutaneously and large doses intraperitoneally or intravenously produced scarcely noticeable effects. The subcutaneous injections were followed by nodular indurations at the site of the inoculations. These reactions lessened after the animals received several treatments. In no case did necrosis occur.

It was noted, however, that during the course of the work some of the guinea-pigs developed lesions that deserve attention. Thus, it was observed that 2 guinea-pigs which had received injections of culture 1875, 3 which had received injections of culture B-370-1 and 2 which had received injections of culture B-1746 after several weeks developed either a right-sided or a left-sided torticollis, which gradually became more pronounced. All these animals finally died of pneumonia. One guinea-pig which had received prolonged injections of culture 6391 developed complete paralysis of both hind legs, from which it did not recover. The possibility that the so-called avirulent diphtheria bacilli may have pathogenic properties is to be considered. Lesieur,[2] in fact, claims that certain strains of pseudodiphtheria bacilli, although non-virulent, may cause fatal paralysis in guinea-pigs similar to that due to diphtheria toxone. No such effects, however, were observed in our series.

Practically all the guinea-pigs that developed symptoms during life showed interesting lesions at necropsy. Five guinea-pigs which had received injections with culture B-370-1, four which received injections of B-196-1, and one each with cultures 6391, 1875 and B-1746 showed a striking condition of the liver, spleen and lungs. The livers of these animals were much enlarged and filled with yellowish-white nodules 1 mm. to 1 cm. in diameter. The spleens were from 2 to 6 times the normal size, and presented much the same appearance. In most of these guinea-pigs the lungs also showed focal lesions, resembling in some respects miliary tubercles. These lesions are being studied. It is evident that some so-called avirulent diphtheria bacilli have pathologic properties when repeatedly injected in massive doses. These results were not constant and seem to depend on individual susceptibility. Neither the symptoms nor the lesions in these guinea-pigs resembled the toxic action of diphtheria bacilli.

THE SCHICK TEST ON GUINEA-PIGS

Guinea-pigs react with striking uniformity to the Schick test. Of more than 350 tested, all reacted positively and gave a uniform picture. The local reaction can best be seen on white guinea-pigs, which were therefore used in these experiments. The test was made on the skin of the abdomen, which was shaved the day before the injection.

A typical reaction in a guinea-pig runs a characteristic course very much like that seen on the skin of a child. The skin of the guinea-pig,

[2] Compt. rend. Soc. de biol., 1901, 53, p. 817.

however, seems to be more sensitive to diphtheria toxin than that of the child; at least, it reacts to smaller amounts of toxin. We found that 1/1,000 MLD produces a slight reaction; 1/500, a definite reaction, but without noticeable edema or induration; 1/250, a typical reaction; 1/50, a severe reaction with necrosis. Glenny and Allen[3] found 1/500 MLD to be the minimum reacting dose of diptheria toxin injected intradermally into guinea-pigs. We selected 1/250 MLD diluted with salt solution so that the test dose is contained in 0.1 c c. The same lot of toxin (MLD 0.017) was used throughout all the work here represented, except the final injection with an MLD to test immunity (table 6).

As a rule, when the Schick test is performed on 100 or more guinea-pigs, a few of them show a slight or no reaction, but when retested a few days later, those with negative reactions give clear-cut positive tests. This indicates that in a series of Schick tests something happens with the technic in a small percentage of cases—perhaps the toxin leaks out. We soon learned never to call a guinea-pig's Schick test negative until two or more successive tests had been made.

In the course of the work it was noted that pregnant guinea-pigs are more likely to show slight or even negative reactions, probably due to mechanical stretching and thinning of the skin over the abdomen, leading to relatively deeper injections of the toxin solution and greater local diffusion. Weak reactions were also more common in sick animals, such as those with pneumonia, and is in agreement with the principle that local reactions may be inhibited by severe systemic ones.

Guinea-pigs react like children whose reaction to the Schick test is positive, but, unlike most children, guinea-pigs react positively to the Schick test throughout their lives unless immunized in some artificial way. In other words, guinea-pigs appear to have no antitoxin in their blood to start with and remain antitoxin-free unless immunized. They vary in the ease with which the Schick test may be rendered negative by the repeated injection of diphtheria toxin. For example, guinea-pigs 76 and 79 in table 3, were started when approximately half-grown, and were given the same number of injections of the same toxin in the same amounts over a period of a year or more. They were kept in the same cage, were given the same food, and as far as can be determined had the same environment. Nevertheless, one guinea-pig's Schick test remained persistently positive, and when tested 15 months after begin-

[3] Jour. Path. & Bacteriol., 1921, 24, p. 61.

TABLE 3

RESULTS OF INJECTION OF TOXIN

Guinea-Pigs	Sex	Weight, Initial-Final	Toxin Injected			Schick Tests										Remarks
			Total Amount	Over Period of	Number and Amount of Injections	1922	1923							1924		
						12/16	1/23	2/14	3/20	5/2	7/23	9/19	10/7	2/12	6/18	
76	F	695–1065	1.944 MLD	15 mos.	39 injections 1/125–1/8 MLD	..	..	+	+	+	+	+	+	+	+	Tested 6/19 MLD; died 52 hrs.
77	F	580	1.694 MLD	13½ mos.	36 injections 1/125–1/8 MLD	..	..	+	+	±	0	0	0	0	..	Died 5/3/24; pneumonia
78	F	590	1,364 MLD	12½ mos.	31 injections 1/125–1/8 MLD	..	..	+	+	±	+	±	+	+	..	Died 4/6/24; pneumonia
79	F	560–1020	1.944 MLD	15 mos.	39 injections 1/125–1/8 MLD	..	..	+	+	±	0	0	0	0	0	Tested 6/19 MLD; lived; no reaction
172	M	395	0.127 MLD	4 mos.	7 injections 1/125–1/25 MLD	+	+	+	±	±	..	..	..	..	..	Died 8/23; pneumonia

0, no reaction; +, positive; ±, slight reaction.

ning the experiment with a MLD diphtheria toxin, it died in 52 hours of characteristic lesions; whereas, the companion guinea-pig's Schick test became negative after 3 months, and it showed no local reaction nor any other ill effects from subcutaneous injection of an MLD diphtheria toxin. It is therefore evident that in experiments of this kind it takes 3 or 4 months to develop immunity under favorable circumstances, and were it practicable to continue observations over a series of years, as is possible in human beings, a different story might develop.

PSEUDOREACTIONS

Living Cultures.—As we had a large number of guinea-pigs sensitized with various substances, we made a study of the problem of the pseudoreaction. It is noteworthy that none of the guinea-pigs throughout our study showed a reaction that could be interpreted as a pseudoreaction following the intracutaneous injection of diphtheria toxin. Experiments were therefore planned to determine how the skin of our sensitized guinea-pigs would react to the various antigens with which they were sensitized. The pseudoreaction is usually interpreted as a reaction to the antigens in the bacillary substance or to foreign proteins other than the toxin.

We first tested the guinea-pigs with the same cultures with which they had been sensitized, and later tested them for cross reactions with heterologous cultures. These tests were first made by injecting 0.1 c c. of living cultures, 7-days growth in broth; later, various filtrates and extracts were used. It at once became clear that the guinea-pigs were indeed sensitized, for they reacted, while control guinea-pigs that had not been treated showed little or no reaction to the different cultures used in these skin tests. The controls at most showed a trifling and transient redness. These tests were repeated a number of times, using the same antigen and also different antigens, to determine the specificity of the reaction. It soon became clear that the guinea-pigs reacted rather indiscriminately when tested with the cultures used, so that no specificity within the group could be determined. The pseudoreaction usually consisted of a pinkish area at the point of injection, with edema and little or no induration. The reaction appeared in about half an hour, leaving redness and edema, which gradually subsided and practically disappeared in 24 hours, and often could not be detected in 48 hours.

Extracts.—When the nonspecificity of the living cultures was determined, a number of filtrates and extracts were used, of which the following are selected as examples:

Extracts 1875, B-370, K-L 8D: Grown 3 days on 10 Loeffler's slants at 37 C. Removed with loop. Washed with normal salt solution and centrifuged 3 times; sediment taken up in 6 c c. N/10NaOH. Incubated 48 hours at 37 C. Shaken 4 hours; centrifuged. Supernatant fluid titrated with N/10 HCl and phenol red indicator to P_H 7.6. The extracts all gave a slight cloudiness with heat and nitric acid. The results of tests on sensitized and control guinea-pigs are shown in table 4.

Table 4 shows the nonspecificity of the skin reaction within the group of avirulent diphtheria organisms tested. A number of extracts were made by different methods, and it was noted that those extracts that contained demonstrable amounts of protein with the heat and acid tests also caused a reaction.

The extracts that did not give a chemical test for protein gave little or no skin reaction.

The nonspecificity of bacterial proteins of this nature is emphasized by the fact that we obtained reactions in guinea-pigs sensitized with avirulent diphtheria cultures and tested with extracts of B. coli, B. subtilis and the pneumococcus.

Extracts of B-370-1, B. subtilis, Staphylococcus albus, B. typhosus, pneumococcus type 1 and sarcina. All except pneumococci were grown in 10 Loeffler's slants. Pneumococci were grown in 10 blood-agar tubes and washed off in 7 c c. of salt solution. The suspensions in salt solution were frozen and thawed

TABLE 4

PSEUDOREACTIONS—BACTERIAL EXTRACTS

Guinea-Pigs	Previous Treatment	Tested with Extracts			
		1875	B-196-1	B-370-1	Park 8
109	1875	+	+	+	+
110	1875	+	+	+	+
111	1875	+	+	+	+
112	1875	+	+	+	+
113	1875	+	+	+	+
129	B-196-1	+	±	+	±
130	B-196-1	+	+	+	±
131	B-196-1	+	+	+	+
132	B-196-1	+	+	+	±
133	B-196-1	±	±	+	±
28	B-370-1	+	+	+	+
42	B-370-1	+	+	+	+
43	B-370-1	+	+	+	+
44	B-370-1	+	+	+	+
76	Toxin	—	—	—	—
79	Toxin	—	—	—	±
Control	None	—	—	—	—
Control	None	—	—	—	—
Control	None	—	—	—	—
Control	None	—	—	—	—
Control	None	—	—	—	—
Control	None	—	—	—	—

20 times—average about 3 times a day over a period of a week. Temperature of freezing—mixture of salt and ice; temperature of thawing—37.5 C. Finally shaken 4 hours, adjusted to P_H 7.6; centrifuged; supernatant fluid placed in icebox over night and allowed to settle. Clear supernatant fluid-extract.

Nitric acid ring test—B-370-1, B. subtilis, Staphylococcus albus, sarcina showed a slight opalescence. B. typhosus and pneumococcus showed no reaction.

Bacterial Extracts.—Grown same as preceding. Sediment which had been frozen and thawed 20 times treated with 6 c c. of N/10 NaOH and incubated 4 days; shaken 4 hours; centrifuged, and supernatant fluid titrated with N-HCl to P_H 7.6.

Tests with HNO_3 showed slight cloudiness at the ring, except in the case of the pneumococcus.

It was soon noticed that the reactions sometimes appeared in 5 minutes, developed rapidly as a red areola, and became purplish or bluish in the center. When this occurred, it usually subsided normally, but sometimes left a little necrotic superficial scab in the center, which was interpreted as a modified Arthus' phenomenon. The pseudoreaction occurs earlier, develops more quickly and fades more rapidly than the true Schick reaction.

RELATION BETWEEN SCHICK TEST AND IMMUNITY

It is now taken for granted that the Schick test is a reliable index of the presence or absence of antitoxin in the blood and therefore of the presence or absence of immunity. We had a good opportunity to try out this correlation by testing all the surviving guinea-pigs at the end of the experiment with an MLD diphtheria toxin. All the guinea-pigs that responded positively to the Schick test reacted characteristically and died of an acute condition, whereas the guinea-pigs that gave a negative Schick showed no demonstrable effects.

TABLE 5

MLD FOR GUINEA-PIGS OF VARIOUS WEIGHTS

Weight, Gm.	Amount of Toxin, C c.	Time of Death, Days
250	0.011	5½
690	0.011	30
875	0.015	6½
1,145	0.02	9
690	0.022	4
810	0.023	3½
780	0.024	2½
940	0.025	4

RELATION OF WEIGHT TO DIPHTHERIA TOXIN

Graham-Smith [4] states that the lethal dose per gram of weight of guinea-pigs varies somewhat with the age of the animal and also with the stock, young guinea-pigs being relatively more susceptible. All our animals were albino stock obtained from the same breeder and therefore of the same stock.

In table 5 are shown preliminary tests made in order to learn the approximate MLD for guinea-pigs of variable weights.

From this series it appears that the dose is not a direct function of the weight, for twice the minimal lethal dose for guinea-pigs weighing 250 gm. produces death in an acute condition in guinea-pigs weighing 4 times as much. We selected 0.04 c c. as the test dose in order to bring out clearly any immunity that might be present in the residual guinea-pigs under question. In all, 114 guinea-pigs were tested, as shown in table 6.

It will be noted in table 6 that the weights of the guinea-pigs varied from 400 to 1200 gms., and the time of death from 20 to 120 hours, with the exception of one animal weighing 1,050 gm., which lived 7½ days. It will be observed that the time of death of 107 of the 114

[4] Bacteriology of Diphtheria, 1908, p. 176.

guinea-pigs was 40 to 80 hours. Within these limits, however, the frequencies tend to follow a linear distribution when the weights in grams are plotted against the hours of death. This is clear from the table without plotting a curve. It is therefore evident that there is a definite relation between the weights of guinea-pigs and the time of death against a constant but lethal dose of diphtheria toxin. Otherwise expressed, there is a relation with individual variation between the weight of a guinea-pig and its minimal lethal dose of diphtheria toxin.

TABLE 6

SUBCUTANEOUS INJECTION OF 0.04 C C. DIPHTHERIA TOXIN TO TEST IMMUNITY

Weight in Gm.	Hours of Death									Totals
	10-20	30-40	40-50	50-60	60-70	70-80	90-100	100-120	120+	
1,200	..	..	..	..	..	1	..	..	..	1
1,100	..	..	..	..	..	2	..	..	..	2
1,050	..	..	2	1	3	1	1	..	1*	9
1,000	..	..	..	..	5	5	2	..	..	12
950	..	..	..	2	3	1	..	..	..	6
900	1	..	3	5	14	1	..	..	..	24
850	..	..	2	3	7	1	..	..	..	13
800	..	..	3	7	9	1	..	1	..	21
750	..	..	1	..	..	..	..	..	..	1
700	..	..	3	4	4	2	..	..	..	13
650	..	..	4	2	..	..	..	..	..	6
600	..	1	1	1	..	..	..	..	..	3
550	..	..	2	..	..	..	..	..	..	2
400	..	..	1	..	..	..	..	..	..	1
Totals	1	1	22	25	45	15	3	1	1	114

* Died in 7½ days.
The figures in the table are the number of guinea-pigs dying in the specified time.

SUMMARY AND DISCUSSION

The object of these experiments was to determine whether avirulent diphtheria bacilli are able to stimulate antitoxin production and thus account for the acquired immunity to diphtheria which most persons develop with maturity. Seventeen different strains of avirulent cultures and also cultures of related organisms, such as B. hofmanni and B. xerosis, were injected into guinea-pigs over a long period of time. The Schick test remained positive for all these guinea-pigs, and when the final test was made they showed no immunity to diphtheria toxin. It was found that there is considerable individual variation in guinea-pigs so far as their response to injections of diphtheria toxin is concerned. Usually the Schick test becomes negative for guinea-pigs in three months, and they then are immune. The Schick test in one animal remained positive after 39 injections of small doses of diphtheria toxin (1/125 to 1/8 MLD) over a period of 15 months. This guinea-pig received a total of 1.94 MLD. If experiments such as ours, with avirulent cultures, could be continued over a series of years, it is possible that some immunizing effects might be manifest.

Our studies emphasize the essential difference between the so-called avirulent diphtheria bacilli and the true Klebs-Loeffler organism. Not only did the avirulent strains fail to induce immunity, but their agglutination reactions showed that there is a wide immunologic gap separating them from the diphtheria bacillus. Some of these so-called avirulent strains have pathogenic properties. We found that a few of our guinea-pigs that received repeated massive injections of live cultures, developed disseminated focal lesions, which are being studied.

No change in virulence was observed in cultures of avirulent diphtheria bacilli or B. hofmanni or B. xerosis under observation for 18 months, and transferred for 36 generations on Loeffler's blood serum.

Guinea-pigs react with striking uniformity to the Schick test. All guinea-pigs appear to be like some children in that they are persistently positive. The guinea-pig's skin seems to be more sensitive than the human skin, for a typical reaction is produced by the intradermal injection of $\frac{1}{250}$ MLD. Pregnancy and general systemic infections appear to inhibit the local skin reaction.

Pseudoreactions were not observed in our studies as a result of the injection of diphtheria toxin; but sensitized guinea-pigs responded to the injection of bacterial antigens, although this reaction is not specific. With certain bacterial extracts containing bacterial protein, a local necrotic action of the skin was produced which was interpreted as a modified Arthus phenomenon.

Experimental confirmation was obtained of the correlation between a positive Schick test and susceptibility and a negative Schick test and immunity. In a series of guinea-pigs it was furthermore found that a definite relation exists between the weight of the animal and the MLD of diphtheria toxin. It takes about twice as much diphtheria toxin to kill a guinea-pig weighing 4 times as much as the standard control; in other words, if the MLD for a 250 gm. guinea-pig is 0.011, it will take 0.022 for a guinea-pig weighing 1,000 gm.

Morphologically the avirulent diphtheria bacillus resembles the true Klebs-Loeffler organism, but the results recorded above emphasize the fundamental difference between the two groups, and throw doubt on the appropriateness of the name "avirulent diphtheria bacilli."

BACTERIAL FACTORS IN PYORRHEA ALVEOLARIS

IV. MICROCOCCUS GAZOGENES, A MINUTE GRAM-NEGATIVE, NON-SPORULATING ANAEROBE PREVALENT IN HUMAN SALIVA

Ivan C. Hall and Beatrice Howitt

From Cornell University, Ithaca, N. Y., and University of California, Berkeley

Early in our effort [1] to isolate sporulating anaerobes from saliva, it was noticed that unheated specimens almost invariably produced abundant gas in primary brain cultures, whereas those heated to 80 C. rarely did so. And since gas-forming aerobes were isolated only occasionally from saliva, we concluded that obligate anaerobes must be responsible. The relative infrequence of anaerobic spores suggested that such organisms might be either the vegetative forms of sporulating species, or species incapable of sporulation. The latter proved to be the case; 35 unheated specimens of saliva yielded 24 strains of a minute, gram-negative, nonsporulating, gas-forming anaerobe, whose high frequency, peculiar properties, significance, nomenclature, and taxonomy form the basis of this report. We strongly suspect that it plays an important rôle in the precipitation of salivary calculus, and thus contributes to irritations which are directly or indirectly responsible for pyorrhea; but further study will be required to establish this.

HISTORICAL

Holman and Krock [2] have recently isolated the same germ from the mouths of 13 people, 3 rabbits, and 1 guinea-pig, as shown not only by our inspection of their papers but also by direct comparison of 2 strains kindly supplied by Dr. Holman. We are convinced of the essential identity of species represented by their strains and ours, but we disagree as to their filtrability and nomenclature.

Holman and Krock found that cultures in certain mediums passed through Berkefeld and Mandler filters, and for that reason suspected a relation to B. pneumosintes of Olitsky and Gates [3] and suggested their possible confusion. Our own experiments, to be discussed in more detail, have failed to show that either Holman's or our own strains are filtrable; the fact that they produce abundant gas, whereas this property has not been recorded for B. pneumosintes, clearly indicates that they are distinct. Furthermore, Olitsky and Gates [4]

Received for publication, Jan. 27, 1925.

[1] Hall: Jour. Infect. Dis., 1925, 37, p. 87.

[2] Proc. Soc. Exper. Biol. and Med., 1923, 20, p. 280; Am. Jour. Hygiene, 1923, 3, p. 487.

[3] Jour. Exper. Med., 1921-1923.

[4] Ibid., 1922, 35, p. 813.

recorded acid production "without gas" for B. pneumosintes, though in an earlier paper[5] "no observable amounts of acid or gas were produced" in dextrose, maltrose, lactose, saccharose, inulin, and mannitol. We have been unable to study B. pneumosintes, but our cultures never produce acid.

Holman and Krock thought their organism "closely related to Staphylococcus parvulus of Veillon and Zuber,"[6] and Olitsky and Gates[7] used this designation for anaerobic gas-producing cocci from rabbits. But there is no excuse for confusing these organisms, because they never produce the fetid odor ascribed to Staphylococcus parvulus; furthermore, S. parvulus was found to produce only a slight amount of gas, and was somewhat pathogenic for laboratory animals.

We believe that our cultures and Holman's are the same as Lewkowicz's[8] Micrococcus gazogenes alcalescens anaerobius, first described in 1901, which was taken from the mouth of a healthy infant 8 days old. That this writer did not confuse his strain with Staphylococcus parvulus may be explained easily; he was working under Veillon's direction in Grancher's laboratory in Cracow. Is it likely that a student working in the same laboratory with his instructor would publish a description of the same species under a new name in the same journal only three years later? Surely there is no reason for confusion here.

However, Jungano and Distaso[9] regarded these two forms as identical, and Ozaki[10] was uncertain which designation should be used for certain cultures isolated by him from the mouth, though to us now his description seems to fit Lewkowicz's germ quite well. We suspect, however, that Ozaki's[11] second micrococcus was contaminated, because of the foul odor and rods in old cultures.

If we admit the originality of Lewkowicz's record, we are then confronted with the priority of a quadrinomial which is contrary to the rules of scientific nomenclature. We, therefore suggest the name Micrococcus gazogenes (Lewkowicz), and shall so use it in this paper.

SOURCE OF MATERIAL

Thirty-five specimens of saliva were collected at various times from 23 persons, of whom 19 were male prisoners in San Quentin, while 4 were members of the senior writer's family. All specimens but the first were among those already reported for reaction changes[12] and for sporulating anaerobes.[1] The subjects were not selected for any particular type of dental condition; several were practically free from dental defects, while others were seriously afflicted in varying stages of dental caries and pyorrhea. No record was kept of the dental condition of the person from whom the first culture was isolated; the remaining 22 were examined by Dr. Clayton Westbay and the senior author,

[5] Ibid., 1921, 33, p. 713.
[6] Arch. de med. exper., 1898, 10, p. 517.
[7] Proc. Soc. Exper. Biol. & Med., 1924, 21, p. 392.
[8] Arch. de med. exper., 1901, 13, p. 633.
[9] Les Anaerobies, 1910.
[10] Centrbl. f. Bakteriol., 1, O., 1912, 62, p. 76.
[11] Ibid., 1, O., 1915, 76, p. 118.
[12] Hall and Westbay: Dental Cosmos, 1925, 67, p. 115.

and their dental defects noted, as in table 1, together with the age and nativity of the subjects, the cultural numbers and the number of attempts required to isolate M. gazogenes.

We were impressed by the great variety of dental conditions in persons from a single specimen of whose saliva it was possible to recover this organism, and by its presence in juvenile as well as in adult mouths. Isolation was duplicated in samples from 3 men, while in 5 instances a second sample, and in 1 case a third had to be secured. There were only 2 donors from whom M. gazogenes could not be isolated, and there was presumptive evidence of it in their saliva, namely, gas formation in the primary brain cultures, although in one of them the gas might have been due to Bact. coli. Unfortunately, repeated samples could not be secured in these 2 cases.

The clinical data show that all but one of those in which isolation did not succeed on first trial presented few or no gingival lesions; but, on the other hand, there were several equally good mouths from which this germ was readily recovered.

We have also isolated one strain from the lung of a rabbit at necropsy for comparison with our human strains and those received from Dr. Holman. All were morphologically and culturally identical.

M. gazogenes is not only present in almost every sample of saliva, it is also often present in tremendous numbers. These two facts justify the conclusion that it is not merely accidental but truly indigenous in the mouth. One c c. of a 1 : 1,000,000 dilution of fresh saliva frequently suffices to inoculate brain medium with M. gazogenes, but a few experiments with serial dilution failed to show that it was the most abundant mouth organism, as we at first suspected; it is generally exceeded in numbers by streptococci. Comparative tests with deep agar for primary cultures have shown the superiority of brain medium for this type of experiment.

COLLECTION OF SAMPLES AND METHODS OF ISOLATION

Our method of collecting salivary samples has been described before (1, 12), and the time involved in transportation from the prison to the laboratory was also mentioned, about 1½ hours, though in some cases the primary inoculations were made at the prison; 1 c c. of mixed saliva was transferred into the depths of a freshly boiled and cooled tube of brain medium and incubated at 37 C. We have never found a specimen of human saliva in which such cultures did not show abundant gas production at 24 hours, and we consider this strong presumptive evidence of a practically universal distribution of M. gazogenes in the mouth.

TABLE 1

DENTAL CONDITIONS OF SUBJECTS WHOSE SALIVA WAS EXAMINED FOR M. GAZOGENES

Number	Nativity	Age	Recession of Gums	Detachment of Gums	Pockets	Pus	Loose Teeth	Inflammation	Hypertrophy	Serumal Calculus	Salivary Calculus	Detritus	Caries	Fillings	Missing Teeth	Micrococcus Gazogenes Numbers*	Number of Attempts
—	—	—	—	—	—	—	—	—	—	—	—	—	—	—	—	1	1
3	Am.	24	+	+	+	0	0	0	0	0	0	+	+	15	6	10, 28	2
4	Am.	25	0	0	0	0	0	0	0	0	0	+	+	0	2	11, 34	2
7	Am.	55	+	+	+	0	0	+	0	+	+	+	+	0	14	14	1
11	Am.	31	0	+	+	0	0	0	0	+	0	++	0	+	0	15	2
15	Am.	43	+++	+++	+	+	+++	+	0	+	++	+	0	++	+++	16	1†
16	Am.	42	+++	+++	+++	+++	+	++	++	+++	+++	++	0	0	8	17	1
18	Am.	25	0	++	++	+	0	+	++	++	+	+	0	0	3	19, 36	2
19	Am	33	+	+	+	0	0	+	0	++	++	++	++	0	11	20	1
26	Am.	48	+++	+++	+	+	++	+	0	+++	+++	+++	0	+	9	21	2
27	Ital.	50	+	++	++	+++	0	+++	+++	+++	+++	+++	0	0	1	22	1
28	Am.	9	0	0	0	0	0	0	0	0	0	0	++	0	0	23	1
29	Am.	13	0	0	0	0	0	0	0	0	0	+	+	3	0	24	1
30	Am.	11	0	0	0	0	0	0	0	0	+	+	+	3	0	25	1
-31	Am.	54	+	+	0	0	0	0	0	0	0	+	0	8	1	26	3
32	Am.	24	0	++	+	+	0	++	+	+	+	+	0	0	1	27	2
34	Am.	31	+	+	+	+	0	+	0	++	+++	+++	0	0	3	29	1
35	Am.	25	0	+	0	0	0	0	0	0	0	+	0	2	0	..	2
36	Am.	26	0	0	0	+	0	+++	++	+	+	+++	0	8	4	..	1
42	Mex.	29	+	++	++	+++	0	+++	+++	+++	+	+++	0	0	0	37	1
43	Am.	38	0	+	++	0	0	0	0	0	++	0	0	2	5	38	2
45	Am.	34	+	0	0	0	0	0	+	+	0	+	+	1	5	40	2
46	Am.	43	0	0	0	0	0	0	0	+	0	0	+	5	3	41	2

* In addition to these were studied 2 strains isolated by Dr. Holman (42 from a rabbit's mouth and 43 from human saliva); we also isolated one strain (44) from a rabbit's lung.

† Treated by instruments 2 years.

These primary brain cultures were always stained by Gram's method; but it is difficult to recognize M. gazogenes in an impure culture, owing to its negative reaction and its extremely small size. Gram-positive cocci in groups, pairs, or chains were always present, while many cultures contained in addition gram-positive rods, long slender filamentous rods, short gram-negative rods and diplococci. Brain medium serves splendidly in the primary culture of many micro-organisms of the mouth.

In the early part of our work, we tried to apply the principle of selective bacteriostasis, using gentian violet; but the streptococci of the mouth are only a little more susceptible than M. gazogenes, and we were not very successful. The best results were secured by making serial dilutions of brain cultures in 1% nutrient agar in meat infusion with 2% peptone, adjusted to P_H 7, and isolating by the well-known deep agar culture method. At first we isolated many facultative aerobes, particularly of streptococcus, and had to rely on the chance of recovering M. gazogenes from among many colonies picked, until we observed that those of M. gazogenes are distinctive in their resemblance to a tiny buckwheat, so that with the aid of a hand lens, the desired species can generally be selected readily by an experienced person. Picked colonies were transferred to brain medium, incubated at 37 C., and checked up for purity by observation of gas production, by microscopic examination using Gram's stain, by attempted aerobic cultures on blood-agar slants, and by deep culture in 1% agar. It was necessary in some cases to make several successive attempts at purification before absolute purity could be assumed.

MORPHOLOGIC AND CULTURAL PROPERTIES OF MICROCOCCUS GAZOGENES

M. gazogenes is less than 0.5 mikron in length and breadth, gram-negative, nonsporulating, nonmotile, and obligately anaerobic. The rarity of visible gas formation among the cocci caused us to question the propriety of its designation as a micrococcus. While staining so poorly by Gram's method that it is almost invisible in pure cultures and likely to be entirely overlooked in mixed cultures, it stains well by dilute fuchsin as a simple stain. Even so, and with a high power binocular microscope using special illumination, it is a matter of personal opinion as to whether it should be called a coccus or a rod. It occurs in pairs, in tetrads, in small clumps, and occasionally in short chains; pairs and clumps are most common.

Hoping to find a clue through involution forms, we examined a 6 months old brain culture, a deep agar colony of the same age, a 2 months milk culture, a 3 months glucose broth culture, an 8 months blood-agar slant kept under alkaline pyrogallol, and a month old meat mash culture, with no evidence of rodlike involution forms.

Pure cultures in brain medium produce abundant gas, reaching a maximum in 24-48 hours at 37 C., and the clear supernatant fluid becomes turbid. Cultures incubated at 20 C. show the same changes, but require a longer time. No visible digestion of the brain tissue occurs, nor is there any blackening either with or without added iron. Evidently no sulphuretted hydrogen is produced. Brain medium is not only the best for enrichment, but viability persists in it for several months.

Growth in Holman's [13] meat mash is similar to that in brain medium. Neither brain nor meat cultures ever develop a fetid or disagreeable odor.

The colonies in deep 1% agar are dense, opaque, grayish white when young, with a more yellowish tinge later. When well separated, they frequently attain a diameter of 1 mm., and show much uniformity in shape, resembling closely a small buckwheat. Familiarity with the form of colony is an important asset in the successful isolation of this organism.

Surface colonies on blood-agar slants under alkaline pyrogallol at 37 C. are small, round, moist appearing, raised, grayish white and nonhemolytic. No growth occurs on the surface of blood or plain agar under aerobic conditions.

Gelatin under vaspar [14] seal becomes turbid and produces gas at 37 C. within 24 hours and at room temperature within 48 hours, but without blackening or permanent liquefaction, as tested by placing such cultures in the ice chest.

Milk in constricted tubes with marble seal or under vaspar produces gas within 24 hours at 37 C., but no other visible change within 2 months.

Broth cultures under marble seal at 37 C. become turbid and produce gas, varying in quantity at the time of maximum collection (usually on the third day) from 12 to 26% of the closed arm of Hall's constricted fermentation tube.[15] In tests of 10 strains with glucose, levulose, sucrose, lactose, maltose, inulin, mannitol, glycerol, and salicin, differing quantities of gas varying from 11 to 38% were produced, but there is no evidence that the gas was derived through fermentation, as it was produced also by sugar-free broth. Furthermore, no acid was formed; the reaction in all sugar or nonsugar mediums became progressively alkaline to brom-thymol blue.

Crude tests for carbon dioxide were made in several fermentation tubes, using the familiar method of absorption with 10% NaOH, with negative results.

[13] Jour. Bacteriol., 1919, 4, p. 149.

[14] Vaspar is a term we apply to a mixture of equal parts of petrolatum and paraffin. It sticks to the glass better than paraffin, and is stiffer than petrolatum.

[15] Jour. Infect. Dis., 1921, 29, p. 317.

FILTRATION EXPERIMENTS

We have already mentioned our inability to confirm Holman and Krock's filtration experiments. Although these authors justly emphasize the desirability of uniform methods in testing and using bacterial filters, their own procedure is open to the criticism that Ps. pyocyaneus is an inferior test organism, not only because of its large size but also because its suspensions become mucoid. The test organism should be of small size and should not exhibit this sticky property. Serratia marcescens (Bizio) (Bact. prodigiosum) meets these requirements, and like Ps. pyocyaneus forms a distinctive pigment.

Prior to our main experiments, preliminary tests had failed to demonstrate the passage through Mandler filters of glucose broth cultures of M. gazogenes grown in constricted tubes. But Holman and Krock[2] also failed to filter any but cooked meat cultures, and we therefore undertook a critical study of the filtrability of our 24 strains, including the 2 from Dr. Holman. To insure comparable results, a uniform procedure was established as follows:

Each strain was grown in a constricted tube of glucose broth with marble seal, and in Holman's meat medium[15] at 37 C. for 48 hours.

The broth culture was then well shaken and inoculated with Serratia marcescens (Bizio) as a filter control. Subcultures by loop to freshly boiled and cooled brain medium and to aerobic agar slant were then made, the former to show the viability of M. gazogenes, the latter of S. macescens. These check cultures never failed to show positive results. The cooked meat culture was inoculated with S. marcescens, shaken for 5 minutes with glass beads and sterile 0.85% NaCl sufficient to make 45 c c., and centrifugalized for ½ minute at low speed to throw down large clumps. Subcultures to brain medium and plain agar slants were then made as for the broth cultures, with identical results.

The corresponding broth and meat cultures of each strain thus prepared were then filtered simultaneously at the same pressure and for the same time into separate flasks connected by means of a T tube with a mercury manometer and a water aspirator. The filters used were ⅝ by 2½ inches Mandler bougies; a record was kept of the behavior of each, so that it might be discarded in case the test organism came through, for filters frequently become permeable on continued use, and the test cultures must be included every time for accurate control. In no instance, however, did any bacteria pass in this series; the filters were new to start with, and we had a sufficient number (15) so that only 3 were used as many as 6 times; the average was 3.2 times.

We always used glass capsules over the bougies to insure the liquid's covering the whole surface and to avoid aspiration to air with resultant loss in efficiency. About 20 c c. of fluid were placed in each filter case, and filtration was continued for 5 minutes after the manometer registered the maximum pressure. The time required to reach the maximum pressure was generally about 1 minute. The pressures varied from 637.5 mm. to 675.0 mm.; the average was 659.4 mm. With the time factor constant and the pressure fairly so, it is still not surpising that the amounts of filtrate varied greatly—for the broth cultures from 3 c c. to 20 c c. (average 12.2 c c.) and for the meat cultures from 2 c c. to 19 c c. (average 11.8 c c.). Inspection of our unpublished data shows that variation of individual filters is largely responsible for the wide range in the amounts of filtrate; and in the later part of these experiments, it was possible to pair slow filters, or fast filters, for a single strain, so that the filtrate from the meat culture was often within 1-2 c c. of that secured from the broth culture. The averages suggest, however, that the meat cultures actually filter a little less rapidly than the broth cultures, as would be expected.

Tests were made for M. gazogenes in the filtrates by inoculation of 1 c c. into brain medium, and for Serratia marcescens by inoculation of 3 loops on agar slants. These cultures were incubated at 37 C., with daily observation for 6 days. In no case was gas produced in any of the brain cultures. They were then stained by Gram's method and transplanted to plain agar slants as a further check. In no case did Serratia marcescens appear, although aerobic contaminations by gram-positive rods were encountered twice. But none of the primary agar slants made from the filtrates showed any bacterial growth.

These experiments, involving as they did, the filtration of 48 separate cultures under the most meticulous control possible failed utterly to indicate the filtrability of M. gazogenes through filters capable of retaining the considerably larger Serratia marcescens.

Further filtration experiments were made on 16-day old cultures of M. gazogenes nos. 42 and 43 (Holman's strains), with similarly negative results. Both new and old bougies were used in these tests.

Only in a single experiment with strains 42 and 43 in which the filtrates were collected fractionally (4 parts) did the first portions of no. 42 show a culture of M. gazogenes; but S. marcescens also appeared, so that this result must be interpreted as being due to a faulty filter which became plugged to both germs as the experiment progressed.

We conclude therefore that these 24 strains, including those from Dr. Holman, are nonfiltrable; whether new or old bougies, young or old cultures, glucose broth or meat mediums are used, makes no difference.

PATHOGENICITY

Most of our data failed to indicate any direct pathogenicity of M. gazogenes for rabbits, guinea-pigs or mice.

Ten strains were selected for the preparation of agglutinating serums as follows: nos. 42 and 43 from Dr. Holman, nos. 23 and 25 from children with healthy gums, nos. 28 and 34 from adults with healthy mouths, nos. 16 and 21 from adults with exceptionally bad mouths, and nos. 22 and 26 for a serologic difference observed in testing their antigens against earlier serums.

Forty-eight hour glucose broth cultures of these were injected intravenously into rabbits in 3 doses of 2 c c. each on alternate days followed by a week's rest generally terminated by a test bleeding. This schedule was twice repeated in each case. These 10 rabbits weighed from 2,270 to 4,080 gm. (average—3,047 gm.) at the beginning, and showed no adverse symptoms of any kind; they weighed from 2,290 to 3,850 gm. (average 3,034 gm.) at the close. Several even gained weight during immunization.

In addition to these, a rabbit (866) that received injections with 2 c c. of a 48-hour glucose broth culture of M. gazogenes 42 (Holman's rabbit strain) died during the following night, with pericardial edema and pulmonary congestion indicating pneumonia. Brain medium cultures from the right and from the left ventricular blood were sterile, but M. gazogenes (44) was isolated from one lung. However, intravenous injection of 2 c c. of a 48-hour glucose broth culture 44 failed to produce symptoms in another rabbit, so that its responsibility for the death of the first animal is indeed doubtful.

A few days later, another intravenous injection of 2 c c. of a 48-hour glucose broth culture of M. gazogenes 42 was made into an apparently healthy rabbit (683). Next morning, this animal appeared weak, huddled in a corner, and breathed with difficulty. At noon, it was prostrate, and was suffering from diarrhea; at 3 p. m., it died. Necropsy showed an enlarged heart, a slight pericardial hemorrhage and a rather larger peritoneal clot of blood over the liver. Brain medium cultures from the heart blood produced gas and showed the presence of gram-negative anaerobic filamentous rods; M. gazogenes may also have been present, but this culture was unfortunately lost before either could be isolated.

At this time, we raised a question without actual proof as to the purity of strain 42. A repurified culture was therefore tested on 3 additional rabbits in doses of 0.1 c c., 0.5 c c. and 2.0 c c. The first two were unaffected, but the one received the largest dose developed diarrhea and seemed ill for a few days, but it recovered and was later used for the production of serum agglutinin for this strain.

Two c c. of strain 42 were also injected subcutaneously into a guinea-pig, without visible effect.

Strain 22 was also apparently pathogenic for certain rabbits. After intravenous injection of 2 c c. of a 48-hour glucose broth culture, a rabbit (182) was quite ill the following day with symptoms of diarrhea, difficult breathing, and intoxication. Its pitiful condition caused us to chloroform it on the second day. The thoracic viscera were apparently normal, but the liver was full of white patches, which were shown by microscopic examination to contain coccidial oocytes. Heart blood cultures in brain medium were negative.

A small piece of lung tissue was ground in sterile 0.85% NaCl and filtered through a Mandler bougie. Five c c. of the filtrate (apparently sterile by cultural test) were injected intravenously into a fresh rabbit (166) as a test for a possible filtrable agent, without result; this animal was later used in the production of agglutinin for strain 22, repeated injection of which produced no untoward effects until 3 days after the 7th dose, when it was unexpectedly found dead over a week end. In this instance, postmortem decomposition prevented a satisfactory necropsy.

About this time, we discovered that strains 22 and 26 were serologically distinct from the others, and later that these 2 evidently belonged to the same agglutination group. A rabbit (179) therefore received injections of 2 c c. of glucose broth culture 26; it was slightly ill next day, but recovered, and later received repeated injections without harm.

Strains 15, 22 and 43 were also injected subcutaneously into white mice in doses of 1.0 to 1.5 c c., without effect.

On the whole, it would seem that certain strains of M. gazogenes possess some degree of pathogenicity for rabbits, but we suspect that this consists in reducing resistance toward other infectious agents which these animals carry. It is almost impossible in California to secure rabbits entirely free from dormant snuffles and coccidiosis. The latter is especially prevalent; it is not uncommon for all but one or two of a litter to be lost at weaning time from intestinal coccidiosis. The survivors generally, perhaps always, become carriers, developing hepatic coccidiosis. These animals may appear normal, but the injection of various known pathogenic bacteria often lights up the characteristic diarrhea in which the parasites may be found, and the livers tell the tale as in the instance above. It is possible that essentially nonpathogenic or slightly pathogenic bacteria may have a similar effect. This indeed is the supposed action of Bact. pneumosintes; perhaps this property is dependent in some way on the extremely small size of these species.

SEROLOGIC AGGLUTINATION

Our study of the agglutination reaction of M. gazogenes showed (1) that rabbits respond to intravenous injection of live cultures by production of highly potent agglutinins; (2) that there are 2 main serologic groups; (3) that though normal rabbits may harbor M. gazogenes, their blood serum does not agglutinate M. gazogenes at a dilution of 1:10; (4) that the blood serum of certain human beings agglutinates M. gazogenes in low dilutions.

The antigens used for immunization and for the agglutination test were living, 48-hour glucose broth cultures tested for purity by microscopic examination and aerobic agar slant, and filtered through sterile absorbent cotton to remove clumps. The schedule of injection has been mentioned under pathogenicity; 8 or 9 doses were given each rabbit in 3 series of 3 doses each at 48-hour intervals, with a week's rest between each 2 series and a test bleeding from the ear at the end of each rest. Final bleedings were made a week after the last dose by ventricular puncture with an 18 gage needle, withdrawing 25 to 60 c c. of blood, but we found that taking more than 40 c c. of blood endangers the life of a rabbit. Serums were separated from the clots by centrifugalization.

Our procedure in the tests was essentially like that employed by Hall and Stark [16] with B. sporogenes, except that incubation (37 C.) was for 4 hours.

The results of the tests with each serum against the 24 strains are shown in table 2. It will be seen that the titer limits were unusually

[16] Ibid., 1923, 33, p. 240.

high, 1 : 10,240 in 2 cases, 1 : 20,480 in 6 cases, and 1 : 40,960 in 2 cases. Each test was carefully controlled with suspensions of each strain without serum; none of them flocculated.

It is evident that strains 22 and 26 are serologically distinct from all the rest in their agglutinability, although their antiserums agglutinated certain other strains in low dilutions. Curiously, these 2 antiserums did not correspond in their behavior toward heterologous strains.

TABLE 2

Serologic Agglutination of M. gazogenes by Rabbit Serums

M. gazogenes Strains	Agglutinating Serums									
	Rabbit 888 Anti Strain 16	Rabbit 677 Anti Strain 21	Rabbit 861 Anti Strain 23	Rabbit 872 Anti Strain 25	Rabbit 624 Anti Strain 28	Rabbit 601 Anti Strain 34	Rabbit 632 Anti Strain 42	Rabbit 863 Anti Strain 43	Rabbit 176 Anti Strain 22	Rabbit 180 Anti Strain 26
1	10240	5120	10240	5120	5120	20480	5120	10240	0	20
10	10240	5120	10240	10240	10240	20480	1280	10240	0	0
11	10240	10240	10240	10240	5120	20480	2560	10240	80	20
14	10240	10240	10240	20480	10240	10240	1280	10240	40*	0
15	10240	10240	20480	10240	5120	20480	2560	10240	320	0
16	10240	1280*	5120*	2560	640*	320*	40*	640*	0	0
17	10240	10240	20480	20480	10240	20480	640	10240	0	0
19	10240	10240	20480	5120	10240	20480	640	10240	160*	20*
20	10240	10240	20480	10240	10240	10240	640	10240	160*	20*
21	10240	10240	10240	10240	10240	10240	1280	1280	20*	20*
22	0	0	0	0	#	0	0	0	20480	320
23	5720	10240	10240	10240	10240	10240	2560	10240	0	20*
24	20480	10240	20480	40960	#	10240	1280	20480	160*	40*
25	10240	5120	5120	20480	5120	10240	1280	10240	0	0
26	0	0	0	0	0	0	0	0	10240	10240
27	20480	10240	10240	20480	#	5120	1280	5120	0	10*
29	80*	40	160	320*	#	160	80	40	0	0
37	10240	10240	10240	5120	20480	10240	1280	10240	0	10*
38	320	160	640	640	#	640	160	160	0	20*
40	20480	20480	10240	20480	#	20480	1280	20480	80*	40*
41	20480	20480	20480	10240	#	10240	1280	5120	160	20*
42	1280	1280	1280	2560	1280	1280	10240	2560	0	0
43	1280	2560	2560	1280	2560	2560	320	10240	0	20
44	2560	1280	2560	1280	#	2560	10240	2560	0	0

The numbers indicate the highest dilutions of serums giving a positive result. All tests were carefully controlled for spontaneous agglutination of the suspensions without serum; none of the controls was positive.

0 Negative in all dilutions, including 1:10.

* Incomplete in all dilutions, including 1:10.

Not tested for lack of serum.

There are apparently 2 main agglutinogenic groups of M. gazogenes, the larger of which, here designated group A, contains 22 of our strains, while the smaller, group B, contains 2 strains. Both of Dr. Holman's strains belong to group A, although one was derived from a rabbit and one from a human source. There is evidence that group A might be subdivided if serum were made from certain strains that flocculated only in lower dilutions, 29 and 38 for example. However, strain 16 always failed to react with any but its own serum as strongly or in as high dilutions as other strains, yet its own serum totally excluded only strains 22 and 26. This suggests that these group A strains differ merely in quantitative agglutinability, not in antigenic quality. It was impossible to correlate strains 22 and 26 with any peculiarity in dental condition; 22 came from one of the worst cases, 26 from one of the best.

Control agglutination tests were also made using 2 of the M. gazogenes serums (rabbit 176 anti 22 and rabbit 601 anti 34) against several other anaerobes (B. bifermentans 50, B. botulinus 119, B. sporogenes 52, and B. putrificus 22) at 1:10, with entirely negative results. Likewise a serum specific for B. putrificus 38 was tested at 1:10 against M. gazogenes strains 23, 25, 37, and 42, without positive

TABLE 3

SEROLOGIC AGGLUTINATION OF M. GAZOGENES STRAINS BY HOMOLOGOUS HUMAN SERUM

Number of Subject	M. gazogenes Number	Dilutions of Serum				Control, No Serum
		1:10	1:20	1:40	1:80	
11	15	++	+?	0	0	0
15	16	0	0	0	0	0
16	17	+?	0	0	0	0
18	19	0	0	0	0	0
19	20	+	0	0	0	0
26	21	++	+?	0	0	0
27	22	0	0	0	0	0
28	23	++++	++++	++	0	0
29	24	++++	++++	+	0	0
30	25	0	0	0	0	0
31	26	0	0	0	0	0
32	27	0	0	0	0	0
33	28	+++	+?	0	0	0
34	29	0	0	0	0	0
42	37	++	+	0	0	0
43	38	0	0	0	0	0
45	40	++++	+++	0	0	0
46	41	0	0	0	0	0

results. Furthermore, serums from 9 normal rabbits were tested at 1:10 against various strains of M. gazogenes as follows, with totally negative results:

Rabbits 1 and 2 tested against M. gazogenes 16, 21, 23, 25, 28, 34.
Rabbit 3 tested against M. gazogenes 10, 42, 44.
Rabbit 115 tested against M. gazogenes 21, 44
Rabbit 161 tested against M. gazogenes 29, 42, 44.
Rabbit 166 tested against M. gazogenes 22, 36, 42.
Rabbit 173 tested against M. gazogenes 42, 44.
Rabbit 179, tested against M. gazogenes 26, 37, 44.
Rabbit 180 tested against M. gazogenes 22, 25, 26, 42.

Although normal rabbits may harbor M. gazogenes yet produce no agglutinins except under inoculation, human beings not infrequently produce low grade agglutinating serums.

Five c c. of blood were secured from the median basilic vein of 18 of the subjects from whose saliva M. gazogenes had been isolated. The serums were tested against their homologous strains. The results of these tests are shown in table 3.

Just 9 (50%) of these serums agglutinated their homologous cultures at 1:10 or higher dilutions. The two highest titers were 1:40, while only 2 others were clear cut at 1:20. We were frankly surprised to secure even this evidence of natural immunologic response in human beings, though we doubt whether it necessarily implies invasion of the tissues by M. gazogenes.

We note that neither of the group B serums agglutinated its homologous strain, that among the donors whose serums failed to agglutinate, 5 out of 9 would be classed as having bad mouth conditions, and that among those donors whose serum showed agglutination, 5 out of 9 would be classed as having good mouth conditions. This perhaps means nothing. But those serums (subjects 28, 29 and 45) that gave complete or nearly complete agglutination at 1:20 all came from subjects whose mouths were free or practically free from gingival lesions, and this causes us to suspect that there may be an immunologic factor relating to this organism in pyorrhea. Two of these 3 strongest serums came from children. We consider our data too scanty, however, to serve as a basis for conclusions, and offer them for their suggestive implications.

SUMMARY

This paper emphasizes the frequent occurrence in human saliva of a minute, gram-negative, nonsporulating, gas-forming, obligate anaerobe. This organism is mainly responsible for the abundant gas generally seen in primary brain medium cultures from unheated saliva. It is identical with the so-called Staph. parvulus (Veillon) recently recovered by Holman and Krock, which they thought resembled Bact. pneumosintes in filtrability. But we disagree both as to its nomenclature and its ability to pass through carefully controlled Mandler filters.

It differs from Staph. parvulus in its lack of fetid odor and in producing abundant gas. It was first discovered by Lewkowicz, working with Veillon in Cracow, in 1901, in the mouth of an 8-day old baby, and described under the name Micrococcus gazogenes alcalescens anaerobius; in accord with modern scientific usage, we suggest the name Micrococcus gazogenes (Lewkowicz).

M. gazogenes is a minute diplococcus less than 0.5μ in length and breadth, gram-negative, nonsporulating, nonmotile, and obligately anaerobic. These properties have caused it to be overlooked in most of the modern work on the mouth flora.

Deep brain is the best medium; no blackening or digestion occurs with or without added iron. Deep agar colonies resemble a tiny buckwheat. Blood-agar surface colonies are small, round, moist appearing, raised, grayish white and nonhemolytic. Gelatin is neither liquefied nor blackened. The only visible change in milk is gas production. Broth cultures become turbid and gassy. No acid is formed from glucose, levulose, sucrose, lactose, maltose, inulin, mannitol, glycerol or salicin. It does not pass through the Berkefeld filter.

It is nonpathogenic directly for rabbits, guinea-pigs and mice, but it appears to reduce the resistance of rabbits toward other pathogenic microbes.

Ten rabbits, immunized by intravenous injection of live cultures, produced powerful agglutinins (all over 1:10,000) which distinguished 2 serologic groups. Group A contained 22 strains, group B, 2 strains. Holman's cultures fell into group A. Normal rabbits harbor M. gazogenes, yet produce no agglutinins except under inoculation, but human beings not infrequently produce low grade agglutinating serums (1:40). The strongest serum came from persons free or practically free from gingival lesions, suggesting an immunologic factor relating to this organism in pyorrhea alveolaris.

OBSERVATIONS ON D'HERELLE'S BACTERIOPHAGE

TWO PLATES

MAX S. MARSHALL

From the University of Michigan, Ann Arbor, and Michigan Department of Health, Lansing

INTRODUCTION

The bacteriophage of d'Herelle is, at the present time, defined by a limited number of properties. We are unable to make, without equivocation, even the first fundamental step in its classification, namely, assignment either to the chemical sciences or to the biologic sciences. We may say only that if the bacteriophage falls within the realms of chemistry, it should be classified with the enzymes; if it falls within the realms of biology, it should be classified with the filtrable viruses. Neither the enzyme, the filtrable virus, nor the bacteriophage is defined by any vast number of specific properties.

D'Herelle has, from the time of his original work, claimed that the bacteriophage was a living, ultramicroscopic organism, Bacteriophagum intestinale. His most recent and perhaps strongest argument for the truth of his contention might be summarized as follows: If any one characteristic of living things could be positively stated to be a property of all living things and the property of no nonliving substance, it would be necessary to show only that the bacteriophage possesses, or does not possess, this property. After a study of this question, he concludes that there is such a characteristic—namely, the ability of living matter to incorporate the inanimate material of a medium in which it is placed into its own living substance—or, to put the matter in his own words, the "power of assimilation in a heterogeneous medium." There is also a second criterion, the power of adaptation. Although the evidence is not wholly incontrovertible, it seems more than probable that the bacteriophage possesses these properties.

Perhaps the greatest obstacle in the way of fixing the properties of these substances, and one which, if overcome, might aid us in fitting them into their proper niches in science, is the difficulty in securing unequivocal quantitative data. Qualitative data are a necessary prelude, but quantitative data must follow closely.

Received for publication, Feb. 20, 1925.

It is the aim of the present work, started in 1922, to study some of the properties of the bacteriophage as closely as possible from the quantitative point of view. It is necessary, as one phase in the study of the action of the bacteriophage, to observe its influence on living cells. Thus, to the bacteriophage, which we must regard as a variable, and which may or may not be a living thing, we are forced to add another variable, which is living—the bacterial cell. Although the study of such variables may not be characterized by the accuracy justly demanded by the chemist, it is the study of the influence of the living cell on the bacteriophage and the influence of the bacteriophage on the living cell which involves the crucial point of the whole problem, and this has formed the primary object of our study. Corollary to this, certain investigations have been carried out on the absorption of bacteriophage by bacterial cells, on the diffusion of the bacteriophage through semipermeable membranes, on the resistance of the bacterial cell to the lytic action of the bacteriophage, and on the specific antigenic properties of the lysed bacterial cell.

The original work of d'Herelle has been set forth at length in his book,[1] and has been extended somewhat in the English translation,[2] and further by his more recent work.[3] D'Herelle's first observations were made in 1912 in connection with his studies of a locust disease. The work probably received an added stimulus through the work of Twort[4] in 1915. D'Herelle has worked steadily on the bacteriophage since 1917, and his work is so well known that no space will be devoted to it. Bibliographic summaries of the work done have been given by Davison,[5] Pico,[6] Rhodes,[7] and Kuttner.[8] Since 1922, papers dealing with the bacteriophage have been numerous, and have added a great deal to our knowledge of the details of its mode of action and the influence of environmental conditions. A number of papers have been written on the nature of bacteriophage, some claiming proof of the enzymatic nature of the active agent, others supporting the theory of the living nature of the agent. The bacteriophage has been found to be so ubiquitous that the fact that it was only recently discovered is a credit to the astute mind of d'Herelle. Different types of bacteriophage exhibiting lytic properties for a large variety of bacteria have been reported, among the most recent being a bacteriophage active against the Klebs-Loeffler bacillus, reported by Blair.[9] Evidence has been given to show that there are many types or strains of bacteriophage differing in their action against different species of bacteria, as well as against different strains of the same species. This has been made especially clear by Asheshov[10] in a recent paper. These differences in

[1] Le Bacteriophage, son Rôle dans l'Immunité, 1921.
[2] The Bacteriophage, 1922.
[3] Immunity in Natural Infectious Disease, 1924.
[4] Lancet, 1915, 189, p. 1241.
[5] Abst. Bacteriol., 1922, 4, p. 159.
[6] Semana méd., 1922, 19, p. 415.
[7] Jour. Lab. & Clin. Med., 1922, 7, p. 288.
[8] Jour. Bacteriol., 1923, 8, p. 49.
[9] Jour. Infect. Dis., 1924, 35, p. 401.
[10] Jour. Infect. Dis., 1924, 34, p. 356.

the mode of action of different types of bacteriophage are of much significance, and it is only by the accumulation of data relating to these differences that it may be ascertained how far the data on one bacteriophage are fundamentally applicable to all.

EXPERIMENTAL

Quantitative Measurement.—Quantitative measurement of the potency, "virulence," or lytic action of a liquid endowed with the properties of the bacteriophage might conceivably be made by physical, chemical, or bacteriologic means. It is possible that chemical means will in time be devised for such measurement, and that physical measurements will follow. At present, however, because our knowledge of the bacteriophage is built around the lytic activity toward the bacterial cell, bacteriologic means of measurement are alone open to experimental use.

A suspension of living bacterial cells in which the cells are present in considerable concentration will, when inoculated on the surface of agar culture medium and incubated, form on the inoculated surface a solid mass of organisms piled perhaps a millimeter high. If, however, broth culturally sterile but containing bacteriophage in proper concentration be added to the suspension with which the agar is to be inoculated, and from this the growth of organisms be secured on an agar surface, there will result (provided the bacteriophage employed is active against the strain of bacteria used) a solid mass of organisms with here and there cleared zones or areas where there appears to have been no growth. To all outward appearances, there is a circular area on the agar to which no organisms had been inoculated. We know, however, from repeated experimentation, that the areas, as they will hereafter be designated, are due, not to lack of adequate inoculation, but to the lytic action exhibited at these foci by the bacteriophage. The number of such areas produced on a given field, taking into consideration the amount of bacteriophage-containing liquid used and the area of the field over which this number occurs, offers an index to the bacteriophage concentration in the original material.

D'Herelle, Maitland [11] and others have used this principle in making quantitative measurements of bacteriophage concentrations by streaking such mixtures of bacteriophage and bacteria to agar slants in more or less known concentrations. The resulting areas may be counted, and the bacteriophage concentration calculated accordingly.

There is another method, devised by d'Herelle, which has been variously used, involving the measurement of bacteriophage concentration by the use of the circumstance that even a single bacteriophage unit, if present in a tube of broth culture medium, will inhibit the growth or cause the eventual lysis of bacteria in that broth, provided that the bacteriophage is active against the bacterial strain used. Thus, a series of dilutions of the liquid containing bacteriophage may be made in a broth medium, the series inoculated with bacteria, and the highest dilution of the original bacteriophage-containing liquid inhibiting or causing the final destruction of the bacterial development ascertained.

Agar plates instead of slants for the demonstration and enumeration of areas have been used to some extent, and this method is most recently and beautifully developed by Asheshov.[10]

Much of the quantitative work which has been done has been directed toward the securing of relative and comparative data for qualitative information. It is

[11] Brit. Jour. Exper. Pathol., 1922, 3, p. 173.

thus necessary, as this study is directed at more intimate quantitative data concerning one type of bacteriophage, that we take cognizance of certain errors in the foregoing methods as pertinent to the present work.

The use of drops, or of the amount of liquid taken up by a platinum loop, has been a procedure frequently followed in the elicitation of comparative quantitative information. In spite of the painstaking work of Miller,[12] it was our own experience that the same loop (2.2 mm.) might take up from 0.01 c c. to 0.002 c c., and that the amount taken up is dependent on viscosity and surface tension, which in turn are variable with physical factors ordinarily uncontrolled, notably the temperature. Furthermore, although the amount taken up by the loop when removed from a liquid into which it has been introduced might be neglected on account of the dilution secured, the amount removed when an agar surface is inoculated is uncertain. Volumes have been written concerning the drop as a unit of measurement.[13] The size of a drop is primarily a function of the size of the opening, of the surface tension, and of the density of the liquid used. To be accurately duplicated, drops must fall at a slow rate from a definite opening "wet" only at the surface at which the drop is formed, the temperature must be constant, and the liquids must have similar densities and surface tensions. Any duplication secured without taking these precautions must be regarded as accidental. Using the ordinary precautions in a preliminary experiment in which drops were expected to give relatively correct results, the variation was from 20 to 37 drops per c c.

Little need be said concerning the fallacy inherent in the use of turbidity as a criterion of bacterial growth from a quantitative standpoint. Experiments revealed that a bacterial concentration of 8×10^6 per c c. was necessary before slight turbidity could be noticed; and that a very heavy turbidity represented from 175×10^6 to 400×10^6 organisms per c c., beyond which only a marked difference could be detected with any degree of accuracy. This represents obviously only a small portion of the growth curve of bacteria. The nephelometer is not convenient when protection to the worker against infection is necessary, and does not allow of any measurement of the first few hours of bacterial growth, which are the most important.

An error in the dilution method for the estimation of bacteriophage concentration became apparent after making a considerable number of such estimations. By using tubes of broth containing just 9 c c., a consecutive series of dilutions of a bacteriophage-containing liquid may be made, 1:10 or 10^{-1}, 1:100 or 10^{-2}, 10^{-3}, 10^{-3}, etc., the series inoculated with sensitive bacteria, incubated, and the end-point determined by a clear-cut reading of the growth; the inhibited and lysed tubes are perfectly clear, and subsequent dilutions show normal growth. This means a convenient and clear-cut procedure for a first approximation. However, in itself it is insufficient. A tube containing 8 bacteriophage units will exhibit the same complete inhibition as will a tube containing one bacteriophage unit. In a series: 10^{-1} 10^{-2} 10^{-3} 10^{-4} 10^{-5} 10^{-6} 10^{-7} 10^{-8} 10^{-9} dilutions of bacteriophage in which the 10^{-8} tube and all lower dilutions are clear after inoculation and incubation, and the 10^{-9} tube shows normal growth, one would say off-hand that there are between 100,000,000 and 1,000,000,000 bacteriophage units per c c. in the original liquid. This is not legitimate, for

[12] Jour. Lab. & Clin. Med., 1924, 9, p. 404.

[13] Harkins: Jour. Am. Chem. Soc., 1916, 38, Pt. 1, p. 228; Willows and Hatschek: Surface Tension and Surface Energy, 1923.

let us assume that there are only 20,000,000 units per c c. in the original. In the 10^{-1} tube there would be 2,000,000 units per c c., in the 10^{-2}, 200,000, in the 10^{-3}, 20,000, in the 10^{-4}, 2,000, in the 10^{-5}, 200, and in the 10^{-6}, 20. We are constantly decreasing the number of units handled, and thus putting more and more confidence in the laws of probability as applied to a small number of cases. In the 10^{-6} tube, we have 20 units in 10 c c. of thoroughly mixed liquid. We remove 1 c c. for the 10^{-7} tube. Perhaps we secure the most probable number of units, namely 2. It is not inconceivable that we secure only 1, or as many as 5. The 10^{-7} tube, then, will contain from 1 to 5 units. If there is 1, in taking 1 c c. for the 10^{-8} tube once in every 10 times we carried out the procedure, we should secure 1 unit for the 10^{-8} tube; the probability that it happens is 1: 10. If 5 units are present in the 10^{-7} tube, the probability is 5: 10 (more exactly, 715:2002) of carrying at least 1 unit to the 10^{-8} tube, and for that matter the probability is not small for carrying 2 units to the 10^{-8} tube, whence there would be approximately a 2: 10 chance of carrying the bacteriophage over the 10^{-9} tube. And, looking back, had there been 1 unit in the 10^{-7} tube, and had it been carried to the 10^{-8} tube by the tenth chance, the 10^{-7} tube would have been left with no bacteriophage units, and would have grown following inoculation, whereas the 10^{-8} tube would not have done so. We have observed this apparently paradoxic error in an "inhibition-titration" on several occasions, not due to the accidental contamination of organisms not sensitive to the lytic action of the bacteriophage. Thus, even by conservative estimate, our results have suggested merely that the bacteriophage concentration sought is between 10,000,000 and 1,000,000,000 per c c., and the difference is too great to be of more than rough quantitative value.

Although there can be no gross difference between enumeration of areas by means of slants and by means of plates as procedures for giving agar surfaces, there are reasons for favoring the plate. In our preliminary experimentation, it was brought out that it is difficult to secure a dilution of bacteriophage which will give a number of areas easily counted on a slant. This is not true of the plate. Because of the difficulty in accurately measuring an amount of liquid deposited on an agar slant, the plate becomes superior. Furthermore, the conditions on all parts of the surface of an agar slant are not uniform, whereas a plate gives uniform conditions. This is particularly true of the moisture, which, in an agar slant, unless precautions are taken, distributes itself according to gravity. The top of the slant will be dry, giving small areas, whereas the moisture in the lower part of the slant may be so great as to cause slurred areas, or areas which have run together. Finally, we found it necessary to take a number of special precautions with an agar slant with a view to counteracting the foregoing faults, and in order to give comparable results with slant and plate methods of enumeration.

There is a further important point regarding the measurement of bacteriophage concentration, based on the fact that the two essential factors, the organisms and the bacteriophage, are mutually interactive. On exposure to organisms, the bacteriophage increases. It is hence imperative that the bacteriophage and the organisms be kept separate until such time as they may be fixed in space, and the bacteriophage, by means of organisms, forced to show its presence. In an inhibition-titration series, the tubes must not be inoculated before the serial dilution is made. In an area enumeration, the organisms should not be mixed with bacteriophage previous to inoculation to an agar surface, at least for any length of time.

Having developed in their broader aspects some of the factors involved in quantitative measurement, it becomes necessary to investigate some of the more specific questions involved.

The bacteriophage under investigation was an original d'Herelle type sent by him to Dr. F. G. Novy in 1921. The original activity of this bacteriophage was against Eberthella dysenteriae (Shiga), Escherichia coli, and Salmonella paratyphi (beta type), and subsequent enhancement of its activity was effected against the first named.

The question of what strain of Eberthella dysenteriae (Shiga) to use in the study of the phenomena was important. Although Eberthella dysenteriae (Shiga) is supposedly a true bacterial species, and as such should be similar in its receptivity to the bacteriophage regardless of the source of the bacterial strains, it became evident at the outset that no such assumption was safe. A study of the character of the areas produced by 3 different specimens of the d'Herelle bacteriophage, all from the same stated source but having received different treatment and being of different age, revealed not only a difference in the type of area against a single strain of Eberthella dysenteriae (Shiga), but the same bacteriophage specimen gave different types of areas and to some extent different numbers of areas with different strains of the Shiga dysentery bacillus. Three strains were used; the original Shiga strain from the Japanese epidemic, a Pasteur Institute strain, and a local strain, all true to type as judged by the ordinary biologic and biochemical tests. The types of areas were definitely divided into 2 classes, a large and small area, respectively, 2 to 5 mm. in diameter, and 0.5 to 1.0 mm. in diameter. One specimen of bacteriophage gave only the small type of area with any strain used. Among all the strains of the dysentery bacillus, the local strain proved the most sensitive, and very consistent in its activity with the specimen of bacteriophage giving only small areas. The consistency of interaction between these two variables, and the fact that we were unable by any means tried to demonstrate a greater bacteriophage concentration in any tube of this bacteriophage than could be demonstrated with this strain of Eberthella dysenteriae (Shiga) led us to employ it for subsequent experimentation. The variation of activity of a given bacteriophage against different bacterial strains supposedly of the same species has been noted by Davison,[14] Janzen and Wolff,[15] Bruynoghe and Appelmans,[16] Pico,[17] and others. It is not uncommon to find that a bacteriophage is active against one bacterial strain to a marked degree, but with no apparent effect on another strain of the same species.

There must be a reasonable degree of permanence of bacteriophage concentration in a culturally sterile broth filtrate containing bacteriophage; or, failing this, there would be another variation to study, and the pursuance of the variables, bacteriophage and organisms would be greatly complicated. D'Herelle's work would indicate an extreme of permanence of bacteriophage concentration in broth over a considerable period of time. Experimental investigation with the particular bacteriophage of our work over a period of 54 days revealed no change in the concentration. The experiment was terminated by an accident at this point, but we have recently had occasion to examine bacteriophage sealed for a year with the result that the concentration appears only

[14] Jour. Bacteriol., 1922, 7, p. 475.
[15] Konink. Akad. v. Wetenschr., 1922, 25, p. 31; abst., Bacteriol., 1923, 7, p. 167.
[16] Compt. rend. Soc. de biol., 1922, 87, p. 96.
[17] Ibid., 86, p. 1106.

slightly reduced, together with a slight reduction in the activity of the bacteriophage unit as indicated by slightly smaller areas.

Bordet and Ciuca[18] made intraperitoneal injections of Escherichia coli into a guinea-pig. Some hours later the peritoneal exudate was found to contain a principle lysogenic for Escherichia coli. From their experiments they concluded that, under the influence of a product secreted by the leukocytes, the bacteria undergo a "nutritive vitiation" resulting in lysis. But, since the leukocytic principle disappears in the course of successive transfers in vitro, without loss of the lysogenic power, they assume that the nutritive vitiation is hereditary.[19] D'Herelle has variously contended that this hypothesis is "purement verbale." He adds a small amount of filtrate containing the lytic principle to a bacterial suspension, and brings about lysis. He then filters this lysed bacterial suspension through a filter impermeable to bacteria. A small amount of this filtrate is added to a second bacterial suspension, and lysis brought about. This is filtered, and the series carried ad infinitum. Where, says d'Herelle,[20] is there place in this process for the transmission of an acquired characteristic, since he has allowed no bacteria to enter a filtrate which will be lysed if they possess the hereditary qualification? And how, he adds, can one invoke heredity when there are no descendants? Since our bacteriophage represents an infinite dilution of the original bacteriophage brought about by a procedure similar to that described, it may be stated with certainty that our bacteriophage falls in line with this argument of d'Herelle's. Two other experiments were carried out by d'Herelle in support of his contention that the phenomenon is not due to hereditary factors set up within certain bacteria. In the first, he used a definite concentration of bacterial suspension and varying amounts of bacteriophage, noting the areas produced when fixed amounts of the mixtures were inoculated to agar slants. Were Bordet's hypothesis, implying a definite proportion of organisms capable of the nutritive vitiation, correct, an equal number of areas should result on all slants. D'Herelle, however, found that the number was proportional to the amount of bacteriophage represented. In the second experiment, he added fixed amounts of bacteriophage to bacterial suspensions of varying concentration. Bordet's hypothesis would demand that the number of areas be proportional to the bacterial concentration; d'Herelle found that the number of areas was the same throughout. To ascertain whether the experimental grounds of Bordet's hypothesis might be applicable to our bacteriophage and bacterial strain, although not applicable to the combination used by d'Herelle, we repeated each of these experiments three times, with the result that d'Herelle's observations were fully confirmed. Asheshov, working with the types of bacteriophage isolated by himself, found corresponding results. It is, therefore, not necessary to consider the number of bacteria used in area enumeration work.

In the course of our study of methods of enumeration, a "live" agar medium was developed consisting of a 4% beef infusion agar to which, in the melted state at 45 C., was added an equal volume of 10 to 18 hour infusion broth culture of the sensitive organism. It was hoped that this medium would develop colonies sufficiently close together to reach any bacteriophage present, which would then demonstrate itself by clearing the agar at that point. Neither the addition of the bacteriophage to the melted agar, nor the pouring of the "live"

[18] Compt. rend. Soc. de biol., 1920, 83, p. 1293.

[19] Bordet and Ciuca: Compt. rend. Soc. de biol., 1920, 83, p. 1296.

[20] Rev. de Path. Comp. et d'Hyg. Gen., Oct. 5, 1923, 238.

agar and subsequent inoculation of the bacteriophage to the surface of the plate gave satisfactory results. Although each colony was estimated to have a working volume of only 20 to 30 microns cubed of agar, it was found that the areas produced in this manner did not account for all the bacteriophage units present; there were apparently some bacteriophage units not reached by bacterial cells in such a manner as to form visible areas. The use of indicator stains did not add to the value of a medium for enumeration. A 30% "live" gelatin treated similarly to the "live" agar failed completely; other authors have found gelatin unsuitable for bacteriophage work.[21]

The final procedure adopted for the enumeration of bacteriophage units, or the measurement of bacteriophage concentration, was as follows. The culture medium was a beef infusion 2% agar of P_H 7.4. Plates were poured, using 10 to 12 c c. of agar, and dried, either for 24 hours or longer inverted, at room temperature, or at 37 C., for a shorter period of time, preferably not less than 10 hours. A proper degree of moisture was found to be essential, as an excess results in washed noncircular areas (plate 2, fig. 1), and too little moisture is not only undesirable for good growth of the bacteria, but also results in minute areas, so that one cannot be sure that all areas which may be present are apparent. To the properly dried, sterile plate was inoculated 3 drops of a rejuvenated beef infusion broth culture of Eberthella dysenteriae (Shiga) from 6 to 16 hours old, and spread with a glass rod. Since the number of areas produced by a given amount of bacteriophage is not affected by the number of organisms present, the amount of inoculum is not important; provided the culture be rejuvenated by frequent transfer and the culture from which the plate is made be still in, or near, the logarithmic phase of growth. D'Herelle has pointed out the necessity for the use of young cells for lysis by the bacteriophage, a point which we have checked. Calculation shows that at least 4 frequent transfers, at least twice a day, should be followed to eliminate any organisms irregular in their growth and not capable of keeping up with the regular logarithmic increase in concentration. The plate inoculated with organisms was incubated for from 2.5 to 5 hours at 37 C. for the dual purpose of drying and of allowing development of the culture, it being necessary to have a solid growth as a background for the bacteriophage areas. The plate was then ready for inoculation with the bacteriophage. This was made by adding a known, carefully measured amount of the suspension to be measured in the proper dilution to secure approximately a hundred areas to the surface of the plate. The amount should be not less than 0.05 c c., and not more than 0.10 c c.: less than 0.05 c c. is difficult to spread properly, and more than 0.10 c c. introduces too much moisture. The liquid is spread with a sterile glass rod to all but the extreme edges at two opposite points, these serving to touch off the rod before finally removing it. The spreading can be done with several rapid sweeping motions; it is not necessary to rub it in. The minute colonies are spread with the bacteriophage, so that following incubation there is a solid mass of culture surface in which the bacteriophage units may form lysed areas (plate 1). By this procedure, the bacteriophage unit is immediately fixed at a point where it must demonstrate itself, the conditions are uniform, and, of great importance, the organisms and bacteriophage are separated and have no opportunity to interact in any way before they are individually fixed at definite points. Incubation of the plates appeared to be reasonably unimportant; the usual procedure was to incubate at 37 C. overnight. Longer incubation, either at

[21] Nakamura: Wien. klin. Wchnschr., 1923, 36, p. 86.

37 C. or at room temperature, caused neither an overgrowth of lysed areas nor the development of previously unseen areas.

The inhibition-titration method of estimating bacteriophage concentration is useful, provided the possible fallacies of the method are considered. In the first place, it forms a convenient method for making approximations where such information would be of use. In the second place, when dilutions of bacteriophage are made in broth for the purpose of securing the desired number of areas on a plate, several higher dilutions may easily be made, and the series of dilutions be inoculated with young rejuvenated culture, thus giving an inhibition-titration as a rough control for the results given by the plate.

The Variables: Bacteriophage and Organisms.—Normal Multiplication of Eberthella dysenteriae (Shiga): The normal rate in beef infusion broth is of interest not only here where it is essential as a standard whereby comparison may be made on the rate as influenced by the bacteriophage, but also perhaps because of the widespread use of this organism in bacteriophage work.

It has been shown by Chesney,[22], Sherman,[23] and others that there need be no lag period in the growth of young cultures, provided the inocualtion is made from the culture still in the logarithmic phase of growth into a similar medium at incubator temperature. If, with this precaution, we inoculate N organisms per c c. into a medium, and the organism divides by binary fission every t hours, then at the end of any time T, taken in hours from the time of inoculation, the bacteria per c c. considered as concentration C is

$$C = N\ 2T/t$$

Thus, if we inoculate 2 organisms per c c. (=N) multiplying every half hour (=t), then at the end of 2 hours (=T) there should be

$$C = 2 \times 2^{2/0.5}$$
$$= 32 \text{ organisms per c c.}$$

If $C = N\ 2^{T/t}$, then $\log C = \log N + T/t \log 2$, in which C and T are variables, and T plotted against log C is a straight line. (Log 2)/t is the slope, whence t is easily determined.

The results of a number of experiments in which the increase in bacterial concentration was followed by plating methods are given in a chart in a paper by the author.[24] With Eberthella dysenteriae (Shiga) plating methods were found to be adequate in studying the logarithmic phase of growth. The cells exist singly in broth culture, and there is evidence that cells in the dividing state, that is, actively reproducing, grow uniformly. Averaging the figures for t, the time of binary fission, as calculated from the slope of the curve in each experiment, the result

[22] Jour. Exper. Med., 1916, 24, p. 387.
[23] Sherman and Albus: Proc. Soc. Am. Bacteriol., abst. Bacteriol., 1924, 8, p. 6.
[24] Jour. Infect. Dis., 1924, 35, p. 532.

indicated a division every 31.3 minutes. In the experiments shown, which were not selected especially for this purpose, the range of binary fission was between 29.4 and 34.0 minutes. The results pertain to the multiplication of Eberthella dysenteriae (Shiga) in beef infusion broth of P_H 7.4 at 37 C.

Organism Multiplication as Influenced by the Bacteriophage: How, then, is the normal rate of development of this organism influenced by the bacteriophage actively lytic for the strain? Since the ultimate bacterial concentration is zero, there must be a reduction in bacterial concentration from even the small number of the original inoculation. In order to throw light on this question, the following experiment was performed:

Data are given from 4 typical experiments, tabulated as A, B, C, and D. In each case, plating methods were applied in order to follow the progress of organisms growing in broth which contained bacteriophage. Known dilutions of bacteriophage were made in beef infusion broth, so that dilution 1 of experiment A represented a bacteriophage dilution of 10^{-5} of a concentrated bacteriophage filtrate; dilution 2 of this experiment, 2×10^{-6} of the same bacteriophage, and dilution 3, 10^{-6} of the same bacteriophage. The bacteriophage dilution of experiment B was 10^{-5} of a weaker filtrate than used in experiment A; in experiment C, the dilution was $4 \times - 10^{-3}$; in experiment D, it was 1:300. The bacteriophage concentrations represented were:

Experiment A,	Dil.1	2,200 units per c c.
	Dil.2	440 units per c c.
	Dil.3	220 units per c c.
Experiment B	....	100 units per c c.
Experiment C	....	18,000 units per c c.
Experiment D	....	580,000 units per c c.

These dilutions of bacteriophage, together with a control broth containing no bacteriophage, were incubated to acquire a temperature of 37 C. Inoculations with Eberthella dysenteriae (Shiga) were made by adding known amounts of rejuvenated broth culture at 37 C. while still in its logarithmic phase of growth, so that, as far as possible, the control at least would continue to show the normal logarithmic rate of increase of bacterial concentration. The suspensions were incubated at 37 C. continuously for 12 hours, except for momentary removal at intervals for sampling and plating to determine the bacterial concentration. The results of these tests are shown numerically in table 1, and graphically represented in chart 1, in which the logarithm of the bacterial concentration is plotted against the time interval between inoculation and the time this concentration was determined.

A broth containing bacteriophage will allow a continuance of the logarithmic phase of growth of culture inoculated into it, under the proper conditions, for a greater or lesser period of time, after which lysis occurs rapidly.

From the results presented in table 1 and in chart 1, it appears that the development of organisms in the presence of bacteriophage follows a normal, logarithmic progression to a marked degree (considering that the bacteriophage might be expected to be active, to at least some degree, from the start) before there occurs a phase of rapid lysis. The age of

TABLE 1

GROWTH OF CULTURE EXPOSED TO BACTERIOPHAGE

Experiment	Age of Culture in Hours	Dilution 1 of Bacteriophage		Dilution 2 of Bacteriophage		Dilution 3 of Bacteriophage		Control (No Bacteriophage)	
		Bacteria per C c.	Log	Bacteria per C c.	Log	Bacteria per C c.	Log	Bacteria per C c.	Log
A	0.00	1.206	3.08	1,206	3.08	1,206	3.08	1,206	3.08
	1.67	1,960	3.29	2,510	3.40	2,300	3.36	2,410	3.38
	3.50	12,382	4.09	20,600	4.31	21,400	4.33	—	—
	7.00	1,481,000	6.17	1,497,000	6.18	1,960,000	6.29	2,000,000	6.30
	12.00	10,740	4.03	200	2.30	3,900	3.59	274,000,000	8.44
B	0.00	1,413	3.15	....	....	....	....	220	2.34
	2.00	2,640	3.42	....	....	....	....	3,420	3.53
	4.00	36,900	4.57	....	....	....	....	36.500	4.56
	6.00	630,000	5.80	....	....	....	....	770,000	5.89
	8.00	10,700,000	7.03	....	....	....	....	18,700,000	7.27
	10.00	<1,000	3.00	....	....	....	....	300,000,000	8.48
	11.00	<100	2.00	....	....	....	....	—	—
	12.00	40	1.60	....	....	....	....	581,000,000	8.76
C	0.17	—	—	....	....	....	....	1,680	3.23
	0.75	1,940	3.29	....	....	....	....	—	—
	3.00	18,600	4.27	....	....	....	....	20,100	4.30
	5.50	571,000	5.76	....	....	....	....	627,000	5.80
	7.00	< or =100,000	5.00	....	....	....	....	—	—
	8.00	< or =1,000	3.00	....	....	....	....	—	—
	9.00	< or = 30	1.48	....	....	....	....	98,000,000	7.99
D	0.00	1,800	3.26						
	2.50	19,000	4.28						
	3.40	50,600	4.70						
	5.00	56,000	4.75						
	6.00	146	2.16						

the culture growing in the presence of the bacteriophage at the time when the phase of rapid lysis begins is not constant; nor, corollary to that, is the organism concentration constant at this point where rapid lysis begins. It may be concluded only that the progress of the bacterial concentration is dependent on the original concentrations of bacteria and of bacteriophage. It will be shown later that this is reasonable, and the manner of this dependence will be discussed.

It is first necessary to take up a study of the change in bacteriophage concentration during the interval in which the bacterial concentration changed in the manner just studied.

Bacteriophage Concentration as Influenced by the Organisms: During the time that the bacterial concentration is being influenced by the presence of bacteriophage, there must be a change in bacteriophage concentration, for we know that a minute amount of bacteriophage may be introduced into a bacterial suspension, and after time has been allowed for lysis, the liquid will contain a high concentration of bacteriophage. The following experiment was performed to give some data on this point:

Dilutions of a potent bacteriophage were made in beef infusion broth, having the concentrations noted below in table 2. The suspensions were set in the incubator to acquire a temperature of 37 C., after which they were inoculated lightly with infusion broth culture at 37 C., rejuvenated so as to be

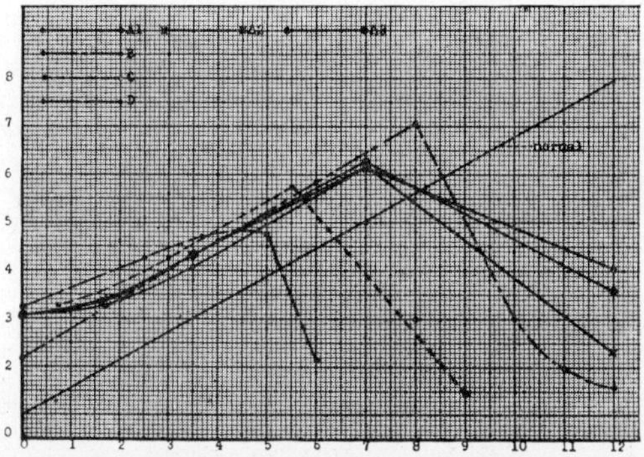

Chart 1.—Influence of bacteriophage on *Eberthella dysenteriae* (Shiga). The figures on the ordinate in this chart and in chart 2 indicate log bacteria per c c.; the figures on the abscissa, the time in hours.

multiplying at the normal logarithmic rate. The inoculated suspensions were held at 37 C. throughout the experiment to determine the bacteriophage concentration, being removed from the incubator only to make dilutions and plates by the standard method for the enumeration of areas.

The results of two typical experiments, called A and B, are given in table 2, and graphically represented in chart 2, in which the logarithms of the bacteriophage concentrations are plotted against the age of the suspension following inoculation. The bacterial concentration is also represented over a synchronous period in order to show the relationship.

As the general trend of the bacterial concentration is to decrease, the general trend of the bacteriophage concentrations under the same conditions is to increase; and the period of increase is more or less synchronous with the decrease in bacterial concentration.

From the data presented, we observe that as the bacteria have been shown to follow for a certain length of time the normal logarithmic rate of multiplication, the bacteriophage concentration over approximately the same length of time is stable. Following this, there occurs what might be called a definite phase of rapid lysis of the bacteria and a definite phase of rapid increase of the bacteriophage concentration. The ultimate bacterial concentration is zero, and the ultimate bacteriophage concentration appears to reach a maximum at approximately 500,000,000 units per c c.

A theory might be formulated as an explanation of the occurrence of a phase of rapid bacterial lysis and of rapid increase in bacteriophage concentration to the effect that cultures of a certain age represent a definite set of conditions as regards age of cells, presence of enzymatic action, or other unspecified conditions pertinent to a culture of a certain

TABLE 2

BACTERIOPHAGE INCREASE WITH LYSIS OF BACTERIA

Experiment	Time at Which Concentration Was Measured, Hours	Bacteriophage per C c.	Logarithm of Bacteriophage per C c.
A	0.00	18,000	4.26
	1.22	18,900	4.28
	3.33	13,858	4.14
	5.93	2,086,920	6.32
	7.38	99,262,800	8.00
	8.47	58,836,000	7.77
	9.58	129,870,000	8.11
B	0.00	580,000	5.76
	2.50	548,000	5.74
	3.67	2,548,000	6.41
	5.00	28,200,000	7.45
	6.00	113,500,000	8.06

age. There has been a tendency to explain some of the bacteriophage phenomena on such a basis—that of cellular condition as a function of time. We cannot believe, however, that the cellular condition is any but a continuous function of the age of the culture—that there is no sudden change of the conditions of the cells and their environment. On this basis there would be no evidence of conditions favoring a more or less sudden stimulation of lytic action. This should more especially appear logical since we are dealing as much as possible with organisms in their logarithmic phase of growth, the organisms multiplying in normal geometric progression with no evidence of any inhibitory agent or cellular eccentricity.

It would appear more logical perhaps to offer as an explanation of the phase of rapid lysis of bacteria, and of rapid increase in bacteriophage concentration, a theory based on the actual physical proximity of the bacterial cells and the bacteriophage units; to say that the phenomena are due to the dispersion of the respective units.

The period of time elapsing between the inoculation of the bacteriophage dilution and the phase of rapid lysis of the bacteria decreases as the bacteriophage concentration of the original dilution increases. For example, from chart 1 it is apparent that the intervals between inoculation and the beginning of rapid lysis were respectively 5.0, 5.5, 7.0, and 8.0 hours; the corresponding original bacteriophage concentrations were 580,000 units per c c., 18,000 units per c c., 2,200 units per c c., and 100 units per c c., respectively. If the original bacteriophage concentration was 2,200 units per c c., a rapid drop in baterial concentration originated

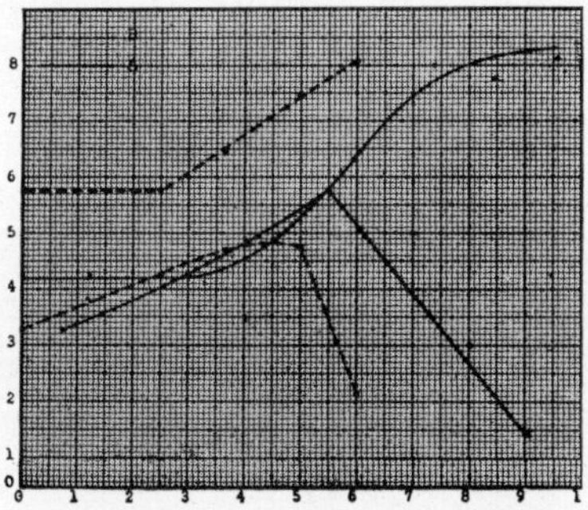

Chart 2.—Rate of increase of bacteriophage.

at or about the point where the bacterial concentration was 10,000,000 organisms per c c. When the bacteriophage concentration was originally greater, as 18,000 units per c c., the phase of rapid lysis began when the bacterial concentration had reached only about 600,000 per c c.

In a suspension containing a few organisms per c c. and a very few bacteriophage units per c c., under stable conditions which do not exist, the elements would in time probably get together and bring about lysis. However, the young culture under such conditions in reality proceeds to multiply apparently normally. The bacteriophage would seem to lie dormant until the organisms reach a certain proximity brought about by the increased bacterial concentration. At that time lysis begins with more than transient rapidity, and although the organisms constantly become fewer and thus more dispersed, the lysis has increased the concentration of bacteriophage units; hence the proximal relationship of the reacting elements is not so much altered, and lysis proceeds to completion. This view of the matter puts the time element of lysis as a function of the dispersion of the two elements.

One might assume that if y were the concentration of bacteriophage units and x the concentration of organisms, that $x + y$ need only reach a certain figure to bring about rapid and complete lysis. If the organisms were present in a concentration of 10,000,000 per c c. and the bacteriophage were present in a concentration of y in one case at the beginning of rapid lysis, then in another case in which the bacterial concentration was only 600,000 per c c., the bacteriophage concentration might be assumed to be close to $y + 9{,}400{,}000$ per c.c. However, it is probable that the difference in size between the bacterial cell and the bacteriophage unit—which it is safe to say is considerable—enters into the matter, for an increase in bacterial concentration means a much larger surface for forming contacts than would a corresponding increase in the number of bacteriophage units. Examination of the data reveals no such simple rule as when $x + y = k$ rapid lysis occurs. On the other hand, it is apparent from chart 2 that although the organisms inoculated to the bacteriophage suspensions were nearly the same in both A and B, the period of rapid lysis of bacteria and increase in bacteriophage concentration began in a much shorter time when the original bacteriophage concentration was greater.

Maximum Concentration of Bacteriophage in Broth: Will the addition of n organisms to b bacteriophage units produce a final bacteriophage suspension containing k bacteriophage units? We should certainly be justified in predicting that, provided n and b were not too large, no constant number of bacteriophage units would result, for neither the bacteria nor the bacteriophage remain fixed; although lysis of one bacterial cell brought about by one bacteriophage unit may result in 15 or 20 bacteriophage units after lysis, we have seen that the addition of n organisms to b bacteriophage units results actually in the lysis of a much larger number of cells. Furthermore, the bacteriophage concentration in a tube of broth in which lysis has occurred seems to be more or less the same, whether the initial concentration of either bacteria or bacteriophage, or both, were high or low. Consequently, we might expect no great increase in bacteriophage concentration if b were very high. What actually happens under such experimental conditions is shown in the following tests:

Into a large sterile tube were placed 24 c c. of a potent bacteriophage filtrate containing 226,000,000 units per c c. To this was added 1 c c. of rejuvenated broth culture, and lysis allowed to proceed at 37 C. for 24 hours, or, strictly speaking, beyond the point of lysis. Five c c. were removed, and the bacteriophage concentration determined by the enumeration of areas. After standing several days at room temperature, the bacteriophage concentration was again measured, further organisms added, and lysis again brought about at 37 C. over a period of 24 hours. The bacteriophage concentration was measured, the tube allowed to stand several days at room temperature, and the operation repeated for a third time. These are tabulated in table 3 as "feeding" A, B and C. Following the third "feeding," the bacteriophage concentration was determined at 5 and 7 days as additional checking. The organisms added were counted by plating methods, so that the exact number might be known.

The results are shown in table 3.

TABLE 3

MAXIMUM CONCENTRATION OF BACTERIOPHAGE

"Feeding"	Date	Bacteria Added	Measurement of Concentration Before or After Lysis	Bacteriophage Units per C c.
A	11/28/23 11/29/23	869.500 in 25 c c.	Before After	226×10^6 162×10^6
B	12/ 3/23 12/ 4/23	10,250,000 in 20 c c.	Before After	50×10^6 145×10^6
C	12/ 6/23 12/ 7/23	300,000 in 15 c c.	Before After	$2,358 \times 10^6$ 221×10^6
(D)	12/11/23 12/13/23	None	After After	$5,824 \times 10^6$ $5,360 \times 10^6$

There was a gradual development of a flocculent débris in the bottom of the tube after the C feeding, in part, at least, due to the development of a resistant, or R, strain, as shown by the microscopic entity of the cells, and by the definite increase in the flocculent precipitate for a period of a week following the feeding C. Continued attempt at culturing the strain resulted only in sterile slants and plates.

From these data one observes that after a certain maximum concentration is reached, bacteria may be lysed without appreciably increasing the bacteriophage concentration. It is also apparent that there appears to be a superconcentrated bacteriophage coincident with the development of the resistant strain. This, as will be brought out in connection with a discussion of the resistant strain, is consistent with the properties of such a strain.

Corollary to the above experiment the following experiment, which was repeated a number of times, is pertinent.

An inhibition-titration was made on a potent bacteriophage. Dilutions up to and including 10^{-8} of this bacteriophage gave no growth following inoculation with rejuvenated culture, and incubation at 37 C. Dilutions of 10^{-9} or higher gave normal growth. After 48 hours of incubation of the inoculated dilutions of this bacteriophage, the dilutions themselves were titrated by a similar inhibition-titration.

It was consistently found that the maximum dilution giving complete inhibition was the same, whether the original tube represented a 10^{-1} dilution of the original bacteriophage, or any higher dilution giving inhibition and lysis.

It is logical to find demonstrated a maximum concentration of bacteriophage in broth, for if there resulted an infinite number of liberated bacteriophage units, even though lysis may continue to occur, chemical laws would require that such infinite concentration result in the separation of bacteriophage in its pure state. If we assume that the bacteriophage unit is a sphere 20 millimicrons in diameter, the maximum concentration is only 0.0000000009% actual bacteriophage material, whatever that may be. This maximum concentration does not take into consideration the concentration in or on a lysed area of bacterial growth on agar when a continuity of bacteriophage units might logically occur in much the same way as the continuity of bacterial cells grown on solid mediums.

Cellular Absorption of Bacteriophage.—There must inevitably occur either absorption or adsorption of the bacteriophage by living bacterial cells against which the bacteriophage is active, under the proper conditions. In order to bring about lysis, there must be some sort of physical contact between the bacteriophage unit and the bacterial cell. Even a theory based on an electrical field of force would not harmonize with the activity within the bacterial cell having a diameter of several microns, due to a force originating at any distance greater than that from the center of the cell to the outer cell wall. D'Herelle postulates the entry of a bacteriophage into a cell, multiplication there, and subsequent liberation of the units following lysis. Adsorption or absorption by dead bacterial cells has been demonstrated,[25] as well as adsorption by colloidal metals, serum, and charcoal.[26] We have attempted the study of absorption by living and dead homologous bacteria, by heterologous bacteria, and by the resistant or R strain of homologous bacteria.

Absorption by Living Homologous Bacteria: The following experiment gives some insight into the rate of absorption by living homologous culture, in spite of the fact that such experimentation requires the mixing of bacteria and bacteriophage in liquid suspension, thereby not fixing the two elements as constants on which to base interpretation.

[25] Jaumain and Meuleman: Compt. rend. Soc. de biol., 1922, 87, p. 364.
[26] De Necker: Ibid.

A 16.5 hour culture of Eberthella dysenteriae (Shiga) in 40 c c. of beef infusion broth was used. Ten c c. of bacteriophage of a concentration of 174,300,000 units per c c. was added, making 34,860,000 units per c c. in the mixed suspension. The experiment was carried out at room temperature. The suspensions were filtered, 15 and 30 minutes, respectively, following the addition of the bacteriophage, enumeration of areas being made both before and after filtration in each case. The results are shown in the following tabulation:

Time	Bacteriophage per C c.
0.00 hrs.	34.86×10^6
0.25 hrs., unfiltered	22.90×10^6
0.25 hrs., filtered	3.83×10^6
0.50 hrs., unfiltered	30.40×10^6
0.50 hrs., filtered	3.69×10^6

There appears to be a definite absorption of the bacteriophage by the bacteria, as well as, probably, by the filter in this experiment.

Bearing on the same point is the following experiment.

Two flasks containing 150 c c. each of beef infusion broth were incubated at 37 C. to acquire that temperature. One was inoculated with young rejuvenated broth culture of Eberthella dysenteriae (Shiga), and allowed to develop to an approximate turbidity of 100,000,000 organisms per c c.—i. e., not beyond the logarithmic phase of growth. To the control flask not containing bacteria was added a small measured amount of bacteriophage. The flask was shaken and filtered to saturate the filter with bacteriophage and to secure a control. Filtration was performed at 37 C. The culture was then mixed with a similar amount of bacteriophage, and held at 37 C., with filtrations made at 0, 15, 30, 45, and 60 minutes. Filtrate remaining in the candle and passing into the subsequent filtrate was taken care of by calculation as well as possible. The results were as follows:

Subject	Bacteriophage per C c.
Unfiltered control	1,240,000
Filtered control	1,150,000
0′ filtrate	1,050,000
15′ filtrate	462,000
30′ filtrate	810,000
45′ filtrate	11,300,000
60′ filtrate	25,400,000

There appears to be a marked absorption during the first 15 minutes, followed undoubtedly by further absorption, the results of which are masked by the natural increase in bacteriophage following lysis.

In these data there is apparent corroboration of the absorption of the bacteriophage by the bacteria during the initial stages of the lytic phenomena. Equally apparent is the liberation from lysed cells of bacteriophage units which are, if one considers the bacteriophage a living agent, the offspring of the absorbed units—all within less than 45 minutes. To say more than this would not be justifiable, for we have no means of ascertaining from the data presented, at just what period each bacteriophage unit was absorbed by a cell. Although the period between ingestion or absorption and the expulsion of the multiplied bacteriophage units should, under similar conditions, be nearly the same, the results gave only average figures of a large number of individual reactions, presumably starting at different times. In broad terms, we may say that during the first 15 minutes, under the conditions of the experiment, there occurs some sort of absorption of the bacteriophage units by the cells, the extent of absorption depending on the concentration of both elements. During the interval between 15 and 30 minutes some of the absorbed bacteriophage units, presumably those first coming in contact with the cells and thus first going through the multiplying phase, have acted on the bacterial cell, with subsequent lysis and liberation of more bacteriophage units than were absorbed. During the interval between 30 and 45 minutes most of the first bacteriophage units absorbed have passed through one cycle, and beyond much doubt many of them have been reabsorbed by bacteria. It is not improbable that some units have been through one cycle, been reabsorbed, and passed through another complete cycle at the end of 45 minutes. Beyond 45 minutes the results become confused, as speculation allows the presence of two or three cycles, with the probability that there are still some of the original bacteriophage units not yet through one complete cycle, since lysis had not occurred completely at the end of the experiment.

Absorption by Dead Homologous Bacteria: The following experiment was performed in order to throw some light on the rate of absorption by dead homologous bacteria, since we may assume from the work of previous authors that absorption should occur with such organisms.

A flask culture of Eberthella dysenteriae (Shiga) in 150 c c. of beef infusion broth was subjected to a temperature of 62 C. for 15 minutes at such time as the bacterial concentration was approximately 100,000,000 per c c. This time was allowed on account of the volume of liquid to be heated. Checks on the sterility demonstrated the absence of living cells. The cells remained in suspension without agglutination and without settling for 48 hours, when the experiment was performed. Duplicating the conditions of the absorption experiment with living cells, bacteriophage was added to a flask of sterile broth so as to have a concentration of 1,130,000 units per c c. This was filtered at 37 C., making enumeration counts before filtration, and the first and second fractions of the filtrate. The same amount of bacteriophage was added to the killed culture suspension at 37 C., and this was filtered at 0, 15, 30, 45 and 60 minutes. Filtrate remaining in the candle was accounted for by calculation. The results are shown in the following tabulation.

Subject	Bacteriophage per C c.
Original bacteriophage	1,130,000
1st fraction, control	690.000
2nd fraction, control	840,000
0′ absorption filtrate	650,000
15′ absorption filtrate	599,000
30′ absorption filtrate	380,000
45′ absorption filtrate	230,000
60′ absorption filtrate	190,000

There is clearly indicated an absorption by dead homologous cells, progressive with time.

The results of the preceding experiment, clearly indicating absorption, do not permit an absolute statement that there is no increase in bacteriophage concentration from exposure to dead homologous bacteria. If, however, there is such an increase, it is certainly slight. The decrease in bacteriophage concentration in the first fraction of the control filtrate is no doubt due to adsorption by the filter. If this be true, the amount of bacteriophage adsorbed by the filter would depend on many factors, such as the porosity of the filter, finer filters presenting more surface than coarse ones, the H-ion concentration, the electrical charge of the micellae being directly concerned, and other physical factors. It has been demonstrated by Mudd [27] that serums when filtered lose some of their immune bodies, and methylene blue, for example, may be filtered out for some time before the surface, originally electronegative to the liquid, becomes electrically neutral or perhaps electropositive through saturation. On this basis, a demonstration of adsorption of bacteriophage by a filter implies that the units are electropositive to the filter surface in broth. These explanations suffice to explain adequately the presence of more bacteriophage per c c. in the second fraction of the control filtrate than in the first, saturation having been approximately completed in the filtration of the first few c c.

Absorption by Living Heterologous Bacteria: We may, for our present purpose, define heterologous bacteria as including all species except the normal sensitive Eberthella dysenteriae (Shiga). The following experiments were performed to ascertain the facts regarding the possible absorption by living cells of Escherichia coli, Eberthella typhi, Eberthella paradysenteriae (Flexner), Eberthella dysenteriae

[27] Am. Jour. of Physiol., 1923, 63, Feb.

(Shiga) (not the standard sensitive strain), and a resistant or R strain isolated from the homologous Eberthella dysenteriae (Shiga).

In testing for possible absorption by Escherichia coli, 12 hour flask cultures were allowed to develop in beef infusion broth following inoculation from a well rejuvenated culture. A small amount of bacteriophage was added to this culture at 37 C., so that the bacteriophage concentration was 800,000 per c c. A control flask containing the same amount of broth as the culture flask, but no organisms, was used, keeping the flask at 37 C., and adding the bacteriophage to the same concentration. Similar amounts of culture—bacteriophage mixture and of control broth containing bacteriophage were filtered through similar filters. The absorption period was 15 minutes at 37 C. The results showed:

Subject	Bacteriophage per C c.
Original unfiltered	800,000
Control filtered	714,000
Absorption filtrate	274,000

There thus appears to be a definite absorption of the bacteriophage by this strain of Escherichia coli.

In the case of absorption by Eberthella typhi (Eberth) the same technic was followed as in the test with Escherichia coli. The following results were obtained:

Subject	Bacteriophage per C c.
Original unfiltered	287,000
Control filtered	256,000
Absorption filtrate	267,000

In this case there would seem to be a conclusive lack of absorption by this culture of the typhoid bacillus.

Application of the same technic to a strain of Eberthella paradysenteriae (Flexner) gave the following:

Subject	Bacteriophage per C c.
Original unfiltered	287,000
Control filtered	256,000
Absorption filtrate	167,000

This culture apparently shows some absorption of the bacteriophage.

Similar technic was applied to a strain of Eberthella dysenteriae (Shiga), not the Shiga type against which the bacteriophage activity had been built up. This might be considered homologous absorption, except for the fact that at the time of the experiment the bacteriophage was only slightly active against this strain. The results follow:

Subject	Bacteriophage per C c.
Original unfiltered	180,000
Control filtered	128,000
Absorption filtrate	210,000

The bacteriophage, being somewhat active against this strain, is undoubtedly absorbed to some extent. The fact that it is not apparent from the results is presumably due to the increase in bacteriophage units owing to lysis of some of the cells.

The absorption of the anti-Shiga bacteriophage was also attempted by the use of the resistant homologous strain of Eberthella dysenteriae (Shiga). The technic of the previous tests was applied, with the one exception that the bacterial suspension was made by washing off agar slants with broth, for the reason that such resistant strains do not grow well in broth. The results were as follows:

Subject	Bacteriophage per C c.
Original unfiltered	287,000
Control filtered	256,000
Absorption filtrate	6,000,000

It is apparent not only that no absorption occurs, but that the number of bacteriophage units in the "absorption filtrate" had actually increased many times. The result clearly indicates the presence of a large amount of bacteriophage closely correlated with and constantly present with an R strain. To demonstrate absorption would necessitate the removal of the bacteriophage thus carried along with the strain, and it is our belief that, could this actually be accomplished, a normal strain would result.

Summarizing as a group the experiments with absorption by heterologous but not distantly related bacterial strains, there appears to be no particular specificity of reaction as regards the ordinary bacteriologic grouping by serologic and biochemical reactions. From the serologic reactions, one would expect Eberthella typhi and Eberthella paradysenteriae (Flexner) to be as closely related to Eberthella dysenteriae (Shiga) as is Escherichia coli, although the results of the absorption tests might indicate the reverse. Judging by the adsorption by inanimate substances and by the lack of specificity of the bacteriophage in lysis of strains presumably identical, it is questionable whether specificity of this type can logically be expected.

There is, however, another type of specificity of absorption which might be considered—absorption by bacterial cells susceptible to the specific lytic action of the particular bacteriophage to a greater or less extent. Regarding the matter from the point of view of the bacteriophage, this would be specific absorption. The results of the preceding experiments do not indicate a specificity of this sort. Absorption by the R strain must be omitted from consideration, but the bacteriophage used was slightly active against Eberthella dysenteriae (Shiga) of this heterologous series, and was originally active against the strain of Escherichia coli used, although we could secure no signs of areas at the time of the absorption experiment. The absorption tests do not correlate with the bacteriophage activity in this particular series, in spite of the fact that specific absorption of this type is extremely probable.

Absorption or Adsorption: In the case of the living cell, the probability is that the focus of reaction is within the cell rather than at its surface. With the dead cell, however, we may very well have adsorption. The only reason for this statement thus far apparent would be the analogy between possible adsorption by the dead cell and the definite adsorption by substances such as filter surfaces, colloidal metals, and the like. If the bacteriophage unit is absorbed by a dead cell, it should not be free to produce areas in living cultures on an agar plate, whereas if adsorption occurs merely at the surface of the dead cell, there should be active contact between the bacteriophage and living cells when opportunity is offered on an agar surface by the usual procedure for the formation of lytic areas. The following experiment is pertinent.

A tube of beef infusion broth, 20 c c., was inoculated with rejuvenated *Eberthella dysenteriae* (Shiga). When, following incubation at 37 C., the bacterial concentration had reached approximately 100,000,000 per c c., the organisms were killed by exposure to a temperature of 62 C. for 10 minutes. To this killed culture suspension, as well as to a control tube containing the same amount of broth but no organisms, was added a definite amount of bacteriophage. The bacteriophage concentration of the control was measured by plate enumeration of areas. The killed culture was exposed to the bacteriophage for 2 hours at 37 C., counts of the bacteriophage concentration being made at 15 minutes, 1 hour, and 2 hours (whether or not this really is a measurement of the bacteriophage concentration is, of course, the point of the experiment). The results follow:

Subject	Bacteriophage per C c.
Control	12,000
Adsorbed 15′	10,300
Adsorbed 1 hr.	16,600
Adsorbed 2 hrs.	17,400

It appears that the bacteriophage in the presence of killed bacterial cells, although previously demonstrated to be taken up by such cells, was still so situated as to come in contact with living cells inoculated to a plate for area enumeration.

Thus, if our reasoning is correct, adsorption of bacteriophage by dead cells would be indicated, and not absorption. We should not consider the apparent slight increase in bacteriophage concentration to be of any significance.

Diffusion of Bacteriophage.—Through Agar: It was observed in the course of experimentation that in several instances in which moist plates were used the culture had run underneath the agar and developed between it and the glass. In such plates, the surface growth might be completely lysed with no effect on the culture underneath. The diffusion of the bacteriophage in agar would seem to be limited to a distance less than the thickness of an agar plate. The following experiment was performed in order to demonstrate the presence or absence of diffusion in agar under controlled conditions.

Small sterile tubes of 4 mm. internal diameter were made and filled with "live" agar, that is, a 4% agar mixed in equal parts with a young broth culture. This was allowed to harden, and a drop of concentrated suspension of bacteriophage was dropped on the surface. The diffusion could be noted in the small tube by the clearing of the agar due to the lysis of the small closely associated colonies.

Diffusion took place to a depth of 1 mm. gradually over a period of 48 hours, beyond which, of course, there was no change, owing to the increased age of the bacteria. Partial anaerobic conditions might have had some slight influence. Various dyes under similar conditions diffused a centimeter or more in the same length of time.

Diffusion of the bacteriophage in agar is borne out by the work of Arnold.[28]

Diffusion Through Parchmentized Membranes: The possible diffusion of bacteriophage through parchmentized membranes was studied by means of dialysis of a broth suspension of bacteriophage with distilled water.

Parchmentized thimbles 2 x 9 cm. were sealed to short glass tubes 2 cm. in external diameter by means of a rubber band and collodion. The tubes were not plugged with cotton, but were placed in larger tubes, which were plugged and sterilized in the autoclave. Distilled water dialysis was carried out at room temperature, about 23 C. Five wash waters were used in 2½ days, all wash waters being saved and measured for bacteriophage concentration by the usual plate method. The concentration of the original suspension was determined, and of the dialysate after the final washing. 12 c c. of suspension were originally placed in each tube, resulting in about 14 c c. in the final dialysate through osmosis; 14 c c. of sterile distilled water were used for each washing. The results were as follows:

Subject	Bacteriophage per C c.
Original concentration	1,240,000
First dialysate	686,000
Second dialysate	754,000
1st wash water, 0-20 hrs.	25,100
2nd wash water, 20-25 hrs.	17,900
3rd wash water, 25-44 hrs.	19,350
4th wash water, 44-49 hrs.	21,500
5th wash water, 49-68 hrs.	28,500

From these data one may conclude that the bacteriophage is diffusible through parchmentized membranes, and that diffusion occurs as a continuous function of time.

These data, besides presenting evidence of diffusion of the bacteriophage through parchmentized membranes, appear to show a considerable adsorption by the membrane, for all of the bacteriophage is not accounted for, and the only condition which would cause one to suspect destruction of the bacteriophage is exposure to distilled water. Although not impos-

[28] Jour. Lab. & Clin. Med., 1923, 8, p. 720.

sible, it is not probable in this experiment, for there was no tendency for the bacteriophage units to produce areas diminished in size, such as might indicate an intermediate step in diminished "virulence" between no effect as a result of exposure to distilled water and complete destruction. The total number of bacteriophage units originally present less the sum of the bacteriophage units of all the wash waters might be expected to equal the total number of bacteriophage units present in the dialysate. That this is not so is apparent from the following:

Original bacteriophage units: 12 c c. x 1,240,000 or......		14,880,000
Dialysate bacteriophage units: 14 c c. x 700,000 or......		9,800,000
Lost		5,080,000
Wash water 1:	376,000	
Wash water 2:	168,500	
Wash water 3:	290,250	
Wash water 4:	322,500	
Wash water 5:	427,500	
		1,584,750
Apparent loss unaccounted for......................		3,495,250

The discrepancy is marked. The figures used for volume of liquid are inexact, but liberal allowance was made where there was doubt, with a view to securing a minimum figure for the bacteriophage "unaccounted for." Thus the result, although it may be somewhat too small, is not too large.

Diffusion Through Collodion Membranes: Dialysis of a broth filtrate containing bacteriophage was carried out both with running tap water and with distilled water. The details of the experiments were as follows.

Tap water. Fat extraction thimbles 2 x 8 cm., made of hardened filter paper, were sealed to short blass tubes of 2 cm. external diameter by means of a rubber band and collodion. The thimbles were then plunged 5 times into collodion, allowing a minute to elapse between immersions, and placed in water. The glass tubes were then plugged with cotton, and sterilized in the autoclave. A broth filtrate suspension of bacteriophage was introduced into the sterile tube, the whole inserted in a beaker filled with tap water, and running tap water allowed to flow over it for 3 days. Bacteriophage concentrations before and after dialysis were determined by area enumeration, with the following results, shown for 2 duplicate tubes:

Subject	Bacteriophage per C c.
Original concentration	4,040,000
Dialysate No. 1............................	1,760,000
Dialysate No. 2............................	1,360,000

The results would seem to indicate a definite diffusion of the bacteriophage through a heavy collodion membrane.

Distilled water. Thimbles were prepared in a manner similar to those used in the experiment with tap water, but with only two immersions in collodion, making a membrane of lesser thickness. These tubes were not plugged with cotton, but were placed within larger tubes, the larger tubes being plugged, and the whole sterilized in the autoclave. The bacteriophage filtrate in broth was introduced into the collodion thimbles in 10 c c. amounts, and sterile distilled water (5 c c.) into the larger tube. The bacteriophage used had a concentration of 24,200,000 units per c c. Dialysis was allowed to proceed at room temperature. From the large tubes the first wash waters were removed after 4 hours and in 2 experiments found to contain 14,600 and 40,000 units per c c., respectively.

Dialysis through thin collodion membranes was thus shown to occur, but further attempts to carry through the enumeration exactly were frustrated by the fact that the size of the areas became so small that it was impossible to say with any certainty how many were present on a plate. This diminution in the size of the bacteriophage area possesses special significance which will be referred to on a later page.

No attempt has been made to calculate the approximate size of the bacteriophage unit from these diffusion data. It is apparent that such units in their narrowest dimension must fall within the realm of colloidal micellae, that is, between 0.14 and 0.00016 microns, the former limits representing the limits of resolving power of the ordinary microscope, and the lower representing the size of the hydrogen molecule. We feel that any further analysis of the probable size from the foregoing diffusion data is not justifiable because of the great probability that adsorption is an important, unmeasured factor, and because our technic lacks the great and carefully checked precision that should precede estimation by this means.

Resistant Strains.—Certain strains of bacteria against which a bacteriophage is active may be exposed to the bacteriophage, under the proper conditions, and variant strains resistant to the lytic action of the bacteriophage isolated. D'Herelle described several procedures whereby this may be accomplished, both of which could be easily duplicated with our bacteriophage and strain of Eberthella dysenteriae (Shiga). One procedure involves the preparation of a plate as for the production of areas, and the addition of an excessive amount of bacteriophage, so that at least part of the growth is entirely cleared. On this cleared zone, there will appear in 24 to 48 hours, small, perfectly symmetrical colonies, granular, dry, and cohesive, as shown by the fact that they may be moved as an unbroken colony along the surface of the agar with a platinum needle. These colonies may be subcultured to agar, on which they will present a similar dry, granular, and very irregular growth (plate 2; fig. 3). It has been our experience that not more than 50% of such subcultures are likely to develop, and that when once a subculture is secured, further transplantation is beset with difficulties, most strains having a tendency to run out entirely. Another procedure for the isolation of resistant strains involves excessive feeding of a bacteriophage with living, lysable cells, following which there occurs a flocculent débris in which the cells are intact, somewhat granular occasionally, usually more oval than the typical dysentery bacillus, and undoubtedly living in the presence of the bacteriophage and multiplying there, as is manifested by the marked increase in amount of flocculent débris. Isolation of this strain, however, is difficult.

The resistant strain presents no biochemical abnormalities. All sugar fermentations are normal, although very slow, owing to the slow rate of growth. Several strains carried over a period of a year lost no characteristics, nor did they gain new ones. During a month of that time transfers were made at least once, and often twice, daily, transferring always from the top of the slants where growth is ordinarily most regular, with no recurrence of the strains to normal growth. Broth cultures give a flocculent growth settling to the bottom of the tube, similar in every respect to the direct production of resistant strains in bacteriophage suspensions. They are capable of only several subcultures in broth, and are difficult to reisolate on agar. Serologic agglutination tests showed that a normal sensitive strain gave good agglutination both with a Mulford immune serum and with our local immune serum, whereas in no case did the resistant strains agglutinate with these serums.

The tendency toward autoagglutination of the resistant strains in broth caused us to look for a specific agglutinating substance. Filtration of both broth cultures and washings from agar slants, however, in no concentration used gave agglutination on incubation with a normal culture antigen.

The water of condensation of an agar slant culture of a resistant strain contains a considerable amount of bacteriophage. It was also found that a bacteria-free filtrate from a suspension of resistant organisms possessed a considerable concentration of bacteriophage units. There is ample evidence of the existence of the bacteriophage outside of the cells of an agar culture of the resistant strain. There is presumably in a resistant culture also a more or less variable amount of bacteriophage enclosed by the walls of various resistant cells. An attempt to wash off the external bacteriophage from the cells of a resistant culture suspended in salt solution, by means of successive centrifugings, taking off the supernatant fluid each time and resuspending in salt solution, failed to separate the external and internal bacteriophage. The supernatant fluids of each of 4 successive centrifugings contained virtually the same amount of bacteriophage, and plating for enumeration of areas of the sediment resuspended to the original volume showed no appreciable reduction over a similar plating of the original suspension. Whether the results were due to an uncontrolled disintegration, or to the fact that continued resuspension of the sediment even with the most violent agitation did not give properly homogeneous results for washing, it is difficult to say. Homogeneous suspension of the bacteriophage from the concentration in which it is present on an agar slant is in itself perhaps parellel to suspending bacteria from such a surface growth—a complex physical problem. In this case, it is further complicated by the presence of the resistant organisms and their associated bacteriophage. A further attempt to locate the focus of the associated bacteriophage was made by heating a suspension of resistant culture at 60 C. for 10 minutes, killing the organisms but not killing the bacteriophage. Thus the absorbed bacteriophage in the resistant cells should be barred from the production of areas, whereas adsorbed or free bacteriophage would be free to form areas. A control suspension of bacteria-free bacteriophage was similarly heated. An average of a number of plates gave 18.5 areas for a certain volume of the unheated bacteria-free bacteriophage, and 20 areas for the same volume of heated bacteriophage; thus, the heating was not too great for the bacteriophage. Plating the unheated resistant strain suspension gave approximately 100 times as many areas as did a similar amount of the heated suspensions.

Thus, although we have no quantitative data on the exact relationship between free and absorbed bacteriophage in a resistant culture, there is good evidence that there is an abundance of each in such a culture. The relationship is, in our experience, too intimate for quantitative resolution except perhaps by very detailed micro-methods; for the marked irregularity of growth and the fact that disintegration of certain cells is bound to occur would indicate beyond much doubt that the free and absorbed bacteriophage are variables with a number of conditions, uncontrollable unless single cells might be used.

It is our belief that the resistant strain consists of normal cells exposed to the bacteriophage, but which, through unfavorable conditions, are never completely lysed. The resistant strains may be plated by streaking in high dilution, and from such plates regular normal colonies may be picked, resulting in normal cultures, as well as irregular, typically resistant strains. Such resistant strains may be replated, and both strains reisolated. Again, the water of condensation of an agar slant culture of a resistant strain may be shown to possess a high concentration of bacteriophage units. The results of the experiment on absorption of bacteriophage by resistant cultures demonstrates the presence of a high concentration of bacteriophage with the dry growth on an agar slant. Subcultures in broth would seem to fail because of the carrying along of the multiplying bacteriophage, lysing all normal cells as they are produced, and leaving behind the slowly reproducing cells with an acquired resistance. The slow growth of the resistant strain would indicate that age is an important factor, for it is well established that an old cell is not especially well adapted to lysis by the bacteriophage. However, this would not seem to tell the whole story, for an old cell in the presence of bacteriophage must reproduce, even though slowly, thereby offering younger cells for lysis. We should thus picture the resistant strain as having adsorbed and absorbed bacteriophage, certain more or less normal cells, and a large proportion of old cells with an acquired resistance. Under proper conditions of isolation, such as on an agar surface or through separation in a liquid medium, certain cells are enabled to reproduce with sufficient rapidity to make them susceptible to lysis in broth, or to produce a normal strain on agar. Certain other cells are too closely associated with bacteriophage to become separated, and the slow development of a resistant colony may be viewed as a resistant cell dividing, producing two cells still possessing much the same relationship to the bacteriophage as the original cell and having the same acquired resistance, these cells reaching gradually the same conditions through aging as the original cell, whence four are produced, and so on.

This view of the typical resistant strain does not explain a variation in a susceptibility of different strains of bacteria, presumably of the same species, to the action of the bacteriophage. We made repeated efforts to adapt a bacteriophage isolated from a case of chronic colitis, and active against a strain of Eberthella typhi (Eberth), to lytic action against a biochemically and serologically identical Rawling's strain, without success. Adaptation of various types of bacteriophage from activity against one bacterial species has been reported in many instances, but in most cases it is not clear whether a single bacteriophage type or several mixed varieties are involved. The fact that some reports note a loss of activity of the bacteriophage for the original culture in acquiring activity against another culture might seem to indicate association of several varieties of bacteriophage. The possibilities of associative action with mixed bacteriophages is not well worked out, but a review of the literature would indicate that as much care is necessary in using mixed types of bacteriophage as in working with mixed bacterial cultures; and the problems of associative action may be equally complicated in the two cases.

Lysed Culture as Antigen Material.—Reports in the literature reveal a lack of consistency of results as regards the specificity of the lysed cell protein, some supporting such specificity, others failing to demonstrate it.

Working with the anti-Eberthella typhi (Eberth) bacteriophage previously mentioned, we inoculated 3 guinea-pigs with lysed culture antigen, and 3 with ordinary killed culture antigen. Four injections were made at 3-day intervals, using 0.5 c c. subcutaneously, 0.25 c c. intravenously, and 0.5 and 0.5 c c. subcutaneously, in their respective order. The lysed culture antigen was potent, having a bacteriophage concentration of 500,000,000 per c c. The killed culture antigen had a similar concentration of killed bacterial cells. One week after the last injection, 2 c c. of blood was removed from the heart of each animal, the serum taken off, and the antibody content determined by the following tests:

The agglutination titer of the serum of the 3 animals receiving the regular killed culture antigen was 1:640, as tested with a fresh homologous culture antigen. The agglutination titer of the 3 animals' serum receiving lysed culture antigen was 0 against a similar antigen. The serums of all 6 animals, as well as other antityphoid serums, were tested for the presence of specific precipitins for lysed Eberthella typhi (Eberth), but in no case could such precipitins be shown. We did not succeed in gaining sufficient virulence for the Eberthella typhi (Eberth) to determine, by means of protection experiments, the relative immunity acquired by animals inoculated with normal culture as compared with animals inoculated with lysed culture.

As a result of our experiments, we are inclined to view the lysed cell protein as lacking the specificity of the protein of the intact or mechanically disintegrated cell. This does not agree with the work of d'Herelle on barbonne, which seems to indicate specificity, or with other workers with various types of bacteriophage and other bacteria. The problem offers, however, so many varied angles that a further accumulation of data from all sources, with a variety of types of bacteriophage, bacterial strains, and serologic technics should be awaited.

DISCUSSION

This study of the bacteriophage of d'Herelle has not been undertaken with a view toward the solution of the question of the nature of the lytic agent. Nevertheless, it has been impossible to observe various manifestations of the activity of the bacteriophage over a period of two years without gaining some impressions as to the nature of the bacteriophage activity.

There can be little doubt that the instigating agent of the lytic phenomena of the bacteriophage exists in a corpuscular state, as well separated and well organized units. The production of lysed areas in mass culture growth implies a localization at the focus of each area of some instigating agent in itself an entity, and it is, incidentally, difficult to conceive of any ionizable chemical substance possessing such a property. The presence of bacteriophage in a broth dilution of 10^{-9} of a filtrate of maximum concentration implies a colloidal suspension. A bacterial or colloidal suspension may be diluted greatly and subsequently shown to be present in the high dilution; a dilution of normal HCl to 10^{-7} is considered to be no more acid than the water in which it is contained. Under proper conditions, a dilution of a colloidal solution may be a mechanical procedure; a dilution of other solutions is not.

The production of "pie-shaped" or cresent-shaped colonies bears out the unit structure of the bacteriophage. We were invariably successful in producing these colonies by adding to melted agar at 45 C. a small amount of bacteriophage, slanting the agar, and inoculating the surface with culture in such a manner as to produce colonies rather than solid growth (plate 2; figs. 4 and 5). If a single bacillus is sufficiently close to a bacteriophage unit, no growth becomes apparent; but if a colony of bacteria is fairly started, and in spreading to an increasing diameter meets a bacteriophage unit, there occurs lysis on that side of the colony and subsequent inhibition to further growth in that direction. Inoculation of such a slant so as to produce heavy growth verifies the explanation, for areas are produced in such frequency as the number of crescent shaped colonies found would indicate. Colonies on such slants vary from large colonies with very small niches at the extreme edge, the original organisms or organism of the colony having been several millimeters from the nearest bacteriophage unit in the surface, to colonies with deep niches on three or more sides.

This method for the production of pie-shaped colonies affords a rough method for estimation of the size of the bacteriophage unit. Organisms to be lysed must come in contact with the bacteriophage units, and the organisms are spread only on the surface of the agar. If a definite number of bacteriophage units are placed in a definite quantity of agar, the number of those units appearing in the surface is a function of the concentration of the units, their size, and the area exposed. This area, the number of units introduced, and the number of active units in the surface may all be determined. Calculation on this basis has given us results roughly between 10 and 100 millimicrons for the size of the bacteriophage unit. This procedure is not accurate in view of the complexity of the phenomena and the small size of the particles, and would not, unsupported, bear too close analysis. It is, however, of interest because of the fact that results thus given agree with those of other investigators,[29] who place the size in the neighborhood of 20 millimicrons in diameter. The matter is further complicated by the fact that we do not know whether the bacteriophage unit has a longer and shorter dimension, or whether it is spherical.

D'Herelle claims to have established a certain relationship between the potency of a bacteriophage filtrate and the number of ultramicroscopic granules of a uniform size as observed by actual ultramicroscopic examination. We have examined suspensions under the ultramicroscope and have seen the granules of uniform size, presumably the granules referred to. The observation would not lead me to make any more definite statements than those made by d'Herelle; and indeed the complex nature of the broth medium renders any definite statements of this nature of somewhat doubtful value.

The definite evidence in favor of a unity of structure, together with the oft-repeated argument based on the fact that lytic action is transmissible by repeated transfer of bacteriophage and exposure to organisms to what would be infinite dilution of the original bacteriophage filtrate, are, in my opinion, strong arguments in favor of the living nature of the agent. The fact that the bacteriophage gives evidence of assimilation of heterogeneous inanimate material into its own substance is, as mentioned in the introduction, strong evidence of the living nature. We have some evidence of the diminishing of the virulence or potency of the lytic activity, both by storage over long periods, and in one case with dialysis with distilled water. Variation of this sort is a property of living matter. The adaptation of a bacteriophage to a culture strain not that against which the lytic activity was built up would, if accepted, definitely favor a theory that the agent is living.

Our picture of the bacteriophage would, then, be an instigating agent of an organized, living, ultramicroscopic nature. We should picture this

[29] Prausnitz: Centralbl. f. Bakteriol., I, O., 1922, 89, p. 187.

cellular unit as attacking a lysable bacterial cell and elaborating, either at the surface of the cell or within its walls, a substance which acts on the cell and brings about its lysis. Since there results coincident with lysis an increasing number of bacteriophage units, there is, be the agent living or inanimate, an increase at or in the cell. Such increase must be at the expense of the cell, unless anabolism is stimulated by contact with the cell and comes from the medium, which seems improbable. Because of quantitative considerations, on the basis of an elaboration of approximately 20 bacteriophage units, say 20 millimicrons cubed from one such unit within the cell, it is not logical to assume that anabolism alone is responsible for the lysis of the cell, and thus the postulate of the elaboration of a ferment, as perhaps a proteolytic enzyme, becomes an essential feature of a theory.

The data presented offer no clues as to the nature of the more intimate reaction between metabolic products of the bacteriophage, if it be living, and the bacterial cell. It is merely our purpose to state a theory compatible with the data, presenting our picture of the mechanism of the phenomena. The details of the nature of the lytic activity of the bacteriophage will, in the course of time, develop naturally from accumulated information, and to state any theory with undue vehemence at this stage of development is unwise and unnecessary.

SUMMARY

The purpose of the present work was the study of the phenomena of a d'Herelle type or strain of bacteriophage from a quantitative point of view, particularly as regards the mutual relationship between bacterial cells and bacteriophage. Studies of certain corollary features were also made from a quantitative point of view, specifically as regards the absorption of bacteriophage by bacterial cells, the diffusion of bacteriophage through agar and semipermeable membranes, the resistant strains, and the lysed culture as antigen.

A technic was developed for the quantitative estimation of bacteriophage concentration, using an original type isolated by d'Herelle.

The normal rate of multiplication of Eberthella dysenteriae (Shiga) during the logarithmic phase of growth was determined, the rate of fission being once every 31.3 minutes in beef infusion broth at 37 C.

The effect of the bacteriophage on this normal logarithmic rate is such as to cause no variation from the normal for a greater or lesser period of time, depending on the concentrations both of the bacteriophage and of the organisms; following this there is a period of rapid lysis.

During this exposure of organisms to bacteriophage, a period of stability in bacteriophage concentration occurs, followed by a period of rapid increase, to some extent synchronous with the period of rapid bacterial lysis.

There was found to be a maximum concentration of bacteriophage in beef infusion broth, beyond which further lysis of bacterial cells seemed to cause no increase. This point of concentration was approximately 225,000,000 units per c c.

Experimental results on cellular absorption of the bacteriophage showed the following:

1. Living bacterial cells sensitive to the lytic action of the bacteriophage absorb bacteriophage from a broth suspension within a period of 15 minutes at 37 C. Dead cells of the same strain. bring about progressive adsorption over a period of at least one hour. It was shown that such dead cells probably adsorb bacteriophage rather than absorb it.

2. Tests involving the absorption of bacteriophage by heterologous bacteria indicated absorption from a broth suspension within a period of 15 minutes at 37 C. with some bacterial strains and none with others.

3. It is concluded that there is no specificity of bacteriophage absorption from the point of view of the accepted bacteriologic grouping, but that there is a specificity from the point of view of susceptibility to lysis by the bacteriophage.

The bacteriophage was found to diffuse 1 mm. in 2% agar in 48 hours, and to diffuse through parchmentized and collodion membranes. It is indicated that adsorption plays a rôle in the diffusion through parchmentized membranes.

Evidence is given to indicate a probability that our resistant or R strains are combinations of normal cells, and older cells with a natural (possibly acquired) resistance, all associated with adsorbed and absorbed bacteriophage.

Attempts at adaptation of an antityphoid (Eberth) bacteriophage to a Rawling's strain of the typhoid bacillus were unsuccessful.

The use of typhoid culture subjected to lysis by bacteriophage as antigen in animal inoculation experiments did not result in a specific antityphoid serum when tested for the presence of agglutinins and precipitins against the normal antigen and the lysed antigen.

Normal antityphoid immune serum, although having a high agglutinin concentration specific for our Eberth strain of the typhoid bacillus, was not found to have precipitins giving specific precipitation with bacteriophage-lysed Eberthella typhi (Eberth) antigen.

A discussion of the unity of structure of the bacteriophage is presented, and the theory that the agent responsible for transmissible bacteriolysis is a living ultramicroscopic entity is concurred in.

PLATE 1

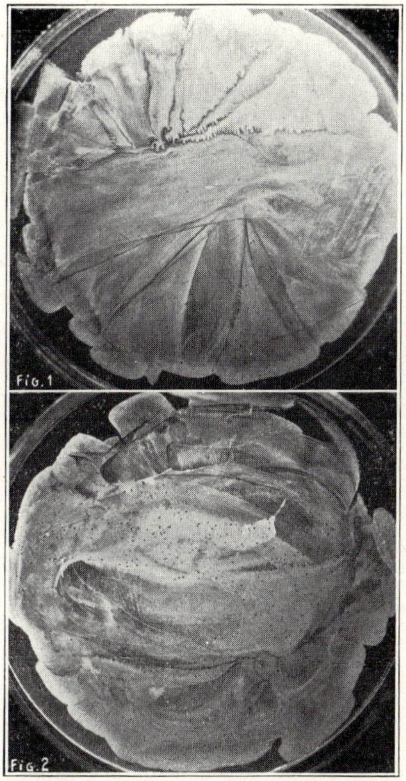

Fig. 1.—A standard plate used in enumeration of areas for determination of bacteriophage concentration. (× 0.6.)

Fig. 2.—Same as figure 1, with a dilution 0.1 as great. (× 0.6.)

Plate II

PLATE 2

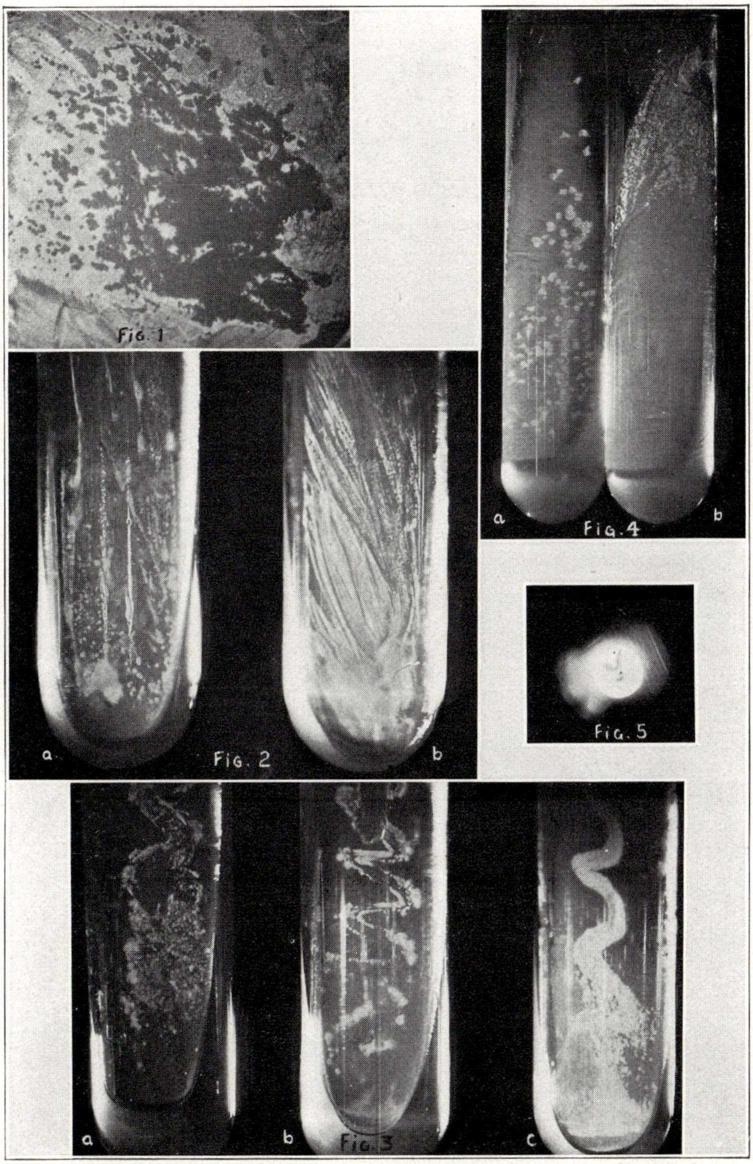

Fig. 1.—Washed areas resulting from excessive moisture on a plate used for enumeration work. (Natural size.)

Fig. 2.—(*a*) Agar slant culture of an R strain; (*b*) an agar slant on which a very young R strain culture was streaked over with normal culture, illustrating the presence of a large amount of bacteriophage on an R strain culture. (× 1.4.)

Fig. 3.—(*a*) and (*b*) Irregular growth of R strain; (*c*) normal strain. (× 1.2.)

Fig. 4.—(*a*) Production of "pie shaped" colonies by method described; (*b*) a similar agar slant heavily inoculated. (× 0.8.)

Fig. 5.—Typical "pie-shaped" colony. (× 2.)

ANALYSIS OF THE FECAL FLORA IN THIRTY-THREE CASES OF PERNICIOUS ANEMIA

WITH PARTICULAR REFERENCE TO B. WELCHII

L. Mary Moench, Morton C. Kahn
AND
John C. Torrey

From the Mayo Clinic, Rochester, Minn., and the Department of Hygiene, Cornell University Medical College, New York City

In view of the recent revival of interest in Germany in the rôle of intestinal toxins in pernicious anemia, based on clinical and bacteriologic studies of recent years, it would seem desirable to review in brief the work prior to and contemporaneous with this development, and to recapitulate the arguments, clinical as well as pathologic, which hitherto have supported this theory. Following Addison's [1] original description in 1855, in which the disease was regarded as strictly "idiopathic," Flint,[2] as early as 1860, noted changes in the mucous membrane of the stomach, as did Fenwick,[3] also later Henry and Osler,[4] Quincke,[5] Nothnagel [6] and others, described similar lesions. Organic changes of like nature have been noted recently in the walls of the small intestine by Wallgren.[7] Faber and Block,[8] as well as most recent authorities, consider gastric lesions, which are now recognized as a constant feature of the disease, due to a common cause (Bunting [9]) with the cord and blood changes. William Hunter [10] went farther than others in outlining a theory of causation of the disease. He regarded the excessive amount of iron in the liver as evidence of destruction of red blood cells in the field of the portal circulation, probably caused by a toxin elaborated in the intestine. In the Ehrlich-Lazarus [11] theory is recognized the probability of the presence of some hemolytic substance having a qualitative (megalo-

Received for publication, Feb. 10, 1925.

[1] On the Constitutional and Local Effects of Disease of the Suprarenal Capsules, 1855, 8, p. 43.
[2] Med. Times, 1860, 1, p. 181.
[3] Lancet, 1877, 2, p. 77.
[4] Am. Jour. Med. Sc., n. s., 91, p. 498.
[5] Samml. klin. Vortr., 1876, 100, p. 798.
[6] Deutsch. Arch. f. klin. Med., 1879, 24, p. 353.
[7] Ueber der Veränderungen des Verdauungskanals bei der perniziosen Anämia, 1923.
[8] Ztschr. f. klin. Med., 1900, 40, p. 98.
[9] Bull. Johns Hopkins Hosp., 1905, 16, p. 222.
[10] Lancet, 1888, 2, pp. 556, 608, 654; 1900, 1, p. 221; 1903, 1, p. 367.
[11] Nothnagel: Spec. Path. u. Therapie, 1901, 8, pp. 163-185.

blastic) stimulation similar to that which occurs in Bothriocephalus anemia. The case for the toxic theory is well summarized by Bunting,[9] who himself succeeded in producing stimulation of the bone marrow in rabbits with intravenous doses of ricin, and blood changes suggestive of the crises in pernicious anemia. He regards the true explanation of the etiology of pernicious anemia as that of the absorption of a toxic substance, probably of intestinal origin, which acts on the circulating blood producing the hemolysis, and through the circulation also on the marrow, resulting in faulty hyperplasia. That this toxin is a result of gastro-intestinal origin as suggested by Hunter seems not improbable. There are other evidences of a toxic substance circulating in the blood, notably, the symmetrical lesions found at times in the spinal cord, which practically all investigators agree are the result of toxin and not of the anemia per se, as they are not found in even the severest types of secondary anemia. According to Minnich,[12] they resemble the lesions of ergotism, pellagra and lathyrismus. The atrophy and degeneration of the gastric tubules may possibly be attributed to the action of a circulating poison, if not to an inflammatory process. Finally, in the multiple capillary hemorrhages resembling the hemorrhages with such intoxications as those due to snake venoms, where they are, according to Flexner, the result of an endotheliolytic principle or "hemorrhagin," one has evidence of further toxic action.

The possibility that specific intestinal bacteria or a bacterial flora with either qualitative or quantitative abnormalities may be responsible for a toxic or infective principle in pernicious anemia has led to various attempts to analyze the intestinal bacteria. An increase in the bacterial content in the duodenum in all cases of achylia has been fairly consistently reported. Faber, in 1913,[13] demonstrated an abnormal flora in the duodenum in pernicious anemia. Kiralyfi,[14] Grassman,[15] and Hoefert[16] reported the rather constant finding of large numbers of colon bacilli in the duodenum in cases of pernicious anemia, and Gorke[17] reported similar findings for the upper small intestine, whereas Bogendörfer,[18] and later Bogendörfer and Bucholz[19] recovered vegetation characteristic of the colon, especially Bacillus coli, at varying levels

12 Ztschr. f. klin. Med., 1893, 21, p. 264.
13 Berl. klin. Wchnschr., 1913, 1, p. 958.
14 Ibid., 1912, 11, p. 1985.
15 Arch. f. Verdauungskr., 1917, 23, p. 477.
16 Ztschr. f. klin. Med., 1921, 92, p. 221.
17 Mitt. a. d. Grenzgeb. d. Med. u. Chir., 1922, 35, p. 279.
18 Deutsch. Arch. f. klin. Med., 1922, 140, p. 257.
19 Ibid., 1923, 142, p. 318.

below the pylorus in cases of achylia. The highest numbers of these organisms occurred in pernicious anemia. Bogendörfer states that in normal controls, Bacillus coli was never found within 2.5 mm. of the pylorus. In one case of pernicious anemia cited, in which these bacilli were 2 mm. from the pylorus, the colonies were so numerous that they could not be counted; Bacillus coli communis occurred in predominating numbers. The study of the organisms in the lower levels of the small intestine was made possible by the ingenious "Darmpatronene" method of Ganther and van der Reis [20] (perfected by van der Reis [21]) by means of which the contents of the lower jejunum and ileum could be recovered. Van der Reis [22] has from time to time reported bacterial findings in normal and pathologic conditions in the small intestine. In 1923, he [23] reported the bacterial growth recovered from the small intestine in 19 cases of pernicious anemia. In the upper intestine he found a marked quantitative but not a qualitative change in the flora, which he regards as normal for this portion of the tract, but in the middle and lower jejunum in these cases he reports an invasion of organisms which normally appear only in the large intestine. The lowest level of the small intestine contained many obligate anaerobes, among which Bacillus putrificus of Bienstock and other unnamed proteolytic organisms were recovered.

Coates [24] believes that the delayed protein digestion occurring in pernicious anemia allows an undue proportion of food residue to remain in the lower part of the ileum in a form suited to bacterial decomposition, thus providing a material from which toxins, possibly of a hemolytic nature, may be formed; also products of a neurotoxic nature may be developed, causing subacute, combined degeneration of the spinal cord and other toxic substances stimulating the bone marrow to produce abnormal types of erythrocytes. He observed ulceration of the intestine in a number of cases of pernicious anemia, and pointed out that abraded surfaces are more permeable to toxic substances than is the intact mucous membrane. He did not report on the types of bacteria present in these ulcers.

Goldman [25] studied material, collected by means of a modified Einhorn tube technic, from the jejunal region (about 75 inches from the

[20] Deutsch. med. Wchnschr., 1920, 46, p. 236; Deutsch. Arch. f. klin. Med., 1921, 137, p. 348.
[21] Klin. Wchnschr., 1922, 1, p. 570.
[22] Klin. Wchnschr., 1922, 1, p. 950; Ztschr. f. d. ges. exper. Med., 1923, 34, p. 384.
[23] Ibid., 1923, 35, p. 296.
[24] Brit. Med. Jour., 1923, 1, p. 677.
[25] Jour. Infect. Dis., 1924, 35, p. 459.

teeth) in a considerable variety of pathologic conditions. In 2 cases of severe anemia, one of them pernicious in type, she found unusually large numbers of viable bacteria (32 to 50 million per c c. of material). In the pernicious case, the predominating organisms were B. coli and streptococci of the gamma type. The other case, in which a gastrojejunostomy operation had been performed, showed meat digesting, spore-bearing organisms, very large numbers of B. coli and some aerobic peptonizing types.

Seyderhelm,[26] on the basis of van der Reis' results, and confirmatory results of his own and of his co-worker Oelsner, for the purpose of obtaining further evidence for the enteric origin of pernicious anemia, established an ileostomy in 10 cases of pernicious anemia between 10 and 20 cm. above the ileocecal valve. He reports that a brown fluid resembling stool was evacuated which could not be distinguished from stool in appearance, odor, or bacterial content. In 3 cases the character of the contents evacuated was changed in from 1 to 2 days. Following the isolation of the small intestine from the cecum, a process of automatic sterilization appeared to have occurred, the mucous membrane of the small intestine overwhelming the remainder of the fecal flora. The number of bacteria greatly decreased, and the clinical condition of the patient, including the blood picture, returned rapidly to normal. In the remaining cases, with the exception of one in which there was a transitory improvement, the fecal character of the evacuation did not change, and the clinical picture remained as before. The author's interpretation of this failure of the small intestine to clear itself of the fecal character of its contents is that the bactericidal power of the mucous membrane had become so depleted that it was insufficient to destroy the bacteria from the colon which were already lodged within it.

The results of this experiment seemed significant as suggesting the colon as the source of the intoxication. "Although normal in the colon," the author states, "the poison becomes of pathologic significance when it extends into the small intestine where absorptive conditions are optimal." Seyderhelm, as the result of earlier bacteriologic analyses, seems inclined to look to the colon bacillus as the most probable pathogenic agent. However, no description is given of the flora as a whole in these cases, either aerobic or anaerobic, but with respect to the colon bacillus, he remarks,

[26] Ergeb. d. inn. Med. u. Kinderh., 1922, 21, p. 361; Klin. Wchnschr., 1924, 3, p. 568; Deutsch. med. Wchnschr., 1924, 1, p. 827.

"the number of colon bacilli was very high, and finally after a suitable diet the bacilli disappeared."

If we may indeed conclude that the colon may be the source of the pathogenic agent in pernicious anemia, it would seem of great importance to determine the fecal organism or group of organisms which finds its way, as an invading and possibly a proliferating growth, from the cecum into the small intestine. An analysis of such organisms to determine their percentage representation and more especially their biologic characteristics as regards adaptability to environment, elaboration of growth products, and the production of a soluble toxin capable of permeating the mucous membrane of the small intestine, would seem urgently indicated. Undoubtedly an analysis of the contents of the ileum itself would be most advantageous for such study, but assuming that the colon may be the source of the invading organisms a clue to such representative forms might, it would seem, be designated by the character of the fecal flora.

Material and Methods.—Through the kind cooperation of Dr. Conner of the Mayo Clinic, stool specimens were secured in a series of 31 cases of pernicious anemia of various periods of duration and observations made on several specimens from each patient in an attempt to obtain an adequate appreciation of the flora in each case. A few additional cases from other sources were examined. The study fell naturally into two parts: the first, a general survey of all of the types represented, a rough classification of the aerobic flora and a quantitative estimate of the colon-aerogenes, streptococcic and aciduric groups; and the second, a more detailed classification and grouping of the anaerobic spore-bearing types. The emphasis of this paper falls on the second division, on the anaerobic organisms characteristic of flora of stools in cases of pernicious anemia. The technic followed for the first portion of the study is as follows:

The methods employed were certain of those which had been found useful by one of us (Torrey) in bacterial analyses of intestinal material and which permitted the recognition of the more important bacterial types and an estimate in regard to their relative numbers.

Dilutions: The specimens were always examined within a few hours of passage and in the interval were kept chilled. An amount of the fecal material was brought into even suspension in about 15 c c. of sterile saline in a test tube 16-17 mm. inside diameter sufficient to produce a density equal to an accepted standard. This was such that the shadow of a black wax pencil mark on the tube could just be detected in looking through the suspension toward a strong light, the observation being made after the coarser material had settled. This tube was labeled no. 1 and graded dilutions of 10 times each were then prepared, using a series of 4 tubes each containing 9 c c. of saline. These were labeled, respectively, 2, 3, 4 and 5, the last tube (5) constituting thus a 1:10,000 dilution of the primary suspension. If properly prepared, the no. 3 tube showed a very faint clouding when observed against a dark surface in a good light.

Films: These were prepared from the no. 1 suspension after the coarser particles had settled. One large loop was spread over an area of about 2 sq. cm. on a clean glass slide. After drying and fixing by moderate heat they were stained by the Kopeloff and Beerman's [27] modification of the Gram stain technic, which gives a particularly sharp differentiation between the gram-positive and gram-negative organisms. The stained films were examined particularly for determination of the relative numbers of free spores, B. welchii-like rods and spirochetes.

Purple Lactose Agar Plates: This medium was prepared from the Difco product by dissolving 30 gm. of this dehydrated powder and 5 gm. of flaked agar in 1 liter of water in the Arnold sterilizer and adjusting the reaction to P_H 7.2. Two large sized (12 cm. diameter) petri dishes of the medium were used, the surface of one being seeded with a large loop (5 mm. diameter) from the no. 4 and the other with a like amount of the no. 3 fecal dilutions. It is necessary to dry off the surface of the medium by inverting the plates uncovered in the incubator for a few minutes either before or after seeding, to prevent spreading of growth. This medium permitted the recognition and estimation of the relative numbers of the B. coli-aerogenes group, B. mucosus, streptococci, staphylococci, alkali-producing organisms and other types. The plates were examined after 24-48 hours' incubation at 37 C.

Ayer and Rupp [28] Agar Plates: This is a synthetic solid medium, devised by the originators to permit the growth only of such organisms as can obtain requisite energy from lactose and inorganic phosphates (sodium ammonium phosphate and potassium phosphate). They found it useful as a practically selective medium for the B. coli group in water analyses. It was first applied to stool examinations by Cannon.[29] We have also found it useful for this purpose, as it inhibits the growth of all aerobic fecal bacteria except the colon group and occasional strains of streptococci; the latter, however, are readily recognizable as the colonies are very small. The originators added a sodium sulphite-fuchsin indicator to this medium, but we have found it unnecessary as the total count of easily observed colonies may be taken as representing that of the B. coli group. A poured plate was prepared with a seeding of 1 c c. of the no. 4 fecal dilution and a count made after 48 hours' incubation at 37 C.

Acid Whey Agar Plates: This is the solid medium which was recommended by Rettger and Cheplin [30] for bringing B. acidophilus to development, but which has been made to a greater degree selective for this group by bringing the final reaction to + 3 acid to phenolphthalein. This acidity checks entirely the colon group but rather encourages the B. acidophilus group, thus permitting seeding with low dilutions of the fecal material which would otherwise give an overgrowth with B. coli. It is not, however, strictly selective for B. acidophilus, as certain intestinal streptococci of aciduric properties also find conditions favorable. These last may generally be recognized under the low power of the microscope by their distinctive type of colony, and thus differential counts may be made. Poured plates, seeded with 1 c c. of the no. 3 fecal dilution, were prepared and incubated at 37 C. for 48 hours.

Cooked Meat Medium: The most important cultural component for the purposes of this study was the cooked meat medium of Robertson,[31] somewhat modified. Holman [32] confirms the claims of the originator in regard to the

[27] Proc. Soc. Exper. Biol. & Med., 1922, 20, p. 71.
[28] Jour. Bacteriol., 1918, 3, p. 433.
[29] Jour. Infect. Dis., 1921, 29, p. 369.
[30] A Treatise on the Transformation of the Intestinal Flora, 1921, p. 114.
[31] Jour. Path. & Bacteriol., 1916, 20, p. 327.
[32] Jour. Bacteriol., 1919, 4, p. 282.

value of this medium in the differentiation of the spore-bearing anaerobes through characteristic changes in reaction, color of the meat and varying degrees of digestion. He also determined that its buffer action permitted the simultaneous growth of acid-producing fermentative types and proteolytic forms unless the former are present in large majority. It is thus well adapted to bringing to development such members of this group as may be present in fecal specimens. Our mode of preparing this medium is similar to that described by Robertson, except that 1% of peptone was added to the final reaction adjusted to P_H 7.2. It is tubed in test tubes with an inside diameter of 16-17 mm. and so that the height of the minced meat column equals about 5 cm. and the supernatant broth, 1 to 2 cm.

Just before seeding, the 5 tubes required for an examination are placed in the Arnold sterilizer for about 10 minutes. When cooled, one tube is seeded with 1 c c. of the no. 5 unheated fecal dilution, placing the tip of the pipet rather deep in the meat column and one tube with 1 c c. from the no. 1 suspension. The 3 other tubes are seeded respectively with 1 c c. each from nos. 5, 3 and 1 heated (80 C. for 10 minutes) suspensions. All of these tubes are then immediately provided with a cap of sterile melted petrolatum about three-fourths inches in thickness.

These tubes were examined after 1 day, 3 or 4, and 7 days' incubation at 37 C., and at each observation the amount of gas formation, the degree of digestion and any changes in color and constitution of the meat were noted. The changes produced by B. welchii are particularly characteristic. Gas is produced in such large amounts that the petrolatum cap is blown to the top or out of the tube within 24 to 48 hours, and the column of meat is also frequently disrupted and partially carried upward. After a few days, the meat acquired a typical terra cotta color. No digestion of the meat is observable within 3 or 4 days, but later the column is found to have decreased in height, due possibly to a certain extent to digestion of connective tissue. No other spore-bearing anaerobe produces just this picture. If proteolytic spore bearers are also present, the foregoing phenomena are combined with marked digestion and subsequent darkening of the meat.

In addition, as an aid to the study of colonies formed by the spore-bearing anaerobes, deep agar tubes enriched with Wolff's casein digest fluid were seeded with the heated dilutions of the stool and capped with petrolatum. Also a poured agar plate seeded with 1 c c. of the no. 2 heated stool suspension was prepared to determine the count of the aererobic spore bearers.

Table 1 details the cultural findings and brief clinical notes in regard to 25 of these cases of pernicious anemia.

A noteworthy feature in the cultural examination of these cases of pernicious anemia, as is illustrated in table 1, is the uniformity in the predominant bacterial types and their numbers. A rather extensive experience on the part of one of us in this type of examination justifies the statement that this uniformity is much greater as regards pernicious anemia than for any other pathologic condition. The flora of the large intestine, as revealed by stool analyses, is of a nonproteolytic fermentative type in which streptococci and B. welchii (B. perfringens) are

TABLE 1

Bacterial Analyses of the Fecal Flora in Twenty-Six Cases of Pernicious Anemia, with Clinical Notes

Case No.	Number of Examinations and Dates	Purple Lactose Agar Plate; Bacterial Types and Average Colony Counts	Ayer and Rupp Agar Plate; Stool Dilution No. 4. B. coli (Average Colony Count)	Acid Whey Agar Plate; Stool Dilution No. 3. Aciduric Organisms (Average Colony Count)	Cooked Meat Medium: Highest Heated Dilution Giving B. welchii Reaction	Cooked Meat Medium: Digestion	Clinical Notes
1	3 March 24, 28, 29, 1923	Streptoc.........1500 B. coli............ 30	1,500	13	3	None	Age, 58 years; advanced case; first symptoms noted 5 years previously; hemoglobin index, 1.08; erythrocytes, 1,310,000
2	2 March 27, 29, 1923	Streptoc.........1000+ B. coli............ 40	1,300	∞	5	None	Age, 43 years; first symptoms noted Oct. 1, 1922; occasional diarrhea; early case
3	2 March 28, April 4, 1923	Streptoc......... 600 B. coli............ 130 B. mucosus...... 2	1,300	∞ B. acidophilus 580	5	None	Age, 26 years; onset September, 1922; occasional diarrhea; early case
4	4 April 4, 13, 25, May 5, 1923	Streptoc......... 410 B. coli............ 375 Alkali producers. 15	1,400	7,000 (B. acidophilus mostly)	3	None	Age, 51 years; first complaint noted May, 1922; diarrhea for 13 years; advanced case
5	1 May 5, 1923	Streptoc.........2100 B. coli............ 140 Alkali producers. 15	3,100	28,000 (Streptococci and B. acidophilus)	3	None	Age, 48 years; onset (?) following influenza, May, 1922; gastric irregularities; hemoglobin index, 0.77; erythrocytes, 2,610,000
6	3 April 5, 8, 12, 1923	Streptoc.........2700 B. coli............ 60	630	35	3 (?)	Moderate	Age, 54 years; weakness and anemia periodically since 1911; hemoglobin index, 1.36; erythrocytes, 1,480,000
7	2 April 5, May 2, 1923	B. coli............4000	22,000	3,400 (Streptococci) 700+ (B. acidophilus)	3–5	None	Age, 57 years; six months starting February, 1918, also during summer, 1922; advanced and rapidly progressing case; hemoglobin index, 1.18; erythrocytes, 1,910,000
8	1 April 9, 1923	....	100	7,000 (B. acidophilus)	5	None	Age, 42 years; symptoms for 4 years; weakness and diarrhea; advanced case; hemoglobin index, 1.47; erythrocytes, 1,710,000
9	1 April 10, 1923	B. coli............1270 Staphyloc........ 69	9,100	17,000	1 (?)	None	Age, 55 years; attacks of diarrhea for 30 years; hemoglobin index, 1.25; erythrocytes, 1,610,000
10	2 April 11, 12, 1923	B. coli............ 120 Streptoc......... 43	2,100	1,450	5	None	Age, 52 years; first symptoms noted November, 1922; epigastric pain, weakness; early case
11	2 April 17, 20, 1923	....	3,550	1,860 (Streptococci) 36 (B. acidophilus)	5	Slight	Age, 32 years; first symptoms noted 2 years before; diarrhea and nausea; hemoglobin index, 1; erythrocytes, 800,000.

13	1 April 18, 1923	B. coli........... 560 Streptoc.........2400	1,960	1,360 (Streptococci) 15 (B. acidophilus)	5	None	Age, 59 years; duration 1 year; anorexia, constipation
14	2 May 6, 9, 1923	B. coli........... 83 Streptoc......... 470 Alkali producers. 10	2,750	1,360 (B. acidophilus)	1–5	None	Age, 34 years; "stomach trouble, 1916"; constipation; hemoglobin index, 0.99; erythrocytes, 3,140,000
15	1 March 1, 1923	B. coli...........1000 Streptoc......... 150	14,000	5,600	5	None	Age, 25 years; Onset (?) August, 1922; general weakness, headache; hemoglobin index, 1.5; erythrocytes, 670,000
16	4 April 25, 26, May 2, July 19, 1923	....	14,800	(Probably Streptococci) 1,400 (B. acidophilus)	2–5	None	Age, 55 years; indefinite onset; definite diagnosis in the spring of 1923; hemoglobin index, 1.16; erythrocytes, 2,830,000; rapidly progressing; death in January, 1924
17	2 May 6, 8, 1923	B. coli........... 365 Streptoc......... 770	7,350	9,460 (B. acidophilus)	3	None	Age, 52 years; onset 18 months before; diarrhea alternating with constipation; hemoglobin index, 0.90; erythrocytes, 2,210,000
18	2 May 6, 11, 1923	B. coli........... 390 Streptoc.........1200 Alkali producers. 5	2,700	25,000 (Streptococci) 360 (B. acidophilus)	5	Slight	Age, 31 years; onset following influenza in 1918; constipated; hemoglobin index, 0.93; erythrocytes, 3,010,000
19	2 May 9, 21, 1923	B. coli........... 515 Streptoc......... 19 B. mucosus...... 10	3,900	1,400 (Streptococci) 80 (B. acidophilus)	5	None	Age, 68 years; onset following attack of grip in 1922; hemoglobin index, 1.6; erythrocytes, 1,090,000; advanced case
21	1 May 23, 1923	Streptoc......... 100	680	13,400	5	None	Age, 67 years; onset January, 1923; weakness, dyspnea, anorexia; hemoglobin index, 1.4; erythrocytes, 1,090,000
22	2 May 23, 1923	B. mucosus....+++	5,880	3,200 (Streptococci) 1,000 (B. acidophilus)	3	None	Age, 59 years; entameba histolytica, October, 1914; negative, 1916; stomatitis, 1919; hemoglobin index, 0.6; erythrocytes, 2,490,000
26	2 June 11, 16, 1923	....	1,280	640 (B. acidophilus)	1	None	Age, 48 years; symptoms for 10 years; constipation and recurring diarrhea; hemoglobin index, 1.23; erythrocytes, 1,310,000
27	3 June 13, 23, July 14, 1923	B. coli........... 15 Streptoc......... 110	2,100	0	1–5	None	Age, 57 years; onset, November, 1922; diarrhea; similar symptoms in 1918; hemoglobin index, 1.4; erythrocytes, 990,000
28	2 June 28, July 14, 1923	B. coli........... 200 Streptoc......... 60	9,000	9,200	5	None	Age, 50 years; dyspepsia for 4 years; hemoglobin index, 1.04; erythrocytes, 1,180,000
29	3 June 30, July 11, 1923	B. coli........... 70 Streptoc......... 115 B. mucosus......	4,200	200 (Stretpococci) 500 (B. acidophilus)	5	None	Age, 52 years; onset, September, 1922; progressive weakness; hemoglobin index, 0.87; erythrocytes, 1,280,000
30	2 July 10, 20, 1923	B. coli........... 200 B. mucosus...... 30	700	100 (Streptococci) 980 (B. acidophilus)	5	None	Age, 39 years; duration 1 year; hemoglobin index, 1; erythrocytes, 1,400,000

particularly prominent. Herter,[33] many years ago, designated this combination, when predominant in the intestine, as a saccharo-butyric type of putrefaction. He was in error, however, in designating B. welchii as a putrefactive organism, as subsequent studies by Kahn[34] and others have shown that it belongs in the nonproteolytic group of the spore-bearing anaerobes. Herter[33] claimed that the harboring of this type of flora was likely sooner or later to produce an anemic condition which might continue to the stage of the progressive pernicious type. His work, however, is open to the criticism that unwarranted dependence was placed on morphology in the identification of the elements of a flora, especially in reference to the spore-bearing anaerobes. In the present study no dependence was placed on microscopic identification, but rather the various components have been demonstrated by differential cultural tests.

The examination of these stool specimens from pernicious anemia cases revealed, almost without exception, unusually large numbers of viable bacteria, of which the most prominent aerobic elements were B. coli, streptococci and, at times, B. acidophilus. These results taken in connection with those of other investigators indicate clearly that in this disease there is an unusually active growth of bacteria throughout the intestinal canal. It seems probable that this condition is largely the result of the archylia gastrica which is so prominent a clinical feature in these cases, a condition which not only favors the passage of viable bacteria through the stomach, but also the active multiplication of the cecal forms in the duodenum.

As is shown in the tabulation, the colony count for B. coli in the no. 4 dilution plate ranged from 100 to 22,000 with an average of 4,800 and only 37% below 2,000. One of us has found in examinations of a series of 47 gastro-intestinal cases of various types that 43% gave B. coli count at this stool dilution of 2,000 or above and 57% below 2,000, with an average considerably lower than that noted above; in 14 normal persons, 32% gave a B. coli count above 2,000 and 68% below that number. The B. coli counts in these cases of pernicious anemia thus seem to be well above the average. Streptococci colony counts were also generally very high, and in about 50% of the cases higher than that for B. coli. In no instance, however, was a true hemolytic (beta type) isolated. Such of these strains as were sub-

[33] The Common Bacterial Infections of the Intestinal Tract, 1907.
[34] Jour. Med. Res., 1922, 43, p. 155.

jected culturally to typing tests conformed to the intestinal variety of streptococcus. In blood agar they produced no change (gamma type) or a dull greenish-brown discoloration (methemoglobin), with sometimes a later partial hemolysis. They exhibited a relatively marked resistance to heat (60 C. for 30 minutes) and generally the ability to ferment mannite. Many also showed aciduric properties sufficient to permit their growth in + 3 acid agar medium. With the exception of one case (16), long chain streptococcic types were not encountered. Staphylococci (albus type) were found in appreciable numbers in only 3 cases. B. acidophilus colonies appeared in large numbers on the no. 3 dilution + 3 whey agar plate in 16 of the 25 cases tabulated. These counts are very much higher than is usually the case with normal persons on ordinary diet. The diet in these cases was not such as would be likely to encourage the growth of these organisms in normal intestines to the degree noted in these cases; accordingly, the high courts may reasonably be ascribed to the gastro-intestinal abnormalities which are characteristic of this disease, particularly the gastric hypo-acidity, favoring their growth as well as that of streptococci and B. coli.

Aerobic proteolytic bacteria of the B. proteus and B. pyocyaneous groups were rarely encountered in fecal specimens from these cases, and it seems probable that they occur in negligible numbers, if at all, in the large bowel of sufferers from this disease. Another organism rather more frequently associated with putrefactive than with fermentative conditions in the human intestine is a gram-negative spirochete which has recently been studied by L. W. Parr [35] and designated by him Spirochaeta enrygyrata. As this organism does not appear to be cultivable, its presence is detectable only through microscopic examinations of stained films. It was noted in only 2 of the 33 cases of pernicious anemia, which is much less frequently than it has been found by one of us to occur in stool specimens from normal persons (46% positive) or in abnormal gastro-intestinal conditions (17.6% positive in 68 examinations). There is no evidence, then, that intestinal spirochetes play any part in the etiology of this disease.

The most significant feature revealed in these examinations is, we believe, the uniformity of results with the cooked meat tubes; these anaerobic cultures showing, frequently with high dilutions of the fecal material, rapid and marked evolution of gas and a copper-red coloration of the meat, a reaction characteristic of the B. welchii (B. perfringens).

[35] Jour. Infect. Dis., 1923, 33, p. 369.

The presence of this organism in the cooked meat cultures showing this reaction was fully confirmed through isolation studies by one of us (Kahn), as is described in the following section. It should be noted also that these culture tubes were seeded with heated fecal dilutions, so that the growth was restricted to the spore stages of this organism; and as B. welchii seems to form spores with difficulty, at least under artificial cultural conditions, it may reasonably be assumed that this bacillus was present in the intestine in far greater numbers than the cultures would seem to indicate. Although the morphology of B. welchii cannot be said to be entirely distinctive, it is perhaps worthy of note that organisms resembling this bacillus were considerably more numerous in most of the Gram stained fecal films prepared from these cases than have been observed in such preparations from normal persons. These several findings are certainly suggestive of an active multiplication of B. welchii within the intestines of patients with pernicious anemia.

In order to demonstrate the striking prevalence of the B. welchii reaction in these cases, as indicated by the cooked meat tube cultures, a table is presented in which the percentages of positive findings in graded dilutions of stool specimens in 33 cases of pernicious anemia is compared with those for 48 cases of gastro-intestinal disorders of various types and for 17 normal persons (table 2).

TABLE 2

PERCENTAGE OCCURRENCE OF B. WELCHII REACTIONS IN COOKED MEAT MEDIUM SEEDED WITH GRADED DILUTIONS OF FECAL MATERIAL FROM CASES OF PERNICIOUS ANEMIA, GASTRO-INTESTINAL CASES AND NORMAL PERSONS

Stool Dilutions	Pernicious Anemia, 33 Cases	Gastro-Intestinal Disorders, 48 Cases	Normal, 17 Cases
Negative in no. 1	0.0	16.6	41.2
Positive in no. 1 only	6.2	37.5	47.0
Positive in nos. 1 and 3 only	27.2	29.2	11.8
Positive in nos. 1, 3 and 5	66.6	16.7	0.0

TYPES OF B. WELCHII OCCURRING IN 26 CASES OF PERNICIOUS ANEMIA

Isolations of B. welchii were effected in 26 of these cases of pernicious anemia. A detailed account of the methods employed for cultivating, identifying and the manipulation of anaerobic spore-bearing bacteria has been published by one of us (Kahn [34]). As these were followed in general in this study, only a brief description of the essential procedures will be given here.

As a preliminary step, the cooked meat cultures from the cases were tested for the presence of aerobic spore-bearing organisms by placing a few drops from each tube on nutrient agar slants. If no growth occurred after 72 hours' incubation, the culture in question was considered free from aerobic forms. If growth was obtained, the aerobic spore bearers were eliminated by inoculating gentian violet agar from the cooked meat culture, in accordance with the technic of Hall.[36] In surprisingly few instances were these types encountered. No attempt, however, was made to identify the anaerobic spore bearers until the aerobic types had been proved eliminated.

Pure cultures were obtained from each of the cooked meat tubes seeded from the heated stool dilutions which showed growth. In making these isolations the following method was employed:

Twenty tubes of 1% casein digest agar were boiled for 15 minutes, and after cooking to about 60 C. were placed in a rack. One c c. of the fluid from a well stirred, original cooked meat, heated stool dilution culture was inoculated into tube 1 and thoroughly mixed, 1 c c. from tube 1 was transferred to tube 2, and so forth, until the entire 20 tubes were seeded in graded dilutions. These tubes were made anaerobic by petrolatum caps, and incubated for 48 hours. The tubes showing the most favorable distribution of colonies were cracked open just at the lower level of the petrolatum, and the agar column expelled into a petri dish. Individual colonies were then picked up with fine Pasteur pipets and planted into melted casein digest 0.5% agar, capped with petrolatum and incubated for 48 hours. Several colonies were thus isolated from each case, care being taken to fish representatives of all types. In the identification of B. welchii much weight was given to the occurrence of the characteristic "stormy fermentation" with distinct butyric acid odor produced in milk tubes, for apparently no other other anaerobe produces just this type of reaction. This, together with the typical cooked meat culture reaction, morphology as revealed in Gram stained films and carbohydrate fermentation tests, when necessary, permitted the identification of the strains isolated.

In the great majority of instances, B. welchii was found alone; in fact, in only 2 cases of the total 26 was there evidence of the presence of a proteolytic type (B. sporogenes). Rottger [37] has also noted a lack of putrefactive anaerobes in the stools of persons with pernicious anemia.

Simonds [38] has recognized 4 types of B. welchii based on their ability to ferment inulin or glycerol: type 1, fermenting glycerol and inulin; type 2, glycerol but not inulin; type 3, inulin but not glycerol; and type 4, neither of these substances. The strains isolated from these cases have been subjected to these differential tests with the following

[36] Jour. Am. Med. Assn., 1919, 72, p. 224.
[37] Jour. Biol. Chem., 1906, 2, p. 71.
[38] Monograph 5, Rockefeller Inst.

results: type 1, twelve cases; type 2, two cases; type 3, four cases; and type 4, six cases. It was thus evident that the strains of B. welchii which may be encountered in pernicious anemia are not of a specific type but are distributed through the 4 fermentative groups. Although type 1 was found most frequently, namely, in about 50%, the occurrence of representatives of the other 3 types in the remaining cases unassociated with type 1 justifies hesitation in attaching any significance to the more frequent presence of this variety in the intestines of persons with pernicious anemia.

Hemolytic Activities of B. welchii Strains.—In view of the possible relationship between the potent hemolysins of B. welchii and the destruction of erythrocytes, which is such a prominent clinical feature in pernicious anemia, it seemed desirable to make quantitative tests of the hemolysin production of these strains of pernicious anemia to determine whether they differed in this characteristic from B. welchii strains of normal intestines. It was thought possible that the former might show greater activity in this respect.

The technic of Lyall [39] was used for this purpose. This consists essentially of growing the organism for 18 hours in a highly buffered medium and then adding graded amounts of the culture to tubes containing a mixture of washed, fresh sheep erythrocytes and normal salt solution. The tubes are incubated in a water bath at 37 C. for 1 hour and then examined for evidence of hemolysis. The results have been recorded according to the degree of hemolysis taking place, making use of the Wassermann reaction symbols.

As may be seen in table 3, the various strains of B. welchii from cases of pernicious anemia varied markedly as regards their hemolysin producing propensities. When a fairly large dosage of the Lyall medium culture was used in making this test, say 0.5 c c., a 4-plus hemolysis could usually be obtained with each of these strains of pernicious anemia. When, however, smaller quantities were employed, a clear-cut difference in this reaction could be demonstrated. While it may be seen that most of the strains isolated from cases of pernicious anemia were strongly hemolytic, this was not always the case; nor could it be shown that the majority of the strains from normal human stool specimens or from other sources (monkeys) showed any weaker hemolytic activity than did the types isolated from this pathologic source. Incidentally, this table also shows that there is no correlation between fermentation types

[39] Jour. Med. Res., 1914, 30, p. 487.

and the degree of hemolysis produced. If, then, intestinal B. welchii are to be brought into etiologic relationship with pernicious anemia, it must be only on the ground of their excessive numbers and activity in the intestine, or the unusual levels at which they are growing or unusual permeability of the intestinal walls to their toxins, rather than on any peculiarity of type associated with this disease.

TABLE 3

HEMOLYTIC PROPERTIES OF STRAINS OF B. WELCHII ISOLATED IN CASES OF PERNICIOUS ANEMIA AND FROM NORMAL PERSONS AND MONKEYS USED AS CONTROLS

Case Number	Amount of Culture Added to Washed Sheep Erythrocytes in Cubic Centimeters to Produce Hemolysis as Indicated					Fermentative Group Simond's Method
	0.5	0.2	0.1	0.05	0.025	
1	++++	++++	++++	++++	+++	4
2	++++	+++	++	+	—	4
3	++++	++++	++++	+	+	4
4	++++	++++	++++	++++	++	1
7	++++	++++	+++	+++	++	1
8	++++	++++	++++	+++	++	1
9	+++	++	++	+	0	4
10	++++	++++	+++	++	++	1
11	++++	+++	++	+	0	4
12	+++	+++	++	1	1	3
14	++++	++++	++++	+++	++++	1
15	++++	+++	+++	+	0	1
16	++++	++++	+++	+++	++	4
17	++++	++++	++	++	0	1
18	++++	++++	++++	++++	++++	2
19	++++	++++	+++	+++	++	2
22	+++	++	0	0	0	3
32	++++	++++	+++	+++	1	1
23	+++	++	0	0	0	1
24	+++	+	0	0	0	1
34	++	+	+	0	0	1
25	++++	++++	++++	++++	+++	1
31	++++	++++	++	+	+	3
33	++++	+++	++	0	0	3
Control A	+++	++	+	0	0	1
Control B	++++	+++	+	+	0	1
Control C	++++	++++	++++	++++	++	4
Control D	++++	++	++	0	0	3
Control E	++++	++++	++++	+++	+++	3
Control F	++++	++++	++++	++	+	3
Control G	++++	+++	+++	+++	+++	3
Monkey A	++++	++++	++++	++++	++++	3
Monkey B	++++	++++	++++	++++	+++	3
Monkey C	++++	++++	++++	+++	+++	4
Monkey D	++++	++++	++++	+++	0	3

Pathogenicity of the B. welchii Strains.—Hall [40] has recently distributed B. welchii strains into the strongly pathogenic, the moderately pathogenic and the nonpathogenic groups. He inoculated guinea-pigs subcutaneously in these tests. We have tested the virulence of representative strains (9 in all) of B. welchii recovered from these cases of pernicious anemia and have found them all fully as virulent as the

[40] Jour. Infect. Dis., 1922, 30, p. 141.

Bull and Pritchett toxic strain. The strains tested included representatives of the 4 fermenting groups and also of those exhibiting the different degrees of hemolysis. The dosage was 0.25 c c. of a 24-hour casein digest broth culture. The inoculations were made into the adductor muscles of guinea-pigs. In every instance the animal died within 24 to 48 hours, and it exhibited the lesions typical for this organism.

DISCUSSION OF POSSIBLE RELATIONSHIP OF TOXIN OF B. WELCHII TO LESIONS OF PERNICIOUS ANEMIA

That the pathologic and the advanced clinical findings in pernicious anemia can best be interpreted as manifestations of a degeneration of selected tissues, has been widely accepted. The qualitative effect on the blood and blood-forming organs, the symmetrical cord lesions, the inflammatory or degenerative atrophy of the gastric mucous membrane and indeed the degeneration of the mucous membrane of the whole small intestine, the endotheliolytic manifestations, all without conspicuous loss of weight, seem to be evidence of some undiscovered toxic agent assailing continuously and over a long period of time tissues which give rise to symptoms only when seriously and irreparably damaged. The vagueness of the history of early pernicious anemia characteristically a syndrome of increasing listlessness, indefinite nervous symptoms, such as transitory headaches, irregular digestive disorders, parathesias indistinguishable in every respect from those that are purely functional, complaints occurring in the fourth or fifth decade and in association with an achylia, has been observed often enough in the early course of the disease to suggest pernicious anemia, even without the characteristic blood changes. An onset of this character, out of which the features of the disease eventually emerge, in itself suggests a toxic influence, unremitting and of extreme chronicity, to which the body reacts ineffectually, with occasional febrile periods and with megaloblastic crises until these resources of the bone marrow and of the body become exhausted.

That there is toxic intestinal absorption in pernicious anemia seems clearly indicated by the work of Seyderhelm and his associates. Whether this toxic factor produces the degenerative lesions of pernicious anemia, whether, furthermore, such a poison is formed by normal fecal bacteria energetically growing in a part of the intestine where they are not normally present in large numbers and where absorption is active, or whether it is of the nature of a specific toxin emanating from a predominate fecal bacterial group or from a single organism either entirely alien or indigenous but predominant in it, remains to be determined.

In this study no other microbe with hemolytic properties in any way approaching that of the Welch bacillus has been encountered in the fecal specimens. It is well known that hemolytic streptococci are rarely isolated from the human intestine, and this investigation has indicated that pernicious anemia offers no exception to this rule; in no one of the many stool specimens examined was Streptococcus hemolyticus encountered. Dudgeon, Wordley and Braintree[41] have recently directed attention to the hemolytic varieties of the colon bacillus, particularly in relation to infection of the urinary tract. Their tests indicate, however, that the degree of hemolysis effected by these B. coli strains is not marked, and it would thus seem in no way comparable to that produced by B. welchii. Unfortunately, no data were obtained during the study of these cases of pernicious anemia as regards the presence of such hemolytic B. coli strains. Dudgeon and his co-workers, however, found them in only 1 out of 3 cases of this disease.

In this connection it is significant to note that Leroy,[42] and later Klotz and Holman,[43] have pointed out the marked anemia and evidence of destruction of erythrocytes in persons suffering from gas gangrene due to infection with B. welchii, and also that Schumm[44] found that the serums of persons with B. welchii bacteremia gave positive spectroscopic tests for hemoglobin. Further, in view of the apparent active growth of B. welchii in the intestinal tract of sufferers from pernicious anemia, reference may again be permitted to Hunter's observation that hemolysis occurs chiefly in the portal circulation in these cases.

Aside from its hemolysin, B. welchii elaborates under favorable conditions a potent exotoxin and large amounts of gas and butyric acid. It has been suggested by Herter that the latter in the form of ammonium butyrate might prove irritating to the mucous membrane, and it seems possible that it might also, in association with other bacterial products, exert a degenerative effect on the same after long exposure. As regards the soluble toxin and hemolysin of B. welchii, the objection might be raised that, granting these products may be elaborated when this bacillus is actively growing in the higher levels of the intestine,

41 Jour. Hyg., 1921, 20, p. 137.
42 Jour. Am. Med. Assn., 1903, 41, p. 1009.
43 Jour. Infect. Dis., 1911, 9, p. 251.
44 Berl. klin. Wchnschr., 1913, 1, p. 517.

there is no evidence that it may be absorbed. In reply to such a criticism, the observations of Ten Broeck and Bauer [45] may be cited. These investigators recovered B. tetani from 34% of stool specimens from 79 persons examined at the Union Medical College, Pekin, China, and later were able to demonstrate tetanus antitoxin in the blood stream of a large majority of persons harboring this bacillus in the intestine, whereas, in cases in which B. tetani was not found, the blood was almost uniformly negative for this antitoxin. Van der Reis [46] also has made a similar observation in the finding of tetanus antitoxin in the blood of a patient with a severe grade of anemia, the source of which was traced to tetanus bacilli present in large numbers in the ileum. These findings, as applied to the possible absorption of the B. welchii toxin, indicate not only that conditions in the intestine, particularly the small intestine, may be such as to permit the elaboration of an exotoxin of neurotropic propensities, but also that the intestinal mucosa at some levels, at least, is permeable to such bacterial products.

As has been demonstrated in a preceding section, bacterial analyses of stool specimens from pernicious anemia cases reveal the presence of unusually large numbers of B. welchii. This phenomenon had previously been noted by Herter [47] who reported B. welchii as much more numerous in fecal specimens from cases of anemia than in those of normal persons. Simond also found, as the result of a study of stool specimens from four cases of pernicious anemia, that B. welchii were more numerous than in any others examined by him. Our study, however, has included a much larger series of cases of this type than has been investigated from this standpoint heretofore. It may be objected that these findings have little significance as they refer to bacterial conditions in the lower large intestine rather than to the higher levels at which absorption of toxic products would be more likely to occur. Although, unfortunately, material from the lower ileum and cecum of persons with pernicious anemia has not been available for study, it has been the experience of one of us that B. welchii finds conditions favorable for growth at these levels. Reference may be made to the findings of Torrey [48] as regards the distribution of B. welchii in the intestinal tract of a dog on a fairly well balanced diet. In this animal they were found all the way from the duodenum to the rectum with

[45] Jour. Exper. Med., 1922, 36, p. 261; 1913, 37, p. 479.
[46] Ztschr. f. d. ges. exper. Med., 1923, 35, p. 296.
[47] Jour. Biol. Chem., 1906-07, 2, p. 1.
[48] Torrey, J. C.: Jour. Med. Res., 1919, 39, p. 415.

the largest numbers in the colon. In several human large intestines, removed at colectomy operations, we have found evidence that this bacillus thrives best in the proximal region of the colon but also is present quite regularly in the lower end of the ileum. Goldman, however, recovered it from the middle region of the jejunum in only 4 of 20 hospital patients. In the one case of pernicious anemia examined by her, no B. welchii were reported from this locality. On the other hand, it would seem probable in view of the findings of van der Reis [23] of the invasion of the small intestine in these cases by bacterial types which are normally characteristic of the large intestine and of our findings as regards the flora of the large intestine in this disease, that B. welchii would be found in unusual numbers at least as high as the distal region of the ileum.

In laying particular stress on the unusual numbers of B. welchii which we have found to characterize the fecal flora in pernicious anemia, we do not wish to commit ourselves in any way to the theory that this bacillus is of primary significance in the etiology of this disease, but we do believe that oiur findings in these cases justify further inquiry as to its possible relationship, particularly through the medium of experimental studies.

SUMMARY

A bacteriologic analysis of 72 stool specimens from 33 cases of pernicious anemia of various durations showed in practically every case an unusually large number of viable organisms, of which B. coli, streptococci, B. welchii and, at times, B. acidophilus were the most prominent types. These findings indicated that the flora of the large intestine is of an actively growing, nonproteolytic, fermentative type.

The most significant feature revealed by these examinations would seem to be the uniformly high counts for B. coli and B. welchii. The numbers of both these organisms averaged much higher than for normal persons or for other pathologic conditions. Although streptococci were also very numerous, they conformed to the normal intestinal types, no representative of the hemolytic group being encountered.

Pure cultures of B. welchii strains were isolated from 26 of these cases, and subjected to differential tests. Representatives of the 4 fermentative types of Simond were encountered, but type 1 occurred with the greatest frequency (50%). These several strains differed also in the amount of hemolysin produced. Although most of them were strongly hemolytic, it could not be said that they exhibited in general greater potency in this respect than did strains from normal human intestines. All of the strains tested showed a high degree of pathogenicity, but this is also frequently true for strains from normal sources. It would seem, then, that if these intestinal strains of B. welchii are to be brought into etiologic relationship to pernicious anemia, it must be on the basis of their excessive numbers and activities, particularly at levels of the intestine where absorption is active and where they are not commonly found only in negligible numbers. In view of Seyder helm's finding that the flora of the large intestine tends to invade the small intestine in this disease, there is some ground for the latter supposition.

Speculation is offered as to the possible significance of active growth of B. welchii at the higher levels of the intestine in the production of the pernicious anemia syndrome in view of its well-known capacity to elaborate a potent hemolysin, an irritating acid and neurotoxic substances.

THE GERMICIDAL PROPERTIES OF SOAP

John E. Walker

From the Laboratory Service, Army and Navy General Hospital, Hot Springs, Ark.

In a recent report [1] on the germicidal activity of the sodium and potassium salts of various fatty acids, I pointed out that these differ considerably in this respect and that there was marked evidence of selective action for the several organisms tested. Sodium and potassium laurate seemed to possess the most general germicidal properties, in that they killed pneumococci and streptococci in high dilutions, and at the same time had an appreciable effect on typhoid bacilli. The salts of the unsaturated acids (oleic, linolic, and linolenic) were highly bactericidal toward the pneumococcus and streptococcus, but seemed to be entirely inert against typhoid bacilli. A strain of Staphylococcus aureus was completely resistant to all of the soaps tested.

This work on chemically pure substances was regarded as being of interest chiefly from theoretical considerations, especially in view of the large amount of information regarding soaps now being collected by colloid chemists, for instance Fischer [2] and McBain,[3] though it was also intended as preliminary to a more practical study of the germicidal properties of soaps in ordinary use. The principal substances entering into the manufacture of commercial soaps are the following: tallow, olive oil, cottonseed oil, coconut oil, linseed oil, palm oil, and resin. These with the exception of resin, are composed chiefly of mixtures of the glycerides of the fatty acids previously studied. The approximate composition of each one of these naturally occurring substances is given by Lewkowitsch.[4] Resin has a chemical composition entirely different from that of the fats and oils, though it is used extensively in the manufacture of yellow or brown bar soap.

Therefore, owing to the impossibility of making any direct hygienic application of the work previously reported, it was determined to make an investigation of the activity of soap prepared in the laboratory from known glycerides, as well as that of representative soaps purchased in the market. For this purpose, the saponification numbers of several fats

Received for publication, March 7, 1925.

1 Jour. Infect. Dis., 1924, 35, p. 557.

2 Soaps and Proteins: Their Colloid Chemistry in Theory and Practice, 1921.

3 Third Report on Colloid Chemistry, Brit. Assn. Adv. Sc., 1920.

4 Oils, Fats and Waxes, 1921.

and oils, and of resin, were determined, and soap made by saponification with a chemically equivalent amount of alkali, thus forming a "neutral" soap. The theoretical amount of soap formed was calculated from the amount of glyceride and of alkali used and then diluted to a convenient strength. No attempt was made to remove the small amount of glycerin formed. Potassium tallow soap was used in these experiments rather than sodium tallow soap, on account of the inconveniently high gelation capacity of the latter. This was felt to be permissible, despite the more widespread use of sodium tallow soap, because the former work had shown that the difference between the sodium and potassium salts of the same fatty acids was not great. Four well-known brands of commercial soaps each representing a different type of soap were purchased and solutions or gels of known strength prepared from them. In making these solutions no allowance was made for the moisture content of the commercial soaps. The figures in the tables showing the dilutions therefore represent the proportion of dry soap in the case of the preparations made in the laboratory, and the proportion of the soap as purchased in the case of the commercial soaps. The moisture content of the soaps purchased was found to be as follows: white floating soap, 16.3%; perfumed toilet, 7.3%; sapo mollis, 47.7%; brown bar, 19.4%.

The most important applications of soaps where their germicidal properties might be of value are three, namely laundering, dish-washing, and hand-washing. Nichols [5] has previously shown that ordinary brown bar soap such as is commonly used in dish-washing can be relied on to prevent the spread by eating utensils of diseases due to pneumococci and streptococci when used in the water at the concentration of 0.5%. The present study was confined to test-tube experiments, to experiments simulating the conditions of hand-washing, and to one experiment relating to the general action of soap on mouth organisms.

EXPERIMENTS

In a general way, the technic given by Anderson and McClintic [6] for the determination of phenol co-efficients was followed. Successive dilutions of the soap differed by one half. Each tube contained 5 c c. of the soap solution, and to it was added 0.1 c c. of a broth culture of the organism to be tested. After the time interval a 4 mm. loopful was transferred from the test-tube to the same sort of medium in which the organism had been grown. The typhoid bacillus was grown in beef extract broth, the diphtheria bacillus in meat

[5] Jour. Lab. & Clin. Med., 1920, 5, p. 502.
[6] Jour. Infect. Dis., 1911, 8, p. 1.

infusion broth, and the streptococcus in "hormone" broth, made according to the formula of Fisk and Burky.[7] The broth cultures of the typhoid bacillus and diphtheria bacillus were 24 hours old when used, and the streptococcus 18 hours. It was not considered necessary to run experiments with the pneumococcus, since the previous study showed it to be acted on by the same soaps as the streptococcus, and to a much greater degree. Phenol was used in all tests in the concentrations of 2%, 1%, 0.5% and 0.25% as a control germicide. The experiments were carried out in a water bath at the temperature stated. The broth to which transfers were made was incubated for 48 hours before being discarded.

TABLE 1

EXPERIMENTS SHOWING THE KILLING STRENGTH OF THE VARIOUS SOAPS

Soaps Prepared in Laboratory	B. diphtheriae			Strep. hem.		B. typhosus			Staph. aureus	
	20 C.		35 C.	20 C.		20 C.		35 C.	20 C.	35 C.
	2½ Min.	15 Min.	15 Min.	2½ Min.	15 Min.	2½ Min.	15 Min.	15 Min.	15 Min.	15 Min.
Coconut oil (sodium)	1:320	1:640	1:5120	1:320	1:640	1:40	1:80	1:160	—	—
Beef tallow (potassium)	1:160	1:1280	1:2560	1:160	1:640	—	1:10	1:160	—	—
Olive oil (sodium)	1:640	1:2560	1:20480	1:160	1:640	—	—	1:80	—	—
Cottonseed oil (sodium)	1:640	1:2560		1:320	1:640	*	*	1:20	*	—
Linseed oil (potassium)	1:640			1:160	1:320	—	1:10	1:160	—	—
Resin (sodium)	1:160	1:640	1:1280	1:160	1:160	1:10	1:40	1:160	1:40	1:80
Commercial Soaps										
White floating		1:1280		1:320	1:640	†	†	1:160	†	—
Perfumed toilet		1:2560		1:160	1:640	†	†	1:160	†	—
Sapo mollis (U. S. P.)		1:1280		1:160	1:320	—	—	1:20	—	—
Brown bar		1:1280		1:80	1:160	†	†	1:160	†	1:10
Phenol	2%	1%	½%	2%	1%	2%	1%	½%	2%	1%

The minus sign indicates that the strongest solution prepared (1:10 for all soaps except sapo mollis, in which it was 1:25) did not kill the organisms.

No determinations were made for the spaces left blank.

* This soap at 20 C. formed gels too firm to be tested in dilutions stronger than 1:40. 1:40 did not kill.

† These soaps form gels at 20 C. in dilution stronger than 1:160.

The results are shown in table 1. Since these soaps were prepared from mixtures of the glycerides of the different fatty acids, no marked evidence of any selective action was to be expected. It is evident that the diphtheria bacillus is to be classified along with the pneumococcus and streptococcus as organisms very susceptible to the action of soap. A 1 : 160 solution of any of the soaps tested will kill these 3 organisms in 2½ minutes at 20 C.

Coconut oil soap is, however, definitely more active against the typhoid bacillus at 20 degrees than any of the other soaps, and this is in thorough agreement with work reported by Hamilton.[8]

[7] Ibid., 1922, 30, p. 128.

[8] Jour. Ind. and Eng. Chemistry, 1912, 3, p. 582.

Staphylococcus aureus, as previously found, is completely resistant to the action of all of the soaps, even at 35 degrees, except that of sodium resin soap. This great resistance of staphylococci to soaps has been previously observed by Reithofer.[9]

The increased efficiency of all of the soaps at 35 degrees as compared to 20 degrees is striking. The high germicidal activity of most of these soaps is realized by comparing the concentration given for them with the killing strength of phenol under the same conditions.

It may be stated that similar determinations were carried out at 50 C., and it was found that a 1 : 1,280 solution of most of the soaps killed the typhoid bacillus in 15 minutes. The typhoid bacillus in distilled water survived this higher temperature for a period of at least 1 hour.

PERCENTAGE OF SOAP IN LATHER

Before attempting to apply the foregoing experiments, it would be desirable to know something about the percentage of soap present in the lather ordinarily formed on the hands in handwashing. This was done by collecting the lather from the hands in a tared watch crystal, weighing rapidly before further loss from evaporation, and again weighing after drying to constant weight, the residue being considered the amount of soap in the lather. The amount of soap present in the average thorough washing of the hands for the purpose of actually cleaning them, rather than for the psychologic effect, was found to be about 8% for the several soaps investigated. With prolonged washing, accompanied by the addition of more soap without washing off the lather, the concentration became as high as 20%, and would have been even higher, due to evaporation of water from the hands, had the experiment continued further. It was found, however, that with a hasty insufficient washing of the hands lasting over only a few seconds with the formation of only a few large bubbles of lather, with much free water on the hands, the concentration might be as low as 0.3%. Pilod,[10] using the same method, found that 15% was the highest concentration of soap in ordinary lather. It is believed therefore, that the figure of 8% can be safely taken to represent the concentration of soap whenever the hands are washed with a fair degree of care, and this is evidently far in excess of the killing strengths of all of the soaps tested for pneumococci, streptococci, and diphtheria bacilli.

[9] Arch. f. Hyg., 1896, 27, p. 350.
[10] Presse méd., 1912, 20, p. 587.

THE EFFECT OF SOAP ON ORGANISMS NORMALLY PRESENT ON THE SKIN

The hands were thoroughly scrubbed in sterile water with a sterile nail brush over a period of 5 minutes, forming a very stiff lather containing at least 20% of soap. This lather was washed off with sterile water, and a fresh sterile brush used to make up a new lather. This process was repeated 3 times, a loop of lather being transferred to broth each time just previous to its being washed off. Staphylococcus albus grew in all these tubes, regardless of the kind of soap used. No organisms other than Staphylococcus albus were encountered, however, on plating out these cultures. This shows clearly that soaps cannot be relied on for the bacteriologic or surgical sterility of the hands, even when their germicidal activity is combined with repeated mechanical removal of the bacteria set free from the skin by scrubbing with a nail brush.

EXPERIMENTS WITH STREPTOCOCCUS HEMOLYTICUS

Since the test-tube experiments had shown that Streptococcus hemolyticus was more resistant to soaps than either the pneumococcus or diphtheria bacillus, it was felt that the streptococcus could safely be used as an index for this group of 3 organisms in hand-washing experiments.

TABLE 2

HAND-WASHING EXPERIMENTS AFTER SMEARING HANDS COVERED WITH STERILE GLOVES WITH STREPTOCOCCUS HEMOLYTICUS

	Time Interval			Concentration of Soap at End	Remarks
	1 Min.	2½ Min.	5 Min.		
White floating	—	—	—	10%	
Sapo mollis	—	—	—	18%	
Sodium resinate	—	—	—	8%	
Brown bar	—	—	—	6%	
Brown bar	+	+	+	0.2%	Almost no lather formed
Scented toilet	—	—	—		
Scented toilet	+	+	—	0.3%	Poor lather
Tallow (potassium)	—	—	—	9%	
Tallow (potassium)	—	—	—	2%	Only moderate lather
Tallow (potassium)	+	—	—	0.5%	Poor lather
Tallow (potassium)	+	+	—	0.3%	Poor lather

The plus sign indicates survival of the organism.

The experiment was carried out as follows: 10 c c. of an 18-hour "hormone" broth culture were concentrated, by centrifuging at high speed, to a volume of 3 c c. The sediment was then thoroughly mixed in this remaining 3 c c. by drawing to and fro in a capillary pipet, and then pipetted by an assistant on to the hands, which had previously been covered with sterile gloves. It was felt necessary to use gloves in order to prevent the overgrowth of any surviving streptococci by Staphylococcus albus, in view of the findings of the experiment just cited. The hands were rubbed together until the broth had evaporated. Lather was then made by using a cake of soap (previously washed rapidly in boiling water) and pouring on sterile water, or else simply pouring on a soap solution. All of the lather formed was allowed to remain on the hands, and care was exercised to ensure that there was no dripping of excess water. In this manner the germicidal properties of the soap were tested without any confusion due to the mechanical removal of bacteria. Sterile water was dropped on from time to time in cases in which it was desired to keep the concentration of the soap low.

Cultures were made by transferring a loop of the lather to "hormone" broth at intervals of 1, 2½ and 5 minutes after the beginning of the formation of the lather (Table 2).

Control experiments, keeping the hands wet with sterile water, instead of with soap solution showed that the streptococcus could be recovered as long as 15 minutes, the longest time interval tested. Table 2 shows that under the conditions of these experiments Streptococcus hemolyticus was destroyed in less than one minute, regardless of the kind of soap, except in those cases in which the lather was noticeably poorly formed. The concentration of the soap in the lather was determined at the end of the experiment in the manner already described. These experiments were carried out at room temperature and with water at room temperature, that is, about 20 C.

EXPERIMENTS WITH B. COLI

During the course of the experiments with Streptococcus hemolyticus, it was observed that a certain amount of flying away of particles of soap lather from the hands could not be prevented. It was therefore decided to use, if possible, a strain of B. coli for further experiments, since this would avoid

TABLE 3

Comparison of Action of Chemically Pure Soaps on B. typhosus and B. coli Killing Strength, 15 Minutes, 20 C.

	Sodium Laurate	Potassium Palmitate	Sodium Oleate	Sodium Linolate
B. coli	N/10	N/10	—	—
B. typhosus	N/20	N/40	—	—

The minus sign indicates that the organisms were not killed in the strongest solution made (N/5, that is, 4.5% to 6.1%).

any danger of infection. It was first necesary to compare the resistance of B. coli to soaps with that of B. typhosus in order to determine whether the former could safely be used as an index of what would happen to B. typhosus under the same conditions.

A recently isolated strain of B. coli was tested along with B. typhosus against several chemically pure soaps (table 3).

Table 3 shows that any difference in susceptibility to the action of soap favors B. coli as being more resistant. Moreover, since Reichenbach,[11] working

[11] Ztschr. f. Hyg. u. Infektionskr., 1908, 59, p. 296.

with B. coli as the test organism, obtained practically the same results that I obtained with B. typhosus, it was felt to be perfectly permissible to substitute the use of B. coli for B. typhosus in these experiments.

Also the choice of B. coli permitted rubber gloves to be dispensed with. The following technic was followed: 10 c c. of a 24-hour broth culture of B. coli were concentrated as described for the streptococcus. The culture was then dropped on the bare hands, rubbed until dry, and lather made as in the previous experiment. Transfers of lather were made to lactose broth fermentation tubes at intervals of 1, 2½, 5 and 10 minutes. Those tubes showing gas formation after 48 hours' incubation were considered positive, that is, to represent the survival of the organisms.

TABLE 4

HAND-WASHING EXPERIMENTS USING B. COLI AS THE TEST ORGANISM. BARE HANDS

Kind of Soap	Time Interval				Concentration of Soap at End
	1 Min.	2½ Min.	5 Min.	10 Min.	
Coconut oil (sodium)	—	—	—	—	
Coconut oil (sodium)	—	—	—	—	15%
Coconut oil (sodium)	+	+	—	—	8%
Coconut oil (potassium)	+	+	—	—	6%
Coconut oil shampoo soap	+	—	—	—	10%
Coconut oil soap*	+	—	—	—	9%
All other soaps†	+	+	+	+	Stiffest possible lather

* A commercial soap, the wrapper of which stated that it was made from coconut oil, olive oil, and benne oil.

† This includes the soaps listed in table 1, except coconut oil (sodium) soap.

The results are shown in table 4. The concentration of the soap given in the final column probably errs on the side of being too concentrated, since the determinations were made at the end of the experiment. Water, however, was added from time to time in most of the experiments in order to make up for that lost by evaporation. As was to be expected from previous test-tube experiments, these soaps are considerably less active against B. coli than against the streptococcus, pneumococcus, and diphtheria bacillus. Coconut oil soap is the only one capable of killing the organism, and this in 2½ minutes only when the lather is very concentrated. Only 2 soaps were available for which the manufacturers claimed that coconut oil was used in their manufacture (coconut oil shampoo soap, and the soap labeled "coconut oil soap"). It is to be remarked that these showed considerable germicidal activity toward the organism, far in excess of that showed by other commercial soaps, or the soaps not made from coconut oil. It would be interesting to test salt water soap in this manner, since coconut oil is extensively used in its manufacture.

RELATION OF THE GERMICIDAL ACTIVITY OF SOAPS TO THEIR CHEMICAL COMPOSITION

Lewkowitsch [4] gives the following analysis of coconut oil: *

Capric acid	19.5%
Lauric acid	40.0%
Myristic acid	24.0%
Palmitic acid	10.6%
Oleic acid	5.4%

The first 4 acids, comprising 94% of the total, have been shown in the previous work [1] to have an appreciable germicidal effect on the typhoid bacillus, and it was to be anticipated that soap made from coconut oil would prove to be more germicidal against this organism and B. coli than the other soaps. Oleic acid, the soaps of which have no effect on the typhoid bacillus at ordinary temperatures, is present in the proportion of only 5.4%.

The following analysis is given for tallow:

Palmitic acid	28.4%
Stearic acid	23.2%
Oleic acid	48.4%

Palmitic and stearic acids form soaps which are germicidal against the typhoid bacillus, and though present in considerable amounts, tallow soap was found to be almost totally lacking in germicidal activity against the typhoid bacillus. It is to be noted, however, that oleic acid comprises nearly 50% of the total. This would suggest that, at 20 degrees, the soaps of oleic acid are not only lacking in germicidal activity against the typhoid bacillus, but might even depress the germicidal activity of other soaps present. A few preliminary tests already made would seem to confirm this opinion. The results given by olive oil, cottonseed oil, and linseed oil soaps correspond closely to what would have been expected from their composition. They all contain very large amounts of the unsaturated acids and relatively small quantities of the solid saturated acids.

The exact composition of the commercial soaps, with the exception of sapo mollis, is not known. The manufacturers of the white floating soap inform me that it satisfies the requirements of the Bureau of Standards Circular No. 123, that is, it contains from 25 to 30% of

* Acids present in very small amounts have been omitted.

coconut oil. This indicates that a soap must contain a much greater proportion of coconut oil if it is to be germicidal against the typhoid bacillus.

The brown bar soap was purchased under the specifications of Bureau of Standards Circular No. 129, and hence contains not more than 25% of sodium resinate. The perfumed toilet soap was probably made chiefly from tallow.

EFFECT OF SOAP ON MOUTH ORGANISMS AS A WHOLE

In view of the results previously reported by Nichols,[5] it seemed of interest to obtain more data in regard to the effect of soap on the organisms in the mouth, since these organisms were especially apt to contaminate the hands, eating utensils, etc. Five c c. of saliva were collected from 5 individuals and diluted to a volume of 1,000 c c. with sterile tap water. This, after thorough mixing, was divided into 2 equal portions. One portion served as a control. The other portion was made to contain 0.5% soap by the addition of a strong solution of brown bar soap. At intervals, 0.1 c c. of solution was removed and plated in agar containing 1 c c. of sterile defibrinated blood. These plates were incubated 24 hours, and then the colonies were counted. Another control showed that the soap carried over in the 0.1 c c. of fluid plated had no influence in preventing the development of colonies.

The results are given in table 5, and show that soaps have a strong sterilizing effect on the organisms commonly occurring in the mouth. The great proportion of the colonies developing in the control plates were of the type formed by Streptococcus viridans.

TABLE 5

EFFECT OF A 0.5% SOLUTION OF BROWN BAR SOAP ON BACTERIA IN SALIVA

	Number of Colonies Developing	
	Tests	Controls
Before adding soap	650	630
One-half minute after adding soap	24	...
One minute after adding soap	3	...
Five minutes after adding soap	0	...
Ten minutes after adding soap	0	520

COMMENT

Hamilton,[8] found coconut oil soap to be appreciably germicidal against the typhoid bacillus, although he later concluded that,[12] "no soap can be considered an effective disinfectant unless associated with some other more active agent"; this is, of course, true if by "disinfec-

[12] Am. Jour. Public Health, 1917, 7, p. 282.

tant" one understands a germicide killing all forms of micro-organisms. Norton[13] has made an investigation of soaps in their relation to washing of the hands. His work is especially important in showing that various special soaps put out by manufacturers with extravagant claims for their antiseptic value possessed no special advantage over ordinary soaps. Norton, however, makes no attempt to take advantage of the selective activity of soaps for various special organisms when he gives one the impression that the hygienic importance of soaps is due solely to the fact that they aid in the mechanical removal of bacteria.

Weaver and Murchie,[14] working in a ward where only soap and water were used for cleaning the hands after caring for diphtheria patients, was able to recover diphtheria bacilli and hemolytic streptococci from the hands of pupil nurses with a fair degree of ease. These organisms (with a single exception) were not obtained from the hands of graduate nurses, and this is attributed to the more thorough training of the latter. The organisms were obtained especially from underneath the nails, and it is, of course, easy to conceive that bacteria in this position might be protected from the action of any germicide. The use of a nail-brush therefore seems to be imperative if one is to rely on the use of soaps for disinfecting the hands in hospital practice.

The following recent work favorable to the germicidal activity of soap may be cited: Lamar,[15] who found sodium oleate, linolate, and linolenate germicidal for the pneumococcus and streptococcus, and Nichols,[5] who extended Lamar's observations to include sodium resinate, and made a practical application of the work as it relates to the washing of eating utensils. As far as the author knows, the present paper is the first to call attention of the marked susceptibility of the diphtheria bacillus to the action of soaps, and it would, of course, be desirable to confirm this observation using other strains of the organism.

It is felt that a certain amount of conservatism should be used in the application of the work here reported, despite the fact that the test-tube experiments show certain of the soaps to be much more active than phenol against some of the organisms. No attempt should be made to take advantage of the germicidal properties of soaps except under conditions in which they would also be used for their detergent properties.. Foreign substances (serum, broth, salt, acid) interfere markedly with their action, and it would, of course, be futile to attempt to disinfect

[13] Jour. Am. Med. Assn., 1920, 75, p. 302.
[14] Ibid., 1919, 73, p. 1921.
[15] Jour. Exper. Med., 1911, 13, p. 380.

sputum or feces by pouring soap solution over them. Noguchi [16] found vegetative forms of the anthrax bacillus to be susceptible to the action of soap, yet the rather large number of cases of anthrax which have resulted from shaving brushes certaintly show that shaving soap has no effect on anthrax spores.

At the same time, it may be pointed out that the conditions under which some of these experiments were carried out are believed to be much more rigorous than those occurring in actual practice. The number of organisms used in the hand-washing experiments was overwhelming, and no attempt was made to take advantage of higher temperatures, at which the test-tube experiments had shown soaps to be considerably more active. Moreover, special precautions were taken to prevent confusion due to the mechanical removal of bacteria.

It is possible that this work may be extended to include other bacteria, though it is evident that each micro-organism must be taken separately. The work of Reithofer,[9] Noguchi,[16] and Rasp,[17] would indicate that the cholera vibrio is to be regarded as susceptible to the action of soap, while Reasoner [18] has observed that soap destroys Spirochaeta pallida. It would be especially desirable to determine the action of soap on the meningococcus and gonococcus.

The question arises as to what changes would be desirable in the composition of commercial soaps in view of the work here reported. It is evident that the soaps already available and in general use are highly germicidal against the pneumococcus, streptococcus, and diphtheria bacillus. The soap in greatest use around hospitals is the official sapo mollis. The substitution of coconut oil for the linseed oil used in its preparation would render it germicidal against the typhoid bacillus as well as against the other three organisms. Such a change would seem desirable, though possibly the soap so formed would be more irritating to the skin than the present soap. Also, the use of a soap made from a base containing a large proportion of coconut oil would be useful in connection with typhoid epidemics, and for general use at all times for washing the hands after going to stool.

CONCLUSIONS

Soaps are not to be regarded as general germicides, but in using them for their detergent properties, advantage may be taken of their germicidal

[16] Bioch. Ztschr., 1907, 6, p. 327.
[17] Ztschr. f. Hyg. u. Infektionskr., 1907-8, 58, p. 45.
[18] Jour. Am. Med. Assn., 1917, 68, p. 973.

activity against the streptococcus, pneumococcus, diphtheria bacillus, and, to a lesser extent, against the typhoid bacillus.

The thorough washing of the hands with the formation of a good lather will destroy any adhering diphtheria bacilli, streptococci, and pneumococci. Any ordinary soap will serve for this purpose.

Coconut oil soap is the only soap appreciably active against the typhoid bacillus at ordinary temperatures. In order to kill typhoid bacilli on the hands, the washing should extend over a period of at least 3 minutes, with the formation of an exceedingly stiff lather.

The use of a nail brush in washing the hands in order to render the surface underneath the nails accessible to the action of soap is desirable.

The activity of soap is greatly enhanced by raising the temperature.

This germicidal activity of soap is in addition to any sterilizing effect brought about by them due to the mechanical removal of bacteria.

The activity of coconut oil soap against the typhoid bacillus seems to be due to its high content of the saturated fatty acids, and the very low proportion of unsaturated acids.

Foreign substances interfere markedly with the germicidal activity of soap.

It is suggested that linseed oil or cottonseed oil used in the manufacture of the official sapo mollis might be advantageously replaced by coconut oil. The greater use of coconut oil soap would aid in the prevention of the spread of typhoid fever by hand contamination.

FURTHER STUDIES ON A DIPLOCOCCUS IN MEASLES

A MEASLES SKIN REACTION

Ruth Tunnicliff

From the John McCormick Institute for Infectious Diseases, Chicago

That the virus of measles may be present in the blood was shown by Hektoen,[1] who produced the disease in man by injecting blood from measles patients. Anderson and Goldberger [2] found the rhesus monkey susceptible to inoculation with measles materials collected just before or early in the eruptive stage, and also that the virus passed through a Berkefeld filter. Later, Nevin and Bittman [3] demonstrated that rabbits, and Duval and D'Aunoy [4] that guinea-pigs, react to the injection of measles virus.

In previous articles I [5] have described a small gram-positive diplococcus that I have isolated from the blood, eyes, nose, throat and sputum of patients with measles during the preeruptive and early eruptive stages. The organism has been cultivated only in anaerobic cultures from the blood, but it generally grows aerobically in the second generation; it is cultivated readily from the respiratory tract, producing small green colonies on aerobic blood agar plates. When first isolated and small, the cocci generally pass through a tested Berkefeld N filter. Diplococci like those in cultures can be demonstrated, often in large numbers, in smears from the tonsils, nose, sputum and eye in measles.

The blood of measles patients gives a distinct increase in specific agglutinins and opsonins for this diplococcus from the third to the eighth day following the appearance of the eruption. Complement fixing bodies seem to be present only to a slight extent as the symptoms subside. Rabbits immunized with this coccus have been found to acquire specific opsonic and agglutinating power not only for the strains used in immunization but for other strains of the measles diplococcus.

Received for publication, March 1, 1925.

[1] Jour. Infect. Dis., 1905, 2, p. 238.
[2] Pub. Health Rep., 1911, 26, pp. 847, 887; Jour. Am. Med. Assn., 1911, 57, p. 113.
[3] Jour. Infect. Dis., 1921, 29, p. 429.
[4] Jour. Exper. Med., 1922, 35, p. 257.
[5] Jour. Am. Med. Assn., 1917, 68, p. 1028; Jour. Infect. Dis., 1918, 22, p. 402; Jour. Am. Med. Assn., 1918, 71, p. 104. Tunnicliff, Ruth; and Brown, M. W.: Jour. Infect. Dis., 1918, 23, p. 572. Tunnicliff, Ruth: ibid., 1919, 24, p. 76; p. 181. Tunnicliff, Ruth; and Moody, W. B.: ibid., 1922, 31, p. 1.

The same symptoms and lesions as are produced by the inoculation of washings of the nose and throat of patients with measles have been observed to follow the inoculation of the measles diplococcus in monkeys, guinea-pigs and rabbits. Rabbits successfully inoculated with the diplococcus have shown no symptoms when reinoculated with fresh measles material. Green-producing diplococci isolated from the blood and lungs of rabbits successfully inoculated with the measles diplococcus also gave rise to Koplik spots and exanthem when injected into other rabbits.

The chance of the selective transfer of an unknown virus by only the green-producing diplococcus appear small because diplococcus cultures, originally isolated from single colonies, have produced a reaction in rabbits in the seventh generation, while rabbits similarly inoculated with the second generation of cultures of staphylococci, green and hemolyzing streptococci from the same plates developed no symptoms of measles.

The cocci in pairs and short chains, observed by Babes [6] in 1880, in the secretions from the nose, conjunctiva and bronchi of measles patients, the diplostreptococci isolated from the sputum by Menschikow,[6] and the green cocci isolated by Donges [7] from the blood in measles may be the same cocci as those cultivated by me.

At the height of the attack of measles, gram-positive bacilli and other organisms were sometimes isolated from the blood, but as I did not find them in the preeruptive stage, when the blood is known to be infective, and as no opsonins, agglutinins or complement fixing bodies could be demonstrated for them, they were not considered to be of any etiologic significance. Some of these bacilli may be the same as those isolated by Sellards and Bigelow [8] from the blood of measles patients, and by Kusama, Yokoyama and Ito [9] from the kidneys of monkeys infected with measles blood. The filter-passing diplococcus, recently isolated by Caronia [10] from measles, differs from my organism in being gram-negative and always anaerobic. The ascites tissue medium used by him is unfavorable for the growth of my diplococcus, and after several generations the cocci become almost invisible and many become gram-negative. Caronia not only isolated the cocci he describes from measles material but also from the blood of rabbits inoculated with measles blood. Ritossa [11] reports agglutinins, opsonins and amboceptor for this organism

[6] Cited by Hektoen: Jour. Am. Med. Assn., 1918, 71, p. 1201.
[7] Centralbl. f. Bakteriol. I, O., 1924, 91, p. 45.
[8] Jour. Med. Research, 1921, 42, p. 241.
[9] The Japan Medical World, 1925, 5, p. 1.
[10] Pediatra, 1923, 31, p. 801.
[11] Pediatra, 1924, 32, p. 784.

in the serum of measles patients. De Villa,[12] on intracutaneous injection of killed cultures of Caronia's coccus, observed a reaction in 65% of the persons without a history of measles, but no reaction in any stage of the disease in children vaccinated with the cultures, or in 75% of children who had had measles before.

Selma Meyer,[13] who worked with Caronia and studied his technic, reports that the bodies similar to those described by him as the cause of measles and scarlet fever, were found by her also in uninoculated culture mediums and in blood cultures from chickenpox, chorea, polyarthritis and from other diseases, as well as from normal blood. Rabbits injected with uninoculated culture medium showed the same bodies in the liver and spleen as those injected with scarlet fever and measles blood. In her hands, complement fixation with the serum of rabbits injected with measles and scarlet fever blood was not specific, neither were skin reactions with filtrates of scarlet fever cultures.

The skin reaction to the diplococcus found by me in measles has been studied with a view to obtaining light on its relation to measles.

Berkefeld W filtrates of aerobic and anaerobic cultures, grown from 24 hours to six days in broth with and without ascites fluid, failed to produce any reaction. Killed organisms suspended in salt solution also failed to give convincing reactions. I then tried a method similar to that used by Gabritschewsky [14] in his streptococcus immunization against scarlet fever, which produced skin reactions in persons who had not had scarlet fever. A few drops of ascitic fluid was added to each 5 c c. of 1% dextrose broth and cultures grown anaerobically under oil; the cocci in the broth were then killed by the addition of 0.5% phenol (carbolic acid) at room temperature. Usually the cocci were killed in 24 hours, 48 hours were required to kill one strain. Anaerobic cultures produced better results than aerobic and twenty-four hour cultures gave better antigens than five or six day growths.

Since I had observed rashes in rabbits after inoculation of the measles diplococcus, it seemed probable that they would respond to injection of the antigen and accordingly 0.2 c c. of full strength antigen was injected intracutaneously into the back or side of rabbits after shaving. Normal rabbits reacted with circumscribed indurated red areas from 1 to 4 cm. in diameter in from 4 to 24 hours after injection. In some instances the area was topped by a white necrotic spot. The

[12] Pediatra, 1924, 32, p. 769.
[13] Monatschr. f. Kinderh., 1925, 29, p. 524.
[14] Smith, R. M.: Boston Med. & Surg. Jour., 1910, 162, p. 242.

reaction persisted from 24 hours to 3 days and was generally followed by pigmentation and desquamation. One rabbit that 6 months previously had been injected with infective human measles material after having received the serum of a goat immunized with the measles diplococcus, showed no reaction to the measles antigen. A rabbit, after receiving many doses of measles antigen as well as convalescent human measles serum and antidiplococcus goat serum, failed to respond to further injections of the measles antigen; another normal rabbit, which gave a well marked reaction, in rabbits both immune and not immune to the measles subcutaneous injection of 2 c c. of the antidiplococcus goat serum.

Twenty-one strains of bile insoluble green-producing diplococci have been tested on rabbits. Five strains were isolated at the onset of measles, one from the blood, and four from the respiratory tract; one strain was isolated from the blood of a goat inoculated intravenously with measles diplococci; fifteen strains were isolated from late cases of measles, from scarlet fever, german measles, acute tonsillitis, the mouth of a normal goat and the normal human throat. The six measles antigens gave marked reactions in normal rabbits but no reactions in rabbits immune to measles. One strain from a normal throat, two from measles late in the disease gave slight reactions, and one from an acute tonsillitis gave marked reactions in rabbits, whether immune or not immune to the measles diplococcus. The other strains failed to produce any reactions. Some of the antigens became inactive after 6 weeks in the icebox.

NEUTRALIZATION EXPERIMENTS

Neutralization experiments have been made with the strains that gave positive tests. The measles antigens were mixed with equal parts of salt solution, of normal goat serum, of antidiplococcus goat serum and of convalescent human measles serum. The serum of two normal rabbits and of one rabbit immunized with the measles coccus was tested with one measles antigen, prepared from the same organisms used in immunization. The culture medium was also used as a control. Antigens from other sources were mixed with salt solution and convalescent human measles serum. After incubation for 3 hours, 0.2 c c. of the mixture was injected intracutaneously in normal rabbits. Normal goat serum did not neutralize the measles antigens. Both convalescent human measles serum and antidiplococcus goat serum neutralized the measles antigens. The two strains isolated late in measles, the strain from the normal throat and the one from tonsillitis were not neutralized by convalescent human measles serum. The serum of the two normal rabbits tested neutralized the measles antigen partly, while the immune rabbit serum completely neutralized it. Some rabbits could not be used because they were sensitive to human and goat serum, and ascitic fluid.

Since the measles diplococcus antigen gave definite cutaneous reactions in normal rabbits, similar tests were made in human beings. Two different measles strains were used, but most of the experiments were made with a culture isolated two years previously with which Koplik spots, eruptions and fever had been produced in rabbits. The antigen was diluted with salt solution to a point that gave no reaction in persons who had previously had measles, and generally a dilution of 1:40 was suitable. No reaction occurred with the control anaerobic ascites broth culture mediums, to which phenol (carbolic acid) and salt solution were added as in the antigens except sometimes a redness 0.3 cm. in diameter at the site of the needle prick. Twenty-eight persons who gave a history of measles or were convalescing from measles showed no reaction to the measles antigen except occasionally the same redness as caused by the control injection of culture mediums. One person with a history of measles reacted positively. A patient with the measles eruption just out on the face gave no reaction. Twenty-six persons, who had not had measles, gave a definite reaction in from 4 to 48 hours, generally in 24 hours, in the form of a circumscribed area of erythema of varying intensity, from 1 to 2 cm. in diameter, as a rule with slight infiltration. The reaction in some instances has been followed by pigmentation and desquamation; generally it disappeared in from 24 to 48 hours, but occasionally it persisted for four or five days.

The ages of the persons tested who have a history of having had measles varied from 19 months to 50 years, of those not having measles from 6 months to 10 years. The sexes were practically the same in both groups.

A few neutralization experiments were tried on persons who had not had measles. To get complete neutralization with convalescent human measles serum in human beings, great care must be taken to get the correct dilution of the antigen and to inject exactly the same amounts of each mixture. Serum from a person with a negative history of measles who showed a positive skin reaction was used as the control serum. The measles antigen was mixed with equal parts of salt solution, control serum and convalescent human measles serum. The mixtures were incubated and injected as previously described. In 20 hours the mixtures with salt solution and control serum produced a circumscribed area of erythema 1.5 cm. in diameter; the mixture with convalescent serum produced no reaction.

CONCLUSIONS

Anaerobic dextrose broth cultures of the green-producing diplococcus found in measles killed by 0.5% carbolic acid, appear to produce a skin reaction in persons who have not had measles, but not in measles patients after the appearance of the eruption, or in 96% of persons who give a history of measles. The measles antigen is neutralized in persons who have not had measles, by convalescent human measles serum, but not by the serum of a person with a negative history of measles. Reaction occurs also in normal rabbits, while rabbits immunized against measles fail to react. The measles antigens are neutralized in rabbits by convalescent human measles serum and by the serum of goats recovering from the reaction produced by measles diplococci, but not by normal goat serum. Green-producing cocci from other sources generally give no reactions in rabbits, but the strains that do, produce similar reactions in both immune and in nonimmune rabbits and are not neutralized by convalescent human measles serum. Normal rabbit serum neutralizes measles antigen partly, immune rabbit serum completely neutralizes it.

These results indicate that the gram-positive, green-producing diplococcus found in measles is of etiologic significance.

THE PROTECTIVE SUBSTANCE IN ANTI-PNEUMOCOCCIC SERUM

1.—TYPE 1 SERUM

Lloyd D. Felton

From the Department of Preventive Medicine and Hygiene, Harvard Medical School, Boston

A number of investigators have shown that the protective substances present in the serum from immunized animals are associated with the globulin portions of the serum—either with the so-called euglobulin, the pseudoglobulin, or with both, depending on the antigen and also on the experimental animal.

In the case of antipneumococcus serum, antibodies have been studied especially by Avery,[1] Gay and Chickering,[2] and Huntoon.[3] To Avery belongs the credit of adding the pneumococcus to the list of bacteria that give rise to immune bodies in the globulin portion of horse serum. He found the protective substance both in the water-soluble and in the water-insoluble fractions of the globulin. The water-insoluble portion possesses the greater agglutinating power for pneumococci. Avery reported no attempts to concentrate the antibodies by precipitation methods but found that complete precipitation of the protective bodies took place on 38% saturation of the immune serum with ammonium sulphate. It is interesting to note that this concentration was that which Pick[4] previously found to be best for the precipitation of antibodies from other bacterial immune serums.

Another method was reported by Gay and Chickering, who were able to bring about a complete precipitation of the protective substance by means of dissolved pneumococci. In similar fashion, Huntoon separated the protective body by precipitation, not with dissolved pneumococci, but with living organisms, and then by one of several methods dissociated the antigen-antibody complex thus formed. He found that the resulting solution contained but little nitrogen, not sufficient to give the usual protein color reactions, and only a trace of phosphorus. It has been possible by the application of this method to type 1 antipneumococcus serum to obtain a solution of such potency that from 0.2 to 0.4 c c. protects against one million MLD of pneumococci.

Received for publication, March 14, 1925.

[1] Jour. Exper. Med., 1915, 21, p. 133.
[2] Ibid., p. 389.
[3] Jour. Immunol., 1921, 6, p. 117.
[4] Beitr. z. chem. Physiol. u. Pathol., 1902, 1, p. 351.

Heretofore several methods have been in use for isolating the water-insoluble globulin fraction from serum: (*a*) by addition of a relatively high concentration of a neutral salt (e. g., ammonium sulphate); (*b*) by the use of salts of heavy metals; (*c*) by saturation of the diluted serum with carbon dioxide; (*d*) by acidifying the diluted serum with one of many acids, and (*e*) by dialysis. To these methods may be added precipitation in the cold by alcohol and by acetone.[5] Obviously in these diverse methods, the principle is the same. Each is designed to alter the conditions of the serum under which the solubility of the globulin fraction is at a minimum.

Recently, in the course of experiments with type 1 antipneumococcus serum, I noted [6] that simple dilution of the serum with distilled water caused a precipitate which contained a large part of the protective bodies. This method presented an excellent opportunity for an extensive study of the antibodies of this and other types of pneumococci. The results of these studies will be reported in a series of papers of which this is the first.

Simple dilution with distilled water of type 1 antipneumococcus horse serum causes the precipitation of a water-insoluble globulin having about 80% of the protective power of the serum from which it is derived. Normal horse serum, when diluted, yields but little precipitate. These facts indicate either that, in such immune serum this protein possesses characteristics different from those of the classical euglobulin, which has its iso-electric point at P_H 5.44, or that in antipneumococcus horse serum there is an increase in the euglobulin fraction, just as the pseudoglobulin fraction is increased in the serum of horses immunized against diphtheria or tetanus toxin. Data bearing on the relative quantities of the pseudoglobulin and the euglobulin and the iso-electric point of the protective globulin in antipneumococcus horse serum will be reported in another paper.

In this study attention is directed to the following points concerning only type 1 antipneumococcus serum:

1. The optimum H-ion concentration at which maximum precipitation of the protective substance takes place.

2. The effect of various acids on precipitation.

3. The effect of phosphate buffer mixtures of various molecular and hydrogen ion concentrations on precipitation.

[5] Villa, A.: Comp. rend. de Soc. de biol., 1922, 175, p. 728.
[6] Boston Med. & Surg. Jour., 1924, 190, p. 819.

4. The percentage of recovery of the protective substance from serum of different horses.

5. The effect of phosphate buffer solutions on yield of protective globulin.

6. A comparison of the amount of protective substance obtained (*a*) by precipitation with ammonium sulphate; (*b*) by dilution with water.

7. The effect of various preservatives on the potency of the protective substance.

8. The effect of heat both on precipitation and on protection.

9. The relation between the yield of precipitate and its protective power.

YIELD OF PROTECTIVE SUBSTANCE FROM TYPE 1 PNEUMOCOCCUS SERUM AT VARIOUS HYDROGEN ION CONCENTRATIONS

The object was to determine the optimum hydrogen ion concentration for the maximum yield in protective precipitate from type 1 pneumococcus serum. Ten c c. portions of serum were diluted with 100 c c. of distilled water, containing varying amounts of a N/20 solution of o-phthalic acid. The mixture remained over night in the icebox, whereupon the clear supernatant fluid was decanted and the precipitate collected by rapid centrifugation and dissolved in 1% solution of sodium chlorid. The hydrogen ion concentration of the supernatant was then determined in duplicate at room temperature by the gas-chain method, using Clark's vessel, proper temperature correction being made. Nitrogen determinations in 3 c c. portions were made in duplicate by the Arnold-Gunning modification of Kjeldahl's method on the dissolved precipitate. Tests of the protective power both of the supernatant and of the dissolved precipitate were made in duplicate, with a standard dose of pneumococci, namely, 0.5 c c. of a 1% horse serum broth culture. The protective power of the supernatant (table 2) was estimated from dilutions equivalent, respectively, to 1:10, 1:20, 1:40, 1:80, and 1:160 of original serum. Table 1 shows that the optimum hydrogen ion concentration for precipitation of the protective substance cannot be deduced with precision from this experiment.

The inconclusive results as to the optimum hydrogen ion concentration for precipitation in this single test seemed to me to be due possibly to the great difference in the series, that is, the steps between the dilutions were too great. To determine this point, reestimation was made on the same globulin solution by using a single dilution of 1:200 and varying the dose of the organisms. Mice in duplicate received injections of 0.5 cc. of globulin solution and 0.5 cc. of culture as follows: 1:5, 1:10, 1:20, and 1:40. Table 3 shows the results of this test from which, as in the previous case, the inference is plain that precipitation of a large part of the protective globulin occurs through a range of hydrogen ion concentration from PH 5.5 to PH 7.8 when the serum is diluted 1:10. Thus the optimum hydrogen ion concentration for precipitation is not definitely shown in these instances.

TABLE 1

YIELD OF PROTECTIVE SUBSTANCE AT DIFFERENT HYDROGEN ION CONCENTRATIONS ESTIMATED BY VARIATION IN DILUTION OF DISSOLVED PRECIPITATE AGAINST CONSTANT DOSE OF CULTURE

(All mice received injections of 0.5 c c. of a 16-hour broth culture diluted 1: 10)

Volume N/20 o-phthalic Acid in 100 C c. Water, C c.	Hydrogen Ion Concentration of Supernatant	Milligrams Nitrogen Per C c. in Dissolved Precipitate	Dilution of Dissolved Precipitate						Milligrams Nitrogen in Protective Dose
			Undiluted	1:10	1:20	1:40	1:80	1:160	
20	4.6	0.06	36	18	20	18	18	18	No protection
			108	22	22	36	18	36	
15	4.9	0.3	84	36	60	36	18	18	0.15
			S	S	84	36	60	18	
10	5.5	1.8	S	S	S	S	60	36	0.045
			S	S	S	S	S	60	
8	5.9	0.95	S	S	S	S	S	60	0.0079
			S	S	S	S	S	S	
6	6.5	1.06	S	S	S	S	S	36	0.013
			S	S	S	S	S	96	
4	6.8	1.43	S	S	S	S	60	60	0.035
			S	S	S	S	S	74	
2	7.3	1.15	S	S	S	S	S	36	0.014
			S	S	S	S	S	S	
0	7.7	1.25	S	S	76	S	84	84	0.031
			S	S	S	S	S	S	
Original serum	7.8	10.5	S	..	S	108	S	60	0.13
			S	..	S	S	S	108	

	1:10,000,000	1:1,000,000	1:100,000
Control of organism	60	36	36
	36	36	24

Numbers indicate hours of life.
S indicates survived.

TABLE 2

PROTECTION OF SUPERNATANT (SEE TABLE 1)

(All mice received injections of 0.5 c c. of a 16-hour broth culture diluted 1: 10)

Hydrogen Ion Concentration	Dilution of Supernatant				
	Undiluted	1:2	1:4	1:8	1:16
4.6	S	S	S	S	S
	S	S	S	S	S
4.9	S	S	132	S	S
	S	S	S	S	S
5.5	S	S	S	36	48
	S	S	36	36	36
5.9	84	60	36	...	...
	S	S	36	...	...
6.5	S	S	36	...	...
	S	S	36	...	...
6.8	108	60	36	...	...
	S	132	96	...	...
7.3	S	116	72	...	...
	S	S	84	...	...
7.7	S	S	44	...	...
	S	108	96	...	...

	1:10,000,000	1:1,000,000	1:100,000
Control of organism	36	36	36

Numbers indicate hours of life.
S indicates survived.
Obviously, undiluted, 1:2, 1:4, 1:8, 1:16 are equivalents respectively of dilutions 1:10, 1:20, 1:40, 1:80, and 1:160 of original serum.

A repetition of the experiment was made in which N/20 phosphoric acid was substituted for o-phthalic acid by testing the protective power of the precipitate against varying doses of organisms. For each test, solutions of the antibody were diluted 1:200, and the varying dilutions of culture injected into mice in duplicate. Two series of determinations were made, each of which gave practically the same results. One of these is reported in table 4. Only an occasional animal survived that had received injections of a dilution of 1:5 culture. It is worth noting, as shown by the foregoing experiment, that simple dilution with 10 volumes of distilled water gave practically the same yield of protective globulin as the same dilution when the hydrogen ion concentration was varied.

TABLE 3

YIELD OF PROTECTIVE SUBSTANCE AT DIFFERENT HYDROGEN ION CONCENTRATIONS ESTIMATED BY VARIATION IN DOSE OF CULTURE WITH CONSTANT DILUTION OF GLOBULIN SOLUTION

(All mice received injections of 0.5 c c. of antibody solution diluted 1: 200)

Volume N/20 o-phthalic Acid in 100 C c. Water, C c.	Hydrogen Ion Concentration	Dilution of Culture			
		1:5	1:10	1:20	1:40
10	5.5	36, S	108, S	S, S	S, S
8	5.9	72, 96	S, S	S, S	S, S
6	6.5	96, S	S, S	S, S	S, S
4	6.8	36, 36	S, S	S, S	S, S
2	7.3	36, 48	S, S	S, S	S, S
0	7.7	84, S	S, S	S, S	S, S
Original serum	7.8	36, 84	84, S	S, S	S, S

	1:10,000,000	1:1,000,000	1:100,000
Control of organism	36	36	36

Numbers indicate hours of life.
S indicates survived.

An interesting fact is revealed, as shown in table 1, by a comparison between the resulting protective value of the precipitate and the residuum in the supernatant, and of the original serum. The precipitate exhibited as high protective value as the original serum; although some protection was still present in the supernatant. As yet no explanation of this phenomenon has been found; but many collateral experiments indicate the presence in antipneumococcus serum of a substance antagonistic to the protective antibody. It is conceivable that this antagonistic substance disappeared from the precipitate during the process of precipitation, but was present in reduced amounts in the supernatant.

The next experiment, designed to ascertain the optimum quantity of acetic acid for precipitation of serum diluted 1:15 in liter lots, fell short of its purpose for the reason that denaturization of the globulin occurred in the more acid range, and also because of failure of the precipitate to settle in the less acid range, when attempts were made to wash it. Therefore the following modification was made. The precipitate in each bottle was washed three times with 15 liters of

TABLE 4

YIELD OF PROTECTIVE SUBSTANCE AT DIFFERENT HYDROGEN ION CONCENTRATIONS ESTIMATED BY VARIATION IN DOSE OF CULTURE WITH CONSTANT DILUTION OF GLOBULIN SOLUTION

(All mice received injections of 0.5 c c. of antibody solution diluted 1: 200)

Volume N/20 Phosphoric Acid in 100 C c. Water, C c.	Hydrogen Ion Concentration	Dilution of Culture				
		1:5	1:10	1:20	1:40	1:80
20	5.53	20 18	26 20	36 36	S 66	S
18	5.83	S 36	S 120	S S	S S	S
16	5.96	S 48	108 84	S S	S S	S
14	6.22	S 36	S 36	S 84	S S	S
12	6.42	36 36	60 36	S S	S 60	S
10	6.53	36 36	S 60	S 60	S S	S
8	6.75	96 36	84 96	S S	S S	S
6	6.92	84 60	60 50	S 60	S S	S
[illegible]	7.13	50 24	48 44	S 50	S 60	S
2	7.39	120 60	60 48	S S	S S	S
0	7.78	96 36	S 60	S S	S S	S

Control of organis u	1:10,000,000	1:1,000,000
	50	36

Numbers indicate hovrs of life.
S indicates survived.

M/500 phosphate buffer of hydrogen ion concentration of that made by acetic acid. The washed precipitate from each sample was dissolved in 150 c.c. of 3% sodium chloride. As shown in table 5, there is not sufficient variation in protective value of the precipitates washed in the P_H range P_H 5.5 to 6.5 to fix the iso-electric point. It is evident that a hydrogen ion concentration of P_H 6 is near the point of least solubility of the protective antibody of type 1 antipneumococcus serum; nevertheless, the results are adequate for orientation, and indicate further work along this line.

EFFECT OF VARIOUS ACIDS ON PRECIPITATION

It had been observed [6] that the addition of small amounts of citric and tartaric acids appeared to aid the precipitation of the protective globulin. Acetic acid gave good results in small lots, but when the precipitate was allowed to stand a considerable length of time in its presence, not only was there pronounced loss of protective potency, but also denaturization of globulin. This circumstance led to the trial of various acids over a range of P_H values. From a study of table 6, it

TABLE 5

PRECIPITATION OF LITER LOTS WITH ACETIC ACID WITH SUBSEQUENT WASHING WITH M/500 PHOSPHATE BUFFER

(All mice received injections of 0.5 c c. of a 16-hour broth culture diluted 1: 10)

Hydrogen Ion Concentration	Dilutions of Globulin Solution					
	1:10	1:50	1:100	1:200	1:400	1:800
4.5	18	18	18	18	18	18
	36	18	60	18	18	24
5.0	S	24	18	18	18	18
	S	S	120	24	36	36
5.5	18	S	84	36	S	18
	S	S	S	S	S	18
6.0	S	S	S	S	24	24
	S	S	S	S	84	36
6.5	S	S	24	7 da	36	18
	S	S	48	S	44	18
7.0	18	S	48	18	18	18
	120	48	84	18	24	36
7.5	S	S	24	18	18	18
	S	S	36	18	24	18
8.0	48	36	18	18	18	18
	108	S	36	24	24	36

Numbers indicate hours of life.
S indicates survived.

One liter of serum was precipitated in 15 liters of water with addition of sufficient N/10 acetic acid to make the foregoing hydrogen ion concentrations.

can be clearly seen that at given hydrogen ion concentration in the case of phosphoric, o-phthalic, and hydrochloric acids, there appeared to be little difference. Acetic acid behaved in this experiment as it has in many others: much of the precipitate was denatured; this may explain the irregularity of the nitrogen determinations of the precipitates with this acid. In addition to these, citric and tartaric acids were also tried, with the same results. It thus appears from these experiments that when the serum is diluted 10 times, there is no sharply defined hydrogen ion concentration, but a wide zone at which most of the protective globulins are precipitated.

TABLE 6

EFFECT OF VARIOUS ACIDS ON PRECIPITATION

(Acetic, phosphoric, o-phthalic, and hydrochloric acids)

Volume of Acid in 100 C c. of Water, C c.	N/20 Acetic			N/20 Phosphoric			N/20 o-Phthalic			N/20 Hydrochloric		
	Hydrogen Ion Concentration	Protective Dose in C c.	Milligrams Nitrogen per C c.	Hydrogen Ion Concentration	Protective Dose in C c.	Milligrams Nitrogen per C c.	Hydrogen Ion Concentration	Protective Dose in C c.	Milligrams Nitrogen per C c.	Hydrogen Ion Concentration	Protective Dose in C c.	Milligrams Nitrogen per C c.
15	Not done	0.5	0.15	6.2	0.0125	0.80	4.5	0.5	0.2			
13	Not done	0.5	0.3	6.25	0.0125	0.91	4.7	0.2	0.3			
11	Not done	0.5	0.54	6.4	0.0125	0.97	5.3	0.2	0.56			
10	Not done	0.05	0.7	6.5	0.0125	0.85	5.5	0.0125	0.61	4.8	0.0	0.64
8	Not done	0.025	1.01	6.7	0.0125	0.85	5.95	0.0125	0.91	5.4	0.025	0.57
6	Not done	0.025	0.77	6.8	0.025	0.83	6.5	0.0125	0.92	6.4	0.0125	0.91
4	Not done	0.05	1.0	7.1	0.0125	0.84	6.8	0.0125	0.89	6.8	0.0125	0.89
2	Not done	0.025	0.84	7.4	0.025	0.82	7.3	0.0125	0.91	7.5	0.0125	0.88
0	Not done	0.025	0.7	7.6	0.0125	0.81	7.6	0.0125	0.78	7.6	0.0125	0.71
Original serum	Not done	0.025	11.5	7.8	0.0125	11.5	7.8	0.0125	11.5	7.8	0.0125	11.5

Ten c c. of serum (the same in all) precipitated in 100 c c.; mixture allowed to stand over night in icebox. After decanting, precipitate was centrifugalized and then dissolved in 10 c c. of 1% sodium chloride.

EFFECT OF FOUR MEMBERS OF THE FATTY ACID SERIES

As stated, acetic acid was found to denature the protective globulin with a resultant loss in potency. The effect of other members of this fatty acid group, propionic, valeric, and butyric, was studied in a preliminary way.

Amounts of the several diluted acids sufficient to bring the PH of the supernatant serum 6.8 was mixed with distilled water to make a volume of 100 c c., and 10 c c. of serum were added. The precipitate was allowed to settle over night, centrifugalized, and dissolved in 10 c c. of physiologic salt solution. In order to obtain the optimum yield, the precipitate was not washed. In addition, as a control one sample of serum was diluted with water only.

TABLE 7

EFFECT OF FOUR MEMBERS OF THE FATTY ACID SERIES

(All mice received injections of 0.5 c c. of a 16-hour broth culture diluted 1: 10)

Name of Acid	Dilution of Globulin Solution					
	1:10	1:20	1:40	1:80	1:160	1:320
Acetic	S	S	S	S	S	84
	S	S	S	S	S	S
Propionic	S	S	S	S	70	24
	S	S	S	S	S	36
Butyric	S	36	S	S	36	24
	S	S	S	S	S	S
Valeric	S	S	S	S	S	36
	S	S	S	S	S	66
Water control	S	S	S	66	24	30
	S	S	S	S	S	44
Control of organism	1:10,000,000		1:1,000,000			
	36		36			

Sufficient of each acid was added to make a resultant PH of 6.8 in supernatant serum diluted 1:10.

Table 7 shows that there was little, if any, difference in the results obtained with the various acids, but with this serum the acids used in these concentrations produced slightly more protective substance than did water alone. These results are similar to those obtained by the use of citric, tartaric, hydrochloric, phosphoric, and o-phthalic acids. It should be mentioned that considerable variation has been found in the way various samples of serums behave toward dilution with water and toward acidulated water, due either to difference in buffer action or perhaps to variation in globulin content. Although careful comparison with a sufficient number of serums has not yet been made of the action of the different acids, results obtained indicate that precipitation with phosphoric acid leaves the least amount of protective substance in the supernatant. If true, this is due to the fact that the globulin in question is less soluble in phosphates than in salts of other acids used.[7]

[7] Hardy, W. B.: Proc. Roy. Soc., 1907, 79 B, p. 413.

EFFECT OF MOLECULAR CONCENTRATION OF PHOSPHATE BUFFERS ON THE PRECIPITATION OF PROTECTIVE SUBSTANCE

In the beginning of these studies on the influence of hydrogen ion concentration, buffer mixtures were used because of the relative insolubility of euglobulin in phosphate (Hardy [7]). The following experiment is reported to emphasize the necessity of using diluted phosphate mixtures to favor complete precipitation in subsequent washing of the precipitated globulin. Hardy has shown that globulin free from salts does not precipitate completely in water. This fact became of importance in our studies on antibodies. From table 8 it can be seen that a phosphate buffer mixture of P_H 6.2 in a concentration of M/400 or

TABLE 8

EFFECT OF MOLECULAR CONCENTRATION OF PHOSPHATE BUFFERS ON THE PRECIPITATION OF PROTECTIVE SUBSTANCE

(All mice received injections of 0.5 c c. of a 16-hour broth culture diluted 1: 10)

Molecular Concentration	Dilutions of Globulin Solution				
	Undiluted	1:10	1:20	1:30	1:40
M/25	S	20	18	60	18
	S	60	S	S	36
M/50	S	60	30	30	44
	S	S	46	47	S
M/100	S	S	60	36	24
	S	S	S	60	S
M/400	S	S	S	46	60
	S	S	S	46	84
M/1000	S	S	72	36	36
	S	S	S	S	36
Water control	S	S	36	36	47
	S	S	S	48	72

Ten c c. of serum precipitated in 100 c c. of the phosphate mixtures indicated above. Precipitate dissolved in 10 c c. of physiologic salt solution.

less does not interfere with a quantitative collection of the globulin from serum diluted 1 : 10. An M/500 phosphate buffer solution was found to have an ideal concentration for washing with a minimum loss of antibody suspensions from type 1 serum.

EFFECT OF HYDROGEN ION CONCENTRATION OF PHOSPHATE BUFFERS ON THE PRECIPITATION OF PROTECTIVE SUBSTANCE

In the foregoing, it has been shown that M/400 phosphate mixtures reported in table 8, having a hydrogen ion concentration of P_H 6.2, gave optimum conditions for the precipitation of the protective globulin. This experiment was planned to show the influence of the hydrogen ion concentration of phosphate buffers on precipitation of diluted serum.

M/100 was chosen instead of M/400 or M/500 so that the end-point might be more definite. It must be borne in mind that the final hydrogen ion concentration of the serum diluted 1:10 in buffer solutions of various P_H has not the same reaction as the buffer salts, due to the stabilizing buffer action of the serum. However, serum diluted with relatively alkaline buffer solutions approaches the hydrogen ion concentration of these buffers more closely than it does those on the acid side. The results, shown in table 9, are interesting. Apparently there was maximum precipitation of protective substance both in an

TABLE 9

EFFECT OF HYDROGEN ION CONCENTRATION OF PHOSPHATE BUFFERS ON THE PRECIPITATION OF PROTECTIVE SUBSTANCE

(All mice received injections of 0.5 c c. of a 16-hour broth culture diluted 1: 10)

Hydrogen Ion Concentration	Dilutions of Globulin Solution		
	Undiluted	1:10	1:20
5	S	23	22
	S	S	84
5.5	S	60	36
	S	S	46
6	S	S	S
	S	S	S
6.5	S	60	46
	S	S	84
7	S	36	22
	S	36	36
7.5	20	36	36
	36	60	36
8	S	S	S
	S	S	S
8.5	S	36	23
	S	96	22

Ten c c. samples serum A18 precipitated in M/100 phosphate buffer solution at varying P_H. Precipitate washed once in 40 c c. of M/200 of respective P_H solutions, centrifugalized, and taken up in 10 c c. of physiologic salt solution.

acid and also in an alkaline range. The hydrogen ion concentration of antipneumococcus serum diluted 1:10 averages P_H 7.8. Considering this in connection with the fact shown above, i. e., that maximum precipitation occurs both on the acid and on the alkaline side, it seems that the protective globulin posesses two zones of hydrogen ion concentration in which there is low solubility, thus pointing toward a relatively high basic nature of type 1 antibody.

PERCENTAGE OF RECOVERY FROM SERUM FROM DIFFERENT HORSES

In the previous experiments in which 10 c c. of serum was the experimental amount, it was seen that a very high percentage of the protective substance was found in the precipitate, despite the fact that the supernatant still had considerable protective value. In certain large lots of serum it was observed that the yield of protective globulin was relatively smaller than in small lots. It became essential to confirm this observation by an experiment of sufficient magnitude to verify the evidence on this point.

In this experiment, precipitation was brought about by pouring 1 liter of serum into 15 liters of distilled water containing 40 c c. of phosphoric acid. On the average, the resultant hydrogen ion concentration of the supernatant of all lots of serum gave P_H 6.78. The precipitate obtained with each lot was washed once with the same volume of distilled water as that of the first diluent. Instead of collecting in a Sharples centrifuge, the precipitate after first settling was poured into tall graduates and allowed to settle for 48 hours in the icebox at 4 C. At the end of that time, sufficient sodium chloride to make 3% con-

TABLE 10

PERCENTAGE OF RECOVERY OF PROTECTIVE SUBSTANCE ON DILUTION WITH WATER ACIDULATED WITH PHOSPHORIC ACID

(All mice received injections of 0.5 c c. of a 16-hour broth culture diluted 1: 5)

Horse	Date Bled	Serum		Supernatant		Precipitate		
		Volume	Protective Dose	Hydrogen Ion Concentration	Protective Dose	Volume	Protective Dose	Milligrams Nitrogen per C c.
008	8/12	3,200	1:20	6.83	1:10 (+)	1,150	1:80	3.32
994	8/12	3,400	1:80	6.89	1:10 (+)	550	1:160	3.5
994	7/29	3,500	1:40	6.86	1:10 (+)	1,300	1:80	2.22
A32	8/13	3,200	1:20	6.87	1:10 (—)	1,400	1:40	2.22
352	....	3,750	1:20	6.78	1:10 (—)	2,150	1:80	2.24
A17	8/ 5	1,500	1:20	6.77	1:10 (—)	350	1:60	2.26
993	7/29	1,600	1:40	6.80	1:10 (—)	800	1:50	2.1
A17	8/20	1,500	1:20	6.76	1:10 (—)	300	1:40	2.35
356	7/29	3,900	1:10	6.76	1:10 (+)	1,600	1:10	2.37
994	7/15	2,000	1:20	6.75	1:10 (+)	620	1:60	2.02
A23	7/29	3,800	1:10	6.73	1:10 (—)	1,500	1:20	1.23
A23	8/13	1,400	1:20	6.78	1:10 (+)	300	1:40	2.16
A32	7/28	2,200	1:20	6.65	1:10 (—)	900	1:40	2.00

(+) indicates protection; (—) indicates failure to protect.

centration was added to each precipitate. This procedure was followed throughout with the exception of serums A and B. In this instance, these were centrifugalized in order to reduce the volume of the precipitate. Otherwise, as may be judged by the nitrogen content of each, 48 hours' settling yielded a nearly uniform precipitate.

The total number of protective units (table 10) in the 35 liters of serum used was 1,860,000, as calculated by multiplying that dilution which protected against a million MLD by the total number of cubic centimeters of serum, and again by 2 (since 0.5 c c. was the dose injected). The total number of units in the concentrate was 1,372,400, which was 74% of its total number. Thus the loss in protective units was 26%. In a parallel experiment, the loss was reduced to 20%. A calculation of the total nitrogen in the combined lots of serum, which has on an average 11.5 mg. of nitrogen per c c., and in the mixed concentrate shows that the former contained 402.075 gm. and the latter 29.80 gm. If correction is made so that the volume of concentrate is increased to a volume which would contain the same number of units as the original serum, the ratio then becomes 402.77 : 37.77; in other words, the serum has 10.7 times more nitrogen per unit of protection than does the concentrate.

At this point it should be emphasized that with the type 1 pneumococcus (Neufeld) used as the test organism throughout this work, although of such virulence that 3 to 30 organisms caused the death of a mouse in from 36 to 48 hours, a larger number of units per c c. both with the serum and with the dissolved precipitate was found than in parallel tests with other strains of penumococcus (e. g., the Park and Wadsworth strains) of like virulence. However, as the same strain was used in testing both the serum and the concentrate, the validity of the comparison is not effected, although the number of protective units in both serum and concentrate is higher than would be the case had some other strain been employed.

It has been quite evident throughout this work that the unit value of antipneumococcus serum or its antibody solution varies, depending on the strain of pneumococcus used to determine its titer. Even when the same pneumococcus is used under standard conditions, there is a variation. In other words, it is not possible at present to determine the strength of antipneumococcus serum with anything like the accuracy of the tests used for diphtheria antitoxin.

COMPARISON OF AMOUNT OF PROTECTIVE SUBSTANCE OBTAINED FROM SINGLE SAMPLE OF SERUM BY AMMONIUM SULPHATE AND BY DILUTION METHOD

One experiment will be reported of a comparison between the amount of protective globulin separated (*a*) by simple dilution with 10 volumes of water, and (*b*) by dilution with an equal volume of saturated ammonium sulphate solution. This percentage of saturation of the serum with ammonium sulphate was used because it precipitates the pseudoglobulin as well as the euglobulin fraction. In the precipitation by ammonium sulphate, serum was first diluted with 10 volumes of water. By the use of 30% and 38% saturation (the percentage Avery [1] found optimum for pneumococcus serums) with ammonium sulphate, in addition to the comparison of the yields by the two methods, an attempt was made to precipitate the residual protective substance in the supernatant after precipitation by dilution with water. The usual procedure of precipitation with ammonium sulphate and separation of the salt by subsequent dialysis was employed. As can be seen from table 11, the original serum in the volume used in the experiment (200 c c.) contained 16,000 units, while the number of units in the dissolved precipitate by the method of water dilution was 12,000. In the precipitate obtained by ammonium sulphate it was 5,280. In the total of the supernatant (estimation from 500 c c. sample) precipitated by

TABLE 11

COMPARISON OF AMOUNT OF PROTECTIVE SUBSTANCE OBTAINED FROM A SINGLE SAMPLE OF SERUM BY AMMONIUM SULPHATE AND BY DILUTION METHOD

Fractions	Dilution Protecting Against 0.5 C c. Culture Diluted 1:10	Total Volume in Separate Fractions	Total Number of Units in Separate Fractions	Units Adjusted to 200 C c. of Serum
(1) Precipitate from 200 c c. serum diluted with 2,000 c c. distilled water	0.002	24	12,000	12,000
(2) Supernatant serum after precipitate collected	1.0	2,200	1,100	1,100
(3) Precipitate from 500 c c. supernatant with ammonium sulphate				
(a) 30% saturation	1.0	135	67.5	230
(b) 38% saturation	0.5	85	85	340
(c) 50% saturation	0.5	230	230	1,040
(4) 50 c c. serum diluted to 550 with water and precipitated with 50% saturated ammonium sulphate	0.25	330	1,320	5,280
Original serum	0.0125	200	16,000	16,000

	1:10,000,000	1:1,000,000	1:100,000
Control of organism	36	36	36
Number of organisms injected (plate method)	3	13	148

30% and also 38% saturation with ammonium sulphate, there were, respectively, 230 and 340 units. It can thus be seen, after precipitation by dilution, that approximately one third (1,100 units) of the protective substance remaining in the supernatant was recovered by 38% saturation and one-fourth by 30% saturation with ammonium sulphate. The total number of units obtained by the dilution method added to the number in the supernatant was 13,100. This is 3,000 less than the number in the original serum, a loss of 18%. Since 12,000 units were obtained by dilution method, the yield was 75%.

It would be unwise at this time and from this single sample of serum to make general deductions concerning the relative value of the two methods. To decide this point, much work will be required on serums from many horses. However, the foregoing results indicate that the separation of the protective globulin from type 1 antipneumococcus serum by the dilution method compares favorably with the more difficult ammonium sulphate technic.

EFFECT OF VARIOUS PRESERVATIVES ON THE POTENCY OF TYPE 1 ANTIBODY CHLOROFORM

The effect of different preservatives on type 1 antibodies has been studied, and although the work is not complete, a few experiments will be reported. Chloroform coagulates the water-insoluble globulin. That is, it changes it so that not only is it no longer soluble in neutral salts, but also in dilute acid and alkali. The first experiment is given in table 12.

TABLE 12

INFLUENCE OF CHLOROFORM ON PROTECTIVE SUBSTANCE, ONE AND SIX HOUR EXPOSURES

(All mice received injections of 0.5 c c. of a 16-hour broth culture diluted 1: 10)

Samples	Milligrams of Nitrogen per C c.	Dilutions of Globulin Solution						
		Undiluted	1:5	1:10	1:20	1:40	1:80	1:160
Control	1.9	S	..	S	S	S	84	46
		S		S	S	S	S	S
1 hour	0.09	S	S	S	36			
		S	S	S	24			
6 hours	±	24	18	36	24			

A sample of protective globulin dissolved in sodium chloride was divided in six 10 c c. portions, and to each was added an equal volume of chloroform. The mixtures were then shaken for a specified time, namely, 1, 2, 3, 4, 5, and 6 hours. Because of an accident, only the supernatant from the 1 and 6 hour samples were tested. Before testing, the chloroform was reduced as much as possible by suction. As indicated in table 11, all the protective globulin when extracted for 6 hours with chloroform was completely precipitated, and the supernatant was practically free from protein.

The foregoing experiment was repeated, the time of shaking being reduced to 5 instead of 6 hours. Moreover, 3 other portions, respectively dissolved in sodium hydroxide, in hydrochloric acid, and suspended in water, were treated in the same manner. A study of table 13 reveals results which might have been expected. About 80% of the globulin dissolved in sodium chloride was denatured; i. e., became insoluble in neutral salts. On the other hand, the globulin dissolved in hydrochloric acid and in sodium hydroxide precipitated only after coagulation, since denatured globulin is soluble in these solvents, and thus more remained in solution; while the suspension in water was affected much less rapidly, due undoubtedly to the slow penetration of chloroform.

In addition to the observation that globulin in the various extracts was gradually precipitated by 5 hour extraction with chloroform, it was found (table 13) that the precipitated globulin was devoid of protective properties, i. e., the globulin was so modified by chloroform that it was no longer soluble in neutral salts and also had lost its protective power. An interesting corollary is found by comparing the protective value of the globulin which remained in solution after chloroform extraction with its nitrogen content. While there is considerable variation in nitrogen content, the amount of nitrogen required to protect against a million MLD is very constant. This furnishes additional evidence of the protein nature of antibodies.

TABLE 13

INFLUENCE OF CHLOROFORM ON PROTECTIVE SUBSTANCE IN DIFFERENT SOLVENTS—5 HOUR EXPOSURE

(All mice received injections of 0.5 c c. of a 16-hour broth culture diluted 1: 10)

Solution	Dilution of Supernatant						Milligrams Nitrogen per C c.	Nitrogen in Protective Dose
	1:1	1:5	1:10	1:20	1:40	1:80		
I. Sodium chloride.......	S	96	36	36	18	36	0.25	0.05
	S	9 da.	132	S	S	132		
II. Hydrochloric acid.....	S	S	S	S	132	96	0.89	0.045
	S	S	S	S	S	9 da.		
III. Sodium hydroxide....	S	S	S	72	36	36	0.58	0.058
	S	S	S	S	30	72		
IV. Water suspension, dissolved in sodium chloride	S	S	72	24	36	20	0.30	0.03
	S	S	S	S	48	36		
V. Precipitate from sodium chloride soluble in hydrochloric acid	36	36	96	20	20	20	0.25	
	72	72	144	36	20	36		
Control..................	S	..	S	S	S	96	1.27	0.032
	S	..	S	S	S			

Control of organism	1:10,000,000	1:1,000,000	1:100,000
	72	72	36

EFFECT OF ETHER

In a fashion similar to the foregoing, the effect of ether was estimated on portions of the same lot of globulin as used in the chloroform experiment. Moreover, in addition to the supernatant, the precipitated globulin and the ether-soluble portions were tested. Equal parts of ether and solution were shaken for 5 hours. This procedure was possible because the globulin is but slowly denatured by ether, and is not coagulated after exposure for 5 hours. The results observed (see table 14) may be summarized as follows:

1. The ether-soluble fraction of the globulin dissolved in sodium hydroxide, sodium chloride, hydrochloric acid and also suspended in

TABLE 14

EFFECT OF ETHER ON THE PROTECTIVE SUBSTANCE IN DIFFERENT SOLVENTS

(All mice received injections of 0.5 c c. of a 16-hour broth culture diluted 1: 10)

Solution	Dilutions					Milligrams Nitrogen per C c.	Nitrogen in Protective Dose
	1:5	1:10	1:20	1:40	1:80		
I. (a) Sodium chloride supernatant	S S	96 S	S	72	48	1.29	0.129
(b) Sodium chloride precipitate in ether	S S	36	36	36	20	0.17	0.085
(c) Sodium chloride ether soluble	18 18	18 24	24	18	18	0.07	
II. (a) Hydrochloric acid supernatant	S S	S S	96	36	120	1.18	0.118
(b) Hydrochloric acid precipitate in ether	36 96	96 96	18	18	18	0.28	
(c) Hydrochloric acid ether soluble	20 36	18 18	18	18	36	0.08	
III. (a) Sodium hydroxide supernatant	S S	11 da. S	S S	S S	S S	1.01	0.012
(b) Sodium hydroxide precipitate in ether	S S	S S	20 S	S 18	20 S	0.38	0.038
(c) Sodium hydroxide ether soluble	18 20	18 20	18	18	18	0.03	
IV. (a) Water precipitate in ether	S S	S S	72	36	36	1.37	0.137
(b) Water ether soluble	18 36	18 36	18	18	20	0.08	
V. Untreated control	S S	S S	S S	S S	96	1.27	0.032
Control of organism	1:10,000,000			1:1,000,000			
	36			36			

Precipitate from serum 993, type 1, washed 3 times with 3 volumes of water, dissolved in same volume of sodium chloride, hydrochloric acid, and sodium hydroxide, and suspended in water. Each extracted in an equal volume of ether 4 hours in shaker. Divided into: (a) supernatant; (b) precipitate insoluble in ether; (c) soluble in ether; (b) and(c) dissolved in 10 c c. of sodium chloride.

water, when freed from ether by suction and emulsified in sodium chloride solution, not only had no protective power, but even hastened the death of mice.

2. In portions dissolved both in sodium chloride and in hydrochloric acid, in the supernatant as well as in the precipitate, a definite destruction of the protective action was observed. Similar results were noted in the case of the water suspension but to a lesser extent.

3. The globulin dissolved in alkali was stable even after 5 hours' extraction with ether, showing no material change in protective value.

Moreover, in the precipitate from the globulins dissolved in sodium chloride, and hydrochloric acid, the precipitate from water suspension and the alkaline precipitate showed constant protective value.

Although no intensive study has been made to determine the best preservative to use in the concentrating of pneumococcus antibodies, for the original serum and the prepared concentrate, in working with serum preserved with ether, chloroform, phenol, and trikresol, the serum preserved in the latter unquestionably gives the product easiest to handle and of greatest protective power. It has been found possible to use as much as 0.4% trikresols of certain makes in the concentrated antibody solution.

The ease with which the euglobulin fraction of serum becomes denatured is the difficulty in using any preservative. This tendency may be almost completely overcome by adjusting the concentrated antibodies from P_H 7.4 to 7.8 with sodium hydroxide before the trikresol has been added. Trikresols do not coagulate the globulin as rapidly as chloroform, so that it becomes feasible to add sufficient alkali to dissolve any globulin that may become denatured by long standing in contact with the preservative.

VARIABLE BEHAVIOR OF DIFFERENT SERUMS BY DILUTION WITH WATER AT VARIOUS HYDROGEN ION CONCENTRATIONS

Avery [1] found that the protective antibody of types 1 and 2 antipneumococcus serum is about equally divided between the euglobulin and the pseudoglobulin fractions. Although it has not been possible in these studies fully to confirm his findings, yet a great difference with different horse serums has been noted in this respect. As an example the experiment reported in table 15 is given. The original serum, as shown by the table, protected in a dilution of 1 : 40 as did likewise the supernatant fluid freed from a major portion of the water-insoluble globulin. However, the precipitates protected but slightly with the exception of the one obtained by addition of 4 c c. of N/10 phosphoric acid. Although hydrogen ion concentration determinations were not made in this case, this amount of phosphoric acid with the average fresh horse serum gives a P_H of from 6.6 to 6.8. It is worthy of note that the supernatant of this particular sample, like the original serum, protected also in a dilution 1 : 40. The fact that the original serum, the supernatant, and one sample of the precipitate (about P_H 6.8) all protected in a dilution 1 : 40 seemed to indicate in the case of this particular serum at this stage of immunization that the protective substance was present to a pronounced degree in the pseudoglobulin fraction only, or that substances were present in the serum antagonistic to the protective antibody and precipitated along with it.

That there is a substance in antipneumococcus horse serum antagonistic to the protective antibody has been indicated many times in the course of this work. Thus, it frequently happens that when a series of mice receive injections of pneumococci and of concentrated antibody

TABLE 15

Variable Behavior of Different Serums Toward Precipitation by Dilution with Water at Various Hydrogen Ion Concentrations

(All mice received injections of 0.5 c c. of a 16-hour broth culture diluted 1: 10)

Volume of N/20 Phosphoric Acid, C c.	Dilutions							
	Supernatant			Precipitate				
	Undiluted	1:2	1:4	1:10	1:20	1:40	1:80	1:160
12	S	S	S	84	60	36	108	18
	S	S	S	S	60	60	S	84
10	S	44	24	S	S	60	36	24
	S	S	S	S	S	120	36	48
8	S	S	S	84	S	S	108	24
	S	S	S	S	S	S	S	120
6	S	36	72	11 da.	44	18	24	18
	S	S	84	S	S	44	36	S
4	S	S	44	36	36	36	36	24
	S	S	S	S	7 da.	48	S	24
2	84	S	60	84	44	36	24	24
	S	S	S	108	84	36	S	S
1	S	S	S	S	44	36	24	24
	S	S	S	S	S	S	24	24
0	S	S	84	96	36	36	24	24
	S	S	S	12 da.	S	36	36	36
Control serum	..	..	..	S	S	S	96	
				S	S	S	S	
Control of organism	1:10,000,000			1:1,000,000				
	36			80				

Serum A17 type 1, 10 c c. precipitated with varying amounts of phosphoric acid, precipitate washed once with equal volume (100 c c.) of cold water and taken up in 10 c c. of 1% sodium chloride.

solution, those receiving the concentrated solution die, while those receiving the weaker dilutions survive up to the limit of its unit strength. For example, a series of mice receive injections of one million MLD of pneumococci and at the same time are given the antibody solution undiluted and in dilutions 1 : 5, 1 : 10, 1 : 20, 1 : 40, 1 : 80 and 1 : 160. Those receiving the undiluted serum and the dilution 1 : 5 die, while all the others are protected until a dilution of 1 : 160 is reached.

Further, if a type 2 concentrate having the properties just described is mixed with an equal portion of a type 1 concentrate which does not possess this characteristic in high concentration, it was found that all except the weakest protect mice injected with one million MLD. However, if type 2 organism is substituted for type 1 organism, the two strongest concentrations and the weakest fail to protect as before. It has not been possible to demonstrate a toxic substance in the concentrated solution, for the concentrated solution is harmless even when very large doses are injected into mice, rabbits, monkeys, and man. So that the failure to protect observed in the strong dilution must be due to some action between the antibody and the infecting organism, and it is found that this inhibition is specific to type.

TABLE 16

RELATIONSHIP OF THE AMOUNT OF PRECIPITATE TO ITS NITROGEN CONTENT AND PROTECTIVE VALUE

Number of Horse	Volume of Precipitate from 10 C c. of Serum, C c.	Milligrams Nitrogen per C c. (Duplicate)	Protective Dose (Dilution)	Nitrogen in Protective Dose
993	8	1.05 1.11	1:50	0.021
994	7	0.91 0.89	1:50	0.019
A32	10	1.20 1.19	1:60	0.020
256 3/28	4.5	0.32 0.34	1:20	0.017
256 5/27	2.6	0.22 0.21	1:5	0.042
256 B 15*	2.0	0.39 0.43	1:10	0.043
256 B 17	2.5	0.68 0.61	1:10	0.068
256 B 18	3.2	0.53 0.59	1:10	0.059

* B indicates bleeding number.

RELATIONSHIP OF THE AMOUNT OF PRECIPITATE TO ITS NITROGEN CONTENT AND PROTECTIVE VALUE

In studying the serum from a large number of horses producing type 1 antipneumococcus, results indicate that there is a relation between the yield obtained by diluting the serum with 10 volumes of water and the protective power. If, for example, before immunization a serum of a horse yields but little precipitate on dilution with water, after immunization the proportionate volume of the precipitate obtained from serum by the water dilution method appears to bear a more or less direct relation to the yield of the precipitate. This is unquestionably borne out, if the precipitate from 10 c c. of serum diluted by 100 c c. of water in a 100 c c. graduate after standing from 16 to 18 hours yields as much as 5 c c. precipitate. As is shown in table 16, horses 993, 994 and A32 producing a very good serum gave more than 5 c c. of precipitate. The protective power of the several precipitates was remarkably constant, as evidenced by the amount of nitrogen in a protective dose (0.021, 0.019, 0.020 mg. of nitrogen against one million MLD). On the other hand, horse 256 producing an average serum, which always gave less than 5 c c. of precipitate from 10 c c. of serum, yielded variable products. The first specimen (3/28) giving 4.5 c c. of precipitate was the only one which approached the quality of the products obtained from horses 993, 994 and A32. From a practical standpoint, it has been found that when the type 1 antipneumococcus serum diluted with 100 c c. of distilled water in a 1 inch 100 c c. graduate making the total volume 110 c c. gave 5 c c. precipitate or more, it was well worth concentrating. No exception to this rule has been found in a large number of serums with which we have worked. On the other hand, serums have been encountered which gave little protective precipitate on dilution while the supernatant remained highly protective. That is, some serums were found in which the protective antibody seemed to be associated with a water-soluble globulin fraction to a greater extent than with the water-insoluble fraction.

PROTECTIVE SUBSTANCE IN SERUM FROM HORSES AFTER VARYING PERIODS OF IMMUNIZATION

Although a complete series of tests during different stages of immunization of the same horses has not been carried out, yet the impression was gained that in the earlier stages of immunization, although the serum produced might be sufficiently potent to pass the government tests, nevertheless the true protective qualities of the precipitate were not as great as they were when the immunization had been continued over a longer period of time. The truth of this impression was tested by examining the serum from 2 horses which had been producing for more than a year (993 and 994), and the serums from horses just beginning to produce (A52, A60, A68 and A53). The details of the results of this experiment are given in table 17.

As in the previous experiment, in all cases 10 c c. of serum were added to 100 c c. of distilled water in a 100 c c. graduate approximately 1 inch in diameter. The following morning the precipitate, after the amount was measured, was collected in a centrifuge, then dissolved in 10 c c. of 1% sodium chloride. The amount of nitrogen both in the serum and the dissolved precipitate was estimated. Tests in triplicate for protection were carried out on (1) the supernatant, on (2) the dissolved precipitate, and on (3) the original serum.

Serums from horses 993 and 994 in this experiment and the preceding one gave similar results, for in both instances, the milligrams of nitrogen in a protective dose was 0.02. With the serum from the horses which were only in the earliest period of production, 3 (A68, A52 and A60) gave a precipitate in which at least twice as much protein was required to protect against a million MLD of pneumococci as in the case of the precipitates from serums 993 and 994. The serum from horse A53 is an exception. In this case, the precipitate had the same protective power as the serum from the 2 horses which had been immunized over a long period.

TABLE 17

PROTECTIVE SUBSTANCE IN SERUMS FROM HORSES AFTER VARYING PERIODS * OF IMMUNIZATION

Number of Horse	Volume of Precipitate, C c.	Milligrams Nitrogen per C c.		Protective Dose (Dilution)			Nitrogen in Protective Dose
		Serum	Globulin	Serum	Globulin	Supernatant 1:10	
993	8	10.9	1.35	1:60	1:60	**—0.5 c c.	0.022
994	8	12.6	1.25	1:80	1:60	+0.5 c c.	0.0208
A68	2.5	11.39	0.488	1:10	1:10	—0.5 c c.	0.048
A52	2.0	11.68	1.1	1:40	1:20	+0.5 c c.	0.055
A60	4.5	11.43	0.71	1:20	1:20	—0.5 c c.	0.035
A53	4.5	12.3	0.722	1:60	1:30	+0.5 c c.	0.024

	1:10,000,000	1:1,000,000	1:100,000
Control of organism	36 48	36 48	36 50

* Horses 993 and 994 immunized over a long period; A68, A52, A60, and A53 over a short period.

** — or + respectively 0.5 c c. of supernatant (1:10 serum) failed to protect or did protect mice in triplicate.

EFFECT OF HEATING ON THE YIELD OF THE PROTECTIVE SUBSTANCE BY DILUTION 1: 10 AT VARIOUS HYDROGEN ION CONCENTRATIONS

As previously shown, when a 10 c c. sample of fresh, potent type 1 serum is diluted 1 : 10 in distilled water in the ordinary 100 c c. graduate, a precipitate amounting to 3 to 11 c c. consisting of protective globulin may be obtained. However, if this same volume of serum is heated at 56 C. for one hour and then diluted to the same volume, no precipitation will occur. Instead the serum takes on the pearly sheen of an alkali serum in solution. The hydrogen ion concentration of the heated serum moves about 0.3 of a P_H toward the alkaline side during the process. Yet it was found in many tests that the protective power of the serum was but slightly decreased when subjected to a temperature of 56 C. for one hour.

The striking internal change of the serum as evidenced by the failure to give a precipitate when diluted 10 times with distilled water suggested a study of the heated serum at various hydrogen ion concentrations. If the explanation of this phenomenon were assumed with the formation of an alkali globulin, it might be expected that the addition of sufficient acid would neutralize the alkali globulin and precipitation would then occur. Accordingly, an experiment was conducted with portions of serum, respectively, of unheated serum, serum heated one-half hour at 56 C., and also one hour at 56 C., 10 c c. samples being diluted 10 times with varying amounts of N/20 phosphoric acid. The resulting precipitates were dissolved in the same volume of the serum before dilution (10 c c.) of 1% sodium chloride. Although no nitrogen

TABLE 18

EFFECT OF HEATING ON THE YIELD OF THE PROTECTIVE SUBSTANCE BY DILUTION 1:10 AT VARIOUS HYDROGEN ION CONCENTRATIONS

Volume of N/20 Phosphoric Acid to 10 C.c. Serum Diluted to 100 C c. in Water, C c.	Period of Exposure to Heat (56 C.)		
	One-half Hour	One Hour	Unheated
	Dilution Protecting Against 1 Million M L D		
0.0	1:40	No precipitate	1:80
7.5	1:40	No precipitate	1:80
10.0	1:40	1:40	1:80
13.5	1:40	1:40	1:80
15.0	1:40	1:20	1:10
17.5	1:20	1:10	1:5
20.0	1:20	1:10	
22.5	1:5	1:10	

determinations were made, the precipitates obtained by addition of acid appeared to be more abundant in the heated than in the unheated specimens. The sample heated one-half hour still gave a precipitate when diluted with water. The sample heated one hour failed to yield a precipitate either on simple dilution or with water containing 7.5 c c. of N/20 phosphoric acid to 100 c c. Although the precipitate was abundant when more acid was added, in both instances the protective power of the precipitate was definitely decreased, as shown in table 18, when there was a reduction in potency of approximately 50%. But it was observed that the precipitate at high acid concentrations (15 to 22.5 c c. of N/20 phosphoric acid) from the heated samples had a higher protective value than in the unheated samples with the same acid concentration. Since the supernatant serum was not tested, it is impossible to say whether the water-insoluble globulin was changed by heat into a soluble globulin, or whether actual destruction of antibody had occurred.

In addition to this experiment, the effect of heat on serum was measured by a change in the hydrogen ion concentration after the addition of relatively large amounts of phosphoric acid, and by the amount of protective substance precipitated at the various hydrogen ion concentrations. Samples of the serum were heated one-half, 1, 2 and 4 hours. The precipitate obtained by dilution of 10 c c. of serum with, respectively, 20, 22, 24, 26 c c. of N/20 phosphoric acid in 100 c c. of distilled water was redissolved in 10 c c. of 1% sodium chloride. As can be seen from table 19, the hydrogen ion concentration of the supernatant was observed to shift definitely to the alkaline side, and also the protective power of the precipitate obtained from the one-half hour, 1 hour and 2 hour

TABLE 19

EFFECT OF HEAT ON THE YIELD OF PROTECTIVE SUBSTANCE AND ON THE HYDROGEN ION CONCENTRATION OF THE SUPERNATANT

Volume of N/20 Phosphoric Acid to 10 C c. of Serum, C c.	Period of Exposure to Heat (56 C.)									
	Unheated		One-half Hour		One Hour		Two Hours		Four Hours	
	Hydrogen Ion Concentration	Protection	Hydrogen Ion Concentration	Protection	Hydrogen Ion Concentration	Protection	Hydrogen Ion Concentration	Protection	Hydrogen Ion Concentration	Protection
20	5.6	1:10	5.64	1:5	5.79	1:2	5.80	1:10	5.81	1:5
22	5.4	1:5	5.41	1:10	5.55	1:10	5.52	1:10	5.61	1:5
24	5.1	0	5.12	1:5	5.25	1:10	5.25	1:10	5.35	0
26	4.8	0	4.86	1:2	4.91	1:5	4.98	1:5	5.02	0

specimens is greater in the heated serum than in the unheated control; while, in the case of the serum heated for 4 hours, destruction of protective power was noted.

DISCUSSION

A full discussion of the results reported in this paper will be reserved until other work, now in progress, shall have been published. In this connection, mention should be made of the work of Caruso and Izar [8] because it presents points of similarity with the work which has just been described. These investigators reported studies in which precipitates were obtained, by simple dilution with water, with and without the addition of the specific antigen, from the serum of rabbits immunized against ox cells, ox serum, a number of syphilitic serums, and serum from patients with Malta fever. In this case, the presence

[8] Riforma med., 1922, 38, p. 145.

of antibodies in the precipitate was inferred by positive complement-fixation tests, and, in the case of Malta fever because micrococcus melitensis was agglutinated by the dissolved precipitate. Their work on the syphilitic serum confirms that of the writer in 1916,[9] in which the complement-fixing antibody was shown to be associated with the water-insoluble globulin fraction of syphilitic cerebrospinal fluid, and also of serum which gave a positive Wassermann reaction.

Recently, Harold [10] by diluting syphilitic serum with water acidulated with acetic acid also has shown that the syphilitic complement-fixing antibody is associated with the euglobulin fraction of the serum. In a similar fashion, the results of yet unpublished experiments by the writer show that, in the case of antimeningococcus serum and in the case of serum against certain streptococci (veridans and other nonhemolyzing strains) the antibodies, as determined by protection tests, are present in the water-insoluble fraction of the serum. It would seem that this and similar work render possible the isolation and purification of the antibodies of immune serum, and may well point the way to important advances in our knowledge of immunity.

SUMMARY

The protective antibody in type 1 antipneumococcic serum, so far studied, is, to say the least, in large part associated with a water-insoluble globulin, which is precipitated by dilution 1 : 10 in water or with water acidulated by varying amounts of hydrochloric, o-phthalic, phosphoric, tartaric, citric acids in a range of hydrogen ion concentrations between P_H 5.5 and P_H 7.8. The optimum hydrogen ion concentration for precipitation when the serum is diluted 1 : 10 has not been definitely determined.

The amount of protective substance obtained in diluting serum 1 : 10 is apparently increased by the use, in concentration of M/200 to M/400, of phosphate buffers.

With the single sample of serum precipitation of type 1 antibody by 50% saturation with ammonium sulphate failed to give a yield as high as simple dilution with water 1 : 10.

Chloroform denatures globulin and destroys the protective action of antibody to a degree corresponding to the extent of the removal of protein from the solution.

[9] Tr. Sect. Path. & Physiol., Am. Med. Assn., 1917, p. 73.
[10] Jour. Royal Army Med. Corps, 1922, 39, p. 83.

Extraction with ether in acid or sodium chloride solution destroys a considerable part of the protective value of this globulin, while in alkaline solution 5 hour extraction has little or no effect.

An apparent exception to the association of the protective body with the water-insoluble fraction of serum is given in the case of a sample of horse serum possessing protective value, but yielding little protective precipitate.

In relatively abundant precipitates, there seems to be a direct relation between the protective value of the precipitate and the yield.

The precipitate obtained by dilution of serum from horses immunized but a short time has less protective value per milligram of nitrogen than the precipitate from horses immunized over a longer period.

Heat alters the type 1 antipneumococcus serum so that no precipitate results from dilution with 10 volumes of distilled water. On the addition of acid, a precipitate is formed which has less protective power than the unheated control.

QUANTITATIVE CHANGES IN BLOOD SUGAR AND IN BLOOD LACTIC ACID IN CANINE ANAPHYLAXIS

MARGERY McCULLOUGH
AND
FRANCIS I. O'NEILL

From the Laboratory of Bacteriology and Experimental Pathology, and the Laboratory of Biochemistry, Stanford University, California

Changes in blood sugar and blood lactic acid during anaphylactic shock have been noted in certain animal species. Hiersch and Williams,[1] for example, found blood sugar increased in about half of their anaphylactic rabbits. Zunz and La Barre[2] report a marked hyperglycemia in the initial stages of guinea-pig anaphylaxis, accompanied by an increase in blood lactic acid. This was followed by a hypoglycemia with decreased blood lactic acid.

Blood sugar and blood lactic acid determinations have apparently not been made in canine anaphylaxis. The only study of carbohydrate changes in canine anaphylaxis is that of O'Neill,[3] who noted that glycogen disappears almost quantitatively from the canine liver during the first 15 minutes of typical anaphylactic shock.

METHODS

Our dogs were sensitized by a subcutaneous injection of 0.3 to 0.5 c c. horse serum per kg. of body weight, followed 2 days later by an intracardiac injection of the same dose. The anaphylactic tests were made under morphine-ether anesthesia, between the 21st and 24th day after the intracardiac injection. The dose which usually produced shock was from 1 to 2 c c. horse serum per kg. of body weight, injected intravenously.

Blood sugar determinations were made by the Meyer-Bailey[4] modification of the Lewis-Benedict technic. Lactic acid was determined by the method of Harrop.[5]

CHANGES IN BLOOD SUGAR

Morphine-Ether Anesthesia.—Since Epstein, Reiss and Branower[6] and others report a hyperglycemia during ether anesthesia, we have made control tests of the effects on blood sugar of the morphine-ether anes-

Received for publication, March 16, 1925.

[1] Jour. Infect. Dis., 1922, 30, p. 175.
[2] Compt. rend. Soc. de biol., 1924, III, p. 121.
[3] Proc. Soc. Exper. Biol. & Med., 1924, 22, p. 124.
[4] The Chemical Analysis of Blood, 1924, p. 92.
[5] Proc. Soc. Exper. Biol. & Med., 1921, 17, p. 162.
[6] Jour. Biochem., 1916, 26, p. 25.

thesia used. Dogs were bled intracardially, then given the customary anesthetic. Composite data thus obtained are recorded in *B,* fig. 1.

Morphine-ether anesthesia causes a rise in blood sugar from the initial 0.11% to 0.17%. The blood sugar is maintained at this level for about 15 minutes, then gradually decreases to about 0.14% by the end of one hour. This blood sugar curve constitutes the base line for the interpretation of the following results.

Normal Dogs.—When 1 to 2 c c. horse serum per kg. of body weight are injected intravenously into normal dogs, the blood sugar remains fairly constant within the limits of the experimental error during the first hour, then slowly increases, reaching 0.25% by the end of the second hour (*N,* fig. 1).

This increase shows that horse serum is toxic for normal dogs, a toxicity not revealed by changes in arterial blood pressure, the currently used index in canine anaphylaxis.

"Negatively Sensitized" Dogs.—After the usual sensitizing doses of horse serum, about 10% of our dogs failed to become hypersensitive, showing no fall in arterial blood pressure on intravenous injection with horse serum, three weeks later. These dogs are referred to as "negatively sensitized."

When 1 to 2 c c. horse serum per kg. of body weight are injected intravenously into "negatively sensitized" dogs, no changes in the blood sugar are observed within the limits of the experimental error other than those due to the anesthetic (*I,* fig. 1). These dogs are, therefore, resistant to the normal toxicity of horse serum, and should be regarded as immune.

Typical Anaphylactic Shock.—Intravenous injection of 1 to 2 c c. horse serum per kg. of body weight into typically sensitized dogs (kymograph control) causes a rapid rise in blood sugar, the sugar concentration reaching about 0.25% by the end of the first 20 minutes (*A,* fig. 2). The percentage then gradually decreases to about 0.17% by the end of 2 hours.

Glucose Injections.—Glucose injected intravenously into normal dogs in amounts equivalent to the estimated total glycogen content of the liver (1.5 gm. per kg. of body weight) reproduces within the limits of the experimental error the blood sugar curve of typical anaphylaxis after the first 15 minutes (*C,* fig. 2). This finding is in line with O'Neill's observation that glycogen disappears quantitatively from the liver during the first 15 minutes of canine anaphylaxis.

CHANGES IN BLOOD LACTIC ACID

Morphine-ether anesthesia causes a 15% increase in blood lactic acid during the first 15 minutes, the lactic acid gradually falling to normal by the end of 2 hours (*B*, fig. 3).

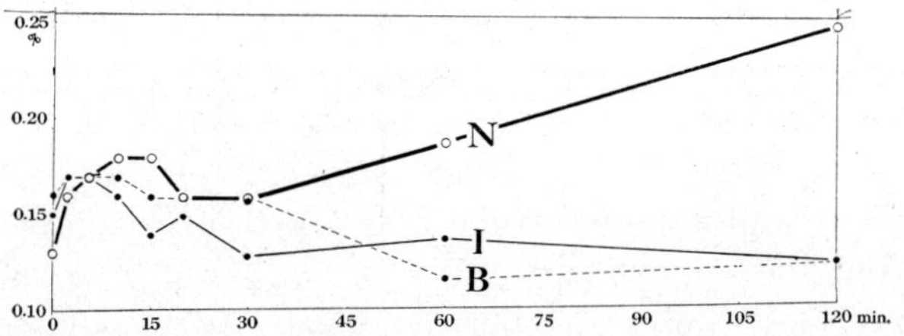

Fig. 1.—Quantitative changes in blood sugar. Composite data obtained from three normal dogs concerning: *B*, morphine-ether anesthesia; *N*, horse serum injection; *I*, horse serum injection into "negatively sensitized" dogs.

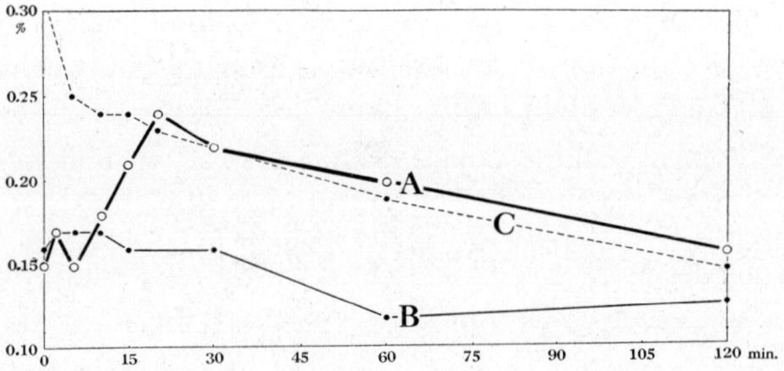

Fig. 2.—Quantitative changes in blood sugar. *B*, morphine-ether anesthesia; composite data, 3 normal dogs. *A*, typical anaphylactic shock (kymograph control); composite data, 7 dogs; *C*, glucose injection; composite data, 3 normal dogs.

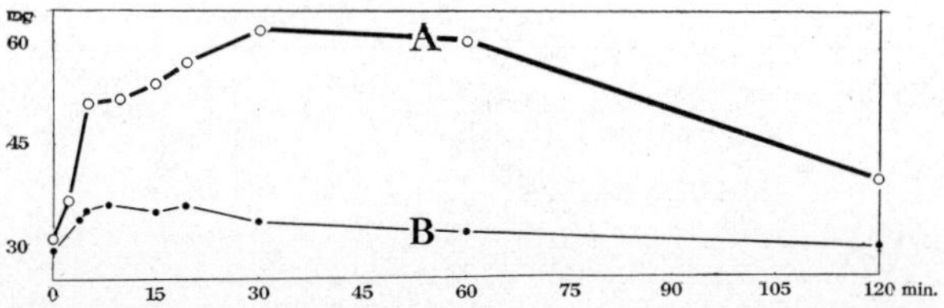

Fig. 3.—Quantitative changes in blood lactic acid. *A*, typical anaphylactic shock (kymograph control); composite data, 6 dogs; readings in mg. per 100 c c.; *B*, morphine-ether anesthesia, normal dogs; composite data, 4 dogs.

Typical anaphylactic shock causes the blood lactic acid to increase 100% during the first 30 minutes, gradually decreasing to about 40% above normal by the end of 2 hours (*A*, fig. 3).

SUMMARY

Horse serum injected intravenously into normal dogs causes a gradual increase in the sugar content of the blood, the blood sugar rising to about twice the normal percentage by the end of two hours. This increase indicates a toxic action of horse serum on normal dogs, not shown by changes in arterial blood pressure, the currently used index in canine anaphylaxis.

Horse serum injected intravenously into "negatively sensitized" dogs causes no changes in blood sugar during the first two hours. These dogs, therefore, are resistant to the normal toxicity of horse serum, and should be regarded as immune.

During typical canine anaphylactic shock, the blood sugar increases rapidly, reaching nearly twice the normal concentration by the end of 20 minutes. The blood sugar then gradually decreases, being but slightly above normal by the end of 2 hours. After the first 15 minutes, the curve thus obtained is identical with the blood sugar curve obtained by intravenous injection of an amount of glucose equivalent to the total estimated glycogen content of the liver.

During typical canine anaphylactic shock, the blood lactic acid increases to twice the normal concentration within the first 30 minutes, gradually falling to about 40% above normal by the end of 2 hours.

QUANTITATIVE CHANGES IN TISSUE GLYCOGEN, BLOOD SUGAR, PLASMA, INORGANIC PHOSPHATES AND IN BLOOD LACTIC ACID IN CANINE HISTAMINE SHOCK

Eleanor K. Chambers and K. W. Thompson

From the Laboratory of Biochemistry, and the Laboratory of Bacteriology and Experimental Pathology, Stanford University, California

Parallel with the studies by O'Neill [1] and McCullough [2] on quantitative changes in hepatic glycogen and blood sugar in canine anaphylaxis, we have followed the quantitative changes in these substances during canine histamine shock.

Methods.—Dogs were studied under morphine-ether anesthesia. Shock was produced by intravenous injection of 3 mg. histamine per kg. of body weight. Tissue glycogen was determined by the official method of the American Association of Agricultural Chemists,[3] blood sugar by the method of Folin and Wu,[4] blood lactic acid by Clausen's method,[5] plasma inorganic phosphates by the method of Benedict.[6]

CHANGES IN TISSUE GLYCOGEN

O'Neill found that glycogen disappears almost quantitatively from the canine liver during the first 15 minutes of anaphylactic shock. We have, therefore, determined the glycogen content of canine tissues at the 15 minute stage of histamine shock, with control determinations of the glycogen content of normal tissues after 15 minutes of morphine-ether anesthesia. Our data are recorded in table 1.

The table shows that liver glycogen decreases nearly 80% during the first 15 minutes of histamine shock. Heart muscle and skeletal muscle glycogen decrease about 60%.

CHANGES IN BLOOD SUGAR

Changes in blood sugar were followed during the first hour of histamine shock, parallel determinations being made in normal dogs under control morphine-ether anesthesia.

Received for publication, March 24, 1925.

1 Proc. Soc. Exper. Biol. & Med., 1924, 22, p. 124.
2 Jour. Infect. Dis., 1925, 37, p. 225.
3 A. A. A. C., Methods of Analyses, 1920.
4 Jour. Biol. Chem., 1920, 41, p. 367.
5 Ibid., 1922, 52, p. 263.
6 Meyers: Chemical Analysis of Blood, 1924, p. 176.

During the first 50 minutes of morphine-ether anesthesia, there is a gradual rise in blood sugar from the initial 0.12% to 0.18% (*N*, fig. 1). This blood sugar curve constitutes the base line for the interpretation of the changes in histamine shock.

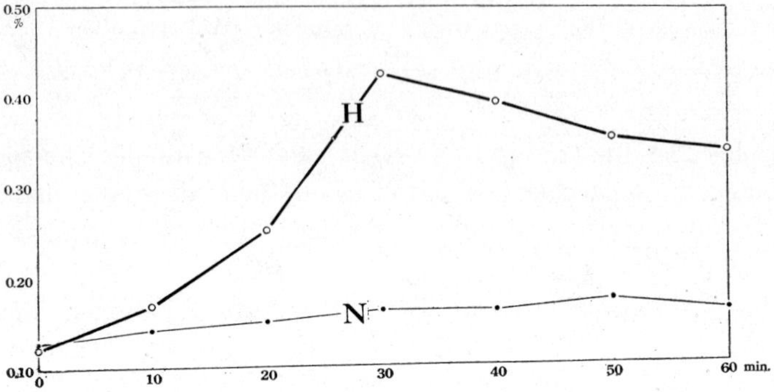

Fig. 1.—Quantitative changes in blood sugar. *N*, normal dogs, morphine-ether anesthesia; composite data, 4 dogs; *H*, histamine shock; composite data, 5 dogs.

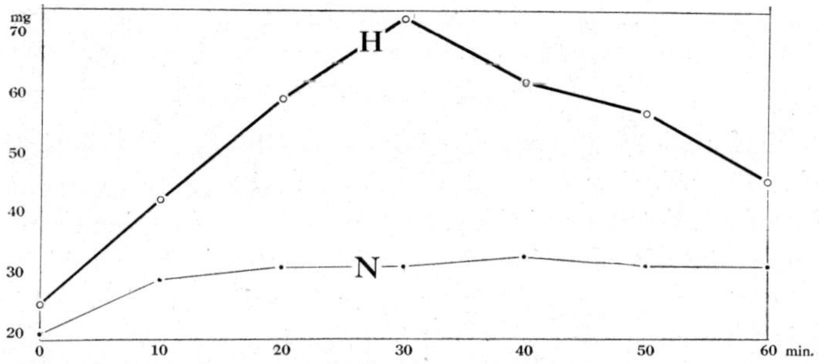

Fig. 2.—Quantitative changes in blood lactic acid, recorded in mg. per 100 c c. of blood. *N*, normal dogs, morphine-ether anesthesia; composite data, 4 dogs. *H*, histamine shock; composite data, 5 dogs.

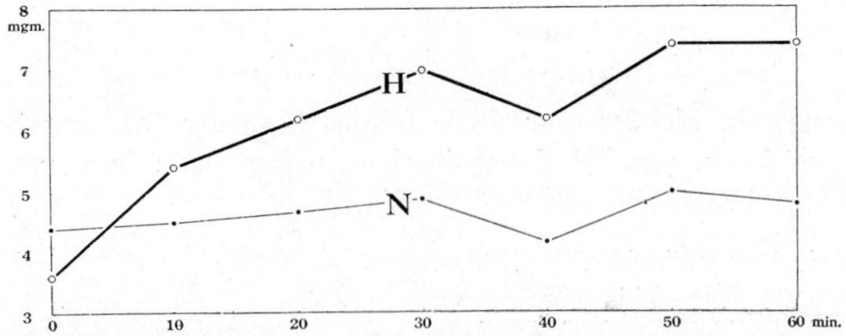

Fig. 3.—Quantitative changes in plasma inorganic phosphates, recorded in mg. per 100 c c. of plasma. *N*, normal dogs, morphine-ether anesthesia; composite data, 4 dogs; *H*, histamine shock; composite data, 5 dogs.

During the first 30 minutes of histamine shock, there is a rapid increase in blood sugar to over 0.40% (*H,* fig. 1), followed by a gradual fall to about 0.30% by the end of 60 minutes.

CHANGES IN BLOOD LACTIC ACID

Parallel determinations of blood lactic acid during morphine-ether anesthesia and histamine shock are recorded in fig. 2. Blood lactic acid increases 133% during the first 30 minutes of histamine shock, followed by a fall to about 66% above normal by the end of 60 minutes.

TABLE 1

GLYCOGEN CONTENT OF FIXED TISSUES

No.	Normal Dogs			Histamine Shock		
	Liver %	Heart Muscle %	Skeletal Muscle %	Liver %	Heart Muscle %	Skeletal Muscle %
1	3.355	2.038	1.945	1.020	0.640	0.693
2	3.190	2.832	2.170	0.750	1.010	0.730
3	3.220	1.821	2.171	0.760	0.861	0.880
4	3.950	1.946	1.880	0.529	0.764	0.801
Average	3.428	2.159	2.044	0.764	0.818	0.776
Decrease in percentage				77.7%	62.1%	62.0%

CHANGES IN PLASMA INORGANIC PHOSPHATES

Parallel determinations of plasma inorganic phosphates are recorded in fig. 3. The curve shows a 50% increase in plasma inorganic phosphates during the first 30 minutes of histamine shock, rising to a maximum of about 60% above normal by the end of 60 minutes.

SUMMARY

During the first 15 minutes of canine histamine shock, there is a decrease of nearly 80% in the glycogen content of the liver, and a 60% decrease in the glycogen content of heart muscle and skeletal muscle.

During the first 30 minutes of canine histamine shock, blood sugar increases about 200%, blood lactic acid about 133%, plasma inorganic phosphates about 50%.

These changes are similar to the changes reported by O'Neill and McCullough in canine anaphylaxis, and differ from them mainly in that the maximum changes are not reached until the end of 30 minutes, instead of at the end of 15 minutes as in anaphylaxis.

CLASSIFICATION OF SPORE-FREE GRAM-NEGATIVE, AEROBIC RODS

WITH SPECIAL REFERENCE TO FERMENTATION AND PROTEOLYSIS

ROGER G. PERKINS

From the Department of Hygiene and Bacteriology, School of Medicine, Western Reserve University, Cleveland, Ohio

There are few tribes among bacteria which have been so discussed. The number of apparent strains, the diversity of chemical activities, the variety and variability of pathogenic activities, and the importance of certain groups as indicators, have led to the publication of many articles which while they agree in certain fundamentals, disagree sufficiently to cause much confusion. After various arrangements, authors are fairly well agreed on the following grouping:

Typhoid group, including both typhoid and dysentery (Eberthella, Bergey)
Paratyphoid group (Salmonella, Bergey)
Colon group, including also such paracolon organisms as do not fall under typhoid and paratyphoid (Escherichia, Bergey)
Proteus group (Proteus, Bergey)
Mucosus capsulates group (Encapsulata, Bergey)
Nonfermenters (Alcaligenes, Bergey)

There is also an "aerobacter" group, invented by Beijerinck and variously peopled by different authors. This has not received universal acceptance.

Comparative familiarity with the colon-aerogenes-capsulatus series automatically confines my efforts to these. While my suggested revision of classification bases makes reference to the other groups necessary, both as concerns their position in the scheme and the inclusion of certain varieties in one or the other group, there is no attempt at their internal rearrangement.

In the study of colon-aerogenes-capsulatus, there are at least three different points of view, each with variations dependent on the personal equation and interests. The morphologist and the chemist have based their schemes on morphology and on chemistry, and of late the bacteriologists in charge of water supplies have sought to determine whether the organisms which passed filters or disinfectors indicated sewage pollution.

Received for publication, March 25, 1925.

It is owing to the stimulus from these last that much recent research has been done. Ever since it was first shown that the presence of fecal organisms in water was an indication of danger, the sanitarian has naturally been suspicious of waters containing such organisms, and the burden of proof of safety has been placed on the water operators. Driven by the economic necessity for a clear and palatable water at a reasonable price, their natural reaction was to find such proof. All agree that no human intestinal organisms should appear in a domestic water supply, but the tendency is to try to show that the organisms in their particular supply might come from animals or plants rather than from man, thus modifying the interpretation of the findings. This of course is an entirely correct thesis, though it remains essential that the proof should be satisfactory.

The investigations of the last 10 years or so have been largely chemical in character, and have determined many valuable factors. Any acceptance of these factors as fundamental bases for classification has caused trouble, partly because there is difference of opinion as to their intrinsic value, partly because there is actual disagreement as to findings, and partly because so many organisms are no longer available, and can therefore be classified on this basis by guess only. It was primarily on account of these difficulties that the present attempt has been made to determine essential bases for a classification which shall place strains formerly described but no longer accessible as well as strains still extant descriptions of organisms have led me inevitably to certain fundamentals.

1. Unless the evidence is satisfactory that we are dealing with lineal descendants of original strains, or unless the organism is so frequently found and well studied that we can be reasonably sure of its identity (as for instance B. typhosus), we can neither speak of the organism by the name originally given, nor can we add to its differential description and identifiable.

Careful analysis of the newer studies and comparisons with original attributes we ourselves have noted.

2. Varieties now in the literature, in which the foregoing has not been conformed to, have no right to the original titles.

3. Many more or less recently described characters, while in the main constant and extremely valuable, have sufficient variation in themselves or in different strains to make it necessary to place them well down the line of classification, lest we find what are probably merely varieties separated into different species or even genera.

REVIEW OF CURRENT BASES

Let us begin with a review of the classification bases now in use, to ascertain (1) which are the most stable and accurate, and (2) what sequence of chemical and morphologic distinctions will best bring together organisms which we believe to be otherwise closely related.

Virulence, pathogenicity, resistance and immunologic reactions have been uniformly unsatisfactory in the colon-aerogenes group, except for certain group reactions which have not reached smaller divisions than the genus.

Morphology.—Practically all biologic classifications are based on morphology, but it must be kept in mind that the morphologic differences in plants and animals are sufficient for a more or less complete classification, whereas in the case of bacteria we are limited to a very few.

In fact, we have only 3 main heads, form, spores, and organelles of motility, on which we can base our classification, and 2 of these are already used, since primary distinctions of our group are rod-form and absence of spores.

This forces us to sequences of morphologic and chemical characteristics, and the main complications are the determination of the relative importance, and the selection of the order.

It is agreed that some are motile and some are nonmotile, but there is no agreement as to the importance of this. Winslow [1] considers motility as unimportant and only valuable as an end point to determine varieties, while Bergey,[2] Weldin and Levine [3] and others do not agree.

Discussion with biologists and students of genetics indicates that in their belief the acquisition of organelles of motility is a more important evolutional event than the acquisition of special metabolic powers, and a strong argument in favor of that idea is the comparative permanence of the flagella as against that of the fermentative activities. Many authors have been able to change—usually temporarily, it is true—the fermentative powers of certain organisms, but I find no evidence of experiments turning a motile into a nonmotile organism as indicated by the disappearance of flagella. The variations in degree of motility, and the technical difficulties in flagella staining have tended to make observers neglect this point, and it is probable that some organisms which were

[1] Jour. Bacteriol., 1919, 4, p. 429.
[2] Manual of Determinative Bacteriology, 1923.
[3] Absts. of Bacteriol., 1923, 7, p. 13.

originally described as nonmotile would be found capable of motility under favorable conditions, if the cultures were still available.

The real key to this situation is the development of a satisfactory flagella stain, for while there are many in the literature for which the inventors claim a high percentage of success, there certainly are none which can be placed in the hands of a class or even of the average bacteriologist with hope of success, and until the diagnosis of motility is more certain, its value as a determinant is not great.

Capsules.—There is still some disagreement as to whether capsules are morphologic characteristics or are merely chemical reactions to the need of protection from outside influences. The fact of their absence under ordinary conditions of laboratory cultivation and their presence under parasitic conditions would indicate the probable justice of the latter point of view, although evidence that they actually have any protective influence when the organism is in the animal body is incomplete.[4] In any case, however, the power to form capsules seems to be an inherent character of many organisms, usually under a well controlled set of conditions, and if this be true, it is a valuable factor in classification. As a usual thing it has been thought that the presence of capsules was not consistent with motility, but Mounce[5] has described a motile capsulated bacillus, and Darling[6] finds all of the colon-aerogenes group in the mouse both motile and capsulated, so that it may be necessary to revise this idea if these observations are confirmed.

Here again, as in the case of flagella, it is in part due to the difficulty of staining capsules, and in part to the fact that they appear chiefly in animal exudates, fairly frequently in milk and serum mediums and scarcely at all in other mediums or after a number of transfers, that we shy off from the capsule as a classification basis.

Chemical Activities.—Perhaps the only strictly chemical differentiation admitted by all to be common to the group is the lack of power of retaining stain when treated by Gram's method. This is placed together with the rod-form and the absence of spores as an intrinsic character.

For a time the indol test was believed to be of importance, and various detailed methods were invented to standardize it. In Europe it still carries much weight, but the best that is ordinarily said of it here is that "organisms of this type usually do (or do not) form indol." It is interesting in this connection to note that whereas organisms of the

[4] Centralbl. f. Bakteriol., I, O., 1921, 86, p. 177.
[5] Absts. of Bacteriol., 1923, 7, p. 18.
[6] Am. Jour. Publ. Health, 1923, 13, p. 822.

capsulated group studied by Perkins and others in 1900-1907 were almost without exception good indol formers by the best technic of that time, one of the habitual statements in recent papers is that present day isolations do not (usually) have this characteristic.

Fermentation of Carbohydrates.—The widest discussion of all has centered around the metabolic activities, and notably the fermentation of a large variety of carbohydrates, with the formation of various cleavage products, most conspicuous among which are acids and gases.

Since Theobald Smith first showed how to collect the gas from fermentation so as to analyze it and to make at least a rough quantitation, the principle has been widely extended. At first only a few sugars were used, and fundamental groupings made on the relations to dextrose, lactose, and sucrose. The addition of new sugars and of carbohydrates other than sugars resulted in the formation of so many groups that imagination staggers at the possibilities. If there were any data to indicate that these fermentative activities bore some special relation to the evolution of the species from the earlier common form, we would have something to go on, but even though from time to time we are apparently able to start new activities in individual species, we have not much to go on as yet, since, as noted below, we cannot be sure whether we are establishing new powers or reestablishing powers in abeyance.

Selection of Types.—It has been the custom in group descriptions to select one member as the type, and various influences have moved the selectors. Similar considerations of heredity as those already referred to in connection with motility should be considered. It has been rather the habit to choose the most active fermenter as the type of the group. This was my own idea in connection with the capsulated group, and is also common to many other observers. But from an evolutionary standpoint it would appear that the bacteria first developed power to break down substances from which they had to draw food, and at the beginning these must have been simple, and more or less scattered. While biologists state that the power to attack any one member of a chemical group probably means the potential power to develop an attack on any other member of the group, these individual powers were acquired one by one, and lost one by one when the need disappeared, with an almost infinite series of possibilities. One can speculate indefinitely, but in the absence of knowledge as to the exact forms of food present at the birth of the bacteria, the general principle is all that is safe. It would therefore appear that an organism which can attack so great a variety of substances as B. aerogenes, or B. communior is probably a later and more experienced member of the community.

Relative Values of the Individual Carbohydrates.—Some 20 fermentable substances have been studied, with tabulations and cross-tabulations, emphasis being laid on the special carbohydrates under consideration, or the association of certain group fermentations with other chemical tests, or with habitat.

A brief summary of the historical changes of opinion as to the values of special carbohydrates as differentiating species or varieties in the colon-aerogenes-capsulatus series by their ease of fermentation is more or less as follows:

At first dextrose was the only one much used, but in view of activities in milk, one of the early standard mediums, lactose was investigated also. This set of single and double sugars naturally led to the inclusion of other single and double sugars, with equally logical extension, as methods became standardized, to various other carbohydrates. Nowadays opinions in this country have simmered down to certain definite agreements, as well as a goodly fringe of disagreements.

An organism which can break down any carbohydrate with acid or acid and gas formation can break down dextrose, so that the fermentation of this sugar may be considered an intrinsic character of a large group.

Study of the other monosaccharides indicates that while some of them are not fermented by organisms which ferment dextrose, there is not sufficient consistency to make them of value, so that galactose, mannose, levulose, sorbose, arabinose and xylose have for some time ceased to be considered as of differential value.

It is now thought that among the disaccharides, lactose and sucrose show constant reactions, though of course it is known that intensive cultivation under special conditions may change such reactions. The conditions needed are sufficiently unusual to make these variations negligible. Perkins [7] and Winslow [1] have shown that lactose and saccharose fermentations are at times delayed, and that acid and gas may not appear for several days. This must be kept in mind when dealing with organisms described only once, and noted as atypical with these sugars. Maltose, however, (a double glucose) follows dextrose so closely as to be no longer seriously considered. The action on the trisaccharide raffinose is also without differential value.

[7] Jour. Infect. Dis., 1904, 1, p. 241; 1907, 4, p. 51.

Among the colloidal polysaccharides, attempted use has been made of dextrin, starch and inulin, but as concerns this particular bacterial group they have certainly not shown up as valuable primary or even secondary differentiators.

Among the higher alcohols, glycerol has long been known as a fermentable substance. It is apparently rather refractory, so that different organisms vary in the time needed for the fermentation, and the actual power is frequently lost. Accordingly, this carbohydrate also has been given up as an essential.

Among the hexatomic alcohols, mannitol, sorbitol and dulcitol have been used. Sorbitol has been abandoned, but there are many observers who feel that mannitol, dulcitol and also a near relative, the pentatomic alcohol adonitol, are of great value especially in the typhoid, dysentery and paratyphoid groups.

Among the glucosides the only one found of value has been salicin.

Summarizing the studies on the varied group of carbohydrates, we then find that with the exception of dextrose, lactose, sucrose, mannitol, dulcitol, adonitol, and salicin, none is sufficiently constant or sufficiently correlated with other characteristics to be of any final value in classification.

In other words, by the use of these fermentable substances, following the essential morphologic classification above noted, we can get in the first place a fairly coherent group and in the second place a finer classification within the group which should bring organisms obviously related into end-groups.

On the basis of these fermentations and of the intrinsic characters noted, we have a primary division:

Common Characters, Apparently Instrinsic and Stable

Gram-negative rods, no spores, grow aerobically.

Group 1. Ferment dextrose with acid and gas. (*a*) Colon (Escherichia), (*b*) Proteus, (*c*) Paratyphoid (Salmonella).

Group 2. Ferment dextrose with acid but no gas. Typhoid-dysentery (Eberthella).

Group 3. Do not ferment dextrose or other carbohydrates. (Alcaligenes).

Group 4. Encapsulata (separate morphologic and immunologic group).

This arrangement appears satisfactory so far and may be carried farther on the same lines. Groups 1 (*a*) and 4 include all organisms which are the object of the present study, and what follows refers particularly to these groups.

Taking lactose as the next differential point and omitting the Encapsulata as a genus set aside morphologically, we find two immediate divisions:

A. Lactose fermented with acid and gas—colon group (Escherichia).
B. Lactose not fermented—(1) proteus, (2) paratyphoid (Salmonella).

This is still satisfactory, as the colon group (Escherichia) have long been noted as lactose-fermenters, and we may now come to the finer divisions within that group.

Sucrose fermentation gives us two groups:

1. B. communior and varieties, fermenting S.
   B. cloacae and varieties, fermenting S.
2. B. coli and varieties, not fermenting S.

This was long the more or less accepted basis, but as a result of the valuable chemical studies of the last few years, much uncertainty and discussion arose. The main investigations fell into two groups, those related to the methyl-red test, or high and low ratio, and to the utilization of citrates and of uric acid. These will be taken up separately with a view to determining whether they influence the classification noted so far, and if so, at what point and to what degree.

MR and VP Tests.—(Fecal vs. nonfecal, discussion.) The work of Rogers and others [8] brought in a new element, with their discovery of organisms apparently of this "intestinal" group, but found in places apparently free from pollution.

With the study of the high ratio and low ratio types, and the MR test, together with the application of the older VP test (found to be usually opposite to the MR reaction), a combination of these with certain fermentations and details as to habitat was brought out as indicating the probability of a "fecal" and a "nonfecal" group. Though at best it gave us a "probably nonfecal" group, it was much worked on and even got a temporary foothold in Standard Methods. It left us with a surely fecal B. coli, a surely fecal B. aerogenes, and a probably nonfecal B. aerogenes, together with a doubtful B. cloacae. It had of course long been appreciated that there is no known distinction between B. coli or B. aerogenes of human vs. animal digestive tracts.

Citrate and Uric Acid Utilization.—Koser,[9] with his uric acid and citrate mediums, added much of value. The indication that some organ-

[8] Rogers, Clark and Evans: Ibid., 1914, 15, p. 99. Rogers, Clark and Davis: Ibid., 1914, 14, p. 411. Rogers, Clark and Evans: Ibid., 1915, 17, p. 137. Rogers, Clark & Lubs: Jour. Bacteriol., 1918, 3, p. 231.

[9] Jour. Bacteriol., 1923, 8, p. 493; 9, p. 59.

isms otherwise indistinguishable can be sharply differentiated by their ability to obtain their living from certain simple mediums, and his observations that most of the citrate users may be found apparently apart from human and animal feces, like many VP+ and MR— forms, while most of the citrate nonusers are fecal in origin, like the low ratio forms, is a possible indication that we are dealing in the former case with organisms which have become accustomed to so varied a life that they must be able to handle anything and have not lost activities by parasitism. But, on the other hand, we find some citrate users in the digestive tract and some citrate nonusers in nature; and as the citrate users are able to flourish in feces, we are still unable to say with certainty whether a given isolation has a fecal history, and if so how recent.

Discussion of these Characterizations.—Leaving aside any detail as to actual disagreements in Voges Proskauer and methyl red reactions in the reports of different observers on what are supposed to be the same organisms, Burton and Rettger [10] state that VP is apparently more reliable than MR, and that VP+ is given by MR— organisms when acid production places them in the low acid mode, but when acid production is high the reaction is + —. They also state that it is necessary to use their special medium with its buffer. In addition, they say that variation in acid production is so great as to cast doubt on the value of biometric data in this connection. Rogers, Clark and Lubs [11] state that both the B. coli group and the aerogenes group are carbinol + — and that any but Witte's peptone is useless in the MR test. Chen and Rettger [12] state that "from the above cited observations it appears very clear that acid production even when determined by the biometric method does not furnish a sound basis for the classification of the colon-aerogenes group of bacteria." Perry and Montfort [13] show that VP and MR are not always opposite. Koser, in 1923,[9] showed marked variations in VP and MR necessitating numerous repeats, some of which resulted in stabilization while others did not. He found that the MR+ did not develop in citrate, while Chen and Rettger found that half of their MR+ cultures from soil grew in uric acid. Koser states "MR and VP appear to have lost ground in recent years; some believe them without significance in routine." Bahlman and Sohn [14] found 15% atypical

[10] Jour. Infect. Dis., 1917, 21, p. 162.
[11] Jour. Bacteriol., 1918, 3, p. 231.
[12] Ibid., 1920, 5, p. 253.
[13] Ibid., 1921, 6, p. 53.
[14] Jour. Am. Water Works Assn., 1924, 11, p. 416.

in 1223 cultures from water and in the atypicals all possible VP and MR combinations.

Summarizing such opinions of competent bacteriologists, it seems clear that while typical B. coli is almost constant in its reactions to the VP and MR tests, there are exceptions, and in the aerogenes group there is wide diversity although it is also evident that the majority of varieties found in soil have reactions opposite to B. coli. If then we use these tests as primary differentiators, the variables may start anywhere or nowhere, and may end up in brackets where they obviously do not belong. For this reason I do not believe in Bergey and Weldin and Levine's place for carbinol.

PLACE FOR GELATIN LIQUEFACTION

The classification carried to this point brings us to a choice between sucrose fermentation and gelatin liquefaction as the next differentiator. The question involves cloacae only, as Proteus has been excluded by the lactose fermentation. From its habitat and all its other characteristics, B. cloacae appears to belong with the intestinal group, and the closely allied forms noted by Ford [15] were also isolated from the digestive tract.

With gelatin liquefaction, followed by sucrose fermentation, we get the following brackets:

Gelatin liquefiers

- Gelatin liquefiers ....
  - S +
    - Cloacae VP + Jordan
    - Entericus VP ? Ford
    - Plebeius VP ? Ford
  - S — Subentericus VP ? Ford
- Gelatin non-liquefiers ....
  - S +
    - M + —
      - B. communior VP — (VP +) Durham
      - B. pseudo colloides VP — Castellani
      - B. wesenbergi VP — Castellani
      - B. alcalescens VP ? } Ford
      - B. gastrica VP ? } Ford
      - B. perturbans VP ? Klotz
    - M —
      - B. neapolitanae VP ? Emmerich
      - B. astheniae VP ? Dawson
      - B. galactophila VP ? Ford
  - S —
    - M +
      - B. communis VP — (VP +) Escherich
      - B. vekanda VP — } Castellani
      - B. archibaldi VP + } Castellani
      - B. shafferi VP Shaffer
      - B. paragrünthali VP ? Castellani
    - M —
      - B. coli immobilis VP ?
      - B. coscoroba (pseudo) VP ? Tretrop

[15] Studies from Royal Victoria Hospital, Montreal, 1903.

Every one of these comes from the digestive tract, and most were found many times. But if we take the VP tests as noted on the chart, we find that instead of being in the same brackets, several of these organisms would be in quite other company. Moreover, as noted above, the variables and atypicals would also be scattered, whereas in their present conjunction further differentiation of varieties which are still extant, by VP, MR, or by citrates and uric acid, is quite easy, and shows us at once, as the authors who exploited those tests told us clearly, that some varieties of B. coli and B. communior differ in these respects, but that these characters, possibly due to long biologic environment, determine variety rather than species, as the organisms apparently do not differ otherwise.

Using these various characters in suitable sequence, we have a combination which makes it possible to bring all the organisms we know into definite small groups which, if the classification be a good one, should appear to be otherwise closely related, as for instance in their usual habitat.

As already noted, there is a certain chronologic order in the discovery of these characteristics, and of course there is also a chronologic order in the naming of bacteria. In other words, organisms discovered, described and deceased before we knew of some of the later refinements can by no stroke of the imagination be endowed with them.

It has been more or less the habit to make a series of isolations from a given source and to name the varieties according to their apparent agreement with some previously described but no longer available organism. This is at first appearance all right, but the organism once named is then endowed with the additional characters found by the new observer, and the next person adds these as though they were in the primary description. Thus many organisms about which there was little information have become endowed with many characters which they may or may not have had. This is dangerous if we wish names to mean anything. The human throat may harbor at least 4 varieties of pneumococcus, and one case of rhinoscleroma [7] gave 3 varieties of Encapsulata, with identical colonies. Thus a single selection may assuredly belong to a definite group, but cannot be described as a variety of a named organism unless we know that the original did not have the character which marks the supposed variety.

Of the organisms of the colon-aerogenes-capsulatus series which have been recorded in literature, and many of which are firmly entrenched in our classifications, many are so incompletely described that one can go no farther than to say that they are probably members of some main subdivision. Others have sufficient to classify them by their fermentation and proteolysis, but not by these later tests. The author has been at some pains to look up the original descriptions in these, and to note as far as possible such descriptions by subsequent authors as indicate that they believed themselves to be using lineal descendants.

DISCUSSION OF ORGANISMS KNOWN LINEAL DESCENDANTS OF WHICH DO NOT EXIST

Only where the description of the organisms and the notes as to their habitat are such that we can be reasonably sure that even though we have lost the original we are dealing with an identical form, may exceptions be made. This for instance is the case with Escherich's B. coli and his B. aerogenes. With regard to certain others the proof is less satisfactory.

Study of the original descriptions shows that the following forms come under this category:

B. neapolitanus was described by Emmerich in 1885 and 1886 as the probable cause of Asiatic cholera. As far as the description goes, it appears to be a nonmotile B. coli, and similar forms are still found. From its first descriptions until 1900, I can find no mention of it in the literature, except that Flügge, 1886 (Sydenham translation) says it is not the cause of cholera, and differs immaterially from Escherich's B. coli. In 1900, Mayer [16] compares it with typhoid and colon on Piorkowski's urine agar. No mention is made of the source of the culture, nor are there any notations of value other than that it resembled colon and alcaligenes in its growth on solid medium.

None of the German bacteriologists in my possession, Migula, Lehman-Neuman, Kolle and Wassermann, or Friedberger and Pfeiffer, mention it. McFarland (9th edition) and Muir and Ritchie (1903) quote it as identical with the colon bacillus. Abbott, in 1902, said the same, and Hewlett, 1902, (both quoted by Winslow [1]), says that B. coli communis has been described as B. neapolitanus.

MacConkey, in 1905,[17] first mentioned it as forming gas in sucrose. He obtained the organism (20 years old) from Kral, supposedly a lineal descendant. It answers exactly to MacConkey's B. coli communis

[16] Centralbl. f. Bakteriol., I, O., 1900, 28, p. 125.
[17] J. Hyg., 1905, 5, p. 333.

except for the sucrose fermentation and the motility. MacConkey adds that it is VP+. In 1909, MacConkey [18] found 15 organisms isolated by himself which he called Neapolitanus from the reactions. He has no B. coli communior, but his Neapolitanus group is identical, except in motility. Winslow,[1] 1919, apparently on the basis of organisms accepted as Neapolitanus but with no known relationship to the original, said that it differs from B. communior in that it does not ferment salicin and is sluggishly motile. It is apparently a nonmotile variety of B. communior.

B. coscoroba was described by Tretrop [19] in a fatal epidemic of swans in Antwerp. Castellani [20] says it must be called pseudo-coscoroba, as there is already a coscoroba of the hemorrhagic septicemia group. Tretrop describes it as bipolar in staining, coagulating milk, forming indol, nonliquefying, apparently nonmotile (oscillation sur place), and from its resistance, apparently non spore-forming. There are no remarks on Gram stain. There are no remarks on gas formation. No further references could be found until 1909 when MacConkey [18] adds it to his list, taking his own isolations and giving some of them this name. There is no claim that they bore any relation to the original. He adds to Tretrop that it is gram-negative and forms acid and gas in lactose and sucrose. He had already mentioned it in a footnote in his 1905 article as conforming to a subgroup B. coli?—but had given no information as to source. This subgroup is said to be VP—, but whether he means coscoroba is VP— is doubtful. No references have been found in French or German to indicate any work with this organism. Winslow,[1] evidently on the basis of previous articles, says it is a nonmotile variety of B. coli communior. He also refers to others as thinking it an aerogenes VP— MR+. Kligler,[21] in 1914, used coscoroba laboratory strains at least 2 years old (isolated in America from a variety of sources). In fine, there is no evidence that any one since Tretrop has worked with his organism, though all sorts of fermentative and other activities are attributed to strains to which this name is given. So far as we know, they may be all right or all wrong. Since fermentation of lactose indicates fermentation of dextrose, we may infer that the original did ferment dextrose, though no mention is made of this, but this is as far as we can go, and the organism is not classifiable.

[18] Jour. Hyg., 1909, 9, p. 87.
[19] Ann. de l'Inst. Pasteur, 1900, 14, p. 224.
[20] Ibid., 1920, 34, p. 600.
[21] Jour. Infect. Dis., 1914, 15, p. 187.

B. vekanda, B. pseudo-entericus, B. archibaldi are 3 organisms described by Castellani,[20] and they differ from B. coli only in their relation to milk and lactose. As they have never been described by any one else, and only on one occasion by Castellani himself, there appears to be no good reason why they should not be grouped as variants of B. coli. Castellani named the second entericus, but Ford [15] has the priority, with a variety of B. cloacae and the name must be changed to pseudoentericus.

B. wesenbergi is another Castellani organism, differing from the last 3 in that it ferments sucrose, and belongs accordingly among the variants of B. communior. All these organisms were found in the intestines in healthy persons in the tropics and had no demonstrated relation to disease. It may be noted also that a large number of organisms similarly isolated were described by Castellani, usually on a single finding, but these are the only ones which have been included in the various classifications. The others are in the main variants on B. coli, B. communior, and B. cloacae.

B. grünthali (Fischer [22]) was isolated in a food epidemic at Grünthal in 1902. It is recorded in some detail as fermenting dextrose but not lactose or sucrose. On page 470 Fischer states:

> In Milch wuchsen die Stäbchen üppig, ohne dass es jedoch zu einer Gerinnung derselben kam. Dagegen nahm die Milch mit der Zeit eine schwach alkalische Reaction an, und wurde sie nach einbis zwei wochentlichen Stehen in Brutapparat durchscheinend, indem zugleich die weisse Farbe durch eine schmützige graugelbe ersetzt wurde.

Further along he says:

> In Lackmusmolke war in der ersten Tagen eine schwache Röthung zu constatiren, dann trat Entfarbung ein, und weiterhin zeigte sich Blaufarbung, die von der Oberflache beginnend sich allmählich über die ganze Milch sich erstreckte.

And again later:

> Wie spätere Untersuchungen ergaben, sind dieselben nicht im Stande Milch- oder Rohrzucker zu vergähren.

This seems clear enough.

Fischer evidently places it with the paratyphoids, as its source and description warrant, but MacConkey, in 1909, states that it ferments lactose with gas formation, and since that time it has been included among the colon group!

B. para-grünthali, which ferments dextrose and lactose and differs from MacConkey's grünthali only in maltose fermentation, is accordingly a B. coli variant, scarcely worth a separate name.

[22] Ztschr. f. Hyg. u. Infektionskr., 1902, 39, p. 447.

Other organisms, such as B. oxytocum,[23] are not sufficiently described to discuss them.

B. levans [24] is a nonlactose fermenter, but otherwise a gas former. It certainly does not belong in this group.

Freudenreich's B. schafferi [25] is insufficiently described, and cannot now be placed.

B. astheniae,[26] found in an epidemic among chickens, could not be made to reproduce the disease, and was almost without pathogenesis for birds. It is described as gram-positive, and does not stain with acid or alkaline methylene blue, carbol fuchsin or in alcoholic solutions of stains. It does, however, stain in aqueous fuschsin, methylene blue, Bismarck brown, and night blue. Aside from this, it is a fairly typical B. communior, forming acid and gas in dextrose, lactose and sucrose, and coagulating milk. There is no mention of motility. Gelatin is not liquefied. If the Gram record is correct, it differs from any known organism, but we know that the Gram technic of 1898 does not always give the same results as the more modern methods. All one can say definitely is that it is fairly probably a variety of B. communior.

B. pseudo-dysenteriae Kruse [27] in the original is said not to make any gas in any sugar; and though Castellani mentions it as forming gas in dextrose, the organism was one of his own finding and not Kruse's.

ENCAPSULATA

A group which can be set aside before proceeding to a final classification of the colon group is that of the capsulated organisms. There appears to be little argument against the formation of a capsulated section, but there is very much argument about what goes into it, and what are the characteristics of the individuals. Castellani [28] has formed the group "Encapsulatus," and this has mostly been taken over by Bergey.[2] There is general agreement that the various capsulated organisms described by various authors, such as Friedländer's bacillus, B. ozenae, B. rhinoscleromae, etc., should belong here, although observers differ as to the chemical activities of the individuals.

The same difficulty has also arisen here with regard to attribution of characters to historic names. The errors noted with grünthali and

[23] Flügge: Die Mikroorganismen, 1886, 2, p. 268.
[24] Lehman: Centralbl. f. Bakteriol., 1894, 15, p. 350. Holliger: Ibid., II, 1902, 9, p. 305.
[25] Ann. de l'Inst. Pasteur, 1920-, 34, p. 600.
[26] Dawson: Bur. Animal Industry, 1898.
[27] Deutsch. med. Wchnschr., 1900, 40, p. 637.
[28] Ann. de l'Inst. Pasteur, 1920, 34, p. 600.

coscoroba have been repeated. Even when one sends for an original it is not certain what will come back. Migula states, mourning over his own troubles, that of the 600 varieties he actually acquired, which were all supposed to be lineal descendants of the originals, he found less than half which answered to the original descriptions! When one considers that the cultural details and metabolic activities taken up by Migula in 1900 were far fewer than those that now concern us, it seems probable that the variation was even greater.

Of the group taken up by Clairmont,[29] Strong,[30] Perkins,[7] and others, there is general agreement that the organisms noted by Friedländer in bronchopneumonia, Abel in ozena, Frisch in rhinoscleroma, and certain others evidently closely allied, should be included among the Encapsulata. As brought out by these authors, there were many duplicates described under different names, and the total varieties were not many.

On the other hand, there has been much disagreement about two especially, B. acidi lactici of Hueppe and B. lactis aerogenes of Escherich. These have been placed in various and usually totally different groups, probably in large part because the organisms described were the describer's idea of what Escherich and Hueppe really thought but did not say.

In connection with B. acidi lactici, one must at once admit that if Hueppe's original description [31] was correct, the organism does not belong in any group with which this paper is concerned, as he noted carefully the presence of spores! On the other hand, Perkins [7] and several others used the Kral culture (probably the same one) and invariably found capsules and no spores. It is clear therefore that either Hueppe was wrong or the cultures were mixed, and when we consider that Gaffky in his original studies of the typhoid bacillus described spores, it seems possible that Hueppe in the early stages of bacteriology may have made a similar error.

There is in my mind no question that this Kral culture was nonmotile, capsulated, and failed to ferment sucrose, and that almost identical forms have been found by others.

Since none of the organisms now described as B. acidi lactici Hueppe can be identified with the original description, and since careful search shows no written record that Hueppe ever revised his description, it would be better to drop this name and substitute that of B. duodenale,

[29] Ztschr. f. Hyg. u. Infektionsk., 1902, 39, p. 1 (Bibliography complete to date.)
[30] Centralbl. f. Bakteriol., 1899, 25, p. 49.
[31] Mitt. kaiserl. Gesundheitsamte, 1884, 2, p. 1837.

Ford, 1903;[15] his description is exact and complete and the only one in which a name has been given to an organism with its characters. Further, his descriptions have been confirmed by the independent isolations of Blumer, Perkins and others. Apparently, B. chinense[32] from Chinese ink is also identical.

The discussion over B. aerogenes (B. lactis aerogenes Escherich) has been far more active. Although no capsules were mentioned in the original description, Escherich's assistant Pfandler notes them in his joint article with Escherich in Kolle and Wassermann's book. As far as I could find, every one working with cultures from Kral prior to 1904 (including myself) had found them, though admitting or urging, as the case might be, that they were harder to demonstrate than those of other members of the capsulated group. Buchanan, in 1921, says they are capsulated; Castellani places them in the Encapsulata, and Coulter[33] says that the organisms decribed by Perkins (including aerogenes) when tested by immunologic tests, "form a single biological group."

There seems therefore to be no valid reason for excluding it from the capsulated group, and consequently no reason for the establishment of an "aerobacter" group.

CLASSIFICATION OF THE CAPSULATED GROUP

The classification made in 1904 by Perkins has met with a certain degree of acceptance, but after this lapse of years there are certain modifications which should be made. A capsulated organism obtained from the upper respiratory passage cannot without further examination be named Friedländer, as has already been indicated, nor B. rhinoscleromae. B. aerogenes is frequent in this location, and it is worthy of note in this connection that Page[34] has obtained from a rhinitis a single strain which answers to B. aerogenes, and which may or may not have been the cause. Friedländer's original article does not show how the organism acted on milk or on lactose, and it is interesting to note that various observers, each believing himself to be working with a lineal descendant of the original, have had different results. In the main, these differences referred to the fermentation of lactose; and since it has been shown that there may be a single sugar present in milk capable of being broken down by nonlactose fermenters, some of the errors

[32] Hamilton: Centralbl. f. Bakteriol., II, 1898, 4, p. 230.
[33] Jour. Exper. Med., 1917, 26, p. 763.
[34] Jour. Med. Res., 1912, 26, p. 489.

may be due to this. Whether the original of Friedländer did or did not make gas in lactose, there appears to be no doubt that such organisms do exist, as even those who have never seen them admit, and two strains have been isolated in Cleveland within a few months. Accordingly, we may use the fact as a classification basis.

The original three groups of Perkins were as follows:

1. Acid and gas in dextrose, lactose, and sucrose. B. aerogenes. It is evident that organisms of this type found in sour milk, as well as others found in pathologic conditions, such as B. pfeifferi, and B. inguinalis, are identical.

2. Acid and gas in dextrose and sucrose, none in lactose. B. pneumonicum. This group apparently includes many but not all of the organisms of this type found in ozena, rhinitis, etc. They are far less frequently isolated than the first group.

3. Acid and gas in dextrose and lactose but not in sucrose. B. duodenale (B. acidi lactici). This type has been found in various pathologic conditions, though the evidence that it is directly concerned is not always adequate. Isolations are infrequent.

It now appears that a fourth group should be added, in which none of the carbohydrates are attacked. Perkins believed that although he found certain organisms which failed to ferment, this was due to degeneration rather than to inherent characters. This opinion was based on his success in reactivating some apparent nonfermenters received from Kral, as well as the strains described by Edwards [35] as nonfermenting. But it would appear from Frisch's [36] original and from subsequent personal observations that there are some strains which are either definitely and intrinsically unable to break down carbohydrates, or are so far degenerated that it requires more special treatment than they are likely to receive to bring them back to their early vigor. From the standpoint of classification, it therefore appears better to admit this group:

4. Ferments no carbohydrates. B. rhinoscleromae Frisch. B. ciprinicida Plehn.[37] B. viscosum.

(The latter organism is placed by Bergey among the lactobacilli, and Weldin and Levine place it with alcaligenes, but there appears to be no reason for displacing a typically capsulated organism with the same habitat [milk] as many of the other capsulated forms.)

In connection with the wide distribution and the limited pathogenic action of the group, it is interesting that Koser [9] should note that all he has studied are Voges Proskauer positive and methyl red negative.

[35] Jour. Infect. Dis., 1905, 2, p. 431.
[36] Quoted by Migula, 1889, 32, p. 352.
[37] Centralbl. f. Bakteriol., 1904, 35, p. 461.

The only objection to the capsulated group appears to be the difficulty of staining the capsules, and the fact that these appear only under certain circumstances. In the large series studied in 1904, it was possible to obtain capsules in all, though with varying ease, and in a recent series of isolations from Lake Erie water capsules were found in milk in many of the nonmotile forms. Darling,[6] in his isolations from animal feces, also records capsule findings in a high percentage of cases.

In sum, the objections to the capsulated group as a distinct entity, and to the inclusion therein of B. aerogenes seem to me inadequate, and I believe the group, with its 4 divisions, is justified.

NONCAPSULATED GROUP

Passing next to the noncapsulated organisms of the original group, we have already noted that there are several divisions, known as the colon group (Escherichia, Bergey), the paratyphoid group (Salmonella, Bergey), the proteus group (Proteus, Bergey), the typhoid-dysentery group (Eberthella, Bergey), and the nonfermenters (Alcaligenes, Bergey).

As noted under "Fermentation and Proteolysis," the group that ferments dextrose and lactose with acid and gas includes B. coli and B. communior and variants, and B. cloacae and variants, while the others lie outside our province.

In the colon group are at present also included most of the atypical forms and those hard to identify. Since it is agreed that the fermentation of lactose is an intrinsic character of the group, the only discussion here relates to the degree of fermentation. If the requirement of this paper that acid and gas be noted is accepted, we have certain of Castellani's isolations to consider which are said to make acid and gas in dextrose and acid but no gas in lactose, and which he has put into a class of their own. As noted earlier, the facts that no one else has noted organisms of this sort and that Winslow and Perkins have found gas formation in lactose frequently delayed do not warrant this, and accordingly these organisms have been set down as possible varieties.

There are also some organisms described by Ford [14] which, while apparently otherwise identical with B. cloacae, form alkali in milk some time after a primary acid formation, confusion due to a small amount of single sugar in the milk apparently being eliminated by the ability to break down lactose with gas formation. Therefore unless we are able to show that the lactose was not pure, we must consider these as varieties with a strong secondary alkali fermentation. All were isolated from the intestine, and none was identified as the cause of disease. Though rarely described, the careful work of Ford suggests that a reasonable number actually exist, and must be recognized.

Terminal Character Differentiations.—It is apparent that by the use of the fermentation of dextrose, glucose and sucrose, and the proteolysis of gelatin, the organisms of the colon group fall into simple and easily recognized divisions.

Although as noted, certain other carbohydrates are more or less consistent in their special relations, they are certainly more valuable in other groups than here. I definitely question whether the evidence shows that they are needed here. Recent work with many organisms has shown that not only is it true that no culture is assuredly pure except by single cell isolation, but even that single cells have a varied heredity and show variations in action on carbohydrates. Thus varieties of B. coli or B. communior which depend for a name on some single character, unless this character can be proved of value are scarcely worthy of a name. Where, however, a character may indicate the source of the organism, we have a question which must be carefully considered —as in the following discussion.

Value of MR, VP, High and Low Ratio, Uric Acid and Citrate Utilization.—The most active discussion of these characters deals with the possible differentiation of a fecal from a nonfecal group. It has been shown that in general a negative methyl-red test, a positive Voges-Proskauer, a high ratio, and the utilization of the simpler organic compounds have gone together, while the reverse has also been true. On the other hand, it has been shown that while in the methyl-red positive, low ratio, etc., group there has been a remarkable constancy, this has not been the case in the other set, so that a variety of combinations has been recorded.

The sources of the organisms to be differentiated have been mainly water and food, together with such areas and materials as might be considered as possible sources of infection for these substances. The classification offered in this paper brings together the possible offenders, in a series which really consists only of B. communior, B. coli, B. cloacae and B. aerogenes, each with minor variants. It is at this point that it appears to me most logical to introduce the various special tests which in connection with the source of the organisms may be considered as evidence of a parasitic or saprophytic habit. Thus, for instance, an organism diagnosed as B. coli may be further differentiated as MR+ VP— citrate—, showing that it belongs to what has been called the fecal type. Moreover, as previously noted, organisms which show atypical combination of these tests fall into an intermediate final group, and in many cases can probably be standardized by single cell isolation, which may show the presence of several variants.

DIFFICULTIES INVOLVED

Before concluding, it is proper to note what appear to be the main difficulties in the classification of this group.

If the author's scheme be followed, we end with B. coli and varieties, B. communior and varieties, and B. cloacae and varieties. In the Encapsulata, the organisms most frequently in question are B. aerogenes and varieties.

On account of the difficulties of definite determination of motility, this has been made an accessory factor, so that both B. coli and B communior have motile and nonmotile varieties. Strictly speaking, B. cloacae and varieties are all motile, B. aerogenes and varieties all nonmotile.

With the technic available, and especially with the use of eosin-methylene blue plates, the nonmotile B. coli and B. communior can be readily distinguished from B. aerogenes and B. duodenale by their development of a heavy precipitate and a metallic sheen, both of which characters are absent in the Encapsulata. So far as our own studies, now in progress, have shown, this is constant; but we have not had sufficient atypical forms to be certain. We do believe, however, that motile organisms described as aerogenes are incorrectly named. It seems likely that further work with MR, VP and citrate, strictly confined to single cell isolations, and combined with careful plating on EMB and crystal violet, may give us a clearer view.

SUMMARY

Classifications of bacteria on the basis of fermentation of dextrose, lactose, sucrose, and liquefaction of gelatin form groupings which bring together organisms closely related in habitat and biology.

Classifications on the primary basis of Voges-Proskauer, methyl-red or citrate tests fail, because there are many organisms now in the literature, but not available, on which these tests have not been made and cannot be made, and because even with those now available there is sufficient disagreement to prevent complete grouping.

These same tests are, however, of great value in distinguishing varieties, especially in regard to the so-called "fecal and nonfecal" colon group organisms.

Review of the literature justifies the genus "Encapsulata," and also seems to justify the inclusion of B. aerogenes therein. This makes the genus "Aerobacter" (Bergey) unnecessary.

Review of the literature shows that certain organisms now described under names given to new varieties by their original discoverers have no right to these names, and that others are almost certainly in the same case.

CONCLUSIONS

It is more consistent to modify the Bergey classification of the Bacteria according to the present suggestions than to keep it as it is.

Organisms which are no longer accessible can have no more attributes referred to them than are absolutely proved to be their property.

Classification factors which cannot be applied to the whole group, or which are subjects of disagreement, should be used to differentiate varieties rather than genera or species.

APPENDIXES

Two appendixes have been added showing the essential and variable characters of each group and species considered, and the key which developed from this. I confess difficulties with the genus names. The eponymic system with its rather arbitrary glorification of selected authors does not appeal, but apparently the familiar names, such as colon, typhoid and paratyphoid are technically improper, though they will probably be found in the current literature 50 years hence. All that remains is to use the old group names, some of which, incidentally, have been adopted in the systemic classifications.

APPENDIX 1

TRIBE, GENUS AND SPECIES CHARACTERS

TRIBE. *Bacteria.* Spore-free rods, growing aerobically, gram-negative.

I. GENUS. *Colon Group (Escherichia,* Bergey).—Fermenting dextrose and lactose, and various other carbohydrates, with the formation of acid or with acid and gas; VP + — MR + — ; citrate fermentation usually — ; motility variable.

1. Species. *B. cloacae.*—Fermenting dextrose and lactose and sometimes sucrose, and various other carboyhydrates, with the formation of acid and gas, and liquefying gelatin; VP + MR —; citrate usually +; motile.

2. Species. *B. communior.*—Fermenting dextrose, lactose and sucrose, and some other carbohydrates, with the formation of acid and gas, no liquefaction of gelatin. VP — usually, MR + usually; citrate usually —; motility variable.

3. Species. *B. coli.*—Fermenting dextrose and lactose and various other carbohydrates, with acid and gas formation, but not sucrose; no liquefaction of gelatin; VP usually —; MR usually +; citrate usually —; motility variable.

II. GENUS. *Proteus.*—Fermenting dextrose and sucrose and some other carbohydrates, with acid and gas formation, but not lactose; gelatin liquefaction variable; morphology and colony formation typical; VP +; MR —; citrate +.

III. GENUS. *Paratyphoid Group* (*Salmonella,* Bergey).—Fermenting dextrose and some other carbohydrates with acid and gas, but not lactose; no liquefaction of gelatin; VP —; MR +; citrate +.

IV. GENUS. *Typhoid-Dysentery Group* (*Eberthella,* Bergey). — Fermenting dextrose and some other carbohydrates with acid but no gas; not atacking lactose; no liquefaction of gelatin; VP —; MR +; citrate —.

V. GENUS. *Alcaligenes.*—Does not attack any of the carbohydrates. Liquefaction of gelatin variable. VP —; MR—. Citrate?

VI. GENUS. *Encapsulata.*—Capsulated, non-motile, gelatin not liquefied.

1. Species. *B. aerogenes.*—Fermentation of dextrose, lactose, sucrose and various other carbohydrates with formation of acid and gas. VP usually +; MR usually —; Citrate usually +.

2. Species. *B. pneumonicum.*—Fermentation of dextrose, sucrose and various other carbohydrates with formation of acid and gas, but no fermentation of lactose. VP usually + ; MR usually — ; Citrate usually +.

3. Species. *B. duodenale* (Former B. acidi lactici).—Fermentation of dextrose and lactose and various other carbohydrates with formaation of acid and gas, but no fermentation of sucrose. VP ususally +; MR usually — ; Citrate usually +.

4. Species. *B. rhinoscleromae.*—No fermentation of carbohydrates. VP usually +; MR usually —; Citrate usually +.

APPENDIX 2

KEY TO COLON AEROGENES CAPSULATUS GROUP

ENCAPSULATA. Dextrose, acid +, gas +.

A. Lactose, acid +, gas +.

B. Sucrose, acid +, gas +; B. aerogenes; B. Pfeifferi, etc.
B. inguinalis.

BB. Sucrose, acid —, gas —; B. duodenale, B. chinense Hamilton.

AA. Lactose, acid —, gas —.

B. Sucrose, acid +, gas +;B. pneumonicum.

Dextrose, acid —, gas —.

A. Lactose, acid —, gas —.

B. Sucrose, acid —, gas —; B. rhinoscleromae, B. ciprinicidus Plehm, B. viscosum.

Colon Typhoid Group.

Group including colon, proteus, typhoid, dysentery, paratyphoid and alcaligenes.

Dextrose, acid +, gas +.

A. Lactose, acid +, gas +.
B. Gelatin liquefied.
C. Sucrose, acid +, gas +; B. cloacae, B. entericus Ford, B. plebeius Ford (19).
CC. Sucrose, acid —, gas —; subentericus Ford (19).
BB. Gelatin not liquefied.
C. Sucrose, acid +, gas +.
D. Motile; B. communior, motile varieties.
DD. Nonmotile; B. communior, nonmotile varieties.
CC. Sucrose, acid +, gas +.
D. Motile; B. coli, motile varieties.
DD. Nonmotile; B. coli, nonmotile varieties.
AA. Lactose, acid —, gas —.
B. Gelatin variable.
C. Sucrose, acid +, gas +; proteus group.
BB. Gelatin not liquefied.
C. Sucrose, no gas; paratyphoid group.

Dextrose, acid +, gas —.

A. Lactose, acid —, gas —.
B. Gelatin not liquefied.
C. Sucrose, no gas; typhoid group.

Dextrose, acid —, gas —; no fermentation; alcaligenes group.

EXTRACTS OF NORMAL TISSUES IN EXPERIMENTAL TUBERCULOSIS

Richard S. Austin

From the Department of Pathology, University of Cincinnati and Cincinnati General Hospital

The places of residence and of production of the substances that contribute to the defense of the host in tuberculosis have been the subject of many investigations for several decades. Cellular and non-cellular elements have been demonstrated to play more or less important rôles, and it is evident that the mechanism of defense is complex. A large proportion of the work on the subject deals with the humoral factors in the defense of the host, a considerable proportion with the parts played by the free-moving cells, especially lymphocytes and large mononuclear cells (of many names), while a smaller number of articles, but by no means a small number, is concerned with the relation of the fixed tissues to defensive processes. In the latter connection, perhaps more attention has been paid to the occurrence of protective or bactericidal substances in tuberculous tissues than in normal tissues.

Bartel and Stein[1] found that virulent tubercule bacilli kept in tuberculous tissue in vitro at body temperature probably do not multiply and suffer a distinct loss of virulence in less than one week. Webb, Ryder and Gilbert[2] in confirming this, attributed the loss of virulence to the development of tuberculotoxic substances in tuberculous tissues kept at body temperature. More recently, Corper, Lurie and Kretschmer,[3] in an interesting series of in vitro experiments, arrived at the same conclusion and added the observation that in normal, as well as tuberculous tissues, a tuberculotoxic substance develops at 37 C. in from one day to a week or more, according to the type of tissue or organ used. These authors have found the developed substance to be thermostabile, unaffected by aeration and unrelated to hydrogen-ion concentration. They consider this substance to be the result of autolysis and comparable to the bactericidal substances produced by Conradi,[4] by aseptic autolysis of various tissues.

The attempts at protection of animals against the development of experimental tuberculosis by the use of injections of tuberculous tissues, or of their extracts, have resulted in various degrees of success and failure. For example, Bartel and his associates,[5] reported good results in guinea-pigs, but Trudeau and Krause,[6] using extracts of homologous lymph nodes and extracts of human

Received for publication, March 26, 1925.

[1] Centralbl. f. Bakteriol., I, O., 1905, 38, p. 154.
[2] Am. Rev. Tuberc., 1921, 5, p. 388.
[3] Am. J. Hyg., 1924, 4, p. 77.
[4] Beitr. z. chem. Physiol. u. Path., 1902, 1, p. 193.
[5] Centralbl. f. Bakteriol., I, O., 1909, 48, p. 657 and p. 667.
[6] Jour. Med. Res., 1910, 22, p. 277.

tuberculous nodes, were unable to protect guinea-pigs against experimental tuberculosis. Their extracts, however, were apparently not taken from well autolyzed tissues. It therefore remains doubtful as to how much defensive power resides in tuberculous tissue in vivo, how much is possessed by the fixed elements and how much by the mobile elements, cellular or fluid.

Turning now to a consideration of the tissues of the nontuberculous animal, some evidence is to be found for the belief that various of these tissues possess a well marked "native" defensive power against the tubercle bacillus. When the fact that the different organs of an animal present great variation in incidence of lesions of tuberculosis is considered in connection with the significant observations recently mentioned by Krause and Willis [7] that living virulent tubercle bacilli after one cutaneous injection are recoverable almost anywhere in the body before the lesion at the site of inoculation has developed and in places in which lesions will not later develop as well as in places where they will, it would seem reasonable to believe that certain types of normal tissue possess greater resistance to the tubercle bacillus than do others and hence presumably possess "native" defensive powers.

EXPERIMENTAL METHODS

The studies reported here are concerned with the effects of fresh extracts of various organs of normal animals on animals infected with tuberculosis. Rabbits were used because of the fairly consistent distribution and extent of lesions produced in the control animals by the strains of tubercle bacillus employed when injected in proper dosage subcutaneously between the shoulder blades. Two strains of tubercle bacillus were used, a bovine culture of marked virulence for rabbits and a human culture which in the dosage employed rarely produced other than local, pulmonary and associated lesions. A few intravenous inoculations of bacilli were made, but the resulting lesions in the control animals, even with careful dosage, were not as consistent in distribution and extent as were the lesions in animals inoculated subcutaneously between the scapulae. For subcutaneous injection, 10 mg. of 3 to 4 weeks old culture on glycerol-agar, a fine suspension in salt solution, was used, the weights of the rabbits varying from 1,600 to 2,300 gm. For intravenous inoculation, 0.1 mg. of culture for each kilo of body weight was employed.

[7] Tr. Nat. Tuberc. Assn., 1924, p. 277.

The organs chosen for the experiments were lung, kidney, spleen, liver, suprarenal and heart. These represent wide variations as to incidence and extent of lesions of tuberculosis produced by the methods used in these experiments, the lung being most commonly the site of demonstrable disease, while the heart is involved with extreme rarity. The organs were removed from normal rabbits immediately after killing by a sharp blow below the base of the skull (to avoid any possible effect of anesthetics). Four animals were used as sources of organs, all being free from disease as determined by necropsy. Each organ on removal was rapidly but thoroughly washed in sterile distilled water to remove as much blood as possible, and was then ground to a pulp and mixed thoroughly with an approximately equal volume of salt solution. The mixture was then filtered through fairly coarse filter-paper, still maintaining aseptic precautions, the filtrate being collected in sterile tubes. The tubes were then tightly stoppered and kept in the icebox, the filtrates being used for inoculation in from 1 to 9 days after preparation. All of the filtrates from the organs of one animal, with the exception of that from the suprarenal, developed bacterial growth, and one other filtrate, from the spleen, also showed bacterial contamination, but all of the other filtrates remained sterile. The filtrates were injected subcutaneously in the anterior abdominal wall, 0.2 c c. or 0.25 c c. being inoculated, larger amounts sometimes producing local changes which resulted in abscess formation.

A number of animals received organ extract on the eighth day before injection of bovine bacilli subcutaneously, followed by a second inoculation of extract on the same day that tubercle bacilli were injected (table 1). Another smaller group of animals was treated with organ extract the day following intravenous injection of bovine bacilli, a second inoculation of organ extract being given 8 days later (table 2). The largest number of animals was inoculated with organ extracts 1 day and 8 days after subcutaneous injection of tubercle bacilli (table 3). This table represents 2 experiments, the second partially repeating the first, 2 animals being employed for each kind of organ extract, all receiving the bovine type of the tubercle bacillus in the first experiment, while in the second only extracts from lung, suprarenal, liver and heart were used, as these promised more definite results than did extracts from kidney and spleen. The results with the use of the human type of bacillus are presented in tables 4, 5 and 6, corresponding respectively to tables 1, 2 and 3. Fewer animals were included in the

TABLE 1

RABBITS INOCULATED WITH SALINE EXTRACTS OF NORMAL ORGANS ON THE EIGHTH DAY BEFORE SUBCUTANEOUS INJECTION OF BOVINE TUBERCLE BACILLI AND AGAIN ON THE SAME DAY AS THE BACILLI

Organ Extracts	Rabbits	Days Before Death	Died or Killed	Change in Weight	Lesions
Suprarenal....	1	43	D	....	Local, lungs (moderate), kidneys
	2	228	K	Slight loss	Local (healing), lungs (moderate), kidneys, liver, spleen
Lung..........	1	39	D	Loss	Local, lungs (moderate), kidneys, spleen
	2	71	D	....	Local, lungs (moderate), kidneys, spleen
Heart..........	1	35	K	Loss	Local, lungs (moderate), kidney, liver (killed because of fracture of femur)
	2	61	D	....	Local, lungs (marked), general
Liver..........	1	42	D	Loss	Local, lungs (marked), kidneys, spleen
	2	100	D	Marked loss	Local, lungs (marked), general
Spleen..........	1	54	D	....	Local, lungs (massive), general
	2	34	D	Marked loss	Local, lungs (marked), general
Kidney..........	1	13	D	Loss	Local only; nontuberculous death
	2	24	D	Marked loss	Local, lungs (marked), general
Controls.......	1	48	D	Marked loss	Local, lungs (massive), general
	2	39	D	Loss	Local, lungs (marked), general
	3	33	D	Marked loss	Local, lungs (massive), general

Controls in tables 1 and 3 are controls for either group, being divided simply for ready comparison; the same holds for the controls in tables 4 and 6.

Nontuberculous death indicates that death was evidently due to other causes than tuberculosis.

"Local" lesions refer to those at the site of injection of bacilli, including changes in the lymph nodes of immediate drainage.

"General" lesions refer to involvement of kidneys, liver, spleen, usually pleura, often peritoneum, as well as "local" lesions (with subcutaneous injection of bacilli) and marked or massive lesions in the lungs; the lymph nodes generally are usually more or less involved. The peribronchial lymph nodes, of course, are found involved when definite pulmonary lesions are present.

Microscopic sections of the principal organs were prepared from a number of animals, but study of these sections revealed nothing of added interest except the occasional presence of unsuspected lesions which, however, do not demand inclusion in the tabulated results of the experiments. No peculiarities of reaction or architecture in the lesions in animals inoculated with organ extracts have as yet been detected.

TABLE 2

RABBITS INOCULATED WITH SALINE EXTRACTS OF NORMAL ORGANS 1 AND 8 DAYS AFTER INTRAVENOUS INJECTIONS OF BOVINE TUBERCLE BACILLI

Organ Extracts	Rabbits	Days Before Death	Died or Killed	Change in Weight	Lesions
Suprarenal....	1	14	D	Loss	Lungs (moderate) only
Lung..........	1	69	D	Marked loss	Lungs (marked), kidneys, liver, spleen
Heart..........	1	18	D	Loss	Lungs (moderate), spleen
Liver..........	1	15	D	Loss	Lungs (moderate), spleen
Spleen..........	1	18	D	Loss	Lungs (moderate), spleen, liver
Kidney..........	1	14	D	Loss	Lungs, (moderate), spleen
Controls.......	1	17	D	Loss	Lungs (marked), kidneys
	2	24	D	Marked loss	Lungs (marked), kidneys, spleen, liver
	3	14	D	Loss	Lungs (moderate), spleen

experiments employing the human bacillus, because the control animals injected with this type of the tubercle bacillus do not present as widely distributed or extensive lesions as do those inoculated with the bovine type, and they commonly live very much longer. The rabbits inoculated with organ extracts but not given any injection of tubercle bacilli ("extract controls") are not listed; they all tolerated the inoculations in 0.2 c c. or 2.5 c c. amounts of filtrate, with repetition of inoculation a week later. In larger doses some of the extracts appeared to exercise a toxic effect, especially those from spleen and kidney.

TABLE 3

RABBITS INOCULATED WITH SALINE EXTRACTS OF NORMAL ORGANS 1 AND 8 DAYS AFTER SUBCUTANEOUS INJECTION OF BOVINE TUBERCLE BACILLI

Organ Extracts	Rabbits	Days Before Death	Died or Killed	Change in Weight	Lesions
Suprarenal....	1	72	D	Loss	Local, lungs (marked), kidneys, liver
	2	121	D	Loss	Local, lungs (moderate), kidneys (slight)
	3	163	D	Loss	Local, lungs (marked), kidneys
	4	191	K	Slight loss	Local, lungs (marked), kidneys, spleen
Lung..........	1	64	D	Slight loss	Local (slight), lungs (slight)
	2	104	D	Slight loss	Local (slight), lungs (marked), kidneys
	3	228	K	Loss	Local, lungs (moderate), kidneys, spleen
	4	191	K	Loss	Local, lungs (moderate), kidneys, spleen
Heart..........	1	50	D	....	Local, lungs (marked), kidneys
	2	72	D	Marked loss	Local, lungs (marked), kidneys, liver
	3	56	D	Loss	Local, lungs (marked), kidneys
	4	98	D	Marked loss	Local, lungs (marked), kidneys, liver
Liver..........	1	39	D	....	Local, lungs (marked), kidneys, spleen
	2	51	D	Loss	Local, lungs (marked), kidneys, spleen, liver
	3	64	D	Marked loss	Local, lungs (moderate), kidneys, spleen, liver
	4	112	D	Marked loss	Local, lungs (massive), general
Spleen.........	1	38	D	....	Local, lungs (massive), general
	2	51	D	Marked loss	Local, lungs (massive), general
Kidney.........	1	29	D	....	Local, lungs (massive), general
	2	43	D	Marked loss	Local, lungs (massive), general
Controls.......	1	49	D	Marked loss	Local, lungs (massive), general
	2	37	D	Marked loss	Local, lungs (massive), general
	3	31	D	Marked loss	Local, lungs (massive), general

COMMENT

In deciding how much the inoculations of extracts of normal organs influence the development of experimental tuberculosis, it is necessary to take into account the records in the 3 columns: "Days Before Death," "Change in Weight" and "Lesions." Considering these 3 sets of results together, it would appear that under certain conditions extracts of suprarenal and of lung retard the development of tuberculosis, in a few cases exercising a definite effect. Extracts of heart and of liver less often and less evidently influence the development of the disease, while extracts of spleen and of kidney produce almost no effect. In comparing the results of injections of bovine and of human bacilli, the marked differences in the disease produced in rabbits by

TABLE 4

RABBITS INOCULATED WITH SALINE EXTRACTS OF NORMAL ORGANS ON THE EIGHTH DAY BEFORE SUBCUTANEOUS INJECTION OF HUMAN TUBERCLE BACILLI AND AGAIN ON THE SAME DAY AS THE BACILLI

Organ Extracts	Rabbits	Days Before Death	Died or Killed	Change in Weight	Lesions
Suprarenal....	1	9	D	Slight loss	Local only; nontuberculous death
	2	228	K	Marked gain	Local (healing), lungs (slight)
Lung..........	1	53	D	....	Local only; nontuberculous death
	2	228	K	Gain	Local (healing), lungs (slight)
Heart..........	1	...	..	Gain	(Alive, 267 days)
	2	208	D	Slight gain	Local (slight), lungs (slight)
Liver..........	1	137	D	Gain	Local (slight), lungs (slight); nontuberculous death
	2	198	D	Slight gain	Local only but marked
Spleen.........	1	147	D	Slight loss	Local (marked), lungs (moderate)
	2	119	D	Slight loss	Local (moderate), lungs (moderate)
Kidney.........	1	9	D	Slight loss	Local only; nontuberculous death
	2	139	D	Loss	Local, lungs (marked), kidneys
Controls.......	1	208	D	Loss	Local, lungs (marked)
	2	167	D	Slight loss	Local, lungs (moderate
	3	193	D	Slight loss	Local, lungs (moderate)

TABLE 5

RABBITS INOCULATED WITH SALINE EXTRACTS OF NORMAL ORGANS 1 AND 8 DAYS AFTER INTRAVENOUS INJECTION OF HUMAN TUBERCLE BACILLI

Organ Extracts	Rabbits	Days Before Death	Died or Killed	Change in Weight	Lesions
Suprarenal....	1	...	..	Gain	(Alive, 267 days)
Lung..........	1	...	..	Gain	(Alive, 267 days)
Heart..........	1	108	D	Loss	Lungs (slight), kidneys; nontuberculous death
Liver..........	1	14	D	Slight loss	No tuberculosis; nontuberculous death
Spleen.........	1	31	D	Slight gain	Lungs (slight), kidneys
Kidney.........	1	12	D	Slight loss	No tuberculosis; nontuberculous death
Controls.......	1	179	D	Slight loss	Lungs (moderate), kidneys
	2	132	D	Slight loss	Lungs (moderate), kidneys, spleen
	3	160	D	Loss	Lungs (moderate), kidneys, liver, spleen

these two types of the tubercle bacillus must be kept in mind. In this connection, the results here presented using bovine bacilli might be considered more significant than those using human bacilli. However, in both series of experiments comparison of the results in treated animals with those in control animals reveals in both cases the tendency of suprarenal and lung extracts to influence the course of tuberculosis much more than the other extracts, liver and heart producing less effect and spleen and kidney virtually none. Two spontaneous epidemics carried off a few of the rabbits, but the results in these animals are included in the record because in most cases they still possess some significance.

The intravenous inoculations of organ extracts were made in a limited number of animals, so deductions may not be as safely drawn from these results as in the case of the rabbits receiving subcutaneous inoculations. Nevertheless, even here some evidence is found for the greater effect of lung and suprarenal extracts compared with those of the other organs used, especially with the human bacillus.

TABLE 6

RABBITS INOCULATED WITH SALINE EXTRACTS OF NORMAL ORGANS 1 AND 8 DAYS AFTER SUBCUTANEOUS INJECTION OF HUMAN TUBERCLE BACILLI

Organ Extracts	Rabbits	Days Before Death	Died or Killed	Change in Weight	Lesions
Suprarenal....	1	228	K	Marked gain	Local only (healing)
	2	...	..	Marked gain	(Alive, 240 days)
	3	...	..	Marked gain	(Alive, 240 days
Lung.........	1	...	..	Marked gain	(Alive, 240 days)
	2	240	K	Marked gain	Local only (slight)
	3	5	D	....	Local only; nontuberculous death
Heart..........	1	191	D	Gain	Local only; nontuberculous death
	2	150	D	Slight loss	Local, lungs (few large foci)
	3	56	D	....	Local only; nontuberculous death
Liver..........	1	172	D	Slight loss	Local, lungs (numerous foci)
	2	108	D	Gain	Local, lungs (slight); nontuberculous death
	3	83	D	Slight loss	Local, lungs (moderate); nontuberculous death
Controls.......	1	201	D	Loss	Local, lungs (marked), kidneys
	2	178	D	Loss	Local, lungs (moderate)
	3	141	D	Slight loss	Local, lungs (moderate); nontuberculous death

The effect of the organ extracts on rabbits infected with either human or bovine bacilli, if the organisms are injected subcutaneously, would appear on the whole to be more often evident and more conspicuous when the extracts are inoculated following the injection of the bacilli than when given preceding the infection of the animals. Whether this be due to the transient existence of the protective substances after inoculation, or to the greater stimulating effect in the production of defensive power in the animal when infection is present, is not clear. In many instances in which apparent restraining effect is to be observed after inoculation of organ extracts this effect on the infection is largely temporary, although, on the other hand, a few animals appear to obtain relatively lasting protection. It has been recognized, as emphasized by Theobald Smith,[8] that the defense of the host in tuberculosis is directed more against multiplication of the bacilli than toward their destruction.

The more or less protective substances whose existence is indicated by these studies are probably not identical with the tuberculotoxic substances reported by Bartel and Stein,[1] by Webb, Ryder and Gilbert [2] and by Corper, Lurie and Kretschmer.[3] The latter substances developed in tissues and organs kept at body temperature for several days as a rule. Corper and his co-workers report the occurrence of these substances in normal organs, but only after incubation, the only tissue in which they developed in less than 2 days in the incubator being voluntary muscle, in which case the substances were once present after but one day. Furthermore, a few experiments in connection with the studies here reported suggest that the protective substances present in fresh saline extracts of organs are possibly destroyed or inhibited by incubation of the extracts for 1 to 2 days. It should be noted that the order of organs in effectiveness in the present studies is not the order of normal organs, as reported by Corper and his co-workers, in the rapidity with which tuberculotoxic substances are developed at incubator temperature. In the former case the order is: suprarenal and lung, then heart and liver, then spleen and kidney; in the latter the order is: liver, lung and spleen, in about 4 days, then heart, kidney and brain, in about a week or more. To be sure, in one case the experimental animal is the rabbit, in the other, the guinea-pig.

The order of the organ extracts in effectiveness does not correspond with the order of the organs in the control animals as to relative lack of susceptibility to tuberculosis. Were it not for the high position of the lung extract such a correspondence would exist. An explanation of this position of the lung extract might be found in the fact that the lung, because of anatomic, and especially circulatory, peculiarities, is exposed to more of a bombardment by bacilli than are the other organs, the supposition being that the lung possesses a higher degree of natural resistance to tuberculosis than most of the other organs, but that this resistance is put to more of a strain. Certainly lung tissue has been found to have a high degree of inhibitory effect on cultures of other bacteria than the tubercle bacillus. Other explanations of this high

[8] Jour. Am. Med. Assn., 1917, 68, p. 669.

position of lung extract, such as those based on conditions of oxygen and carbon dioxide content of different organs, would perhaps carry the question too far into the realm of speculation.

SUMMARY

In summary it may be stated that the inoculation of simple extracts, not incubated, of certain fresh normal organs of the rabbit appears to influence the development of experimental tuberculosis in rabbits. The extracts of different kinds of organs vary considerably as to the amount of influence displayed. Extracts of suprarenal and lung frequently would seem to retard the development of the disease, those of heart and liver produce less effect as a rule, while extracts of spleen and kidney exert little or no influence. The freshness of the organs used, the short time utilized in preparing the extracts, the avoidance of incubation and the preservation of the extracts, between inoculations, at icebox temperature make it seem possible that the more or less protective substances present in some of the organ extracts exist in the organs before removal from the animal.

INDUCED AND NATURAL TRANSMISSION OF BLACKHEAD IN THE ABSENCE OF HETERAKIS

Ernest Edward Tyzzer and Jane Collier

From the Department of Comparative Pathology, Harvard Medical School, Boston

Although it has been possible by experimental work carried on through successive seasons to establish certain facts bearing on the transmission of blackhead in turkeys, there are some points that still remain obscure. Undoubtedly any knowledge of the distribution in nature of the parasite of blackhead will prove useful in the control of this disease.

Since the ceca are primarily affected, it is natural to assume that the disease is transmitted directly by the ingestion of food contaminated with freshly passed fecal material. That the infection is regularly transmitted in this manner has never been conclusively demonstrated, however, and evidence is at hand indicating that it is often transmitted in a much less direct manner. Thus the disease appears in young birds that have never been in contact with older turkeys or fowls.

In earlier experiments [1] planned to test the efficacy of a certain drug, the attempt was made to infect normal turkeys by direct exposure to birds infected with blackhead. In a group of 13 turkeys thus exposed, one showed symptoms of blackhead 14 days and another 15 days from the beginning of the exposure, i. e., after what is known to be the incubation period of the disease. However, additional attempts to infect the remaining 11 turkeys of this group by feeding lesions and discharges from infected turkeys failed.

In a subsequent experiment,[2] blackhead was produced artificially in young turkeys by feeding fresh active liver lesions.

Following the demonstration by Graybill and Smith [3] that blackhead could be produced experimentally by feeding normal turkeys the embryonated eggs of Heterakis gallinae (=papillosa), the question arose whether it is possible for the disease to be transmitted by the direct exposure of normal to infected turkeys. These authors did not conclude that infection took place only through the agency of Heterakis,

Received for publication, March 28, 1925.

[1] Tyzzer, E. E.: Jour. Med. Res., 1920, 41, p. 212.
[2] Tyzzer, E. E., and Fabyan, M.: Jour. Exper. Med., 1922, 35, p. 791.
[3] Ibid., 1920, 31, p. 647.

but on the contrary pointed out that the development of this worm in overwhelming numbers might so lower the resistance of the host as to allow the invasion of the tissues by the protozoon of blackhead, which they suggested might be generally distributed in turkeys.

It has not only been possible to confirm the results of Graybill and Smith, but also in carefully conducted experiments [2] to produce blackhead by feeding young incubator turkeys with embryonated Heterakis eggs which had been kept throughout their development in 1.5% nitric acid for the purpose of destroying all organisms external to the egg membrane. These turkeys on removal from the incubator were isolated in clean insect-proof compartments and fed thereafter on sterilized food. Our earlier experiment was perhaps open to criticism in that the compartment in which the Heterakis-fed turkeys were kept was separated only by a partition from 2½ to 3 feet in height from turkeys which were fed blackhead lesions. However, several repetitions of this experiment in which the turkeys were carefully isolated in separate rooms have always yielded positive results.

The experimental production of blackhead by the feeding of Heterakis gallinae material that has been kept for weeks in dilute nitric acid thus indicates the occurrence of a resistant or protected form of the blackhead protozoon, which evidently is in some way commonly associated with this worm. The sporadic cases of the disease which appear in young turkeys kept entirely separate from old turkeys and other poultry doubtless arise from such resistant forms of the infectious agent picked up from the soil, for it has been found that newly hatched turkeys are invariably free from any blackhead infection. The importance of contaminated soil as a source of infection in blackhead has already been demonstrated experimentally.[3] Thus a series of 23 young turkeys fed on a mash to which a small amount of hen-yard dirt had been added, all contracted the disease.

Previous investigations made in the course of the transmission of the disease by inoculation have failed, however, to furnish any indication of a resistant form of the blackhead protozoon in Heterakis-free material. In lesions kept at room temperature, this organism has never been found to survive more than 24 hours and at lower temperatures no more than four days.[4]

The experiments here recorded were planned to demonstrate whether under natural conditions blackhead may be transmitted directly from

[4] Tyzzer, E. E., and Fabyan, M.: Jour. Infect. Dis., 1920, 27, p. 207.

infected to normal turkeys in the absence of Heterakis and also to show how long worm-free fecal material may remain infectious after being discharged from the body.

MATERIAL AND METHODS

For these experiments 41 turkeys hatched on July 5 and 107 on July 30, 1923, were used. Those hatched on July 5, on removal from the incubator were placed in 4 compartments constructed on a table top with partitions of wire mosquito netting.

In order to determine whether blackhead may be transmitted by the contaminative method in the absence of Heterakis, it was first important without this worm to produce an infection similar to the spontaneous disease. It had already been shown that infection might occasionally be produced by feeding active liver lesions to young turkeys. In one of two cases in which infection occurred in this way, the initial lesion appeared in the cecum, in the other in the proventriculus.[2] The attempt was therefore again made in the present investigation to infect a series of young turkeys through the ingestion of fresh liver lesions.

The posibility of producing infection of the ceca by the rectal injection of suitable material was suggested by the report of Hall and Shillinger[5] on the rectal administration of anthelmintics for the removal of Heterakis in chickens. This method of introducing material into the ceca of birds was discovered by Browne,[6] who found that fluid injected into the large intestine of chickens is driven immediately along the entire length of the ceca.

Since these measures for the production of blackhead without employing Heterakis were successful, the normal turkeys kept in the adjoining compartment and separated only by wire netting from the infected ones were thus more or less exposed.

A number of turkeys hatched July 30, immediately on removal from the incubator were placed in the quarters contaminated by the infected turkeys of the July 5 hatch. The remainder of this lot was placed in new compartments in a separate room and served as controls until employed for special experiments. There was thus a large number of stock birds to serve as controls for those under experiment.

A somewhat disturbing factor was furnished in the early appearance of coccidiosis in the birds of both hatches although kept in carefully isolated quarters. From its occurrence in turkeys under experiment, it was at first thought that the material used to produce infection might possibly have contained coccidium oocysts, but its early appearance in great numbers in one of the control birds of the July 30 hatch indicated that the infection was contracted before the birds were removed from the incubator, possibly from eating bits of shells of the eggs from which they hatched. This infection became general, but among the large number of turkeys on hand only 2 or 3 showed any ill effects that could be attributed to this organism, and only 1 died. With the exception of the blackhead organism in the experimentally infected turkeys and the above mentioned coccidium, the birds were free from protozoa until late in the season when through accident or negligence a swarm of flies was

[5] Jour. Am. Vet. Med. Assn., 1923, 62, p. 623.
[6] Comp. Path. & Therap., 1922, 35, p. 12.

admitted to the room where the food was prepared. A chilomastix, a trichomonas and a small amoeba subsequently appeared in the cecal discharges of the turkeys on hand at that time.

INGESTION OF VIRUS FROM FRESH LIVER LESIONS

In this investigation several groups of turkeys were fed fresh liver lesions (table 1). The ingestion of such material by turkeys at the age of 5 days produced infection in 7 of a group of 11; another turkey of this group died too early to show infection. Later attempts to produce blackhead by feeding fresh lesions to 7 slightly older poults failed. Thus in a total of 18 turkeys fed freshly obtained virus,

TABLE 1
INGESTION OF FRESH LIVER LESIONS

Turkeys	Age, Days	Procedure	Result	Anatomic Findings
1	5	July 10, fed fresh liver lesions.......	July 13, dead.........	Ruptured yolk sac
2	5	July 11, fed liver lesions kept for 24 hrs. at about 21 C.	July 24, dead.........	Typical blackhead *
			July 20, dead.........	Typical blackhead
4	5		July 26, dead.........	Typical blackhead
5	5	July 10, fed fresh liver lesions.......	July 21, dying, killed	Typical blackhead
6	5	July 11, fed liver lesions kept for 24 hrs. at about 21 C.	July 23, dead.........	Typical blackhead
7	5		July 22, dead.........	Typical blackhead
8	5	July 17, fed fresh liver lesions.......	July 25, dead.........	Typical blackhead
9	5		Aug. 14, alive, normal	
10	5		Aug. 14, alive, normal	
11	5		Aug. 14, alive, normal	
12	5		Aug. 14, alive, normal	
27	16	July 21, fed fresh liver lesions.......	Aug. 14, alive, normal	
28	16		Aug. 14, alive, normal	
43	15	Aug. 14, fed fresh liver lesions.......	Sept. 24, dead..........	Organs normal
44	15		Sept. 28, killed.........	Organs normal
45	15		Oct. 15, killed.........	Organs normal
46	15		Oct. 15, killed.........	Organs normal
47	15		Oct. 6, killed.........	Organs normal

* Coccidium oocysts found in small intestine.

7 became infected. All of these showed disease of the type which occurs spontaneously. Coccidium oocysts were found in one of these turkeys which died of blackhead at the age of 19 days. The remaining birds showed no protozoon other than the blackhead parasite.

RECTAL INJECTION OF VIRUS FROM FRESH LIVER LESIONS

For this purpose, a suspension of finely comminuted liver lesions in salt solution was injected into the rectum by means of a blunt tipped pipet slightly larger than an ordinary medicine dropper. The injection was made rather gradually, and the anal opening was held firmly during the withdrawal of the pipet and thereafter for at least 2 minutes. The dose was graded from 1 to 2 c c., according to the age of the turkey, and was in some cases repeated after a number of hours or on the following day.

This procedure resulted in infection much more frequently than was the case with the ingestion of virus. Thus in 20 turkeys receiving fresh liver lesions by rectum, 16 became infected (see table 2). Only a single rectal infection was made in 2 of the negative cases, and material of questionable activity was used in another negative case. The deaths of those becoming infected occurred between the 10th and the 20th day after the 1st injection. The disease produced by rectal

TABLE 2

RECTAL INJECTION OF FRESH LIVER LESIONS

Turkeys	Age, Days	Procedure	Result	Anatomic Findings
13	5	July 10, fresh liver lesions injected rectally	July 21, dead..........	Typical blackhead ‡
14	5	July 11, liver lesions kept at about	July 22, dead..........	Typical blackhead
15	5	21 C. for 24 hrs. injected rectally	July 22, dead..........	Typical blackhead
16	5		July 23, dead..........	Typical blackhead ‡
17	5	July 10, fresh liver lesions injected	July 20, dead..........	Typical blackhead ‡
18	5	rectally	July 21, dead..........	Typical blackhead ‡
19	5	July 11, liver lesions kept at about	July 23, dead..........	Typical blackhead
20	5	21 C. for 24 hrs. injected rectally	July 23, killed..........	Typical blackhead ‡
21	5	July 17, fresh liver lesions injected	July 23, dead..........	Typical blackhead ‡
22	5	rectally	July 26, dead..........	Typical blackhead ‡
23	5		July 27, killed..........	Typical blackhead ‡
24	5		July 30, killed..........	Organs normal
29	22	July 27, fresh liver lesions injected rectally	Aug. 14, alive, normal*	
30	22		Aug. 14, alive, normal†	
52	58	Sept. 26, fresh liver and lung lesions injected rectally, 2 doses at intervals of 4 hours	Oct. 11, dead..........	Typical blackhead
53	58	Sept. 27 and 28, fresh subcutaneous lesion injected rectally, 3 doses at intervals	Oct. 15, killed..........	Organs normal
56	28	Aug. 27 and 28, fresh liver lesions	Sept. 7, dead..........	Typical blackhead ‡
57	28	injected rectally	Sept. 10, dead..........	Typical blackhead ‡
58	28		Sept. 17, dead..........	Typical blackhead ‡
59	28		Sept. 17, dead..........	Typical blackhead

* Died Sept. 30, 1923, showing no evidence of blackhead.
† Subsequently showed no symptoms of blackhead.
‡ No protozoa other than Histomonas found on examination of cecal contents, others not examined for protozoa.

injection was the type which occurs spontaneously, although both ceca were in all cases extensively diseased, whereas in spontaneous cases the involvement of a single cecum is of frequent occurrence, and the initial lesion is often confined to a small area of the cecal wall.

EXPOSURE TO INFECTED TURKEYS THROUGH WIRE NETTING

Seventeen of a lot of turkeys hatched in the incubator on July 5 were kept in compartments on the same table with, and separated only by ordinary wire mosquito netting from 24 others that at the age of

5 days received blackhead virus either by mouth or by rectum. Although 18 of the latter died of blackhead between July 20 and 27, none of the birds exposed to them through the wire partition became infected. Coccidiosis on the contrary was observed to spread readily from one compartment to another.

EXPOSURE IN CAGES PREVIOUSLY OCCUPIED BY INFECTED BIRDS

Eighteen newly hatched turkeys were, on August 2 and 3, placed in compartments previously occupied by infected birds. The last of these had died 7 days previously, and the compartments had not been cleaned at any time during the experiment. None of these turkeys, exposed from an early age to old fecal material from infected birds, contracted blackhead. Later the experiment was repeated, 3 normal turkeys being placed, at the age of 56 days, in a contaminated cage immediately after the removal of the last of several turkeys dying of blackhead. Two days later, 3 more normal turkeys of the same age were introduced. In order that any virus present should not be buried under accumulating dejecta and surplus food, the material on the floor of the cage was stirred each day and new food thrown directly on it at feeding time. Under such conditions, none of the turkeys showed any evidence of blackhead infection, but all those that died or were killed showed coccidiosis.

DIRECT EXPOSURE TO INFECTED TURKEYS

On 3 occasions normal turkeys were placed in cages occupied at the time by others infected either by the feeding or by rectal injection of blackhead lesions (see table 3). Two turkeys whose exposure to turkeys receiving rectal injections of liver lesions commenced on the day of the injection, succumbed to blackhead after 14 and 21 days, respectively. However, this result is perhaps open to the criticism that the infection may have been brought about by the ingestion of material discharged immediately after its injection into the rectum of the other turkeys.

The most striking result was obtained in the infection of 6 of a group of 8 turkeys exposed to infected turkeys that had received a rectal injection 9 days previously. In this instance the material in the bottom of the cage was stirred each day and the food scattered on it. The failure in a previous experiment of a number of turkeys to contract blackhead when placed in a compartment immediately after the removal of the last of 5 turkeys dying of blackhead indicates that the protozoon persists for only a short time in dejecta from infected birds. From the results obtained in the latter 2 experiments, it is evident that infection may be brought about by the transference of the protozoon of blackhead from sick to normal turkeys through the medium of food contaminated with the cecal discharges of the former. By this mode of transmission, infection apparently results only from the direct transference of freshly passed organisms.

TABLE 3

DIRECT EXPOSURE TO INFECTED TURKEYS

Turkeys	Age, Days	Procedure	Result	Anatomic Findings	Protozoa Other Than Histomonas in Caeca
54*	28	Aug. 27, 1923, exposed to 4 turkeys injected rectally on same date with fresh liver lesions	Sept. 10, dead	Typical blackhead	None
55*	28		Sept. 17, dead	Typical blackhead	
60	37	Sept. 5, exposed to 4 turkeys infected rectally on Aug. 27, with fresh liver lesions and also to 2 turkeys nos. 54 and 55 infected by exposure	Sept. 15, dead	Acute cecal blackhead	Eimeria sp.
61	37		Sept. 17, dead	Early cecal blackhead	None
62	37		Sept. 21, dead	Typical blackhead	Eimeria sp.
63	37		Sept. 20, dead	Early blackhead	None
64	37		Sept. 21, dead	Blackhead, microscopic lesions in liver	
65	37		Sept. 28, killed	Early blackhead	Eimeria sp.—Chilomastix gallinarum
66	37		Oct. 20, alive, normal		
67	37		Oct. 20, alive, normal		
50	58	Sept. 26, exposed to 2 turkeys injected rectally on same date with fresh liver lesions	Oct. 14. dead	Typical blackhead	
51	58		Oct. 11, killed	Ceca normal	

* On Aug. 23, nos. 54 and 55 had been inoculated on the breast with liver lesions without success. At the time of their exposure, Aug. 27, they were again inoculated on the breast, but no active infection was found locally at the time of death.

THE INFECTIVITY OF VIRUS KEPT FROM 1 TO 5 DAYS AT ROOM TEMPERATURE

Liver lesions kept for 24 hours at room temperature were administered to 2 turkeys by mouth and by rectum. Samples of the same material were given after intervals of 3 and 5 days at room temperature to 2 other turkeys. None of the 6 turkeys receiving virus kept for 24 hours or longer became infected. Unfortunately, the demonstration of the infectivity of this virus when fresh was neglected, but since it was obtained from 2 cases of acute blackhead, it was in all probability potent when fresh. The results obtained at least indicate that as compared with virus occurring in the cecal discharges that present in liver lesions is similarly nonresistant.

THE INFECTIVITY OF VIRUS KEPT IN 1.5% NITRIC ACID

Large amounts of material consisting of liver lesions and diseased ceca were finely chopped and placed in 1.5% nitric acid in which it was kept from 13 to 15 days, at which time it was first washed in several changes of normal salt solution and then given both by mouth and by rectum to 6 normal turkeys. None of these developed blackhead.

CONTROL TURKEYS

A large number of stock turkeys isolated in new clean quarters on removal from the incubator and fed thereafter on sterilized food, served as controls for the foregoing experiments. There were in all 61 such turkeys that served as controls for various periods, after which, in many instances, they were used for special experiments. Thus 16 served as controls for 28 days, 10 for 37 days, 4 for 43 days, 2 for 47 days, 2 for 48 days, 1 for 50 days, 6 for 52 days, 4 for 56 days, 2 for 58 days, 5 for 68 days, 1 for 75 days, 3 for 77 days, and 5 for 82 days. The absence of blackhead in so large a number over so long periods of time practically precludes the possibility of its transmission through the turkey's egg, especially since the present experiments show that the mere introduction of the virus into the ceca without local injury is sufficient to produce the disease. Furthermore, of the considerable numbers of turkeys employed in previous investigations, none of those reared in isolation has developed blackhead. That serious pathologic conditions may occur in the ceca of young isolated turkeys without producing blackhead has already been pointed out.[3, 7]

EXAMINATION OF CECAL CONTENTS

The routine examination of the cecal contents of turkeys killed or dying of disease, for protozoa and intestinal worms, has served as an additional check in the foregoing experiments. The cecal discharges from living birds were also examined from time to time throughout the investigation. The early appearance of a coccidium of the type of Eimeria avium, especially since it occurred in isolated control turkeys,

[7] Tyzzer, E. E., Fabyan, M., and Foot, N. C.: Jour. Infect. Dis., 1921, 29, p. 1.

may be explained only by its transmission through the egg or by its acquisition before leaving the incubator through the ingestion of small fragments of egg shells by the newly hatched turkeys. No other protozoon, except the organism of blackhead in the infected birds, was found in any of the turkeys of the July 5 hatch. Those of the July 30 hatch, some of which were placed in the uncleaned compartments from which the previous hatch had been removed, showed no other protozoa up to September 28, when Chilomastix gallinarum was found on post-mortem examination. The exemption of the experimental stock from the common intestinal flagellates and amebae for a period of nearly 2 months serves as an index of the efficacy of the precautions taken to prevent any adventitious introduction of blackhead virus.

Throughout these experiments the cecal contents of all turkeys dying of blackhead or other causes were with few exceptions carefully examined for Heterakis gallinae, but no worm was found. The entire cecal contents were diluted with water and then examined in thin layers for worms. Scrapings of the mucosa were also examined microscopically for worms in early stages of development, but with negative results.

The present series of experiments show that a type of blackhead infection similar to that which occurs naturally follows the entrance of the protozoon, Histomonas meleagridis, into one or both ceca of the turkey. Lowered resistance or local injury are not essential factors in the etiology of the disease in young turkeys, for the mere ingestion of material containing the protozoon is sufficient in a certain proportion of cases, while the introduction of such material into the rectum is even more effective, having produced infection in 80% of the birds thus treated. In the latter procedure, it is neither necessary to inject a large amount of material nor to exert pressure, for, as Browne and others have already shown, fluid introduced into the rectum usually passes into the ceca evidently through the action of peristalsis. Failures following rectal injection may possibly be due to the evacuation of the injected material without its passing into the ceca. It is also possible that when only a small number of the protozoa reach the ceca, all may become eliminated before they have an opportunity to establish themselves through multiplication.

Apparently the chances of the virus reaching the ceca are much less when given by mouth than when given by rectum. Whether it is to a large extent destroyed en route or whether it passes directly through the large intestine without entering the ceca has not been determined.

The rarity of initial infection elsewhere than in the ceca is of considerable interest. Infection commencing in the proventriculus of a young turkey fed large doses of blackhead material has already been reported.[3] One case of spontaneous blackhead has more recently come under observation which presented a large lesion of the small intestine at a considerable distance from a smaller localized lesion of one cecum as well as the usual lesions of the liver. This is the only one in a large series of cases of natural infection in which there has been any question of the cecum representing the initial site of invasion. Evidently under ordinary circumstances the conditions necessary for invasion are met with only in the cecum. That this is due to conditions within the alimentary tract rather than those within the tissues is shown by the fact that the organism on becoming disseminated from a local lesion develops in various tissues and organs, including the proventriculus and small intestine.[4]

Whereas the mere introduction of the blackhead protozoon into the ceca without injury to the latter is sufficient to cause infection in young turkeys, previous observations have shown that injury of the ceca does not produce blackhead. Thus neither the obstruction of the cecum by the injection of soft paraffin nor the inflammatory processes that sometimes occur in the ceca of young laboratory reared turkeys result in blackhead. These facts taken together with the nonoccurrence of the disease in turkeys reared in clean quarters indicate that the infection is not transmitted through the egg, as is the case with Bacillus pullorum. Up to the present time, no case of blackhead has occurred in turkeys kept from the time of hatching in clean quarters in the laboratory even though large numbers have been under observation each summer for several years.

Although some writers on the subject of rearing turkeys attach great importance to indigestion supposed to result from eating unripe corn, etc., no convincing evidence is at hand that such factors themselves actually increase the incidence of blackhead. The importance of such conditions as warm, dry quarters during the first 3 months of life, as well as wholesome, well balanced diet at all times are not denied, and failure to provide them may result in the loss of large numbers of turkeys without the occurrence of any blackhead infection. However, assertions that chilling, improper diet, etc., result in blackhead, only serve to confuse the question, since the more important point relative to the manner in which the blackhead protozoon is acquired is not taken into account. That this organism is not generally present in turkeys is shown by the fact that it is only necessary to introduce it into the alimentary tract to produce disease. The health and vigor of young turkeys in no way protects them from infection.

The experimental production of blackhead of the natural type, in the absence of Heterakis, has served to make clear certain biologic peculiarities of the protozoon of this disease. If this organism produced resistant forms which were discharged from such infected birds, it should be possible to transmit the disease by indirect exposure. No case has occurred, however, as the result of the exposure of normal turkeys in a compartment in which they were separated from infected turkeys only by a partition of ordinary wire mosquito netting. Exposure in a contaminated cage after various periods following the removal of infected turkeys has also furnished only negative results. With direct exposure of normal to infected birds, i. e., living in the same compartment under conditions such that the food becomes contaminated with cecal discharges, a considerable proportion—75%—of the exposed turkeys have become infected. As these results indicate, Histomonas meleagridis occurs in the cecal discharges of infected turkeys, and large numbers of this organism are frequently demonstrable microscopically, especially in discharges consisting of blood-tinged exudate. Thus at least at times during the acute infection, the protozoon is discharged in a form that is incapable of surviving long outside the body, but which may produce infection if immediately ingested.

The possibility of the direct transmission of blackhead from infected to normal turkeys should be taken into account in the practical control of blackhead, for conditions such as those provided in the experiment are frequently found on the farm. Whereas the sporadic cases may be contracted through the ingestion of some resistant or protected form distributed over the soil, it is not improbable that certain acute epidemics destroying in a short time an entire flock are brought about by direct exposure of healthy poults to infected ones, with the resulting contamination of food. There is thus basis for the belief that the association of healthy with infected turkeys is undesirable, and on this account, the safer procedure is to isolate all sick turkeys in a separate yard where in case of recovery, they should be kept until late in the season.

SUMMARY

No case of blackhead has developed in large numbers of incubator hatched turkeys kept in clean compartments and fed on sterilized food, so that there is no indication that the infection is transmitted through the egg.

Turkeys reared under such conditions remain free from intestinal amebae and flagellates for long periods.

The early appearance of coccidiosis under conditions of strict isolation indicates that the coccidium of the turkey is transmitted either through the turkey's egg or on the shell of the latter.

Blackhead of the type which occurs naturally may result from feeding material from active liver lesions but is produced more regularly by the rectal injection of such material.

The passage of the blackhead protozoon into the turkey's cecum in sufficient numbers for it to become established appears to be the only condition necessary for the invasion of the tissues in young turkeys, so that lowered resistance and local injury are without etiologic significance.

It is apparent from the present experiments that the blackhead protozoon is discharged from acutely infected turkeys in a form which is capable of producing infection if ingested at once, but which persists for only a short time outside the body.

The possibility of the direct transmission of the disease from infected to healthy stock indicates the importance of the isolation of the former.

EFFECT OF MEDIUM ON RATE OF MULTIPLICATION, VIRULENCE AND HEAT SUSCEPTIBILITY OF HEMOLYTIC STREPTOCOCCUS

T. D. Beckwith and E. J. Rose

From the Department of Bacteriology, University of California, Berkeley

Beckwith and Eddie have shown [1] that there is a definite relationship between the mode of cultivation of a certain streptococcus and its susceptibility to heat. This hemolytic streptococcus "H" has been carried as follows: One portion is transferred always upon blood agar slants. This is known as the stock culture. The other method is to pass it monthly from rabbit to rabbit by intrapleural injection. The animal thus inoculated dies in 4 or 5 days. The resulting exudate is pipetted from the pleural cavity and sealed hermetically in a test tube. A 24-hour beef infusion broth culture from this fluid is used for the next animal inoculation. The exudate remains a pure culture of the hemolytic streptococcus as noted by Gay and Stone [2] provided ordinary care is exercised. This culture thus maintained within the body fluids is known as the passage culture. Originally this streptococcus was isolated from a fatal infection in man. The work of Beckwith and Eddie [1] indicates that the stock culture is more resistant to heat than the passage portion by approximately 5 degrees, time factors and mediums being equal and identical. Counts of the numbers of organisms exposed to heat were not made, however, at that time.

It is difficult to ascribe a reason for this difference in susceptibility to heat. Possibly it has some connection with the metabolism of these two strains of the same streptococcus, for Foster,[3] working with the same form showed that there is "a marked difference between a passage strain and a laboratory strain of Streptococcus hemolyticus during the first 3 hours in glucose serum broth. Whereas the passage strain shows a definite decrease in amino acid output coupled with an increased ammonia excretion, the laboratory strain exhibits a decided increase in amino acid output coincident with a slight decrease in ammonia formation." Thus the former may be interpreted to be somewhat more active

Received for publication, April 29, 1925.

[1] Jour. Lab. & Clin. Med., 1924, 9, p. 316.
[2] Jour. Infect. Dis., 1920, 26, p. 265.
[3] Jour. Bacteriol., 1921, 6, p. 211.

physiologically than the latter, and thus more easily susceptible to deleterious influences.

The virulence of an organism may have close connection with its adaptability, and thus, in part at least, with its physiologic activity. We determined to attempt to ascertain the relative virulence of the stock culture and the passage culture of this streptococcus. When this was done, it was decided to expose similar numbers of the organisms to the effects of heat in an endeavor to determine whether there is any relationship between virulence and heat resistance.

Gay and Morrison [4] already have computed the virulence of this passage streptococcus for rabbits, but their work was done some months ago. In the meantime, the culture has been passed through additional animals, a total of 67, and presumably, therefore, its virulence has become increased. We have followed the same method which has proved so dependable in the hands of Gay and Morrison. First, a count was made of the numbers of living organisms in a culture, and second, from this count we estimated the numbers of organisms necessary to kill a 3,500-4,000 gm. rabbit by intrapleural injection.

The initial experiment was to find the numbers of organisms in such 24-hour beef infusion broth cultures. Following is the procedure given by Gay and Morrison.

1. A series of dilutions is made in 9.9 c c. of beef infusion broth from the original 24-hour culture, beginning with 1: 100 and extending in multiples of 10 to one billion. A fresh sterile pipet must be used for each.

2. Of fresh sterile defibrinated rabbit blood 0.5 c c. is placed in each of a series of sterile tubes marked to correspond to the culture dilution series. One c c. of each broth dilution is added to its respective blood tube.

3. Fifteen c c. of melted and cooled fluid beef infusion agar is added to each blood-broth dilution tube. This is then rolled and poured into a sterile Petri dish.

By this method, we have made counts of ten 24-hour beef infusion broth cultures made from pleural fluid passage culture and also from 10 similar cultures prepared from the blood agar stock strain of the streptococcus. Our results were as follows: passage culture (in terms of millions per c c.), 240, 289, 258, 262, 272, 267, 264, 256, 265, 257. The average was 264 millions per c c., which coincides closely with the 266 millions obtained by Gay and Morrison. Stock culture, 160, 151, 156, 203, 156, 175, 163, 159, 171, 164, and with a final average of 166 millions per c c. Multiplication on even the same batch of medium differs greatly therefore, since the passage portion proliferates more

[4] Jour. Infect. Dis., 1923, 33, p. 338.

rapidly than the organisms which have been maintained on ordinary blood agar. The physiologic activity, therefore, of these two portions again is shown to be different.

Having determined the bacterial content of the broth culture, our next endeavor was to estimate the numbers of organisms of each of these two strains of hemolytic streptococcus necessary to kill rabbits.

Two series of normal rabbits with weights between 3,500 and 4,000 gm. were used for each strain. Again a 24-hour beef infusion broth culture was diluted as before in sterile broth, using multiples of 10 from 1:10 to 1:10,000,000. One c c. of the diluted material was introduced intrapleurally into each rabbit. Of the passage culture, one one-millionth killed in each of the two instances. Two different tubes of the 24-hour beef infusion broth passage culture were used. Of these, one showed a count of 268 million per c c., while the other gave a count of 289 million. Thus in each instance less than 300 organisms proved fatal. On the other hand, the stock culture proved to be easily overcome by its rabbit host, since 0.1 c c. was not fatal, and the animals soon recovered. Later it was shown that 1 c c. of a 24-hour beef broth infusion culture counting 165 million organisms per c c. was not fatal in each of 3 trials.

Thus we come to the conclusion that the virulence of these two strains of hemolytic streptococcus, one being maintained in body fluids and the other on blood agar, differs tremendously. In fact, the minimum lethal dose of the passage culture is considerably less than that determined by Gay and Morrison,[4] but this difference we ascribe to a longer period of passage through animals and possibly to individual differences in the animals themselves.

Our next step was to expose known numbers of the organisms to heat to learn whether they are all killed at a certain temperature and after a known time. Our procedure here was nearly the same as that outlined by Beckwith and Eddie.[1] Fresh milk was separated and pasteurized with care at 75 C. for one-half hour. This was then placed in 15 c c. amounts in thin glass test tubes with precautions for sterility maintained throughout. The period of time necessary for such a tube of milk to warm up to the temperature of the surrounding water in a bath was then observed by use of two tested thermometers, one placed in the bath and the other immersed in the milk. It was found to vary from 3 minutes at 50 C. to 9 minutes at 75 C. Having determined previously that a 24-hour broth culture of the stock culture contains 166 millions of organisms per c c., while the expectancy is that the passage culture will have a count of 264 millions as the result of 10 trials with each, we were enabled to add to each tube of milk amounts of culture presumably containing equal numbers of organisms. By means of a sterile 1 c c. pipet graduated to hundredths, we added 0.1 c c. of a 24-hour broth culture of the stock strain or 16,600,000 organisms to a 15 c c. tube of milk. To a second milk tube was added an equivalent amount of passage culture to contain a similar number of cocci. These were then rolled carefully for thorough mixing, and preliminary streaks of the inoculated milk made on blood agar plates with a 3 mm. platinum loop as a control. The tubes were then heated at 50 C.; the lag period was allowed to elapse, after which

TABLE 1

THE EFFECT OF HEAT ON KNOWN NUMBERS OF THE STOCK STRAIN OF HEMOLYTIC STREPTOCOCCUS IN MILK

Temperature	Immediate	10 Min.	15 Min.	20 Min.	25 Min.	30 Min.
50	++++	++++	++++	++++	++++	++++
55	++++	++++	++++	++++	++++	+++
60	++++	+++	+++	+++	+++	++
65	++++	++	++	++	++	++
70	++++	—	—	—	—	—

++++ very heavy growth, +++ heavy growth, ++ good growth, + light growth, — no growth.

TABLE 2

THE EFFECTS OF HEAT ON KNOWN NUMBERS OF THE PASSAGE STRAIN OF HEMOLYTIC STREPTOCOCCUS IN MILK

Temperature	Immediate	10 Min.	15 Min.	20 Min.	25 Min.	30 Min.
50	++++	++++	++++	++++	++++	++++
55	++++	++++	++++	++++	++++	++
60	++++	+++	++	++	—	—
65	++++	++	—	—	—	—
70	++++	—	—	—	—	—

TABLE 3

EFFECTS OF HEAT ON THE STOCK STRAIN AT VARYING POINTS OF HYDROGEN ION CONCENTRATION

Temperature	PH Values						
	5.8	6.2	6.6	7.0	7.6	8.2	8.8
55	+++ 30	+++ 30	+++ 30	+++ 30	+++ 30	+++ 30	+++ 30
60	++ 30	++ 30	++ 30	++ 30	++ 30	++ 30	++ 30
65	++ 30	++ 30	++ 30	++ 30	++ 30	++ 30	++ 30
70	— 10	— 10	— 10	— 10	— 10	— 10	— 10

Numbers represent minutes heating.

TABLE 4

EFFECTS OF HEAT ON THE PASSAGE STRAIN AT VARYING POINTS OF HYDROGEN ION CONCENTRATION

Temperature	PH Values						
	5.8	6.2	6.6	7.0	7.6	8.2	8.8
55	++ 30	++ 30	++ 30	++ 30	++ 30	++ 30	++ 30
60	— 25	— 25	— 25	— 25	— 25	— 25	— 25
65	— 15	— 15	— 15	— 15	— 15	— 15	— 15
70	— 10	— 10	— 10	— 10	— 10	— 10	— 10

streaks with the same loop were made on blood agar plates at the expiration of 101, 15, 20, 25 and 30 minutes. A like method was followed for temperatures of 55, 60, 65 and 70 C. This entire procedure was followed through to conclusion on three different occasions with identical results each time. The tables show the outcome.

It is well understood that the curve of death for an organism exposed to heat or to other unfavorable environment at first slopes in an acute angle to the vertical. In turn this slant tends soon to become more nearly parallel to the horizontal, with the result that a certain remainder, possibly very small in numbers, persist. They may be so few as to be absent even in a fraction of a single c c. Account of this possibility was taken by Beckwith and Eddie,[1] and thus the milk tubes after heating were incubated in order that any remainder might have opportunity to proliferate and thus later to become sufficiently numerous to be recognized by culture. The importance of such a small resistant fraction of organisms in relationship to pasteurization of milk has been stressed recently by Ayers and Johnson[5] in their consideration of the absolute death points of micro-organisms. In order that we might be assured then that all of the organisms of the inoculum had been killed by the heating processes, the milk tubes were cooled at once after heating and then incubated for 24 hours. Subsequent streaking on blood plates proved that they were sterile.

The milk used in these experiments had been shown to be at or close to the point of neutrality electrometrically. Our next attempt, therefore, was to determine whether a change in hydrogen ion concentration in milk would result in any difference in the relative susceptibility of the stock strain and of the passage strain to heat. In this connection it should be noted that Brown and Peiser[6] have stated that the addition of small amounts of lactic acid to a milk suspension of bacteria does not change their thermal death point. For this purpose, then, the reaction of the milk was altered artificially so that there resulted a range varying from P_H 5.8 to P_H 8.8 by the addition of lactic acid or of sodium hydroxide as the case might be. All determinations were made electrometrically rather than colorimetrically because of the difficulty of accurate color comparisons in milk. Heat tests were made immediately after the addition of the acid or alkali. The technic was otherwise the same as that used previously (tables 3 and 4).

Again, it appears that throughout the range utilized here, there persists a relative difference in heat susceptibility between the two fractions, the stock portion being always more resistant than the passage portion. An amount of the lactic acid sufficient to produce curdling of the milk kills within 3 hours without heat.

From this experiment it becomes evident that when the same numbers of streptococci are placed in equal quantities of milk, the thermal death point of the stock strain of this streptococcus is higher than that of the passage strain. It is possible that a similar difference may be found when other protein suspension and solution is used. We, therefore, tested the comparative susceptibility of these two forms in similar

[5] Jour. Bacteriol., 1924, 11, p. 279.
[6] Mich. Agric. Exper. Station, Technical Bull., 1916, 30.

numbers in a mixture of equal parts of inactivated rabbit serum and sterile beef infusion broth which had been carefully neutralized. The results obtained were identical with those in tables 1 and 2. Thus, these differences in heat susceptibility are not due to the effect of the milk.

Our next attempt was to discover whether the two portions of this strain of streptococcus which are unequally susceptible to heat show the same difference with regard to certain germicides. Phenol is the generally accepted standard although its importance has been greatly diminished in later years through the discovery of other compounds with coefficiency much higher and with toxicity greatly decreased. Acriflavine is an exception to most of the germicides. Its coefficiency, which is very great with protein absent, is still further increased by the presence of serum. Its dispersion is very high, but its action is slow in velocity. Crystal violet is decidedly rapid in effect, but is ephemeral and is inactivated by protein.

These substances were tested against the two fractions of the streptococcus in freshly prepared Ringer's solution. All glassware was cleansed with cleaning fluid, rinsed with distilled water and sterilized. Equal numbers of organisms computed as outlined were used in each instance. Streaks were made immediately after preparation on blood-agar plates with a 3 mm. loop, and thereafter at intervals for 24 hours. All preparations were maintained at 37 C. in the incubator.

For germicidal tests with protein we used rabbit serum heated at 56 C. for 30 minutes in order to inactivate alexin. This was used with equal parts of normal salt solution containing the germicide.

As a result of this series of trials, which were carried through 3 times for the sake of accuracy, we have been unable to determine any difference in susceptibility of equal numbers of the two portions of this strain of streptococcus to phenol, acriflavine or crystal violet. This is true whether serum protein is present or absent. Phenol reached its greatest efficiency in 2 hours in the absence of protein and killed at 1:250 but not at 1:300. With serum present, it again reached its maximum effectiveness in 2 hours and was germicidal at a dilution of 1:200 but not at 1:250. Acriflavine killed at a dilution of 1:50,000 without serum and was most effective at 24 hours, while with the presence of serum this critical dilution with a like time factor was 1:350,000. Crystal violet showed its maximum effect in 4 hours at 1:50,000 in Ringer's solution, but with the addition of rabbit serum the highest germicidal dilution was 1:15,000 in each instance, and the time necessary to produce the greatest effectiveness was lengthened to 6 hours. In order to conserve space, the full tabulations of all of these results have been omitted.

We must conclude, therefore, that the susceptibility of the passage strain varies with regard to heat exposure in comparison to that portion which has been propagated continuously on blood agar. It is more susceptible. On the other hand, this difference in susceptibility vanishes when certain chemical compounds rather than heat are used. We cannot explain this difference, but suspect that it will be found to be connected with varying metabolic rates of the two portions.

SUMMARY

A certain strain of hemolytic streptococcus has been maintained in a twofold manner over a period of at least 5 years. It has been cultured continuously in rabbits by intrapleural injection. This is the passage strain. It has been carried on blood agar. The latter is the stock strain.

Proliferation of the passage strain in infusion broth is much more active than that of the stock strain in the same medium.

The minimum lethal dose for normal rabbits of 3,500 to 4,000 gm. weight by intrapleural injection of these two strains differs greatly. Three hundred organisms of the passage culture kill, while 166,000,000 organisms of the stock culture are not fatal.

The thermal death point of the passage culture is lower than that of the stock culture by approximately 5 C. when the numbers of organisms thus treated are approximately the same in both instances. A similar difference is noted also when inactivated serum with broth is substituted for the milk.

This same difference in heat susceptibility persists when the reaction of the medium is altered through a range of P_H 5.8 to P_H 8.8.

This difference in relative susceptibility disappears when chemical germicides are used.

ANTIGENIC PROPERTIES OF CERTAIN GLUCOPROTEINS

KENNETH GOODNER

From the Department of Bacteriology and Immunology, University of Kansas, Lawrence

The small amount of work on the antigenic properties of glucoproteins would seem to warrant further investigations. Wells,[1] using the anaphylaxis reaction, found that hog stomach mucin showed a well developed independent biologic specificity against the serum and tissues of the same species. On the other hand, Elliott,[2] working with swine stomach mucin, ox tendon mucin and ox submaxillary mucin, found that each gave rise to an antiserum that reacted with itself in comparitively high dilutions, with the blood serum of the same species to a less degree, and with the other mucins almost as well as with the blood serum. His results also indicated that the glucoproteins are not as powerful in their antigenic properties as the simple proteins. Wells [3] has distinguished between ovomucoid and ovomucin (ovoglobulin) of the hen's egg by means of the anaphylaxis reaction. Hektoen and Schulhof [4] have recently studied the antigenic properties of extracts of the digestive mucosa and found little inter-reaction with serum proteins. It may be that their antigenic substance was composed, in part, of glucoprotein.

Our purposes in this study have been to test the anaphylactic work of Wells by using the precipitin method; to repeat, in part, the work of Elliott, in order to determine whether the proteins could be so prepared as to eliminate the serum reactions; and with serum reactions eliminated, to study the immunologic properties and inter-relationships of these proteins.

Levene [5] found that chemically the glucoproteins could be arranged in two classes, the prosthetic groups in which were mucoitin-sulphuric acid and chondroitin-sulphuric acid, respectively. To represent the first group (true mucins) we used the mucins prepared from beef submaxillary glands and from hog stomach linings. From the second group (mucoids) we chose chondromucoid from beef nasal septums and tendomucoid from beef tendon (Achilles). We also prepared a gluco-

Received for publication, March 30, 1925.

[1] Jour. Infect. Dis., 1911, 9, p. 168.
[2] Ibid., 1914, 15, p. 501.
[3] Ibid., 1911, 9, p. 147.
[4] Jour. Am. Med. Assn., 1924, 83, p. 1300.
[5] Monograph 18, Rockefeller Inst. for Med. Research, 1922.

protein from beef trachea with the expectation that it would contain a more or less natural mixture of the two types. In order to determine whether a relationship existed between the glucoproteins from two classes of animals we selected ovomucoid and ovomucin from the hen's egg. These proteins, because of certain properties, cannot be exactly classified in either of the great groups.

Beef submaxillary mucin was prepared after the method of Hammarsten.[6] Fresh beef submaxillary glands were cleaned, hashed, and extracted with distilled water for 30 hours, using 2 parts of water to 1 of tissue. The filtrate from this was treated with 10% HCl until the concentration of acid in the liquid was approximately 0.15%. Four volumes of distilled water were then added, and the mucin thereby precipitated. This was repeatedly purified by washing in water of a P_H of approximately 6 and then redissolving in 0.15% HCl, filtering, and reprecipitating by the addition of distilled water.

Swine stomach mucin was prepared according to a method adapted from Elliott's [2] method. Fresh hog stomach linings were finely hashed, and 2 liters of distilled water were added to each kilogram of tissue. After 24 hours the aqueous extract was removed, and the same quantity of 10% NaCl was added. At the end of another similar period this extract was also discarded, and the material washed in running water until free from salt. Then an extraction was made for 24 hours with half saturated lime water, in the same proportion as above. This extract was filtered through paper and the mucin precipitated by the addition of 0.2% HCl. The point of maximum flocculation for this product was at about neutral to methyl red, that is, between P_H 4.4 and 5. This precipitate was washed twice with 0.05% HCl, then dissolved in a minimal quantity of 0.5% Na_2CO_3 and filtered through paper. Sufficient 10% HCl was added to bring the reaction to neutral to litmus, and 0.2% HCl added to the point of maximum precipitation as determined above. This reprecipitation was repeated twice, and then the precipitate was washed free from acid by means of distilled water.

Chondromucoid was prepared from beef nasal septum. The material was carefully freed from adhering tissue, so that the source represented only pure cartilage. This was hashed, and preliminary extractions were carried out with distilled water and 10% NaCl. The tissue was then washed free from salt, and 2 parts, by weight, of half saturated lime water was added. After 72 hours, this was filtered off and the mucoid

[6] Ztschr. f. phys. Chemie, 1888, 12, p. 163.

precipitated from the filtrate by the addition of large quantities of 0.2% HCl. This precipitate was washed twice with 0.2% HCl and then dissolved in a minimal quantity of 0.5% Na_2CO_3 and filtered through paper. To the filtrate enough 10% HCl was added to bring the reaction to neutral to litmus, and then a large amount of 0.2% HCl was added to precipitate the mucoid. This reprecipitation was repeated twice, and finally the mucoid was washed free from acid by means of distilled water.

Tendomucoid was prepared from beef Achilles' tendons by the same method as described for chondromucoid. This is essentially the method of Chittenden and Gies.[7]

Glucoproteins were extracted from beef trachea in the same manner, except that we purposely avoided cleaning the tracheas.

Ovomucin is more often called ovoglobulin and is that fraction of the protein of egg white which separates on half saturation with ammonium sulphate. It is essentially a glucoprotein, yielding about 11% glucosamine on acid hydrolysis,[8] but differs from the general type in being heat coagulable. According to the best chemical evidence, this protein is a definite individual and not composed of 4 fractions as had been previously claimed.[9] To the whites of fresh eggs we added an equal quantity of saturated ammonium sulphate solution, and the precipitate so obtained was washed repeatedly with half saturated ammonium sulphate solution and several times with 0.05% HCl until free from ammonium sulphate.

Ovomucoid is that protein of egg white which is not coagulated by heat, but which redissolves in water after precipitation in alcohol. It is a typical mucoid as regards its composition, but in its chemical behavior it is more of a pseudopeptone. In the preparation of this substance, the method of Robertson[10] was employed. Egg white was diluted, slightly acidified with acetic acid, and boiled for at least 10 minutes. The coagulum was filtered off and the filtrate concentrated by evaporation. To this was added a large quantity of alcohol. The precipitate of ovomucoid was then washed with alcohol twice, dissolved in water, filtered, the filtrate concentrated, and, finally, the mucoid precipitated with large volumes of alcohol.

All extraction was carried out at low temperature and very small quantities of chloroform were used to guard against putrefactive changes.

[7] Jour. Exper. Med., 1896, 1, p. 186.
[8] Matthews, A. P.: Physiol. Chemistry, 1922, p. 316.
[9] Osborne and Campbell: Jour. Am. Chem. Soc., 1900, 22, p. 413.
[10] Physical Chemistry of Proteins, 1918, p. 49.

For the demonstration of immune reactions, we chose the precipitin test alone for the following reasons:

1. Although not as delicate, quantitatively, as the complement-fixation test, this reaction was less likely to be influenced by a slightly alkaline antigenic solution such as was unavoidable in part of this work. We have confirmed Hirsch's statement [11] that a P_H as strongly alkaline as 9.6 does not interfere with the reaction.

2. The results of the precipitin reaction are generally more clear-cut than those in gross anaphylaxis, and this would be especially true in this case because of the chemical resemblance of some of these substances to the peptones. Our experience with Dale's excised uterine strip method of anaphylactic determination would point to the inadvisability of using it unless each reagent could be had in neutral solution.

Rabbits were given successive intraperitoneal inoculations of increasing amounts of the protein in rather concentrated solution at 2 to 3 day intervals. The test bleeding was made on the fifth or sixth day after the last inoculation. This method has given a high degree of satisfactory results in these laboratories when the simpler proteins were used.

The glucoproteins tend to become less soluble if carried through a desiccating series of alcohols and ether, and hence the moist precipitate was used as a basis for all solutions. In preparing solutions of glucoproteins from nonmammalian sources a special technic was employed. The moist precipitate was packed by high speed centrifugalization, and the volume of this material formed the rough but constant basis for dilutions. The first dilution was made by adding 3 parts of 1.7% NaCl, then sufficient 0.5% Na_2CO_3 to bring the solution to approximately P_H 9 (at which point most of the glucoproteins are soluble) and then making up to the full 5 parts with 1.7% NaCl. Other dilutions were made from this using the same reagent. The use of this "double strength" salt solution was based on the original observation of Hammarsten,[12] who found that a solution of glucoprotein could be slightly acidified without the mucin precipitating, provided NaCl had first been added up to 5 or 10%. Since there was some objection to even 5% NaCl, it was determined that 1.7% NaCl (P_H 7) could be used satisfactorily. The mixing of this and the slightly alkaline primary solution tended to make the new solution less alkaline, so that the higher the dilution the more nearly the reaction approached neutrality.

[11] Jour. Infect. Dis., 1923, 33, p. 470.
[12] Textbook of Physiological Chemistry, 1914, p. 170.

In the case of the two proteins from egg white, a plan was adopted to give an accurate comparison with whole egg white. The yield of a known volume of egg white for each of these substances was determined, and in making up the dilutions the basis was obtained by making a packed precipitate up to a volume that would correspond to the original volume of the egg white. Distilled water was used in making the primary solution for both ovomucin and ovomucoid.

The usual stratification method was used in demonstrating the presence of precipitins. Readings were made after two hours, and confirmatory readings after standing overnight in the icebox.

It was found exceedingly difficult to elicit the production of precipitins against glucoproteins. These proteins had been prepared with extreme care, and except for the ovomucin, none contained even a trace

TABLE 1

RESULTS OF CROSS TITRATIONS

Antigens	Serums of Rabbits Immunized with						
	Beef Serum	Beef Chondromucoid	Beef Submaxillary Mucin	Hog Stomach Mucin	Ovomucin	Ovomucoid	Egg White
Beef serum	100,000	0	0	0	0	0	0
Beef chondromucoid	0	50	0	0	0	0	0
Beef tendomucoid	0	0	0	0	0	0	0
Beef trachea mucoid	0	0	0	0	0	0	0
Beef submaxillary mucin	0	0	100	0	0	0	0
Hog stomach mucin	0	0	0	200	0	0	0
Ovomucin	0	0	0	0	1600	50	3200
Ovomucoid	0	0	0	0	50	200	10
Egg white	0	0	0	0	800	25	100,000

of heat coagulable matter, and it might possibly be assumed that they were free from the more prominent serum proteins, at least as regards any considerable amounts. The production of even low titered immune serum following repeated injections of large amounts of protein (which proved to be comparatively nontoxic) was the exception rather than the rule in the many different rabbits employed, and precipitins appeared in the serum of the animal most often only after several courses of injections. We never did succeed in obtaining antibody production against tendomucoid and against the glucoprotein from beef trachea.

The combined results are shown in table 1. The figures indicate the highest dilution of antigen which gave a definite precipitate with the antiserum dilutions being based on the volume of the moist precipitate.

Although at first glance the figures above may seem low, it must be remembered that the dilutions were based on the moist precipitated substance, and if calculated from the dry material would obviously run considerably higher.

In comparing these results with those of Elliott, one notes that the serum reactions have been eliminated. This is not surprising considering the many recent developments in the field of biologic specificity.

Along with the loss of the serum reactions we have been unable to secure cross precipitation among the mammalian glucoproteins, and as a matter of fact, there is no chemical evidence that points to any relationship of these proteins outside of the nonprotein grouping.

The failure of the glucoproteins to show strong antigenic properties may possibly be explained by the amount of extraproteinous matter present in the molecule, for it seems that the greater the amount of this material, the less potent is the substance antigenically. Thus ovomucin has been shown to yield about 11% glucosamine on acid hydrolysis,[8] and is at the same time the best antigen in our series, while ovomucoid yields about 35% and submaxillary mucin about 24% glucosamine,[13] and they are weak antigens.

Since the glucosamine makes up only a part of the prosthetic group, it may be reasoned that a considerable proportion of the molecule is of a nonprotein nature.

It seems evident that this holds for all of the conjugated proteins. Hemoglobin, which has a large proportion of true protein, has been shown by Hektoen and Schulhof [14] to be potent antigenically, while the alpha nucleoproteins, which are largely composed of nucleic acid, were found by Wells [15] to be scarcely, if at all, antigenic. Midway between these two extremes we might place the glucoproteins and Mills' phospho-lipo-protein (the active element of tissue fibrinogen [16]) the antigenic value of which Downs [17] has recently found to be rather low, which might be expected considering the 41.6% of nonprotein matter.

SUMMARY

The results seem to show the complete independent biologic specificity for certain glucoproteins isolated from mammalian sources, but that a certain amount of relationship seems to exist between two glucoproteins of the hen's egg.

[13] Seeman, cited by Müller: Ztschr. f. Biol., 1901, 42, p. 489.
[14] Jour. Infect. Dis., 1922, 31, p. 1.
[15] Ztschr. f. Immunitätsforsch., 1913, 19, p. 599.
[16] Jour. Biol. Chem., 1921, 46, p. 135.
[17] Jour. Infect. Dis., 1925, 37, p. 49.

TOXIC PRODUCTS OF BACTERIUM ENTERITIDIS AND OF RELATED MICRO-ORGANISMS

Sara Elizabeth Branham

From the Department of Hygiene and Bacteriology of the University of Chicago

HISTORICAL

Gaertner,[1] in 1888, the first to attribute meat poisoning to an infection and the first to isolate and describe an organism responsible for it, found that boiled cultures of Bact. enteritidis which he isolated from the flesh of a cow were toxic for guinea-pigs and rabbits when inoculated intraperitoneally. Since then thermostable toxic substances have been reported frequently, especially in connection with outbreaks of food poisoning. A summary of this work may be seen in table 1.

Although most workers have agreed that toxic substances are present in broth cultures of paratyphoid organisms, there has been great difference of opinion concerning the properties of these poisons. Some have emphasized their inconstancy of production and their instability; while others have found the toxicity of filtrates kept in the icebox to persist indefinitely. Different degrees of heat resistance have been reported; most investigators have found a definite thermostability.

The production of serum that neutralized the toxicity of broth filtrates has been reported by Kraus and Stenitzer, Ecker, Aronovitch, Wherry and Butterfield, and Franchetti. Both Franchetti and Ecker found agglutinins in their immune serum, and Franchetti reported complement-fixation.

Precipitation of the toxic substances with ammonium sulphate was obtained by Aronovitch and by Ecker, and with alcohol by Ecker.

The purpose of this work was to gain information about the toxicity of cultures of the paratyphoid group, and about their nature and action in the animal body. Interest centered around the following questions: Are the toxic properties of broth cultures due to the production of true soluble exotoxins by the bacteria? Can antitoxins be prepared to protect animals against their action? Or are the poisonous qualities of cultures due to the so-called "endotoxins"? Are these inherent in the bacterial cell, or are they protein split products which result from enzyme action? Are these poisons simple chemical substances?

STRAINS OF BACTERIA USED

The work was done chiefly with Bact. enteritidis, but other organisms were included in some of the experiments. All of the paratyphoid

Received for publication, April 8, 1925.

[1] Korrespondensbl. d. allg. ärtzl., Vereins von Thüringen, 1888.

TABLE 1

A SUMMARY OF INVESTIGATIONS ON TOXIN PRODUCTION BY THE PARATYPHOID AND TYPHOID GROUPS OF BACTERIA

Name	Organism	Material Used	Toxicity	Thermostability
Gaertner [1]	Bact. enteritidis	Boiled broth cultures	+	+
van Ermengem [2]	Bact. enteritidis	Boiled broth cultures	+	+
Holst [3]	Bact. enteritidis	Boiled broth cultures	+	+
Kaensche [4]	Bact. enteritidis	Boiled broth cultures	+	+
Brion and Kayser [5]	Bact. paratyphosum A	Boiled broth cultures	+	+
Bonhoff [6]	Bact. typhi murium	Boiled broth cultures	+	+
Schottmüller [7]	....	Boiled broth cultures	+	+
Vagedes [8]	....	Boiled broth cultures	+	+
Lochman [16]	Bact. enteritidis	Boiled broth cultures	+	+
Rolly [9]	Bact. paratyphosum B	Boiled broth cultures	+	+
Sacquépée [10]	Bact. enteritidis	Boiled broth cultures	+	+
Gaffky and Paak [11]	....	Boiled broth cultures	0	0
Kurth [12]	....	Boiled broth cultures	0	0
Korte [13]	....	Boiled broth cultures	0	0
Conradi, V. Drigalski, Jurgens [14]	....	Broth culture killed with chloroform	0	
Fischer [15]	Bact. enteritidis	Boiled broth culture	+	+
		Broth culture killed with chloroform	+	
		Suspension heat killed washed cells	+	+
		Broth filtrates heated	+	+
		Broth filtrates unheated	+	+
Trautmann [16]	....	Heated broth cultures	+	+
		Unheated broth filtrate	+	
Uhlenhuth [17]	....	Heated broth culture	+	+
Konrich [18]	....	Heated broth culture	+	
		Heated broth cultures	+	+
Morgan [19]	Bact. paratyphosum A Bact. enteritidis	Filtrates of 5-day broth cultures	+	
Kraus and Stenitzer [20]	Bact. typhi murium Bact. paratyphosum A Bact. paratyphosum B Bact. suipestifer	Filtrates of 11-27 day broth cultures	+	
Yamanouchi [21]	Bact. typhosum Bact. paratyphosum A Bact. paratyphosum B Bact. enteritidis	Filtrates of 3-day broth cultures	+ + +	
Zwick and Weichel [22]	....	Filtrates of 48-hour broth cultures	+	0
Schern [23]	Bact. paratyphosum B	Filtrates of 4-weeks broth cultures	+	+

[2] Bull. d. l'Acad. de méd. de Belgique, 1892, p. 1095.
[3] Baumgarten Jahresb., 19, p. 326.
[4] Ztschr. f. Hyg. u. Infectionskrankh., 1896, 22, p. 53.
[5] München. med. Wchnchr., 1902, 49, 611.
[6] Arch. f. Hyg., 1904, 50, p. 222.
[7] München. med. Wchnschr., 1905, 51, p. 349.
[8] Klin. Jahrb., 1905, 14, p. 517.
[9] Deutsch. Arch. f. klin. Med., 1906, 87, p. 595.
[10] Compt. rend. Soc. de biol., 1907, 63, p. 328.
[11] Arb. a. d. k. Gsndsamte, 1890, 6, p. 159.
[12] Deutsch. med. Wchnschr., 1901, 27, p. 501.
[13] Ztschr. f. Hyg. u. Infectionskrankh., 1903, 44, p. 243.
[14] Ibid., 1903, 42, p. 141.
[15] Ibid., 1902, 39, p. 447.
[16] Ibid., 1903, 45, p. 139.
[17] Gedenkschrift f. von Leuthold, 1906, p. 1.
[18] Klin. Jahrb., 1908, 19, p. 247.
[19] Brit. Med. Jour., 1905, 1, p. 1257.
[20] Wien. klin. Wchnschr., 1907, 20, p. 753.
[21] Compt. rend. Soc. de biol., 1909, 66, p. 1050.
[22] Arb. a. d. k. Gsndhtsamte, 1901, 34, p. 391.
[23] Centralbl. f. Bakteriol., I., O., 1912, 34, p. 391.

TABLE 1—*(Continued)*

A SUMMARY OF INVESTIGATIONS ON TOXIN PRODUCTION BY THE PARATYPHOID AND TYPHOID GROUPS OF BACTERIA

Name	Organism	Material Used	Toxicity	Thermostability
Hoffmann[24]	Bact. paratyphosum B	Broth culture filtrates	+	
Messerschmidt[25]	...	Filtrates of 5-day broth cultures	+	+
Smith and TenBroeck[26]	Bact. of fowl typh.	Filtrates of broth cultures	+	+
	Bact. typhosum		+	
	Bact. suipestifer		+	
	B. dysenteriae		+	
	Proteus vulgaris		+	
Ecker[27]	Bact. paratyphosum B	Filtrates of 24-hour broth cultures	+	+
Aronovitch[28]	Bact. suipestifer	Filtrates of broth cultures	+	+
	Bact. enteritidis		+	+
	Bact. dysenteriae		+	+
	Bact. paratyphosum A		+	+
	Bact. paratyphosum B		+	+
	Bact. typhosum		+	+
	Bact. coli		+	+
	Proteus vulgaris			
Wherry and Butterfield[29]	Bact. enteritidis	Filtrates of broth cultures	0	
Kutscher[30]	...	Filtrates of broth cultures	0	
Bidault[31]	...	Filtrates of broth cultures	0	
Kutscher and Meinicke[32]	...	Filtrates of broth cultures	0	
Levy and Fornet[33]	Bact. paratyphosum B	48-hour broth filtrates	0	
Glaser[34]	Bact. paratyphosum B	48-hour broth filtrates	0	
Bernstein and Fish[35]	Bact. paratyphosum B	48-hour broth filtrates	0	
Cathcart[36]	...	Broth culture filtrates	+	+
		Autolyzed bacteria	+	+
Franchetti[37]	...	Filtrates of broth cultures	+	+
		Autolyzed bacteria		
Heller[38]	Bact. dysenteriae	Broth culture filtrates	+	
		Extracts of cells	+	
Olitsky and Kligler[39]	Bact. dysenteriae	Broth culture filtrates	+	0
		Autolyzed cells	+	+

strains came from Professor Jordan's collection. They were obtained originally from widely separated sources.

51—Bact. enteritidis. Laboratory culture, The University of Chicago.

52—Bact. enteritidis I. Sent to Johns Hopkins Pathological Laboratory from Durham, University of Cambridge, 1900. Probably a very old strain.

53—Bact. enteritidis, Hunt. From human feces in "an epidemic of para B infection," 1911.

[24] Inaug. Diss., Heidelberg, 1912. Abstract in Centralbl. f. Bakteriol., I., Ref., 1912-13, 55, p. 335.
[25] Ibid., I., Orig., 1912, 66, p. 35.
[26] Jour. Med. Res., 1915, 31, p. 523.
[27] Jour. Infec. Dis., 1917, 21, p. 541.
[28] Proc. Soc. Am. Bacteriol., Abstracts Bacteriol., 1920, 4, p. 9.
[29] Jour. Infect. Dis., 1920, 27, p. 317.
[30] Ztschr. f. Hyg. u. Infectionskrankh., 1906-07, 55, p. 331.
[31] Compt. rend. Soc. de biol., 1914, 76, p. 422.
[32] Ztschr. f. Hyg. u. Infectionskrankh., 1906, 52, p. 301.
[33] Centralbl. f. Bakteriol., I, O., 1906, 41, p. 161.
[34] Ztschr. f. Hyg. u. Infectionskrankh., 1910, 67, p. 459.
[35] Jour. Am. Med. Assn., 1916, 66, p. 167.
[36] Jour. Hyg., 1906, 6, p. 112.
[37] Ztschr. f. Hyg. u. Infectionskrankh., 1908, 60, p. 127.
[38] Centralbl. f. Bakteriol., 1908-09, 42, p. 13.
[39] Jour. Exper. Med., 1920, 31, p. 19.

206—Bact. enteriditis. Isolated by Cumming, 1914, from feces of man who attended calves during an epidemic.
226—Bact. enteriditis. From McWeeney, University College, Dublin, 1916. Originally isolated in Alexandria, Egypt, 1916.
228—Bact. enteritidis. Limerick strain isolated by McWeeney, 1909.
323—Bact. enteritidis. Isolated by Wherry and Butterfield from mice inoculated with influenza material, 1920. Reported by them to produce a soluble toxin.
390—Bact. enteritidis. Isolated by Yuri from the heart blood of a rat during an epidemic among rats and mice in Rickets Laboratory, 1922.
180—Bact. paratyphosum B. (Type aertrycki). Isolated by Bernstein and Fish from a pie mixture involved in a food poisoning outbreak in Westerly, R. I. Reported by Ecker to produce a soluble toxin.
379—Bact. paratyphosum B. (Type Schottmüller). Reported by Jordan and Geiger Isolated from a meat sandwich incriminated in a food poisoning outbreak in the Birmingham, Ala., High Schools, 1923.
339—Bact. paratyphosum A. Reported by Jordan and Geiger. Isolated from milk involved in a food poisoning outbreak at Rockford College, Ill., 1923.
290—Bact. suipestifer. From the liver of a pig.

In addition, 3 strains of Bact. coli from the laboratory stock were included; one of them was Bact. coli Y, which has been widely used in many experiments on bacterial metabolism. Bact. dysenteriae Flexner was isolated by Davison during an epidemic among infants in Baltimore. Staph. aureus was of unusual virulence. The last 2 strains were received from Dr. David T. Smith at the Rockfeller Institute. The strains of B. subtilis and Erythrobacillus prodigiosus were taken from the laboratory collection.

TECHNIC

The broth filtrates were prepared by inoculating 200 c c. in liter flasks with a loopful of organisms from 24-hour agar slant cultures. In the case of the synthetic medium adopted later, 500 c c. amounts were used, and a larger inoculum was necessary. After incubation for the desired length of time, these cultures were filtered through Berkefeld N filters, and a small amount of each filtrate was incubated to test its sterility.

Thirty-two different lots of mediums were used. There were wide variations in the toxicity of the filtrates obtained with these even when they were made alike. On the whole, sugar-free broth seemed to have no advantage over unaltered veal infusion broth. The addition of 0.1 to 1% dextrose proved undesirable. The omission of NaCl[40] appeared to be favorable to the quick development of toxicity. The brand of peptone seemed to be important. Bacto, Merck, Difco, Armour and Witte were used in 1% concentration, and invariably Witte proved best. Control experiments were made with every medium used, and they were all without effect when given to rabbits intravenously.

The best autolysates were obtained by modifications of Rosenow's[41] method with pneumococci. Kolle flasks containing veal infusion agar were inoculated, the 24-hour growth washed off into flasks with 0.8% salt solution, the cells washed and then resuspended in salt solution in autolysis 2 and in distilled water in 3 and 4. The bacteria in the suspension were killed — in 2 and 3 by heat, and in 4 with chloroform which was evaporated. The absence of living cells was determined by plate cultures. The suspensions were then incubated

[40] Schoenholz, P., and Meyer, K. F.: Jour. Infec. Dis., 1921, 28, p. 384.
[41] Jour. Am. Med. Assn., 1910, 54, p. 1943.

at 37 C., and from time to time small amounts were removed and centrifugalized; both the supernatant fluid and the washed sediment were used in experiments. The use of distilled water did not seem to introduce complications when animals were inoculated intravenously with the supernatant liquid.

In attempting to find a method that would break up the cells quickly without allowing time for enzyme action, rapid freezing and thawing by the use of liquid air and hot water as described by Melick[42] was tried. The organisms were grown 24 hours on the surface of agar in Kolle flasks, scraped off and washed 3 times in salt solution, suspended finally in distilled water, placed in special silver tubes, and alternately frozen and thawed from 11 to 13 times in rapid succession. Then the material containing the disintegrated cells was centrifugalized at high speed, and the toxicity of the clear supernatant fluid tested in various dilutions. The sediment and the washings from the cells before they were broken up were also tested.

Injections were made into the marginal ear veins of rabbits; into the caudal veins of mice; and into the jugular veins of guinea-pigs.

Variation in the susceptibility of individual rabbits, instability of the toxins, and fluctuations in their production have made the determination of minimum lethal doses unsatisfactory and impossible except within wide limits. Therefore a purely arbitrary standard dose of 2 c c. was chosen, and as far as possible work was done with filtrates, 2 c c. of which would kill a rabbit weighing 1 kilogram within 2 hours.

THE ACTION OF BROTH CULTURE FILTRATES

Symptoms Produced in Rabbits by the Filtrates.—To determine toxic properties in cultures of Bact. enteritidis, 24-hour filtrates of the 8 strains of this organism described were injected intravenously into rabbits. After about 35 minutes some of the animals showed symptoms of severe intoxication. Those that received injections with filtrates from strains 51 and 52 died within 40 minutes, the ones with 226, 323 and 390 died within one hour, and the one with 228 was found dead the next morning. The rabbits receiving filtrates from 53 and 206, as well as from the uninoculated control, remained perfectly well. From the 6 strains that yielded the toxic filtrates, 52 was chosen for use throughout the following experiments.

About 200 rabbits received intravenous injections with toxic filtrates. The injections were followed by a definite incubation period from 30 minutes to 1 hour and 15 minutes in length, the average being about 40 minutes. At the end of that time the rabbits became restless and moved about uneasily. Dyspnea, loss of muscle tone, and prostration soon followed. These symptoms were sometimes accompanied by diarrhea. In fatal cases the animals usually died in convulsions within from 40 minutes to 2 or 3 hours after injection. The body became rigid, with the head drawn back and the limbs extended. Diarrhea was generally

[42] Jour. Med. Res., 1922, 43, p. 405.

absent, but it was nearly always present in nonfatal cases. Animals that lived through the stage of diarrhea and acute prostration usually began to recover during the second hour and often recovered completely, although sometimes they were found dead in their cages the next day. The resistance of these animals was much lowered for the time being, and often secondary infections set in, snuffles being most common. For this reason deaths later than 24 hours after injection were not considered definitely to be due to the effect of the toxic filtrates.

Pathologic Changes.—Necropsy of animals that had just died showed little that was abnormal. There was a marked general vasodilation. The lungs were often almost vermilion. Both large and small intestines were usually filled with a yellowish fluid. Sections from lungs were stained with hematoxylin and eosin. The rabbits from which this material was taken had died at intervals of from 2½ to 15 hours after injection with toxic filtrates. Microscopic examination revealed engorgement of the capillaries and edema in the alveoli in all the lungs. The amount of edema was proportional to the length of time between inoculation and death. The animals dying within 2½ to 3 hours showed this much less markedly than those surviving for 12 to 15 hours. In about 50% edema was conspicuous in the perivascular spaces. Hemorrhage into the alveoli was noted in about 25%. In 60% there were agglutination thrombi in the capillaries. In about 50% there were platelet thrombi. Wright's stain and the anilin blue method for collagen fibrils were used, but they showed nothing significant. The series of rabbit lungs studied was small. Although edema and distention of the capillaries were constant, agglutination and platelet thrombi were not found in all. These observations were confirmed by Dr. H. G. Wells. It is of interest that Hanzlik and Karner [43] have described hemorrhage and thrombi in the lungs of rabbits receiving intravenous injections with a number of different substances.

Results with Other Animals and with Other Methods of Inoculation.—A number of the earlier workers in this field used mice or guinea-pigs inoculated subcutaneously and intraperitoneally.

Series of mice and guinea-pigs received intravenous injections with 0.5 to 2 c c. of toxic filtrates, 2 c c. of which killed the rabbits used as controls within 2 hours. The mice, after about 40 minutes, showed typical intoxication which in 3 of 12 resulted in death—2 within 2 hours and the other within 12 hours; the others recovered. Mice given 1 c c.

[43] Jour. Pharm. & Exper. Therapy, 1920, 14, p. 379; 1924, 23, p. 173.

pigs remained entirely unaffected though some of the 300 gm. animals intraperitoneally seemed a little ill for a time, but recovered. All guinea-received an amount that was fatal to a 1,500 gm. rabbit within 2 hours. Not once have other than the most transient symptoms been produced in either guinea-pigs or mice by subcutaneous or intraperitoneal inoculation with sterile toxic filtrates, nor has the intraperitoneal inoculation of rabbits ever led to noticeable symptoms. All striking results have been obtained with the intravenous injection of rabbits (table 2).

TABLE 2

EFFECT ON MICE AND GUINEA-PIGS OF INOCULATIONS WITH 24-HOUR BROTH CULTURE FILTRATES OF BACT. ENTERITIDIS

Animal	Amount of Filtrate, C c.	Manner Given	Results	Death
Mouse 1	0.5	Intravenously	Dyspnea, prostration, paralysis	In 1 hr.
Mouse 2	0.5	Intravenously	Dyspnea, prostration	
Mouse 3	0.25	Intravenously	Dyspnea, prostration	
Mouse 4	0.25	Intravenously	Dyspnea, prostration	
Mouse 5	0.5	Intravenously	Dyspnea, prostration, paralysis	In 12 hrs.
Mouse 6	0.5	Intravenously	Dyspnea, prostration, paralysis	
Mouse 7	0.5	Intravenously	Dyspnea, prostration, paralysis	In 2 hrs.
Mouse 8	0.5	Intravenously	Dyspnea, prostration, paralysis	
Mouse 9	1.0	Intraperitoneal	Apparent slight discomfort	
Mouse 10	1.0	Intraperitoneal	Apparent slight discomfort	
Mouse 11	1.0	Intraperitoneal	Apparent slight discomfort	
Mouse 12	1.0	Intraperitoneal	Apparent slight discomfort	
Guinea-pig 1	1.0	Intravenously	No effect	
Guinea-pig 2	1.0	Intravenously	No effect	
Guinea-pig 3	1.5	Intravenously	No effect	
Guinea-pig 4	1.5	Intravenously	No effect	
Guinea-pig 5	2.0	Intravenously	No effect	
Guinea-pig 6	2.0	Intravenously	No effect	
Guinea-pig 7	3.0	Intraperitoneal	No effect	
Guinea-pig 8	3.0	Intraperitoneal	No effect	
Guinea-pig 9	3.0	Intraperitoneal	No effect	
Guinea-pig 10	3.0	Intraperitoneal	No effect	
Rabbit 1	2.0	Intravenously	Marked dyspnea, prostration	In 3 hrs.
Rabbit 2	2.0	Intravenously	Dyspnea, prostration, diarrhea	In 1¼ hrs.
Rabbit 3	2.0	Intravenously	Diarrhea and prostration	
Rabbit 4	2.0	Intravenously	Diarrhea and prostration	In 2 hrs.

Feeding experiments with the toxic filtrates were made with rabbits, guinea-pigs, and mice, using 12 of each, but with no positive results. Sometimes the rabbits showed a rise of temperature and some had diarrhea, but there was no evidence that this was due to the ingestion of the filtrates.

PROPERTIES OF THE FILTRATES

The optimum incubation time for obtaining the maximum toxicity was inconstant.

It has been pointed out that the instability of the toxic property of paratyphoid culture filtrates has been mentioned by many. In some of the experiments reported here there was great difficulty in getting filtrates that retained their toxicity. One that seemed strong would be nontoxic the next time it was tested. Thus it was necessary to use a number of control animals with every experiment. This instability may have been more apparent than real, on account of a possible variation in susceptibility of individual animals. With a relatively weak toxin, such variation may be conspicuous. Some poisonous filtrates kept their full strength for as long as two months, and might have kept it longer.

Do these filtrates contain true soluble toxins? According to usually accepted ideas, such toxins are thermolabile. Fourteen toxic filtrates were tested for thermolability by boiling 10 minutes and by autoclaving 10 minutes at 15 pounds pressure. In only 2 was the toxicity completely destroyed by the boiling, and in 8 it resisted the autoclaving. The toxicity seemed, on the whole, rather lessened after heating. The symptoms of the animals given the heated material were the same as those caused by the unheated; and they seemed to be in no way different from those caused by the two filtrates with thermolabile toxicity.

The intoxication produced in rabbits by these filtrates of Bact. enteritidis was in some ways suggestive of the action of histamine. A quantitative determination of the histamine present was made by the methods of Hanke and Koessler,[44] under the direction of Dr. Hanke. A maximum of 0.000625 gm. of histamine was found in the 200 c c. sample of the filtrate. This was too little to have any but the most transient effect on a rabbit. Inoculation of material containing this trace of histamine, enough to equal the usual 2 c c. given, produced no effect in rabbits.

POISON PRODUCTION IN SIMPLER MEDIUMS

It was considered that the more simple the culture medium in which the poison might be produced, the better might be the chance of isolating it. The first step was the substitution of a simple 1% peptone solution for the veal infusion broth. The formation of the toxic material occurred as well here as in the broth previously used.

In order to determine whether or not a simple mixture of amino-acids would serve as well, a medium was made by hydrolyzing Witte peptone. Tryptophane is destroyed in such a hydrolysis. Hence 0.1 gm. was added to a volume that gave an amino-acid content of about 1%. There was abundant poison production in this medium.

[44] Jour. Biol. Chem., 1920, 43, p. 567.

The following medium was finally chosen because it was the simplest, and the organisms grew well in it:[45]

Ammonium lactate	0.6%
K_2HPO_4	0.2%
NaCl	0.5%

This was used at a P_H of 6.8 to 7.2. Growth and poison production were slower in this medium than in those used previously. Filtrates from 6-day cultures were usually very toxic, and their effect on rabbits, both in regard to symptoms and pathology, seemed no different from those of the broth filtrates. Evidently, the presence of protein, peptone, and even amino-acids was unnecessary for the production of toxic material in cultures of Bact. enteritidis.

No precipitate was obtained in these filtrates of cultures in synthetic medium, either with absolute alcohol or with ammonium sulphate. Others have reported precipitating the toxin in this way, but they used peptone broth filtrates, and the toxic elements came down with the protein fractions contained therein. In these filtrates of synthetic medium cultures no bacterial protein could be detected by the methods used. They were toxic, yet not only the biuret reaction, but also the Millon, vanillin, Ehrlich, and ninhydrin tests were negative.

RELATION OF TOXICITY OF CULTURES TO THE NUMBER OF VIABLE CELLS

Comparison of the toxicity of cultures with the number of viable bacteria at different periods of incubation yielded interesting results.[26] This experiment was made with both veal infusion peptone broth and the synthetic medium described. At intervals of several days a small amount of each culture was withdrawn, plate counts made, and the remainder of the sample filtered and tested for toxicity by inoculation into rabbits in duplicate.

In the case of the synthetic medium there was no effect on rabbits until the 7th day, at which time 2 c c. of the filtrate killed a rabbit in 3 hours. After this the toxicity remained constant until the 30th day. On the 37th day and thereafter it seemed nontoxic. The number of bacteria increased rapidly to 3,400,000,000 on the 4th day. This was the maximum, and after this it decreased steadily, though on the 61st day it was still 10,000,000. The toxic properties of this culture did not appear until the cells had begun to die off and disintegrate. The broth

[45] Braun, H., and Cahn-Bronner, C. E.: Centralbl. f. Bakteriol., I., O., 1921, 86, p. 1.

filtrate began to be toxic on the 3rd day. This toxicity increased and remained fairly constant. It was still toxic when last tested on the 61st day. The maximum count of 10,490,000,000 was reached on the 4th day also and fell gradually to 21,000,000 on the 61st. In neither medium was the toxicity appreciable until the cells began to die off. This would indicate that cell destruction and autolysis are more closely related to the occurrence of the poison in the cultures than the active life processes of the cells (table 3 and chart 1).

TOXIC PRODUCTS OF AUTOLYSIS

Autolyzed cultures were studied in order to compare their action with that of the poisonous substances in the filtrates. Autolysates 2,

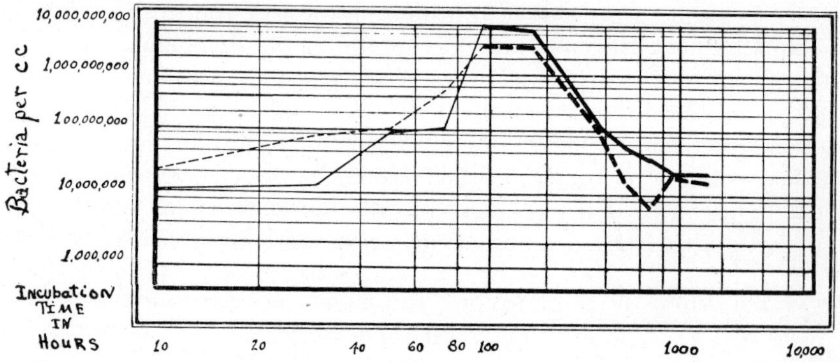

Chart 1.—Relation of toxicity of cultures to number of viable cells. The solid line is the curve of the culture in broth; the broken line represents the synthetic medium; the narrow parts represent the nontoxic portions; the wide parts, the toxic.

3 and 4 were prepared as described, allowed to stand at 37 C., and tested for toxicity from time to time. Very early a toxicity appeared which increased rapidly for a few days, the maximum occurring from the 6th to 10th days, though this optimum incubation time varied with each autolysate. After nearly a year at room temperature, 2 c c. of autolysate 2 still killed rabbits within 2 hours.

The poison was highly soluble, and, as a rule, the supernatant fluid was more toxic than the sediment. Although the toxicity of this material was greater than that of the filtrates, a minimum lethal dose was equally hard to determine. Even with large doses the incubation period was the same as that with the filtrates. The symptoms produced seemed identical. Diarrhea was a more constant symptom than with the filtrates.

Many animals recovered completely, in spite of large doses, but often they died within a few hours.

The activity of these toxic autolysates was never destroyed by autoclaving at 15 pounds for 10 minutes.

Feeding experiments with the autolysates yielded negative results as with the filtrates. Guinea-pigs seemed unaffected by injections except with very large doses, but a number of mice died within a few hours after intraperitoneal injections of 1 c c. Organisms which resembled Bact. enteritidis were isolated from a great many of these mice. For this reason their use in this work was discontinued.

The usual methods of autolysis have not settled the question as to whether the so-called "endotoxin" is native bacterial protein, inheritently

TABLE 3

A COMPARISON OF THE TOTAL BACTERIAL COUNT IN CULTURES OF BACT. ENTERITIDIS WITH THE TOXICITY OF THE FILTRATES FROM THESE CULTURES

Time Incubated	Broth		Synthetic Medium	
	Cell Count	Effect	Cell Count	Effect
10 hours	12,630,000	0	21,400,000	0
24 hours	17,300,000	0	66,000,000	0
48 hours	86,500,000	0	97,350,000	0
72 hours	111,200,000	+	511,000,000	0
4 days	10,490,000,000	++	3,420,000,000	+++
7 days	7,500,000,000	+++	3,015,000,000	++
15 days	114,500,000	++	100,000,000	++
21 days	51,500,000	++	15,500,000	+++
28 days	33,850,000	++	6,400,000	++
37 days	23,000,000	++	19,000,000	0
61 days	21,000,000	++	11,000,000	0

In the table + indicates symptoms of intoxication in the rabbit used, as shown by dyspnea, prostration and usually diarrhea; ++ shows that these symptoms were more severe, and +++ means that the animal died within several hours at least.

a part of the cell, and simply set free on its disintegration, or a protein split product, the result of enzyme action. A method which would break up these cells quickly without allowing time for enzyme action was advisable. Rapid freezing and thawing by the use of liquid air and hot water as described by Melick was tried. The clear bacterial solution thus obtained was inoculated intravenously into rabbits in triplicate in an undiluted state and in dilutions of 1:10, 1:20, 1:40, 1:80, 1:100.

The effects were similar to those produced by the filtrates and autolysates. All rabbits were affected, and the 1:100 dilution produced symptoms as marked as those of the straight undiluted material. Most of these animals recovered. The material obtained by alternate freezing and thawing was apparently identical with that found in the filtrates and autolysates, but was not more toxic in this form than it was usually in a 24-hour broth culture filtrate or a 6-day synthetic medium filtrate. The washings of the cells also proved to be toxic. Animals receiving injections of these did not develop diarrhea, but within the usual definite time showed dyspnea and marked prostration. Rabbits receiving injections with the sediment showed typical symptoms of dyspnea, prostration, and diarrhea, as would be expected since the sediment contained every part of the bacterial cell that had not gone into solution. These animals died within a few hours.

In a later repetition of this experiment parts of the solutions of disintegrated cells were filtered through Berkefeld N. filters in order to remove any bacteria present and were then given to rabbits intravenously in dilutions of 1 : 10 and 1 : 40. The unfiltered material was given in the same dilutions, as were also the cell washings. The 1 : 10 dilutions were more toxic than the 1 : 40, and the unfiltered material was more toxic than the filtered, though all produced characteristic symptoms within the usual incubation period. Material obtained in this same way from Bact. coli was as toxic as that from Bact. enteritidis, but whereas the cell washings of Bact. enteritidis were also toxic, those of Bact. coli were not.

All of the bacteria in the suspensions were not broken up by this method. Much of the material contained some living organisms, so no special significance was attached to the death of animals after a period that would allow multiplication of organisms enough to produce infection. Deaths occurring later than 24 hours after injection are not included.

Young cells of Bact. enteritidis, quickly broken up by freezing and thawing, without opportunity for enzyme action, evidently contained a toxic substance which had an action similar to that of filtrates of cultures and to autolysates prepared in other ways. Washings from such cells before autolysis were also toxic. It seems likely that this poison exists in the bacterial cell, is set free when the cell is broken up, and that it is not a protein split product resulting from enzyme action. That this poison is not peculiar to Bact. enteritidis is evident from the parallel experiments with Bact. coli.

The effect of the intact organisms was next investigated. Rabbits were inoculated intravenously with 2 c c. of suspensions of 24-hour agar slant cultures of Bact. enteritidis, some being given the living suspension, and others the same material after it had been boiled 10 minutes. With these large doses results were obtained similar to those with filtrates and autolysates. The immediate effects were less marked with the living organisms than with the killed, and less with both than with autolysates and filtrates, for none of the animals died from the effect of the poison. The animals that were given the living organisms died within 2 or 3 days.

Apparently the same effects have been produced in rabbits by the intravenous inoculation of filtrates, autolysates of different kinds, cell washings, and by both living and heat-killed organisms. It seems reasonable to assume that the active principle, if it be an integral part of the bacterial cell, would be more concentrated in autolysates than in washings or in filtrates. But the effects of such materials have not been proportionately greater, and the size of the dose has seemed of much less importance than the individual susceptibility of the animals used. The size of the dose has not controlled the incubation period, if this term is used to denote the period elapsing before symptoms appear; this interval has remained constantly about 40 minutes, no matter what amount has been given. If the inoculum was sufficient to produce any symptoms, they occurred within 40 to 50 minutes, even though these symptoms were slight and soon passed away. If the material was sufficiently toxic, the symptoms were more violent and death occurred usually within from 1 to 3 hours. With a sublethal dose the effects began to wear off about ½ hour after the onset of the acute attack, but the animals were left in a much weakened condition, and complete recovery was slow. This constancy of the incubation period, irrespective of the size of the dose, is contrary to what would be expected if a soluble toxin were the chief factor involved. It is further significant to call attention to the essential similarity between the effects produced in the animal body by the extract obtained from Bact. coli and by the toxic materials obtained from Bact. enteritidis by various methods.

PRODUCTION OF PROTECTIVE SERUM WITH TOXIC CULTURE FILTRATES

The production of antitoxins against the toxic substances produced by Bact. enteritidis was undertaken. The first series of large rabbits was treated according to the method of Ecker, but no immunity was produced. By the method of Wherry and Butterfield two series of rabbits were immunized, one with a toxic filtrate prepared from a peptone broth and the other with a filtrate from a synthetic medium culture. The serums of these animals were tested for power to protect other rabbits against both the synthetic medium and the peptone broth filtrates. The serums were not pooled, but each was tested individually, because of the possibility that some animals might not respond to inoculation by the production of antitoxin as well as others. The toxin-antitoxin mixtures were incubated for one hour at 37 C. and then injected intravenously (tables 4, 5 and 6).

TABLE 4

PROTECTIVE ACTION OF SERUM OF RABBITS IMMUNIZED WITH SYNTHETIC MEDIUM FILTRATES

Weight of Rabbit, Kg.	Kind of Toxin	Amount of Toxin, C c.	Amount of Serum, C c.	Source of Serum	Symptoms Produced	Death
1.040	Synthetic	2	...	....	In 40 min., dyspnea, prostration, diarrhea	In 10 hrs.
2.700	Peptone broth	2	...	....	In 30 min., dyspnea, prostration, convulsions	In 1¼ hrs.
1.370	Peptone broth	2	6	Normal rabbit	In 30 min., dyspnea, prostration	In 10 hrs.
1.020	Synthetic	2	6	Normal rabbit	Marked diarrhea	
1.050	Synthetic	2	6	Rabbit 164	No effect	
1.190	Peptone broth	2	5	Rabbit 164	No effect	
1.080	Synthetic	2	6	Rabbit 167	No effect	
1.220	Peptone broth	2	6	Rabbit 167	No effect	
1.680	Synthetic	2	4	Rabbit 169	Marked diarrhea	

TABLE 5

PROTECTION AFFORDED BY SERUM OF RABBITS IMMUNIZED WITH A BROTH FILTRATE AGAINST THIS SAME FILTRATE

Weight of Rabbit, Kg.	Amount of Toxin, C c.	Amount of Serum, C c.	Source of Serum	Symptoms Produced	Death
1.500	3	...	....	In 30 min., prostration, diarrhea	In 5 hrs.
1.200	3	...	....	In 1 hr., prostration, dyspnea, diarrhea	In 3 hrs.
0.720	3	2	Normal rabbit	In 45 min., dyspnea, prostration, diarrhea	
1.070	3	3	Normal rabbit	In 30 min., diarrhea, prostration	
1.040	3	2	Rabbit 207	No effect	
1.800	3	2.5	Rabbit 311	No effect	
2.450	3	3	Rabbit 220	No effect	
0.700	3	1.5	Rabbit 221	No effect	

Table 4 shows the protective action of the serum of animals immunized with synthetic medium filtrates against both peptone broth and synthetic medium filtrates. The serums of rabbits 164 and 167 protected other rabbits perfectly. That from rabbit 169 did not protect at all. The controls given toxin alone were all very ill, and the one given the broth filtrate died within 1¼ hours. The animals given the normal serum were as much affected by the toxin as those that received the toxin alone.

Table 5 shows the protection against a toxic peptone broth filtrate by the serum of rabbits immunized with this filtrate. A toxic 48-hour broth filtrate known as no. 18 was used in immunizing these animals. Serum from each of the 6 rabbits was tested for its protective properties aginst this filtrate. Equal amounts of toxin and serum were used for the test. All serums from treated animals protected against the toxin perfectly, whereas the toxin alone killed the control rabbits within 3 hours.

The serum of these rabbits were tested with a filtrate of a 6-day synthetic medium culture. Two control animals were given the filtrate alone. Both were very ill, with the usual syndrome, but finally recovered. Those given filtrate plus normal serum were affected similarly. Of 4 given filtrate plus immune serum, 2 were completely protected and 2 had some diarrhea and dyspnea, but recovered quickly. Table 6 shows the details of this experiment. Undoubtedly there was

TABLE 6

PROTECTION AFFORDED BY SERUM OF RABBITS IMMUNIZED WITH BROTH FILTRATES AGAINST FILTRATES OF SYNTHETIC MEDIUM CULTURES

Weight of Rabbit, Kg.	Amount of Toxin, Cc.	Amount of Serum, Cc.	Source of Serum	Symptoms Produced	Death
0.760	2	...	....	In 1 hr., prostration, severe diarrhea	
1.080	2	...	....	In 45 min., dyspnea, prostration, diarrhea	In 24 hrs.
1.140	2	2	Normal rabbit	In 1 hr. and 20 min., dyspnea, severe diarrhea	
1.250	2	2	Rabbit 208	No effect	
1.300	2	2	Rabbit 211	In 1½ hrs., slight diarrhea, quick recovery	
1.170	2	2	Rabbit 220	No effect	
1.500	2	2	Rabbit 221	In 1 hr., prostration and slight diarrhea, quick recovery	

protection afforded by the serum of the immunized rabbits. Sometimes this protection was complete and sometimes only partial.

There are many difficulties in immunizing animals with toxic filtrates. If one stable filtrate could be used throughout the experiment the task would be relatively simple, for its approximate strength could be determined and would be a fairly dependable factor. It has not been possible to do this, and several have been used in the same experiment. These always differed in strength, and variation in the resistance of animals made exact determination of a minimum lethal dose impossible. Consequently, many animals were lost during the process by being given more toxin than they could tolerate.

The similarity of action between the autolysates and the filtrates demanded that an attempt be made to determine whether the serum of the animals immunized with the filtrates could protect other rabbits against autolysate. The supernatant fluid of autolysate 4, 2 c c. of which killed a control rabbits within 3 hours, was used for this experiment. Five different immune serums and one normal serum were used. All of these animals became ill within 45 minutes. All recovered, including those given the normal serum. There was no definite protection offered against this autolysate by the immune serum any more

TABLE 7

EFFECT ON RABBITS OF INTRAVENOUS INOCULATION WITH 2 C C. OF 24-HOUR BROTH FILTRATES OF VARIOUS BACTERIA

Strain	Organism	Effect	Death
339	Bact. paratyphosum A	In 50 min., dyspnea, prostration, paralysis	In 5 hrs.
339	Bact. paratyphosum A	In 50 min., dyspnea, prostration	
180	Bact. paratyphosum B	In 50 min., dyspnea, prostration	
180	Bact. paratyphosum B	In 40 min., dyspnea, prostration	In 1 hr.
379	Bact. paratyphosum B	In 1 hr., dyspnea, prostration	In 2 hrs.
379	Bact. paratyphosum B	In 40 min., dyspnea, prostration	In 12 hrs.
290	Bact. suipestifer	In 40 min., dyspnea, prostration	
290	Bact. suipestifer	In 40 min., dyspnea, prostration	
390	Bact. enteritidis	In 45 min., dyspnea, prostration	
390	Bact. enteritidis	In 40 min., dyspnea, prostration, diarrhea	In 12 hrs.
323	Bact. enteritidis	In 40 min., dyspnea, prostration, diarrhea	
323	Bact. enteritidis	In 40 min., dyspnea, prostration, diarrhea	In 12 hrs.
52	Bact. enteritidis	In 40 min., dyspnea, prostration, diarrhea	
52	Bact. enteritidis	In 35 min., dyspnea, prostration, diarrhea	In 12 hrs.
	Bact. dysenteriae, F	In 40 min., dyspnea, prostration, diarrhea	
	Bact. dysenteriae, F	In 40 min., dyspnea, prostration	
	Bact. coli	In 45 min., dyspnea, prostration, diarrhea	
	Bact. coli	In 45 min., dyspnea, prostration, diarrhea	
	Bact. coli	In 40 min., slight diarrhea	
	Bact. coli Y	In 1 hr., dyspnea and diarrhea	
	Bact. coli Y	In 50 min., dyspnea and diarrhea	
	B. subtilis	No effect	
	B. subtilis	No effect	
	Eryth. prodigiosus	No effect	
	Eryth. prodigiosus	No effect	
	Staph. aureus	No effect	
	Staph. aureus	No effect	

than by the normal serum. Normal serum has consistently seemed to have some slight protective action.

The failure of serum from rabbits immunized with toxic filtrates to protect other rabbits against the poisonous substances in autolysate is not to be taken as proof that the toxins are different. The antitoxic strength of the serum was weak and often did not protect completely against the amount of filtrate given. The toxic action of the autolysates was greater than that of the filtrates, and the variabiliy in individual resistance among the animals used prevented a determination of a minimum lethal dose, so that the amounts of serum used might have been insufficient to afford protection.

The possibility must not be overlooked that a true soluble toxin may have been present in small amounts in many or in all of the filtrates, but that the protective action of the immune serum was masked by the larger proportion of endotoxin present. The thermolability of some markedly toxic filtrates of young cultures (not more than 24 hours old), the toxicity of cell washings, and the complete protection afforded by some of the immune serums have indicated that this may be the case. The methods used by Olitsky and Kligler [39] in demonstrating two toxins in Bact. dysenteriae, Shiga have not been applicable to this work with Bact. enteritidis, as the incubation period is too short to allow the production of characteristic lesions. So far it has not been possible to separate the two toxins.

Antibodies other than the specific protective antibodies were found in the blood of these immunized animals. The results of these experiments will be reported in detail in a paper now in preparation.

TOXIC PRODUCTS OF OTHER MEMBERS OF THE COLON-TYPHOID GROUP

The group included strains of other members of the colon-typhoid group: Bact. paratyphosum A, Bact. paratyphosum B, Bact. suipestifer, Bact. dysenteriae Flexner, and Bact. coli. Also several other common bacteria were used: Erythrobacillus prodigiosus, B. subtilis, and Staph. aureus. Three strains of Bact. enteritidis from which toxic filtrates had been constantly obtained were included here as controls.

Twenty-four hour broth filtrates of these were given intravenously to rabbits (table 7). All members of the colon-typhoid group tested produced toxic substances, the difference being apparently one of degree and not of kind. The toxicity of these filtrates in every case survived boiling for 10 minutes. No other organisms tested yielded a poison under the conditions of these experiments, but the evidence is insufficient to warrant the statement that such a property is peculiar to the colon-typhoid group.

GENERAL SUMMARY

Filtrates of fluid cultures of Bact. enteritidis usually are toxic for rabbits and mice, but not for guinea-pigs, when injected intravenously, but are apparently harmless when given by other routes.

The time between the introduction of the poisonous fluids into the blood stream and symptoms of intoxication seems to bear no relation to the size of the dose, but is constantly about 40 to 45 minutes, whether the amount given be lethal or sublethal.

The symptoms are restlessness, dyspnea, prostration, often diarrhea, and either death within 1 to 12 hours or slow recovery. The acute stage lasts about from 30 minutes to 1 hour.

The most conspicuous finding at necropsy is a marked general vasodilation, with edema of the lungs, and in many animals, both agglutination and platelet thrombi in the capillaries.

The occurrence of toxicity in cultures is variable, but it may be found in any medium in which the organism grows. The poisons are thermostabile. Toxicity of broth and synthetic medium cultures appears after the number of living cells has reached its maximum and has begun to decrease.

The toxic properties are demonstrable not only in filtrates of fluid cultures, but in autolysates, and with dead and living bacteria.

Toxic materials, in dilutions in which no protein could be detected, stimulate the production of antibodies. The serum of rabbits immunized with them bestows definite protection on other rabbits when injected intravenously.

Similar poisons are demonstrable with other members of the colon-typhoid group.

The results appear to indicate that the poison demonstrated by these experiments is within the bacterial cells, is set free on cell disintegration, and probably is not a true soluble toxin.

THE PROTECTIVE SUBSTANCE IN ANTI-PNEUMOCOCCIC SERUM

II. EFFECT OF CERTAIN CHEMICAL MANIPULATIONS ON THE STABILITY OF THE PROTECTIVE SUBSTANCE IN TYPE 1 ANTIPNEUMOCOCCUS SERUM

LLOYD D. FELTON

From the Department of Preventive Medicine and Hygiene, Harvard Medical School, Boston

Simple dilution of type 1 antipneumococcus serum with water caused a precipitate of a water-insoluble globulin which contained the major portion of the protective substance of the original serum.[1] It was shown also that chloroform or ether under prescribed conditions caused a denaturization of this globulin with a destruction of its protective properties, and further, an example was given in which denaturization occurred by solution of a sample of protective globulin in hydrochloric acid and precipitation by neutralization with sodium hydroxide. Loss of protective power of the globulin was noted as it became denatured (insoluble in neutral salts). It consequently became important to determine what kind of manipulations could be employed in a further study of the nature of antibodies.

Accordingly this study on the antibody in type 1 pneumococcus serum deals primarily with the effect of certain chemical manipulations on the stability of its protective power. It was thought that the results would serve as a guide in developing methods for precipitation, and aid in the isolation of the antibody. Two procedures were adopted: first, reprecipitation by dilution in water of globulin dissolved in neutral salts (sodium chloride); and second, precipitation of globulin at various hydrogen ion concentrations in a hydrochloric acid—sodium hydroxide mixture.

The relation between the protective power of globulin and the percentage of protein present in solution seemed an important consideration. This relationship was studied by comparing the nitrogen content of the various samples with their protective value.

The same technic for protection tests in mice as in the first study was carried out. The pneumococcus strain used was type 1 Neufeld of such virulence that 0.000,000,1 c c. of a 12-hour broth culture, or 3-30

Received for publication, April 15, 1925.

[1] Felton, Lloyd D.: Jour. Infect. Dis., 1925, 37, p. 199.

organisms, produced a fatal infection in a mouse in 36 to 48 hours. All estimations of protective power were made in duplicate with the exception of one experiment in which more mice were used, and repeated at least once.

EFFECT ON THE PROTECTIVE VALUE OF REPRECIPITATION FROM SODIUM CHLORIDE BY DILUTION IN WATER

Exper. 1.—This experiment is concerned with the reprecipitation, by dilution in water, of a solution of protective globulin in sodium chloride. The material was obtained from 1 liter of type 1 serum precipitated in 15 liters of distilled water. The precipitate was washed once with 5 liters of water, and then dissolved in 200 c c. of 3% sodium chloride. The material so obtained is the number 1 in table 1. After taking out 5 c c. for tests, the remaining 195 c c. were precipitated in 5 liters of fresh distilled water. The precipitate was allowed to collect over night, centrifugalized, and dissolved again in 200 c c. of 3% sodium chloride. The reprecipitation process was carried out 7 times in all. Samples of the dissolved precipitate and of the supernatant from each were saved, and, in a single experiment, tested for protective power. A study of the table reveals that in all instances the supernatant in the quantities used possessed no protective properties, and that after second reprecipitation the dissolved precipitate gradually decreased in protective value. Because the supernatant, which is a dilution of approximately 1:25, had little or no protective power, and the final precipitate only protected in a dilution of 1:10, the conclusion is drawn that the protective substance itself is destroyed. The manner of this destruction is not clear, especially since it is not known whether the protective substance is a chemical attached to the globulin, an enzyme, or a modification of the globulin radical per se. There was undoubtedly some loss of globulin during the reprecipitation; nevertheless, judging from other experiments, the final precipitate must have contained at least 50% as much substance as the original solution.

Therefore, from this experiment, it is inferred, since the water-insoluble globulin present lacked protective properties, and since the supernatant had no determinate protective value, that reprecipitation from sodium chloride by dilution in water causes destruction, not of the globulin, but of its protective property.

RELATION BETWEEN THE PHOSPHORUS CONTENT AND PROTECTION

Exper. 2.—In studying the phosphorus content of protective globulin as compared with that of normal globulin, it appeared that there was more phosphorus in the globulin from the immune than from the normal serum. Reprecipitation of globulin dissolved in sodium chloride by dilution in water reduces the phosphorus content of globulin. The use of this method afforded an opportunity of following, after each reprecipitation, the variation in amounts of phosphorus and nitrogen in relation to the protective value. Accordingly, another sample of precipitate, prepared as in exper. 1, was dissolved in 3% sodium chloride and reprecipitated by dilution with water, the volumes of which are given in table 2. Number 1 sample is the original dissolved precipitate. The results show that the phosphorus content, as tested in 25 c c. amounts, decreased from a maximum of 0.77 mg. in this quantity to a mere trace after the fifth reprecipitation. Such globulin could be thought of as essentially phosphorus-free. On the other hand, the nitrogen in this series of globulins decreased only from

TABLE 1

EFFECT OF REPRECIPITATION FROM SODIUM CHLORIDE BY DILUTION IN WATER ON THE PROTECTIVE VALUE

All mice received injections of 0.5 c c. of a 16-hour broth culture diluted 1: 10

Number of Reprecipitation	Dilutions					
	Supernatant Undiluted	Precipitate				
		1:10	1:50	1:100	1:200	1:400
1	18 18	S S	S S	S S	60 S	22 36
2	36 36	S S	S S	S S	S S	S S
3	18 36	S S	S S	S S	36 60	18 36
4	18 36	S S	48 S	36 S	18 36	36 48
5	22 36	S S	68 84	36 84	36 48	18 36
6	18 36	S S	48 S	84 S	22 84	18 36
7	18 36	S S	36 48	20 36	18 20	20 20

Numbers indicate hours of life; S indicates survival.

TABLE 2

THE RELATION BETWEEN THE PHOSPHORUS CONTENT AND PROTECTION

Number of Reprecipitation	Volume of Diluent, C c.	Protection		Titer of Agglutination	Milligrams Phosphorus in 25 C c.	Milligrams Nitrogen per C c.	Nitrogen in Protective Dose
		Supernatant*	Precipitate				
1	15,000	1,000	1:160	1:80	0.77 0.74	2.80 2.81	0.0175
2	10,000	10,000	1:80	1:60	Less than 0.1	2.83	0.035
3	6,000	1,000	1:40	1:40	Less than 0.01	1.62	0.040
4	6,000	.....	....	Not done	Trace	1.76	
5	......	1,000	1:40	Not done	Trace	1.56	0.039

* Figures given in this column mean the dilution of organism against which 0.5 c c. of supernatant protects mice.

2.8 mg. per c c. to 1.56 mg., a reduction of 44%. The protective value dropped from a dilution of 1: 160 to a dilution of 1: 40, a reduction of 75%. Yet the decrease in phosphorus content was more rapid than the decrease in nitrogen and also in the protective value of the reprecipitated globulin. As seen in the last column of the table, the number of milligrams of nitrogen necessary for protecting against a milliom MLD remains quite constant. From this study, it may be inferred that the phosphorus content does not parallel the protective power of the globulin; but, on the other hand, protective value bears a direct relationship to the amount of nitrogen. Since in exper. 1 the protective antibody was destroyed after 7 reprecipitations, it is necessary to limit the statements to this single experiment. For, had nitrogen determinations been made on the globulin of exper. 1, a parallelism between the nitrogen content and the protective power of the globulin would not have been found throughout the entire number of reprecipitation.

EFFECT OF REPEATED PRECIPITATION FROM HYDROCHLORIC ACID SOLUTION BY NEUTRALIZATION WITH SODIUM HYDROXIDE

Exper. 3.—Exper. 3 consisted of reprecipitation of a sample of globulin dissolved in hydrochloric acid by neutralizing with sodium hydroxide to that point

TABLE 3A

EFFECT OF REPEATED PRECIPITATION FROM HYDROCHLORIC ACID SOLUTION BY NEUTRALIZATION WITH SODIUM HYDROXIDE

Hydrogen Ion Concentration of Supernatant	Milligrams Nitrogen per 10 C c. Supernatant	Volume Used		Protection Supernatant Dilution of Culture	Milligrams Nitrogen per C c. Precipitate	Average Protection 17 Mice Dilutions 60, 70, 80, 100	Nitrogen in Protective Dose	Nitrogen in Protective Dose Calculated to 100%
		Hydrochloric Acid (C c.)	Sodium Hydroxide (C c.)					
	2.135	50	40	1:500	1.85	83	0.0210	0.0266
6.6	0.448	35	35	1:500	1.51	66	0.0172	0.026
6.3	0.742	30	30	1:500	1.50	66	0.0170	0.026
6.2	0.280	30	30	1:5,000	1.44	78	0.0164	0.021
6.0	0.189	20	20	1:5,000	1.43	78	0.0163	0.021
6.3	0.196	20	20	*1:5,000(—)	1.34	81	0.0152	0.019
6.2	0.161	20	20	1:5,000(—)	1.29	86	0.0147	0.017
6.2	0.147	20	20	1:5,000(—)	1.275	58	0.0145	0.025
6.0	0.140	20	20	1:5,000	1.27	51	0.0144	0.028
6.0	0.184	20	20	1:500	1.257	60	0.0143	0.024
5.9	0.236	0	0	1:500	1.250	65	0.0143	0.022

* (—) indicates failure to protect against a dilution of 1:5,000 culture. No mark indicates survival with that dilution of culture when the mice received injections with 0.5 c c. of the undiluted supernatant.

which gave maximum precipitation, that is, near the iso electric point. The protective globulin was obtained by precipitation of serum in dilute phosphoric acid. Thus 1 liter of serum was poured into 15 liters of distilled water acidulated with 40 c c. of normal phosphoric acid, and the resultant precipitate was washed once with distilled water. The globulin thus prepared was suspended in 400 c c. of water and then dissolved by the addition of 50 c c. of N/20 hydrochloric acid. This acid solution of globulin was neutralized with 40 c c. of N/20 sodium hydroxide, and the precipitate formed thereby was thrown down in a centrifuge. The supernatant was carefully decanted, and the precipitate was again suspended in 400 c c. of distilled water, and dissolved by the addition of 35 c c. of N/20 hydrochloric acid. The process of dissolving in acid and precipitating by neutralization with alkali was repeated 10 times in alternation with the amounts of acid and of alkali for each operation given in table 3a. Samples of 10 c c. were taken out after the precipitate had been made to a volume of 400 c c. with water, and dissolved in 10 c c. of 3% sodium chloride. The 10 reprecipitations were carried out in two stages, and the solutions kept in the icebox between operations so that at no time was the solution above room temperature. The hydrogen ion concentration at which precipitation occurred ranged from P_H 6.6 down to P_H 5.9, the concentration in all samples being above P_H 5.4, the isoelectric point of the classical euglobulin. The eleventh precipitate, as shown in the table, was washed with water, centrifugalized, and dissolved by adding sufficient sodium chloride crystals. The protective value for each specimen was estimated from the average of 17 mice, from dilutions 1: 100, 1: 80, 1: 70, and 1: 60. An example of the estimation at a dilution of 1: 100 is given in table *3,b*. The average protective value of the globulin samples in these dilutions was considered the end-point. The calculation of the amount of nitrogen necessary for protection which is given in the eighth column of table *3,a,* is based on this average. As a matter of interest also, the amount of nitrogen which would be necessary to assume 100% protection with the individual samples is given in the last column of table *3,a*. This table suggests certain inferences. In the first place, the hydrogen ion concentration at which precipitation occurred is P_H 6 or above. Second, after the third precipitation, the supernatant maintains

TABLE 3B

EFFECT OF REPEATED PRECIPITATION FROM HYDROCHLORIC ACID SOLUTION BY NEUTRALIZATION WITH SODIUM HYDROXIDE
(An example of the 1: 100 dilution)

Allmice received injections of 0.5 c c. of a 16-hour broth culture diluted 1: 10

Number of Reprecipitation	Record of Injected Mice				
	1	2	3	4	5
1	S	S	S	S	S
2	S	S	S	S	S
3	S	S	S	S	S
4	108	S	S	S	S
5	60	S	S	S	S
6	66	108	S	S	S
7	18	S	S	S	S
8	36	36	60	84	S
9	36	60	S	S	S
10	36	84	84	S	S
11	18	108	S	S	S
Control of organism	1:10,000,000 36 36		1:1,000,000 18 48		1:100,000 36 36

Numbers indicate hours of life; S indicates survival.

a rather constant nitrogen, suggesting thus a uniform product. Third, there is a gradual decrease of the nitrogen content of the precipitate, but up to the seventh reprecipitation, apparently an increase in the protective power of this precipitate, with a fall in value in the eighth, ninth, and tenth samples. Fourth, the calculation of the amount of nitrogen in a protective dose based on the average number of animals surviving when receiving injections with amounts of protective globulin in dilutions of 1: 100, 1: 80, 1: 70, and 1: 60 reveals a uniformity of dosage, and only when calculation is based on 100% protection does it become apparent that there is a decrease in potency of the globulin of the last 4 samples. The final precipitate which was dissolved with sodium chloride crystals contained 7.34 mg. per c c. of nitrogen, and when diluted 1: 400 protected each of four mice that received injections with 0.5 c c. of a 1: 10 culture in which the duplicate control died in 1: 10,000,000 dilution of culture.

Accordingly, it would seem that, contrary to the results of reprecipitation with sodium chloride in the previous experiment, reprecipitation by neutralization with sodium hydroxide from a hydrochloric acid solution of globulin causes no great loss of the protective antibody.

DENATURIZATION OF THE PROTECTIVE GLOBULIN IN RELATION TO ITS PROTECTIVE POWER

Exper. 4.—Exper. 4 is a repetition of exper. 3. It reveals interesting facts, for this particular lot of globulin became denatured (that is, became insoluble in sodium chloride) as reprecipitation was carried out, and thus presented the opportunity of studying the effect of denaturization on the protective value of globulin. This was done by estimation of the protective value of these 3 fractions: (1) supernatant; (2) sodium chloride soluble; (3) sodium hydroxide soluble but sodium chloride insoluble. The protective value was based on the nitrogen content of the several fractions, as shown in table 4. The supernatant

TABLE 4

DENATURIZATION OF THE PROTECTIVE GLOBULIN IN RELATION TO ITS PROTECTIVE POWER

Number of Reprecipitation	Supernatant			Precipitate: Soluble in 1% NaCl			Precipitate: Soluble in NaOH Insoluble in 1% NaCl		
	Protection	Milligrams Nitrogen per C c.	Nitrogen in Protective Dose	Protection	Milligrams Nitrogen per C c.	Nitrogen in Protective Dose	Protection	Milligrams Nitrogen per C c.	Nitrogen in Protective Dose
1	0.5	0.63	0.315	1:80	1.68	0.021	1:80	0.3	0.004
2	0.5	0.20	0.10	1:80	0.74	0.009	1:80	1.65	0.0206
3	0.5	0.08	0.04	1:80	1.10	0.014	1:80	0.81*	0.0101
4	1.0	0.1	0.044	1:20	0.28	0.014	0	0.78	0
5	0.5	0.088	0	0.2	0.11	0.022	0	0.40	0
6	0	0.094	0	0	0.08	0	0	0.58	0
7	0	0.046	0	0	0.11	0	0	0.43	0
8	0	0.014	0	0	0.03	0	0	0.47	0
9	0	0.056	0	0	0.08	0	0	0.40	0
10	0	0.042	0	0	0.087	0	0	0.46	0

0 signifies failure to protect.

* At this stage and after each subsequent reprecipitation some of the globulin became insoluble in hydrochloric acid and was filtered from the solution. This acounts for the discrepancy in nitrogen content of the three fractions.

fluid was found to protect to the fourth reprecipitation; and the salt-soluble seemingly as long as the solution of the globulin contained as much as 0.1 mg. of nitrogen per c c., while the fraction insoluble in salt but soluble in sodium hydroxide protected only through the third reprecipitation.

Since all the samples insoluble in sodium chloride but soluble in alkali contained considerable nitrogen, the decrease in protective value of this fraction of globulin insoluble in a neutral salt, is a confirmation of the work [1] in which it was shown that under specified conditions protective globulin was denatured and made inert by the action of chloroform and of ether. Indeed, it has been observed in general that agents which render the protective globulin insoluble in neutral salts cause destruction of its protective property.

EFFECT OF RAPID PRECIPITATION AT VARIOUS HYDROGEN ION CONCENTRATIONS

Exper. 5.—The object was to determine the effect on the protective value of the antibody of rapid and repeated precipitation at various hydrogen ion concentrations in a hydrochloric acid — sodium hydroxide mixture. By "rapid" is meant immediate centrifugalization after adding to the hydrochloric acid — globulin solution sufficient sodium hydroxide to assure the desired hydrogen ion concentration. Reprecipitation was done twice with each of 6 aliquot portions, adjusted respectively to P_H 5.4, 6, 6.4, 7, 7.6, 8.6. For example, the precipitate of the sample adjusted to a hydrogen ion concentration of P_H 5.4 was dissolved in hydrochloric acid and reprecipitated by neutralizing with sodium hydroxide to the same hydrogen ion concentration. Thus for each of the 6 portions there were 4 samples for testing, i. e., first and second supernatant, and first and second precipitate. The results show in the case of the 2 supernatants (table 5) that (1) the major portion of the globulin precipitate at the various hydrogen ion concentrations was thrown down in the first operation. For the hydrogen ion concentration in each sample was constant and the globulin in the second supernatant might well be the amount which is soluble in the sodium chloride made by the neutralization of hydrochloric acid by sodium hydroxide. (2) The greatest amount of protection remained in the first supernatant at P_H 5.4, the least at P_H 7 and above. (3) So far as results on animals can be relied on to estimate small differences, the amount of globulin present is, in the main, an index of protective value of any given fraction. However, there was an exception in the case of the first supernatant at P_H 6.4. Here the amount of nitrogen in a protective dose was at least three times that of any of the other supernatants. A study of the results of the first and second precipitates reveals a fairly close relationship between their nitrogen content and their protective value. The second precipitate, in a case of hydrogen ion concentrations at P_H 5.4 and at P_H 6, contained more protein in a protective dose than in those of a higher hydrogen ion concentration, and about one-half as much nitrogen as that of the first precipitate.

TABLE 5

EFFECT OF RAPID PRECIPITATION AT VARIOUS HYDROGEN ION CONCENTRATIONS

Hydrogen Ion Concentration at Precipitation	First Precipitate						Second Precipitate					
	Supernatant			Precipitate			Supernatant			Precipitate		
	Milligrams Nitrogen per C c.	Protective Dose	Nitrogen in Protective Dose	Milligrams Nitrogen per C c.	Protective Dose	Nitrogen in Protective Dose	Milligrams Nitrogen per C c.	Protective Dose	Nitrogen in Protective Dose	Milligrams Nitrogen per C c.	Protective Dose	Nitrogen in Protective Dose
5.4	1.83	1:80	0.023	0.34	1:10	0.034	±	±	—	0.25	0.5	0.125
6.0	0.64	1:10	0.064	1.93	1:80	0.024	0.06	±	—	1.20	1:20	0.060
6.4	0.37	0.5	0.185	2.29	1:60	0.038	0.06	0.5	0.03	2.0	1:100	0.020
7.0	0.08	0.5	0.04	2.45	1:60	0.041	0.06	0.5	0.03	2.16	1:100	0.0216
7.6	0.11	0.5	0.055	2.86	1:80	0.036	0.09	0.5	0.045	2.39	1:100	0.0239
8.6	0.06	±	—	2.86	1:60	0.048	0.08	0.5	0.04	2.02	1:100	0.0202

It may be inferred, therefore, since the supernatant lacked measurable protective value, that rapid reprecipitation at a hydrogen ion concentration below P_H 6 causes some destruction of the protective substance, while, on the other hand, reprecipitation at higher P_H values results in a decrease in the amount of nitrogen to a protective dose. Care must be exercised in making deductions from this experiment in regard to the iso-electric point of the protective globulin; for the relative difference in rate of solubility of euglobulins in acid and alkali must be considered as well as the time for establishment of solution equilibrium.

FRACTIONAL PRECIPITATION AT VARIOUS HYDROGEN ION CONCENTRATIONS: SHAKEN FOR TWO HOURS

Exper. 6.—Expers. 6 and 7 represent attempts to separate globulins of different physicochemical properties through their solubilities at various hydrogen ion concentrations. The first was carried out as follows: a sample of type 1 precipitate obtained by a tenfold dilution with water was dissolved in N/20 hydrochloric acid, and the volume made up to a liter. Sodium hydroxide was then added until a slight but definite flocculation occurred, and the mixture

TABLE 6

FRACTIONAL PRECIPITATION AT VARIOUS HYDROGEN ION CONCENTRATIONS: SHAKEN FOR TWO HOURS

Fraction	Volume, C c.	Hydrogen Ion Concentration of Various Fractions	Total Nitrogen	Protective Dose	Total Units	Nitrogen in Protective Dose
Original solution....	1,000	....	460	1:40	40,000	0.0115
Precipitates						
1................	15	5.01	7.65	1:10	150	0.051
2................	100	5.49	136	1:60	6,000	0.0226
3................	180	6.4	270	1:40	7,200	0.037
4................	700	7.0	84	1:5	3,500	0.024

was shaken at room temperature for 2 hours, centrifugalized, and the precipitate dissolved in 15 c c. of 3% sodium chloride. To the clear supernatant another increment of sodium hydroxide sufficient to cause definite precipitation was added. In all, 4 reprecipitations were made, and samples of each precipitate were saved for determination of nitrogen content and for estimation of protective value. The results (table 6) are somewhat indefinite, perhaps in part due to variation in length of time of shaking between the first and last precipitate; also because shaking was not continued a sufficient length of time to establish acid-base equilibrium. The decrease of antibody strength by shaking so far has proved an uncontrollable factor; for some samples of globulin when reprecipitated lose their protective property under apparently the same conditions which do not affect others. The inference is plain for this experiment, that the protective water-insoluble globulin obtained by simple dilution in water of type 1 antipneumococcus serum is comparatively a pure substance. For, regardless of the hydrogen ion concentration at which the precipitate was obtained, the amount of protein, as judged by nitrogen content, in a protective dose was rather uniform. Furthermore, if it be assumed that the globulin of this experiment is uniform, then the range of total solubility is greater than that of the classical euglobulin, which is completely soluble first at P_H 4.8, and then at P_H 6.8 to 6.9. This experiment shows that the type 1 antibody is sufficiently stable to enable an exhaustive study of its chemical nature.

FRACTIONAL PRECIPITATION AT VARIOUS HYDROGEN ION CONCENTRATIONS: SHAKEN FOR FOUR HOURS

Exper. 7.—Table 7 represents a repetition of the preceding experiment in which shaking, to establish a better acid-base equilibrium, was continued for 4 instead of 2 hours. Also, smaller amounts of alkali were used, so that the changes in hydrogen ion concentration would be less. In other ways, the technic of the experiments is identical.

The results, however, are more definite in this than in the preceding experiment. By comparing the total nitrogen content of the different samples, the hydrogen ion concentration of least solubility is found to be at P_H 5.86. If the protective value or number of units is used as a basis for comparison, the hydrogen ion concentration of the lowest solubility of the protective substance is nearer P_H 5.93. A consideration of these

TABLE 7

FRACTIONAL PRECIPITATION AT VARIOUS HYDROGEN ION CONCENTRATIONS: SHAKEN FOR FOUR HOURS

Fraction	Volume, C c.	Hydrogen Ion Concentration of Precipitate	Total Nitrogen	Protective Dose	Total Units	Volume N/100 NaOH, C c.	Nitrogen in Protective Dose
Original solution..	1,000	....	826	1:80	80,000	..	0.0103
Precipitates							
1.............	100	5.14	49	1:40	4,000	2	0.01225
2.............	150	5.4	150	1:40	6,000	5	0.025
3.............	100	5.86	293	1:80	8,000	10	0.0366
4.............	200	5.93	196	1:160	32,000	40	0.0061
5.............	50	6.4	19	1:20	1,000	50	0.019

two facts suggests the possibility that there are two globulins of different iso-electric points in this sample of precipitate, the one having an iso-electric point on the alkaline side of the other.

PRECIPITATION AT VARIOUS HYDROGEN ION CONCENTRATIONS WITH HYDROCHLORIC ACID AND SODIUM HYDROXIDE MIXTURES SHAKEN FOR TWO HOURS

Exper. 8.—Expers. 8 and 9 were for the purpose of estimating the effect of the chemical procedure used on the protective value of the antibody, as well as to serve as a possible guide in determining the iso-electric point of the protective substance in type 1 pneumococcus serum. In numerous instances it has been observed that apparent variation of action of the protective globulin from that of the classical euglobulin could be explained only on the assumption of different iso-electric points for the two globulins. The proof of this hypothesis cannot yet be given, but these experiments indicate that the protective globulin, at least of type 1 pneumococcus serum, has an iso-electric point on the alkaline side of the euglobulin derived from normal horse serum. The experiments here described consisted in dissolving a sample of protective globulin in dilute hydrochloric acid, dividing it into aliquot parts, and adjusting to various hydrogen ion concentrations by the addition of graded amounts of sodium hydroxide. The amount of sodium hydroxide to be added was calculated by dividing the amount of alkali needed to dissolve the precipitate by the number of samples.

In the first experiment, a sample of globulin which had been precipitated by dilution with water and subsequently washed once with half the volume used in dilution, was dissolved in N/20 hydrochloric acid and then divided into 10 equal parts. To the first sample, 4.5 c c. of N/10 sodium hydroxide was added, or a sufficient amount to form a precipitate. In each of the succeeding tubes in turn was added an increment of 0.59 c c. of alkali. Sufficient water was added

TABLE 8

PRECIPITATION AT VARIOUS HYDROGEN ION CONCENTRATIONS WITH HYDROCHLORIC ACID AND SODIUM HYDROXIDE MIXTURES, SHAKEN FOR TWO HOURS

Hydrogen Ion Concentration of Supernatant	Volume N/10 NaOH, C c.	Milligrams Nitrogen per C c.		Protective Dose		Nitrogen in Protective Dose	
		Supernatant	Precipitate	Supernatant	Precipitate	Supernatant	Precipitate
4.96	4.5	0.86	0.09	1:40	1:2	0.0215	0.045
5.49	5.09	0.79	0.28	1:40	1:5	0.01975	0.056
5.95	5.68	0.42	0.51	1:40	1:10	0.0105	0.051
6.22	6.25	0.34	0.61	1:30	1:10	0.0113	0.061
6.57	6.86	0.24	0.72	1:2	1:40	0.12	0.018
6.67	7.45	0.11	0.87	1:2	1:40	0.055	0.0217
6.95	8.04	0.03	0.91	1:2	1:40	0.015	0.0222
7.49	8.63	0.28	0.67	1:20	1:20	0.014	0.0335
7.70	9.22	0.41	0.54	1:20	1:20	0.0205	0.027
8.45	9.81	0.61	0.30	1:20	1:5	0.0305	0.06

to make the volume in all tubes the same. The tubes were shaken for 2 hours, the precipitates collected by centrifugalization, and finally dissolved in the original volume of 2% sodium chloride. Nitrogen determinations and protection tests were made both on the dissolved precipitate and on the supernatant. When possible, after a 2 hours' shaking, hydrogen ion concentrations were determined on the supernatant by means of the gas chain, using Clark's electrode. Colorimetric estimations were made when the protein content was low.

In the study of the results (table 8), there are 3 items to be considered, both in the precipitate and the supernatant: (1) the hydrogen ion concentration of least solubility; (2) the hydrogen ion concentration of least protective value; (3) the hydrogen ion concentration of least amount of globulin necessary to protect a unit dose of organism. The first of these shows from the standpoint of both the supernatant fluid (minimum nitrogen) and the precipitate (maximum nitrogen) that a hydrogen ion concentration of P_H 6.95 approaches the iso-electric point of the globulin in this sample. The second factor, or the hydrogen ion concentration of the least content of protection, is apparently not so definite; for the zone extends from a hydrogen ion concentration of P_H 6.57 to P_H 6.95. In like manner, at the hydrogen ion concentration in which the protection is the least per milligram of nitrogen, the same zone (P_H 6.57 to 6.95) is found.

PRECIPITATION AT VARIOUS HYDROGEN ION CONCENTRATIONS WITH HYDROCHLORIC ACID AND SODIUM HYDROXIDE MIXTURES, SHAKEN FOR EIGHT HOURS

Exper. 9.—In exper. 8 the samples were shaken for only 2 hours after addition of the desired amount of alkali. The work of Cohn[2] has emphasized the necessity of longer exposure of globulins to solvent to establish equilibrium. For this reason, a repetition of the former study was made in which shaking was continued for 8 instead of 2 hours. Furthermore, the sample of precipitate was divided into 13 instead of 10 aliquot parts. The results (table 9) are in accord with those obtained in the study in which shaking was continued for 2 hours. A study of the nitrogen content in the precipitates, their relative protective value, and the amount of nitrogen in a protective dose, indicates that the protective globulin is least soluble at a hydrogen ion concentration between P_H 6.6 and P_H 7. The method, or the degree of purity of the globulin, does not permit of a more definite estimation of the iso-electric condition. That there were globulins in this sample having different iso-electric points is indicated from the fact that the greatest amount of precipitate was obtained at a hydrogen ion concentration of P_H 6.3, but that the globulin of the greatest protective value was found at a hydrogen ion concentration of P_H 6.6 to P_H 7.

TABLE 9

PRECIPITATION AT VARIOUS HYDROGEN ION CONCENTRATIONS WITH HYDROCHLORIC ACID AND SODIUM HYDROXIDE MIXTURES, SHAKEN FOR EIGHT HOURS

Hydrogen Ion Concentration of Supernatant	Volume N/100 NaOH, C c.	Volume Water, C c.	Milligrams Nitrogen per C c. of Precipitate	Protective Dose of Precipitate	Nitrogen in Protective Dose
5.0	0.8	3.0	0.24	1:10	0.024
5.2	1.0	2.8	0.34	1:15	0.0202
5.4	1.2	2.6	0.32	1:20	0.016
5.5	1.4	2.4	0.56	1:40	0.014
5.8	1.6	2.2	0.53	1:50	0.0106
6.2	1.8	2.0	0.61	1:50	0.0122
6.3	2.0	1.8	0.65	1:50	0.013
6.4	2.2	1.6	0.63	1:50	0.0126
6.6	2.4	1.4	0.64	1:70	0.0092
6.8	2.6	1.2	0.59	1:70	0.0084
7.0	2.8	1.0	0.58	1:70	0.0083
7.3	3.2	0.6	0.61	1:40	0.0152
7.8	3.6	0.2	0.28	1:15	0.0186

Protective power did not run parallel to nitrogen content, a fact which indicates, providing antibodies are protein, the presence of globulins of different iso-electric points. Further study along this line is being done in an endeavor to isolate the globulin which alone possesses protective properties and to determine its iso-electric point.

[2] Jour. Gen. Physiol., 1922, 4, p. 697.

SUMMARY AND DISCUSSION

The results of these experiments have served two purposes, the one an orientation as to the possible iso-electric zone of the antibody of type 1 pneumococci and the other showing the possibility of a physico-chemical study of protective globulin with the assurance of the persistence of its protective properties. Certain inferences, however, may be made. In the first place, the protective water-insoluble globulin contained in type 1 antipneumococcus serum loses its protective power when the process of dissolving in sodium chloride and precipitating by dilution in water in alternation is often repeated (at room temperature). This process causes a loss in protection as determined by nitrogen content and also frees the protein almost completely of phosphorus. As the phosphorus-free globulin possesses protective properties, it is assumed that the protective substance contains no essential phosphorus or that its content is extremely small. However, protective globulin dissolved and reprecipitated respectively by dilute hydrochloric acid (N/20) and by sodium hydroxide, so long as it does not become insoluble in neutral salts, maintains its protective power for at least 10 reprecipitations. Fractional precipitation at various hydrogen ion concentrations in hydrochloric acid-sodium hydroxide mixtures yields variable results, doubtless due in part to long continued shaking at room temperature. This is particularly the case for the last fraction in which in one experiment shaking was continued for 28 hours. However, in the main it may be stated that the greater part of the protective substance is precipitated at a hydrogen ion concentration of between P_H 6 and 7. These results with the fractional precipitation method are confirmed by the two experiments in which precipitation at various hydrogen ion concentrations was carried out but once on each sample in a hydrochloric acid-sodium hydroxide mixture.

It must be emphasized that the experiments in this paper are preliminary and are reported only to give some idea of the stability of the antibody of type 1 serum, to show the probability of more exact chemical studies. Although the iso-electric zone has been rather definitely shown, the iso-electric point of the protective globulin has not been exactly determined by the methods used in this work.

QUANTITATIVE RELATIONS BETWEEN ANTIGEN AND ANTIBODY IN THE PRECIPITIN REACTION

H. W. Cromwell

From the Laboratory of Medical Bacteriology, University of Wisconsin, Madison

The practical applications of the precipitin reaction have been, for the most part, the qualitative or quantitative determination of unknown blood and other proteins. The work of Ramon [1] on the standardization of diphtheria toxin and antitoxin by this method has shown the desirability of a more thorough knowledge of the quantitative relations of the reaction. Such a knowledge would be valuable, not only because of its practical possibilities, but also because of the light it might throw on the subject of antigen-antibody reactions in general.

The researches of Opie [2] have cleared up obscure points concerning the reaction and emphasized the importance of optimal proportions of antigen and antiserum, and the different results obtained with simple and complex antigens. He has shown beyond doubt that the alleged coexistence of uncombined antigen and antibody in the blood and in the test-tube can be explained by the complexity of the antigen, and that when purified proteins are used one constituent of the reaction may be in excess, but never both in more than negligible quantities.

The purpose of the experiments here reported was to study the quantitative relations in the precipitin reaction with complex and simple antigens. So far as the work has been carried, it confirms the findings of Opie, and presents a few additional points of interest.

The antigens used were crystalline egg albumin, and sheep, human, and chicken hemoglobin, as simple antigens, and sheep serum as a complex antigen. The egg albumin was recrystallized three times according to the method of Hopkins and Pinkus, filtered through a Mandler filter for sterilization, and stored in the icebox without preservative. The blood samples for obtaining hemoglobin were collected in citrate and the cells washed repeatedly in large volumes of salt solution to free them from plasma. The cells were then laked with 25 times the original blood volume of water and centrifuged again at high speed to remove the stroma. To the hemoglobin was added an equal volume of 1.8% NaCl and the solution filtered through a Mandler filter. The best results in titration were obtained when freshly prepared hemoglobin solution was used because of its tendency to precipitate gradually in storage.

The immune serums were obtained from rabbits, and the flocculation method was used for the study of the antigen-antibody relations. By this method the antigen was tested in graded dilutions with various dilutions of the antiserum.

Received for publication, April 24, 1925.

[1] Ann. de l'Inst. Pasteur, 1923, 37, p. 1001; 1924, 38, p. 1.
[2] Jour. Immunol., 1923, 8, pp. 19 and 55.

The smallest reacting amounts of both antigen and antiserum were determined. Readings were made after 18 to 24 hours at room temperature. An artificial light arrangement for making readings was used, which was essentially the same as that described by Dreyer and Ward.[3] The apparatus consisted of a small box, lined inside with black velvet, and containing a long frosted electric lamp which illuminated a slit in the front of the box. The lamp was located so that it illuminated the tubes held in front of the slit but was not visible to the observer. By this arrangement small amounts of precipitate were detected which would otherwise have been overlooked. Table 1 shows the method and the results obtained in one complete titration of an immune serum against sheep hemoglobin.

TABLE 1

FLOCCULATION TEST OF IMMUNE SERUM AGAINST SHEEP HEMOGLOBIN

Antiserum Dilutions	Sheep Hemoglobin Dilutions (in Terms of Whole Blood)								
	400	1,000	2,000	4,000	10,000	20,000	40,000	100,000	200,000
1:20	3+	4+	3+	3+	2+	2+	+	+	0
1:40	+	+	3+	2+	+	+	+	+	0
1:100	0	+	+	2+	+	+	+	+	0
1:200	0	0	+	+	+	+	+	+	0
1:500	0	0	0	0	+	+	+	+	0
1:1,000	0	0	0	0	0	±	+	+	0
1:2,000	0	0	0	0	0	0	±	+	0
1:4,000	0	0	0	0	0	0	0	0	0

TABLE 2

FLOCCULATION TEST OF SERUM AGAINST CRYSTALLINE EGG ALBUMIN

Antiserum Dilutions	Dilutions of Crystalline Egg Albumin											
	400	1,000	2,000	4,000	10,000	20,000	40,000	100,000	200,000	400,000	1,000,000	2,000,000
1:20	2+	3+	4±	4+	3+	3+	2+	2+	+	+	+	0
1:100	+	+	+	+	2+	3+	2+	2+	+	+	+	0
1:400	...	...	...	...	+	+	+	+	+	+	+	0
1:1,000	...	..	...	...	0	0	±	+	+	+	+	0
1:2,000	...	..	...	...	...	...	0	±	+	+	+	0
1:4,000	...	..	...	...	...	...	0	0	0	±	+	0
1:8,000	...	...	...	...	...	...	0	0	0	0	0	0

The ring test was also made on many of the serums. Glass tubing of about 3 mm. inside diameter was cut into 4 cm. lengths and the pieces sealed off at one end in a flame. The small tubes conserved materials and facilitated the making of a sharp plane of contact between the fluids. With a fine capillary pipet small amounts of antiserum were delivered into the tubes and the antigen dilutions carefully floated over the antiserum. The tubes were kept under observation at room temperature for 2 hours.

The ring test, however, proved less suitable than the flocculation method for quantitative work of this nature. Differences in amount of precipitate are not so easily read, and the lack of delicacy of the method is revealed in tables 3, 4 and 5. The antigen can be detected in about 10 times as high a dilution by the flocculation test as by the ring test. Furthermore, in these experiments the amounts of antigen and antibody actually in contact must be known, and from the nature of the ring test it is hardly possible to know or control the amount of diffusion of the fluids. No attempt was made, therefore, to use the ring test in the study of the quantitative relations of the antigen and antibody.

[3] Great Britain, Medical Research Council, Special Report Series No. 78.

TABLE 3

TITRATIONS OF HEMOGLOBIN AS ANTIGEN

Antigens	Antigen Titer		Antibody Titer		Remarks
	Ring	Flocculation	Observed	Calculated	
Sheep hemoglobin..........	10,000	100,000	200	200	Same antigen against different serums
Sheep hemoglobin..........	......	100,000	2,000	2,000	
Sheep hemoglobin..........	......	100,000	100	100	
Sheep hemoglobin..........	10,000	100,000	100	100	
Sheep hemoglobin..........	......	200,000	100	100	Same antigen against different serums
Sheep hemoglobin..........	......	200,000	400	400	
Sheep hemoglobin..........	......	200,000	400	500	
Human hemoglobin.......	20,000	200,000	200	200	
Human hemoglobin.......	10,000	200,000	100	100	
Human hemoglobin.......	20,000	200,000	100	200	
Chicken hemoglobin.......	20,000	200,000	400	500	
Chicken hemoglobin.......	20,000	200,000	200	200	
Chicken hemoglobin.......	20,000	200,000	200	200	
Chicken hemoglobin.......	20,000	200,000	50	200	

TABLE 4

TITRATION OF CRYSTALLINE EGG ALBUMIN AS ANTIGEN

Antigen Titer		Antiserum Titer		Remarks
Ring	Flocculation	Observed	Calculated	
10,000	40,000	300	400	
......	100,000	200	200	Same antigen against different serums
10,000	100,000	200	200	
10,000	100,000	200	100	
......	100,000	200	400	
20,000	1,000,000	10,000	10,000	Same antigen against different serums
20,000	1,000,000	4,000	5,000	
20,000	1,000,000	1,000	1,000	
20,000	1,000,000	4,000	5,000	
......	100,000	......	200	Same antigen against different serums
......	100,000	......	100	
......	100,000	400	400	
......	100,000	40	40	
......	100,000	......	200	
......	100,000	40	40	
......	100,000	......	200	
......	100,000	1,000	1,000	

TABLE 5

FLOCCULATION TEST OF ANTISHEEP SERUM AGAINST SHEEP SERUM

Antiserum Dilutions	Antigen Dilutions											
	20	100	200	400	1,000	2,000	4,000	10,000	20,000	40,000	100,000	200,000
1:2..................	4+	4+	3+	3+	2+	2+	2+	+	+	+	+	0
1:10..................	3+	4+	3+	2+	2+	2+	+	+	+	+	+	0
1:20..................	+	2+	2+	2+	2+	+	+	+	+	+	+	0
1:40..................	+	2+	2+	2+	+	+	+	+	+	+	+	0
1:100..................	+	+	+	+	+	+	+	+	±	0	0	0
1:200..................	+	+	+	+	+	+	+	±	0	0	0	0
1:400..................	±	+	+	+	+	+	+	±	0	0	0	0
1:600..................	0	0	0	±	+	+	±	0	0	0	0	0
1:1,000..................	0	0	0	0	0	0	0	0	0	0	0	0

UNIFORMITY OF ANTIGEN TITERS WITH SIMPLE ANTIGEN

The results of all the titrations with simple antigens are summarized in tables 3 and 4. Here are listed for each test the antigen titer, i. e., the highest reacting dilution of the antigen, and the antibody titer, or the highest reacting dilution of the antiserum. The calculated antibody titers will be referred to later.

It is noteworthy that when the simple antigens are used, the highest dilution of the antigen giving a visible precipitate gives no indication as to the potency of the antiserum. The remarkable fact is the striking uniformity of the antigen titers. In tables 1 and 2 it is seen that all dilutions of the antiserum give a precipitate with the same high dilution of the antigen. Also, with the different serums the antigen titers are remarkably constant, especially when the same lot of antigen is tested against the different lots of antiserum. In table 3, in which the titrations with hemoglobin are recorded, the antibody titers range from 50 to 2,000, while the antigen titers are fairly uniform with all serums. The same point is brought out in table 4 in the titrations with egg albumin. The antibody titers vary from 200 to 10,000 while the antigen titers are exactly the same when the same lot of antigen is used for the different serums.

It is evident, therefore, that when the simple antigens are used, the dilution of the antigen gives no direct evidence as to the antibody content of the serum, since all serums tested against the same lot of antigen give a precipitate with about the same dilution of antigen regardless of their potency.

SIGNIFICANCE OF THE POINT OF MAXIMUM PRECIPITATION

However, if we examine tables 1 and 2, we can see that such a titration with a constant amount of antiserum and graded dilutions of antigen gives fairly accurate if indirect evidence as to the strength of the serum in question. As reported by Opie, there are found to be certain well defined optimal proportions of antigen and antibody at which maximum precipitation occurs. If the smallest reacting amounts of antigen and antiserum are taken as natural units, it is seen on calculation that the units of each at the points of maximum precipitation are approximately equal in number. Thus, in table 1, when a 1 : 20 dilution of immune serum is used, the maximum precipitation occurs with a 1 : 1,000 dilution of sheep hemoglobin, or 100 antigen units, since the antigen titer is 1 : 100,000. Since the antiserum titer is 1 : 2,000 there are also present at this point 100 antibody units. About the same quantitative relations obtain when the 1 : 40 and 1 : 100 dilutions of the immune serum are used. A brief study of table 2 is sufficient to show that the same relations hold in both the antihemoglobin and the anti-egg albumin systems. In each dilution of the serum tested the point of maximum precipitation represents approximately equal amounts of antigen and antibody reckoned in terms of units. The neutralization of antigen and antibody in the precipitin reaction, therefore, seems to follow the law of multiple proportions just as closely as the neutralization of toxin by its specific antitoxin. Is it not possible, therefore, that further study of the other types of antibodies and their antigens will show this relation to be true?

These three points, then, are to be considered in making a flocculation test with a simple antigen: antigen titer, antibody titer, and the proportion of serum to antigen at the point of maximum precipitation. They are in quantitative relation, and if any two are known, the other can be calculated. Thus, in table 1, if the antiserum titer were unknown, we could calculate it according to the formula,

$$\frac{\text{Antigen titer } 100{,}000}{\text{Antigen dilution, at maximum precipitation } 1{,}000} = \frac{\text{Antiserum titer } x}{\text{Antiserum dilution, at maximum precipitation } 20}$$

or $x = 2{,}000$, which is the titer observed experimentally.

In table 2, the proportion would be

$$\frac{1{,}000{,}000}{4{,}000} = \frac{x}{20} \text{ or } x = 5{,}000.$$

The agreement with the experimental result 4,000 is easily within the limit of experimental error. In only one case, table 3, do the calculated and experimental results disagree beyond the probable range of experimental error.

So if one desires to know the antibody content of a given serum, it is necessary to test only one dilution of the antiserum against the various antigen dilutions, and, by noting the antigen titer and the proportion of antigen to antiserum at the point of maximum precipitation, one can calculate the antibody titer with considerable accuracy. This is true provided the antigen is comparatively simple.

The results obtained with the complex antigen, sheep serum, are given in tables 5 and 6. The same exact quantitative relations are not

TABLE 6

TITRATIONS OF SHEEP SERUM AS ANTIGEN

Antigen Titer		Antiserum Titer	
Ring	Flocculation	Observed	Calculated
100	1,000	...	.....
2,000	40,000	600	2,000
5,000	20,000	800	4,000
5,000	100,000	600	4,000
1,000	4,000	100	.....
10,000	40,000	800	.....
10,000	40,000	800	.....
5,000	10,000	100	.....

found as with the simple antigens. The antigen titer is not constant, but varies in a general way with the antibody content of the serum. The higher dilutions of the antiserum, too, tend to react with lower dilutions of the antigen. The maximum precipitation occupies a whole zone in which it is usually impossible to pick out one tube showing heavier flocculation than the others. It is not possible, therefore, to make calculations that would agree even approximately with the experimental results.

COMMENT

Opie [2] suggested the posibility that the maximum precipitate obtained with various dilutions of immune serum might furnish a more accurate measure of the strength of an immune serum than the point of disappearance of a recognizable precipitate with increasing dilution of the antigen. It has been my experience that the reading of the antigen titer is comparatively easy provided the dilution of the antiserum is not too great. On the other hand, the reading of the antiserum titer is a difficult task since one is dealing with high dilutions, then, of both antigen and antiserum. It seems, therefore, that the estimation of the strength of the serum on the basis of the titer of the antigen and the maximum precipitate obtained when one dilution of the antiserum is tested against the various antigen dilutions affords a much easier method of determining the strength of a given serum and in most instances just as accurate as the laborious procedure of testing all dilutions of antiserum against all dilutions of antigen. In view of the fact that the readings are so hard to make when extremely high dilutions of antigen and antiserum are used, it is suggested that the method of estimation may be even more accurate than the visual observations. Of course, as is shown by the experiments mentioned, such estimation is possible only when the antigen used is comparatively simple.

No claim is made as to the degree of simplicity of the antigens used in these experiments. They may each contain only a single antigenic substance or several. In general, however, their reactions with the antiserum compare favorably with what one might reasonably expect if the constituents of the reaction were known to be a single antigen and its specific antibody. And it is obviously true that, when compared to sheep serum, crystalline egg albumin and hemoglobin are comparatively simple antigens.

It seems probable that these quantitative relations can be found to apply to any flocculation test when a simple antigen is used. The experiments of Morgan,[4] in which the precipitin reaction was carried out using the soluble specific substance of the pneumococcus, show essentially the same results as are reported here with crystalline egg albumin and hemoglobin, although he does not report the testing of different serums against one lot of antigen.

SUMMARY

When two or more specific precipitating serums are tested against the same lot of antigen, they all react with the same dilution of the antigen regardless of the strength of the serums, provided a simple antigen is used.

The determination of the point of disappearance of a recognizable precipitate on increasing the dilution of the antigen does not, therefore, give direct evidence as to the strength of the antiserum.

The point of maximum precipitation when a single dilution of the antiserum is tested against the various antigen dilutions represents an approximately equal number of units of antigen and antibody. On the basis of this fact, then, one can calculate the antibody content of the serum with considerable accuracy when, by test, the antigen titer and point of maximum precipitation have been determined with one dilution of the serum. This is true provided a simple antigen is used in the test.

The exact quantitative relations do not obtain when a complex antigen like sheep serum is used. The antigen titer is not constant but varies in a general way with the antibody titer of the serum. The maximum precipitate occupies a whole zone in which it is often impossible to pick out one tube showing heavier flocculation than the others.

[4] J. Immunol., 1923, 8, p. 449.

It is not possible, therefore, to make calculations that would agree even approximately with experimental results.

The neutralization of antigen by its specific antibody in the precipitin reaction seems, like the toxin-antitoxin reaction, to follow the law of multiple proportions. It is not possible that when further study is made other types of antigen-antibody reactions will be found to follow this same law?

NONGLUCOSE-FERMENTING BACTERIA AND INSULIN

STUDIES IN BACTERIAL METABOLISM. LXXIII

Arthur Isaac Kendall

From the Department of Bacteriology and Public Health, Washington University School of Medicine, St. Louis

The striking pharmacologic effect obtained by injecting insulin into a diabetic person, thereby influencing favorably and rapidly his utilization of glucose, suggests that a similar response might be detected in cultures of certain bacteria that fail to manifest any discernible action on this sugar, provided, of course, that insulin alone, with no supplementary factor, is responsible for the phenomenon. Only a few bacteria among the multitude of known types seem to be unable to utilize glucose for energy. It cannot, obviously, be stated that these few microbes are "diabetic"; some of them have been kept on artificial culture mediums for untold generations without the slightest suggestion that their failure to derive energy from glucose in the manner characteristic for most micro-organisms is a pathologic manifestation. Whatever may have been the original cause for their departure from the normal metabolism of glucose, the multitude of succeeding generations has repeated this phenomenon in a regular manner, without any indication that the particular type is lacking in any other aspect of normal development. In other words, these non-glucose-fermenting types are hereditarily fixed, unicellular organisms which neither show any discernible tendency to become glucose fermenters nor manifest any developmental peculiarities that would point toward a retrogression.

Four different organisms that do not ferment glucose in the manner common to almost all known bacteria were tried out with this idea in view. They were: Bacillus alcaligenes, a well-known incitant of an intestinal infection resembling typhoid fever in its general symptomatology; a spiral organism, H/61, isolated from a case of cholera, although not etiologically related to that disease; Micrococcus catarrhalis, occasionally found in infections of the respiratory tract; and a diplococcus, hitherto apparently not described, isolated from intestinal contents.

None of these four microbes produce detectable traces of acid in glucose-containing mediums, and a comparative study of one of them,

Received for publication, May 25, 1925.

alcaligenes, failed to reveal any difference in its nitrogenous metabolism in broth medium with and without glucose.[1] In this respect, the nitrogenous metabolism of B. alcaligenes is unlike that of most other bacteria examined under similar conditions in which glucose exerts a clearly defined "protein sparing action," which may be measured quantitatively.[2]

The metabolism of glucose by most bacteria leads to the production of readily detectable amounts of acid, and, accordingly, the following series of cultures were set up to observe any change in hydrogen-ion concentration that might be produced by these bacteria from glucose under the influence of insulin. Stated differently, these experiments were planned to test the influence of insulin on certain non-glucose-fermenting bacteria in cultural mediums in which, under ordinary conditions, the organisms do not utilize this sugar as a source of energy.

Plain, nutrient broth was prepared. Several 50 c c. portions were set apart to serve as controls; the remainder was dispensed in several 500 c c. flasks, and inoculated respectively with the 4 organisms previously mentioned. Growth was satisfactory after 18 hours' incubation. Following this preliminary incubation, the several broth cultures were subdivided, with suitable precautions to guard against contamination, into smaller flasks. Fifty c c. of medium were placed in each flask. It will be seen that the inoculum was as nearly equal in each flask as could be obtained.

Then 1 c c. of a 10% glucose solution [3] was added to each culture, and to one half of these in turn, 1 c c. of insulin [4] was introduced. The insulin was tested for sterility. The potency of the insulin was not determined by direct experiment: clinical results with insulin of the same lot, however, were known to be satisfactory. It will be noted that the difference in volume of these several flasks was slight, owing to the addition of glucose and insulin, respectively. These slight variations in volume did not perceptibly influence the results.

The reaction of the plain, uninoculated broth was slightly acid, P_H 6.7. After the preliminary incubation of 18 hours, this acid reaction decreased somewhat in each culture. This was to be expected, because the bacteria employed do not utilize carbohydrate in the ordinary way. The exact amount of this change is indicated for each culture in the table. The addition of insulin increased the reaction slightly, indicating that the

[1] Kendall, Day and Walker: Jour. Am. Chem. Soc., 1913, 35, p. 1213.
[2] Kendall: Physiol. Rev., 1923, 3, p. 438.
[3] Sterilized by filtration to guard against the possible effects of heat.
[4] Lilly preparation, 20 units per c c.

insulin solution is of itself slightly acid. The glucose solution, on the other hand, had no appreciable effect on the reaction. The several cultures were almost at the neutral point when the final incubation was started.

Incubation was practiced at 37 C. for 6 and 24 hours, respectively, and the hydrogen-ion concentration was determined at these intervals. It should be stated that separate cultures were used for these several 6 and 24 hour determinations, to avoid the possibility of contamination, which would exist if the same culture were used for successive examinations.

In the table, the reactions indicated by the caption "start" are those at the beginning of the second, or test incubation. The initial reaction of the uninoculated broth was uniformly P_H 6.7, as explained above.

HYDROGEN-ION CONCENTRATIONS AFTER INCUBATION

Mediums	B. alcaligenes			Vibrio H/61			M. catarrhalis			Micrococcus "N"		
	Start	6 Hrs.	24 Hrs.	Start	6 Hrs.	24 Hrs.	Start	6 Hrs.	24 Hrs.	Start	6 Hrs.	24 Hrs.
Plain broth....	6.9	7.0	7.6	7.0	7.2	7.6	6.8	6.8	7.2	6.8	6.9	7.4
Glucose broth..	6.9	7.1	7.4	7.0	7.3	7.5	6.8	6.8	7.3	6.8	6.9	7.5
Glucose insulin broth........	6.8	7.0	7.4	6.9	7.2	7.6	6.7	6.8	7.2	6.7	6.7	7.3

COMMENT

The salient features of this investigation are shown clearly in the table. Insulin, added in considerable amounts to cultures of certain bacteria that have no appreciable action on glucose, failed to induce any change in the conditions of the experiment which resulted in discernible alterations in reaction suggestive of utilization of this sugar by the organisms for energy. In other words, the addition of insulin to these cultures failed to elicit an acid fermentation of the glucose. If this had been demonstrated, the organisms would, temporarily at least, have manifested the same reaction toward glucose as that shown by a multitude of well-known organisms.

The absence of a detectable reaction induced by the insulin might indicate: (*a*) that the change was too slight to be detected with the method employed, (*b*) that the organisms were wholly refractory toward glucose, (*c*) that the organisms destroyed or rendered the insulin inert, or (*d*) that the insulin was carried out of solution with the newly forming organisms.

A fifth possibility, that insulin does not act alone, but requires a supplementary factor, does not enter into this particular case.

With reference to the first possibility, it should be remembered that even very small amounts of glucose (0.01%) are fermented by many bacteria with detectable amounts of acid.[5] On the other hand, it is possible that the bacteria employed in these experiments were unable to utilize the glucose molecule under any conditions supplied by these reagents.

Little is known about the composition of insulin: a recent communication by A. Cruto[6] on the "Chemical Constitution of Insulin" assigns to "insulin sulphate" a highly purified preparation of insulin, the tentative formula C 47.73; H 7.27; N 14.53; S 1.73; O 22.84, H_2SO_4 5.90. It is conceivable that such a compound might be so altered by microbic action that it would fail to react in its altered state in a characteristic manner. If this proves to be the case, this particular type of experiment cannot be relied on to furnish information concerning the mechanism of insulin action.

SUMMARY

The results are wholly negative. There is no suggestion in them that insulin, under the conditions imposed by the method employed, stimulated these several non-glucose-fermenting bacteria to utilize this sugar with the production of acid.

[5] Kendall and Yoshida: Jour. Infect. Dis., 1923, 32, p. 355.
[6] Chemical Abstracts, 1925, 19, p. 1143.

EFFECT OF INSULIN ON CULTURES OF B. BULGARICUS AND B. ACIDOPHILUS

STUDIES IN BACTERIAL METABOLISM. LXXIV

ARTHUR ISAAC KENDALL AND MITZUTERU ISHIKAWA

From the Department of Bacteriology and Public Health, Washington University School of Medicine, St. Louis

A recent, highly interesting communication by Noyes and Estill [1] contains a report of the influence of insulin on the intensity of acid formation in cultures of B. bulgaricus and B. acidophilus. The method used was simple and direct: to a 10% milk culture of the respective organisms in glucose broth, about 24 units of insulin were added, and after 24 hours' incubation at 32 C., the cultures being frequently agitated, the amount of acid produced was measured by direct titration, after removal of the coagulated casein by filtration. The increase in acid was judged by a direct comparison with control cultures, exactly similar in every respect, except that insulin was omitted. The amount of acid formed in the bulgaricus-insulin-glucose-milk medium was stated to be several times (20 to 25%) that produced under similar conditions in parallel mediums from which the insulin was excluded. Cultures of B. acidophilus were less markedly influenced by insulin, although the difference in acid production between insulin and insulin-free mediums was noticeable.

It is of more than academic interest to discover living cells which are simple, all of one kind, and readily procurable, whose sugar metabolism is influenced by insulin. It should be possible, through the utilization of such microbes, to throw much light on the puzzling mechanism through which insulin acts. At the present time, animals and man, but not unicellular organisms, seem to offer the only channels through which insulin activity may be detected, and measured.

In this respect, insulin and bacterial toxins have a common background: they are of unknown chemical composition, and they are assayed for potency through pharmacologic responses elicited in suitable animals. The advantages to be gained by less expensive and more readily controllable methods of assay are perfectly obvious.

Received for publication, May 25, 1925.

[1] Proc. Natl. Acad. Sc., 1924, 10, p. 415.

Two sets of experiments were set up to test the effect of insulin on the glucose metabolism of B. bulgaricus and B. acidophilus. The first set was designed to measure the rate and intensity of acid formation after 4 and 24 hours' incubation in cultures of B. bulgaricus, using mediums with and without insulin, prepared in accordance with the Noyes-Estill formula; the second set was set up in the same manner, but inoculated with cultures of B. bulgaricus and B. acidophilus, respectively, to measure their respective rates of acid formation in insulin and insulin-free mediums.

The strain of B. bulgaricus used was a stock culture, obtained from an authentic sample of Bulgarian milk several years ago. It conformed to the usual reactions of this organism. The culture of B. acidophilus was isolated by one of us (A. I. K.) from a patient undergoing treatment with acidophilus milk, about a year ago. It was of the relatively low acid-producing type.[2] This strain was selected because it was hoped that the acid-producing capacity might be augmented under the influence of insulin.

TABLE 1

COMPOSITION OF MEDIUMS

	A	B	C	D
Milk culture	10 c c.	10 c c.	10 c c.	10 c c.
Broth	90 c c.	90 c c.	90 c c.	90 c c.
Glucose sol	10 c c.	10 c c.	......	......
Insulin	1 c c.	......	1 c c.	......

The insulin was a Lilly preparation, labeled 20 units per c c. This amount was used throughout. The potency was not tested, but it was part of a lot that gave satisfactory clinical results.

The milk cultures, inoculated with the appropriate organisms and incubated for 24 hours, were distributed as outlined in table 1. This procedure insured a uniform inoculum in each test solution.

The glucose solution, 10% in distilled water, was sterilized by passage through a Berkefeld filter, to avoid the effects of heat on the sugar. Plain, nutrient broth was used as the basic medium. All reagents added to the milk cultures, including the insulin, were sterile at the start.

Two complete sets of these mediums were prepared: one set was examined after 4 hours' incubation, the other set, exactly the counterpart of the first, was examined after 24 hours' incubation. Each set was shaken thoroughly about 4 times per hour for 4 hours, and less frequently for the following 4 hours.

[2] Jour. Infect. Dis., 1924, 35, p. 89.

Method of Examination.—The several cultures were heated to the boiling point at the proper time to remove the coagulated protein, and then 10 c c. of the hot filtrate, diluted with 25 c.c. of boiling hot distilled water, were titrated with N/10 NaOH, using phenolphthalein as an indicator. Duplicate determinations were made, with an allowable difference of 0.1 c c. between the two.

Exper. 1.—The results are expressed as c c. of normal caustic soda solution per 100 c c. of the original culture medium, and represent the difference between the initial acidity (which was the same for all cultures) and the final acidity found by titration.

The results are negative so far as they relate to the effect of insulin on the intensity and rate of fermentation of glucose by B. bulgaricus. There is no discernible evidence that this substance had the slightest influence on the utilization of glucose by this microbe. Another experiment was set up, using the same procedure as before, but omitting the 4-hour cultures, and adding B. acidophilus as a second test organism. The cultures were titrated after 24 hours' incubation as 37 C. as before.

TABLE 2

ACIDITY PRODUCED BY B. BULGARICUS AND B. ACIDOPHILUS WITH AND WITHOUT INSULIN

Mediums	B. bulgaricus		B. acidophilus, 24 Hours
	4Hours	24 Hours	
A (insulin)........................	2.05	5.10 5.25	3.95
B.................................	2.15	5.95 6.00	4.00
C (insulin)........................	1.65	4.80 5.00	3.60
D.................................	1.75	4.90 5.10	3.65

COMMENT

The results were wholly negative. The differences in acidity between the insulin-containing and the insulin-free mediums are slight, and may be explained simply on the basis of somewhat unequal rates of growth in the several cultures. Such slight differences are the rule, rather than the exception, in bacteriologic work.

There are several possible explanations for these negative results in the light of the positive evidence obtained by Noyes and Estill. The type of organisms used in the two investigations may have been different, but as the organisms herein reported are typical so far as available methods of identification permit, little can be gleaned from this angle.

The amounts of insulin used differ little; about 24 units were used by Noyes and Estill and 20 by us. If this slight variation in the amount of insulin were the sole cause of the discrepancy, it must be admitted that disproportionately large amounts of insulin must be added to microbic cultures in comparison with the amounts required to affect definite results in human and animal experiments. It is, of course, possible that the potency of the insulin preparations may have been the determining factor, but 20 units of a clinically active insulin solution should be sufficient to induce at least some detectable differences in microbic cultures, even though the preparation be less powerful in its action than usual. It does not seem probable that the organisms destroy the insulin, in the light of the positive results reported by Noyes and Estill, especially in view of the fact that bacteria of the lactic acid type are almost obligately carbohydrophilic. Their action on protein is minimal. However, to obtain some additional evidence, an additional set of experiments was made, adding the insulin to cultures when they were active, namely, after 4 hours' incubation, but no other evidence was obtained than that already described.

SUMMARY

At the present time, with available evidence, the definiteness of the effects of adding insulin to milk-glucose-insulin cultures of B. bulgaricus and B. acidophilus, as shown by detectable increase in titrable acidity, remains an open question.

EFFECT OF INSULIN ON BACTERIAL METABOLISM

STUDIES IN BACTERIAL METABOLISM. LXXV

ARTHUR ISAAC KENDALL AND MITZUTERU ISHIKAWA

From the Department of Bacteriology and Public Health, Washington University School of Medicine, St. Louis

In the preceding study [1] negative results were reported in an attempt to substantiate an observation of Noyes and Estill [2] that insulin, added to cultures of B. bulgaricus and B. acidophilus, increased the amount of acid produced by these organisms in a milk-glucose solution. One of the possible reasons for lack of agreement might well be that the organisms employed in the two laboratories were not the same in actuality, although called by the same names.

The question naturally arises: Do any bacteria, under the conditions imposed in microbic cultures, exhibit qualitative or quantitative evidence of insulin stimulation in their utilization of glucose? Already a certain amount of evidence has been published of an entirely negative character. McGuire and Falk [3] found that insulin had no effect on the metabolism of glucose by B. coli, and Travell and Behre [4] reported similarly that this substance was equally inactive when added to several strains of yeast.

On the other hand, the many advantages to be gained by successful experiments in which insulin stimulates the glucose metabolism of microbes are so apparent that a search was made among a variety of bacterial types to detect such an organism.

The two most probable indications to be expected from bacterial cultures should insulin exert any influence on their glucose metabolism, are changes in the rate and changes in the intensity of acid formation (fermentation). This seems to follow logically from the fact that the most conspicuous chemical result of the utilization of glucose for energy by bacteria in general is to increase the hydrogen ion concentration of the medium [5] in which this reaction takes place.

The procedure to be followed to demonstrate this phenomenon is simple. It consists essentially in measuring the change in hydrogen ion

Received for publication, May 25, 1925.

1 Study LXXIV, Jour. Infect. Dis., 1925, 37, p. 333.
2 Proc. Natl. Acad. Sc., 1924, 10, p. 415.
3 Jour. Biol. Chem., 1924, 60, p. 489.
4 Proc. Soc. Exper. Biol. & Med., 1924, 21, p. 478
5 Certain nonfermenting bacteria are discussed in Study LXXIII, Jour. Infect. Dis., 1925, 37, p. 329.

concentration in appropriately compounded mediums containing glucose, with and without the addition of insulin.

Accordingly, nutrient broth was prepared, and dispensed in several 100 c c. flasks, 50 c c. in each flask. After sterilization, 1 c c. of a 10% glucose solution [6] was added to each, and the entire number was incubated to insure sterility. Then 1 c c. of insulin [7] was introduced into half the number of flasks. Sterility being insured, each pair of flasks (glucose and glucose-insulin) was inoculated with one kind of bacteria, and incubated for 18 hours, with proper controls.

The organisms were chosen partly because of their widely divergent reactions to various carbohydrates, and partly because their nitrogenous metabolisms indicate considerable qualitative and quantitative differences

RESULTS OF SEVERAL SERIES OF EXPERIMENTS

	Glucose Broth P_H	Glucose-Insulin Broth P_H
Control	6.8	6.7
B. dysenteriae Shiga	5.9	5.9
B. dysenteriae Flexner	5.6	5.7
B. typhosus	5.7	5.6
Bacillus of Morgan	6.2	6.1
B. paratyphosus alpha	5.5	5.4
B. paratyphosus beta	5.6	5.6
B. coli	5.5	5.5
B. proteus	5.8	5.7
Strep. hemolyticus	5.9	6.0
Staph. aureus	5.5	5.5
Pneumococcus (type 4)	6.1	6.2
Mic. ovalis	5.5	5.5

in their attack on the protein constituents of the medium. With this variety, there would seem to be a chance that one or more bacteria might exhibit a positive reaction to the insulin stimulation, and, possibly, negative results might show some factor which might render the insulin inert.

After 18 hours' incubation, the cultures were examined for changes in hydrogen ion concentration.

All of the organisms fermented the glucose in the manner characteristic for their type. The amounts of acid produced varied somewhat owing partly to the relative luxuriance of growth, and partly to slight variations inherent in the microbes themselves. The results are in accord with previous studies in this respect as made by many observers.

There seems to be no indication that insulin had an appreciable effect on the glucose metabolism of the bacteria so far as changes in hydrogen

[6] Sterilized by filtration to avoid the effects of heat on the sugar.

[7] Lilly preparation, 20 units per c c., found to be sterile, and satisfactory, clinically, in its results.

ion concentration are concerned. It might be argued, however, that sufficient time was not allowed for an insulin effect to make itself manifest, although experiments on man and animals show almost immediate response. Bacterial cultures, however, require time to develop to a point at which products of metabolism accumulate in considerable quantity. Another series was set up, using the same organisms, and the same broth described above with and without insulin. Examinations were made for evidences of fermentation after 8 hours and also at 24 hour intervals for a period of 3 days. Nothing significant appeared, and the protocols are omitted, because they show no qualitative differences between the glucose and the glucose-insulin mediums at the intervals indicated, except, of course, much less hydrogen ion concentration at the 8 hour period, and somewhat more at the 48 and 72 hour periods. The rates of formation and the quantities of acid formed were parallel in the two mediums at equal intervals of incubation.

SUMMARY

It would appear that insulin, under the conditions imposed by the experiment, had no appreciable effect on the utilization of glucose for energy by a considerable number of bacterial types.

A PATHOGENIC SUBTILIS BACILLUS FROM A PATIENT WITH CHRONIC TUBERCULOSIS

H. C. Sweany and Max Pinner

From the Laboratories of the Municipal Tuberculosis Sanitarium, Chicago

During a tuberculous infection, the patient may be subject to secondary infections by parasites and by saprophytes that may acquire virulence. Sweany [1] has pointed out that tuberculous patients, or those suspected of being tuberculous, may be divided roughly into 4 groups: (1) the nontuberculous or those whose symptoms simulate tuberculosis; (2) the tuberculous who have no complications or other diseases; (3) the tuberculous with secondary infections or conditions such as bronchiectasis, empyema, septic cavities, etc.; (4) those in whom the complicating conditions, such as malignant tumor, syphilis, endocarditis, etc., have no relation to the tuberculosis. In the case now reported there were various associated conditions, but emphasis is placed on the presence of a virulent subtilis bacillus.

B. subtilis has been described a number of times as pathogenic for man, but always in connection with eye lesions. Baenziger and Silberschmidt [2] report two cases of purulent iridocyclitis caused by B. subtilis. Filatow [3] makes an exhaustive report on subtilis infections of the eye. A complete review is given also by Axenfeld.[4] Filatow collected all the cases of eye infection in which B. subtilis was found alone or associated with some of the more usual pathogenic organisms. He enumerates 68 cases of acute conjunctivitis, 5 cases of ulcers of the cornea with hypopyon, and 22 cases of purulent iridochoroiditis and panophthalmia. Stueber [5] reports an acute hemorrhagic panophthalmia, which was first diagnosed as anthrax infection. Seitz [6] reports that he isolated B. subtilis from the feces of a patient with acute enteritis; mice died after the injection of living or killed cultures of this strain; mice fed with the bacillus developed an acute enteritis, and the bacillus was recovered from the spleen and from the heart blood. This result leads to the question of

Received for publication, May 28, 1925

[1] Am. Rev. Tuberc., 1923, 8, p. 40.
[2] Bericht über die 30te Versammlung d. ophthalmologischen Gesellschaft, 1902.
[3] Arch. f. Augenhenheilk., 1912, 70, p. 185.
[4] The Bacteriology of the Eye, 1908.
[5] Ohio State M. J., 1921, 17, p. 175.
[6] Centralbl. f. Bakteriol., I, O., 1913, 70, p. 113.

the pathogenicity of bacilli of the subtilis group for animals. Charrin and De Nitis [7] increased the pathogenicity of B. subtilis by passing it several times through animals. Kayser [8] found B. subtilis pathogenic for the rabbit's eye when injected into the anterior chamber. After peritoneal injection death resulted only from large doses. Filatow's findings were essentially the same, and he observed that intravenous injection would lead to a localized eye infection, if the eye was injured. Kneass and Sailer [9] killed rabbits by injecting large amounts of B. subtilis, the growth of 14 agar plates. Large masses of sclerotic tissue formed in the abdominal wall at the site of injection, and there was a fibrino-purulent pericarditis; the bacillus was recovered from the heart blood. Weil [10] found B. subtilis plus the peritoneal exudate (mouse) caused by intraperitoneal injection of large amounts of the bacillus to be lethal for mice.. Barabaschi [11] describes a goat in which the lesions simulated a miliary tuberculosis of the lung, lymph glands and spleen, but bacteriologic examination revealed B. subtilis and no acid-fast bacilli. An interesting phenomenon was observed by Hobbs and Lafolie: [12] Simultaneous intraperitoneal injection of B. subtilis and staphylococcus in amounts that separately did not affect control animals killed guinea-pigs.

In the case of a patient with acute and chronic tuberculous lesions in the lungs and other organs, and with widely scattered hemorrhages and larger and smaller abscesses, as well as acute inflammatory processes in the endocardium, pericardium, leptomeninges, etc., bacteriologic examination gave the following results: from the heart blood, Streptococcus nonhemolyticus and B. substilis; from the pericardial fluid, Streptococcus nonhemolyticus and B. subtilis; from the pericardial fluid, pneumococcus, Staphylococcus aureus and B. subtilis; from the peritoneal fluid, Staphylococcus aureus and B. subtilis; from brain abscess, B. coli.

Two guinea-pigs into which cheesy material from the abscesses in the kidney had been injected did not present any lesions two months later.

The subtilis bacillus in cultures from 3 different sources, including the heart blood from which the organism was obtained on 4 different mediums, differed from the commonly described forms. In all the primary blood agar cultures the colonies appeared only on the 4th or 5th

[7] Compt. rend. Soc. de biol., 1897, 49, p. 711.
[8] Centralbl. f. Bakteriol., I, 1902, 33, p. 241.
[9] Univer. Pennsylvania Med. Bull., 1903, 16, p. 131.
[10] Wien. klin. Wchnschr., 1905, 18, p. 662.
[11] Gazz. d. osp. Milan, 1910, 31, p. 1081.
[12] XIII Congres Internat. de Med., 1900, Sect. gen. Pathol., p. 315.

day; in broth, the 24-hour growth was sparse; the first 3 or 4 generations grew slowly and only on medium containing blood. Hemolysis was marked; the cleared area was 2.2 cm. wide. The later generations, however, were in no points atypical. The organism eventually grew rapidly and luxuriantly on ordinary mediums, became less hemolytic and did not kill white rats.

One c c. of a 24-hour broth culture was not pathogenic for rabbits and guinea-pigs. One loopful of agar culture injected subcutaneously into a white rat was followed by death 17 days after the injection; both lungs were studded with submiliary abscesses; 2 larger abscesses about 0.3 c c. in diameter were found close to the hilus on either side; there was no change in any other organ, except that at the site of injection was a hard, infiltrated area, 1 cm. in diameter, in the subcutaneous tissue; all the lung abscesses contained caseous purulent material closely resembling the contents of the spleen and kidney abscesses in the patient, and smears from this material revealed B. subtilis in large numbers; from the abscesses and from the heart blood B. subtilis was recovered in pure culture. Subcutaneous injections were made into another white rat with one loopful of agar growth, and the rat was killed 23 days after the injection. The changes were much the same as in the first animal; B. subtilis was recovered in pure cultures from both the lesions in the lung and the heart blood; there was a generalized edema with a moderate number of large phagocytic cells throughout the lungs, and large abscesses composed chiefly of polymorphonuclear leukocytes; in the centers of the abscesses the alveolar structures could not be made out; only strands of connective tissue and remnants of blood vessels and scattered alveolar cells were discernible in addition to the pus cells; the epithelium was desquamated and filled the lumen of the bronchi, and in the bronchioles these cells formed rings of cells in the lumen not unlike giant cells.

After these results the kidneys of the patient were removed from Kaiserling's solution and smears of the necrotic material revealed a few gram-positive rods like B. subtilis.

It appears that in this case B. subtilis developed certain qualities that enabled it to grow and produce lesions in the white rat. This is the second report that B. subtilis has been found to be pathogenic otherwise than by causing eye lesions. Kelemen [13] describes a case of sepsis and pneumonia which was caused by B. subtilis.

[13] Gyo'gya'szat, 1924, 64, pp. 512, 531, 548, 561; abstr., Zentralbl. ges. Tuberkfg., 1925, 24, p. 22.

It may be assumed that in our patient, defensive factors either were lacking or were so low that the subtilis bacillus was able to reproduce itself. This perhaps occurred slowly at first, but, according to the law of survival, the organisms that produced the most hemolysis or other food preparing enzymes, survived and reproduced until a new strain developed capable of semiparasitic (patient) or parasitic (rat) existence. It is conceivable that new diseases may take their origin in some such a way; either by saprophytes becoming parasites or parasites increasing in virulence.

SUMMARY

This appears to be the second time that a subtilis bacillus, pathogenic for animals, has been isolated from human sources other than the eye. This bacillus was isolated from most of the lesions and the principal body fluids; it grew at first only on medium containing blood, where it produced a large hemolytic zone, and it killed white rats. These results suggest that subtilis bacilli in cultures from human sources perhaps should not be discarded offhand as always being due to mere contamination.

TOXIN PRODUCTION BY CLOSTRIDIUM BOTULINUM IN CANNED FOODS

LUTHER THOMPSON WITH F. W. TANNER

From the Department of Bacteriology, University of Illinois, Urbana

This investigation was begun in the summer of 1923, and was primarily intended to test the ability of Clostridium botulinum to grow and produce toxin in canned foods of widely varying composition. It was hoped in this way to indicate those foods that are potentially dangerous, although some of them might never have been reported as the cause of food poisoning. In the fall of the same year the paper by Schoenholz, Esty and Meyer [1] appeared, which treated in detail the problem and gave results corresponding essentially to those obtained in the present investigation. For this and other reasons the work was extended to another phase of the general problem, namely, the explanation of the irregularity of toxin production in certain foods. It often has happened that one or more cans of food from a lot have been poisonous, while the greater number of them have been harmless. This is particularly true of vegetables such as spinach, asparagus, beets, and canned greens.

Although a number of experiments have been performed on inoculation of foods with Clostridium botulinum, few have been comprehensive in scope. For the most part from 1 to 3 or 4 kinds of food were used. Dickson [2] in showing that a meat medium is not necessary for growth and toxin production, inoculated cans of beans and peas as well as pork and beef, and found that all produced strong toxins. Dickson, Burke and Ward [3] used cans of apricots, peaches, and pears inoculated with washed spores, and after incubation for 3 months a toxin was present in such quantity that 1 c c. of the material injected into a guinea-pig would cause death in from 1 to 2 days. In the light of recent experiments these results are less convincing, since the inoculum was not detoxified by heat. Armstrong, Story, and Scott [4] used ground ripe olives as a medium, and stated that a strong toxin was produced in 9 days. Koser, Edmondson, and Giltner [5] inoculated cans of spinach with approximately 800,000 washed, heated spores. They reported that toxin production in spinach was irregular. Of 174 cans of spinach selected from various commercial lots, 6 contained toxin. Bengtson [6] used string beans, peas, spinach, olives, corn, and beets as mediums. On all of these except beets and olives a strong toxin was produced. Here also heated spores were not used in every case. In studying the relation of toxin production to temperature, Edmondson,

Received for publication, May 6, 1925.

[1] Jour. Infect. Dis., 1923, 33, p. 289.
[2] Jour. Am. Med. Assn., 1915, 65, p. 492.
[3] Arch. Int. Med., 1919, 24, p. 581.
[4] Pub. Health Rep., 1919, 34, p. 2877.
[5] Jour. Am. Med. Assn., 1921, 77, p. 1250.
[6] Pub. Health Rep., 1921, 36, p. 1665.

Giltner, and Thom [7] inoculated peas in open flasks and bottles of milk. Their results show that a temperature below 20 C., and lack of anaerobic conditions may retard or prevent toxin production. The first comprehensive attempt to inoculate canned food was made by Schoenholz, Esty, and Meyer.[1] These investigators, using heated spore suspension, inoculated a large series of cans of foods comprising the following varieties: Group 1—corn, peas, sweet potato, salmon; Group 2—sauerkraut, tomato, apricots, cherries, peaches, pears, plums, raspberries, strawberries; Group 3—asparagus, beets, olives, peppers, spinach, string beans, evaporated milk. Group 1 showed marked physical and chemical changes, and were regularly toxic; group 2 rarely showed spoilage or toxin, while group 3 was irregular, both as to signs of spoilage and toxin production, certain foods being very toxic, at times without physical signs of spoilage. For the most part, type A cultures were used for inoculation, each can receiving from 50 million to 17 billion spores, and the incubation of inoculated foods was continued up to 12 months. An attempt was made to correlate the growth and toxin production with the hydrogen ion concentration of the foods at the end of the incubation period. Considerable variation in acidity was noted among cans of the same kind of food, and tables are given showing the relation between acidity and the ability of Clostridium botulinum to grow and produce a toxin. Edmondson, Thom, and Giltner [8] inoculated normal cans of spinach with toxin-free spores, and noted irregularity in growth at the same temperature. They state that some cans may be toxic while showing little physical evidence of spoilage. These authors [9] also inoculated peas, milk, cream cheese, meat balls and mashed potato, which were placed in containers to simulate the conditions in which they would naturally be kept in the household. It is interesting that a strong toxin may be produced under conditions which are not usually considered anaerobic, as for example in the middle of a meat ball, or in the bottom of a dish of mashed potato where no particular precautions are taken to exclude air. Bachmann [10] used as mediums chopped green beans and cabbage packed in test tubes. The beans developed a toxin, while the cabbage did not. Lynn and Sells,[11] in studying the chemical changes produced by Clostridium botulinum in food, used string beans as a medium.

EXPERIMENTS

The cultures used in our experiments comprised 2 type A strains known in this work as A1 and A2, which were received from the Department of Health Laboratories, New York City, and came labeled as "Delbene" and "Bronfenbrenner," respectively; also 2 type B strains, 175 B (Nevin) and 7870 (Graham). All strains have been typed from time to time and have always proved true to name. Before use they were tested for toxin production in canned corn; in all cases the cans developed into "hard swells" in 48 hours, and a potent toxin was formed such that when 1 c c. of the liquor was fed to guinea-pigs, the death time varied from 5 to 18 hours.

These strains were grown in flasks of sugar-free casein digest broth, or coagulated egg broth, covered with paraffin, and incubated at 37 C. until growth apparently had ceased, and the organisms were well sedimented. This varied with the strains from 30 to 60 days. The supernatant fluid was then decanted, and the sediment containing the spores was well washed in salt

[7] Abstr. Bacteriol., 1922, 6, p. 23.
[8] Am. Food Jour., 1923, 18, p. 143.
[9] Ibid., p. 143.
[10] Jour. Infect. Dis., 1924, 34, p. 129.
[11] Abstr. Bacteriol., 1924, 8, p. 31.

solution, suspended in 25 c c. of salt solution and heated in an oil bath at 80 C. for 15 minutes. The use of 150 c c. flasks for this purpose insured quick heat penetration due to the shallow layer of liquid. The spore suspensions were then shaken by machine with glass beads for 15 minutes to break up clumps, and the spores enumerated by the use of anaerobic plates after the method of Krumwiede. The suspensions were then diluted to give between 2,000,000 and 4,000,000 spores per c c.

The foods used were purchased from a local dealer and consisted of the following varieties: fruits—apricots, apples, blackberries, cherries, gooseberries, peaches, pears, plums (green gage), black raspberries and strawberries; vegetables—asparagus, red kidney beans, lima beans, beets, hominy, peas, dill pickles, sweet potato, pumpkin, sauerkraut and spinach; meats—salmon and shrimp, making 23 kinds of food in all. These were given a preliminary incubation at 37 C. for 30 days as a control for sterility, during which time only 2 cans of sauerkraut showed any change, these becoming "springers" due, probably, to hydrogen. This incubation, of course, did not reveal the presence of thermophilic bacteria—those which cause "flat sours" in certain foods. Since there were 18 cans of each kind of food, this indicates that the heating and processing of these 414 cans had probably been adequate so far as organisms which develop at 37 C. are concerned.

Two cans of each food were then inoculated with each of the 4 spore suspensions, making 8 cans of each food in all. One set of 4 cans was held at room temperature for 10 months in a room at about 25 C.; the corresponding set was placed at 37 C. In all cases the cans were examined when they showed physical signs of spoilage by swelling, but otherwise they were incubated for the full 10 month period. The method of making the inoculation was as follows: The tops of the cans were scrubbed with alcohol and a small area was smeared with rosin flux. Through this area a hole was punched with a small nail and 1 c c. of the spore suspension introduced well into the center of the can with a glass syringe equipped with a long needle. The holes were then closed with solder.

Tests for toxicity were made on each of the 184 cans inoculated by feeding approximately 0.5 c c. of the material to a guinea-pig with a pipet. When a strong toxin was present the animals died with typical symptoms in less than 24 hours. In all cases the animals were kept under observations for 3 or 4 weeks before a negative result was recorded. The results have been summarized in table 1. Of the 184 cans inoculated, 61 were toxic and 123 nontoxic. No more cans developed toxin at 37 C. than at room temperature, although the physical signs of spoilage were more evident at 37 C., since 49 cans at this temperature were apparently spoiled compared to 33 at room temperature. Much of this spoilage, which did not show toxin, judged by "swells" or "springers," occurred in acid products such as gooseberries, cherries, strawberries, sauerkraut, etc., in which an inflammable gas could be demonstrated, probably hydrogen. None of the fruits showed toxin production after the full incubation period. All the cans of beans, hominy, peas, sweet potato and shrimp were very toxic, and all cans of salmon except 2 were toxic. One can of pumpkin which was apparently normal contained a weak toxin which killed a guinea-pig in 17 days, the animal showing typical symptoms. In addition 3 cans of pumpkins were spoiled, the contents of one being quite black, while but 2 were toxic. This would place pumpkin in the group of vegetables which might show irregular toxin production, a point which is not in agreement with the results obtained by Schoenholz, Esty and Meyer.[1]

The hydrogen ion concentration of the foods was determined on one or more of the 10 cans which were kept as controls In certain cases both the potentiometer and the indicators of Clark and Lubs were used, the former being necessary when a highly colored liquid was to be tested as in beets, blackberries, raspberries and cherries. It was found that the two methods did not check exactly when tried on clear liquors from cans of spinach, asparagus, apples and apricots, but the variations in most cases did not amount to more than 0.2 of a point on the H-ion scale, and were no greater than the variations found in a series of cans of the same food when tested by the same method. The results of this determination of acidity on control cans are given in table 1. In addition, a number of determinations were made as follows: 8 cans of

TABLE 1

RESULTS OF DETERMINATION OF ACIDITY ON CONTROL CANS

Foods	Room Temperature			37 C.			Total Toxic	Total Non-Toxic	P_H of Control
	Average Incubation	No. Spoiled	No. Toxic	Average Incubation	No. Spoiled	No. Toxic			
Apples	9½ mos.	0	0	9½ mos.	1	0	0	8	3.6
Apricots	9½ mos.	0	0	9½ mos.	0	0	0	8	3.8
Blackberries	9½ mos.	0	0	9½ mos.	0	0	0	8	3.3
Cherries	9½ mos.	0	0	7 mos.	2	0	0	8	3.4
Gooseberries	9½ mos.	0	0	9½ mos.	4	0	0	8	3.0
Peaches	10 mos	0	0	10 mos.	0	0	0	8	4.4
Pears	10 mos.	0	0	10 mos.	0	0	0	8	4.2
Plums (green gage)	10 mos.	0	0	10 mos.	1	0	0	8	3.6
Raspberries (black)	9½ mos.	1	0	6 mos.	2	0	0	8	4.3
Strawberries	10 mos.	0	0	10 mos.	3	0	0	8	3.2
Asparagus	9½ mos.	1	1	9½ mos.	0	0	1	7	4.9
Beans (red kidney)	4½ days	4	4	2½ days	4	4	8	0	5.2
Beans (lima)	2 days	4	4	2 days	4	4	8	0	5.6
Beets	8½ mos.	1	1	10 days-10 mos.	1	1	2	6	5.2
Hominy	12 days	4	4	10 days	4	4	8	0	6.6
Peas	3 days	4	4	2 days	4	4	8	0	5.2
Pickles (dill)	10 mos.	0	0	10 mos.	2	0	0	8	3.6
Potato (sweet)	12 days	4	4	11 days	4	4	8	0	4.6
Pumpkin	9½ mos.	1	2	9½ mos.	2	1	3	5	5.0
Sauerkraut	9½ mos.	1	0	7 mos.	3	0	0	8	3.4
Spinach	9 mos.	0	0	9 mos.	0	1	1	7	4.6
Salmon	4 days	4	3	2-39 days	4	3	6	2	6.6
Shrimp	5 days	4	4	4 days	4	4	8	0	6.8
Total	....	33	31	....	49	30	61	123	

spinach, in which the readings were 4.6 in six, and 4.8 in two; 9 cans of asparagus, in which the readings were 4.8 in six, 5.0 in two, and 5.6 in one. This suggests one possible explanation of why an occasional can of asparagus or spinach shows toxin production while the rest of the lot does not. The cans used appeared to be normal in every respect, and were evidently sterile, since they had been incubated for 30 days at 37 C. and held at room temperature for 10 months thereafter. The reason for this occasional variation in reaction will be discussed later. Four cans of gooseberries which were hydrogen swells were selected from the controls and tested to determine what effect this had on reaction. Three cans gave a reading of 3.6 the same as that of a normal can, while one gave a reading of 4.2. In this case hydrogen swells did not seem to affect the reaction.

The greatest interest in this study attaches to those foods which are irregularly toxic, such as asparagus, beets, pumpkin and spinach. With spinach, particularly, several investigators have had similar results—a few cans of a lot made suitable medium while the remainder did not support growth. This failure to support growth has been correlated with the reaction by Schoenholz, Esty and Meyer,[1] who point out also that other conditions besides acidity are significant. They state also that the limiting acidity will vary with the kind of food. But with a given food. particularly with cans of the same lot, we look to the acidity as the chief factor, and in attempting to explain the variations found in cans of spinach a study of various kinds of natural medium was made. The object of using several kinds of canned foods as mediums was to obtain a comparative idea of their growth promoting abilities, and to be able to compare them with the best known artificial mediums.

Accordingly, liquid culture tubes were made from peas, corn, white potato, salmon and spinach. When possible the liquor from the can was decanted and tubed along with fragments of the solid material, no attempt being made to use a filtered medium in any case. The potato medium was made from the fresh vegetable as follows: After peeling, the pulp was cut in small pieces, covered with water and boiled until it was soft. It was then strained through cheesecloth to remove most of the starch, and the liquid poured into tubes for use. At first the reaction was not adjusted in any of the mediums. After sterilization the mediums showed a fairly clear supernatant fluid and considerable sediment. The corn broth was opalescent, and the salmon broth had a layer of fat at the top. For comparison hormone broth, made according to Huntoon's formula, and brain broth were used. These two have been found to give rapid and profuse growth with Clostridium botulinum.

The results of numerous tests with these various kinds of mediums, using comparative methods, and heavy and light inoculations, with vegetative cells, and with spores both young and old, make it apparent that brain broth, hormone broth, and potato broth are in the same class. All gave rapid and profuse growth, as evidenced by heavy clouding and gas production. It was a little surprising to find potato extract such a good medium. Growth in it seemed to be maintained at a high level for several days, longer in fact than in hormone broth, which began to show sedimenting and clearing by the third day. The potato broth in the same test was still turbid and giving off abundant gas on the fifth day. The corn medium was found inferior to that made from peas, while the unneutralized spinach liquor did not support any visible growth. Potato broth would make a very useful medium for culture of Clostridium botulinum.

When cultures of these various mediums were observed for ability to form spores, it was found that potato broth and corn broth, as well as hormone broth, were not well suited to sporulation. The latter was made with 0.25% dextrose, and the others naturally have an appreciable carbohydrate content. Any medium which produced large amounts of gas, expelling the paraffin caps from the tubes, did not give a satisfactory yield of spores. On the other hand, brain broth and the liquid from a can of peas gave a very good yield with most cultures. The liquor from canned peas is especially useful, since it can be sterilized and the clear supernatant fluid used. This gives a good yield, and there is little débris to interfere.

Since potato broth seemed to rank so highly as a growth producing substrate, several tests were made to discover the chemical nature of the medium. The only positive results were a strong test for starch, as was to be expected, and a small amount of amino nitrogen, about 0.05%. This would make the total nitrogen at least 0.312%. The biuret reaction and tests for trytophane and reducing sugars were negative.

Attention was now directed to the spinach juice which, among the other natural mediums, was the only one which failed to show growth. A normal can was selected and the liquor removed aseptically. The H-ion concentration was about 4.5, using methyl red. It was adjusted to P_H 7 and sterilized. Five days after inoculation there was no growth, and the control tubes showed that the medium had again been made acid by sterilization. In repeating the

TABLE 2

RESULT OF HEATING ON CANS OF SPINACH

	Vacuum	Physical Condition	P_H	Remarks
Grade 1	0	Good, liquor clear	5.0	Seam not tight
Grade 2	14	Soft, liquor cloudy	6.8	
Grade 3	23	Mushy, liquor dark and cloudy	7.2	

test, the medium was neutralized, heated in the autoclave, again neutralized and sterilized in tubes. To a portion 0.5% glucose was added. In this case the reaction remained neutral after the sterilization, and abundant growth was secured after 2 days with a light inoculation. Growth was not long continued, however, and a test showed that the reaction in the inoculated tubes had again become acid, although the control tube, which was incubated with the others, showed little change, a point which will be referred to later.

From this experimentation it seems that spinach is also a good medium for Clostridium botulinum if it has a proper reaction, and that the irregular results from inoculating cans may in part be due to this factor. Attempts were now made to discover if possible why one can of spinach is too acid to support growth while another is a favorable medium.

At this time the fresh spinach on the market was undergoing a soft slimy rot after standing for a day or two. Some spinach was purchased and carefully sorted into 3 grades as follows: (1) all sound leaves; (2) partly sound and partly decomposed leaves, about two-thirds good and one-third affected; (3) poor leaves, most of them affected with rot.

A No. 2 can of each grade was packed and loosely sealed by means of the first roll on a hand closing machine. The cans were then heated at 5 pounds for 45 minutes and sealed while hot. They were then allowed to stand at room temperature for 2 or 3 days before they were examined. The results are given in table 2. As a check on the heating process the vacuum in the cans was determined, the gage readings being in inches.

This experiment showed that the reaction became increasingly alkaline in proportion to the amount of rotted spinach in the can. It showed further that a relatively small amount of poor spinach in a can might reduce the acidity to a point where Clostridium botulinum would grow and produce its toxin.

On several different occasions the flora of rotted spinach obtained in the market was studied to determine the specific cause of the soft slimy rot. For the most part the predominant species were gram-negative nonspore-forming rods, producing a strong alkaline reaction in litmus milk and in sugar broths, showing that they were proteolytic rather than fermentative in action. The odor of decayed spinach indicates the presence of ammonia.

We have then, perhaps, a rational explanation of why certain cans in a pack of spinach become toxic. A portion of poor spinach gets into a can occasionally, thus reducing the natural acidity. If spores of Clostridium botulinum also happen to be introduced two conditions necessary for toxin production are fulfilled. In addition, it can be seen why physical signs of spoilage do not always accompany toxin production. The work of Schoenholz, Esty, and Meyer,[1] as well as our own, has shown that the growth of Clostridium botulinum in spinach causes an increase in acidity. When the initial reaction is near the limiting acidity, this increase due to the metabolism of the bacteria is sufficient to inhibit growth before any marked signs of spoilage have occurred, but not before there has been a considerable multiplication of cells. Since the medium is not well suited to spore formation, the cells formed will slowly autolyze and liberate toxin, and we should expect to find a stronger toxin after 5 months than after a week or 10 days, a fact which was noted by the authors named. Dozier [12] has found that mediums with 1% of glucose are unfavorable for spore formation, and has correlated autolysis with toxin production. This would explain well the results of our observations on spinach.

If we go back now to the results of the food inoculation we can see the relationship of toxin production to reaction. In the case of asparagus, 8 cans were inoculated, and only one was toxic. Of the uninoculated controls, 9 were tested for reaction. Only one showed a reaction above P_H 5.0, and that one was 5.6. It might not always happen that one can out of every 8 or 9 would show such a marked variation in reaction. This is illustrated by the results obtained with spinach. Of

[12] Jour. Infect. Dis., 1924, 35, p. 105.

the 8 cans inoculated, only one was weakly toxic after 8 months' incubation. None of the 8 control cans tested for reaction showed any marked change. If a larger series had been examined, no doubt one could have been found with a reaction less acid than P_H 5.

COMMENT

The results of the inoculations of foods do not differ materially from those obtained by Schoenholz, Esty and Meyer.[1] The same general groups of foods were observed, each group consisting of about the same varieties. The foods used in this investigation and not by the foregoing authors are: apples, blackberries, gooseberries, dill pickles, red kidney beans, lima beans, hominy, and shrimp. The first 4 belong to the acid group of foods showing no toxin; the last 4 belong to the class of foods which are regularly and highly toxic after short incubation, and which show marked physical signs of spoilage. The results of the inoculation of pumpkin place it in the intermediate group of foods which are irregularly toxic. This does not agree with the work cited, in which pumpkin is placed in the groups of foods which are regularly toxic.

In the case of beets, the cans inoculated with culture A1 were toxic, both at room temperature and at 37 C. No other cultures developed a toxin in beets. In this case it seems that beets were a more suitable medium for culture A1 than for the other strains used, although it is possible that these cans may have been less acid in reaction than the others, and happened to be used with the same culture.

The work on food inoculation in conjunction with that in which various food extracts were used as medium serves to emphasize that Clostridium botulinum is not especially fastidious as to food requirements, but grows well on a wide range of substances if a suitable reaction is present. In addition, certain foods, such as spinach, asparagus, beets, and string beans, which have a natural reaction near P_H 5.0 in case a sound product is canned, have all the requirements for promoting good growth except perhaps acidity. If such foods were neutralized before inoculation, it should be possible to get consistent spoilage and toxin production. Since a large share of the outbreaks of botulism reported in this country have been caused by this group of foods, particularly string beans and spinach, some procedure aimed at preserving the protective natural acidity of the food should be valuable.

It is conceivable that the reaction in foods may be rendered less acid after canning by certain bacteria which escape the heating process, and thus make the material in the can suitable for the development of spores of Clostridium botulinum when they are present; this would amount to a bacterial metabiosis, and is less likely than that the alkaline substance is formed previous to canning, since the bacteria found in rotted vegetables are often of the type producing an alkaline rather than an acid reaction on the common artificial mediums.

SUMMARY

Twenty-three kinds of food were inoculated with detoxified spores of 4 strains of Clostridium botulinum. Those found to be regularly toxic with all strains are: red kidney beans, lima beans, hominy, peas, sweet potato, salmon, and shrimp. Those irregularly toxic are: asparagus, beets, pumpkin, and spinach. The acid fruits and the very acid vegetable products, such as sauerkraut and dill pickles, did not become toxic.

Certain extracts and liquors from canned vegetables were used as medium in comparison with brain broth and hormone broth. The extract from white potato was found equal to the best medium for promoting growth. The liquor from cans of peas, corn, and salmon gave lesser growth, while that from spinach gave growth only after being neutralized.

The reaction in cans of asparagus, string beans, beets, pumpkin, and spinach probably explains the irregularity of toxic production so frequently noted in these foods.

The reaction in certain canned vegetables is greatly affected by the quality of the material put in the cans. Experiments with spinach show that a small amount of rotted material will reduce the acidity to a point where Clostridium botulinum can grow and develop a toxin.

ACTUAL TEMPERATURES ATTAINED BY MEDIUMS IN AUTOCLAVE STERILIZATION

Anne Benton and Alan Leighton

From the Research Laboratories, Bureau of Dairying, U. S. Dept. of Agriculture

Autoclave sterilization is apparently a simple process and easily standardized, but occasional failures to secure a sterile product occur, as well as irregular chemical changes in the mediums, which are even more serious, particularly in biochemical identification of species and similar work. These difficulties make it obvious that there must be considerable differences in the temperatures actually attained when medium is "autoclaved at 15 pounds' pressure for 20 minutes." The general impression prevails, and is stated or implied in many laboratory manuals, that 15 pounds' pressure on the gage means 120 C. inside the chamber. In actual practice this can almost never be the case. Saturated steam at that pressure has a temperature of 120.95 C., but the steam in an autoclave usually contains air, and the pressure reading on the gage is the sum of the pressures of the air and the steam. Unless the air outlet is at the bottom of the chamber and proper care is exercised to drive out all the air before closing the cock, some of it will be entrapped. Moreover, steam piped from a central plant or generated from a tank in the sterilizer itself is likely to contain air unless the water from which it came was air-free. The amount of air present varies from day to day, and no trustworthy idea of the temperature inside the autoclave can be obtained from the pressure-gage reading. As the rate of transfer of heat from one substance to another depends on the difference of their temperatures, it is important that the temperature inside the autoclave be considered rather than the pressure.

With a constant temperature maintained inside the autoclave, the time required for attainment of the same degree of heat at the center of a vessel of medium depends on the size of the container, the original temperature and viscosity of the contents, and, more particularly, on the free access of steam to the surface of the container. In order to determine how much time should be allowed for these factors, it was necessary to take accurate measurements, while sterilization was going on, of the temperature in an autoclave and in mediums disposed in various types of containers.

Received for publication, May 16, 1925.

The experiments which follow were made with an ordinary horizontal, cylindrical autoclave with an inside chamber 20 inches in diameter and 30 inches long, heated directly by steam piped under pressure from a central plant. It was wired with a copper-constantan thermocouple with 8 points, which could be disposed at will in different parts of the chamber or within the medium itself. The cold junction, outside the autoclave, was kept at 0 C. by packing it in snow in a thermos bottle. With practice one can develop sufficient dexterity in manipulating the switches and accuracy in reading the millivoltmeter to call off the figures on all 8 points at 1-minute intervals. From the millivolt readings recorded during the experiment, actual temperatures can be calculated at one's leisure, and the theoretical experimental error is only a fraction of a degree. The advantage of this procedure is that it gives a continuous record of the temperature at 8 different points simultaneously, minute by minute, thus enabling one to run duplicates on the autoclave temperature, as well as on that of the mediums. Preliminary experiments showed that while some parts

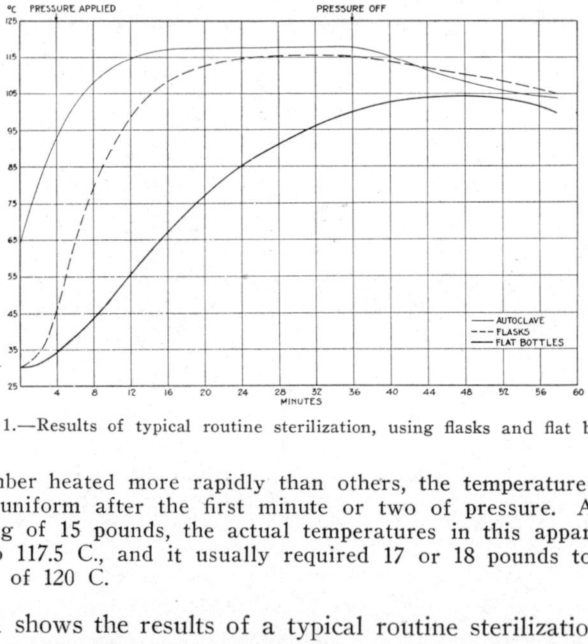

Chart 1.—Results of typical routine sterilization, using flasks and flat bottles.

of the chamber heated more rapidly than others, the temperature throughout was fairly uniform after the first minute or two of pressure. At a steam-gage reading of 15 pounds, the actual temperatures in this apparatus varied from 113 to 117.5 C., and it usually required 17 or 18 pounds to produce a temperature of 120 C.

Chart 1 shows the results of a typical routine sterilization and also illustrates the importance of free access of steam to the surfaces of the containers. The shelf was packed full of 100 c c. water blanks in flat bottles, 118 in all, and the apparatus heated to 15 pounds for 20 minutes. The autoclave temperature, as shown by the fine line, went to 117.5 C., but bottles at the center of the pack (continuous heavy line) attained a maximum of only 105 C. The dotted line records the result when an equal amount of water (11,800 c c.) was distributed in 10 large Florence flasks. The autoclave curve was almost identically the same as before, but the water in the flasks was at or above 115 C. for 11 minutes. The tightly packed flat bottles represent the worst possible conditions, as only those on the outer row are freely exposed to the steam, and convection currents can have but little effect in such small volumes.

The same principle applies to material in test tubes packed in baskets. Tubes only 2 inches from the edge of the basket reached sterilizing temperatures several minutes after those at the edge. It is evident that in order to get sufficient heat at the center of the mass, time was wasted and the outer tubes badly overheated. A basket with a wire top whose mesh will just admit one tube permits spacing. Experiments showed that alternate spaces, checker-board fashion, gave sufficient access to the steam so that all heated uniformly, and wider intervals gave no additional advantage.

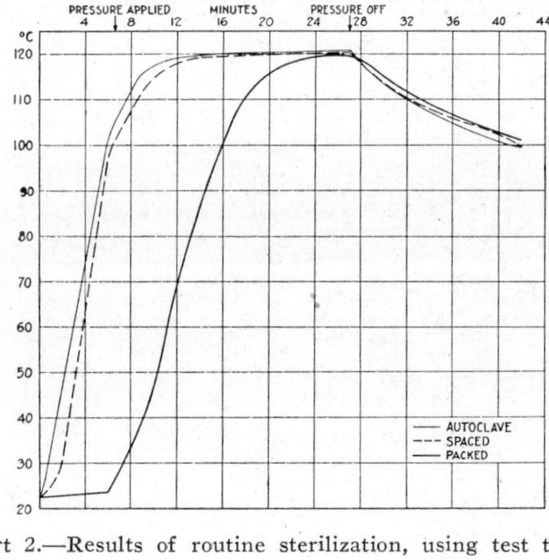

Chart 2.—Results of routine sterilization, using test tubes.

With this arrangement slightly less than half as many tubes can be treated in a given space as when tightly packed.

Chart 2 shows a typical run with tubes 1.5 cm. in diameter, each containing 10 c c. of medium, when the autoclave was brought to 120 C. and kept as nearly as possible at that temperature. The continuous heavy line shows the temperatures in the central ones of 65 tubes packed in a 4.5 x 6 inch basket; the dotted line represents the tubes at the center of one containing an equal number, spaced as described, all sterilized at the same time. The outside tubes in the packed basket followed the curve of the spaced tubes. Note that there is little difference in the rate of cooling. It is evident that the central tubes in even a small basket require

10 minutes longer to come to temperature than do those at the edge, and this discrepancy would be much greater in the larger baskets used in most laboratories, especially if several had been packed in together, as is the custom. Investigators on the heat resistance of spores report that unless they are dealing with abnormally resistant strains or numbers greatly in excess of those ordinarily encountered, 5 minutes at an actual temperature of 120 C. is enough to kill them. This means that when one sterilizes all the tubes in even a small basket, alone in the autoclave, those at the edge must bear the maximum heat 3 times as long as those in the middle.

When mere attainment of sterility is the sole object, as in treating discarded cultures or water blanks, these considerations are of little importance, as no harm is done by prolonging the heating until all the material in the apparatus is sterile. The case is quite different when one is preparing special mediums containing organic compounds sensitive to heat. Several investigators have called attention to the now generally accepted fact that the prolongation of exposure is often more harmful than the intensity of heat itself. Mudge [1] in particular has shown that maltose and lactose mediums are injured less by rapid autoclaving than by treatment in the Arnold apparatus, and in many laboratories intermittent sterilization is no longer practiced. Even when all possible speed consistent with safety is used in operating the autoclave, the lag at the center of a large basket of medium permits considerable chemical change in heat-sensitive materials to take place in the tubes at the edge by the time those at the center are sterile. It is not hard to understand why variable maltose fermentations may apparently be observed on the same strain of bacteria in teaching laboratories if batches of sugar broth are autoclaved in baskets that hold 150 to 200 tubes. Many vexatious inconsistencies and irreguarities in research work have doubtless arisen in the same way. In some of the older work on resistance of bacteria, particularly in reported instances of extraordinary survival in heated material, allowance should be made for possible errors arising from undue reliance on pressure as an indication of temperature, as well as discrepancies due to slowness of heat penetration.

Chart 3 displays an additional advantage from spacing the tubes in that cooling below 100 C. is greatly hastened after the medium is taken from the autoclave, especially if set in cold water. The tempera-

[1] Jour. Bacteriol., 1917, 2, p. 403.

tures in tubes at the centers of packed baskets are indicated by continuous lines; dotted lines represent spaced tubes. Lines *a* and *b* show the slowness of cooling when the material remained in the open autoclave; baskets *c* and *d* were taken out as soon as possible and left at room temperature; baskets *e* and *f* were set in a pan of cold water.

A series of experiments was performed to learn the length of time which should be allowed for heat penetration in containers of different shapes and sizes freely exposed to steam. While 10 c c. amounts in test tubes reach 120 C. only one minute later than the autoclave itself, 100 c c. require about 7 minutes, and 500 c c. at least 10 minutes, to come to temperature. For amounts greater than 500 c c. it is advisable

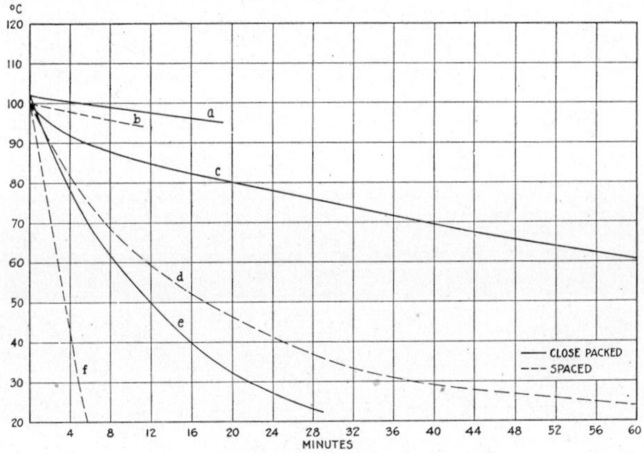

Chart 3.—Rate of cooling in test tubes.

to run the autoclave to a temperature slightly above that desired in the mediums. Note that in Chart 1, with the autoclave maintained at 117.5 C., the large flasks reached a maximum of 116 C., and for the last 6 minutes during which pressure was applied, showed no rise in temperature. In experiments in which the autoclave was allowed to go to 122 C., flasks holding 800 c c. of liquid reached 120 C. about 15 minutes after the autoclave, and the same was observed in volumes up to 1,600 c c. in Florence flasks. The flat layer procured when medium is placed in an Erlenmeyer flask offers little or no advantage over the same volume disposed in a hemispherical shape by half filling a Florence flask, due, perhaps, to the fact that the curving side of the latter permits some contact with the steam on the under side. Increasing the number of flasks treated at once increases the time necessary to bring the autoclave to 120 C., but once that temperature has been reached, the presence of the additional flasks has no effect on the penetration of heat into the contents of any one of them, provided it is not in contact with others.

SUMMARY

Sterilization should be controlled according to temperature, not pressure. Autoclaves should be equipped with reliable thermometers and should have the air outlet at the bottom.

In sterilizing any substance which is easily injured by heat, much time can be saved and injury avoided by disposing the material in small containers, spaced to permit free access of steam to their surfaces.

GERMICIDAL EFFICIENCY OF COCONUT OIL AND LINSEED OIL SOAPS AND OF THEIR MIXTURES WITH CRESOL

F. W. Tilley and J. M. Schaffer

From the Biochemic Division, Bureau of Animal Industry, U. S. Department of Agriculture

Many investigators have studied the bactericidal action of soaps and of mixtures of soaps with cresol or other phenolic compounds, and the literature is extensive. As our work is limited in its scope, we shall not attempt any review of the literature, but shall mention the work of others only so far as may be necessary in presenting the results of our own work.

While investigating soap-cresol solutions made with different kinds of soap, we found that preparations made with coconut oil soap exhibited much greater germicidal activity against B. typhosus than preparations made with linseed oil soap, which is the soap usually employed at the present time. This led us to make a more extended study of the germicidal value of these soaps and of their mixtures with cresol, some of the results of which are presented in this paper.

Our work consisted in part of an investigation of the germicidal value of the soaps of the pure fatty acids of the saturated series from butyric to palmitic, inclusive. As the results obtained were similar to those of Reichenbach [1] and of Walker,[2] we shall not discuss them in detail, but state only that they show that the germicidal value of the soaps of the saturated fatty acids increases regularly with increasing molecular weight. The results which we shall present here are mainly those which seem to us to have practical value in demonstrating the value of coconut oil soap and preparations containing coconut oil soap.

MATERIALS

Since linseed oil from the soap-making point of view has proved to be a rather uniform product and its practical application in the manufacture of saponified cresol solutions also indicates considerable uniformity, we have made use of only one sample of linseed oil.

On the other hand, there are numerous varieties of coconut oil for sale, so it was deemed advisable to work with a number of different samples of

Received for publication, June 18, 1925.

[1] Ztschr. f. Hyg. u. Infektionskr., 1908, 59, p. 296.
[2] Jour. Infect. Dis., 1924, 35, p. 557.

coconut oil and coconut oil fatty acids as they are obtainable from commercial sources. For detailed specifications of the characteristics of the different grades the reader is referred to the circular of the New York Produce Exchange.[3]

The only important characteristic of coconut oils which concerns us here is the saponification value. This tends to identify the oil, for among the soap-making oils available in this country in any considerable quantity, coconut oil is in a class by itself so far as saponification value is concerned. In connection with this work tests were made on 13 different samples of coconut oil obtained from several refiners and representative of the various grades obtainable in commerce. All except one of these samples had saponification values between 254 and 260, which indicates a rather constant composition. This was confirmed by the results of the bacteriologic tests.

According to Lewkowitsch,[4] further research is needed to establish satisfactorily the exact proportions of the various fatty acids in linseed and coconut oils. The best available analyses, however, indicate that linseed oil contains mostly linolenic and linolic acids with small amounts of oleic and other acids, while in coconut oil lauric and myristic acids make up about two-thirds of the total fatty acids and the lower fatty acids a little more than half of the remainder.

In making cresol-soap solutions, three different samples of cresol were used, the chemical composition of which varied as follows:

Cresol 1, a commercial sample of "cresylic acid 97-99," was used in all the saponified cresol solutions mentioned in table 2. Chemical analysis of the saponified cresol solutions indicated that cresol 1 must have contained between 97 and 99% of total phenols. The bacteriologic tests indicate that it must have contained an appreciable amount of the higher-boiling phenols.

Cresol 85 was a sample of redistilled U. S. P. cresol; 48% distilled over between 198 and 200 C. and 52% between 200 and 203 (corrected temperatures); 85, therefore, was composed of nearly equal parts of para and meta cresols.

Cresol 2867 was a sample of commercial cresol. Distillation of a 500 gm. sample showed 1.5% (essentially water) boiling below 200 C., 2.5% from 200 to 205, 17.5% from 205 to 208, 34% from 208 to 212, 26% from 212 to 220, 16% from 220 to 240 and 2.5% remaining in the flask. This indicates the presence of little, if any, cresol, of 60% of meta xylenols, and of about 35% of other high-boiling phenols.

METHODS OF PREPARATION

The soaps of the pure fatty acids were compounded by adding to a definite weight of the fatty acid a chemically equivalent amount of standard sodium hydroxid solution and then bringing to the desired strength by proper adjustment with distilled water.

The soaps of the commercial oils and commercial fatty acids were usually prepared with an excess of about 10% of alkali over the theoretical requirement as indicated by the saponification value in order to insure complete saponification within a reasonable length of time, and to render them comparable in alkalinity to the soap-cresol solutions which in practice contain a similar excess of alkali. Commercial linseed oils with saponification values varying between 187 and 195 would require 18.7 to 19.5 gm., respectively, of

[3] Rules regulating business among members of the New York Produce Exchange in Oils, Waxes and Fats, not otherwise provided for. Effective May 20, 1920.

[4] Chemical Technology of Oils, Fats and Waxes. 1914.

potassium hydroxide, or the chemically equivalent amount of sodium hydroxide, 13.3 to 13.9 gm., to saponify 100 gm. of the linseed oil. The saponification value of the coconut oils indicated that from 25.4 gm. to 26 gm., respectively, of potassium hydroxide, or the chemically equivalent amount of sodium hydroxide, 18.1 to 18.6 gm., would theoretically be necessary to saponify 100 gm. of the various samples of coconut oil, except one recovered coconut oil with the low saponification value of 225, which would require only 22.5 gm. of potassium hydroxide. Analysis of many of our preparations, unless otherwise stated, showed from 8 to 12% more alkali than was theoretically required to combine with the fatty acid, as soap.

The method employed in the preparation of sample 82, a linseed oil soap solution, is illustrative of that which was followed generally in the preparation of soap solutions. To 140 gm. of linseed oil, in a tared beaker, 60 c c. of sodium hydroxide solution, containing 20 gm., NaOH was added, and stirred about 3 minutes, when the mixture appeared to be properly emulsified. This was allowed to remain over night at room temperature, 30 to 35 C. The next day the beaker and its contents were heated on the steam bath for 2 hours; sufficient water was added to bring it approximately to the desired concentration, after which the mixture was stirred until homogeneous, and finally brought to the desired weight of soap solution by the proper addition of water.

In the preparation of coconut oil soap solution, the proportions of oil and alkali used were naturally not the same as when linseed oil was used. No. 84, a coconut oil soap solution containing 20% of sodium soap, was made as follows: To 100 gm. of a Ceylon type of coconut oil was added 59 c c. of sodium hydroxide solution containing 19.7 gm. of NaOH; the mixture was stirred for 3 minutes, at the end of which time it appeared to be properly emulsified. The remaining steps were run parallel with number 82, except that the final concentration was made on the basis of 20% of anhydrous soap. instead of 15%.

Usually when several different soaps were to be compared individually and in combination with cresol, they were prepared at the same time, so as to have the same step in each preparation as closely parallel as possible, and thus obtain finished products which were closely alike.

PREPARATION OF SAPONIFIED CRESOL SOLUTIONS

The term "saponified cresol solution" is used here to denote a product similar to Liquor Cresolis Compositus, U. S. P., differing from it in the following particulars. The commercial product "cresylic acid" is used instead of U. S. P. cresol, in such proportions as to give 50% of "phenols" in the finished product. The amount of soap present is equivalent to not less than 28% of linseed oil, or the chemically equivalent amount of its fatty acids or of other oils or their fatty acids. Either caustic potash, caustic soda, or a mixture of these may be used to form the soap.

The linseed oil soap cresol solutions used in our tests were made so as to contain 28% of linseed oil as soap, caustic soda being the alkali employed unless otherwise specified. Since the saponification value of linseed oils may vary from 187 to 195 and the saponification value of coconut oils from 250 to 260, the amount of coconut oil equivalent to 28% of linseed oil will average 21%, this percentage of coconut oil, therefore, was used in making the coconut oil soap-cresol solutions.

The saponified cresol solutions were made by emulsifying the oil or fatty acid with the alkali solution as described for the preparation of soaps and after standing over night, when oils were used, and 2 hours on the steam bath to soften the soap, the requisite amount of cresol was added. The mixture was stirred until uniform, and was finally brought to the required weight by the addition of water. When the fatty acids are used in making the soaps it is not necessary to let the emulsion stand over night, since the formation of soap takes place more rapidly than when the oils are used.

BACTERIOLOGIC WORK

Almost all of the bacteriologic tests were made by the Rideal-Walker technic, modified as follows: the unadjusted culture medium devised by Wright,[5] made with Armour's peptone, was substituted for the R-W standard broth; instead of a dropping pipet we used a 1 c c. pipet graduated into tenths for measuring out the 0.5 c c. of culture required for the test; the medication temperature was 25 C.; tests were made against Staph aureus and B. pyocyaneus as well as B. typhosus; in many tests sodium chloride, serum, etc., were added; dilutions were made up in sterile Erlenmeyer flasks instead of cylinders, adding fixed amounts of the stock solution of disinfectant to the varying amounts of sterile distilled water required, transfers of stock solution, water, etc., being made with sterile standardized pipet; the scale of dilutions was not based on the phenol dilutions but was varied as seemed necessary to obtain comparable dilutions; finally, although phenol coefficients where obtained are shown in the tables for the benefit of those who may wish to use them, it is intended that comparisons should be based on killing strengths for 10 minutes' exposure.

Although tests were made on a large number of different samples the results obtained were so much alike that it does not seem necessary to do more than present a limited number of representative tests.

Such results for linseed oil soap and for coconut oil soap and various mixtures containing coconut oil soap are shown in table 1. No results are given for linseed oil soap and Staph. aureus, since a 20% solution required 15 minutes to kill that organism. It is evident from the results in the table that coconut oil soap has a greater germicidal efficiency than linseed oil soap. It is also evident that the germicidal efficiency of coconut oil soap is greatly increased by the addition of 2% sodium chloride or 20% more sodium hydroxide than is necessary to saponify the oil.

The results of tests on a number of samples of saponified cresol solution are shown in table 2. These solutions were all made with cresol 1, a commercial cresol with a phenol coefficient of 4. This fact should be considered in making any comparisons with results shown in subsequent tables.

[5] J. Bacteriol., 1917, 2, p. 315.

The tests, the results of which are shown in table 3, were made upon various mixtures of soaps with cresol 85 or cresol 2867. Cresol 85 was a purified cresol containing approximately equal amounts of meta and para cresols. Cresol 2867 was a commercial cresol consisting mostly of xylenols and having a high phenol coefficient.

The results in tables 2 and 3 indicate that the germicidal efficiency of saponified cresol solutions containing soap prepared exclusively from

TABLE 1

KILLING STRENGTHS OF SOAPS FOR DIFFERENT ORGANISMS

Soap	Diluent	S. aureus	B. pyocyaneus	B. typhosus
Coconut oil soap	Water	1:36 (0.45)	1:100 (1.1)	1:200 (1.5)
Coconut oil soap	25% Serum in Water	1:20 (0.25)	1:40 (0.44)	1:75 (0.75)
Coconut oil soap	2% NaCl in Water	1:250 (3.2)	1:150 (1.6)	1:1000 (8.4)
Coconut oil soap with 20% excess NaOH	Water	1:40 (0.5)	1:200 (2.2)	1:300 (2.6)
Linseed oil soap	Water	....	1:35 (0.38)	1:25 (0.2)
Linseed oil soap	2% NaCl in Water	....	1:20 (0.22)	1:30 (0.3)

Killing strengths shown indicate concentration of anhydrous soap.
Phenol coefficients shown in parentheses.

TABLE 2

GERMICIDAL EFFICIENCY OF SAPONIFIED 50% CRESOL 1 SOLUTIONS ON B. TYPHOSUS

Samples	Oil or Fatty Acids Used	% Oil as Soap	Alkali %	Phenol Coefficient
20	Coconut oil	20	NaOH 4.0	4.0
24	Lauric acid	20	NaOH 4.0	5.0
31	Myristic acid	25	NaOH 4.0	5.0
32	Palmitic acid	25.6	NaOH 4.0	3.0
33	Oleic acid	28.2	NaOH 4.0	2.5
61	Ceylon coconut oil	20	NaOH 3.7	5.0
63	Cochin coconut oil	20	NaOH 3.8	5.3
68	Cochin coconut oil	20	NaOH 3.8	4.0
70	Recovered coconut oil	20	NaOH 3.8	4.6
71	Coconut oil	20	NaOH 3.8	4.0
72	Coconut oil	20	KOH 5.3	4.0
74	Coconut oil	20	NaOH 4.5	4.0
75	Coconut oil	20	NaOH 7.6	4.0
67	Linseed oil	28	KOH 5.8	2.6
11	Linseed oil	28	NaOH 4.0	2.1
12	Soy bean oil	28	NaOH 4.0	1.9

coconut oil is greater than that of solutions containing soap prepared exclusively from linseed oil. Since the saponified cresol solutions contain only 50% of cresol their dilutions are really comparable with cresol dilutions only half as strong. An increase of germicidal activity on the addition of sodium chloride occurs with the saponified cresol solutions, as it does with the soaps, this effect being more marked with solutions containing coconut oil soaps than with those containing linseed oil soap.

In addition to the previously described experiments, a few tests were made to determine the effect of the soap and cresol on each other. The results obtained indicate that mixtures containing approximately half as much soap as cresol possess the maximum germicidal efficiency. Larger proportions of soap diminished the germicidal efficiency of the cresol to such an extent that 1% of cresol in a 5% solution of linseed

TABLE 3

KILLING STRENGTHS OF CRESOLS AND OF SAPONIFIED CRESOL SOLUTIONS FOR DIFFERENT TEST ORGANISMS

Test Material	Diluent	S. aureus	B. pyocyaneus	B. typhosus
Cresol 85	Water	1:200 (2.5)	1:225 (2.6)	1:250 (2.5)
	2% NaCl in water	1:225 (2.5)	1:300 (3.3)	1:360 (3.7)
	25% Serum in water	1:160 (1.9)	1:200 (2.2)	1:210 (2.1)
	25% Serum in water plus 2% NaCl	1:180 (2.1)	1:240	1:260
Sap. cres. sol. containing cresol 85 + linseed oil soap	Water	1:150	1:150 (1.6)	1:225 (2.0)
	2% NaCl in water	1:200 (2.6)	1:200 (2.2)	1:325 (3.0)
	25% Serum in water	1:80 (1.0)	1:100 (1.2)	1:120 (1.2)
	25% Serum in water plus 2% NaCl	1:120	1:130	1:200
Sap. cres. sol. containing cresol 85 + coconut oil soap	Water	1:160	1:200 (2.2)	1:275 (2.6)
	2% NaCl in water	1:240	1:350 (3.5)	1:500 (5.0)
	25% Serum in water	1:90	1:130	1:160 (1.6)
	25% Serum in water plus 2% NaCl	1:120	1:160	1:240 (2.4)
Cresol 2867	Water	1:400 (5.0)	1:550	1:650 (6.0)
Sap. cres. sol. containing cresol 2867 + linseed oil soap	Water	1:200	1:300 (3.3)	1:350 (3.5)
Sap. cres. sol. containing cresol 2867 + coconut soap	Water	1:300 (3.5)	1:400 (4.4)	1:600 (6.0)

Phenol coefficients shown in parentheses.

oil soap showed no germicidal efficiency while 0.5% of the same cresol in a 0.25% solution of the same soap killed the organism in less than two and one-half minutes. That the cresol may also act on the soap is suggested by the results with a 3% coconut oil soap solution which showed a greater germicidal activity alone than when mixed with 0.5% of cresol.

Besides the previously described tests by the Rideal-Walker method with B. typhosus, B. pyocyaneus and Staph. aureus as the test organisms, experiments were also made with B. tuberculosis as the test organism, with results which indicated that coconut oil soap alone is not effective against this organism in dilutions up to 10% with exposure varying from 1 to 5 minutes.

DISCUSSION

The work of Reichenbach and, more especially, the recent work of Walker with soaps of the pure fatty acids indicates clearly that the difference in germicidal activity between coconut oil soap and linseed oil soap depends on the difference in chemical composition. Walker has shown that the soaps of the saturated fatty acids of coconut oil have greater germicidal efficiency against B. typhosus than the soaps of the unsaturated fatty acids of linseed oil.

On the other hand, Walker found the soaps of both saturated and unsaturated fatty acids very efficient against the pneumococcus and streptococcus, while neither was efficient against the staphylococcus. Specificity of action is also shown in our own work, not only for coconut and linseed oil soaps against the same test organism, but also for coconut oil soap against different organisms, since it is most efficient against B. typhosus, less efficient against B. pyocyaneus and but slightly efficient against Staph. aureus.

It should be noted here that Hamilton [6] some years ago called attention to the fact that he had found soap made from coconut oil to have somewhat greater germicidal activity against B. typhosus than soaps made from various other oils.

The practical value of the remarkable increase of germicidal activity caused by the addition of sodium chloride to solutions of coconut oil soap is greatly diminished by the fact that the salt has a marked flocculating or gelating effect on the soap solutions. With 4% salt this was so marked as to prevent making the usual tests. With 2% salt it was possible to make the tests and obtain concordant results, but even with this amount of salt flocculation or gelation occurred after the tubes of soap solution had stood for a short time. With less than 2% of salt, the increase in germicidal efficiency was not as great.

Although the addition of sodium chloride to saponified cresol solutions caused more or less clouding, there was no such flocculation or gelation as occurred with the soaps alone. It was noted, however, that with strong concentrations of salt (3 to 10% of sodium chloride) with 3% saponified cresol or 2% salt with the very weak concentrations of

[6] Jour. Ind. & Eng. Chem., 1911, 3, p. 582.

saponified cresol used in some of our tests, there was a tendency to separate into two layers on standing over night. With a 3% solution of saponified cresol and 2% sodium chloride, there was no separation after standing at room temperature for 7 days. In view, then, of the increased germicidal efficiency obtained and its maintenance to a considerable degree in the presence of blood serum, it seems possible that the addition of sodium chloride to saponified cresol solutions may have some practical value.

SUMMARY AND CONCLUSIONS

Coconut oil soap has a greater bactericidal efficiency than linseed oil soap against B. typhosus, B. pyocyaneus and Staph. aureus, both in the absence of added organic matter and in the presence of 25% of horse blood serum.

The bactericidal efficiency of coconut oil soap is increased by the addition of a slight excess of alkali and by the addition of sodium chloride. The practical value of the action of sodium chloride is, however, greatly diminished by the undesirable physical changes produced and by failure to maintain the increased efficiency in the presence of blood serum.

Although its low efficiency against Staph. aureus and B. tuberculosis limits the value of coconut oil soap as a disinfectant, it seems likely that it can be used to advantage against other organisms. It is suggested that if a nonpoisonous antiseptic in the form of soap is desired, this need may be very well met by the use of pure coconut oil soap, which combines some germicidal activity with the detergent properties of soap.

The bactericidal efficiency of cresol-soap mixtures is greatly affected by the proportions of soap and cresol used. Mixtures containing approximately half as much soap as cresol showed maximum efficiency. An increase in the proportion of soap causes a reduction in efficiency. Saponified cresol solutions containing coconut oil soap have a greater germicidal efficiency than those containing linseed oil soap, both in the absence of added organic matter and in the presence of 25% blood serum. The difference in efficiency is most marked when the cresylic acid used contains a large proportion of high-boiling phenols.

The addition of sodium hydroxide in fairly large excess over that needed to saponify the oil does not diminish the bactericidal efficiency of saponified cresol solutions. The addition of sodium chloride to diluted saponified cresol solutions containing coconut oil soap increases bactericidal efficiency without causing such undesirable physical changes as occur with the soaps alone. The increased efficiency is fairly well maintained in the presence of 25% blood serum.

It was found that 21% of coconut oil (or the chemically equivalent amount of its fatty acids) as soap can satisfactorily take the place of 28% of linseed oil as soap for holding in solution the 50% of cresylic acid contained in saponified cresol solutions.

STANDARDIZATION OF TUBERCULIN

ASSAY ON THE BASIS OF THE SPERMATOCYTE REACTION

ESMOND R. LONG
From the Department of Pathology of the University of Chicago and the Otho S. A. Sprague Memorial Institute

The need for a standard by which tuberculin can be measured quantitatively is obvious. Tuberculin in some form is used in enormous quantities in the diagnosis of tuberculosis in man and cattle, and in the treatment of tuberculosis in man. Yet a diagnostic test or therapeutic injection is yet to be made with a measured quantity of the active principle.

The reason for this is that we do not know what the active principle of tuberculin is. No preparation containing the active principle and nothing else has ever been made. We do not know whether there is a single active principle or several responsible for the tuberculin reaction. We are far from sure of the general chemical nature of the substance which is active. In gross chemical fractionation of tuberculin, activity remains with the protein portion. This does not necessarily mean that the active substance is protein. It may be merely absorbed by protein. Furthermore, on finer fractionation protein fractions which are not active can be separated from tuberculin.[1] Hence chemical evaluation, such as is practiced in the assay of opium or belladonna root, is at present an impossibility.

Chemical assay being out of the question, we are forced to fall back on some biologic method. Biologic methods are available for the measurement of active principles in biologically active preparations when the chemical nature of the active principle is imperfectly understood, or chemical analysis is extremely difficult. Biologic assay is officially recognized by the United States Pharmacopeia in the case of several drugs, notably digitalis and aconite, and in the case of the antitoxic serums for diphtheria and tetanus. Another well-known biologic evaluation is that used in the assay of insulin.

The dosage of diphtheria and tetanus antitoxins and diphtheria toxin-antitoxin mixtures, and of insulin, is based on biologically deter-

Received for publication, Aug. 12, 1925.

[1] Long, E. R., and Seibert, F. B.: Am. Rev. Tuberc., in press.

mined units. Comparison between preparations is possible, and accurate administration can be carried out. For tuberculin, on the other hand, a biologic preparation fully as extensively used, no unit has ever been proposed which has met with general acceptance. In the following, several methods by which tuberculin is standardized at present are reviewed, and the advantages and disadvantages of each method are considered.

PRESENT STANDARDIZING METHODS

The standardization of tuberculin is based in most laboratories on the hypersensitiveness of the tuberculous guinea-pig. Both the general and the local reaction have been used in the evaluation. Recently, however, the antigenic capacity of tuberculin in the precipitin and complement-fixation reactions with the serum of tuberculous animals has been proposed as a measure. These methods will be discussed below under the headings summarized in the following outline:

- I. Hypersensitiveness of the Tuberculous Guinea-Pig.
  - 1. The lethal dose. Methods of:
    - Koch.
    - The Institute for Experimental Therapy, Frankfurt a.M.
    - The United States Bureau of Animal Industry.
  - 2. The skin test.
    - Method of Lewis and Aronson.
- II. Antigenic Capacity of Tuberculin in Serum Reactions.
  - 1. The precipitin test.
    - Method of Dreyer and Vollum.
  - 2. The complement-fixation test.
    - Method of Watson and Heath.

The Method of Koch.—Koch[2] was the first to record that extracts of the tubercle bacillus and the medium in which the bacillus had been grown are toxic for the tuberculous animal and nontoxic for the nontuberculous; in other words, he discovered "tuberculin," and he introduced its use in medical practice. He considered a preparation of tuberculin satisfactory if 0.5 c c. or less would kill in from 6 to 30 hours, with characteristic pathologic change, a guinea-pig infected 1 month previously with tuberculosis.

The Method of the Institute for Experimental Therapy, Frankfurt a. M.—This method is the Doenitz modification[3] of the original Koch procedure. Fifty or more guinea-pigs are infected with tubercle bacilli. Of this number certain ones are selected for the test after steady loss of weight indicates that the disease is well under way. Two parallel series of tests are then made with 6 animals in each. One series is injected subcutaneously with decreasing amounts of a government standard tuberculin (Koch method), and in this way the lethal dose in 24 hours is determined. The dilution method is used

[2] Deutsch. med. Wchnschr., 1901, 17, p. 1189.
[3] Arb. a. d. Staatsinst. f. exper. Therap. u. d. Georg Speyer Haus, Frankfurt a. M., 1921, pp. 1-116.

in injecting from 0.5 to 3 c c. of the diluted product. The sample of tuberculin under test is injected in a similar manner into the other set of 6 guinea-pigs. The minimum lethal dose is determined and compared with the M L D of the standard tuberculin. If it is greater than that of the standard the preparation is substandard. If, on the other hand, the tested preparation is more potent than the standard, it is returned with directions for dilution to the standard strength.

The Method of the United States Bureau of Animal Industry.—This method, devised by Schroeder and Brett,[4] is similar in many respects to the Frankfurt method. In a much condensed form it is as follows: Guinea-pigs are infected with tuberculous tissue from guinea-pigs. From time to time the sensitiveness of the infected animals to tuberculin is determined by injecting a standard OT (Old Tuberculin) intraperitoneally. When the degree of sensitization has reached the point at which 0.25 gm. OT per 500 gm. body weight causes death in 24 hours in 4 of 6 guinea-pigs of the series, the remaining pigs are regarded as being suitably sensitive for determining the potency of a tuberculin of unknown strength. They are then divided into groups of 6. One group is injected intraperitoneally with 0.25 gm. per 500 gm. weight of the standard tuberculin, and the other groups similarly with the tuberculins to be tested.

A preparation of tuberculin is considered as passing the test if under the conditions of the experiment it kills at least one-half as many guinea-pigs as the standard tuberculin, with the characteristic lesions of tuberculin death.

The Method of Lewis and Aronson.—The method[5] is based on the intracutaneous test of Roemer. Guinea-pigs ranging in weight from 200 to 300 gm. receive intraperitoneal injections with 0.1 mg. of virulent tubercle bacilli of the bovine type. Three weeks later they are suitable for the intracutaneous test. The animals are divided into groups of 6, and decreasing amounts of tuberculin are injected. In the series reported the amounts injected were 0.02, 0.01, 0.005, 0.002 and 0.001 mg., brought up to a total volume of 0.1 c.c. Readings made after 48 hours are tabulated, and the degree of reaction is recorded on a 1, 2, 3, 4 basis, 4 indicating the most marked reaction.

In this way standard tuberculins and tuberculins of unknown strength can be compared. The authors have not attempted to elaborate a standard method, but believe the method is suitable for the development of one.

The Complement-Fixation Method of Watson and Heath.—This method[6] is based on the fact that during certain stages of tuberculous infection in horses and cattle, complement fixation is given with tuberculin as the antigen. In the preparation of the horse antiserum a horse at intervals receives injections with a virulent culture of tubercle bacilli, 1 mg. moist weight being given intravenously at the first injection, and 2 mg. after 14 days and 3 mg. 21 days later. During the seventh week, the peak of fixation curve is reached. Thereafter the fixation titer drops. At the peak the fixation titer is about 0.0066, or 150 units per c c., titrated against a fixed dose of standard tuberculin. With this standard antiserum at hand, the dose best suited for titrating tuberculins has been determined, and a fixed dose of 20 units found most suitable. Commercial tuberculins are tested in comparison with the standard. The minimum amount of tuberculin, added to 20 units of antiserum, which is capable of fixing the unit of complement completely, is said to represent one active unit of tuberculin.

[4] Jour. Am. Vet. Med. Assn., 1919, 54, p. 357.
[5] Am. Rev. Tuberc., 1923, 7, p. 404.
[6] Jour. Am. Vet. Med. Assn., 124, 66, p. 24.

The Precipitin Method of Dreyer and Vollum.—The method[7] is based on the fact that the serum of horses treated with defatted tubercle bacilli gives a precipitin reaction on mixture with tuberculin. The serum is prepared by giving a horse weekly intravenous injections of "diaplyte" B. tuberculosis vaccine, the amounts injected increasing from 0.1 mg. to 225 mg. in 3 months. Great care is necessary in the technic of the precipitation, as discordant results are obtained unless serum and tuberculin are used in certain definite proportions. The precipitation increases with decreasing amounts of serum when concentrated tuberculin is used, but with high dilutions the reverse is true. The authors therefore give careful and complicated directions for the dilutions to be used in making the test, for which the original must be consulted. The strengths of all tuberculins are expressed in standard units. The Frankfurt standard tuberculin has been chosen as the standard for comparison, and an arbitrary value of 100 units per c c. assigned to it. "The value of any other tuberculin is inversely proportional to the smallest amount required to produce the same degree of precipitation as the standard with the same quantity of serum under the same conditions." The authors found a close parallelism between the strength of a tuberculin preparation as determined by their precipitin method and by a skin test on human subjects.

CRITICISM OF PRESENT METHODS

The advantages and disadvantages of the methods outlined above may be conveniently analyzed under 4 headings: (1) the methods based on the lethal dose for the tuberculous guinea-pig, (2) the method based on the cutaneous test, (3) the complement-fixation method of Watson and Heath, and (4) the precipitin method of Dreyer and Vollum.

Methods Based on the Lethal Dose for the Tuberculous Guinea-Pig.—The original Koch standardization, the Frankfurt method and the method of the United States Bureau of Animal Industry are to some extent similar in their advantages and disadvantages.

The Koch method has the advantage of extreme simplicity. A preparation of tuberculin passes the test or fails according as 0.5 c c. kills or fails to kill a tuberculous guinea-pig. Practically no labor is required, and the test needs only 30 hours for its completion.

The disadvantages, however, are marked. In the first place, the test is too gross. The criticism applies equally to all methods based on the lethal dose for the tuberculous guinea-pig. There are too many unknown factors. A positive result, the death of the guinea-pig, represents the summation of these unknown factors. The first unknown factor is the extent of the tuberculosis itself within the guinea-pig. The animal is already absorbing a great or small amount of poisonous material, as the course of the disease present is rapid or slow. The

[7] Lancet, 1924, 2, p. 1003.

general tuberculin reaction is added to this unknown factor. The general tuberculin reaction includes the summation of the individual tuberculin reactions between sensitized tissue and tuberculin in all parts of the body. Probably all tissues are sensitized to some degree, but the degree for the different tissues is not known. There is evidence that it varies in the different tissues (unpublished observations of the author on the suprarenal, kidney, testis and skin). Perfection in a test based on the strength of the general reaction could not be obtained without a series of animals of the same weight with exactly the same amount of tuberculosis at the time of the test, with livers, spleens, brains, kidneys, etc., of the same size, with the same amount of muscle, the same amount of skin and subcutaneous tissue, etc. This is obviously impossible of attainment. Even when a large series of animals is used, accordingly, and a lethal effect on the majority is considered the basis for a standard, individual variation is so great as to rob the test of much of its value.

There is another weighty objection. The test is quantitative only in a "pass or fail" manner. No unit is established. A unit is very desirable, not only in the diagnostic, but particularly in the therapeutic, use of tuberculin. Two preparations of tuberculin might pass the test, and yet one of them be twice as potent as the other. This opens the possibility of gross error in therapeutic dosage.

The Frankfurt method has the advantage of relative simplicity, and recognizes the variability of animals as respects the lethal dose, without, however, avoiding it. An advance over the Koch procedure is achieved in that an attempt is made to measure the degree by which superstrength preparations surpass the standard, and a basis is set for dilution to a common strength. However, no true unit is established by which the strength of a preparation may be determined without going through the laborious process of comparison with a standard tuberculin on a large series of animals.

The method of the United States Bureau of Animal Industry is an improved lethal dose method in which careful control is exercised with respect to the degree of sensitiveness of the animals used. The actual measurement of tuberculin is made only after extended preliminary tests have led to the selection of animals of suitable and comparable sensitiveness. The method is, however, laborious, and large numbers of animals are required, a great many being killed in the determination of sensitiveness before the test proper is begun.

At the best, even when well controlled and based on averages, methods founded on the lethal dose leave much to be desired, in view of the unquestionable complexity of the general tuberculin reaction. The method of the Bureau of Animal Industry, like the others of this type, sets up a required standard which must be met before a tuberculin is acceptable, but it does not establish a unit which can be used in measuring doses.

In favor of the lethal dose methods in general, in contrast to the serum methods discussed below, is the fact that the allergic state of the tuberculous animal is a factor in the measurement. It is the allergic state of the patient or suspected animal which is of significance in the diagnosis and treatment of tuberculosis by tuberculin. There is therefore in these methods no such dissociation of standardizing principle and diagnostic and therapeutic action as in the serum standardization tests analyzed below.

The Intracutaneous Test of Lewis and Aronson.—This test has the great advantage of close association between the standardizing test and the use to which the product is adapted. The substance is standardized with respect to the skin of an allergic animal and later used on the skin of an allergic patient. Furthermore, it is easy of application, requires no special technic, takes little time, and is economical of animals.

It would perhaps be the most useful method were it not for one serious defect. The reactive capacity of the skin varies tremendously in a series of tuberculous guinea-pigs, even when these are all injected at the same time. Numerous authors have stressed this point, and Lewis and Aronson themselves are careful to state, on the basis of their own protocols: "It is evident that the individual variation in reaction of the animals is wide." Naturally the value of a test in which the strength of reaction is an important measuring factor, is much reduced by such variability. W. Löwenstein-Brill [8] has expressed a similar view, stating that the intracutaneous test is not suitable for the standardization of tuberculin, since in weak concentrations the traumatic reaction cannot be sharply distinguished from the specific reaction.

The Complement-Fixation Method of Watson and Heath.—This method has the primary advantage that it furnishes a unit in terms of which all doses of tuberculin can be measured. It has another great advantage in that a standard reagent, the antiserum, can be prepared in a quantity sufficient for a great number of tests. The antiserum appears

[8] Ztschr. f. d. ges. exper. Med., 1918, 7, p. 103.

to stand aging moderately well, and thus furnishes a reagent of somewhat greater reacting constancy than the tuberculous guinea-pig. It is time saving in that the test may be carried out at once on the receipt of the material to be tested. No delay for the sensitization of guinea-pigs is required.

On the other hand, it suffers from the great defect of complete dissociation of standardizing test and the use to which the material is adapted. This is no evidence that the tuberculin reaction and the antibodies which can be detected in the serum are even related. In fact, Calmette,[9] on the basis of long study, states that purified tuberculin will not act as antigen in the serum test. If this is true, the extraordinarily close agreement obtained by Watson and Heath using the complement-fixation method, and Schroeder using the lethal dose method,[6] is nothing more than a coincidence, and leaves open the possibility that samples of tuberculin might be encountered which would fix complement well in the presence of the antiserum, and yet be low in tuberculin potency. Indeed, if Calmette's contention is correct, a highly purified tuberculin, free from certain extraneous products of the tubercle bacillus which are antigenic to the antiserum, would fail altogether to give the complement-fixation test. Evidence corroborating Calmette's view is cited in discussing the precipitin method of standardization.

The Precipitin Method of Dreyer and Vollum.—Like the fixation method just discussed, the precipitin method has the advantage of establishing a unit in which dosage can be calculated. Similarly, the essential reagent, the antiserum, is one which can be prepared in large quantities and which is of constant potency for a given lot. It has an advantage over the other serum procedure in that the precipitin method requires fewer fresh reagents and is easier of application.

On the other hand, as in the case of the fixation method, no relation has yet been established between the type of reaction in which the substance is actually used and that used in standardizing the product. In this case also the work of others indicates that the two reactions do not measure the same thing (Calmette [10]). The antiserum is not an antituberculin. It is more than possible that potent tuberculins might be encountered giving a weak precipitin test, and vice versa. In this case also highly purified tuberculins might be expected to give a weaker

[9] L'Infection Bacillaire et la Tuberculose, 1922, p. 576.
[10] Ibid., pp. 573-4.

result than crude tuberculins. The reason for this is the simple fact that the serum prepared is an antiserum not to the active principle of tuberculin alone, but to all the antigenic proteins of the tubercle bacillus. Until there is proof that all of these proteins are potent as tuberculin, the use of such a method of standardizing tuberculin is illogical.

The confusion which has existed concerning the relation of the tuberculin skin test and serum antibody reactions in tuberculosis has been considerably reduced by the recent studies of Zinsser and his colleagues, Julia T. Parker, Wayman and Mueller. By a method of extraction of tubercle bacilli, precipitation of the extract with acetic acid, and filtration, they have secured clear solutions antigenic in both the skin test and serum antibody reactions with tuberculosis serum. At first they were inclined to believe that the two actions were due to the same active principle; but in a recent report on the continuation of this work, Mueller [11] states, "It has finally been possible to show definitely that they (precipitin reaction with tuberculosis serum and the tuberculin skin test) are dependent upon entirely different substances in the tuberculin." Mueller is of the opinion that the substance active in the precipitin test is a carbohydrate analogous to the gum found by Dochez and Avery to be active as an antigen with antipneumococcus serum, while he thinks the substance active in the tuberculin skin test is chiefly protein.

A great deal of work has been done on the relation of tuberculin hypersusceptibility and anaphylaxis since the early work of P. A. Lewis,[12] who definitely distinguished the two phenomena, and the exhaustive study of Baldwin.[13] Baldwin found that whereas tuberculous animals are regularly sensitive to the intracutaneous tuberculin test, they are seldom made anaphylactic. Furthermore, he and most other observers find old tuberculin devoid of sensitizing properties for the cutaneous test. As M. I. Smith [14] states, reporting this finding in his own experience, "This fact further fails to lend support to the assumption that the tuberculin reaction is an anaphylactic manifestation." Selter,[15] whose work may be consulted for a review on the relation of the tuberculin skin test to anaphylaxis, states the extreme view: "The tuberculin reaction is not an antibody reaction, since no antibodies can be recognized in the body of a tuberculous organism which enter into

[11] Proc. Soc. Exper. Biol. and Med., 1925, 22, p. 219.
[12] Arch. Int. Med., 1909, 4, p. 528.
[13] Jour. Med. Res., 1910, 22, p. 189.
[14] Ibid., 1922, 43, p. 435.
[15] Ztschr. f. Immunitätsf. u. exper. Therap., 1921, 32, p. 325.

combination with tuberculin." Krause [16] stresses the point that "allergy (used in the sense of the hypersensitiveness of infection) stands alone among all immunological reactions," and he differentiates it sharply from those types of immunity in which precipitins, agglutinins, aggressins, opsonins, complement-fixing bodies and anaphylactic hypersensitiveness are observed.

These views, therefore, support the contention of Calmette, and constitute a fundamental objection to the precipitin method of standardizing tuberculin. In view of the probable identity of the factors concerned in the complement fixation, precipitin and anaphylactic reactions (Wells [17]), they are equally adverse to the complement-fixation method as a test for the biologic activity of tuberculin.

It is possible that pure proteins from tuberculin, which elicit the tuberculin reaction, may some time be prepared and be found to be antigenic in the sense that precipitating antiserums can be developed to them. We can only say that up to the present time attempts to develop antiserums to the active principle of tuberculin by injection of soluble tuberculins like OT have encountered little success. It is significant that antiserums may readily be developed when the whole bacillus or unheated water extracts are used as antigens, but not when purified tuberculin, free from bacilli, is used. It is strongly suggestive that when raw tuberculin does give a precipitate with an antiserum prepared by the injection of defatted or native tubercle bacilli, the reaction is between the antiserum and constituents of the bacilli present in the tuberculin which are antigenic as far as the antiserum is concerned but are not identical with the element which is active in the tuberculin reaction. The latter element can indeed be present and play no part in the serum reaction.[18]

ANALYSIS OF THE TUBERCULIN REACTION

Before proceeding with the description of a new method of standardizing tuberculin which is based on a true tuberculin reaction, it seems desirable to present a brief analysis of the tuberculin reaction. The fundamental nature of the reaction, to be sure, is not well understood.

[16] Tr. Seventeenth Ann. Meeting Nat'l Tuberc. Assn., 1921.

[17] The Chemical Aspects of Immunity, pp. 169, 220.

[18] In two very interesting articles (American Review of Tuberculosis, 1925, 11, pp. 146, 151) Dienes, Schoenheit and Scheff describe experiments in which "a rough parallelism is noted between the potency of preparations in the skin test and complement fixation, and between them and their content of coagulable protein." The antigenic capacity of the coagulable protein is particularly emphasized. The points raised in these articles are too numerous to be discussed in this article, but will be treated elsewhere.

I have discussed some of the problems presented elsewhere.[19] The events which transpire in the course of the reaction are, however, well known. Two broad phases of the reaction may be distinguished. These are: (1) exudation, (2) necrosis. Associated with the exudation, as in other inflammations, there is a marked active hyperemia.

The exudate which pours out when tuberculin is injected into sensitized tissue consists of plasma, the fibrinogen of which often clots, polymorphonuclear leukocytes, eosinophils and great numbers of large mononuclears, probably identical with the monocytes or "transitional cells" of the blood stream. It is this exudation and the associated active hyperemia which leads to the red swelling of the well-known cutaneous test.

Whether or not necrosis occurs depends on a number of factors, including the degree of sensitiveness of the tissue into which the injection is made, the type of tissue and the dose of tuberculin. The tissues of the skin, chiefly connective tissue and squamous epithelium, are relatively resistant, and necrosis occurs only with strong doses. In the testicle, on the other hand, which reacts in an extraordinary manner to be described, typical coagulation of the spermatocytes and their derivatives occurs.

THE SPERMATOCYTE TUBERCULIN REACTION

This reaction has been described in several previous publications [19, 20] as the testicle tuberculin test. As four stages of germ cell are present in the testicle, and of these the spermatocyte is most severely affected, "spermatocyte reaction" is more appropriate, and henceforth this term will be used.

Two phases of the reaction have been studied—the early and the late. In the early stage hyperemia and inflammatory edema of the type described above are observed, and coagulation necrosis of the spermatocytes and spermatids occurs. A notable feature in the microscopic picture is the increase in size of the tubules, with great departure from the normal orderly arrangement of the successive division phases of the germ cells, i. e., spermatogonia, spermatocytes, spermatids and spermatozoa. Swollen spermatocytes and spermatids, with densely staining cytoplasm and pyknotic nuclei, lie in the center of the tubules intimately mingled with the spermatozoa. The spermatogonia or parent

[19] Long, E. R.: Tubercle, 1924, 6, p. 128.
[20] Long, E. R.: Am. Rev. Tuberc., 1924, 9, p. 215. Long, E. R., and Seyfarth, M. H.: Am. Rev. Tuberc., 1924, 9, p. 254.

cells seem the least affected, and it is these which remain after absorption of the necrotic cells.

The late phase of the spermatocyte reaction is best observed after from 3 weeks to a month. Marked atrophy has occurred. The tubules are no more than half the original size. Spermatocytes and spermatids, the cells observed in the necrotic state in the acute reaction, together with the spermatozoa, have disappeared. The tubules remain, lined by

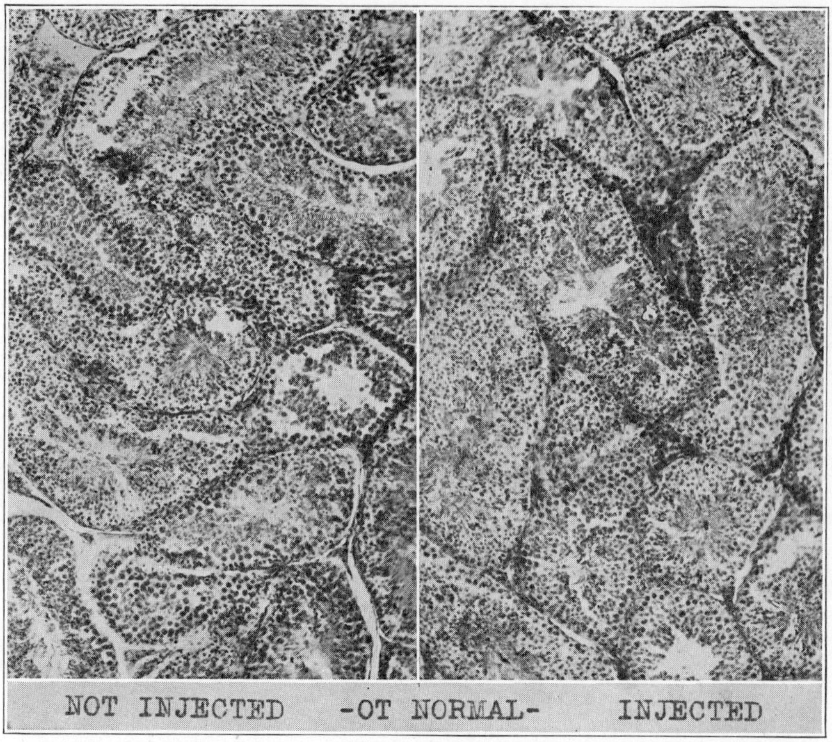

Fig. 1.—One tenth c c. of a 1:10 dilution of Old Tuberculin was injected into the left testis of a normal guinea-pig. The animal was killed one month later. The left testis into which the injection had been made, as well as the right testis into which injections had not been made, which served as control, was found to be normal, as the illustration shows.

their basement membrane and a single layer of epithelial cells. As observations (not previously reported) have shown that in the course of 3 or 4 months regeneration of spermatocytes and the succeeding divisions occurs from these cells, these epithelial cells are certainly to be looked on as spermatogonia. Between the atrophied tubules a marked hyperplasia of the interstitial cells of Leydig is observed.

There can be no question that the reaction just described is a true tuberculin reaction. It is absolutely specific. In at least a hundred experiments in this laboratory in which the testicles of normal animals have been injected with tuberculin, a reaction has never occurred. Tuberculin is nontoxic for the spermatocytes of the normal animal (fig. 1); on the other hand, it has never failed, in suitable dosage, to elicit reaction in the testicle of the tuberculous animal. Furthermore, preparations of bacteria other than the tubercle bacillus (and other acid-fast bacilli), of which several have been injected, do not elicit the reaction. Finally, the type of reaction is histologically identical with that observed in the skin reaction, except that degeneration and necrosis are more pronounced. This is to be explained as a result of the exquisite susceptibility of the delicate germ cells.

This susceptibility of the germ cells makes the spermatocyte reaction superior to the skin reaction. The reaction is more pronounced, for the necrosis is such a conspicuous feature. The spermatocyte reaction is more delicate. Repeated tests indicate that it will detect about one tenth of the minimum quantity detectable by the skin test.

Furthermore, the reaction is much more constant than the skin test. The great lack of uniformity so common in the skin reaction has not been observed in trials of the spermatocyte test when injections have been made in increasing dilution in duplicate. Several series of tests of this character have been made.

Finally, in the microscopic section preserved the spermatocyte reaction permits filing a permanent record of any test.

THE SPERMATOCYTE REACTION APPLIED QUANTITATIVELY

The Method.—Male guinea-pigs weighing approximately 400 gm. are chosen for the test. These are infected in the groin with tubercle bacilli of mild virulence in such dosage that a caseous nodule appears in the regional lymph nodes within one month, but the process does not become generalized. One-half milligram of the Saranac Laboratory strain R_1 has been found suitable. Entirely satisfactory results have, however, been achieved with smaller doses of a more virulent strain.

One month after the injection the animals are suitable for the test. The testicles are pressed into the scrotal sac with the fingers. The overlying skin is swabbed with alcohol, and 0.1 c c. of the tuberculin to be tested is injected into the middle of one testicle. The injection appears to cause no more discomfort than a simple subcutaneous inoculation. The animal is then returned to its cage and killed after 36 hours or 1 month, according as one wishes to observe the early or the late phase of the reaction.

In applying the test quantitatively, dilutions are made so that the 0.1 c c. injected contains 0.1, 0.01, 0.001 and 0.0001 c c. of the original product in the case of unconcentrated tuberculins such as BE. OT, which is concentrated to one tenth of its original volume, is injected in one tenth of these amounts. When solid preparations, such as BE or tuberculoprotein, are being tested, 0.1 c c. of suspensions or solutions is injected. Successive dilutions of the suspension or solution are made so that the actual amounts injected are 0.01, 0.001, 0.0001 and 0.00001 mg.

The injections are made in duplicate for each dilution, and a pair of normal animals are inoculated with the strongest dilution for control. Thus 10 animals are required for testing a single preparation.

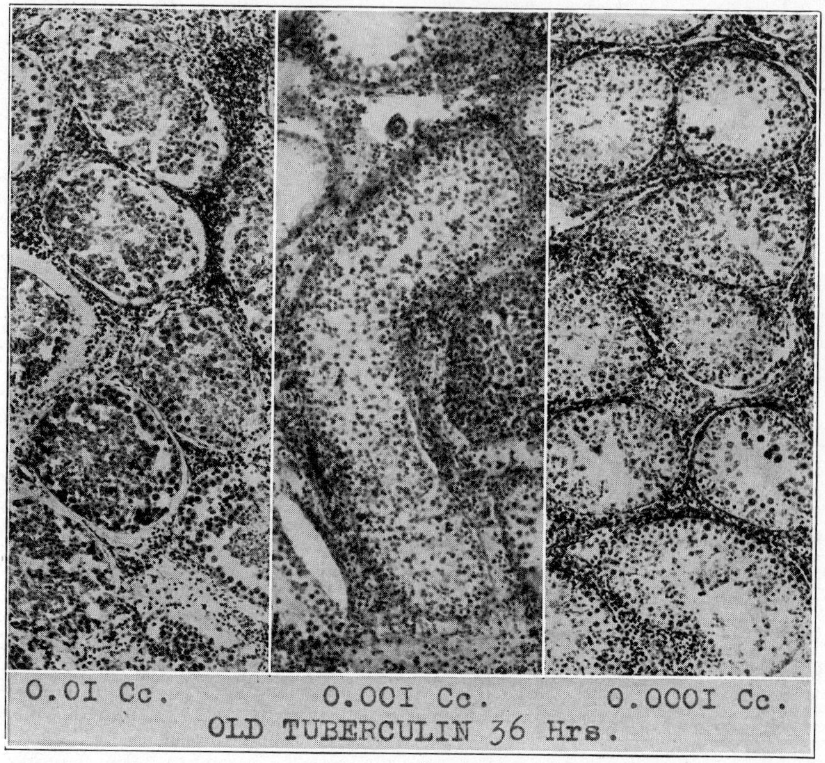

Fig. 2.—Old Tuberculin in increasing dilution was injected into the left testis in a series of tuberculous guinea-pigs. One tenth c c. of a 1:10 dilution was injected into the first animal, and 0.1 c c. of a 1:100 and 0.1 c c. of a 1:1,000 dilution into the other two. The animals were killed 36 hours later. The left testis showed an acute tuberculin reaction in each case. The illustration shows a cross section of each testis into which injections had been made. Degeneration of the tubules and marked intertubular exudation are noted in all, the least effect being seen in the testis receiving injections with the smallest amount.

The reaction may be read after 36 hours, or in from 2 to 4 weeks, the animals being killed, and paraffin or colloidin sections are prepared. The longer period is preferable. Except for the specially trained histologist, the microscopic picture in the acute stage is confusing on account of the quantity of débris in the tubules and the difficulty of distinguishing normal spermatocytes and injured spermatocytes in reactions at the higher dilutions. Probably the most delicate indicator of reaction in the acute phase is the interstitial exudation. No exudation follows the injection of this same dilution into a normal animal, or the introduction of a similarly diluted plain broth into a tuberculous animal. Figure 2 illustrates the effect of OT on the testicle of the tuberculous guinea-pig as observed 36 hours after injection. Unfortunately, the black and white reproduction fails to show fine differences in the normal and degenerating cells, which are well shown in the colored H and E stained specimens. It is plain, however, that the effect decreases in severity with decreasing dosage. Even at 0.0001 c c., however, there is still a noticeable effect, as may be seen by comparison with normal testicles shown in fig. 1. The spermatocytes, the large cells confined in the normal to the middle zone between the basal layer and the center of the tubule (fig. 1), are scattered at random in the tubules of fig. 2, and, as the colored preparation brings out, in various stages of degeneration. The intertubular infiltration of monocytes, conspicuous in the first dilution, is still marked at 0.0001 c c.

The changes shown in the late phase (fig. 3) are more striking. The tubules have decreased in size in the first 3 dilutions, and, except in a few portions of the tubules here and there, the spermatocytes and their derivatives have disappeared. Fig. 3 is taken from a series killed at the end of one month. It shows the limiting concentration at which the reaction was given with the preparation of OT used. Whereas little is to be seen in the tubules representing the first 3 dilutions except the basal layer of spermatogonia, spermatocytes and their derivatives are still numerous in the tubules after injection of the fourth and highest dilution; in other words, at this dilution spermatogenesis has not been completely stopped. The distinction is sharp, and forms a convenient basis for defining a unit. This may be arbitrarily set as that amount which just stops spermatogenesis. On this basis the amount injected in the third dilution of fig. 3 contains 1 unit. As the actual amount injected in this instance was one ten thousandth of a c c., 1 c c. of this sample of OT may be said to contain 10,000 spermatocyte units.

It must not be supposed that the testicle is invariably uniformly affected. As a matter of fact, the effect is almost always practically uniform throughout the organ, but rarely some portions remain normal or nearly normal, as if for mechanical reasons these parts had not come into contact with the injected tuberculin. In view of this fact, the reaction must be read on the basis of the appearance of the majority of the tubules in the section. The section should always be an entire cross section of the center of the organ.

THE SPERMATOCYTE TUBERCULIN UNIT

On the basis of the quantitative test outlined above, a tuberculin unit suitable for measuring doses may now be defined as follows:

The spermatocyte unit is that quantity of tuberculin just sufficient to abolish spermatogenesis in the majority of tubules on injection in a

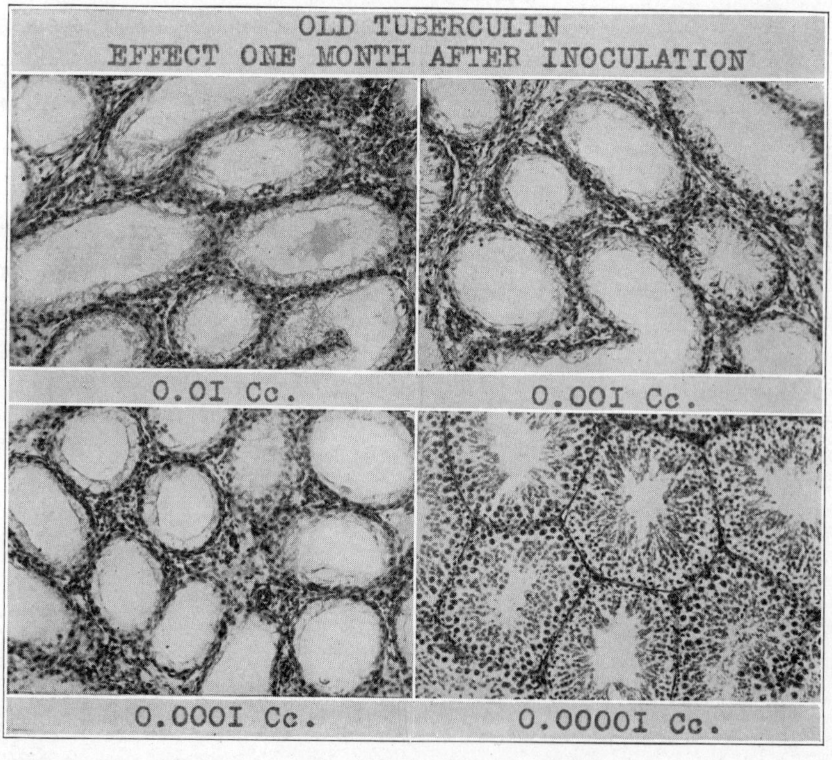

Fig. 3.—Old Tuberculin in increasing dilution was injected into the left testis in a series of tuberculous gunea-pigs, the fluid volume injected being 0.1 c c. in each case. The animals were killed one month later. In each case the right, control, testis was found to be normal. The illustration shows the condition of the left testis into which injections were made. There is profound atrophy of the tubules of the testes receiving injections with 0.01 c c., 0.001 c c. and 0.0001 c c. Spermatocytes, spermatids and spermatozoa have disappeared. Practically no effect is visible at 0.00001 c c., although the tubules in this case were found to be somewhat smaller than in the right testis into which no injections had been made. The smallest amount causing complete abolition of spermatogenesis was thus 0.0001 c c. On the arbitrary scale here developed this represents one spermatocyte unit, and this sample of tuberculin therefore contains 10,000 spermatocyte units per c c.

volume of 0.1 c.c. into the testicle of a 400 gm. guinea-pig with a mild, localized tuberculosis of one month's duration. Microscopic section of the testicle (middle cross section) one month after the injection of one unit or more shows the majority of the tubules atrophic and lined only by spermatogonia. No normal spermatocytes, spermatids or spermatozoa are present. The test is controlled by examination of the noninjected opposite testicle and of the injected testicle of a noninfected animal, both of which should show normal spermatogenesis.

For rapid work, when sufficient time for embedding and cutting sections is not available, a rough approximation of the true result can be obtained by a simple procedure. The testicles into which injections have been made and those into which they have not been made are cut in half and the fresh surfaces rubbed on microscopic slides. The slides smeared with the normal testicles will show numerous spermatozoa. Those smeared with the testicles into which injections have been made show none or few or many spermatozoa in proportion to the degree of change in the testicle. The last slide in which spermatozoa are still hard to find may be considered to represent the injection of one unit.

The unit so defined should be useful in standardizing tuberculin for diagnosis and treatment. Ordinarily unconcentrated tuberculins like BE will be found to contain at least 1,000 spermatocyte units per c c., while OT will contain at least 10,000 units. The potency of solid preparations like BE or tuberculoprotein can be stated in the number of units to the milligram.

ADVANTAGES AND DISADVANTAGES OF THE METHOD BASED ON THE SPERMATOCYTE UNIT

The advantages of the standardization method based on the spermatocyte reaction are: (1) the absolute specificity of the reaction, (2) the great delicacy of the reaction, (3) the sharp picture presented by the positive reaction, (4) the constancy of the reaction (as compared, for example, with the variable skin reaction), and (5) the ease with which a permanent record of the reaction may be preserved.

The chief disadvantages are the length of time desirable before reading the reaction (3-4 weeks) and the necessity of cutting, staining and examining sections. The latter disadvantage may be avoided if a simple examination of smears from the testicle is substituted for the examination of sections, but this opens the method to the possibility of error.

The disadvantages are those of time and moderate technical labor. However, the greater reliability and sharpness of the test far overbalance these disadvantages. The actual manipulation is in no way complicated. Much less technical skill is required than in carrying out the precipitin and fixation reactions. The chances for technical error are no greater than in carrying out the skin test.

SUMMARY

Methods used at present in the standardization of tuberculin may be grouped as (1) those based on the action of tuberculin on the hypersensitive tuberculous animal, and (2) those based on the interaction of tuberculin and serum antibodies in the serum of a tuberculous animal. While each of the methods within these groups has its individual advantages, the disadvantages in all are great. The method by which the minimum lethal dose for a tuberculous guinea-pig is determined is altogether too gross, too many unknown factors being concerned. The method by which the ultimate dilution giving a cutaneous test in a tuberculous guinea-pig is determined is unreliable because of the wide individual variation in skin reaction capacity in tuberculous guinea-pigs of the same series.

The precipitin and fixation reactions between tuberculin and the serum of a tuberculous horse or horse inoculated with dead tubercle bacilli are unsuitable as standardizing methods because we have no assurance that the substance in raw tuberculin which reacts with the serum of the inoculated horse is the active principle of tuberculin. In fact, there is much evidence that it is not, and that the reaction which does take place between raw tuberculin and such serum is the result of interaction between serum antibodies and bacillary substance in the tuberculin, which cannot be properly called the active principle, that is to say, the substance which elicits the tuberculin reaction.

A method is proposed which is based on the hypersensitiveness of the spermatocytes of the tuberculous guinea-pig to the action of tuberculin. The spermatocyte reaction (previously reported as the testicle reaction) is delicate, and when carried out in the manner described above is of greater constancy and reliability than the other methods based on hypersensitiveness of the tuberculous guinea-pig, viz., the minimum lethal dose and the cutaneous test methods. Necrosis and subsequent absorption of the spermatocytes is used as the basis for recognizing a positive reaction, and the limiting dilution at which this is observed under the conditions outlined above is considered to represent one unit of tuberculin.

STANDARDIZATION OF TYPHOID VACCINE

COUNTING CHAMBER METHOD VERSUS WRIGHT'S METHOD

JOSEPH W. SMITH, JR.

From the Department of Laboratories, Army Medical School, Army Medical Center, Washington, D. C.

Various ways of estimating the strengths of bacterial suspensions have been advanced from time to time, among which are Wright's method, the biologic method of Wright, as well as the counting chamber, opacimetric and nephelometric, living or colony count, gravimetric, volumetric, chemical and serologic methods.

These methods are by no means equal in importance or practical value. With the exception of the biologic method of Wright, the serologic method of Lamb and Forster and the living or colony count method, none of which alone is of practical value, there are really but two basic ways in which to standardize vaccines. One is by an actual enumeration of the bacteria and the other is by an actual estimation of the weight of dried bacterial protein from the suspension. Opacimetric and nephelometric methods depend on standards which in turn are determined by either one or both of the basic methods. The chemical methods likewise require for interpretation and practical application correlation with either actual counts or actual dried weights. It might be possible to label a typhoid vaccine, let us say, "Vaccine made from B. typhosus. Total nitrogen 10 milligrams per mil." The dosage would have to be determined by actual trial or by our previous experience, which is in terms of numbers of organisms per mil. The volumetric method of Hopkins [1] also is dependent ultimately on either a count or a weight, otherwise it cannot be said that a given volume represents so many bacilli or so much protein. In fact, we have all become so accustomed to expressing bacterial dosage in terms of numbers of bacilli that perhaps we might consider the actual count the only really practical basic method. The gravimetric method, however, although not practically so applicable as the enumeration method, is of course quite as basic. In fact, it would appear to be more exact. It is a measure of all of the bacterial protein in the suspension. The counting methods

Received for publication, June 17, 1925

[1] Jour. Am. Med. Assn., 1913, 60, p. 1615.

fail to consider the protein which is in solution and that is certainly a factor of importance unless the vaccine is a so-called "washed" vaccine.

WRIGHT'S METHOD

In 1902, Wright[2] presented a "method of determining under the microscope the number of micro-organisms in a bacterial culture." The procedure, which is now so familiar as to need no description is extremely ingenious and simple and has been of great service. It was advanced at a most opportune moment, when bacterial vaccines were just coming into use and when it was necessary to have a rapid, easy and fairly reliable method of estimating the concentration. It was seized on at once wherever vaccines were made, and has been used generally from that day to this. It has had an extensive and also intensive trial, and the verdict appears to be adverse. In 1907, Leishman[3] wrote that, in his hands, Wright's method has not "proved sufficiently accurate in dealing with typhoid germs, since we have found that a certain proportion of these are dissolved by the action of blood fluids and in this way the strength of the vaccine is liable to be underestimated. The modification of this method described by Major Harrison, in which the blood fluids are replaced by an inert fluid, by which the bacteria are not affected, gives much more regular results, and is the method which we at present employ in the standardization of the vaccine." The modification of Wright's method devised by Harrison[4] consists in "(1) preparing a suspension of the cells of a definite volume of blood in a similar fluid to that in which the bacteria to be counted are suspended; (2) mixing the suspension of blood cells with a convenient number of volumes of the culture, the bacteria of which have been previously stained in bulk; (3) placing a sample of the mixture under a cover-glass and luting the specimen with vaseline; (4) counting the red cells and the bacteria in the specimen, field by field, and calculating the bacterial content of the culture from the figures thus obtained. By these means one avoids all fallacies due to the action of the blood fluids, which have been removed during the process of preparing the suspension of blood cells; one gets an even mixture; the red cells and bacteria are evenly distributed in the specimen and are not further interfered with, so that there is no risk of losing bacteria during the process of fixing and staining."

Harrison's technic was modified by him in 1908. Leishman, Harrison, Grattan and Archibald,[5] discussing the standardization of the British Army vaccine, described the modifications, which are technical in the direction of simplification. They then wrote: "The results that have been obtained have been fairly uniform and the error can be easily kept under plus or minus 10% after a short experience of the method; it has, however, been found that, when tried by those unaccustomed to the procedure, the tendency is to underestimate the strength of the culture."

Recently, without reference to the work of Harrison, we have independently devised a modification of Wright's method which we have called the "wet Wright count." Our technic is described later. As a practical method for every-day use our "wet Wright" is probably no improvement on Harrison's method. As a research method the "wet Wright" has several distinct advantages over Harrison's method. For one thing, the chamber being ruled

[2] Lancet, 1902, 2, p. 11.
[3] J. Roy. Army M. C., 1907, 8, p. 463.
[4] Ibid., 1905, 4, p. 313.
[5] Ibid., 1908, 10, p. 583.

and of a standard depth, permits an accurate count of the blood suspension employed with each count, and thus automatically controls the calculation.

Harrison's modification has never come into general use. Wright's original method, however, has been universally employed despite its alleged uncertainties. Callison[6] appears to feel that the fault lies not so much with the method as with the worker, writing: "As the technique is usually carried out the result is little better than a good guess." The experience of Glynn, Powell, Rees and Cox[7] agrees with that of Callison who found that in his average Wright preparation "in the part where the stroke begins there is a heavy deposit of bacteria, whilst in the last part it consists almost wholly of red cells." As early as 1905, Leishman, Harrison, Smallman and Tulloch[8] pointed out that they were "unable to obtain consistent satisfactory results, and in the case of broth cultures errors from 50% to 100% in counts of the same films made by different observers were by no means uncommon. All the devices recommended by Dr. Wright and many others were employed toward securing a perfect blood film which in all its parts should represent accurately the relation of the number of germs to the number of red corpuscles, but without giving us any greater confidence in the results obtained."

It will be noted that most writers not only emphasize the fact that the method gives uncertain and unreliable results, but they also incline strongly to the opinion that bacteria are lost in the process of preparing the specimen for examination, and that bacteria, even when present, may be overlooked in the examination. Until recently we were of the same opinion, but we have succeeded in demonstrating a basic error in Wright's method hitherto apparently overlooked, which makes it evident that suspensions of bacteria counted by Wright's method rather than underestimated are decidedly overestimated.

Although it has a basic error, for comparative purposes Wright's method may still prove useful in a practical clinical laboratory. It has much to recommend it, particularly when one is dealing with vaccines composed of the larger gram-positive cocci, and especially when one is making up only small amounts of autogenous vaccines of such organisms at irregular intervals.

THE COUNTING CHAMBER METHOD

In 1908, Mallory and Wright[9] advanced the counting chamber method of standardizing vaccines. They employed a well 0.02 mm. deep, an optically plane cover-slip, the 1/16 in. dry lens and no staining fluid. Mallory and Wright regarded it as much easier of execution than Wright's method, but they made no statement concerning comparative results. Leith Murray[10] likewise suggested the method as simple and reliable. He employed the 1/12 oil immersion objective, the Thoma-Zeiss hemacytometer with a well 0.1 mm. deep, an ordinary cover-slip and a staining solution of weak Giemsa. He made no mention, either, of comparative results. Callison,[6] expressed his opinion that the method of counting bacteria in the hematcytometer is possible of scientific accuracy and rapid application when finally perfected. He made no mention of using a special shallow chamber nor an especially thin cover-slip. He recommended the use of a diluting fluid composed of hydrochloric acid, bichloride of mercury and acid fuchsin. Callison expressed a lack of

6 J. Med. Res., 1912-13, 27, p. 225.
7 Path. & Bacteriol., 1913-14, 18, p. 379.
8 J. Hygiene, 1905, 5, p. 380.
9 Pathological Technique, 1908, p. 454.
10 Lancet, 1908, 1, p. 790.

confidence in Wright's method and advocated the use of the counting chamber but did not present any comparative results. Glynn, Powell, Rees and Cox[7] presented observations on the standardization of bacterial vaccines by 3 different methods, namely, the Wright method, the hemacytometer and the plate culture method. As the result of a considerable amount of careful research, these workers concluded that Wright's method "does not give consistently satisfactory results." They chose the counting chamber method as the most scientific way of enumerating bacteria and presented a complete technical study of the use of the Helber counting chamber for this purpose. Their paper was not so much a comparative study as a demonstration of the unreliability of the Wright method and a complete exposition of the counting chamber method with an advocacy of its use. Incidentally, they condemn the plate culture method as absolutely unreliable. Glynn and others employed the Helber chamber, the oil immersion lens, an optically plane cover-slip, 0.18 mm. thick, strengthened with a cemented cylindrical glass cell, and a staining solution composed of 1 part of a saturated solution of thionin blue in absolute alcohol and 9 or 10 parts of a 1% solution of phenol in clear tap water. They were troubled at times by agglutination of bacteria in the staining solution, and found that it always occurred when too much thionin was employed. They found that Brownian movement sometimes proved troublesome and could be completely eliminated only when the stain is sufficiently concentrated to produce some agglutination. They felt, however, that agglutination was distinctly undesirable, and preferred the lesser inconvenience of the Brownian movement. They advised that the suspension for counting be so diluted that not more than 6 bacteria occur to the square.

Glynn and his fellow workers found that a certain proportion of the bacteria always adhere to the under surface of the cover-slip, and that this number is increased by overstaining. They indicated also one important point in enumerating bacilli like typhoid or colon. "They not infrequently stand at right angles to the cover slip or the floor of the chamber and consequently appear as round dots." It was advised to allow the chamber to stand for 15 minutes before counting to allow the bacteria to settle. It was pointed out out that all will not settle. Some adhere to the under surface of the cover-slip, and some remain suspended in active Brownian movement.

Macalister[11] employed the Helber counting chamber, a diluting fluid of N/10 hydrochloric acid, a dry 7 mm. objective Zeiss C and a Zeiss compensating ocular 18, carrying a grating micrometer. He adjusted the tube length so that 4 eye-piece squares fitted 1 on the Thoma-Zeiss rulings. His condenser was Beck's old type of Abbe condenser carrying on the under surface of its lower lens a disk of black paper to cut off central rays of light. Without specific mention of any other method, Macalister reported that comparative observations showed that his method gave more constant results, took less time and caused much less fatigue of the eye than any of the other methods in use.

McCoy[12] employed the Helber counting chamber in the preparation of typhoid vaccine at the Hygienic Laboratory of the U. S. Public Health Service. He used a diluting fluid of Ziehl-Nielsen carbol-fuchsin, diluted 400 times with 5% phenol solution.

Brown[13] employed freshly filtered Ziehl-Nielsen's carbol-fuchsin, using equal parts of bacterial suspension and staining solution, and made his further dilutions with distilled water. His results were far from satisfactory to him, and

[11] J. Path. & Bacteriol., 1913-14, 18, p. 411.
[12] Hygienic Lab. Bull., no. 110, 1917.
[13] Indian J. Med. Res., 1919-20, 7, p. 238.

his was the first voice raised in adverse criticism of the cytometer method since 1902 when Wright wrote that the device of the hemocytometer was inapplicable to the case of a bacterial culture. Brown concluded as a result of his efforts that all numerical values, by whatever method obtained, are conditioned by the technic used. Any one who has done much bacterial cytometry will agree with Brown in that statement.

On the basis of a series of comparisons between actual dried weights, opacities and hemocytometer counts, Brown finds that considerable variations in the hemocytometer counts indicate that the method of enumeration by the hemocytometer is capable of giving variable results. Brown then proceeds to advocate the gravimetric method and standardization by means of opacity tubes.

Russell, Nichols and Stimmel[14] published "Directions for Making Triple Typhoid Vaccine" as employed at the U. S. Army Medical School. Under the head of standardization they wrote:

"1. Place well-mixed samples of the suspension from every other section in small sterile conical containers. 2. Dilute a portion of this in a red cell counting pipette. (Diluting fluid: 2% phenol solution, 30 c c.; saturated aqueous solution of thionin, 1 c c. Mix, let stand 15 minutes, filter. This diluting fluid kills the bacilli and stains them a dark blue.) 3. Count the number of bacteria in a Helber counting chamber in the same manner in which red blood cells are counted."

Holker[15] described a method of standardizing vaccines by the use of what he termed an "opacimeter." In his own words, his method "resolves itself into the best means of using a counting chamber in order to get as good a value as possible for the number of bacteria per mil of a diluted suspension." Holker found that very inconsistent results may be obtained with a counting chamber, even of the Helber type. He felt, however, that much depended on correct technic, and he set forth his manner of performing a cytometric estimation thus:

A 24 hours' growth on agar is suspended in 5 mils of normal salt solution, transferred to a clear test-tube and heated at 60 C. for 1 hour. It is then shaken in a shaking machine for 10 minutes. A 1:50 dilution is then made, and 5 mils are transferred at once to each of 3 clear, dry test-tubes. To one of the tubes is then added 5 mils of 1:20 solution of thionin blue, prepared by adding 1 mil of an alcoholic saturated solution of the dye to 19 mils of 1% aqueous solution of phenol. If bacteria do not stain well with this, Holker recommends the use of a 1:10 solution. The preparation is then mixed well and a small drop is transferred to the special counting chamber. Fifteen minutes are allowed for sedimentation. One hundred squares are counted. The second and third tubes are then treated in exactly the same manner, and the average of the 3 counts is taken as the count for the suspension. Holker feels, however, that the accuracy of the counting chamber, even when the most careful technic is employed, is much below that of the opacimeter readings.

The counting chamber method has certain limitations which are obvious. It is impossible, for example, to count organisms such as the Bordet-Gengou bacillus in the counting chamber with any degree of accuracy. It is impossible to see them with sufficient definition to make an accurate count. However, most of our vaccine organisms are sufficiently large to be seen easily and counted in the counting chamber with

[14] Military Surgeon, 1920, 47, p. 359.
[15] J. Path. & Bacteriol., 1921, 24, p. 419.

almost equal ease. But, although the cytometric method does give an accurate count of bacteria, opinion is divided as to the advisability of standardizing vaccines on a basis of numerical count of organisms, rather than on actual weight of bacterial protein. However, this question must be left for discussion at some later date. We come now to a comparison between Wright's method and the counting chamber method.

COMPARISON BETWEEN WRIGHT'S METHOD AND THE COUNTING CHAMBER METHOD

It has always been recognized that Wright's method gives only approximate results, but apparently it has not been realized that underneath the many technical variations there is a basic error—the loss of red cells. This has given rise to a false set of relative standards. We believe that this error has been demonstrated by the experience at the Army Medical School in the manufacture of vaccine over many years. In brief, when we changed from Wright's method to the use of the counting chamber, our vaccines became too toxic and gave severe reactions. It was necessary to reduce the bacterial content, as determined by the new method, to one-half of what it had previously been stated to be, before the reactions fell off again to the degree usually experienced with Wright standardized vaccines.

In the fall of 1924, Dr. Edgar B. Carter, Secretary, Committee on Literature, Biological Section, American Drug Manufacturers' Association, proposed to Major H. J. Nichols, Director of Laboratories, Army Medical School, that samples of a number of commercial vaccines be examined for bacterial content at the school by the newer methods. This work has been done under the direction of Major Nichols. Samples were submitted from 9 different laboratories. The samples of 7 were labeled to contain 2,500 million bacilli per mil; the other two were marked 2,000 million per mil. Two sets of samples were submitted. All of them were examined by our usual technic in the Helber counting chamber, and each sample of the second set was compared in the nephelometer [14, 16] with our own typhoid standard suspension.

The method of making the bacterial count in the Helber chamber is as follows: One mil of vaccine is diluted with 3½ mils of buffered salt solution and one-half mil of carbol methyl violet. The mixture is rapidly heated over an open flame almost to boiling, stoppered tightly

[16] Richards, T. W.: Ztschr. f. anorg. chemie, 1895, 8, p. 269. Richards and Wells: Am. Chem. J., 1915, 31, p. 145. Bloor, W. R.: J. Biol. Chem., 1915, 22, p. 145. Kober, P. A.: Ibid., 1913, 13, p. 485, and 1917, 29, p. 155.

with a rubber stopper and set aside until it has cooled a bit and has ceased to steam. It is then thoroughly agitated, and a small drop is placed in the counting chamber. The counting chamber is a Bureau of Standards certified Helber-Levy chamber. The cover-slip is a Bureau of Standards certified reinforced precision cover-slip.

In nephelometry, the standard employed was our own typhoid standard suspension, made by combining 2 parts of standard suspension of typhoid bacilli, with 1 part of standard suspension of paratyphoid "A" bacilli and 1 part of standard suspension of paratyphoid "B" bacilli. It was made with great care and carefully checked in the Helber chamber and is known to contain 1,000 million bacilli per mil.

The results of our examination are presented in table 1.

TABLE 1

BACTERIAL CONTENT OF SAMPLES OF TYPHOID VACCINES SUBMITTED BY NINE LABORATORIES

	First Set of Samples: Cytometer Counts	Second Set of Samples		Averages of All Readings	Theoretical Strength
		Cytometer Counts	Nephelometer Readings		
1	670	235	200	369	2,500
2	1,050	1,050	1,072	1,058	2,500
3	1,100	1,200	1,095	1,132	2,500
4	725	700	700	709	2,500
5	1,150	1,000	1,020	1,057	2,500
6	1,000	1,000	1,095	1,032	2,000
7	128	150	120	133	2,000
8	No sample submitted, 3 separate stock suspensions	400	375	388	2,500
9	785	1,250	1,252	1,096	2,500
Controls A. M. S.					
308	850				
309	1,050				
310	1,200				
311	950				
312	1,000				
313	800				
312-B-2	.....	950	930	980	1,000

It is obvious from an inspection of these figures that all of the samples examined contain fewer organisms than they are supposed to contain according to the labels. However, samples numbered 2, 3, 5, 6 and 9 all contain 1,000 million bacilli or more per mil, and we feel that 1,000 million bacilli per mil are sufficient. Number 4 is a bit too low. Numbers 1, 7 and 8 contain altogether too little bacterial substance. Refined methods of counting are unnecessary to detect that fact. The unaided eye is sufficient.

The methods of standardization employed by all the various laboratories is not known to us. We do know, however, that Wright's method is used by one of them, and it is probably safe to assume that most of them employ it or its standards.

Wright's method was used at the Army Medical School prior to 1920. The official U. S. Army typhoid prophylactic in the years 1911-1916 inclusive was standardized by Wright's method. This vaccine was composed of typhoid bacilli only—the paratyphoid organisms were not used at that time—and it was supposed to contain 1,000 million bacilli per mil. Several samples of vaccines made in 1913, 1914 and 1915 were selected from among our stock of retained samples and counted by our present methods. They all counted very much below their supposed content, most of them in the neighborhood of 500 million per mil. Then, as a check on these counts, a typhoid vaccine was made exactly as it was made in the old days by the same persons who made the typhoid prophylactic 10 years ago, and standardized by them by Wright's method. This vaccine counted 530 by Helber and 500 by Nephelometer.[17]

It began to look as though vaccines standardized by Wright's method do not contain as many organisms as they are thought to contain. At first this seemed an anomalous situation. It is so easy to see bacteria in the Helber chamber that we felt that in any given suspension we would be more likely to see a larger number per unit volume in the bacteriocytometer than we would see in a Wright preparation. Wright's method is susceptible to many serious errors, most of which seemed to us at first to lie in the direction of low counts. Evidence was presented, however, which pointed in the opposite direction. In order to clear up this point, we decided to investigate further.

The examinations made in this study were two:

1. Wright count.

2. A new counting chamber procedure utilizing the basic principle of Wright's estimation but also employing a Helber counting chamber; a kind of "wet Wright count."

Our red blood cell suspension were made as follows:

1. Whole Blood: By vein puncture of a normal young man, more than 1 mil of blood was obtained.

2. First or Primary Blood Dilution: With an Ostwald volumetric pipet 1 mil of blood was transferred to a tube containing 4 mils of

[17] Am. J. Pub. Health, 1925, 15, p. 433.

0.9% sodium chloride solution with 2% sodium citrate and thoroughly mixed therewith.

3. Secondary Blood Dilution: With an Ostwald volumetric pipet 1 mil of the primary blood dilution was transferred to another tube also containing 4 mils of the salt—citrate solution.

4. With an ordinary hemacytometer chamber and red blood cell pipet, the first blood dilution was counted.

We prepared 7 different sets of blood dilutions. Assuming that each sample of blood containing 5,000 million red cells per mil, each primary dilution would contain 1,000 million. The counts are shown in table 2.

TABLE 2

HEMACYTOMETER COUNTS OF PRIMARY BLOOD DILUTIONS MADE MARCH 27, 1925

	Hall	Smith	Averages
1—H.	1,040	900	970
2—Ca.	960	968	964
3—R.	936	...	
4—U.	800	780	790
5—Si.	920	...	
6—Cu.	808	...	
7—Sm.	904	968; 1,040	970
General average			910

The bacterial suspension used was prepared fresh several times during the experiment, always from the same stock bottle; that is, a formalinized typhoid standard suspension, which had been repeatedly counted and which was definitely known to contain approximately 1,000 million bacilli per mil, was used, and from this the preparation to be counted was made.

THE WRIGHT COUNTS

An exact technic was used in the preparation of the Wright spreads. It is as follows:

1. 0.2 mils of the primary dilution of erythrocytes is mixed with 0.2 mils of standard suspension of typhoid bacilli.

2. A very small drop of the mixture is placed on the right hand end of the slide and quickly drawn across the slide behind another slide held at an angle of 30 degrees to the first slide.

3. The preparation is allowed to dry, stained with Wright's stain, and examined, using the oil immersion objective and no. 10 ocular, and employing a cut-off at the diaphragm of the ocular to reduce the field.

4. Ten fields at left, 10 fields at center and 10 fields at right end are counted and averaged.

The findings in the case of the Wright counts are listed in table 3.

TABLE 3

WRIGHT COUNTS ON AN IDENTICAL SUSPENSION OF TYPHOID BACILLI, USING SEVEN DIFFERENT SAMPLES OF BLOOD

1 Sources of Blood Used	2 Number of Millions of Red Blood Cells per Mil. in Primary Dilution of Blood	3 Number of Red Corpuscles Counted in 30 Fields	4 Number of Bacilli Counted in 30 Fields	5 Bacterial Count of Suspension Based on Figure in col. 2	6 Bacterial Count of Suspension if Red Corpuscles Count Were Assumed to be 1,000	7 Actual Bacterial Count of Suspension
1—Sm	970	304	662	2,100	2,180	1,000
2—H	870	88	282	3,100	3,200	1,000
3—Ca	960	220	478	2,080	2,200	1,000
4—R	936	139	356	2,400	2,560	1,000
5—U	780	69	163	2,000	2,360	1,000
6—Si	920	57	213	3,435	3,730	1,000
7—Cu	808	155	327	1,700	2,100	1,000
8—Sm	970	145	208	1,390	1,430	1,000
9—Sm	970	119	173	1,410	1,450	1,000
Aver.	923	144	318	2,180	2,357	1,000

It will be observed that the average red blood cell count of 7 presumably normal young men was not 1,000 million per mil (first dilution, 1:5), but 910 million per mil. Here at once is a loss of almost 9% of red cells. The differences made by this discrepancy are apparent when the figures in columns 5 and 6 are compared. This is one source of error, which, however, is relatively so small as to be really insignificant when compared with the enormous total error of the method. In the 3rd column is indicated the number of red blood cells counted in 30 microscopic fields. This varied from as low as 57 in one preparation to as high as 304 in another spread. This great variation may be taken as an indication of the difficulty of securing uniform red blood cell distribution. In the 4th column is given the number of bacilli counted in 30 microscopic fields. This number also varied very much, from as low as 163 to as high as 662. The variations in the numbers of bacilli parallels roughly the variations in the numbers of red cells. In the first specimen the ratio between cells and bacilli is as 1:2.14; in the second specimen, 1:3.2; in the third, 1:2.17; in the fourth, 1:2.56; in the fifth, 1:2.36; in the sixth, 1:3.73; in the seventh, 1:2.1; in the eighth, 1:1.43; in the ninth, 1:1.45. The ratio of the average is as 1:2.2. It would therefore appear that although the red cells were not uniformly distributed, the bacteria were not uniformly distributed either, but that the ratio of red blood cells to bacteria was constant in all of the preparations. This is a bit of evidence in opposition to the commonly accepted belief that one great source of error in Wright's method is uneven variation of distribution of red cells and bacteria.

In the 5th and 6th columns of table 3 are given 2 different estimations of the bacterial content of the suspension. In the 5th column is the count based on the figure given in the 2d column, the actual number of red blood cells per mil in the cell suspension used. In the 6th column is the bacterial count of the suspension as it would be expressed if it were assumed that the blood suspensions contained 1,000 million cells per mil. In the 7th column, for purposes of comparison, is the actual number of bacilli per mil in the bacterial suspension. The average figures in columns 5 and 6 vary 8% either way. This error, as has been pointed out, is relatively small when compared with the discrepancy between either of these figures and the proper count—1,000 million.

It may be appropriate to note at this point that the average ratio of 2,357 : 1,000 is almost similar to that which exists between the average of the supposed contents of the vaccines 2, 3, 5, 6 and 9 to 1,000. It is 2,400 : 1,000. This close resemblance is significant.

THE NEW METHOD OR "WET WRIGHT" COUNTS

The technic of the new counting chamber procedure or "wet Wright" is as follows:

1. A bacterial suspension is prepared exactly as is that for the Helber count.

2. Exactly equal volumes of the bacterial suspension so prepared and the secondary dilution of blood cells are mixed.

3. A drop of this mixture is placed in the Helber chamber and examined.

4. The erythrocytes and the bacteria in at least 40 small squares—preferably 100 small squares are counted.

The "wet Wright" gives us a great deal of information in itself, and throws some light on the Wright count in addition. In it we have:

1. An erythrocyte count.
2. A bacterial count.
3. Data for comparison in the manner of Wright.

Now let us study the results of the new method of "wet Wright" counts. The findings by this method are set forth in table 4.

TABLE 4

NEW METHOD OR "WET WRIGHT" COUNTS ON AN IDENTICAL SUSPENSION OF TYPHOID BACILLI, USING SEVEN DIFFERENT SAMPLES OF BLOOD

1 Sources of Blood Used	2 Number of Millions of Red Blood Cells per Mil in Mixture of Secondary Suspension of Blood and Bacterial Suspension	3 Number of Millions of Bacilli per Mil in Same Mixture	4 Number of Red Blood Cells Counted in Preparation	5 Number of Bacteria Counted in Preparation	6 Bacterial Content of Suspension Based on Figure in col. 5 without Reference to Red Blood Cells	7 Bacterial Content of Suspension Derived by Wright's Method Based on Figure in col. 2	8 Bacterial Content of Suspension Derived by Wright's Method Based on Assumed Red Blood Cell Count of 5 million per C.mm.
1—Sm	97	100	84	106	1,060	1,220	1,260
2—H	97	100	60	92	920	1,490	1,530
3—H	97	100	60	92	920	1,490	1,530
4—Ca	96	100	84	134	1,340	1,530	1,600
5—Sm	97	100	98	87	870	860	900
6—R	93.6	100	76	116	1,160	1,430	1,520
7—U	80	100	52	124	1,240	1,900	2,380
8—Si	92	100	80	120	1,200	1,380	1,500
9—Cu	80.8	100	86	121	1,210	1,140	1,400
Aver.	92	100	75	110	1,102	1,404	1,500

In the first column occurs the initial of the man whose blood was used; in the second column, the number of millions of red blood cells per mil in the mixture of secondary suspension of blood and bacterial suspension. The secondary blood dilutions were not actually counted in the hemacytometer prior to use, but as the secondary dilutions were made immediately from the primary dilutions, it is felt that it is safe to assume the counts set forth in column 2. It will be recalled that one mil of the secondary blood dilution was mixed with one mil of the bacterial suspension prepared as for the Helber count. Therefore, theoretically, the number of red blood cells in the mixture should be just one-half of the number assumed to be present in the secondary dilution. The number of bacilli assumed to be present per mil of mixture is 100, indicated in column 3.

The number of millions of red blood cells and of bacteria actually counted in the preparations are shown in columns 4 and 5, respectively. Note that the average number of millions of red blood cells assumed to be present is 92; the average number actually counted was 75. This is an apparent loss of 18%. Now compare the figures in columns 3 and 5. The average number of bacilli assumed to be present is 100 million; the average number actually counted was 110 million. This is a gain of 10%. The total discrepancy reaches the considerable figure of 28%. The greater part of the error appears to be due to the loss of red blood cells.

Column 6 carried the figures which express the bacterial content of the undiluted suspension based on the figures in column 5, without reference to red blood cells. That is, these figures are ordinary Helber chamber counts. In all cases they should be, theoretically, 1,000, i. e., the actual count of the suspension. The variations from that figure are never very great, 1,340 being the greatest above and 870 the greatest below. The average, 1,100, is not very far from the proper figure. It is an error of 10%. It is probable that we must allow as much as 10% or even 15% error to even the most refined and exact method of counting bacteria.

Column 7 in table 4 contains the figures which express the bacterial content of the suspension when estimated after the manner of Wright, using the figures in column 2 as the basis of comparison. The average count in this column is 1,404. In column 8 are given figures which express the bacterial content of the suspension when estimated after the manner of Wright, using the figure 100 as the basis of comparison; that is, proceeding on the assumption that the red blood cell count is always 5 million per c.mm. The average count in this column is 1,500.

On either basis of comparison with red blood cells the count is far from correct. If the number of red blood cells actually counted is used as a basis of comparison, a correct count is, of course, obtained, but there is no advantage gained by this procedure over a simple count of bacteria. Column 7 shows an average error of 40%; column 8, of 50%. The error in the case of counts made in the new manner is not so great as in the case of Wright counts, in which the average error in these experiments is shown to be from 118% to 135%.

DISCUSSION

It is felt that the Wright method of standardizing vaccines or any present known modification of that method is extremely deceptive and should be abandoned in favor of a more accurate method. The basic error of the Wright method, which appears to be unavoidable, is the loss of red blood cells. This means that the estimation of the bacterial content is based on the assumption that the relation between the red blood cells and the bacteria in the mixture may be expressed by the ratio 5 : x, whereas that ratio is more accurately expressed as 2.5 : x or 3 : x. Thus the estimated bacterial count is too high, and the consequent dilution of the vaccine is too great. The error may be as great as 135%.

It seems to be impossible to manipulate blood without losing cells. They settle out of suspension so quickly that it is extremely difficult to keep a suspension uniform. They stick to the sides of pipets and test-tubes. In making a spread it is impossible to distribute the red cells evenly and uniformly.

It is probable that cytolysis plays a minor rôle, but it is a possible factor to be considered. Probably sedimentation and adherence to walls of apparatus account for the greater part of the loss of red cells. At least, in this experiment we have not been able to demonstrate cytolysis. However, whatever may be the cause, the effect is plainly evident. Red blood cells are lost. They are lost to a great degree in the original Wright technic, to a less degree in the new technic. In either case their loss affects a profound influence on the results.

If it seems desirable to adhere to the bacteriometric method we recommend that the bacteria be counted directly in the Helber counting chamber, as is now done at the Army Medical School. It will then be advisable to revise the expression of dosage in accordance with the new standards.

SUMMARY AND CONCLUSIONS

Evidence has been presented that there is a basic error in the Wright method of standardizing vaccines, which is due to the loss of red blood cells. In the usual Wright preparation the cells are lost to a great degree; in the counting chamber or "wet Wright" count, to a less degree. The loss appears to be unavoidable by even the most painstaking technic, and is probably accounted for largely by sedimentation and adherence to walls of apparatus. Hemolysis probably plays a minor rôle.

Because of this loss of red blood cells, the ratio of cells to bacteria is not 5 : x, but 2.5 : x or 3 : x. Consequently, when the ratio 5 : x is employed, the value for x becomes very much too great. In other words, the bacterial content of the suspension is overrated. The suspension is therefore overdiluted, and as a result the final product contains only about one-half as many bacteria as it is thought to contain.

The counting chamber method of standardizing typhoid vaccine gives a count which is only half that obtained with Wright's method.

For purposes of accuracy and uniformity it seems advisable to adopt the counting chamber method of standardization and to revise the expression of dosage to accord with the new standards.

RELATIONSHIP OF ENTERITIDIS-PARATYPHOID B INFECTIONS TO HYPERGLYCEMIA IN RABBITS

Maud L. Menten and Helen M. Manning
From the Pathological Laboratory, University of Pittsburgh, Pittsburgh

Guinea-pigs dying from enteritidis-paratyphoid B infections show various changes, among which hydropic degeneration in the islets of Langerhans may be prominent. As it is difficult to obtain a quantity of blood from guinea-pigs without some injury, only single specimens for glucose determinations were withdrawn from the heart. These single tests indicated that the lesions were accompanied by hyperglycemia. As similar infections are fairly widespread among laboratory animals and especially rodents, it was believed that the varying degrees of hyperglycemia so frequently encountered in rabbits might owe its origin to this cause. The present study, therefore, was undertaken with a view to determining whether the organisms of the enteritidis-paratyphoid B group bore a causal relationship to changes in the blood sugar of these animals. Phases of the problem studied include coincidence of onset and development of hyperglycemia with the lowering of the animal's resistance occasioned by environmental changes (as evidenced by changes in atmospheric temperature), the effect of injections of killed and living bacterial suspensions, the possibility of conferring protection against bacterial invasion by immunization, and, finally, the pathologic changes induced by acute and chronic infections.

METHODS

Studies were made chiefly on rabbits (60). A few experiments were also made on dogs. The animals were housed in a wooden building heated by stoves so that some fluctuation in temperature was unavoidably present. Rabbits were fed on oats and hay with green food at intervals of 4 to 5 days. After the animal had been deprived of food for 20 to 24 hours, slightly more than 1 c.c. of blood was allowed to drop from the marginal ear vein into a graduated centrifuge tube containing 2 mg. of powdered potassium oxalate. Subsequent technic and estimation of dextrose in blood filtrate was that recommended by Folin and Wu.[1] When nonprotein nitrogen determinations were to be made on the same sample, blood slightly in excess of 3 c.c. was withdrawn, and these estimations made on part of the blood filtrate by Folin's method.

Necropsies were made on all animals as soon after death as possible. Between the months of December and April, inclusive, cultures were made of

Received for publication, June 20, 1925.

[1] Lab. Manual Biol. Chem., 1922.

the heart blood and organs of all animals killed or dying spontaneously. The majority of the animals died during January and February. During April, the percentage of rabbits dying spontaneously was markedly reduced, and cultures from these animals were then uniformly negative, so that further culturing of organs was discontinued on the occasional animal dying during the summer months. Small fragments of spleen, liver and kidneys were removed aseptically and transferred to a preliminary differential medium of the following composition:

Fresh ox bile	90 c c.
Infusion broth	10 c c.
Peptone	1 gm.
Lactose	1 gm.

After 20 hours' incubation in this medium, lactose litmus agar plates were streaked, and at the end of 20 hours colonies not showing fermentation were picked and transferred to lactose broth containing Andrade's indicator. From those tubes in which no fermentation occurred, transfers were made to carbohydrate mediums for differentiation. Finally, agglutination tests were made on all bacteria isolated with antiserum obtained by inoculation of animals. Routine microscopic examination of paraffin sections of all the organs except the brain and thyroid stained with hematoxylin and eosin was carried out.

RESULTS

Our findings confirm the wide variations in glycemic values of rabbits which have been encountered by various workers, and, furthermore, a correlation between the hyperglycemia and general condition of the animal has been observed. Repeated blood examinations on animals throughout the year disclosed that a close parallel existed between the weather and the glucose content of the blood. During the warm weather of September, October, May, June and July, glycemia in our rabbits approached a value closely approximating that found normally in man and averaging about 100 mg. per c c. of blood. With the advent of cold autumn weather, a mild intermittent hyperglycemia varying somewhat in individual animals occurred. After a few days of cold weather in November, values of 125 to 140 mg. per c c. of blood were frequently found. As the periods of cold weather became more prolonged and the fall in temperature greater, these values increased from 150 to 165 mg., and during January and February to 180 mg. Rabbits with hyperglycemia at or about 165 mg. of glucose per c c. of blood persisting for many days lost weight; the respirations became noisy and shallow; there was a thin, purulent discharge from the nose, and many animals suffered from diarrhea. It was during such periods that the majority of animals died. A return from cold weather to higher temperatures was invariably accompanied by a fall in blood sugar values and in robust animals by a rapid return to the normal figure. This general correspondence between atmospheric temperature and blood sugar values is indicated by the tables which are representative of the findings in all our animals. Allowing for variations due to slight differences in individuals and such factors as previous infection and crowding of animals, the hyperglycemia is roughly inversely proportional to the temperature. The sort of weather preceding the date of the experiment exerts an influence on the height of the rise in sugar. The hyperglycemia is more marked following sudden onset of cold than when the fall in temperature has been gradual.

TABLE 1

VARIATIONS IN GLYCEMIA IN RELATION TO TEMPERATURE CHANGES, SHOWING MILLIGRAMS OF DEXTROSE PER C C. OF BLOOD IN RABBITS

No. of Rabbit	Dec. 11	Dec. 12	Dec. 18	Dec. 20	Dec. 22	Feb. 22	May 10	June 18	July 2
34	166	149	142	—	117	126	116	95.2	80
86	154	131	158	129	133	160	105	102.6	94
100	167	147	140	119	114	143	119	106	101
55	145	138	124	132	129	129	111	Killed	
Temp. F.	38	46	38	54	54	20	56	70	62

TABLE 2

VARIATIONS IN GLYCEMIA IN RELATION TO TEMPERATURE CHANGES (MILLIGRAMS OF DEXTROSE PER C C. OF BLOOD IN RABBITS)

No. of Rabbit	Nov. 9	Nov. 20	Nov. 27	Dec. 4	Dec. 14	Dec. 17	Feb. 23	May 8	May 14	May 27	June 18	June 26
77	117	105	135	150	128	142	133	105	101	105	94	90
81	129	92	125	133	126	138	141	99	107	111	98	90
149	109	105	121	144	126	126	140	133	117	109	98	98
85	118	93	126	136	124	133	154*					
4	138	118	150	125	158	155	170	105	104	108	103	97
Temp. F.	35	44	36	49	27	36	22	62	53	60	70	66

* Died, April 26.

The temperatures recorded in tables 1 and 2 are the mean of the maximal and minimal temperatures recorded daily in the temperature chart issued by the Weather Bureau for Pittsburgh. When low temperatures persist continuously for a considerable time, and especially when several rabbits are confined in one enclosure, the blood sugar fluctuates between 145 and 170 mg., and many animals die. From a high percentage of such animals, cultures of nonlactose fermenting organisms and Staphylococcus aureus were obtained. That the former were not merely postmortem invaders is indicated by the fact that when rabbits with high hyperglycemia, which has persisted for many days, are killed and cultures immediately taken from the organs, identical organisms are invariably found. Of the 25 rabbits from which cultures were taken, positive findings were obtained in 17, of which number 14 gave the cultural characteristics of the enteritidis-paratyphoid B group. Two other organisms, strains 11 and 184, were identified as B. morgani 1, since they were motile organisms producing acid and gas in dextrose, levulose, xylose, and galactose only, producing terminal alkalinity in milk and blackening lead acetate. Finally one strain, 72, a peritrichous motile bacillus likewise giving a terminal alkalinity in milk and not blackening lead acetate, gave acidity but no gas with dextrose only. While identification by fermentation tests was carried out immediately following the

TABLE 3

AGGLUTINATION TESTS

Bacterial Strains	Limit of Agglutination with				
	Antiserum B. Enteritidis Strain PT 40	Antiserum B. Enteritidis PT 40 Absorbed with P. Paratyphosus B Strain PT 2	Antiserum B. Paratyphosus B Strain PT 2	Antiserum Morgan 1 Stock Culture	Antiserum Bacillus 72 (Producing Acidity without Gas in Dextrose)
Strains 63, 69, 70, 84, 91, 92, 93, 94, 96, 97, 99, 103, 228, 321.........	4,000	4,000	0	0	0
Morgan 1, strains 11 and 184	0	0	0	3,000	0
Bacillus 72 (acid with dextrose)	0	0	0	0	8,000
B. enteritidis (Jordan)	5,000	5,000	0	0	0
B. enteritidis (mouse) (Rockefeller)	4,000+	4,000	0	0	0
B. paratyphosus B (Howell A95)	200	0	800	0	0
B. paratyphosus (hog lung) (Jordan)	200	0	800+	0	0
B. dysenteriae (Shiga and Flexner), B. paradysenteriae (Knox and Hiss-Russell), B. paratyphosus B (R. V. H.) and A (B. J.)	.....	.....	.....	0	0

isolation of the bacilli in pure culture, the final conclusive identification by agglutination of the foregoing closely related nonlactose fermenting organisms was postponed until June, since our previous studies showed that rabbits immunized during the winter months readily succumb to minute injections of suspensions of killed bacteria belonging to this group. Differentiation between B. enteritidis and B. paratyphoid B can be made only by agglutination tests. Table 3 gives the results of the agglutination tests.

In 68% of the animals from which cultures were taken, nonlactose fermenting strains of bacteria were isolated from organs, and the majority of the bacteria belonged to the enteritidis-paratyphoid B group. The most remarkable observation, however, was that all of the organisms of this group proved on agglutination to be B. enteritidis, and at no time did we obtain B. paratyphoid B. In our previous work,[2] in which plain broth instead of a bile broth was employed as a preliminary differential medium, both B. enteritidis and B. paratyphosus B were obtained. The conditions obtaining in the use of bile broth apparently are such as to inhibit the growth of B. paratyphosus B while allowing that of B. enteritidis. This view is strengthened by the fact that in the organs of the 8 animals giving negative cultures pronounced signs of gross and microscopic pathologic changes suggestive of infections of the enteritidis-paratyphoid B group and similar to that found in the 17 animals reacting positively were present and by the fact that rabbits can be readily infected with B. paratyphosus B of animal origin.

Investigations at present being carried out indicate that many factors underlie this difference in reaction to the bile medium displayed by these two bacilli. The presence of several strains of organisms, comprising different forms of the enteritidis-paratyphoid B group and frequently staphylococcus, streptococcus or B. coli as well as the products elaborated by them in the preliminary culture medium contribute to conditions favoring the dominance of B. enteritidis. Addition of bile to broth, with its property of lowering surface tension, must cause considerable alteration at the bacteria-fluid interface in the potential difference which, as Northrup and De Kruif [3] have shown in experiments on agglutination, markedly modifies bacterial activity. The nonlactose-fermenting bacillus producing acid without gas in dextrose remained constant in its cultural characteristics at the end of 10 months. Unlike B. enteritidis, B. morgani and B. paratyphosus B studied, this organism does not show the Theobald and Dorothea Smith phenomenon,[4] but does produce gas following the addition of B. coli to tubes of dextrose broth in which it has been growing for from 4 to 5 days.

Attempts were made to infect animals by giving B. enteritidis and B. paratyphosus B by mouth, but the ingestion of these bacteria in equal dosage per kilo. gave irregular results in different animals, possibly because of the varying numbers of bacteria already existing in the intestinal tract, with more or less derangement of the mucosa. Intrave-

[2] Jour. Infect. Dis., 1924, 35, p. 407.
[3] Jour. Gen. Physiol., 1920-21, 3, p. 21.
[4] Ibid., 1921-22, 4, p. 639.

nous injections of living bacteria in adequate amounts cause foci of infection in the spleen, kidneys and liver with lesions similar to those already reported from this laboratory in guinea-pigs dying with spontaneous infection. The infected animals show rapid loss of weight, pulmonary distress, diarrhea and a rise of blood sugar. Three or four successive doses, varying in concentration between 500,000 and 50,000,000 bacteria per c c. per kilo., depending on the season of the year, at intervals of one week, suffice to give marked results. Smaller doses in winter are as effective as larger dosage in warmer weather. Single massive doses of 1 to 2 billion living bacteria per c c. are similar in effect to single massive doses of killed bacteria and cause the death of the animal in from 2 to 24 hours. The effective dose in this case likewise shows wide fluctuation dependent on the condition of the animal of which the degree of hyperglycemia is a good index. With lethal doses of B. enteritidis, animals invariably die with convulsions. Immediately following the intravenous injection of a lethal dose, there is rapid shallow breathing with increase in the rate of the heart beat, and examination of blood sugar reveals a rise in from 5 to 15 minutes, depending on the dosage. This rise may be considerably above 200 mg. per c c. of blood, and is immediately followed by a precipitate decline reaching the normal level in from 30 to 50 minutes and a hypoglycemia of from 80 mg. to 70 mg. during the next half hour. Death of an animal with a hypoglycemia of from 40 to 50 mg. occurs in from 2 to 4 hours, at which time the blood pressure has become exceedingly low. Thirty minutes before death it is impossible to withdraw blood from the ear veins. With injection of smaller numbers of organisms the curve presents a similar outline, but the initial rise reaches a proportionately lower level, and the subsequent hypoglycemia becomes less and may even fail to occur. For example, with a dose of 1 c c. containing 250,000,000 bacteria injected in May into a vigorous animal with an initial glycemia of 100 mg. per c c. of blood, the resulting hyperglycemia reached 170 to 190 mg. and the maximum hypoglycemia 75 mg.

The most consistent results are obtained in animals whose blood sugar content at the end of 20 hour's deprivation of food is not greater than 110 mg. Rabbits with an initial hyperglycemia always show the most marked and rapid effects, and the degree of individual response in reaction to bacterial injections is closely paralleled by the degree of hyperglycemia at the time of injection. Animals with a blood sugar of

180 mg. per 100 c c. frequently succumb to suspensions containing small numbers of killed bacteria.

It is interesting that the dog possesses considerable resistance to these organisms by whatever route they are administered. It was found impossible to infect healthy dogs by feeding either B. enteritidis or B. paratyphosus B, although massive doses of broth cultures were incorporated with food for many successive days. So far as could be discerned, no deleterious effects were produced. Subcutaneous injections produced large cystlike masses containing a clear fluid from which pure cultures were recovered, but no demonstrable toxic symptoms developed. Intravenous injections containing more than 700,000,000 organisms per c c. per kilo. proved fatal in from 2 to 12 hours. The general effect was similar to that resulting from intravenous injections into rabbits, except that in the dog death was preceded by the vomiting of large quantities of bile.

The acute changes in the vascular endothelium of the glomeruli and the tubular degeneration suggested possible disturbance in the elimination of nitrogenous waste products, and estimations of nonprotein nitrogen were made on about half of the animals. These values, varying between 25 and 80 mg. per c c. of blood, indicated that these changes were not associated with any marked retention of protein. Furthermore, no close parallel between the degree of hyperglycemia and the increase in nonprotein nitrogen of the blood was observed. The main focus of injury was the liver, in which extensive hemorrhage, extreme degeneration and frequently disappearance of the hepatic cells and widespread change in the Kupffer cells lining the sinusoids were found.

Since guinea-pigs, rabbits and white rats continuously harbor in their intestinal tracts organisms of the enteritidis-paratyphoid B group which have been found by us in the internal organs in a high percentage of animals subjected to adverse environmental conditions, it was thought desirable to test the efficacy of immunization procedures. Two outstanding features were noted in these experiments: first, the individual differences in reaction to identical dosage per kilo weight of antigen and, second, the intensity of the reaction following single injections depended in no small measure upon the value of the blood sugar at the time of the initial injection. Both, we believe, are referable to the same cause, namely, the presence of enteritidis-paratyphoid B infection. The influence of the blood sugar values at the time of injection of the antigen is illustrated in table 4.

The intravenous injection of a small dose of killed B. enteritidis into rabbits apparently normal but with a hyperglycemia of 175 or more mg. of glucose per c c. of blood was invariably fatal in a few days. This finding has been confirmed repeatedly, and offers an explanation for the difficulty experienced in attempts to immunize animals during the winter months as compared to the comparative ease with which the same effect may be accomplished in May, June and July. This fact, we believe, explains the extreme variation in susceptibility of animals to varying doses of enteritidis-paratyphoid B organisms as recorded by Schütze.[5] Furthermore, the production of antibodies apparently progresses at a more rapid rate during the warmer months than during the winter. As in the previous study by Thomas,[2] at no time have we

TABLE 4

EFFECTS OF INJECTING KILLED SUSPENSION OF B. ENTERITIDIS INTO ANIMALS WITH HIGH INITIAL GLYCEMIA — MILLIGRAMS OF DEXTROSE PER C C. OF BLOOD

No. of Rabbit	Dec. 1	Dec. 11	Dec. 12	Dec. 13	Dec. 13*	Dec. 15*	Dec. 19	Dec. 21	Feb. 25	May 10	May 23
84	—	186	158	141	....	....	‡				
103	128	175	156	146	....	....	151§				
94	—	197	166	143	....	....	200	235¶			
87	—	155	149	153	....	....	163	149	105	110	87
179	136	141	154	170?	....	....	137	128	122	101#	
Temp. F.	41	38	46	47	47	29	44	57	34	56	60

* Given intravenously 1 c c. = 50,000,000 killed B. enteritidis.
‡ Died Dec. 18.
§ Died Dec. 20.
¶ Died Dec. 22.
# May 23, animal killed by other animal fighting.

been successful even after a prolonged series of injections in producing antiserum against B. paratyphoid B giving agglutination in dilution greater than 1 in 800, although B. enteritidis readily gave antiserum producing agglutination in 1:4,000 in from 3 to 4 weeks. While it is possible to immunize readily against B. enteritidis, this immunity confers little protection against B. paratyphoid B. Injections of mixed cultures proved toxic. Besides these two allied forms, nonlactose-fermenting bacillus morgani 1 and a strain producing only acidity in dextrose against which antiserum of high titer was readily obtained were also isolated from internal organs, so that the problem of spontaneous intestinal infections in rabbits is not limited to the enteritidis-paratyphoid B group.

[5] Jour. Hygiene, 1921, 20, p. 330.

The lesions obtained in acute infections were similar to those found in guinea-pigs and were found mainly in the kidneys, liver, spleen and suprarenals. While karyolysis and fading of the nuclei in the islets of the pancreas were frequently encountered, hydropic degeneration was noted only in those rabbits in which hyperglycemia had persisted continuously for a considerable time. In addition to the acute lesions in organs already reported, we have had the opportunity to study chronic reactions. Of these the most interesting appeared in the kidneys and the liver. In two immunized animals, we noted kidneys with marked irregular scarring in the gross which resembled closely the contracted arteriosclerotic kidney. In many other animals less extensive areas of fibrosis were observed. The progressively developing biliary cirrhosis, which in animals under observation and showing recurrent infections for 14 to 16 months frequently became extensive in the absence of coccidial infection, strongly suggested the enteritidis-paratyphoid B group as the causative agent. In young rabbits, bred in our animal house and free from coccidiosis, the initial stages of biliary cirrhosis could be followed. Atrophy of spleen with extensive scarring as well as fibrosis in the zona glomerulosa and medulla of the suprarenals was present in a large percentage of the animals studied.

DISCUSSION

The figures obtained by us for blood sugar values in rabbits are in close agreement with those of Scott and Ford [6] whose tables indicate a general seasonal variation, the values being low during the summer months and reaching a maximum during January and February. As the temperatures for exact dates on which glycemia estimations were made are not recorded by those authors, it is not possible to determine how closely the variation is related to change in temperature. So wide is the range of variation in rabbits' blood sugar throughout the year that a correct average value must necessarily be calculated from a series extending over the 12 months.

While factors other than the one of spontaneous infection may contribute to the development of hyperglycemia in rodents, the presence of the enteritidis-paratyphoid B infection in rabbits is sufficient to account for the abnormal values of blood sugar so frequently obtained. It is noteworthy that in dogs which are not readily susceptible to enteritidis-paratyphoid infections, there is almost no evidence of hyperglycemia as

[6] Am. Jour. Physiol., 1922-23, 63, p. 520.

compared to its prevalence in rabbits, especially during the winter months when subjected to conditions tending to lower the animals' resistance. The close correlation between variations in the hyperglycemia and the physical condition of the animal as well as a rapid return to normal blood sugar value on the disappearance of deleterious environmental conditions account for the irregular and transitory character of hyperglycemia, and suggests its association mainly with disturbance in storage of dextrose in the liver in the form of glycogen, rather than a relationship to pancreatic derangement. Single intravenous doses of suspensions of killed B. enteritidis or B. paratyphoid B, while they give a rise in blood dextrose, do not produce hydropic degeneration in the islets of Langerhans in rabbits. This histologic change appears in these animals only after prolonged infections, with accompanying hyperglycemia of varying degree. Rabbits killed showing mild hyperglycemia and slight evidence of infection may show little change in the islet cells. When present, these alterations consist of pyknosis, karyorrhexis and karyolysis. We are, therefore, inclined to believe that hydropic degeneration of beta cells is the result of exhaustion of these cells in an effort to relieve the prolonged hyperglycemia resulting primarily from disturbance of liver metabolism, particularly since pathologic changes of varying intensity are always in evidence in the liver of these animals. The hydropic degeneration of the islet cells is apparently not due to postmortem changes, as we have observed this lesion in animals which have been killed and whose tissue has been fixed immediately following death. Furthermore, pancreas removed from the animal and exposed to the air, or left in situ after the death of the animal and subsequently removed at periods varying from 1 to 6 hours and then fixed and stained in a routine manner, show pyknosis, karyorrhexis and karyolysis, the usual autolytic changes occurring in the nucleus; but hydropic degeneration has not been observed. Islet tissue of the different animals shows a varying degree of reactivity to the toxic effects of the enteritidis-paratyphoid organisms. Hydropic degeneration and pyknosis readily occur in the islets of Langerhans in the guinea-pig subjected to the toxic influence of these infections for a brief interval, while the beta cells of the islets of the rabbit are apparently more stable, and well defined lesions are observed only late in the infection. The pancreatic tissue of the white rat lies intermediate in its reaction.

While it has been possible to produce readily antiserum of fairly high titer against B. enteritidis, it has not proved of much practical value in the prevention of a high percentage of fatalities among our rabbits, in all of which the internal organs show traces of the infection. This lack of protection we attribute to the fact that B. paratyphoid B does not readily lend itself to production of immune bodies as evidenced by the low agglutinating power of the antiserum obtained. Furthermore, studies now in progress strongly indicate that many of the pathologic changes observed in the various tissues is due to soluble products elaborated by the B. paratyphoid B.

CONCLUSIONS

Rabbits subjected to adverse environmental conditions develop hyperglycemia. Coincident with a marked hyperglycemia, cultures of organisms of the enteritidis-paratyphoid B group may be recovered from organs of rabbits, which likewise show characteristic morphologic changes.

Similar pathologic conditions can be produced by the injection of killed or living organisms of this group.

Hydropic degeneration in the islets of Langerhans in the rabbit is present only when the hyperglycemia is of prolonged continuous duration.

ISOLATION OF BACTERIOPHAGE FREE FROM BACTERIAL PROTEINS

Lloyd Arnold and Emil Weiss

From the Department of Bacteriology, Pathology and Preventive Medicine, Loyola University School of Medicine, Chicago

The study of the antigenic properties of the Twort-D'Herelle bacteriophagic substance has always been complicated by the presence in the mixture of antigenically active bacterial proteins derived from the dissolved bacteria. We first attempted to remove the bacterial proteins from the bacteriophagic fluid medium by repeated treatment with homologous antibacterial serum. If the bacterial proteins could be quantitatively removed in this way, we could see whether the active lytic principle remained unaltered in the supernatant fluid. A strong bacteriophage (against B. typhosus) was mixed with antityphoid serum (agglutination titer 1:20,000). The technic was varied from a ratio of 5 parts bacteriophage to 1 part antiserum, to 10 parts bacteriophage and 1 part antiserum. Incubation required from 2 to 48 hours, and it remained in the icebox for 24 hours. The supernatant fluid after centrifugation was again handled in the same manner. If there was a visible precipitate formed after incubation and refrigeration, the supernatant fluid was treated again in the same manner. We have varied this technic in many minor ways that would not be of sufficient value to describe in detail. The supernatant fluid, after all of the demonstrable antigen of B. typhosus source had been absorbed, was passed through the Berkefeld filter and used to immunize rabbits. Four rabbits received injections 12 times with increasing doses, at 3 day intervals, with each suspension prepared as mentioned. Eight days after the last injection the agglutination titer of the rabbit serum ran from 1:160 to in some instances as high as 1:640. We concluded that we could not completely absorb the bacterial proteins from our bacteriophage by the use of antibacterial serum.

We tried next to combine a salting out method with the absorption method just mentioned. After the addition of antityphoid serum, the mixture was shaken and concentrated sodium sulphate solution added to make a 14% concentration.[1] This mixture was incubated for 24 hours at 37 C., put in the icebox over night, passed through filter paper

Received for publication, July 22, 1925.

[1] Howe: Jour. Biol. Chem., 1921, 49, pp. 93 and 100.

and then through a Berkefeld candle. The precipitate was redissolved in normal salt solution, corresponding to the original volume of the bacteriophage used; this was then passed through the Berkefeld filter. Both filtrates were injected into 4 rabbits. The filtrate of the supernatant fluid did not produce agglutinins, but contained antibacteriophagic substance. The redissolved precipitate gave an agglutination titer of 1:80 and 1:160 and contained some antibodies against bacteriophage, but not inhibiting to the extent that was found in the filtrate antigen.

We then investigated this question more thoroughly. Antibacterial, antibacteriophagic and normal rabbit serum each were added to bacteriophage in a concentration of 1 part serum to 5 parts bacteriophage. After the mixture was shaken well, concentrated sodium sulphate was added to make a 14% concentration; it then was incubated for 2 hours and placed in the icebox over night. The precipitate was collected on a filter paper and redissolved in normal salt solution. The filtrates and redissolved precipates were passed through Berkefeld candles to insure sterility and then used as antigens for rabbit injections as outlined. Table 1 gives the results of these experiments. The filtrate antigen from all 3 series did not produce agglutinating antibodies against the B. typhosus used in the production of the potent bacteriophage. All of the precipitates caused the production of agglutinins in low titer. The precipitate from the bacteriophage and normal serum contained the highest agglutinin titer. This was expected; the antibacterial and the antibacteriophage [2] serums contained specific antibodies against the bacterial proteins in the original bacteriophagic suspension. Antibacteriophagic bodies were found in the filtrate and to some extent in the precipitate antiserums of the antibacterial and normal serum mixtures. When the antibacteriophagic serum was used in the preparation of the antigen, no antibodies against bacteriophage could be detected. This confirms our previous observations.[2]

Our next step was to determine whether it was necessary to have serum present in the salting out procedure to insure a precipitation of the bacterial proteins from the bacteriophage. We repeated the foregoing experiment, as control, and added distilled water to the bacteriophage (1:4) and brought this mixture to a 14% sodium sulphate concentration as was done with the serum mixtures. It was found that if this bacteriophage and sodium sulphate were incubated at 37 C. for 2 hours and then put in the icebox over night and the filtrate and

[2] Arnold and Weiss: Jour. Infect. Dis., 1924, 34, p. 317; 35, pp. 505 and 603.

precipitate used as antigens as outlined, the results were the same as if serum were present in the mixture. The results are shown in the last columns to the right in table 1. Further experiments showed that the

TABLE 1

PURIFICATION OF BACTERIOPHAGE WITH THE AID OF SODIUM SULPHATE WITH AND WITHOUT SERUM

Rabbits 1 and 2	4 Parts Bacteriophage and 1 Part of							
	Bacterial Antiserum Serum, Agglutination Titer 1:20,000 +		Antibacteriophage Serum, Agglutination Titer 1:640, Antilytic Titer 0.05 C c. +		Normal Serum +		Distilled Water —	
	Redissolved Precipitate	Filtrate	Redissolved Precipitate	Filtrate	Redissolved Precipitate	Filtrate	Redissolved Precipitate	Filtrate
Agglutinins...	1:80 1:160	0 0	1:320 1:80	0 0	1:640 1:1280	0 0	1:60 1:640	0 0
Antilysins*....	0.8 c c. 0.9	0.005 c c. 0.025	0 0	0 0	0.75 c c. 0.6	0.0025 c c. 0.005	0.7 0.4	0.005 0.025

* Titer determined according to the method described in a previous paper (footnote 2).
\+ Sodium sulphate was added to make a 14% concentration (footnote 1).

addition of serum to the bacteriophage before the sodium sulphate caused a complete precipitation of the bacterial proteins in 20 minutes. Without serum, 2 hours was found to be the shortest interval of time. When shorter incubation periods are used, agglutinins against the bacterial proteins are present after the injection of the filtrate antigen.

TABLE 2

THE EFFECT OF THE CONCENTRATION OF PRECIPITANT, TIME AND TEMPERATURE OF BROTH AND SERUM ON THE STRENGTH OF THE PURIFIED BACTERIOPHAGE

Bacteriophage	Na_2SO_4	Time of Contact									
		½ Hour		2 Hours		6 Hours		12 Hours		24 Hours	
		Room Temperature	37 C.	Room Temperature	37 C.	Room Temperature	37 C.	Room Temperature	37 C.	Room Temperature	37 C.
Bacteriophage and water*	14% 32%	100 85	100 80	100 70	85 50	95 40	65 20	70 30	50 20	60 25	45 10
Bacteriophage and broth*	14% 32%	100 90	100 85	100 80	95 60	95 65	85 45	90 50	80 35	85 40	75 25
Bacteriophage and serum*	14% 32%	100 100	100 90	100 85	100 70	100 70	90 60	95 55	85 40	90 45	80 30

* 1 part bacteriophage—1 part serum, broth or water—8 parts of sodium sulphate solution to make the required 14 or 32% concentrations.

We have tried concentrations of sodium sulphate up to 32%, and find that higher than 14% have a toxic effect on the bacteriophage. The more concentrated and the longer the period of contact, the weaker is the active lytic agent.

Table 2 shows the comparative effects of time and temperature on the bacteriophage with and without the addition of serum in the presence of 14% and 32% sodium sulphate. Broth alone was substituted for serum in one series of experiments. The figures represent the percentage of activity of the bacteriophage, i. e., 100% is the same strength as the original untreated control bacteriophage diluted to the same extent with salt solution or broth; 70% represents a decrease of 30% below original activity, etc. It will be seen that the serum exercises a protective influence and that 32% sodium sulphate is more toxic than 14% concentrations.

The bacteriophage used by us has been prepared by the bottom layer agar method.[3] The bacterial proteins are present in much smaller quantities than are found by the use of D'Herelle's method.[2] Pick [4] reviews the literature in regard to the use of neutral salts in the isolation of toxins from bacterial cultures. Many phases of the colloidal chemical nature of such reactions are discussed in this review. The greatest attention was given to the precipitates obtained by salting out with various inorganic salts. Many by-products of bacterial metabolism and most of the bacterial proteins liberated as a result of lysis are eliminated from our bacteriophage by the method used in its preparation.

As all of our antigens contained sodium sulphate, it was necessary to show that the presence of this salt in the concentrations used in the injecting fluid did not account for our lack of antibody response. Living B. typhosus and sheep cells were suspended in normal salt solution and injected into the ear vein of rabbits; bacteriophage was injected directly in the same manner. Eight rabbits each received injections with the same antigen; 2 of these received an injection of 14% sodium sulphate in the vein of the opposite ear; 2 received injections with a 10%, 2 with a 5% and 2 with a 1.5% solution of sodium sulphate in the same manner. The remaining 2 rabbits of each series were used as controls; 24 rabbits were used in the whole experiment; 10 injections, with increasing amounts of antigen, were given at 2 to 3 day intervals, and antibodies examined 8 days after the last injection. Table 3 shows that the 14% sodium sulphate did not influence the anti-

[3] Arnold: Jour. Lab. & Clin. Med., 1923, 8, p. 720.

[4] Kolle-Wassermann: Handb. d. path. Mikroorg., 1912, 1, p. 735.

body response of the rabbits. The lower concentrations of sodium sulphate did not in any way interfere with antibody formation. We feel justified in concluding that the filtrate antigens used by us did not inhibit antibody production. The fact that there were no demonstrable bacterial antibodies was due to the absence in the filtrates of antigenically active bacterial proteins detectable by the agglutination reaction.

We next tried to determine whether it was possible to use a proteolytic enzyme as a means of splitting the bacterial proteins to a nonantigenic stage and leaving the active bacteriophagic substance undamaged. The influence of pancreatic proteolytic enzymes on the bacteriophage phenomenon has received the attention of several investigators,[5] most of whom have included that the bacteriophage in commercial trypsin is a contamination due to a crude process of purification.

TABLE 3

EFFECT OF SODIUM SULPHATE ON THE FORMATION OF ANTIBODIES

Rabbits 1 and 2	Antigens for Immunization			
	Typhoid Bacilli: Agglutination Titer	Typhoid Bacteriophage: Agglutination Titer	Typhoid Bacteriophage: Antilytic* Titer	Sheep Blood Cells: Hemolytic Titer
Antigen and 14% sodium sulphate....	1:20,480 1:40,960	1:2560 1:10,240	0.005 c c. 0.0025	1:10,000 1:4,000
Antigen suspended in salt solution...	1:10,240 1:20,480	1:5120 1:10,240	0.005 0.001	1:6000 1:7000

* Titer determined according to the method described in previous paper (footnote 2).

The lytic and tryptic activity do not in any way run parallel. The two substances seem to be entirely different. We only mention this now to show that trypsin and bacteriophagic substance can exist together without the former destroying the activity of the phage.

One per cent. trypsin (Pfansteil) was added to bacteriophage, this was incubated for 24 hours, filtered and again trypsinized in the same manner. This was repeated 5 times. The resulting fluid did not give a precipitate on the addition of antibacterial serum against the typhoid bacillus used in the propagation of the bacteriophage. This material was then used as an antigen for rabbit injections. The technic was the same as before. The antiserum did not contain bacterial antibodies,

[5] Borchardt: Klin. Wchnschr., 1923, 2, p. 791. Pico: Compt. rend. Soc. de biol., 1922, 86, p. 1106. Cruz: Ibid., 1924, 90, p. 694. Keller: Ztschr. f. Hyg. u. Infektionskr., 1924, 103, p. 177.

but the bacteriophagic antibodies were present. We then determined the shortest period of time of incubation and treatment necessary to render the bacterial proteins nonantigenic. This was found to be 48 hours' incubation of a 1% trypsinized bacteriophage, filtered through paper and then passed through a Berkefeld candle. Such a trypsinized bacteriophage does not produce agglutinins against the corresponding bacteria, but produces antibacteriophagic neutralizing bodies, 0.001 to 0.0025 c c. of such antiserum containing a unit dose. The filtration through paper is necessary before the material can be passed through a Berkefeld filter; both processes remove some trypsin; the antiserum contains a trace of antitryptic activity.

In a previous paper,[2] we concluded that the only antibodies formed as a result of the injection of bacteriophage into an animal were neutralizing antibacteriophagic substances comparable to the antitoxins or antilysins of other antigenic substances. In the antiserum obtained by the injection of our purified bacteriophage there were no agglutinins, precipitins or complement-fixing bodies against the bacteria or bacterial proteins of the homologous strain. The titer of the bacteriophagic antibodies was high. When this purified bacteriophage was used as an antigen, complement fixation was not obtained in any instance with the antiserum prepared by injecting the usual bacteriophage or as a result of the injection of the purified bacteriophage. Even when the bacterial antiserum of the homologous strain is used with the purified bacteriophage as antigen, there are no complement-fixing bodies present. We have used the usual or stock bacteriophage, which contains bacterial proteins, as an antigen and the antiserum obtained from the injection of our purified bacteriophage, and in this case there was no complement fixation. In all of this work we wish to emphasize the importance of careful and accurate titration of the antigen and the serum.[6] The only antibodies produced by the injection of bacteriophage are antibacteriophagic in nature. These antibodies neutralize the lytic activity of the bacteriophage.

CONCLUSIONS

It was not possible to absorb completely the dissolved antigenic bacterial proteins from bacteriophage with the homologous bacterial antiserum.

A filtrate free from antigenic bacterial proteins but containing a strong lytic substance could be prepared from a bacteriophage in the

[6] Weiss and Arnold: Jour. Infect. Dis., 1924, 35, p. 23.

following manner: (1) precipitating with sodium sulphate in 14% concentration; the addition of antibacterial or normal serum hastens the reaction; (2) digesting bacteriophage with trypsin for 48 hours. Antibacteriophagic serum free from bacterial protein antibodies has been obtained by these methods. The only antibodies produced by bacteriophage are neutralizing bodies or antilysins. There are no complement-fixing antibodies present in antibacteriophage serum.

RÔLE OF THE NONGRANULAR BLOOD LEUKOCYTES IN THE FORMATION OF THE TUBERCLE

ONE PLATE

ALEXANDER A. MAXIMOW

From the Department of Anatomy, University of Chicago

In the early stages of the development of our knowledge of the histogenesis of the tuberculous lesions, an important or even exclusive rôle in the formation of the epithelioid cells was attributed by many writers to white blood corpuscles. Koch, as well as Cornil, believed the leukocytes to be the originators of the epithelioid cells of the tubercle, and the French school of Metchnikoff, represented especially by Yersin [1] and Borrel,[2] gave to this idea the real basis of facts. Injecting tubercle bacilli into the venous system of rabbits, they observed the first development of tubercles in the lumen of blood vessels, in the liver, in the lung and in the kidney. The bacilli were first partly phagocytized by the polymorphonuclear leukocytes, but after 2 days the latter began to degenerate, and after 5 days no trace of them could be found. The mononuclear leukocytes, gradually assembling intravascularly around the proliferating bacilli, on the contrary, hypertrophied and became transformed into clusters of epithelioid cells, which phagocytized the bacilli and later fused into multinucleated giant cells. Yersin and Borrel gave exact drawings of the described process, and it is hard to understand why their results were so utterly disregarded by subsequent investigators.

Of the more recent writers, the idea of the active participation of the nongranulated white blood corpuscles in the formation of the elements of the tubercle in experimental tuberculosis was advocated by Buday [3] for the kidney, by Wallgren [4] for the liver, and by Homen [5] for the peripheral nerve trunks. Besides, mention can be made of the work of Orth [6] and Speroni,[7] who claimed that in acute and chronic tuberculous meningitis the exudate cells partly originate from emigrated lymphocytes.

Received for publication, July 10, 1925.

This work was aided by a grant from the Fenger Memorial Association.

1 Ann. Inst. Pasteur, 1888, 2, p. 245.
2 Ibid., 1893, 7, p. 593.
3 Virchows Arch. f. path. Anat., 1906, 186, p. 145.
4 Arb. a. d. path. Inst. d. Univ. Helsingfors, 1911, 3, p. 139.
5 Ibid., 1911, 3.
6 Deutsch. med. Wchnschr., 1906, 32, p. 92.
7 Arb. a. d. path. Inst. Berlin, 1906, p. 160.

The prevailing opinion concerning the histogenesis of the tubercle, however, is in strict accordance with the theory originally expressed by Baumgarten [8] that the epithelioid and giant cells develop exclusively from local fixed elements of the connective tissue.

The special question of the origin and histogenesis of the epithelioid and giant cells of the tubercle cannot be separated from the general question of the development of the mononuclear ameboid phagocytic exudate cells appearing in any type of inflammation—aseptic or purulent—in the tissue surrounding the lesion. These cells, the macrophages of Metchnikoff, which I called polyblasts because of their varying structural aspect, correspond histogenetically to the epithelioid cells of the tubercle. The tuberculous epithelioid cells are merely a variety of the polyblasts, and we know that epithelioid cells, i. e., large phagocytic elements with abundant protoplasm and spherical or polyhedral cell bodies, may be found in various other conditions. The tuberculous giant cells which are known to arise from the epithelioid cells are also merely a special type of the common foreign body giant cells.

The study of the histogenesis of inflammatory lesions led me [9] to the conclusion that for the origin of the polyblasts of aseptic or purulent inflammation and of the epithelioid cells of the tubercle, neither the exclusive histogenous nor the exclusive hematogenous explanation could be adopted. The polyblasts and the epithelioid cells have a double origin. They arise partly from the local resting wandering cells of the connective tissue (clasmatocytes, histiocytes), through rounding off and mobilization. The common endothelium of the blood vessels does not play any rôle in their formation. A part of the polyblasts, however, are nongranulated white blood corpuscles, lymphocytes and monocytes, which emigrate out of the blood vessels or which may be present in the tissue previously. After emigration into the tissue, they undergo rapid hypertrophy and join the local histiocytes in their progressive development into large, ameboid, phagocytic cells, the polyblasts.

The method of tissue cultures offers unusually favorable opportunities for solving histogenetic problems in the experimental way. In vitro we can analyze the reactions of the local fixed or free elements of the explanted tissue toward different factors without the interference of the surrounding parts of the body or of the organism as a whole and of cells coming into the tissue out of the circulation. The transformations

[8] Verhandl. d. deutsch. path. Gesellsch., 1902, 4, p. 2.

[9] Beitr. z. path. Anat. u. z. allg. Path., 1902, Suppl. 5; 1903, 34, p. 153; 1903, 35, p. 93; 1905, 38, p. 301; Verhandl. d. 16 Internat. Mediz. Congr. zu Budapest, 1909, 41, p. 41.

of the different local elements can be easily followed in the living condition. On the other hand, we may try to explant isolated blood elements and test their reactions in the same way. Finally, we may artificially combine blood elements and local tissue elements in a culture and in this way try to produce the picture of inflammation with its histogenous and hematogenous cell type. By inoculating tissue cultures with pathogenic bacteria, we can study in the living condition the interaction of the cells and the micro-organisms.

In a series of previously published papers, I [10] have described the transformations undergone by various types of connective tissue while cultivated outside the body in different mediums. The reactions of the tissue to the abnormal surroundings in many cases proved almost similar to the inflammatory reaction. Whereas the special or other granular leukocytes present in the explant emigrate into the medium but very soon degenerate, the fibroblasts actively proliferate and form a zone of new tissue surrounding the explant. The endothelium of the blood vessels either forms new capillary sprouts or becomes transformed into fibroblasts. The local histiocytes of the tissue (resting wandering cells in the common loose, areolar reticular cells in the lymphoid tissue, etc.) are mobilized and transform themselves into large ameboid phagocytic cells exactly similar to the polyblasts on the field of inflammation. If vital dyes are present in the culture medium, the mobilized cells store them in granular form in their protoplasm. But the most important fact, perhaps, is that the same transformation into ameboid, phagocytic, colloid-storing polyblasts is shown also by a part of the lymphocytes present in the explants of lymphoid tissue.

Recently, I [11] endeavored to attack the problem of the histogenesis of the tubercle with the aid of the method of tissue culture. By inoculating growing tissue cultures with tubercle bacilli, I succeeded in obtaining in vitro a duplication of the tuberculous process with tubercles and giant cells as well as caseation. The clear-cut pictures which can be observed in the living cultures as well as after fixation and staining enabled me to trace back to their source all the elements playing a rôle in the tuberculous process.

The epithelioid cells of the tubercle in vitro were found to originate chiefly from the local fixed elements of the tissue. Contrary to the opinion expressed by Castrén,[12] the fibroblasts seemed not to play any

[10] Archives russes d'Anat., d'Histol. et d'Embryol., 1916, 1, p. 105; Arch. f. mikrosk. Anat., 1922, 96, p. 424; 1923, 97, p. 283; 1923, 97, p. 314.

[11] Jour. Infect. Dis., 1924, 34, p. 549.

[12] Arb. a. d. path. Inst. d. Univ. Helsingfors, 1923, 3, p. 1.

active rôle. The same is true of the endothelium of the blood vessels, which by many investigators (Foot [13]) is believed to produce the mononuclear inflammatory exudate cells (polyblasts) and the epithelioid cells in tuberculosis. In the lymphoid tissue, the local histiocytes—the reticular cells and the "endothelium" of the sinuses, which is the same—were the first to react by hypertrophy, mitotic division and phagocytosis of the bacilli. They gradually became transformed into typical large epithelioid cells, which arranged themselves in clusters and through fusion gave rise to giant cells of the Langhans type. In the explanted omentum and in the subcutaneous tissue, similar transformations were shown by the resting wandering cells (clasmatocytes), here representing the histiocytes.

The lymphocytes in the explanted lymphoid tissue gave rise partly to plasma cells and partly to large, ameboid phagocytic cells, polyblasts, in the same way as in the cultures of the same tissue not inoculated with tubercle bacilli. Many of the polyblasts of lymphocytic origin joined the epithelioid cells of reticular, histiocytic origin and could not be distinguished from them in the later stages. Occasionally a few tubercle bacilli could be seen engulfed by lymphocytes at a very early stage of this transformation, while they were still small and kept their typical basophilic protoplasm. Pronounced phagocytic activity was displayed, however, only when the lymphocyte lost its characteristic features and acquired the aspect of a polyblast.

The ideal way to study the histogenesis of the reaction of a complex tissue to a pathogenic factor by means of the tissue culture method would be to isolate the various cell types in pure strains and to test them.

In the cultures of lymphoid tissue, in which I first studied tuberculosis in vitro,[11] an experienced eye can easily identify the various cell types on fixed and stained preparations and, partly, even in the living culture. The transformations of the reticular cells—especially the histiocytes—are so clear and correspond so closely to what has been described many times for the lymph nodes in the organism (Joest and Emshoff [14] and others), that this part of the problem seems to be settled in a satisfactory way. On the contrary, the presumed active rôle played by the lymphocytes in the construction of the tubercle in the lymphoid tissue cultures still remains open to criticism. As I have shown, the reticular syncytium developing in vitro, through isolation and proliferation of its elements can produce a multitude of small cells

[13] Jour. Exper. Med., 1920, 32, pp. 513, 539; 1921, 33, p. 271

[14] Virchows Arch. f. path. Anat., 1912, 210, p. 188.

which might be mistaken for lymphocytes, although as a rule they have a rather pale, acidophilic protoplasm and a pale nucleus. It might be objected, therefore, that the lymphocytes, which were observed to become transformed into tuberculous epithelioid cells, were, in fact, merely descendants of the local reticular histiocytes.

In order to settle this question cultures of blood leukocytes were studied.

Awrorow and Timofejewsky,[15] in 1914, were the first to show that it is possible to grow nongranulated leukocytes of the human leukemic blood in the blood plasma of a rabbit and to obtain from them large, hypertrophic, phagocytic polyblasts and even fibroblast-like forms. Carrel and Ebeling [16] obtained the same results in 1922 for the monocytes of chicken blood. Recently, I [17] obtained positive results with the leukocytes of the rabbit. Cultures of blood leukocytes of this animal were prepared with a mixture of blood plasma and extracts of embryonic tissues or of inflamed connective tissue of another adult rabbit. In some sets of experiments lithium carmine was added to the medium as vital stain. The granular leukocytes degenerated during the first two days. The monocytes as well as the lymphocytes, on the contrary, remained alive and hypertrophied, sometimes excessively. After 3 or 4 days they became transformed into large, ameboid, fat-containing, carmine-storing and phagocytizing cells, with distinct attraction spheres exactly similar to the polyblasts on the field of inflammation; they proliferated mitotically. M. Lewis,[18] incubating drops of blood taken from various animals, also saw the monocytes hypertrophy and become transformed into large macrophages, which in some cases, through fusion, gave rise to multinucleated giant cells. A. Fischer [19] recently came to similar conclusions.

In this paper I shall present the results obtained by the inoculation of cultures of mammalian blood leukocytes with tubercle bacilli.

MATERIAL AND METHODS

In order to obtain blood leukocytes of the rabbit, the blood of the carotid of adult normal animals was aseptically drawn into an ice cooled paraffinized centrifuge tube and centrifuged for 10 minutes at high speed. The supernatant plasma was pipetted off, and the superficial

[15] Ibid., 1914, 216, p. 184.
[16] Jour. Exper. Med., 1922, 36, p. 365.
[17] Klin. Wchnschr., 1925, 4, p. 1486.
[18] Am. Jour. Pathol., 1925, 1, p. 91.
[19] Compt. rend. Soc. de biol., 1925, 92, p. 109.

white layer lying above the red mass of erythrocytes was coagulated at room temperature by dropping on its surface some drops of freshly prepared embryonic extract. After from 15 to 20 minutes, the coagulated white layer was taken out of the tube, slightly washed in a Ringer dish and then cut into small fragments in a few drops of Ringer's solution on the surface of a sterile slide. The technic for the explantation of these fragments was the same as that I [11, 20] have described on several other occasions. As nutritive medium I used a mixture of diluted blood plasma taken from another young rabbit and embryonic extract in most cases originating from rabbit embryos from 13 to 16 days old. Plasma stained with lithium carmine was used in some cases. Immediately after the clotting of the plasma drop containing the explanted fragment of the white blood layer, the edge of the fragment was inoculated with tubercle bacilli in the same way that I [11] described in a previous paper. A strain of tubercle bacilli of the human type grown for a considerable time on glycerol agar was used.

The inoculated leukocyte cultures were kept growing for varying periods of time, which in the present series of experiments did not exceed 7 days. After every second day they were transplanted into fresh medium. They were observed in the living condition, and, after fixation in Zenker-formol and embedding in celloidin, they were cut in serial sections and stained according to the technic previously described.

It may be mentioned that on serial sections of the white superficial blood film fixed with Zenker-formol and stained with hematoxylin-eosin-azure, the bulk of the explanted mass proves to consist of large quantities of well preserved blood platelets appearing as small, slightly elongated bodies, containing a distinct azurophilic, purple stained granulation. Among the platelets, all the types of leukocytes are seen scattered singly or in small loose groups.

TRANSFORMATIONS OF THE LEUKOCYTES AND THE TUBERCLE BACILLI IN VITRO

The tubercle bacilli begin to proliferate immediately after being explanted into the nutritive medium of the tissue culture. As I used a rather heavy emulsion of bacilli for inoculation, there were usually present from the very beginning, not only single bacilli, but also small clumps of them. This is favorable, as the reaction of the leukocytes had

[20] Virchows Arch. f. path. Anat., 1925, 256, p. 813.

to be studied from its earliest stages, and the presence of a sufficient quantity of bacilli was necessary for this purpose.

Immediately after explantation of the fragment of the platelet layer with the white blood corpuscles, the latter begin to migrate into the surrounding nutritive medium. This can be seen in the living condition; all the different types of white blood corpuscles can easily be identified in the zone surrounding the explant. The transformations in the interior of the latter, on the contrary, remain invisible in the living culture and have to be studied on fixed and stained sections.

The special granular (pseudoeosinophilic) leukocytes display the highest activity in migration. After 24 hours they are seen to scatter over a large area, diminishing in numbers as one proceeds further away from the explant. They are seen to change their form continuously, sometimes being drawn out into a long filament, to accumulate a few fat droplets; otherwise their internal structure, their nucleus and the granules, as seen in fixed preparations, do not show any changes. In the places in which the tubercle bacilli are scattered, the leukocytes sometimes accumulate in larger numbers, and occasional phagocytosis occurs. However, they never engulf large quantities of bacilli.

During the first day in vitro the majority of the special leukocytes appear normal. During the second day they show a rapidly spreading degeneration, and after 48 hours one can hardly find a living special leukocyte in the culture. They are all transformed into small bodies with dark staining, pycnotic, nuclear remains and a vesicular cell body without any trace of the specific granulation (figs. 1 and 2, *a*). In later stages the dead leukocytes gradually disintegrate to granular detritus. The bacilli, which were engulfed by the cells, thus are set free and continue to proliferate. In the clot and in the masses of the platelets the special leukocytes undergo the same degenerative changes as in the surrounding plasma medium.

Thus, the first phenomenon to be observed in vitro closely corresponds to the old findings of Yersin [1] and Borrel.[2] They also saw the polymorphonuclear leukocytes engulf bacilli immediately after the intravenous injection of tubercle bacilli. During the third day (Borrel [2]), they found signs of degeneration of the leukocytes, and after 5 days no trace of the latter could be discovered. The eosinophils degenerate simultaneously with the special leukocytes. The basophils seem sometimes to resist a little longer, but after 3 days they also disappear. No phagocytosis of the bacilli by these cells could be observed.

PLATE 1

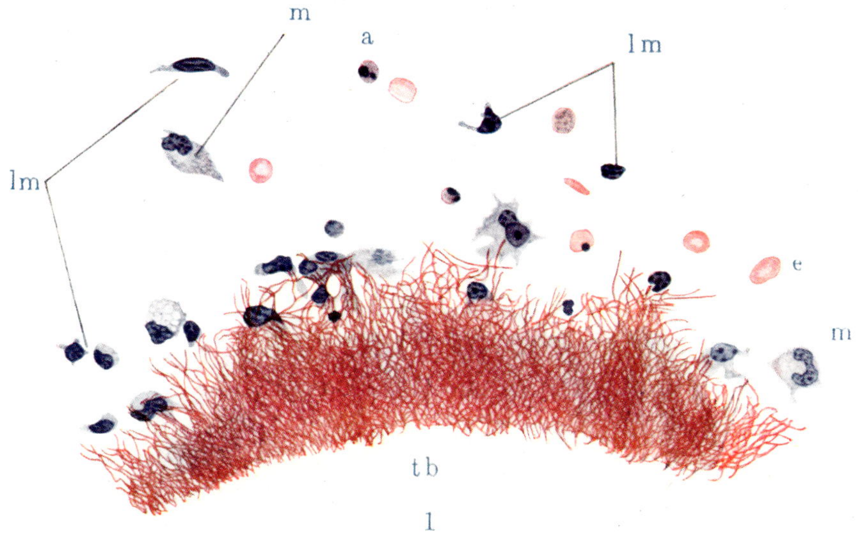

1

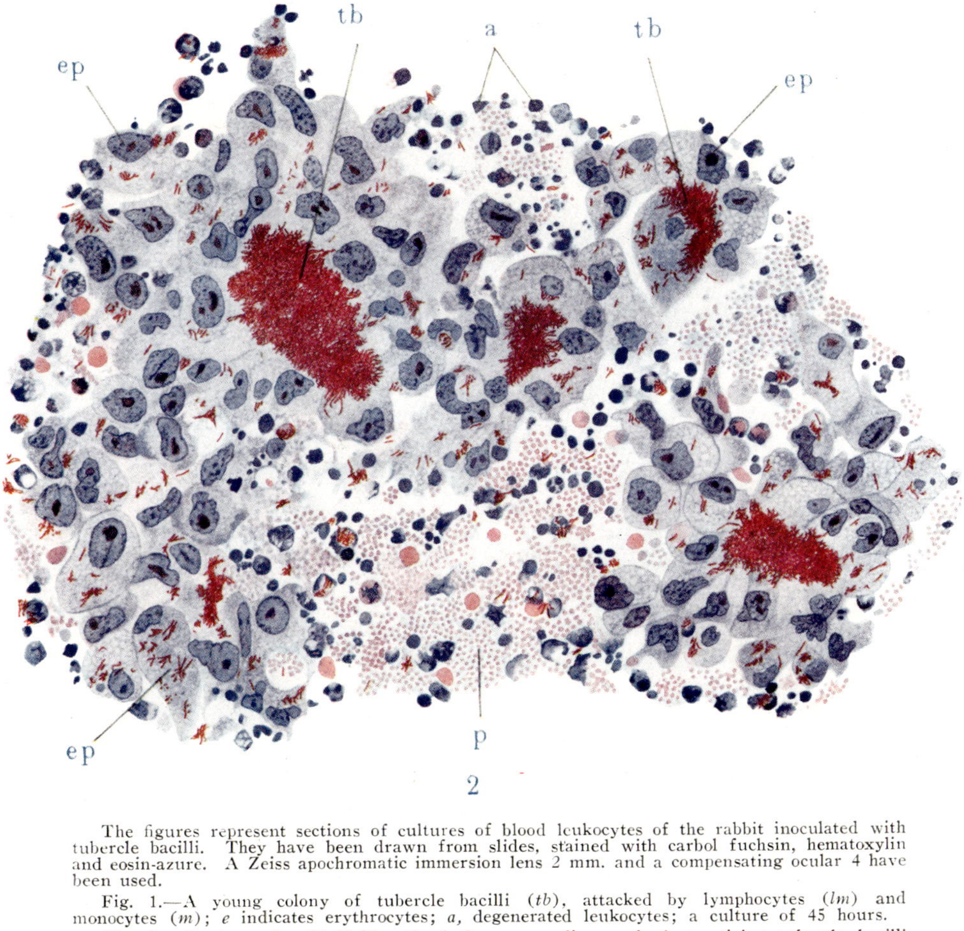

2

The figures represent sections of cultures of blood leukocytes of the rabbit inoculated with tubercle bacilli. They have been drawn from slides, stained with carbol fuchsin, hematoxylin and eosin-azure. A Zeiss apochromatic immersion lens 2 mm. and a compensating ocular 4 have been used.

Fig. 1.—A young colony of tubercle bacilli (*tb*), attacked by lymphocytes (*lm*) and monocytes (*m*); *e* indicates erythrocytes; *a*, degenerated leukocytes; a culture of 45 hours.

Fig. 2.—Clusters of epithelioid cells (*ep*), surrounding and phagocytizing tubercle bacilli (*tb*); *p*, platelets; *a* indicates degenerated leukocytes; culture of 6 days (2 transplantations).

The platelets, as well as the erythrocytes, practically remain unchanged for a long time. They can be easily recognized after 6 days (fig. 2). The platelets form large accumulations mixed with fibrin clots of varying density and texture; later, they slowly swell, become paler and disintegrate.

The nongranulated leukocytes, the monocytes and lymphocytes also migrate into the plasma during the first day of life in vitro. They are, however, slower than the special granular leukocytes. Their transformations can be partly followed in the living cultures. Fixed and stained sections are necessary to obtain an exact idea of these processes.

The monocytes are the more active cells among the agranulocytes. After migration into the plasma they show a great variety of changing forms. Sometimes the whole body is drawn out into two or more pseudopodia. The oval or kidney shaped nucleus may temporarily assume an irregular shape with indentations and constrictions. Although during the second day fat droplets begin to accumulate in their protoplasm, as a rule, the monocytes do not show degeneration in vitro. On the contrary, they at once begin to hypertrophy. This is true for the cells migrating out of the explant into the plasma as well as for the cells remaining in the explant. In the later stages, after 5 or 6 days, the culture usually contains numerous large, sometimes enormous, ameboid elements, attaining a size of 18μ. They are scattered in the plasma medium singly or in small groups, and here display their ameboid character; they are found also in large numbers in the interior of the explanted fragment with its compact masses of blood platelets and dense, homogeneous or granular fibrin clots; here they often are assembled in large, compact masses, and may assume a quiescent, spherical or polyhedral form. Here also they assume the structure of typical epithelioid cells.

The large nucleus of the hypertrophied monocytes usually occupies an excentric position, has an oval, kidney-shaped or irregular form, or develops permanent deep indentations and constrictions. In the largest cells it usually contains a big deeply staining nucleolus. Another characteristic feature of the hypertrophied monocytes is a large acidophilic, homogeneous attraction sphere in the middle of the cell body, containing in its center a distinct group of centrioles. The peripheral layer of the cell body is occupied by fat droplets, giving the protoplasm a foamy appearance after the fat has been dissolved.

The hypertrophic monocytes in the leukocyte cultures are absolutely identical with the polyblasts or macrophages found in the connective tissue during common or purulent inflammation.[9] They display a marked degree of phagocytic activity; they proliferate mitotically—mitotic figures are numerous; this accounts for their surprising increase in number in the later stages; if the medium contains lithium carmine, they store it in granular form in their cytoplasm.

From the beginning of the described transformations of the monocytes, in stages in which they are still small, they are seen moving, together with the lymphocytes, toward the young colonies of the tubercle bacilli with their radiating, filamentous skeins, and to adhere closely to the surface of the latter. A small colony with its radially arranged bacilli on its entire periphery may show loose swarms of monocytes and lymphocytes (fig. 1, *m, lm*). Many of the cells are seen creeping between the skeins far into the interior of the colony. It is self evident that wherever the monocytes on their errands between fibers of fibrin meet isolated tubercle bacilli, they engulf them. This active phagocytosis is found everywhere in the cultures, from the earliest to the latest stages. Some of the larger epithelioid cells may accumulate considerable quantities of bacilli in their protoplasm, but this does not seem to interfere with their vital functions.

In stages of 5 to 6 days the cultures show a remarkable picture (fig. 2). The colonies of bacilli (*tb*) are for the most part surrounded by huge, dense masses of large polyhedral epithelioid cells (*ep*), phagocytizing bacilli and sometimes showing continued mitotic proliferation. In some places beginning fusion of the cells, with the cell outlines disappearing, can be noted. The smallest colonies of bacilli are located in the center of more or less regular spherical clusters of epithelioid cells closely resembling primary tubercles. Often epithelioid cells were seen forming clusters where there were no tubercle bacilli, neither in the interior of the cells nor in their immediate neighborhood.

The described phenomena exactly correspond to the reaction of the mononuclear leukocytes toward the tubercle bacilli in the lumen of the blood vessels caused by the intravenous injection of tubercle bacilli, as observed by Yersin [1] and Borrel [2] and later by Wallgren [4] and Bouday [3] in experimental tuberculosis.

That the monocytes play an important rôle in the formation of the epithelioid and giant cells of the tubercle, as well as in the formation of the polyblasts in common inflammation, seems to be an established fact. There remains the question of the participation of the lymphocytes in this process.

The majority of hematologists, especially the representatives of clinical hematology, believe that the lymphocytes of the circulating blood are mature elements incapable of further development, and that they are sharply separated from the monocytes. The basis of this distinction is given chiefly by the dry smear method and partly by the supravital blood staining method of Pappenheim and Nakanishi, used in various modifications (for instance with Janus green and neutral red by Simpson [21] and Sabin.[22]

It is true that in dry smears of the normal blood of an adult rabbit (as well as in human blood) the small and medium sized lymphocytes in the majority are easily distinguishable from the monocytes. Nevertheless, as Weidenreich [23] has pointed out, one can always find cells which seem to occupy an intermediate position regarding the structure of the nucleus and the width and the basophilia of the protoplasm. In serial celloidin sections of the fixed white platelet leukocyte film on the blood surface after centrifuging, the transitional forms between the lymphocytes and monocytes are prominent. Some large monocytes greatly exceeding the usual size of this cell type also can be found in most of the sections. They probably represent free histiocytes or, according to the new terminology of Ferrata,[24] hemohistioblasts.

The dry smear and the supravital staining method may perhaps be more sensitive than the section method for the discrimination of some minute structural details of the white blood cells; but it is obvious that the picture of a cell as a whole, seen on a well fixed and stained section, when compared with the same cell observed alive in the nearest possible normal surroundings, is far closer to the normal living conditions than the dried, flat, brightly stained cell remnants of a dry smear or the rapidly changing agonal cell structures seen with the supravital method. The latter cannot be considered as reliable in demonstrating such cell organoids as, for instance, the chondriosomes. It is easy to show the presence of these important structures in the clasmatocytes or in the squamous cells of the serosal mesothelium with the ordinary technic, whereas the supravital staining method fails in these cases. I cannot, therefore, attribute to either one of the two methods discussed a decisive importance for the discrimination between the lymphocytes and the monocytes as two independent cell types. The idea of their close

[21] Jour. Med. Res., 1922, 43, p. 77.
[22] Bull. Johns Hopkins Hosp., 1921, 32, p. 314.
[23] Arch. f. mikrosk. Anat., 1909, 73, p. 793.
[24] Haematologica, 1921, 2, p. 242.

interrelationship is confirmed, furthermore, by the study of the development of the cells in the embryo, where, as I [25] have shown, wandering cells of lymphocytic and of histioid or monocytic character freely transform into each other; and by the study of inflammation,[9] in which both monocytes and lymphocytes become transformed into phagocytic polyblasts.

The same is true for the cultures of leukocytes inoculated with tubercle bacilli. In the early stages of the cultures, during the first two days, in the living as well as in fixed condition, the majority of the lymphocytes can easily be differentiated from the monocytes (fig. 1, *lm, m*); in advanced stages, however, after the second day and later, the differences gradually disappear. The lymphocytes also hypertrophy and become transformed into large, phagocytic, epithelioid cells (fig. 2, *ep*).

The monocytes promptly respond to the external stimulus; they are elements predestined to take an active part in the defense reaction of the organism. The lymphocytes are much slower. After having originated in the lymphoid tissue as a result of a long series of mitoses, they remain for a while in a passive, quiescent condition; they are sent into the blood and probably have to circulate there for a certain time before they regain the capacity of displaying their potencies. As Babkina [26] has shown, the lymphocytes in the lymph nodes, in the very place of their development, being young, are far slower in responding to the experimental inflammatory stimulus than the older lymphocytes of the circulating blood.

In our cultures some of the lymphocytes, probably the youngest, which recently have come into the blood from the lymph nodes, degenerate in the course of the first two days; but the others respond to the stimulus much in the same way, as the monocytes. During the first two days, together with the latter, they creep toward the colonies of bacilli and surround and penetrate them. They hypertrophy, and, through a series of transitional stages, with a nucleus, becoming larger, paler and acquiring a kidney shaped form and an eccentric position, and with a protoplasm, steadily growing larger, becoming more ameboid and accumulating a varying quantity of fat droplets, finally join the monocytes in their transformation into epithelioid cells in the same way as they do it in the formation of tubercles in the organism or in cultures of lymphoid tissue inoculated with tubercle bacilli (Maximow [11]). In

[25] Arch. f. mikrosk. Anat., 1909, 73, p. 444.

[26] The changes of the tissues of the blood forming organs in aseptic inflammation, St. Petersburg, Inaug. Dissert., 1910 (in Russian); reviewed in Fol. hämat. Zentralorg., 11, p. 202.

the cell clusters surrounding the bacilli, as described in the foregoing, the epithelioid cells of lymphocytic origin at first can be distinguished by their smaller size and the smaller, darker nucleus. In the later stages, these differences disappear, and a uniform type of epithelioid cell is present.

CONCLUSIONS

The study of in vitro cultures of various tissues and of blood leukocytes inoculated with tubercle bacilli shows that the epithelioid and giant cells of the tuberculous lesions have the same double origin as the polyblasts or mononuclear exudate cells in common or purulent inflammation. They arise partly from local fixed elements—the histiocytes of the respective tissue (resting wandering cells or clasmatocytes, reticular cells, cells of Kupffer, "endothelial" cells of the sinuses in the spleen, etc.), partly from the migrated (or local, if available), nongranulated, i. e., lymphoid white blood corpuscles—both monocytes and lymphocytes. According to the tissue and to the special circumstances of the case, the relative number of the epithelioid cells of histiocytic and of lymphoid descent may vary. If there are no leukocytes available, the epithelioid cells will be of purely local, histiocytic origin. This is, for instance, the case in the cultures of the lung tissue inoculated with tubercle bacilli described by Dr. Lang [27] in a paper from my laboratory published in the present volume of THE JOURNAL OF INFECTIOUS DISEASES. If, on the contrary, as in our cultures of leukocytes, or, for instance, in the early stages of tuberculosis, following the intravenous injection of bacilli, as described by Yersin [1] and Borrel,[2] only leukocytes are available near the bacilli, the primary tubercles will consist only of transformed lymphoid cells, lymphocytes and monocytes. No sharp discrimination between monocytes and lymphocytes could be made regarding their rôle in the formation of the tubercle. The monocytes respond more promptly to the stimulus and, being larger and better prepared for the defense reaction, sooner reach the fully developed epithelioid stage. The lymphocytes are slower, but nevertheless they follow in the same way, and sooner or later joint the monocytes in their transformation into epithelioid cells.

[27] Jour. Infect. Dis., 1925, 37, p. 430.

THE REACTION OF LUNG TISSUE TO TUBERCULOUS INFECTION IN VITRO

TWO PLATES

F. J. Lang

From the Department of Anatomy of the University of Chicago

The method of tissue culture furnishes the possibility of a thorough histologic analysis of the tissues in the living condition as well as after fixation and staining. The prospective potencies and the genetic relationships of the cells manifest themselves more distinctly than in the organism. Furthermore, the reciprocal functional influences of the different cell types can easily be studied. Finally, the problem of the reaction of the tissues to micro-organisms can be attacked experimentally. The fact that there is no circulation in vitro facilitates histogenetic investigations, no hematogenous elements interfering with the clarity of the histologic picture.

Recently I published a paper on the transformations of adult lung tissue in vitro.[1] It sheds new light on the structure of the lung tissue, especially the so-called respiratory epithelium of the alveoli, and elucidates the nature and the origin of the alveolar phagocytes or the so-called "dust cells." The alveolar phagocytes appearing in the cultures of the lung and corresponding to the large exudate cells as found in inflammatory conditions proved to be morphologically and functionally identical with histiocytic connective tissue elements. They belong to the same category of ameboid, phagocytic and dye-storing cells, widely spread all over the organism, as the macrophages of Metchnikoff[2] playing such an important rôle in the defense reactions, as the polyblasts of Maximow[3] on the field of inflammation or as a mobilized reticular cells in cultures of lymphoid tissue (Maximow).[4] This point of view is different from the opinion usually expressed in the literature of the subject that the alveolar phagocytes (dust cells) originate mainly from the so-called "granular," nucleated epithelial cells on the wall of the alveoli. Our experiments have shown, on the contrary, that these

Received for publication, July 10, 1925.

This work was aided by a grant from the Fenger Memorial Association.

[1] Arch. f. experiment. Zellforschung, in press.
[2] L'immunité dans lès maladies infectieuses, 1901.
[3] Beitr. z. path. Anat. u. z. allg. Path., 1902, 5, suppl.
[4] Arch. f. mikr. Anat., 1922, 97, p. 494.

"granular" epithelial cells, although partly arranged after the fashion of epithelium, in reality are not epithelial elements. They are connective tissue cells belonging to the so-called reticulo-endothelial or histiocytic system and provided with embryonic potencies of development. These "septal cells," as we call them, are mobilized under the influence of various normal and abnormal stimulations and appear then as "alveolar phagocytes," as "dust cells" or "exudate cells." We were unable to find any "respiratory epithelium" on the wall of the alveoli, except the well known non-nucleated plates, the limits of which can easily be made visible through the use of silver nitrate.

Maximow [5] recently has studied the reaction of the lymphoid tissue of the omentum and of the common loose connective tissue to tuberculous infection in vitro. This method enabled him to obtain definite results concerning the histogenesis of the tubercle, a problem which—together with the questions of the histogenesis of inflammation in general and of the origin of the mononuclear exudate cells in particular—has been extensively discussed in the literature.

The most active elements in the cultures of lymphoid tissue, inoculated with tubercle bacilli, according to Maximow,[5] are the reticular cells. They mobilize, hypertrophy, divide mitotically and become transformed into large, polyblastic, epithelioid cells that phagocytize bacilli. Local cluster-like accumulations of such cells with subsequent formation of giant cells through fusion closely resemble primary tubercles. The lymphocytes, according to Maximow, also play an active rôle; they hypertrophy and become transformed into large, polyblastic elements, which are identical with the epithelioid cells of reticular origin; they also phagocytize bacilli and take part in the formation of giant cells. In the later stages of his experiments, Maximow succeeded in obtaining typical caseation in vitro. He obtained similar results with the explanted omentum and the common loose connective tissue; in these cases the local histiocytes responded to the stimulus and gave rise to phagocytic epithelioid and giant cells and to tubercles.

The common endothelium of the blood vessels as well as the fibroblasts apparently do not play an active rôle in the construction of the tubercle and the giant cells.

Thus, an exact duplication of the tuberculous process in vitro was obtained and the development of the various phenomena could be easily followed in all their details.

[5] Jour. Infect. Dis., 1924, 34, p. 549.

Timofejewsky and Benewolenskaja,[6] whose work was done without any knowledge of the experiments of Maximow,[5] have confirmed all the principal results of this investigator.

The tuberculous process in the human lung manifests itself either by the appearance of large phagocytic epithelioid exudate cells, which fill the alveoli and phagocytize bacilli, or by the formation of tubercles. In both cases the cellular elements are probably of the same origin.

That the epithelioid cells of the ordinary tubercle originate from the local histiocytes of the involved tissue (resting wandering cells, clasmatocytes, reticular cells, etc.) seems to be an established fact (Aschoff,[7] Maximow [5]). According to Maximow, however, as we have seen, emigrated or local monocytes and lymphocytes seem also to play an important rôle. Regarding the histogenesis of the tuberculous exudate cells filling the cavity of the alveoli in the lung in cases of exudative reaction, no definite information can be found in the literature. Whereas some investigators (Orth,[8] Calmette [9]) trace them back to cells, migrating out of the blood vessels, other authors claim that they originate from fixed cells—the resting wandering cells of the connective tissue or the histiocytes (Kiyono [10]). The method of vital staining, which clearly points out the histiocytes in other parts, in the lungs gives poor results; this may be due to the impossibility of the dye reaching the histiocytes in the lung in sufficient concentration. Foot [11] believes that the exudate cells in the lung are descendants of the endothelium of the capillaries. The majority of the authors, however, (v. Buhl,[12] Rindfleisch,[13] Baumgarten,[14] Marchand,[15] Wiethold [16]), consider them as proliferating, desquamated epithelial cells of the alveoli. The latest paper of Timofejewsky and Benewolenskaja [6] also support this standpoint.

However, the theory of the epithelial origin of the cells of tuberculous exudate in the lung does not seem probable. The cells in question are known to behave and to look exactly like histiocytes. We shall see that the same can be observed in tissue cultures.

In view of the unsettled condition of our knowledge of the histogenesis of the tuberculous lesions of the lungs and especially of the

[6] Virchows Arch. f. path. Anat., 1925, 255, p. 613.
[7] Ergeb. d. Inn. Med. u. Kinderh., 1924, 26, p. 1.
[8] Virchows Festschrift 1891 and Deutsch. med. Wchnschr., 1906, No. 3.
[9] L'infection bacillaire et la tuberculose, Paris, 1922.
[10] Verhandl. d. Japan. path. Gesellsch., 1918, 8, p. 1.
[11] Jour. Exper. Med., 1921, 32, pp. 513 and 533.
[12] Lungenentzündung, Tuberkulose u. Schwindsucht, 1872.
[13] Von Ziemssen: Handbuch d. spec. Path. u. Therap., 1874-1883, 5, p. 2.
[14] Ueber Tuberkel. u. Tuberkulose, 1885.
[15] Verhandl. d. Deutsch. Path. Gesellsch., 1913, p. 64.
[16] Frankf. Ztschr. f. Path., 1922, 26, p. 341.

origin of the cells of the tuberculous exudate, at the suggestion and under the direction of Professor Alexander Maximow I undertook a series of experiments concerning the reaction of the tissue of the lung to tuberculous infection in vitro.

MATERIAL AND METHODS

For explantation I used small fragments of lung tissue from normal adult or young rabbits. They were taken from the peripheral part of the organ, but denuded of their pleural membrane. The method of tissue culture was the usual one, as described by Maximow[17] in his previous papers. Blood plasma from 2 to 3 months old rabbits was used as nutritive medium; it was diluted with Ringer's solution and water in the proportion of 3 (plasma) : 1.5 (Ringer's solution) : 0.75 (water) and mixed with an equal volume of freshly prepared tissue extract from 13 to 15 day old rabbit embryos. In some cases bone marrow extract from an adult (usually pregnant) rabbit was used instead. The tubercle bacilli were inoculated either simultaneously with the explantation of the tissue or they were added to the latter at the first subcultivation. The strain of tubercle bacilli I used was obtained through the courtesy of Dr. E. Long of the Department of Pathology of the University of Chicago; it was of the human type and grown for a long time on glycerol-agar. In some series of cultures sterile lithium carmine solution was added to the medium. Every third or fourth day the cultures were washed in Ringer's solution and provided with fresh medium. There was great inconvenience in many cases through the liquefaction of the fibrin by the bronchial epithelium; the cells, accumulating outside the explant in the plasma and freely floating after the liquefaction of the latter, were mostly washed off in the Ringer's bath. The same difficulty was encountered when the liquefied cultures had to be fixed. In order to avoid the loss of the free cells it proved useful to cover the culture immediately before fixation with some fresh egg albumin. The fixing fluid coagulates the albumin, and the cells are kept in their place. The oldest cultures of the present set of experiments were 21 days old.

The cultures were always carefully watched in the living condition. This, however, is not sufficient for the elucidation of the histogenetic relationships of the cells and of their reaction toward the bacilli. Fixed and stained serial sections are necessary. They were prepared from cultures, fixed with Zenker v-formol and embedded in celloidin accord-

[17] Arch. f. Mikr. Anat., 1922, 96, p. 494; 1923, 97, pp. 283 and 314.

ing to the technic advised by Maximow.[18] The sections were always made parallel to the surface. For staining carbol-fuchsin of Ziehl-Neelsen, with subsequent hematoxylin-eosin-azure (Maximow [19]) counterstain was used. When lithium carmine was used as vital stain, a part of the slides were stained in Delafield's hematoxylin alone.

OBSERVATION IN LIVING CONDITION

The first 48 hours of life in vitro are characterized—in the same way as in lung cultures without tubercle bacilli—by an abundant emigration of various ameboid cells out of the explant into the surrounding nutritive medium. These cells are partly small lymphocytes; the majority, however, are large, ameboid, carmine-storing, septal cells, which rapidly invade the plasma.

After two or three days, the first colonies of tubercle bacilli become visible in the medium surrounding the explant or on its surface. The bacilli developing in the interior of the explant cannot, of course, be seen in the living culture. The aspect of the colonies is typical—they represent spherical, yellowish-gray bodies consisting of a dense feltwork of fine filaments; on the surface of the spheres the twisted, wavy skeins of bacilli are clearly seen radiating into the surrounding medium. They grow rapidly, and after 6 or 7 days they form large continuous masses, sometimes completely concealing the cells between them or even the explant itself. In the latest stages the colonies can be easily distinguished with the naked eye as gray spots.

The small wandering cells of lymphocytic character are seen to increase in size during the fourth, fifth and sixth day. At the same time the cells of the larger type are seen to divide, to accumulate carmine and to gather in looser or denser crowds near the colonies of bacilli. Large clusters of round, ameboid cells, containing coal particles and carmine inclusions, arise on the surface of the explant, around and in the masses of bacilli. It is, of course, difficult to make out the details of the processes in these clusters; at any rate the cell bodies are seen to acquire, through the excessive phagocytosis of tubercle bacilli, a peculiar, opaque yellow-gray aspect. The processes in the interior of the explant remain invisible.

If bronchial epithelium is present in the explanted fragment, it does not grow into the plasma in sheets or membranes, as other epithelial organs usually do in similar conditions. It merely glides over the free

[18] Virchows Arch. f. path. Anat., 1925, 256.
[19] Ztschr. f, wiss. Mikr., 1909, 26.

surface of the explant itself and covers it partially or completely. In the living condition this epithelium on the surface appears as a thinner or thicker, highly refringent, brilliant sheet. In some cases it shows distinctly high columnar cells, provided with cilia on their free surface; the regular, vigorous beating of the cilia could be observed until the latest stages. In the interior of the explant small islands of brilliant epithelium or cysts with a lumen filled with liquid occasionally could be distinguished.

In all cases in which sufficient quantities of epithelium are present on the surface of the explant, the fibrin of the plasma clot undergoes liquefaction. This is known to be of common occurence in cases in which epithelium is cultivated in vitro. In the liquefied areas the cell clusters mentioned above and the colonies of tubercle bacilli are scattered. After each subcultivation many of them are lost. If the whole surface of the explanted tissue fragment is covered with epithelium, the whole explant may float freely in the liquefied medium.

In comparison with lung cultures without tubercle bacilli may be mentioned the rare occurrence of spindle-shaped fibroblasts radially invading the plasma clot in the spaces between the colonies of bacilli.

In the latest stages observed (15 to 21 days) the whole culture was completely overgrown by immense masses of bacilli. In only a few places could clear spaces be seen between them, containing large, round cells, full of phagocytized bacilli and a few transparent spindle-shaped fibroblasts; where the free surface of the explant was visible, it still showed an intact layer of epithelium with a continuous layer or small groups of beating cilia.

FIXED AND STAINED PREPARATIONS

The first 48 hours in the fixed and stained material do not reveal any substantial difference from what is observed in noninoculated cultures of lung tissue. A larger or smaller central area of the explant usually shows necrosis; the larger the explant, the larger the area. Among the necrotic masses, however, some single living cells occasionally can be found. The endothelium of the blood capillaries proves especially resistant.

The afore mentioned transformations of the epithelium on the surface and in the interior of the explant can easily be followed in all their details; but the most striking changes, as in the noninoculated cultures, concern the dust cells and the septal cells. The dust cells, which were previously present in the alveoli in a free condition, rapidly hypertrophy. The dust cells, located in the partitions between the alveoli, become free and also get into the cavity of the latter. Here they hypertrophy, show abundant mitotic figures and migrate to the periphery; on their way to the nutritive medium they are seen storing gradually increasing quantities of carmine. The septal cells attached to the surface of the alveolar wall or located in the interior of the partitions also show considerable swelling. Their cell bodies bulge far into the lumen of the alveoli and finally, after rounding off completely, they also are transformed into free cells. Increasing in size, proliferating mitotically, phagocytizing coal particles and storing carmine, they migrate into the surrounding nutritive medium and join the dust cells in their further development. In the later stages these phagocytic cells are all uniform; they cannot be differentiated as developing from the dust cells previously present in the tissue or from septal cells mobilized after the explantation.

In comparison with noninoculated lung tissue cultures the proliferation of the fibroblasts is very weak and in only a few places are spindle-shaped cells seen to grow out of the explant (fig. 6).

Beginning with the second or third day, together with the progressing multiplication of the bacilli, distinct differences from noninfected cultures gradually develop. The hypertrophy of the ameboid, alveolar phagocytes, originating from the septal cells, is more pronounced. Excessively large spherical or polyhedral epithelioid cells with large centers appear; they accumulate in various quantities in the interior of the alveoli, on the surface of the explant and outside in the nutritive medium. They continue to proliferate mitotically, to phagocytize carbon particles and to store carmine. The most important phenomenon, however, is that they also continue to engulf tubercle bacilli wherever they can. The active phagocytosis where the cells seem to be attracted by the young colonies of bacilli is, as we have seen, especially manifest in the earlier stages. In the later stages now under consideration the same tendency to arrange themselves in dense clusters and to produce tubercle-like structures, as in the cultures of lymphoid tissue described by Maximow,[5] is being displayed (fig. 1). It may be noted that in the center of such cell clusters often no colonies of bacilli can be found; the clustering thus appears to be the general effect of the medium, which has been changed by the presence of tubercle bacilli.

In the interior of the explant the same large ameboid phagocytic cells can be seen everywhere. Here, however, they are found, as a rule, in smaller quantities, scattered singly or in small groups, sometimes in the midst of extensive necrotic masses. Some of them may also attain an exceptional size and contain giant nuclei (fig. 8); this is usually found in the cases in which the bacilli were introduced into the tissue of the explant itself and where, accordingly, small colonies of bacilli are seen scattered in the tissue. Such giant epithelioid cells sometimes contain large numbers of bacilli arranged in convoluted skeins—an evidence of their continuing intracellular multiplication (fig. 8, A, B). On the other hand, the picture occasionally demonstrates an intracellular digestion and destruction of bacilli, as seen by Maximow and Timofejewski and Benewolenskaja in their experiments. In such cases a peculiar yellowish pigment accumulates in the protoplasm of the phagocytes (figs. 1 and 3).

Typical giant cells of the Langhans type could not be found; occasionally, however, exceptionally large epithelioid cells could be located, containing from 8 to 10 nuclei.

In the lung tissue in vitro no such typical tubercle formation with giant cells of the Langhans type takes place as described by Maximow for the lymphoid tissue and the omentum in vitro. The picture in lung cultures reminds one more of the conditions in cultures of loose subcutaneous tissue inoculated with tubercle bacilli. Perhaps this might be associated with the absence of lymphoid elements. When tubercles develop in the lung tissue of the organism, unlimited quantities of hematogenous lymphocytes are available.

Of other important phenomena especially prominent in the older stages (beginning with the eighth day), the following can be noted. The cavities of the alveoli collapse and the partitions show a peculiar diffuse swelling and homogeneity of the intercellular substance.

The unmobilized septal cells, which did not transform themselves into phagocytic, ameboid, epithelioid histiocytes, give rise after from 8 to 10 days to a peculiar loose tissue; it looks like embryonic mesenchyme and consists of small, stellate or spindle-shaped cells, connected with each other by means of their processes and keeping the characteristic nucleus of a septal cell (fig. 2). The spaces between these cells are filled with the swollen intercellular substance, mixed to a larger or smaller extent with homogeneous or finely granular detritus originating from necrotic and disintegrated cells. In many places large areas of this pale, finely granular detritus are seen; they resemble caseous masses. Colonies of bacilli (fig. 5) and occasionally large phagocytes that are still alive are scattered in them (fig. 3). It is remarkable that in these later stages often colonies of bacilli, directly surrounded by living cells in the interior of the explant, do not seem to provoke any reaction on the part of the latter. This might be due to the even concentration of the products of metabolism and the toxins of the bacilli throughout the whole culture; under such circumstances naturally, a local reaction, different from the general reaction in the whole culture, could not possibly be expected to develop.

Besides the phenomena of the more productive type of reaction just described, the explanted lung tissue in some of the cultures may show to a larger or smaller extent pictures of an exudative reaction—of caseous pneumonia. The lumina of the well preserved alveoli are filled with numerous large, spherical exudate cells storing carmine and tubercle bacilli (fig. 7). These elements develop in the same way as the phagocytes in the foci of productive reaction and as the dust cells—they originate from the septal cells (fig. 7). In some cases small giant cells are seen in the cavities of the alveoli. Finally, these exudate cells also disintegrate to a granular detritus, filling the alveoli and mixed with bacilli. Such microscopic pictures remind one closely of the phenomena found in human tuberculosis of the lung, and in virginal or sensitized conditions of the organism, respectively.

If, as is usually the case, the explant contains a bronchus, the bronchial epithelium, sometimes accompanied by small cartilaginous islands, gives rise in the interior of the explant to small irregular, cystlike or angular cavities (fig. 3); the epithelial cells may keep their columnar shape and the cilia. Compact angular or irregularly branched epithelial islands with large, polymorphous cells scattered among necrotic masses, mesenchymal areas, epithelioid cells and colonies of bacilli, are also of common occurrence. At the same time, as a rule, a larger or smaller part of the surface of the explant—in the same way as in cultures without tubercle bacilli—is covered by a layer of squamous or cuboidal epithelium (fig. 5); in places in which the epithelial cells keep their high columnar form, they usually also present vigorously beating cilia.

There is another peculiar transformation characteristic of the epithelium in the presence of tubercle bacilli—its protoplasm often shows a high grade of vacuolization. Large and small irregular vacuoles (fig. 4) distend the cell body and may push the nucleus to the periphery and flatten it; this refers not only to the surface epithelium, but also to the epithelial cells in the interior of the explant.

Large masses of caseous necrotic substance sometimes can be seen covered by a living and active epithelial layer (fig. 5). It not only does not show any signs of degeneration or necrosis, but its cells show mitotic divisions and the cilia are beating up to the latest stages observed. In the protoplasm of such epithelial cells tubercle bacilli may be found (fig. 3); they sometimes proliferate in the interior of an epithelial cell and finally overcrowd and distend its cell body (fig. 6).

The colonies of bacilli located under the epithelium sometimes can break through the thin epithelial sheet and grow into the outside medium (fig. 5).

Where no epithelium is seen on the surface of the explant, more or less necrotic, caseous masses or living mesenchyme-like tissue is seen to represent the outer surface. Whereas, as mentioned above, in the noninfected cultures often an exuberant proliferation of fibroblasts can be seen, the lung cultures, inoculated with tubercle bacilli rarely show at their margins spindle-shaped fibroblasts, radially invading the medium (fig. 6). This is in accordance with the results of Timofejewsky and Benewolenskaja. Nevertheless, in some cultures the explant may surround itself partly with a loose network of fibroblasts; between them histiocytes, phagocytizing bacilli and small free colonies of the latter can be seen (fig. 6). In the protoplasm of the fibroblasts one may also occasionally find a passively engulfed bacillus (fig. 6). A transformation of fibroblasts into histiocytes or into epithelioid cells could not be observed.

The endothelium of the respiratory capillaries did not show reactive phenomena. As long as it remains alive, its dark, sometimes worm-shaped nuclei can be easily distinguished from other cells, and especially from the different phagocytic wandering cells (fig. 7). In the later stages they degenerate; this seems to occur sooner than in aseptic cultures. At any rate, they never were seen to transform themselves into epithelioid cells.

In the latest stages observed (from 15 to 21 days) the explant was practically always rounded off and showed in its interior extensive caseation. In some places the necrotic masses contained islands of mesenchyme-like tissue or of epithelium, large epithelioid, vacuolated phagocytes and small colonies of bacilli (fig. 3). The surface of the explant still kept an uninterrupted sheet of high, columnar or squamous ciliated cells (fig. 5). The surrounding fibrin was usually liquefied, and large colonies of bacilli were floating in it. In some places large and small phagocytic cells were also present, but their quantity in most cases was restricted because the losses inflicted by the bath in Ringer's solution could not be replaced by a sufficient proliferation.

The bronchial cartilage, present in many cultures, may remain unaltered for a long time. In many cases, however, it underwent the same changes as those observed by the author in noninoculated cultures of the lung tissue and by Chlopin,[20] Maximow [21] and Fischer [22] in cultures of other tissues. The basophilic intercellular substance is being dissolved and its fibrillae may become manifest; the most common phenomenon, however, is the lacunar resorption of the cartilage by the septal cells. The cartilaginous cells swell, store carmine and eventually can be set free as large elements, which scatter among the proliferating septal cells and cannot be distinguished from the latter.

CONCLUSIONS

In cultures of lung tissue inoculated with tubercle bacilli, both tissue cells and bacilli can be kept alive for a long time in a state of a peculiar symbiosis (21 days). Like the phenomena observed in human phthisis, the tissue shows, in response to the infection with tubercle bacilli, either a productive (fig. 2) or an exudative reaction. This reaction is connected exclusively with cellular elements of the interstitial connective tissue of the parenchyma of the lung. This tissue contains, the hematogenous cells of the circulating blood being ruled out in cultures, two cell types: (1) the endothelium of the capillaries, and (2) the elements which I have described as "septal cells" (fig. 7), which are identical with the "granular" or "vacuolated" nucleated cells of the authors and are usually supposed to belong to the "respiratory epithelium." The endothelium of the capillaries, contrary to Foot,[11] who believed the epithelioid cells of the lung tubercle and the large exudate cells of the exudative phthisis originated from capillary endothelium, does not play any rôle (fig. 7). The epithelium is of no importance either, as the alveolar wall, according to my previous investigations,[1] is not provided with any special "respiratory" epithelial layer, except the non-nucleated plates.

The septal cells are the real active elements. Together with the cells which were activated previously (dust cells or alveolar phagocytes) and correspond to the mobilized histiocytes in other parts of the body, for instance in the omentum, they are mobilized and furnish the new

[20] Arch. f. Mikr. Anat., 1922, 96, p. 435.
[21] Contributions to Embryology, Carnegie Inst., 1925, 16, p. 47.
[22] Journal of Exper. Med., 1922, 36.

free phagocytic and ameboid cells, engulfing the bacilli and transforming themselves into large epithelioid cells.

The epithelioid cells either accumulate in the alveoli in the form of large exudate cells (fig. 7, exudative reaction) or they become arranged in tubercle-like clusters (fig. 1); in some cases a peculiar diffuse mesenchyme-like transformation of the interstitial tissue takes place (fig. 2). The two latter phenomena may be looked on as the expression of a productive reaction.

I could not find in cultures of lung tissue the typical giant cells seen by Maximow in cultures of lymphoid tissue with tubercle bacilli. Nevertheless, it is certain that in tuberculosis of the lungs the same elements must play the leading rôle as in tuberculosis of the lung in vitro. In the organism, of course, the hematogenous cells also take an active part in the process. We know that they emigrate in all inflammatory processes and become transformed into polyblasts, and, in tubercle formation, furnish a part of the epithelioid cells.

The bronchial epithelium in many cases covers a part of or the whole free surface of the explant (fig. 5); despite the proximity of large masses of tubercle bacilli and of widespread caseation of the underlying tissue, it may remain alive for a long time, and its cilia were seen beating in the latest stages observed. In the interior of the explant it forms cysts or solid islands, embedded in mesenchyme-like tissue or in necrotic masses (fig. 3).

As in the experiments of Maximow with inoculated cultures of lymphoid and subcutaneous tissue and omentum, and in the experiments of Timofejewsky and Benewolenskaja, the tubercle bacilli in the tissue cultures were found to influence the elements of the explanted tissue through their soluble products of metabolism. This influence may manifest itself locally as well as diffusely; to this action may be attributed the extensive mesenchyme-like tissue formation, especially in later stages, in which the toxins must be present everywhere in the culture in a uniform concentration (fig. 2).

In the cultures of lymphoid tissue with tubercle bacilli the fibroblasts and the endothelium of the blood vessels assume an embryonic character. In the cultures of the lung the same is true for the septal cells of the interstitial connective tissue. They must be endowed with unspent embryonic potencies and represent cells of a primitive, undifferentiated nature. They might be compared with the syncytial cellular reticulum of the lymphoid tissue or with the reticulo-endothelial, histiocytic elements of the organism in general. Under the influence of the stimulus originating in the tubercle bacilli, the septal cells which have not been used in the formation of wandering phagocytic elements (histiocytes, epithelioid cells) become transformed into a peculiar tissue, resembling embryonic mesenchyme. Under the conditions prevailing in vitro, they usually do not give rise to fibroblasts. In the organism, however, they might play a decisive rôle in the healing of the tuberculous lesions, in the substitution of the histiocytic reaction by the fibroblastic reaction (Aschoff [7]), as a source of the fibroblasts, forming the scar tissue.

EXPLANATION OF PLATES 1 AND 2

All figures represent sections of cultures of lung tissue, inoculated with tubercle bacilli, stained with carbol v-fuchsin-hematoxylin-eosin-azure. They have been drawn with a camera lucida of Abbe, a Spencer achromatic immersion lens, 4 mm., and a compensating ocular 6.

Epc indicates epithelioid cells originating from the septal cells and forming clusters; they contain particles of coal, tubercle bacilli and a peculiar greenish-yellow pigment, representing remnants of intracellularly digested bacilli; *Sc'* and *Sc''*, phagocytes of the same kind, but single; *Sc,* septal cells, partly located in the partitions between the alveoli, partly bulging into the lumen of the latter; *MSc,* mitosis of a mobilized septal cell; *MEpc,* late stage of a similar mitosis, daughter cells contain bacilli; *Exc,* large exudate cells of septal origin, containing bacilli; *Ctc,* young stellate connective tissue cells; *Fbl,* fibroblasts, partly with bacilli; *MFbl,* mitosis of fibroblast; *Enc,* nucleus of an endothelial cell; *Epcy,* epithelial cyst; *d,* remnants of degenerated cells.

Plate 1

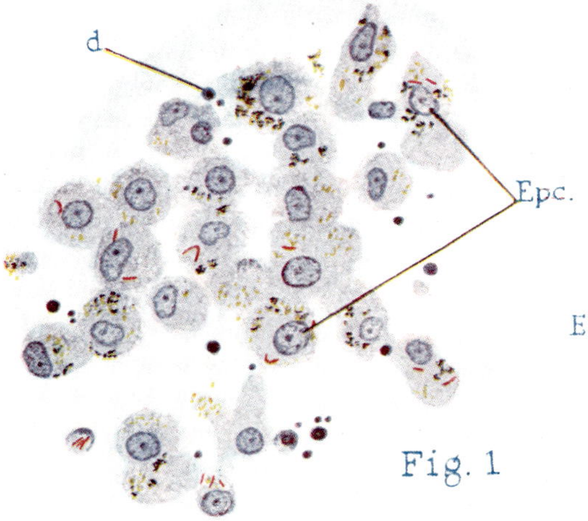

Fig. 1

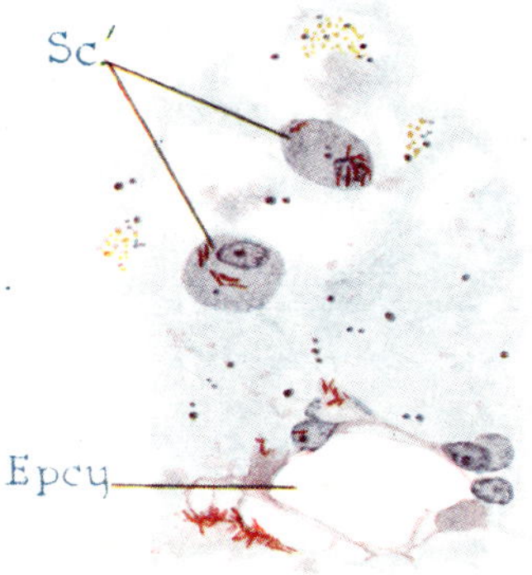

Fig. 3

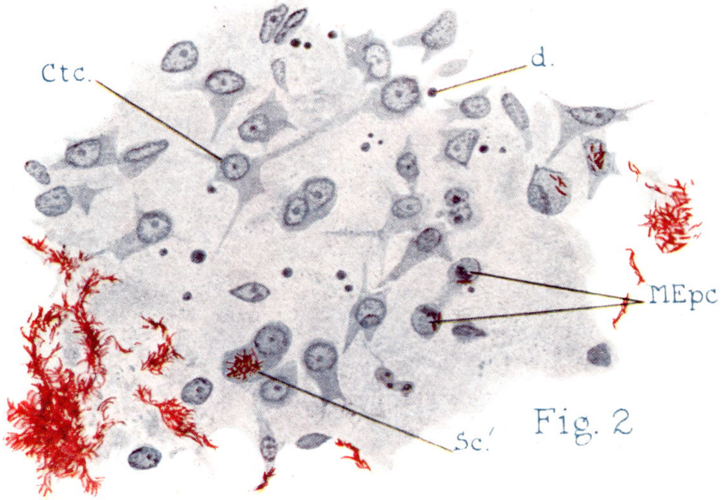

Fig. 2

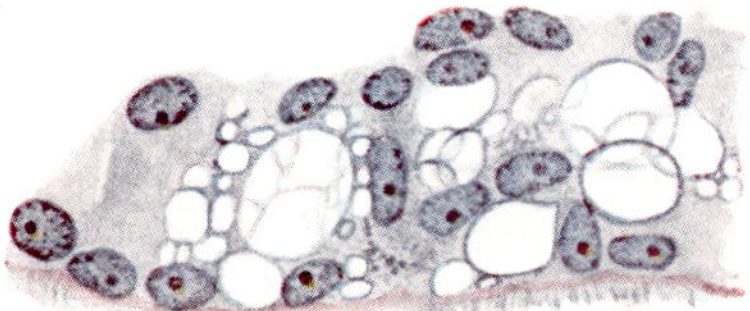

Fig. 4

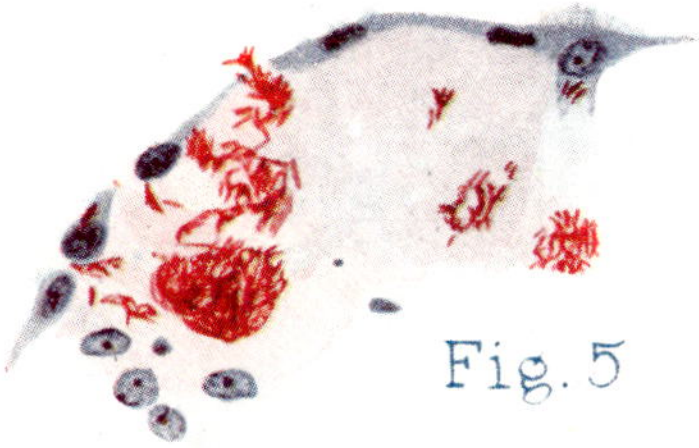

Fig. 5

Fig. 1.—Clustering of epithelioid septal cells to tubercle-like formations; the cells partly contain coal, partly tubercle bacilli and yellowish pigment; culture of 6 days (1 transplantation).

Fig. 2.—Mesenchyme-like transformation of interstitial connective tissue near colonies of tubercle bacilli; culture of 9 days (2 transplantations).

Fig. 3.—Two phagocytic septal cells, with bacilli; the caseous detritus contains yellow pigment, originating from bacilli, destroyed through intracellular digestion; *Epcy,* epithelial cyst, showing bacilli in degenerating epithelium; culture of 12 days (3 transplantations).

Fig. 4.—Vacuolization of the ciliated bronchial epithelium. Culture of 7 days (2 transplantations).

Fig. 5.—Skeins of tubercle bacilli break through a squamous, partly ciliated, epithelial sheet covering the surface of the explant; subepithelial tissue necrotic; culture of 12 days (3 transplantations).

Plate 2

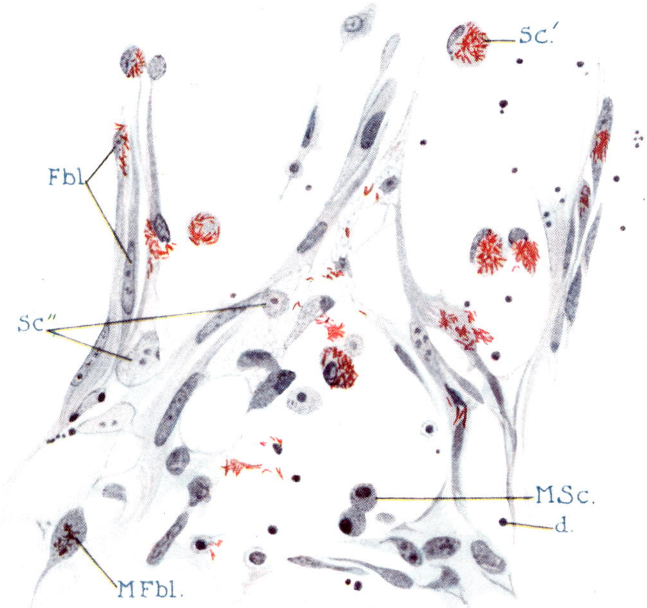

Fig. 6

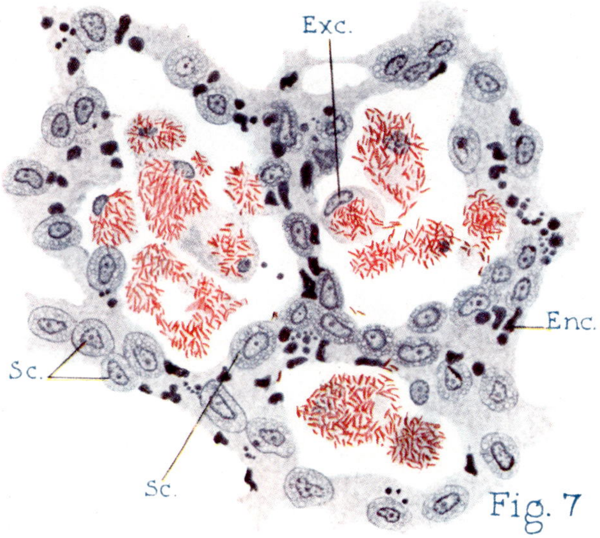

Fig. 7

Fig. 8

Fig. 6.—Fibroblasts growing out from the edge of the explant, partly containing bacilli; between them ameboid phagocytes of septal origin with fat droplets and bacilli; culture of 6 days (1 transplantation).

Fig. 7.—Picture similar to caseous pneumonia with large exudate cells containing bacilli in the lumen of the alveoli; excessive mobilization of septal cells, partly projecting into the lumen; the endothelium of the capillaries distinctly differs from them by its dark nuclei; culture of 6 days (1 transplantation).

Fig. 8.—*A* indicates proliferation of tubercle bacilli, forming convoluted skeins, in the protoplasm of an ameboid epithelioid cell; culture of 9 days (2 transplantations); *B*, multinucleated epithelioid giant cell with bacilli and coal; culture of 7 days (2 transplantations); *C*, giant cell with two nuclei, coal particles and bacilli; culture of 12 days (3 transplantations); *D*, large epithelioid cell with crystaloid inclusions; culture of 9 days (2 transplantations).

EFFECTS OF DIPHTHERIA TOXIN ON THE MYOCARDIUM OF GUINEA-PIGS

Carl W. Appelbach

From the Pathological Laboratory of the Presbyterian Hospital of Chicago

The myocardial changes and the clinical signs of disturbance of the cardiovascular system associated with diphtheria have been the source of much investigation and speculation during the last fifty years. The clinical signs are described with considerable uniformity in most textbooks. The interpretation of the cause of the cardiovascular disturbances, however, has passed through epochs in which paralysis of the vasomotor system, endocarditis, retrogressive changes of the suprarenal glands and myocarditis each has been suggested as the dominant process. Myocardial changes are now accepted by most investigators as the principal cause for the cardiovascular signs and symptoms. Two recent exhaustive reviews [1] completely outline the development of knowledge regarding the cardiac disease in diphtheria, and reference is made to them for the literature on the subject.

Certain fundamental principles are now generally accepted. Some patients with diphtheria die with symptoms of cardiovascular disturbance represented by the signs of myocardial insufficiency and changes in the conduction system. After death from diphtheria, the myocardium in approximately 33% of the cases shows changes that are severe in comparison with those usually found in the myocardium after death from other infectious diseases. The changes in the myocardium are of two types, namely, degenerative (cloudy swelling, fatty changes and necrosis) and inflammatory (infiltration of leukocytes in the interstitial tissue, proliferation of connective tissue and muscle cells and degenerative changes).

Jaffé [1] examined the hearts of 113 guinea-pigs, 75 of which had received injections of diphtheria toxin and 38 inoculated with the diphtheria bacillus. He believes that the changes of the myocardium in experimental diphtheria in guinea-pigs do not differ essentially from those in human diphtheria. Retrogressive changes occur early. Cloudy swelling was found in practically every instance. Fatty degeneration

Received for publication, June 18, 1925.

[1] Jaffé, Rudolf: Pathologisch-anatomische Untersuchungen über das Diphtherieherz, Arb. a. d. Inst. f. Exper. Therapie u. d. Georg Speyer-Hause z. Frankfurt-am-Main, 1920. Warthin, A. S.: The Myocardial Lesions of Diphtheria, Jour. Infect. Dis., 1924, 35, p. 32.

was present in about two thirds of the animals. Myolysis and other severe changes of the muscle were uncommon and never present in a severe degree. True waxy degeneration did not occur. Interstitial changes appeared later than the degenerative changes, and Jaffé believes that they are dependent on the parenchymatous change.

Eppinger [2] described a condition in the myocardium associated with diphtheria that he thought was characteristic and named it myolysis. He claims that the myocardial fibers undergo liquefaction, represented microscopically by breaks in the fibers between which the material is "crumbly"; also that there are large homogenous spaces in some bundles. Jaffé believes that the term myolysis is a fitting one for some of the severer changes described in diphtheria and reported under a variety of names in the past; in other words, such changes are indications of the death of the myocardial fibers, and myolysis is a new name for the stages of necrosis that occur in diphtheria.

Warthin [1] studied 16 hearts from patients that died from diphtheria and in whom definite cardiovascular disturbances existed during life. The essential lesion of the heart, according to Warthin, is a toxic parenchymatous hyaline degeneration or necrosis, associated frequently with fatty (degenerative) infiltration and less frequently with cloudy swelling or simple necrosis, the latter lesions most probably being due to nutritional conditions. Following these lesions there is, if the patient survives, a reparative inflammatory process (myocarditis) accompanied by muscle regeneration.

The severer myocardial changes (necrosis) are in the background in Jaffé's interpretation, and the lesser changes (cloudy swelling and fatty changes) are the common ones. In Warthin's cases the severer changes predominate. Although Jaffé believes that the changes in the animal are of the same kind as those in the human infection, there seems to be a great gap in the severity of the lesions in Jaffé's guinea-pigs and in those described by Warthin in man. A partial explanation for this discrepancy, as well as for many of the disputes of the past about the nature of the myocardial changes in diphtheria, is the lack of control of the changes in the human heart. The presence of other infections in diphtheria in many cases surely may confuse some of the results observed. Bronchopneumonia was present in 9 of Warthin's 16 cases; streptococcus infection of a tracheotomy wound in another, congenital syphilis in another, erysipelas in one and purulent infection of the genito-urinary tract with purulent bronchopneumonia in still another.

[2] See Jaffé, Footnote 1.

This paper is concerned with the changes in guinea-pigs inoculated with diphtheria toxin and especially with the nature of the changes of the myocardium. In order to become acquainted with the changes that may be produced in guinea-pigs by injection of diphtheria toxin, a study was made of 18 animals, in which injection was made subcutaneously, and of 9 in which injection was made into the heart muscle. The hearts of 5 supposedly normal guinea-pigs were examined as controls.

Guinea-pigs weighing between 170 and 312 gm. were used. The diphtheria toxin was obtained from the United Standards Products Company and the L+ dose was about 0.297 c c. Dilutions of the toxin were made according to the tables for diluting toxins described in the Hygienic Laboratory Bulletin 21, 1905. The smallest dose used was 0.5 c c. of a 1 : 1,000 dilution, the largest 0.8 c c. of a 1 : 40 dilution. Injections were made in the subcutaneous tissues of the abdomen in 13, and in the subcutaneous tissues of the chest in 5 animals. The attempt was made to kill and examine the guinea-pigs shortly before it was thought they would die. Such animals were lightly anesthetized with ether and formalin-zenker's fixing solution injected through the femoral or iliac arteries under 20 to 50 mm. of pressure. Complete fixing of the tissues was not obtained in all instances by this method alone; and pieces were removed immediately from the muscles of the thigh and leg, liver and kidneys, and fixed for 24 hours. The whole heart, after opening the ventricles, was also fixed. Some animals died during the night, but necropsies and fixing of tissues were made never later than 6 hours after death.

Frozen sections, stained with sudan 3 and sudan 3 with Delafield's hematoxylin, were made of all tissues. The mercury was removed previous to staining by using Gram's iodine solution and sodium thiosulphite (2% sol.). Paraffin sections were stained with hematoxylin and eosin, phosphotungstic acid hematoxylin, Van Gieson and Giemsa stains.

The following conclusions are drawn from the examination of the microscopic preparations:

1. Fatty changes are the outstanding alteration. The fat is most commonly found in patches with a maximum diameter from 2 to 10 times the width of a muscle bundle, the patches usually in the outer and inner thirds of the walls of the ventricles. The fat is in the form of round minute granules in the muscle bundles, most numerous near the nuclei; in one fiber, there might be from 20 to 50 granules. When the changes

are extensive, about three-fourths of the sections are red. 2. Cloudy swelling is found in most of the hearts. 3. Definite evidence of necrosis is found only in 5 of the 18 guinea-pigs. 4. Interstitial change, in the sense that it is used in the description of diphtheritic myocarditis, was observed in 2 instances. Jaffé describes as the first stage, "Hyperemia and engorgement of small vessels with leucocytes, which collect along the walls." The latter changes are sometimes observed in the sections to a slight degree, but it is also found in one of the controls.

An attempt was made to inoculate the myocardium with diphtheria toxin in 9 guinea-pigs. In 5 instances, necropsy revealed a local lesion resembling a puncture wound. In 4, evidence that the myocardium had been pierced could not be found. In microscopic sections of portions near but outside of the puncture wounds, the changes were like those found with subcutaneous inoculations, but of a more severe degree. In 2 of the 5 hearts, about one-fourth of the sections was made up of patches of myocardium with varying degrees of necrosis, the patches involving 3 or 4 contiguous muscle bundles. Also, hemorrhage was found frequently, together with a minimal amount of infiltration of leukocytes.

The interpretation of the condition in the interstitial tissues in guinea-pig hearts is difficult, because even in the hearts of normal guinea-pigs there is often an abundance of young fibrous tissue about the blood vessels and in the subendocardial tissues.

Frozen sections stained with sudan 3 were made of the skeletal muscle, liver and kidneys. The difference in the amount of fat in these various tissues is striking. The degree of fatty change in the myocardium is preponderant, and it is a marked feature of the alterations in guinea-pigs injected with diphtheria toxin. The explanation for this preponderance of fatty change of the myocardium in comparison with skeletal muscle, liver and kidney is not clear; apparently the myocardium is most directly affected by the diphtheria toxin.

SUMMARY

The changes in the myocardium of guinea-pigs after injection of diphtheria toxin subcutaneously resemble the changes described in the myocardium in human diphtheria, but they are in general not as extensive.

By direct injection of the myocardium, extensive degenerative and inflammatory changes can be produced in the guinea-pig equal in

TABLE 1

THE CHANGES FOUND IN 18 GUINEA-PIGS FOLLOWING SUBCUTANEOUS INJECTION OF DIPHTHERIA TOXIN

No. of Animal, Weight, Gm.	Dose	Hours Between Injection and Death	Location of Injection (Subcutaneous)	Fatty Changes	Cloudy Swelling	Necrosis	Infiltration of Leukocytes	Fatty Changes		
								Skeletal, Mm.	Liver	Kidney
1 278	1 c c. 1/450	24 K*	Abd.	None	+	0	0	0	+	0
2 208	1 c c. 1/300	28 D*	Chest	Slight	?	0	0	+	0	+
3 228	1.5 c c. 1/300	29 D	Abd.	Abundant	+	0	0	+	0	+
4 230	0.8 c c. 1/40	23 K	Abd.	Abundant	+	Shrunken nuclei; striations indistinct	0	+	0	0
5 192	0.6 c c. 1/40	36 to 48 D	Chest	Abundant	+	?	Slight hemorrhage; infiltration of leukocytes	?	0	+
6 170	0.2 c c. 1/40	48 D	Chest	Extensive	+	Striations indistinct; hyaline change in patches	0	+	+	+
7 190	0.5 c c. 1/100	42 K	Abd.	Slight	0	0	0	0	0	0
8 270	2 c c. 1/1,000	48 K	Abd.	Moderate	0	0	0	0	0	0
9 242	1 c c. 1/450	48 K	Abd.	Extensive	?	0	0	+	0	+
10 246	1 c c. 1/450	48 K	Abd.	Extensive	0	?	0	—	—	—
11 186	1 c c. 1/450	72 K	Abd.	Slight	0	Striations indistinct in small patches	0	—	—	—
12 250	1 c c. 1/450	70 K	Abd.	Slight	?	0	0	—	—	—
13 282	1 c c. 1/450	71 K	Abd.	....	+	0	0	+	0	0
14 202	1 c c. 1/300	72 D	Chest	Abundant	+	Nuclei swollen and pale; striations indistinct	0	0	0	0
15 210	1 c c. 1/300	72 D	Chest	....	+	Nuclei pale; striations absent in patches	Leukocytes in subendocardial tissues	+	—	—
16 312	1 c c. 1/450	96 K	Abd.	Slight	?	0	0	—	—	—
17 292	1 c c. 1/450	96 K	Abd.	Slight	0	0	0	—	—	—
18 258	1 c c. 1/450	168 K	Abd.	None	0	0	0	—	—	—

* In the tables, K indicates killed; D, died.

TABLE 2

THE CHANGES FOUND IN 9 GUINEA-PIGS FOLLOWING THE INJECTION OF DIPHTHERIA TOXIN IN THE REGION OF THE HEART

No. of Animal, Weight, Gm.	Dose	Time Between Injection and Death	Location of Injection	Fatty Changes of Myocardium	Necrosis and Infiltration of Myocardium
19 328	0.5 c c. 1/100	23 hours D*	Heart	Extensive	Patchy necrosis; extensive hemorrhage between muscle bundles
20 332	0.4 c c. 1/100	48 hours D	Heart	Abundant	Patchy necrosis
21 244	0.3 c c. 1/100	60 hours D	Heart or mediastinum	Extensive	Extensive necrosis; slight infiltration of leukocytes
22 262	0.2 c c. 1/100	75-80 hours D	Heart	Extensive	Striations indistinct; slight hemorrhage
23 214	0.1 c c. 1/100	12 days K	Heart or mediastinum	None	No change
24 246	0.2 c c. 1/400	5 days K	Heart or mediastinum	Moderate	Slight necrosis in small patches
25 244	0.1 c c. 1/400	7 days D	Heart	Moderate	No change
26 252	0.35 c c. 1/400	5 days K	Heart	None	No change
27 288	0.3 c c. 1/400	5 days K	Heart or mediastinum	Slight	No change
28 275	0.4 c c. normal salt solution	4 days K	Heart	None	No change

intensity to those found in human diphtheria. The outstanding changes are retrogressive (cloudy swelling, fatty change and necrosis). Infiltration of leukocytes with degenerative changes occur, but in the myocardium of guinea-pigs degeneration, proliferation and exudation were not commonly observed together in the same regions.

The degenerative changes in the skeletal muscles, liver and kidneys, as represented by the amount of fat that can be stained with sudan 3, are less than those in the myocardium.

THE ISOLATION OF SUBSTANCES WITH IMMUNE PROPERTIES

Arthur Locke and Edwin F. Hirsch

From the Henry Baird Favill Laboratory of St. Luke's Hospital, Chicago

THE FRACTIONATION OF AMBOCEPTOR PROTEIN BY SELECTIVE ADSORPTION

The purest preparation of hemolysin that we have been able to obtain by the porcess of electrodialysis,[1] unassisted by iso-electric fractionation, contains 0.000,002 gm. of protein and some lipin associated with each hemolytic unit. This, a solid, dry preparation, was found to be unimpaired after a year's storage. The present investigation was undertaken with the purpose of preparing a more pure hemolysin by a method of selective adsorption.

The ideal adsorbent for the separation of its specific hemolysin from amboceptor serum is the erythrocyte itself. One c c. of packed sheep cells is capable of adsorbing more than 300,000 units (see section 5) of rabbit antisheep hemolysin, but can adsorb very little of the inert proteins likewise present in the serum.

The bound hemolysin may be recovered in two ways: by desorption, or by destruction of the binding capacity of the erythrocyte. That desorption can occur is demonstrated by the transfer of hemolysin from one cell to another. The combination of 1 unit of sheep cells with 3 units of antisheep hemolysin will sensitize 2 additional units of sheep cells for complement hemolysis. Desorption of hemolysin from erythrocytes may also be occasioned by shifting the P_H of the suspension to either side of the iso-electric point of the cell.[2] The desorption produced in this way is not considerable. It is not always distinguished from the peptization of hemolysin-saturated, disintegrated cell matter which readily occurs when hemolysin-saturated cells are shaken with acid or alkaline solutions.

There have been several reports of the preparation of highly purified solutions of hemolysin by desorption from the hemolysin-

Received for publication, June 30, 1925.

1 Jour. Infect. Dis., 1924, 35, p. 519.

2 Coulter, Calvin B.: Jour. Gen. Physiol., 1921, 3, p. 309.

erythrocyte combination.[3] The usual procedure for their preparation has been somewhat as follows:

Erythrocytes, saturated with an homologous hemolysin, are washed as free from serum as it is possible to wash agglutinated erythrocytes without lacking or disintegrating them. They are then extracted with a slightly acid or alkaline solution of sodium chloride or sucrose. The hemoglobin is removed from the extract by repeated extraction with ether, when the hemoglobin and stroma material are drawn to the ether-water interphase and removed.

We have found that such extracts, when their hemolysin content is at all appreciable, are cloudy with dispersed, disintegrated stroma, and that ether extraction of such a suspension destroys the capacity of the stroma material to bind hemolysin, thus liberating bound hemolysin to the solution (see section 4).

The ether extraction incorporated into these methods for the removal of hemoglobin was in reality responsible for the hemolysin content of the solutions obtained. But the concentration of hemolysin so obtained was small. The preparations of Liebermann and Fennyvessy had some agglutinating power but contained little hemolysin. Preparations of higher hemolysin content have been made by concentrating the extracts in vacuo (Kosaki [3]). These, dialyzed and separated from flocculated material, have been the purest preparations of hemolysin yet secured.

Two of the major difficulties in the practical use of the method outlined, namely, that experienced in washing agglutinated erythrocytes free from serum protein and that involved in ridding the final extracts from hemoglobin, may be eliminated by using fresh amboceptor serum as the source of the hemolysin and permitting the cells to lake under the influence of the native complement. The cell stroma binds, quantitatively, as much hemolysin as the erythrocyte (table 4), and the hemolysin-saturated stroma may be completely centrifugated from suspension and washed with great efficiency and little loss. The third and foremost difficulty, that of the small yield obtained, may be overcome by making the ether extraction on the entire stroma suspension instead of the small portion of it which can be suspended in a weakly acid or alkaline solution. The amended method is as follows:

Fresh sheep blood is defibrinated, centrifugated, and the cell sediment washed 5 times with 0.9% sodium chloride solution. Fifteen c c. of the packed, washed cell sediment are equally divided, between 2 large centrifuge tubes, and to each portion there is added quickly and with vigorous shaking, 40 c c. of perfectly

[3] Liebermann and Fennyvessy: Centralbl. f. Bakteriol., 1908, 47, p. 274. Kosaki, M.: Jour. Immunol., 1918, 3, p. 109. Kosaki's paper gives an excellent survey and discussion of the literature.

clear, fresh rabbit antisheep serum. After two hours, the cells have completely laked and the stroma has flocculated and settled toward the bottom of the tubes. Centrifugation for 45 minutes completes the separation; 90 to 99% of the hemolysin originally present is found to be bound to the stroma sediment. The brilliantly clear, red supernatant liquid is decanted from the sediment and replaced by an equal volume of 0.9% sodium chloride solution. After the stroma is finely suspended in the wash liquor by prolonged shaking, the suspension is allowed to stand for 20 minutes and is then strongly centrifugated for 30 minutes. The washing process is repeated (about 6 times) until the supernatant liquid has no trace of color and gives no trace of foam when shaken. The stroma obtained is perfectly white and has lost little of the originally bound hemolysin, as may be seen from table 1.

The well washed, hemolysin-saturated stroma is extracted with ether 3 times. The volume of the stroma decreases 90% under this treatment. After the removal of the third ether extract, the ether remaining dissolved in the stroma

TABLE 1

THE YIELD OF HEMOLYSIN SATURATED STROMA

	Total Content of Hemolysin	Protein Associated with One Hemolytic Unit
Amboceptor	87,000 units	0.000,04 gm.
Supernatant	6,500	
1st washing	1,250	
2d washing	600	
3d washing	500	
4th washing	350	0.000,004 gm.
5th washing	250	0.000,002 gm.

Loss in supernatant	6,500 units	7.5%
Loss in washings	2,950 units	3.4%

material is removed by centrifugation in a warm centrifuge. The stroma material packs at the bottom of the tube and the salt solution, which made up the cell volume, may be decanted. The residue is washed twice with 0.9% salt solution and once with distilled water. Considerable hemolysin is lost to the salt solution, but protein impurities, due to surface adsorption, are thereby almost completely removed. The hemolysin of the salt extracts may be recovered by electrodialysis and iso-electric flocculation. The washed residue is extracted repeatedly with N/1000 sulphuric acid, the extracts are pooled, flocculated by neutralization, and the suspension centrifugated. The flocculation is quantitative, as hemolysin is almost insoluble in pure water. The precipitated material is extracted with 0.9% salt solution, and solutions of any desired hemolytic content may be obtained by varying the amount by salt solution used. The hemolytic unit of the extract is associated with from 0.000,125 to 0.000,18 mg. of protein. Further electrodialysis and iso-electric fractionation of these extracts has not yet been attempted. The preparations still contain a small amount of cell globulin, but are probably 30% or more pure hemolysin. Their combining power for erythrocytes far exceeds that of ordinary immune serums, indicating that their content of stroma material is very small. The amount of the original hemolysin which is recovered in these preparations is only 30 to 50%, but it may be seen from table 2 that there is considerable hope for improvement in the matter of yield.

THE PROTEIN-CONTAINING CHARACTER OF IMMUNE HEMOLYSIN

The general belief in the protein-containing character of the antibodies is founded on the experimental fact that they may be precipitated with definite protein fractions of the immune serum, and on the theoretical implication that the proteins, alone of the constituents of animal tissue, have the requisite versatility of chemical and spatial configuration to account for the specificity and multiplicity of immunologic reactions.

Opposed to this are the reports of Salkowski [4] that he obtained, in 1896, a diphtheria antitoxin preparation 20% as potent as the antitoxin serum, and containing no trace of protein. Liebermann and Fennyvessy,[3] Kosaki [3] and many others have obtained more or less potent antibody solutions which give no positive chemical test for the presence of protein.

TABLE 2

THE RECOVERY OF HEMOLYSIN FROM ITS COMBINATION WITH STROMA

Hemolysin	Hemolytic Units
Originally bound to the stroma	28,000
In salt supernatant after ether extraction	8,300
In salt washings	1,932
In first acid extraction	14,000
In second acid extraction	4,000
In third acid extraction	650
Total recovery, 97%	

The limiting dilution at which a solution of protein may just be identified by a chemical test is from 2.5 to 10 parts in 10,000. Solutions of purified hemolysin will sensitize one unit (defined in section 5) of erythrocytes to complement hemolysis in dilutions of 1 part in 8,000,000. The protein character of the hemolysin in these preparations would fail to be recognized by many chemical tests unless the concentration of the solutions exceeded 8,000 hemolytic units per c.c. This concentration exceeds, many times, those of the best preparations which have been reported and may explain their failure to be recognized as containing proteins.

The progress of an investigation into the isolation of an immune substance is necessarily guided by analytic data relative to the content of immune activity associated with the quantity of material obtained. The hemolytic system was chosen for these investigations because its immune activity may be quickly and accurately measured. For a like reason, the nitrogen or protein value was chosen as the measure of the content of substance associated with the hemolysin.

[4] Biochem. Ztschr., 1922, 132, p. 84.

Tests must be made frequently in the course of a fractionation, and a test which requires several thousand hemolytic units to be present for positive protein identification is confiscatory and impossible. For this reason, the following tests were devised. They are reliable when solutions consisting almost entirely of protein are used, and are semiquantiative when control comparisons are made. It is customary to run check tests on two progressive dilutions.

The Ammonium Sulphate Test.—Two-tenths c c. of saturated ammonium sulphate, contained in a micro-test-tube, is covered with 0.2 c c. of the test solution. The tube is held against a dark background and illuminated strongly from below, with proper protection for the eyes. When the protein concentration of the sample exceeds 0.035 mg. per c c., a distinct ring may be observed. The protein is a globulin if the contents of the tube remain visibly turbid when shaken.

The Foam Test.—The glassware used must be clean; 0.2 c c. of the test solution is sealed into a micro-test-tube and shaken vigorously. A momentary foam film is produced when the protein concentration of the sample exceeds 0.006 mg. per c c.

The quantitative determinations were made by the method of Main and Locke,[5] which permits 0.03 mg. of protein to be estimated with fair precision. The determinations were checked frequently by the unmodified method of Folin and Denis [6] to insure their validity.

There is no question but that our highly purified preparations of hemolysin contain protein. The protein is coagulated by alcohol and by heat, and is precipitated from solution on half saturation with ammonium sulphate. It is soluble in 0.9% salt solution and in saturated salt solution, but not in distilled water. It dissolves readily in dilute acids and alkalis, does not pass through a semipermeable membrane and is very sensitive to denaturation. It cannot yet be established whether the protein responsible for these reactions is the hemolysin itself; they may be due in part or entirely to red cell protein admittedly present.

A preparation in which the hemolytic unit was associated with but 0.000,2 mg. of protein definitely sensitized guinea-pigs to anaphylactic response toward rabbit serum as is recorded in table 3. No antirabbit precipitin was found in the pig blood serum. No anaphylactic shock was produced by the intracardial injection of sheep stroma or serum. This last observation was not unexpected. It is extremely difficult to sensitize an animal to anapylactic response to stroma by the injection of stroma extracts.[7] The preparation was known to contain some stroma protein by its iso-electric behavior. The results of anaphylaxis

[5] Jour. Biol. Chem., 1925, 64, p. 75.
[6] Ibid., 1916, 26, p. 473.
[7] Hadjopoulos, L. G.: Arch. Int. Med., 1921, 27, p. 441.

experiments, with our more highly purified preparations, have been somewhat uncertain in character. It is not yet possible to conclude that rabbit antisheep hemolysin is a rabbit protein.

The fact that the sensitization of guinea-pigs is produced only feebly, and sometimes not at all, on the injection of more than a thousand units of the highly purified preparations of hemolysin, is interesting from the clinical angle.

TABLE 3

SENSITIZATION EXPERIMENTS WITH PURIFIED HEMOLYSIN PREPARATIONS

Source of the Hemolysin Injected	Sensitization Dose, Intraperitoneal		Mg. of Protein per Hemolytic Unit	Intracardial Shock Dose	Anaphylactic Response
	Hemolytic Units	Mg. Protein			
Control	0	0	0	2 c c. 1:10 normal rabbit serum	None
Fractionated salt solution supernatant from ether extraction of sheep stroma saturated with rabbit amboceptor	3,000	0.65	0.00022	1 c c. 1:10 normal rabbit serum	Marked
	3,000	0.65	0.00022	1 c c. 1:10 normal rabbit serum	Slight
Acid extract of ether extracted, washed sheep stroma, saturated with 75% rabbit amboceptor and 25% normal dog serum	900	0.11	0.00012	1 c c. 1:10 normal dog serum	None
				1.5 c c. 1:10 normal rabbit serum	Very slight
	1,500	0.24	0.00016	1 c c. 1:10 normal rabbit serum	None
Unfractionated salt solution supernatant from ether extraction of sheeep stroma saturated with 83% rabbit amboceptor and 17% normal dog serum	2,000	1.44	0.00072	1 c c. 1:10 normal dog serum	None
				1.5 c c. 1:10 normal rabbit serum	Marked
	2,000	1.44	0.00072	1 c c. 1:10 normal dog serum	None
				1 c c. 1:10 normal rabbit serum	Slight
	2,000	1.44	0.00072	1 c c. 1:10 normal dog serum	None
				1.5 c c. 1:10 normal rabbit serum	Marked

THE ANTIGENIC CONSTITUENT OF ERYTHROCYTE STROMA

Fractionation of the constituents of an organized cell involves the dissolution of chemical unions and the separation of substances extremely soluble or adsorbable in one another. In attempting to ascertain the constituent alone responsible for the antigenic property of a cell, the difficulty is further complicated because the production of antibodies in response to the injection of antigens is not strictly proportional to the amount of antigen introduced, and usually is enormously greater in comparison. Ostromuislenski[8] reports that one unit of toxin

[8] Jour. Russ. Phys. Chem. Soc., 1915, 47, p. 263.

may cause the production, in a horse, of 100,000 units of antitoxin. Thus a trace of impurity representing the real antigen may readily give a spurious, antigenic character to a nonantigenic fraction.

This fact cannot be overemphasized. Thiele and Embleton [9] in 1913 stressed the fact that the lipin fractions of erythrocyte stroma, when properly freed from adventitiously present proteins, have no antigenic activity. Nevertheless, each year sees the publication of new accounts of alleged antigenic activity in lipin fractions,[10] frequently not at all purified, and in other cases, insufficiently purified. We have observed that emulsions of lecithoprotein will remain dispersed in an ether extract containing large amounts of lipin even after long centrifugation. One may, in fact, readily obtain very stable, solid emulsions of this character. This has been previously observed with chloroform extracts and alcoholic extracts.[9, 11]

On the other hand, there is no good evidence that a completely purified stroma protein has been found antigenic. The preparations of Thiele and Embleton were residues from extractions of dried material and undoubtedly contained considerable of the original lipin content of the stroma.[12] The various alkaline extracts of stroma and of ether extracted stroma that have been investigated [13] are not definitely known to be lipin-free. The so-called cell globulin of Bennett and Schmidt [14] contains large quantities of lecithin and cholesterin and has an iso-electric range of approximately P_H 4.8, characteristic of disintegrated stroma, and not of P_H 6.6, the approximate iso-electric point of the stroma globulin. There has been no clear-cut demonstration that any completely purified constituent of the erythrocyte is able to elicit the production of hemolysins in experimental animals.

It seemed best, to us, to attack the problem from the reverse angle. To this end, erythrocytes saturated with homologous hemolysin were investigated for loss of combining power, as evidenced by a liberation of bound hemolysin, after treatment with various extractive agents.

The effect of complement hemolysis on the capacity of erythrocytes to bind hemolysin was determined in the following experiment, the results of which are in table 4. Identical quantities of erythrocytes were treated with fresh and with inactivated amboceptor serum, respec-

[9] Ztschr. f. Immunitätsf., O., 1913, 16, p. 160.
[10] Heterologous antigens are not considered.
[11] Dean, cited by Wells, H. G.: The Chemical Aspects of Immunity, 1925, p. 50.
[12] Suranyi, E.: Berl. klin. Wchnschr., 1912, p. 409.
[13] Balls and Korns: Jour. Immunol., 1918, 3, p. 375.
[14] Jour. Immunol., 1919, 4, p. 29.

tively. The cells saturated with hemolysin from the fresh serum were completely laked.

It may be seen that the removal of the hemoglobin from an erythrocyte does not affect its combining power for hemolysin; nor does it modify its antigenic capacity, for stroma suspensions are very efficient in the production of hemolysin in animals.[7]

The stroma-hemolysin combination is little affected by extraction with 0.9% sodium chloride solution, sucrose solution, or distilled water, even when these are slightly acid or alkaline. Distilled water disintegrates the stroma and shaking causes a small amount of material to become peptized, especially in acid or alkaline solutions. Practically no hemolysin is liberated to the solutions except the small amount which

TABLE 4

THE RELATIVE CAPACITY OF ERYTHROCYTE AND OF ERYTHROCYTE STROMA TO BIND HOMOLOGOUS HEMOLYSIN

Volume of Cells per C c. of Suspension	Concentration of Hemolysin in Units per C c.			Difference in Binding Capacity of Erythrocyte and Stroma
	Originally Present	Unadsorbed by Erythrocytes from Inactivated Serum	Unadsorbed by Stroma from Fresh Serum	
0.002 c c.	1,225	1,100	1,100	0
0.004 c c.	1,225	1,000	1,000	0
0.008 c c.	1,225	825	825	0
0.016 c c.	1,210	600	600	0
0.032 c c.	1,190	400	400	0
0.062 c c.	1,155	225	225	0

is dispersed but still combined to stroma. Stroma which is not saturated with hemolysin is peptized by alkali almost completely. The "alkaline extracts" of stroma have, therefore, been successful antigens.[13] The stroma-hemolysin combination is tremendously affected by ether extraction, as may be seen from a consideration of the following experiment.

Hemolysin 90,000 units, absorbed by 6 c c. of red cell stroma, were extracted 3 times with ether. The ether extraction disintegrates the stroma, reducing its volume to about 1 c c. The residual volume is a salt solution. The ether-stroma emulsion was vigorously centrifugated for 20 minutes after each extraction, before removing the ether layer. The salt solution supernatant contained 7,000 units of hemolysin, a 40,000% increase over the amount that could be extracted by an equal volume of salt solution without accompanying ether extraction.

Iso-electric precipitation of the salt solution after it had been electrodialyzed free from salt and made slightly acid demonstrated, first, that the precipitated material always contains more protein per hemolytic unit than the supernatant solution, and, second, that there are two fractions of protein present. The one precipitates at approximately P_H 7, and carries down with it some hemolysin which may be extracted with 0.9% sodium chloride solution. The second fraction precipitates at approximately P_H 5, and probably is a mixture. Either the first mentioned fraction is a stroma protein which is not antigenic for hemolysin, or, the ether extraction has rendered the antigen-antibody bond so loose that it has become easily dissociable, permitting the one component to be precipitated relatively free from the other. The latter conclusion is borne out by the fact that the concentration of the P_H 7 fraction is largely proportional to the extent to which the stroma material has become dissolved or peptized. It has an affinity for hemolysin because its partial removal improves the combining power of the preparation for added erythrocytes, as may be seen in table 6 of the next section.

The lipin appears to be a real part of the antigen. The hemolysin is synthesized or formed in the tissue as a result of the presence of a foreign aggregate with an iso-electric point of approximately P_H 5. (The influence of the phosphates, etc., of the blood on the iso-electric point of the stroma, in vivo, is not entirely known at this time). It is significant that the iso-electric point of the hemolysin produced is likewise approximately P_H 5. It is known that a shift of the P_H of a suspension of hemolysin-saturated erythrocytes to either side of P_H 5 [15] causes some dissociation to result. It is possible that a similar and greater dissociation would result when the iso-electric point of the stroma aggregate is shifted to P_H 7 by the extraction of the lecithin with its iso-electric point of P_H 2.7. This conclusion was checked by determining the combining power for hemolysin of normal, disintegrated stroma before and after ether extraction. The method of titration is as follows:

Five-tenths c c. of a 5% suspension of washed sheep red cells is added to a consecutive series of dilutions of the stroma material contained in microtest-tubes. The content of each tube is diluted to 1.5 c c., all dilutions being made with 0.9% sodium chloride solution. A mixture of 2 units (see next section) of amboceptor and 2 units of complement in 0.5 c c. is then quickly added to each tube, with shaking, and the whole is incubated for 1 hour at 38 C. The tube in which hemolysis is just complete indicates the amount of the stroma material which is equivalent to one unit of whole red cells. The disintegrated stroma was prepared by the method of Bennett and Schmidt [14] for "cell globulin" as follows:

Freshly bled, defibrinated sheep blood was centrifugated and the cell sediment washed 9 times with 0.9% sodium chloride solution. The cells were laked by the careful addition of 2 volumes of distilled water, and thereupon the unlaked cells and débris were removed by strong centrifugation. After further dilution with 7 volumes of water, the dispersion of disintegrated stroma was flocculated

[15] Coulter, Calvin B.: Jour. Gen. Physiol., 1921, 3, p. 309.

by saturation with a stream of carbon dioxide, under slight pressure, for 2 hours. The flocculation is comparable to the agglutination of red cells suspended in isotonic sugar solution by the spontaneous absorption of carbon dioxide from the air. The flocculated material was collected by centrifugation and washed 5 times with distilled water. The hemoglobin could not be entirely removed. The final preparation is able to combine practically the same amount of hemolysin as the original cell suspension.

A suspension of the disintegrated stroma in 0.9% sodium chloride solution was extracted repeatedly with ether, whereupon the material collected at the interphase as a waxy solid, difficult to redissolve or resuspend. Neither the solid, the supernatant salt solution, nor the either extract were able to bind any appreciable quantity of amboceptor; nor could the fractions be remixed in any way that would bring back the combining power.

It becomes clear that the lack of harmony in the reported results as to the nature of the antigenic constituent of erythrocyte stroma is due not only to the use of incompletely fractionated material, but also to the fact that the antigenic entity seems not to be a simple protein or lipin but a compound lipoprotein.

The results of these experiments do not preclude the possibility that the cell protein itself when freed by the action of serum enzymes from combined lipin may act antigenically with the production of precipitins. These precipitins may possibly be the hemaglutinins while the true cellular antibody is the hemolysin. The increased formation of agglutins late in the period of rapidly developing immunity,[16] when the concentration of lipin-free cell-protein should be greatest, is indeed suggestive. In fact, Frouin [17] has reported that he obtained only agglutinins on injecting ether-extracted erythrocytes into animals. This possibility is being further investigated on account of its bearing on the preparation of an entirely pure hemolysin.

THE HEMOLYSIN-ERYTHROCYTE EQUILIBRIUM

When a specific antigen is added to an homologous immune serum, the antigen combines with the antibodies present until a condition of equilibrium is reached. It is necessary to think of a state of equilibrium because the combination of antigen with antibody is reversible and incomplete.[18]

An equilibrium is best illustrated from the standpoint of a distribution by an example such as the distribution of iodine between chloroform and water which results when the three are shaken together. The relative amounts of iodine dissolved in the chloroform and in the water

[16] Okell, C. C., and Parish, H. J.: Brit. Jour. Exper. Pathol., 1924, 5, p. 355.
[17] Compt. rend. Soc. biol., 1912, 72, p. 154.
[18] Arrhenius, S.: Immuno-Chemistry, 1907.

have been found to be proportional to the relative solubilities of iodine in these two solvents. Mathematically speaking:

$$\frac{\text{The quantity of iodine dissolved in each c c. of chloroform}}{\text{The quantity of iodine dissolved in each c c. of water}} \propto \frac{\text{The solubility of iodine in chloroform}}{\text{The solubility of iodine in water}} = \text{A constant}$$

The equilibrium between antigen and antibody lends itself especially to this treatment, although the mechanism of their combination is unknown. It has been variously postulated to be[18, 19] a chemical reaction, physical solution, and colloidal adsorption. But the law of distribution is equally valid for all types of equilibrium.

The law of distribution was first applied to the hemolysin-erythrocyte equilibrium by Arrhenius. He stated that when erythrocytes are added to an homologous, immune serum, the hemolysins of the serum become redistributed as follows:

$$\frac{\text{The quantity of hemolysin adsorbed by each c c. of added erythrocytes or (A)}}{\text{The } n^{th} \text{ power of the quantity of hemolysin remaining dissolved in each c c. of the immune serum solution or } (H)^n} = \text{A constant, K}$$

This equation has not been found to conform altogether with experimental findings. There are two possible explanations for this failure: first, that the equation does not correctly describe the hemolysin-erythrocyte equilibrium; second, that the experimental findings are obtained with improperly devised systems which do not avoid the presence of other, complicating equilibriums.

The Arrhenius equation does not correctly describe the equilibrium. The possibility was not considered that the equilibrium may be between hemolysin adsorbed by the added erythrocytes and hemolysin adsorbed by some constituent of the immune serum, rather than as indicated, i. e.,

$$\frac{\text{The quantity of hemolysin adsorbed by each c c. of added erythrocytes or (A)}}{\text{The } n^{th} \text{ power of the quantity of hemolysin remaining adsorbed by each c c. of a constituent of the immune serum or } (H')^n} = \text{A constant, K'}$$

For simplicity, (A) is replaced by A/C, and $(H')^n$ by H^n/I^n, where A is the total quantity of adsorbed hemolysin, H the total quantity unadsorbed, C the volume of added cells, and I the total volume of the hypothetical immune serum constitutuent present. Then:

$$\frac{A}{C} = K'.\frac{H^n}{I^n} \quad \ldots\ldots (1)$$

The volume of the immune serum constituent is a definite fraction of the total volume, S, of immune serum present in the suspension, i. e., $I = p.\ S$, and:

$$\frac{A}{C} = K'.\frac{H^n}{p^n S^n} = K''.\frac{H^n}{S^n} \quad \ldots\ldots (2)$$

Every variable is now capable of measurement.

[19] Ehrlich, Paul: Studies in Immunity, 1910. Bordet, Jules: Studies in Immunity, 1909.

In table 5 are presented 3 series of hemolysin-erythrocyte equilibriums. In the first series, *S*, the volume of immune serum present in the c c. of suspension, was kept as near unity as possible, while *C*, the volume of added cells, was varied. Equal volumes of whole, immune, antisheep serum were treated with increasingly larger volumes of sheep erythrocytes. After equilibrium had been established, the suspensions were strongly centrifugated and the hemolysin content *H* of the supernatant liquid determined. The value *A* was obtained by subtracting the determined value *H* from the original hemolysin content of the serum. A slight dilution of the immune serum was not avoided, as some salt solution was introduced with the cells.

In the second series, *C* was kept as nearly constant as possible, and *S* was varied by progressively diluting the serum. Equal quantities of sheep erythrocytes were added to progressive dilutions of immune antisheep serum. After equilibrium had been established, the suspensions were strongly centrifugated, and the hemolysin content *H* of the supernatant solution was determined as before.

The third series is like that of the second except that the progressive dilutions of the immune serum were made with normal serum instead of with 0.9% sodium chloride solution.

The volume determinations and the hemolysin titrations recorded in table 5 have a precision of approximately 90%. The volume of the added cells was determined by calculation from an actual count and cell measurements made on a known dilution.

The hemolytic unit as expressed in these tables is the smallest volume of serum which will hemolyze 0.5 c c. of a 5% sheep erythrocyte suspension in the presence of one unit of complement. The unit of complement, determined by a previous titration, is added to each of a consecutive series of microtesttubes. After the further addition of progressive dilutions of the serum sample, the mixtures are diluted to 1.5 c c., with 0.9% sodium chloride solution, 0.5 c c. of the 5% sheep cell suspension is then added slowly and evenly distributed by shaking; the racks are partially immersed in a water-bath at 38 C., and readings are made at the end of one-half hour and one hour, respectively. The two readings should agree closely if the complement has been satisfactory. If, for instance, the last tube in which hemolysis was more than 90% represented a 1:500 dilution of the serum, the serum is said to contain 500 units; if there is 90% hemolysis in a dilution of 1:2,000, there are 2,000 units present, etc.

The accuracy of the method has been severely criticized by Manwaring.[20] We have concluded after a study of several hundred of these tests that the method is remarkably accurate, especially since the indicating tube contains hemolysin in a concentration of less than 1 part by weight in 16,000,000. The titration must be properly controlled, triplicate tests made, the range of probable values obtained plotted, and that value selected which falls on a smooth curve drawn through the series. Reasonable care must be taken, of course, that all glassware is well seasoned and chemically clean, and that all dilutions are accurately made. When working with high dilutions, precaution must be taken against loss of material in foams.

[20] Jour. Biol. Chem., 1905, 1, p. 213.

The series of values of K'' in table 5, series 1, are plotted in fig. 1 as ordinates against values of n as abscissas. The point of common intersection of the lines represents the value of n for which K'' is constant, and vice versa. It is seen that n equals unity and that K'', as would be anticipated from its derivation, is

TABLE 5

THE INFLUENCE OF SERUM DILUTION ON THE HEMOLYSIN-ERYTHROCYTE EQUILIBRIUM

Volume of Cells per C c. of Suspension -C-	Concentration of Immune Serum Present -S-	Concentration of Hemolysin in Units per C c. of Suspension: Originally Present	Unadsorbed by Erythrocytes -H-	Adsorbed by Erythrocytes -A-	$K'' = \frac{A}{C} \cdot \frac{S^n}{H^n}$: n = ½	n = 1	n = 2
Series 1. Concentration of Immune Serum Constant, Volume of Red Cells Varied							
0	1.00	1,250	.....	...	.....	......	.....
0.001	0.98	1,230	1,150	80	2,340	68 ± 7	0.058
0.002	0.98	1,225	1,100	125	1,880	56 ± 6	0.050
0.004	0.98	1,225	1,000	225	1,740	55 ± 6	0.054
0.008	0.98	1,225	825	400	1,710	59 ± 6	0.071
0.016	0.97	1,210	600	610	1,580	62 ± 6	0.101
0.032	0.95	1,190	400	790	1,200	59 ± 6	0.140
0.062	0.92	1,155	225	930	960	61 ± 6	0.250
0.117	0.87	1,090	120	970	700	60 ± 6	0.437
Average....	....	....	....	....	....	60 ± 6	
Series 2. Concentration of Immune Serum Varied by Dilution with 0.9% NaCl Solution, Volume of Red Cells Constant							
0	1.00	700	.....	...	.....	......	.....
0.020	0.75	525	225	300	870	50 ± 5	0.17
0.020	0.64	455	180	275	850	49 ± 5	0.17
0.020	0.53	350	125	225	840	48 ± 5	0.20
0.020	0.38	270	80	190	650	45 ± 5	0.22
0.020	0.23	160	30	130	580	50 ± 5	0.38
Average....	....	....	....	....	....	48 ± 5	
Series 3. Concentration of Immune Serum Varied by Dilution with Normal Serum, Volume of Red Cells Constant							
0	1.00	475	.....	...	.....	......	.....
0.020	0.75	355	165	190	630	44 ± 4	0.20
0.020	0.64	300	125	175	640	45 ± 5	0.23
0.020	0.53	250	100	150	550	40 ± 4	0.21
0.020	0.38	180	50	130	570	49 ± 5	0.37
0.020	0.23	105	20	85	460	49 ± 5	0.56
Average....	....	....	....	....	....	46 ± 5	

different for each of the serums used in the 3 series, being 60 in the first, 48 in the second and 46 in the third.

It is further seen that normal serum does not contain the hypothetical constituent I, for the dilutions with normal serum in table 5, series 3, gave practically the same equilibrium values as the dilutions with salt solution in series 2.

The value of unity for n permits the simplification of the equation (1) to:

$$\frac{A}{C} = K'.\frac{H}{I}; \text{ or } \frac{A}{H} = K'.\frac{C}{I} \quad \text{.......} (3)$$

which correctly describes a type of compound absorption equilibrium and corresponds with experimental findings within the limits of experimental precision.

We have found within the limits of error of centrifugation and analysis: (1) that suspensions of hemolysin-saturated stroma, when washed free from adhering immune serum, contain all of their hemo-

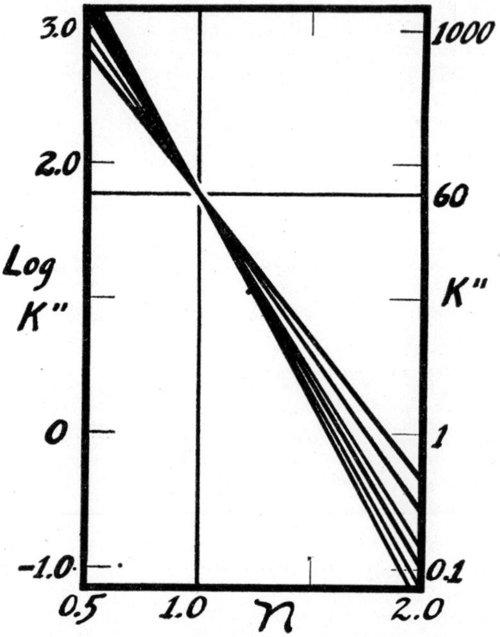

Fig. 1.—The hemolysin-erythrocyte equilibrium. Each plotted line represents the series of values for K" which may be obtained by substituting increasing values for n in the equation: $K'' = \frac{A}{C}.\frac{S^n}{H^n}$, the successive values for A, C, S, and H having been determined experimentally as recorded in table 5.

lysin bound tightly to the erythrocytes; (2) that the hemolysin-erythrocyte equilibrium is correctly described when, and only when, it is regarded as a distribution of hemolysin between two adsorbents—the added cells and a constituent I of the immune serum; and (3) that this constituent is present only in immune serum, being absent from the normal serum. We wish now to present the hypothesis that the constituent *I* is disintegrated erythrocyte material which after injection gradually has become dispersed in the plasma as a consequence of lysis and phagocytosis.

This hypothesis was tested experimentally. Erythrocyte stroma was saturated with homologous hemolysin and washed 6 times with 0.9% sodium chloride solution. The washed material was suspended in salt solution and since less than 3 units of hemolysin were found present in each c c. of the supernatant solution, very little of the serum contituent *I* could have been present. The suspension was extracted with ether as in the preceding section, allowed to stand for some time in the icebox, and then centrifugated strongly. The clear supernatant, containing liberated hemolysin and disintegrated erythrocyte material in almost perfect "solution" was tested for its combining capacity for added erythrocytes (table 6). The mixtures imitate ordinary amboceptor in their combining capacity to an extent which cannot be entirely coincidental.

TABLE 6

THE "COMBINING POWER" OF ARTIFICIAL MIXTURES OF HEMOLYSIN AND STROMA MATERIAL

	Volume of Cells per C c. of Suspension -C-	Concentration of Hemolysin in Units per C c.			$K'' = \frac{A}{H} \cdot \frac{S}{C}$
		Originally Present	Unadsorbed by Erythrocytes -H-	Adsorbed by Erythrocytes -A-	
Fresh amboceptor	0.008	1,225	825	400	60
Salt solution supernatant after ether extraction of hemolysin saturated stroma	0.008	1,000	666	333	65
Fractionated salt solution supernatant after ether extraction of hemolysin saturated stroma	0.008 0.008 0.008	900 1,700 275	450 600 100	450 1,100 175	125 225 220

An identity between the unknown constituent *I* and distintegrated, dispersed antigen demands the important corollary that no hemolysin can be found in the plasma until such distintegration and dispersion occurs. Carrel[21] reports that when artificial cultures of living tissue are injected with goat erythrocytes, phagocytosis of the cells precedes directly the appearance of hemolysin in the plasma.

The source of the antibodies in immune serums becomes, not an overproduction of injured cell receptors as postulated by Ehrlich, but a probably phagocytic destruction of antigen already saturated with antibodies by some preliminary process. The nature of this preliminary process is not known.

SUMMARY

A method has been presented for the preparation of a highly purified hemolysin. Hemolysin is separated from amboceptor serum by

[21] Jour. Exper. Med., 1912, 15, p. 287.

selective adsorption on homologous erythrocytes. It is recovered through a destruction of the combining capacity of the erythrocyte for the bound hemolysin. This is accomplished by means of ether extraction. The procedure outlined permits hemolysin to be obtained in good yield and of a purity such that but 0.000,125 to 0.000,18 mg. of protein are associated with each hemolytic unit.

It is demonstrated that the failure of certain reported preparations of hemolysin to give a positive chemical test for the presence of protein is due to the lack of a sufficient delicacy in the tests employed. Qualitative tests are proposed which, under restricted conditions, permit the detection of protein in concentrations as low as 0.006 to 0.035 mg. per c c.

The stroma-hemolysin combination is loosened and made easily dissociable when the lipins of the stroma are partially removed by ether extraction. This behavior is correlated with the shifting of the iso-electric point of the stroma from P_H 5 to P_H 7, approximately, when the lipins are so removed. It is suggested that while lipin-free stroma protein may be antigenic in the production of hemagglutinin, the antigenic entity in the production of hemolysin is probably the entire lipoprotein complex.

When erythrocytes are added to an homologous immune serum, the hemolysin of the serum becomes redistributed between the added cells and some component of the serum. This component is not present in normal serum. It is probably derived from the disintegration of the erythrocytes used in the immunization. It is suggested that the appearance of antibodies in the blood plasma follows the disintegration, by lysis and phagocytosis, of antigen already saturated with antibody by a primary process.

VIABILITY OF MYCOBACTERIUM TUBERCULOSIS IN A SEMI-ARID ENVIRONMENT

Mary Estill Caldwell

From the Biological Laboratories, University of Arizona, Tucson

It is generally acknowledged that the viability of Mycobacterium tuberculosis in an unfavorable environment is much greater than that of most pathogenic bacteria. Experiments to determine the vitality of this bacillus in sunlight, have been made by means of smears on glass, quartz plates, gelatin films, mica plates and paper (Weinzirl [1]); exposures of cultures (Simmons [2]); smears on linen and woolen cloth (Migneco [3]); smears on sand, dust and beaten snow (Tecon [4]); and in 1921, Mayer [5] reviewed the work of Finsen,[6] Jansen,[7] Treskenskaja,[8] Buchner,[9] Thiele and Wolf,[10] Wiesner,[11] Dorno,[12] Bernhard,[13] Duclaux,[14] and others. However, the procedure followed in these studies is a departure from technic described in the literature, and in no instance do environmental conditions even remotely approach those found in the southwestern part of the United States where the work described in this paper was done.

EXPERIMENTAL WORK

Study of the viability of Mycobacterium tuberculosis was undertaken as follows: Sputum was obtained in the early morning hours from three well advanced typical cases of tuberculosis; these samples, designated as A, B and C, contained approximately the same number of organisms. Amounts approximating those most likely to be expectorated were transferred to Petri dishes containing sterile dust. The plates were placed on the ground in a dry open area, the covers of the dishes removed, and the material exposed to direct sunlight. The dishes were protected from birds by means of large mesh wire screening. The first series of plates inoculated with sputum A was placed in

Received for publication, June 27, 1925.

1 Jour. Infect. Dis., 1907, Suppl. 3, p. 128.
2 Am. Rev. Tuber., 1923, 8, p. 165.
3 Arch. f. Hyg., 1895, 25, p. 361.
4 Paris méd., 1920, 10, p. 33.
5 Am. Rev. Tuber., 1921, 5, p. 75.
6 Allg. Wien. med. Ztschr., 1900, 45, p. 591.
7 Mitt. aus Finsen's med. Lysinst., 1903, p. 127.
8 Centralbl. f. Bakteriol., 1, Abt., 1910, 47, p. 681.
9 Arch. f. Hyg., 1893, 17, p. 179.
10 Ibid., 1907, 60, p. 29.
11 Ibid., 1907, 61, p. 1.
12 Strahlentherap., 1919, 9, p. 467.
13 Ibid., 1917, 8, p. 500.
14 Ann. de l'Inst. Pasteur, 1890, 4, p. 232.

the sun for 2, 3, 4, 5 and 6 hour periods. Also, exposures were made for 12, 16, 20, 25, 30, 48 and 72 hours; and in this second series, sputum samples B and C were used.

At the beginning of each exposure the temperature was recorded as soon as the maximum temperature of the earth was reached and observations continued every hour during the exposure. This was done as follows: The bulbs of 2 accurately calibrated thermometers were buried in dust of the same consistency as that in the inoculated dishes to a depth of about 2 mm. The dust in the plates was sufficiently deep so that its temperature varied only a negligible amount from that noted in dust spread directly on the ground; in other words, the dishes made no appreciable difference in the temperature to which the dust was exposed.

At the end of each period, healthy guinea-pigs were inoculated in duplicate as follows: Hair was clipped on the lower abdomen, and the skin thoroughly disinfected; the animals were anesthetized, and, after making an incision from 4 to 5 mm. in length, a pocket was made subcutaneously on the left side toward the inguinal glands, and the dust introduced into this area. Because of the difficulty of keeping the dust in suspension, a 1 c c. pipet graduated to the tip was filed off at the 0.95 c c. graduation mark to secure a larger opening, and a rubber aspirator was attached. The dust, previously suspended in 1 c c. sterile physiologic salt solution, was drawn up, thoroughly mixed, and about 0.47 c c. aspirated at once into the subcutaneous pockets of each of 2 pigs. At no time did the amount of dust in 0.95 c c. salt solution exceed 0.05 gm., and as a rule it was considerably less. A small piece of sterile gauze was placed over the incision and secured by adhesive tape. All pigs were weighed once a week. Time did not permit the making of temperature records of the pigs other than those in the first series; temperatures were taken daily between 11 and 12 o'clock in the morning.

In order to ascertain possible physiologic effects of the introduction of the dust, 6 guinea-pigs were inoculated with 0.05, 0.1, 0.2, 0.3, 0.4 and 0.5 gm. of sterile dust and 6 other uninoculated guinea-pigs were used as controls. Careful temperature records and weight records were kept of this series of animals.

Due to the great variations in normal temperatures of lower mammals, it was thought that the normal temperatures of guinea-pigs to be used might be of interest; hence records were kept for 1 week prior to inoculation as well as during the 4 following weeks.

When plates were exposed to sunlight on February 21, several were allowed to remain for one week of continuous exposure in the shade on the north side of a building. Here the primary factors involved were those of diffuse light and desiccation; no account was taken of cloudy periods.

All guinea-pigs were kept on a mixed diet of alfalfa hay, carrots, cabbage, and lettuce. No guinea-pigs were killed until after a month from the time of inoculation had elapsed; necropsy was made on each animal when chloroformed or at the time of death.

All inoculated guinea-pigs showed an infection to a greater or less degree. The clinical picture was typical, and microscopically no difficulty was experienced in finding tubercle bacilli at the point of inoculation and in material from caseopurulent inguinal nodes. As a rule the bandage was not removed until the lesion, which showed evidences of previous acute subcutaneous reaction, was entirely covered by a scab and apparently healed; then, since it was only a matter of a few days until the lesion broke down again, the fresh bandage was put on as a matter of protection. When the guinea-pigs were weighed at the end of the first week the superficial inguinal nodes could be felt to be somewhat enlarged, and became more and more so as time advanced—the left glands were naturally the first to be involved palpably. At necropsy, when the lesion at the site of inoculation was not broken down, the removal of the scab always showed the presence of pus, and the tissues of the pocket were usually studded with tubercles. The superficial inguinals, deep inguinals, and iliacs were grossly tuberculous: often they were as large as good sized lima beans, firm, and opaque, with necrotic areas or exhibiting an abscess of the soft tissues. The spleen was frequently involved and nodulated with masses of tubercles; the hepatic lymph nodes were sometimes enlarged; and even several guinea-pigs that had received material which had been exposed for 30 and 48 hours exhibited small yellowish patches in the liver.

The guinea-pigs which received sample C. sputum exposed for 72 hours showed apparent tuberculous infections, but the amount of involvement diminished, and the bacilli had been carried only from the periphery to the next adjacent lymph nodes. The spleen, liver and lungs were all normal, and it is regretted that these guinea-pigs could not have been kept for an indefinite period. Time did not permit of reinoculations, but experiments now in progress will determine whether the response was provoked by living or dead bacilli.

The weight curves are of interest: the animals used were young adults and the tendency of the controls was naturally an upward curve. Since highly virulent human tubercle bacilli were used and present in great numbers, the health of the animal was influenced in the majority of cases from the first.

All sixteen guinea-pigs which received sputum exposed for 2, 3, 4, 5, 6, 12, 16, 20 and 25 hour sunlight exposures together with the pigs which were inoculated with sputum exposed for one week to diffuse light, showed abruptly downward curves.

The pigs which were inoculated with sputum exposed to sunlight for 30 and 36 hours showed a marked loss in weight the first week, and in two instances this continued the second week, after which one of the pigs died while the other gained over 60 grams. All of the other pigs in this series gained weight to a greater or less degree after the first week; two showed no loss or gain from the third to the fourth week.

The pigs which were inoculated with sputum exposed to sunlight for 48 and 72 hours, showed in 4 instances a loss during only the first week; after that, while they did not regain their former weight as the controls did, nevertheless, there was a decided gain for the time being. One guinea-pig died suddenly at the beginning of the fourth week, due to an acute infection; about that time another animal began to suffer from the effects of the tubercle bacillus, and its curve began to descend.

There was no evidence of tuberculosis in any of the control guinea-pigs. During the first week after the injection of sterile dust a loss in weight occurred, but in practically all instances this amount was promptly regained. All the normal guinea-pigs ran a typical weight curve except one, which lost some weight the third week, most likely owing to sudden climatic changes.

COMMENT

The results of this investigation indicate that Mycobacterium tuberculosis is viable in sputum from well advanced cases of tuberculosis for a much longer time than is generally supposed. The general opinion today is that the tubercle bacillus is killed in from 20 or 25 minutes to 2 hours to 2½ days. Widely different circumstances are encountered when sputum is ejected on the ground and covered by more or less dust, especially in gutters where fragments of débris may adhere. The mucoid material is often extremely tenacious and its ability to protect the tubercle bacillus to a greater or less degree is generally recognized. No reference to the exact penetration of ultraviolet rays into mucoid matter such as sputum has been found. All workers agree that bacteria in a dry state are more difficult to kill than when moist. The work of Treskenskaja [8] and von Bergen [15] and others seems to show that desiccation and heat have little or no effect on the destruction of the tubercle bacillus; hence, if drying is accomplished at the same time that the bactericidal rays are inhibited, then the organisms in a more or less desiccated condition may retain their virulence for long periods of time.

It is little wonder that results of different investigators who exposed micro-organisms to sunlight vary so much. The quality and intensity of the light are the effectively destructive factors, and these vary greatly in different environments; likewise, as Mayer [5] points out, the duration of the exposure to light, the amounts of humidity and temperature, the dry or moist condition of the bacilli, their age, number, etc., all have an

[15] Schweiz. med. Wchnschr., 1920, 50, p. 1120.

important bearing. And he refers to variations in time of killing from a few minutes to 2½ days. The results of Tecon [4] most nearly approximate those obtained by me, for at Leysin he found that in from 2 to 52 hours sunlight rendered sterile sputum which contained tubercle bacilli and which was placed in sterilized dust, sand and gravel. It seems strange that his figures are not more widely quoted. Many simply state that "cultures of tubercle bacilli" are killed in from a few minutes to a few hours, and surprisingly few references are made to sputum which harbors these virulent micro-organisms.

It is generally agreed [16] that the bactericidal effect of light has to do with the blue, indigo, violet, ultrared and ultraviolet rays. Bayliss [17] says that "the direct action of ultraviolet light on micro-organisms and tissue cells is a destructive one. The shorter the wave length, the more powerful the effect with equal energy of the radiation." When Mayer [5] mentions the fact that at the seashore and in high altitudes the greatest intensity exists, he incidentally states that "the deserts and prairies may also be rich in ultraviolets."

Since geographic situation, weather conditions, etc., are responsible for the great variations in bactericidal power, the differences in exposures should be emphasized: the 12 hour exposure of sputum B was begun on April 1 at 10:30 a. m., while that of sample C was started the following day at 8:30 a. m. According to the U. S. Weather Bureau Reports, the maximum temperature on April 1 was 26.6 C., while on the second day it was 20 C.—a difference of 6.6 degrees. There was a variation in sunlight temperature of 19 degrees on April 2 and of 36 degrees on April 18 and 19. The plates, which were exposed for one week to diffuse light, did not undergo such extreme variations; for example, on Feb. 21, there was a variation in sunlight temperature of 18 degrees, but in the shade a difference of only 2 degrees.

The following description of typical spring weather conditions is given to emphasize the great variations in climatologic factors. After April 3 inclement weather did not permit exposures to be made for a week—April 4 to April 11. Thus, April 4 was decidedly cloudy, April 5 was a windy, dusty day, and the dust storm persisted all that night and until the following afternoon, when showers cleared the atmosphere. On April 7 the sunlight was intermittent, and no exposures were possible. The following day was hazy, and although plates were

[16] Jordan, E. O.: General Bacteriology, 1922, p. 85. Park, W. H., and Williams, A. W.: Pathogenic Microorganims, 1920, p. 57.

[17] Bayliss, W. M.: Principles of General Physiology, 1918.

exposed, at 11:30 it suddenly began to rain, and time was not reckoned for that morning. The rain continued during April 9; April 10 and 11 were cloudy, but April 12 brought a bright clear still morning with only a few clouds hovering over distant mountain peaks. At 4:30 it became cloudy, and the plates were returned to the laboratory. It must be noted that for an exposure of 72 hours to direct sunlight, sputum was first exposed April 2 and not ready for inoculation until April 23. While not undergoing exposure, the dishes were covered and kept at room temperature in a dark place.

The great temperature variations during a period of 24 hours may not only be noted on inspection of climatologic data, but also on a glance at the weights of the guinea-pigs. After the dust storm on April 16 it became cold, and the effect of severe surrounding storms was obvious. Several apparently normal guinea-pigs in the breeding cages died that night, and 4 tuberculous guinea-pigs died in the cages were experimental animals were kept. On the mornings of April 17 and 18 all guinea-pigs were much affected by the cold—even a control pig lost weight. The maximum temperature on April 17 was 21.6 C., and that night it dropped to — 1.1 C.—a difference of 22.2 degrees. During the following two periods of 24 hours each, there were differences of 27.8 and 27.3 degrees, respectively.

Further study of weights is of interest. It is impossible to account for their trend in all instances. On the whole, they run as might be expected: normal animals of nearly the same age and weight and living under carefully controlled conditions show similar curves. Variations readily occur if the diet is slightly changed, if an acute infection arises, or when such accidental factors as environment and time are concerned. The guinea-pigs which received highly virulent tubercle bacilli together with the irritative dust were decidedly affected from the start, and their curves show a striking resemblance. De Witt [18] points out that guinea-pigs inoculated with the same strain of tubercle bacilli and kept under the same conditions exhibit a fairly regular and typical weight curve; and the reports of the Royal Commission on Tuberculosis, 1917, show that in their reaction to this disease guinea-pigs may differ among themselves. The differences that arise are not as great as might be expected under the transitory atmospheric disturbances often experienced, for it is well known that extreme temperatures do not affect the body as much as abrupt variations.

[18] Jour. Infect. Dis., 1920, 27, p. 503.

As time elapsed and virulence diminished, the curves on the whole eventually assumed an upward trend to a greater or less extent. To be sure, in some cases after an initial loss in weight, the guinea-pigs gained from 10 to 20 gm., and then succeeded in holding their own for the time being. DeWitt [18] found that a generalized infection is not always indicated by a downward curve after an apex has been reached, "since several animals that died or were killed at or near the apex of the curve showed all the internal organs involved in the tuberculous process." Thus, in accordance with the reports of the Royal Commission, the individual resistance of the animal plays an important rôle. Laird [19] found that tuberculous guinea-pigs on which necropsy was performed on an average of about 6 weeks after inoculation frequently showed a gain in weight; other guinea-pigs found to be nontuberculous exhibited a similar increase. Here also, from the nature of his work, it might be suspected that virulence played a part. He remarks that "the question of the viability of the tubercle bacillus and especially of the duration of its existence in water courses has not been settled."

Only after an exposure to direct sunlight for 30 hours do the weight curves indicate a diminution in virulence; not until after 48 hours would the lesions found suggest a decrease. No references to such observations have been seen, and whether this distinction would be true in a much larger number of tuberculous animals would be a matter of considerable interest. Weight determinations for much longer periods of time than those previously used, when more or less attenuated bacilli have been inoculated, will be recorded in future work.

In a study of lymph node distribution, Webb, Ryder and Olcott [20] speak of the possibility of tubercle bacilli with diminished activity still remaining viable in remote nodes, such as the mesenteric and ileocecal, and suggest that this may explain the constancy of the Pirquet test in man. So in the present work, perhaps the bacilli are not sufficiently viable to pass the first defenses of the body. Harbitz,[21] together with Loomis [22] and Spengler,[23] believe that in the lymphatic system diminution of virulence and even death of the bacillus might occur. Several months after inoculation of rabbits and guinea-pigs, Perez [24] and Manfredi and

[18] Jour. Infect. Dis., 1920, 27, p. 503.
[19] Tr. Nat. Assn. Study and Prev. Tuberc., 1917, 13, p. 290.
[20] Amer. Rev. Tuberc., 1922, 6, p. 575.
[21] Jour. Infect. Dis., 1905, 2, p. 143.
[22] Researches of Loomis Lab., Univ. City of N. Y., 1890, 1, p. 75.
[23] Ztschr. f. Hyg. u. Infektionskr., 1893, 13, p. 349.
[24] Centralbl. f. Bakteriol., 1898, 23, p. 404.

Frisco [25] refer to an attenuation and death of the bacillus. Krause [26] showed that subcutaneously a strain of Mycobacterium tuberculosis of weakened virulence was rarely fatal for guinea-pigs, and in his "inheritance experiments" these animals were kept usually for from 2 to 3 years and in one instance 5 years.

It is obvious that more work must be carried on to determine whether there are degrees of attenuation, when these occur, whether a typical or an atypical infection follows, whether the reactions in certain instances are due to living or dead bacilli, etc., and in such experiments guinea-pigs should be allowed to live for 6 or 7 to 12 or 14 months. It is to be kept in mind that the situation may not be exactly the same in the human body—too close analogies should never be drawn between one animal and another; however, similar conditions may be encountered.

CONCLUSIONS AND SUMMARY

Mycobacterium tuberculosis in sputum exposed to direct sunlight and in a manner to simulate as closely as possible actual community conditions is viable for longer periods of time than is generally conceded.

Guinea-pigs inoculated with sputum exposed to sunlight for 2, 3, 4, 5, 6, 12, 16, 20, 25, 30, 48 and 72 hours showed extensive tuberculous infections.

[25] Ibid., 1902, Ref., 32, p. 295.
[26] Amer. Rev. Tuberc., 1922, 6, p. 1.

INFLUENZA STUDIES

XX. IDENTIFICATION OF FIXED TYPE PNEUMOCOCCUS CARRIERS: A STUDY OF TECHNICAL METHODS

WILLIAM B. SHARP AND ELSIE URBANTKE

From the Department of Hygiene and Bacteriology of the University of Chicago, and the Department of Bacteriology and Preventive Medicine of the University of Texas Medical Department

Paths of pneumonia transmission have as yet been defined but roughly; questions continue to arise after examination of all available data. How long after recovery do patients continue to disseminate infective pneumococci, or may dissemination be from healthy carriers having no pneumonic history? Is it practicable to combat pneumonia, like diphtheria, by freeing convalescents from the germs, or are the germs so widely distributed through the community that their numbers could not be affected thereby? Many such questions must remain unsettled until we have reliable means for recognition of the carrier condition.

The germ of pneumonia was formerly thought to live about healthy persons generally, passing readily from one to another, and to infect when temporary depression of the resistance permitted. Laboratory evidence supporting that view was the recovery of pneumococci from a large proportion of the healthy throats examined, from the air of houses and public places, from street dust, etc.[1]

More modern technical methods, while further establishing the fact of a wide distribution of pneumococci, leave doubt as to the nature of the conditions under which these germs cause pneumonia. Our own observations on these points coincide so nearly with those reported by others as to warrant but brief expression here. In one series of nearly 400 unselected persons, including only a few cases of respiratory disease, seven-eighths were found to have in their throats organisms of the pneumococcus-streptococcus group, and nearly one-third, pneumococci. Similar proportions obtained in a series of about 50 persons in apparently perfect health.

On the other hand, there is little reason to think that a majority of these pneumococci could under any circumstances cause pneumonia. A

Received for publication, June 15, 1925.

[1] Burt, S. S.: Med. Rec., 1902, 61, p. 368.

large proportion of the attacks of pneumonia in the locality of this survey are due to infection with fixed type pneumococci, and fixed type pneumococci were found in less than 4% of the persons in our series. The pneumococci recovered from healthy throats have long been known to include fewer strains that are virulent for animals than the pneumococci from pneumonic sputum. They have later been found to fall more often among the type 4 varieties.[2]

Epidemiologic evidence points to carrier transmission as playing some part in the spread of pneumonia.[3] That a carrier condition exists might be inferred also from the occasional finding in healthy throats of fixed type pneumococci. Indication of contact between carriers and persons attacked has been infrequent, however, and no given type of pneumococcus has appeared in healthy throats with sufficient frequency to account for the widely scattered incidence characteristic of the disease. A carrier condition responsible for disease incidence of this character might be expected to exist more extensively than reported observations have indicated.

The wide distribution of persons attacked suggests either a persistent lodgement of infective pneumococci in throats of patients who have recovered, or a ready dissemination among healthy persons. In the instances we were able to follow, the convalescent carrier condition did not appear to be persistent, and while noninfected persons associating with patients occasionally were found to harbor the germ, they did not long continue to do so, and did not pass the germ on to subsequent healthy carriers. For example, in one group of 13 children living together, a type 2 pneumococcus was recovered from 2 who were infected and from 3 who were healthy, but within a few days it had disappeared from the healthy throats, and shortly after their recovery, from the infected children.

We wish now to report some experiments indicating that failures to demonstrate more widespread and persistent carriage are due largely to technical difficulty. After a short time the infecting pneumococcus cannot be found when looked for by the ordinary methods, but its actual disappearance from the throat is not proved. Only when in preponderance over certain other members of the throat flora can a fixed type pneumococcus be expected to appear on such examination.

[2] Eyre, J. W., and Washbourn, J. W.: Lancet, 1899, 1, p. 19. Park, W. H., and Williams, A. W.: Jour. Exper. Med., 1905, 7, p. 403. Meyer, J.: Jour. Am. Med. Assn., 1920, 75, p. 1268.

[3] Duncan, L. C.: Mil. Surgeon, 1918, 42, p. 123.

By ordinary methods, we refer to the various modifications of the mouse technic, which have proved so successful for typing infective pneumococci from patients with pneumonia,[4] and to the isolation of these bacteria by means of blood-agar plates.[5] The larger series of cases mentioned above was examined by the mouse method, and the incidence of pneumococcal carriage arrived at approximates that commonly reported by others. Dextrose blood broth cultures were made from swabbings of nasopharyngeal and tonsillar regions of the throat, incubated from 6 to 8 hours and inoculated into mice. Unless the animals died, they were killed the next day, the peritoneal fluid and blood stained and cultures made, and bacteria centrifuged from the peritoneal washings for agglutination and bile solubility test.

Our aim was to determine the presence or absence of fixed type pneumococci. The fact that virulent type 4 pneumococci might sometimes be present and escape notice seemed inconsequential. A recognition, in suitably selected groups, of all persons carrying pneumococci of the three fixed types—or of one of these types even—would throw light on the main questions of pneumococcal transmission. It would permit conclusions as to whether pneumonia-producing germs are commonly carried by convalescents and for how long, whether they are transmissible from one carrier to another without infection, etc. On the other hand, a recognition of only a portion of the carriers, whether of one or of all types, could afford but little information of any kind.

What our tests actually showed was whether the bulk of the organisms obtained from the respective cases were pneumococci of one of the fixed types, or pneumococci of a type 4 variety, or streptococci. In many of the cases in which the patient harbored more than one of these organisms, the tests proved definitely inadequate. Either of two coexisting types of pneumococcus might be the one found, and similarly either a pneumococcus or a streptococcus.

We had anticipated that the virulent pneumococci would persist after other organisms had been filtered out and lost, as they would grow more readily than others in the mouse. To a degree this has proved to be so in the typing of pneumococci from sputum.[6] The contaminating bacteria that actually were filtered out of our test material by the mouse passage did not include those so confusingly similar to fixed type

[4] Dochez, A. R., and Gillespie, L. G.: Jour. Am. Med. Assn., 1913, 61, p. 727. Cole, R.: Arch. Int. Med., 1914, 14, p. 56. Blake, F. G.: Jour. Exper. Med., 1917, 26, p. 67.

[5] Sailer, J.; Hall, M. W.; Wilson, R. L., and McCoy, C.: Arch. Int. Med., 1919, 24, p. 600.

[6] Avery, O. T.: Jour. Am. Med. Assn., 1918, 70, p. 17.

pneumococci. That member of the pneumococcus-streptococcus group appeared to survive the eliminating process which had originally been present in the greatest numbers.

Streptococci and type 4 pneumococci are as a rule far more prevalent in healthy throats than the fixed type pneumococci. The latter predominated sufficiently to be recognized in less than 4% of our cases, whereas the others did in a large majority. It is therefore the fixed type pneumococcus which is the more commonly obscured in an examination of this sort.

Appropriate study of 40 cases established the points just brought out: that the proportions of streptococci and type 4 pneumococci in the flora are not materially diminished by mouse passage; that the fixed type pneumococci are often intermingled with much greater numbers of one or the other of these; and, finally, that in such a mixture the presence of the fixed type pneumococcus actually is obscured.

In each of the 40 instances, the throat flora was cultivated on 2 blood-agar plates. The one plate was inoculated directly with material swabbed from the throat. The other was inoculated with the peritoneal fluid of a mouse, to which had been injected previously a blood broth culture of the same material. The flora as it developed on the two plates was compared, to find what effect the mouse passage had had. From each plate were picked for typing 13 random colonies with green zones about them, or all in which fewer than 13 developed.

Fixed type pneumococci occurred in only one instance among the colonies picked from the inoculated mouse plate, but were found on 4 of the plates inoculated directly from the throat. The one case positive by the mouse method constituted 3.4% of all having noncontaminated and therefore readable plates, about the same percentage as in the large series before studied. Fixed type pneumococci were shown by the directly inoculated plates to be present in several times as many of the cases examined. Mouse passage had clearly failed in its purpose.

Fixed type pneumococci were recovered in all from 6 of the 40 cases; fewer than 6 entered into the comparisons just made, as a contamination spreading over either plate forestalled one. All 6 yielded green zone streptococci as well, and 3, type 4 pneumococci also. From half of them, 3 cases, only 1 of all the green zoned colonies brought into subculture proved to be a fixed type of pneumococcus, a proportion at times as low as 1/13. It is not improbable that other cases with still smaller proportions of fixed type pneumococci among the flora were missed.

Several times as many colonies would have to be picked for assurance that none was being overlooked. We sometimes found the green streptococcus flora so rich that dozens of colonies must have been picked in order to include the scantily present pneumococci. There is thus a great likelihood of the organism sought being far outnumbered and therefore obscured by other members of the group in ordinary examinations.

The excess in the flora of the throat of the other green zone producers constitutes the practical objection to the picking of plates streaked directly with throat secretions, as a means of identifying the pneumococcus carrier. If all green zone colonies are picked and typed, any fixed type pneumococci among them will of course appear as such, but the typing of a few of the colonies does not point out the carrier any more consistently than the mouse method; findings of ourselves and others are in accord with this.[5] The number of cultures and typing tests necessary for a really dependable survey of the throat's flora is so great that the examination of very many cases would overtax any laboratory.

The principle of a third technical method seems better adapted to the requirements of the carrier problem than either of those already described. Through it we may expect to recognize fixed type pneumococci constituting but a small part of the green zone flora. The authors of that method typed sputum cultures[6] and the sputum direct[7] by dissolving out with bile any pneumococcus proteins, separating from extraneous solids in saline, and precipitating with specific serums. We followed a similar procedure with mixed throat cultures, pneumococci being dissolved away from the bile-insoluble bacteria and their presence determined by specific precipitation. The worst of the difficulties seemed to be overcome by this means.

In the first of our experiments by this method, glucose blood broth was inoculated by throat swab and allowed to incubate over night, for the purpose of bringing into mixed culture any fixed type pneumococci harbored. Experiments with known organisms had shown no practical advantage in using inulin instead of dextrose to favor pneumococci overgrowth of rival organisms, nor in using slants of solid mediums to favor separation from grossly contaminating growths.

The broth culture was separated from the blood cells and treated with beef bile to dissolve any pneumococci present; 6 drops of the bile

[7] Oliver, W. W.: Jour. Infect. Dis., 1920, 27, p. 310.

proved sufficient to clear 2.0 to 2.5 c.c. quantities of pneumococcus culture within 20 minutes, in the 42 C. water bath. Occasional failure of the pneumococci to dissolve completely interfered only in that reactive protein was kept from the test fluid, and except where pneumococcal growth was very scant proved less consequential than in the bile test which is used for differentiation between pneumococci and streptococci. All solids in suspension were removed by centrifugalization, leaving the solution of pneumococcal material in a perfectly clear fluid.

This fluid was tested for precipitable pneumococcus antigens. It was distributed in 0.7 c c. quantities to three 10 mm. serologic tubes, and to each tube was added 3 drops of one of the type antiserums undiluted. Positive reaction led to a cloudiness in one of the tubes, settling later into a definite flocculation at the bottom. Absence of any precipitation by the other 2 serums controlled the reaction sufficiently to permit reliable reading from even a scant precipitate. Some clouding often occurred immediately, but a clear reaction was more constant after incubation in the 42 C. water bath for half an hour and in the icebox over night. Comparative tests with known cultures seemed to establish these as desirable dosages and incubations.

Fixed type pneumococci overgrown greatly by streptococci or other organisms reacted by this method. Known cultures of fixed type pneumococci outnumbered dozens of times by streptococci showed a positive reading. So small a proportion of fixed type pneumococci among other green zone producers had not been recognized in our experiments by the mouse method, and only after laborious technical procedure by direct plating and the picking off of cultures to be typed. As before pointed out, fixed type pneumococci in a throat can easily be outnumbered to this extent by the others.

The experiments made to gage the efficacy of the method were made with dextrose broth cultures of a pneumococcus and a streptococcus, respectively. The 2 suspensions were first shaken with beads for 2 hours by motor to break up bacterial groupings, and then counted and so diluted that they contained equal concentrations of bacterial cells; subsequent control plating developed equally rich growth from them. Mixtures were made with graduated amounts of these suspensions, from 1 to 80 streptococci to each pneumococcus being represented. From each of the mixtures a blood-agar plate was streaked, and with the growth on this plate the test above outlined was carried out. Results indicated that fixed type pneumococci are not to be obscured by 20, and sometimes 80, times their number of other green zone producers.

The method proved defective in that at times some organisms which grew luxuriantly crowded out the pneumococcus-streptococcus group altogether. The mouths of some persons examined are very dirty and heavily contaminated, and even in clean mouths there are forms which greatly outgrow the pneumococcus. We found staphylococci in the throats of 36 out of 48 students, sometimes abundantly, and in occasional cases we found organisms growing far more luxuriantly. A heavy contamination of the broth culture is more serious than one of the plate, for, being unrecognized, it gives no hint that the culture should be discarded and the test repeated. The selective properties by which mouse infection and blood-agar plating had afforded green zone colonies relatively free from other contamination were here lacking.

As a preliminary step to overcome this obstacle, the throat secretions were inoculated first to a blood-agar plate, the material being swabbed on the edge of the medium and then streaked by needle over the rest of the surface. The green zone colonies developing on this plate were picked as in the direct plating method above outlined, except that instead of each colony being picked individually for identification, they were all scraped up together and a culture made.

The green-producing colonies, together with any others unavoidably included, were transferred to a tube of dextrose blood broth and incubated at 37 C. for from 12 to 15 hours. The suspension was then removed from above the blood cells and treated with bile, after which the broth was cleared in the centrifuge and tested with the type serums. As few but green zone colonies are inoculated to the broth for culture, the danger of overgrowth by other organisms is practically done away with.

If practical utility measures up to the experimental promise, the fixed type pneumococcus carrier can be identified as such, through the procedure described, with relative ease and with sufficient accuracy for tracing the transmission routes of pneumonia. Associates have undertaken such a study. The hope that others with similar intent may be aided leads us to report the experiments now, though the method arrived at is still untried in practical work.

SUMMARY

The technical methods commonly used for the typing of pneumococci in infected sputum are not suited for determining the presence of virulent pneumococci in healthy carriers. Pneumococci of a given type are readily obscured by the more abundant members of the throat flora. Dependable methods of separation from these others, and of subsequent identification, are too laborious for use in extended studies. A new, relatively short method is therefore outlined by which it is possible to determine the presence of fixed type pneumococci without isolating them.

The secretion to be tested for the presence of these organisms is streaked over a blood-agar plate. All green zone colonies developing on the plate are transferred to a tube of dextrose blood broth and incubated. The resulting culture is withdrawn from over the blood cells and treated for 20 minutes—at 42 C.—with bile, 2 or 3 drops per c c. of culture. All undissolved matter is then centrifuged out for discard and a precipitin test made on samples of the clear fluid with the 3 type serums. Three drops of the undiluted antiserum are added to about 0.7 c c. of the treated culture fluid. When incubated at 42 C. for 30 minutes and at icebox temperature over night, the antigen of any fixed type pneumococcus present is precipitated by the corresponding serum. The presence of this pneumococcus is thereby readily recognized.

STUDIES ON RESPIRATORY DISEASES

XXI. ELECTROPHORETIC POTENTIAL AND VIRULENCE OF PNEUMOCOCCI (TYPES 1, 2, 3 AND 4)*

I. S. Falk, H. A. Gussin and M. A. Jacobson

From the Department of Hygiene and Bacteriology of the University of Chicago

The dynamics of bacterial virulence still remain essentially obscure in spite of numerous researches which have been directed toward their elucidation during several decades. Indeed, there is no general agreement among writers on this subject as to the scope, the nature or even the precise implications of the term "virulence." In some publications "virulence" means pathogenicity; in others it is coterminal with fatality or lethality of infection or intoxication. The mechanisms of phenomena which may be subsumed under "virulence" are certainly but little understood. It is often recognized that toxigenicity, invasiveness, avidity to fix and localize on specific tissues and capacity to necrotize are or may be distinct phenomena, and that it is often necessary to distinguish among them in attempting to characterize the virulence of a specific parasite for a particular host. It is almost gratuitous to remark that the factors which influence each of these phenomena, whether occurring singly or together in an infection, are largely unknown. The researches reported here are part of an extended series of studies designed to cast some light on the significance of certain forces which appear to affect one or the other of the phenomena of virulence.

It has become evident from studies which will be reported in detail in subsequent publications that the stability of a bacterial suspension (whether the organisms be live or dead) is significantly correlated with the electrophoretic potential of the bacteria. In our laboratory, as in others, it is also recognized that among bacteria of certain generic and species groups there appear to be parallelisms, direct or inverse, between the stability of suspension and such properties as are associated with virulence, specific serum agglutination, colony form and texture, antigenic properties, etc. We present here the results of a series of experiments which were designed to determine more directly the correlation between electrophoretic potentials of bacteria and the virulence of the micro-organisms for susceptible hosts.[1]

Received for publication, July 16, 1925.

* The four articles on respiratory diseases in this issue are part of a series of studies carried out in connection with the Influenza Commission established and financially aided by the Metropolitan Life Insurance Company of New York.

[1] For the present, we are using the term "virulence" to mean the capacity of bacteria to produce death in a host into which they are introduced by the methods detailed below.

ISOLATION OF CULTURES

With one exception,[2] all of the pneumococcus cultures used in these experiments were freshly isolated from patients suffering with acute lobar pneumonia who had been admitted to pneumonia wards of the Cook County Hospital of Chicago. Included in the group were white and colored males and females, generally over 20 years of age, all—with one exception—over 10 years of age. The cultures were unselected, including all that could be obtained from material taken for type determinations from the majority of the patients admitted to the wards of the hospital between October, 1923, and June, 1924. The clinical diagnosis of lobar pneumonia had already been made on the patients before the materials for cultures were obtained. The patients ranged from some in relatively early to others in late stages of pneumonia.

Throat swabs, specimens of blood and sputum were taken from the patients—in many cases all three; in some, one or more. On many of the patients repeated determinations of pneumococcus type were made on successively obtained specimens of blood. In some cases the material taken from a patient yielded more than one type of pneumococcus. Hence, the data which are included in this paper are based on the type determinations made on the pure cultures which were later isolated from these materials.

The material used in the examinations and pneumococcus isolations were obtained within 24 hours—and in most cases within 12 hours—of the patients' admissions to the hospital. The laboratory examinations were conducted according to the following technic:

(*a*) Specimens of sputum were obtained in sterile paper cups, the patient having been instructed to expectorate from the deeper air passages of the lung. The specimens were examined within 6 hours of their collection. On receipt in the laboratory, part of each specimen was used to streak blood-agar plates. The remainder was washed with 0.9% NaCl solution. One half to 1 c c. of the washed sputum was injected intraperitoneally into a white mouse. If the animal had not died from 12 to 20 hours later, it was killed. Cultures were taken with sterile loops from the heart blood and from the peritoneal exudate and were streaked on blood-agar plates.[3] The peritoneum was washed with approximately 10 c c. of salt solution. The washings were centrifugalized at low speed (several hundred revolutions per minute) for 2 or 3 minutes to throw down cells, fibrin and other débris. The supernatent fluid was transferred to another centrifuge

[2] Culture "A1," a type I pneumococcus which was received from Dr. F. G. Blake of the Yale School of Medicine, was included with the others for purposes of comparison because it has been possible to obtain from it certain variant strains.

[3] The blood agar was prepared from veal infusion agar (2%) which had been adjusted to $P_H = 7.8$ and to which had been added from 5 to 10% fresh defibrinated sheep blood.

tube and centrifugalized at 3000 r.p.m. for from 15 to 20 minutes. Type determinations were made on the sediment by the usual agglutination test and were confirmed in same cases by the precipitin test made on the supernatent fluid.[4] In parallel with the agglutination tests all samples were subjected to the bile solubility test. The serum-antigen mixtures were incubated in a water bath at 37.5 C. for from 1 to 2 hours, were read, and the readings were confirmed after the mixtures had been held in the ice chest over night.

(*b*) Sterile swabs were used to obtain test material from the nasopharynx of the patient. After swabbings had been made, the swab with its adherent material was immersed in from 5 to 10 c c. of 1% dextrose veal infusion broth ($P_H = 7.8$). On arrival at the laboratory the tubes containing the swabs were incubated at 37 C. for from 6 to 12 hours. One c c. of culture was then injected into a white mouse and the type determination made by the same procedure described above for the sputum samples.

(*c*) From 1 to 2 c c. of blood were taken from a vein in the arm of the patient with a sterile hypodermic needle and introduced directly into from 5 to 10 c c. of dextrose broth. The cultures were incubated for from 12 to 18 hours at 37 C. As soon as there were evidences of growth, 0.5 c c. was transferred to dextrose broth, incubated for from 12 to 18 hours and examined for pneumococci with the usual agglutination and bile solubility tests. The subculturing into dextrose broth was made in order to avoid the interfering effect of the serum from the patient's blood on the bile solubility test. In addition to the procedures which have been enumerated, blood-agar plates were streaked from the original cultures of the patient's blood in dextrose broth.

All of the cultures used in our experiments were obtained from discrete colonies which had appeared on the blood-agar plates streaked with the blood or peritoneal exudate from a mouse that had received injections or from material taken from the patient. Confirmatory agglutination and bile solubility tests were made on these cultures on the occasion of each experiment reported in this paper. The cultures were carried in stock on blood-agar slants which were kept in the ice chest. Transfers were made at intervals of from 1 to 2 weeks.

MEASUREMENT OF ELECTROPHORETIC POTENTIAL

The electrophoretic (cataphoretic) potentials on pneumococci were measured by a method which has been adequately summarized in a convenient form by Burton[5] and which is described in detail in earlier papers. The form of apparatus used (fig. 1) is a modification of that described by Northrop.[6] In its present design it is less fragile and is more conveniently dismounted and cleaned. This apparatus was prepared for us by Mr. Morgan of the Eimer and Amend Company of New York. From theoretical considerations which have been dis-

[4] For these tests New York State Department of Health typing serum were used.
[5] Physical Properties of Colloidal Solutions, 1921, p. 132.
[6] Jour. Gen. Physiol., 1922, 4, p. 629.

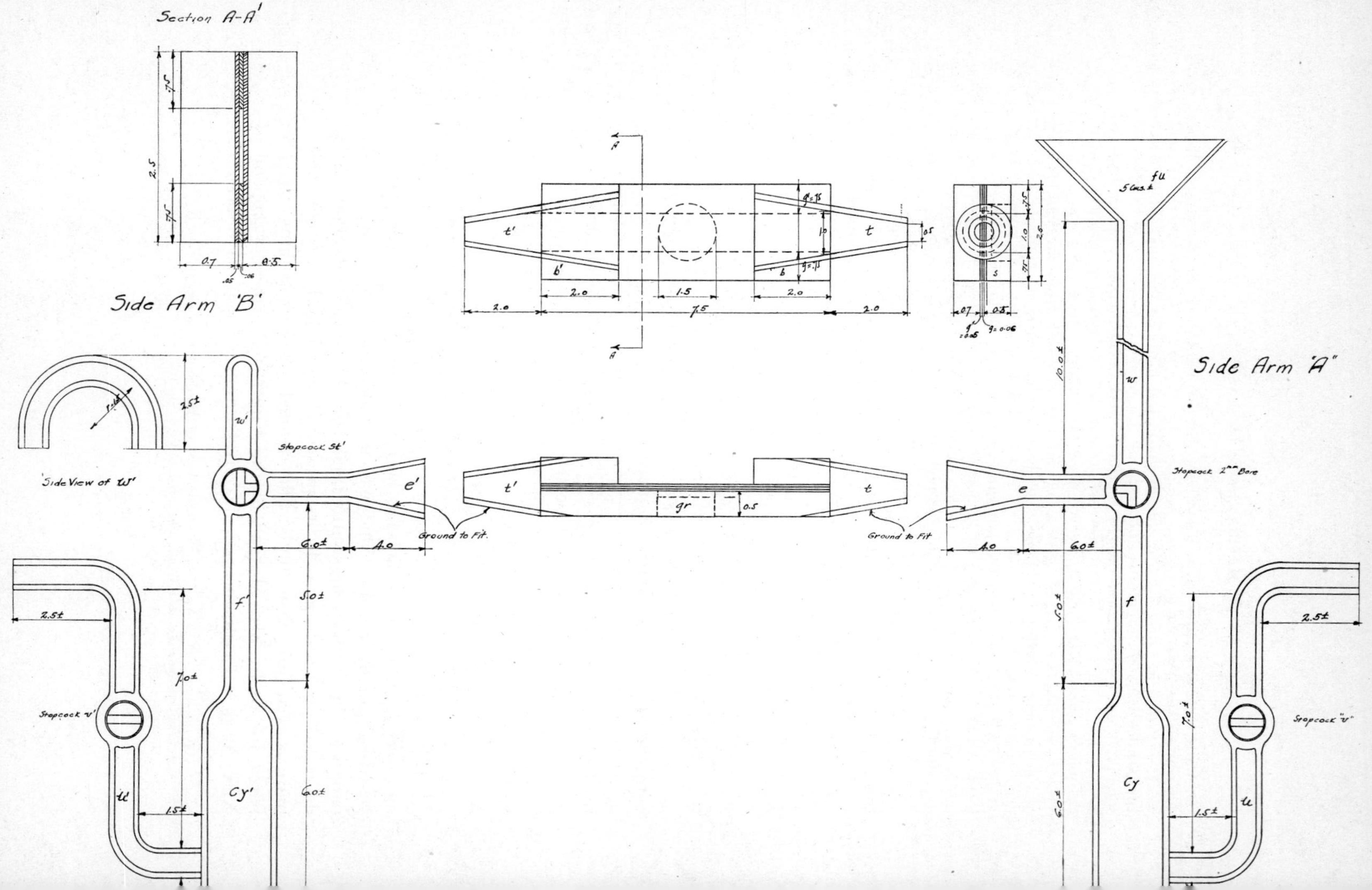
Section A-A'
Side Arm 'B'
Side View of W'
Stopcock St'
Stopcock v'
Ground to Fit.
Ground to Fit
Side Arm "A"
Stopcock 2 mm Bore
Stopcock "v"
5 Cms.±
fu
w
e
f
Cy
u
w'
e'
f'
Cy'
u'
t
t'
b
b'
gr
s

cussed at length by Winslow, Falk and Caulfield,[7] it is considered preferable to express the results of measurements in terms of observed electrophoretic velocities of the migrating bacteria. If it be desirable to convert these velocities to potentials in millivolts, assuming the accuracy and the applicability of the Helmholtz-Lamb equation, it may be recorded that the dimensions of our apparatus were such that, with an impressed voltage of 110 volts for the external field, velocities in microns per second to the anode (μ/sec) may be converted to potentials in millivolts by being multiplied by the constant 1.3.

In our earlier experiments we used the same procedure to eliminate the effect of the endosmotic streaming in the electrophoresis chamber as was used by Ellis,[8] Powis,[9] Northrop[6] and by Winslow, Falk and Caulfield.[7] In our later experiments we have used a more convenient and equally accurate method which is based on the theoretical considerations of Smoluchowski[10] which have recently been amplified by Mooney.[11] Instead of making 10 measurements of velocity (5 with one and 5 with a reversed orientation of the external field) at each of 3, 4, 6 or 8 levels in the cell, we have restricted our mesurements to one or the other of the two levels in the cell at which there is no endosmotic streaming of the water (the so-called "stationary layer—v_s).[12] Our procedure has been to make the usual 10 readings at this level on each of 2 samples of the test suspension of pneumococci. Before each sample was introduced into the apparatus, the cell was flushed first with a liberal quantity (about 200 c c.) of water and then with from 50 to 100 cc. of the bacterial suspension or the sterile medium of the same composition as that in which the bacteria were suspended. All the measurements were made at room temperature. Hydrogen ion concentrations were determined colorimetrically.

The relative accuracy of velocity measurements made in the stationary layers, as confirmed by measurements made at the middles of each sixth or eight portion of the cell depth, is indicated in table 1. Such check experiments have been made a number of times and have indicated the validity of this more convenient procedure which eliminates the necessity for repeated adjustments of the microscope focus.

[7] Ibid., 1923, 6, p. 177.

[8] Ztschr. physik. Chemie, 1912, 78, p. 321; 1912, 80, p. 597.

[9] Ibid., 1915, 89, p. 91.

[10] Graetz' Handbuch d. Elektr. u. d. Magnetismus, 1921, 2, p. 366.

[11] Phys. Rev., 1924, 3, p. 396.

[12] For a cylindrical cell, v_s is located at the distance $R/\sqrt{2}$ from the axis, where R is the radius of the cell; for a rectangular cell, such as was used in these studies, v_s is located at the levels $\frac{1}{2}D/\sqrt{3}$ above and below the middle of the cell, where D is the depth of the channel in the cell.

To eliminate convection currents in the fluid under examination which are due to the absorption of heat waves from the source of illumination for the microscope, we have found that the interposition of a gold reflector is highly efficient.

These reflectors were made for us by the Acme Motion Picture Projector Company of Chicago. They consist of a glass plate on which a very thin layer of gold has been deposited in a splutter arc and another glass plate over it to serve as a protecting cover. The entire reflector

TABLE 1

EXPERIMENTAL VERIFICATION OF THE STATIONARY LAYER (v_s) IN THE ELECTROPHORESIS CELL

Calculations:

Total depth of cell (D)	=	630μ
½D (= R) (= v_0)	=	315μ
$R/\sqrt{3}$	=	315/1.732μ = 182μ

Hence $v_s = 315 \pm 182\mu = 497\mu$; 133μ.

Exper. 35. Measurements on pneumococci (PnA).

Levels μ	Electrophoretic Velocities μ/sec
53	5.5
158	6.9
263	8.1
Avge. for lower half	6.8
368	8.1
473	7.1
578	5.7
Avge. for upper half	7.0
Avge. for entire cell	6.9
$\overline{133}$ (v_s)	$\overline{6.8}$
497 (v_s)	6.9
Avge. (v_s lower and upper)	6.85

was made of such dimensions as permit of its introduction into the carrier for a circle of white or blue glass in the standard substage condenser of a microscope.

MEASUREMENT OF VIRULENCE

In our earliest experiments virulence determinations were made by injecting into white mice measured quantities of 24-hour cultures grown in 1% dextrose broth. It was soon found, however, that duplicate experiments failed to give confirming results. Because exploratory experiments failed to reveal the nature of the uncontrolled variables, this technic was given up. Instead, we conducted our subsequent experiments by the methods suggested by Dr. F. G. Blake of the Yale School of Medicine.

In conducting an experiment to determine the minimum lethal dose of a pneumococcus culture for white mice the procedure was:

1. Prepare a 24-hour culture on a blood-agar slant.
2. Pour 10 c c. of Blake's broth[13] over the slant and incubate for 5 hours.
3. Transfer 0.5 c c. of the broth suspension to a tube containing 10 c c. of Blake's broth and incubate the inoculated tube at 37 C. for from 16 to 18 hours.
4. Prepare decimal dilutions of the culture in sterile broth so that quantities of the culture from 0.1 to 0.000,000,01 c c. are contained in a volume of 0.5 c c.
5. Warm the culture dilutions to 37 C. and inject 0.5 c c. of each intraperitoneally into each of 2 mice.
6. Inject into from 2 to 6 mice each 0.5 c c. of sterile dilution fluid to serve as controls on the technic.
7. Keep the mice under observation for 48 hours.

EXPERIMENTAL FINDINGS

A total of 76 separate strains of pneumococci were studied in the first 40 experiments. Owing to the interference of numerous factors which it is impossible to control without making the conduct of each of a long series of experiments too cumbersome, discrepancies appear in the absolute values of the electrophoretic potentials measured on the same strains in different experiments. The measurements on different strains which are made in a single experiment are more directly comparable. Hence we present separately the results of each of the experiments in which a sufficiently large number of strains were included to give results which can be treated statistically (tables 2-6) and then present (table 7) a summary table which includes the results of all of the electrophoretic measurements made in the first 40 experiments. Electrophoretic potentials are expressed in velocities (μ/sec).

The results of experiments conducted by earlier workers as well as by us have indicated the effects of various organic and inorganic reagents on the electrophoretic potentials on bacteria. Indeed, Winslow, Falk and Caulfield have utilized measurements of such effects to indicate the likelihood that these potentials take their origin, largely if not entirely, in conditions postulated by the type of membrane equilibrium which has been described by Donnan. Hence, it is important to control or eliminate the effects on potential of such substances as appear as constituents of culture medium. The effects of such

[13] Blake's broth was prepared by the following method: One pound of lean, chopped beef was infused with 1 liter of tap water in the ice chest over night. The infusion was boiled for 30 minutes, filtered through paper, and water added to restore the loss by evaporation. One% peptone (Fairchild) and 0.2% sodium phosphate (Na_2HPO_4—anhydr.) were added. The solution was boiled for 20 minutes. The PH was adjusted to 8, and the medium was sterilized in the Arnold sterilizer for 20 minutes on each of 3 successive days. The final PH was 7.8.

reagents are almost invariably in the direction of reducing the potentials on bacteria. The highest potentials which we have ever observed on any strains of bacteria were found on the bacteria which had been suspended in distilled water after repeated sedimentation in the centrifuge and resuspension in distilled water. We have found that from 4 to 6 washings suffice to give potentials which are unaffected by further washings. Owing, however, to the low buffering power of water and, hence, to its easily shifted P_H, duplicate suspensions prepared in this

TABLE 2

ELECTROPHORETIC POTENTIALS ON PNEUMOCOCCI, EXPER. 20

	Type	Number of Strains	Broth Cultures		Washed NaCl Suspensions	
			P_H	μ/sec	P_H	μ/sec
	1	4	5.8	6.2	6.1	6.9
	2, 2a	6	5.5	5.0	6.1	6.3
	3	2	5.7	11.1	6.3	12.3
	4	6	5.6	4.8	6.3	5.6
Totals and averages............	1-4	18	5.7	6.8	6.2	7.8
Totals and weighted averages...	1-4	18	5.6	5.9	6.2	6.9

TABLE 3

ELECTROPHORETIC POTENTIALS ON PNEUMOCOCCI, EXPER. 23

	Type	Number of Strains	Broth Cultures		Washed NaCl Suspensions	
			P_H	μ/sec	P_H	μ/sec
	1	4	5.3	7.9	6.3	10.6
	2, 2a	6	5.4	6.2	6.3	7.7
	3	2	5.3	11.5	6.3	14 0
	4	4	5.5	5.6	6.1	6.8
Totals and averages.............	1-4	16	5.1	7.8	6.3	9.8
Totals and weighted averages....	1-4	16	5.4	7.1	6.3	9.0

manner often show appreciable differences in hydrogen ion concentration. As the potential is known to be a function of the hydrogen ion concentration [7, 14] measurements made on such suspensions are not directly comparable unless the differences in P_H are first demonstrated to be of inconsequential magnitude. We have found that suspensions prepared by repeated washings with from 0.5 to 0.9% NaCl are more constant with respect to both P_H and potential. Hence our tables include data on the electrophoretic potentials on pneumococci in dextrose broth and in NaCl (4 washings).

[14] Northrop, J. H., and De Kruif, P. H.: Jour. Gen. Physiol., 1921-1922, 4, p. 639.

The data from exper. 20 and 23 are presented in tables 2 and 3. From measurements on 18 and 16 strains, respectively, it appears that the potentials on type 3 organisms are distinctly higher than on types 1,

TABLE 4

ELECTROPHORETIC POTENTIALS ON PNEUMOCOCCI, EXPER. 25

	Type	Number of Strains	Broth Cultures		Washed NaCl Suspensions	
			P_H	μ/sec	P_H	μ/sec
	1	6	5.3	3.9	6.3	7.3
	2, 2a	4	5.5	5.8	6.3	6.8
	3	3	5.1	9.7	6.3	11.7
	4	9	5.5	4.7	6.3	6.7
Totals and averages.............	1–4	22	5.4	6.0	6.3	8.1
Totals and weighted averages....	1–4	22	5.4	5.4	6.3	7.6

TABLE 5

ELECTROPHORETIC POTENTIALS ON PNEUMOCOCCI, EXPER. 26

	Type	Number of Strains	Broth Cultures		Washed NaCl Suspensions	
			P_H	μ/sec	P_H	μ/sec
	1	4	5.4	7.4	7.6	8.9
	2, 2a	7	5.7	8.9	7.6	9.7
	3	1	...	....	7.6	11.1
	4	7	5.3	6.5	7.6	10.9
Totals and averages.............	1–4	19	5.5	7.6	7.6	10.2
Totals and weighted averages....	1–4	19	5.5	7.6	7.6	10.0

TABLE 6

ELECTROPHORETIC POTENTIALS ON PNEUMOCOCCI, EXPER. 27

	Type	Number of Strains	Broth Cultures		Washed NaCl Suspensions	
			P_H	μ/sec	P_H	μ/sec
	1	7	5.6	7.6	6.7	11.2
	2	9	5.2	5.8	6.8	9.5
	4	6	5.3	5.2	6.6	9.7
Totals and averages.............	1, 2, 4	22	5.4	6.2	6.7	10.1
Totals and weighted averages....	1, 2, 4	22	5.4	6.2	6.7	10.1

2, and 4. It is also apparent that the gradient of decreasing potential in both broth and NaCl suspensions is 3, 1, 2, 4. In tables 4, 5 and 6 the results are somewhat different. It still remains that type 3 organisms uniformly show higher potentials than the others; but the sequences for types 1, 2 and 4 are not the same. If these differences are significant, they are determined by factors which we have neither recognized nor controlled.

From inspection of the summary table 7, it is clearly evident that type 3 pneumococci have distinctly higher electrophoretic potentials than pneumococci of types 1, 2 and 4. Among the latter, in both broth and NaCl suspension, the sequence of decreasing potential was 1, 4, 2. It is evident, however, from inspection of the average deviations of potentials that the differences between types 1, 2 and 4 are probably insignificant, represent the results of an averaging process only, and

TABLE 7

SUMMARY OF ELECTROPHORETIC POTENTIALS ON PNEUMOCOCCI (ALL EXPERIMENTS)

Type	Number of Strains	Broth Cultures					Washed NaCl Suspensions				
		Number of Measurements	P_H		μ/sec		Number of Measurements	P_H		μ/sec	
			Average	Average Deviation	Average	Average Deviation		Average	Aver. age Deviation	Average	Average Deviation
1	19	35	5.4	±0.2	6.4	±1.6	29	6.5	±0.5	8.9	±2.3
2, 2a	24	38	5.5	±0.3	4.9	±1.5	34	6.7	±0.5	7.0	±2.1
3	7	12	5.5	±0.3	10.8	±0.9	12	6.7	±0.4	12.4	±1.0
4	26	34	5.5	±0.3	5.2	±1.5	31	6.6	±0.4	7.8	±2.1
1–4	76†	119	5.5	±0.3	6.8*		106	6.6	±0.5	9.0*	

* These figures (6.8 and 9) are average averages and are taken to represent the mean potential on pneumococci, assuming equal numerical distribution of the several types. The weighted averages for the data of our experiments are 5.9 and 8.2 for the broth cultures and washed suspensions, respectively.

† A total of 76 different cultures of pneumococci are included in these data. These represent 76 successful isolations. However, they were not obtained from as many successive cases of lobar pneumonia and hence cannot be utilized in their present tabulation to indicate the relative incidence of the various types in pneumonia infections. From a number of patients we obtained more than one culture on repeated examination of blood or other material; and from another number of patients more than one type was obtained from the different materials examined.

do not necessarily predict the results that may be anticipated in any single experiment in which several strains of each type are included. Indeed, there is not in our records a single experiment in which the sequence of potentials is—as in the summary table—3, 1, 4, 2. Indeed, in those experiments in which a sufficient number of strains are included to render comparisons between the types significant, the commonest finding is a sequence like that observed in tables 2 and 3, namely 3, 1, 2, 4. There was a relatively high average potential for all type 4 organisms recorded in table 7, higher than the average potential for the type 1 strains, because in those experiments in which all of the potentials were somewhat above the average values more than an average proportion of type 4 strains were included.

It appears to us that the outstanding finding indicated by the data reported here is the significantly higher as well as less varying potential on the type 3 than on the types 1, 2 and 4 pneumococci. This and the finding that there is little difference between the types 1, 2 and 4 are precisely what might have been anticipated from considerations on the biologic characteristics of these organisms.

As was pointed out in an introductory paragraph of this paper, it had appeared from a priori considerations based on other researches that a parallelism would be found between agglutinability, electrophoretic potential and virulence of different types of organisms in a

TABLE 8

THE VIRULENCE OF PNEUMOCOCCUS CULTURES FOR WHITE MICE (BLAKE'S TECHNIC)

Strain	Type	Fraction of C c. Causing Death
J 106	1	10^{-8}
G 79	2	10^{-6}
M 184	2	10^{-6}
D 73	3	$10^{-8}+$
C 139	4	10^{-2}

TABLE 9

THE VIRULENCE AND ELECTROPHORETIC POTENTIALS ON PNEUMOCOCCI, EXPER. 42

Strain	Type	Fraction of C c. Causing Death	P. D. μ/sec
J 106	1	$10^{-8}+$	9.2
O 46	2	10^{-5}	7.7
N. Y.	3	$10^{-8}+$	13.6
P 35	4	—†	4.7

† No deaths.

single group. We may now proceed to illustrate our findings from experiments on the virulence of pneumococci, measuring virulence in terms of the minimum lethal dose for white mice. In table 8 we present the results of one of many similar experiments on the M L D for mice of one or more representatives of each pneumococcus type. The determinations were made by the technic which has already been described.

It appears from table 8 that the virulence sequence is 3, 1, 2, 4, identical with that which, as we have already indicated, is most commonly found for electrophoretic potentials.

In a number of experiments, electrophoretic potentials were measured on the pneumococci in the same suspensions used for the virulence tests. In table 9 we present a typical experiment in which such measurements were made, one of many showing essentially the same results.

The general parallelism between the virulence and the electrophoretic potential is evident in table 9. The difference in M L D between types 1 and 3 was not marked in this particular experiment, but was not inconsistent with the more common finding which was illustrated in table 8. The failure of culture "P35" (type 4) (table 9) to show any virulence, as contrasted with an M L D of 0.01 (10^{-2}) c c. for culture "C139," type 4 (table 8) is probably to be accounted for by the fact that the former had been carried in stock for about one year before being used in the virulence experiment, whereas "C139" had been used shortly after its isolation from a case of lobar pneumonia.

DISCUSSION

In all the experiments reported here the electrophoretic movement of pneumococci was toward the anode of the external electrical field. Hence, it is presumed that these organisms, like all other bacteria, yeasts, trypanosomes, erythrocytes, etc., on which precise observations have been made, are electronegative to water or other aqueous menstrua in which they are suspended when the P_H is at or near neutrality. When the cultures are carried in stock by the technic described in this paper their potentials do not change. The strict interpretation of these potentials is difficult, owing to uncertainties which attach to their origins, their precise locations and to their exact evaluations. In later papers from this laboratory these problems will receive more detailed consideration. For the present it may suffice to consider them potential differences between the surface films of the bacteria (or of the menstruum immediately contiguous to them) and of the fluid layers which are continuous with the bulk of the menstruum.

In the introductory paragraphs of this paper we remarked on the difficulties inherent in efforts to define the term virulence. For the purposes of these first studies we have used the M L D for mice as the measure of virulence. The technic which we have used has given constantly repeatable results. M L D determinations on cultures which were isolated in the course of these studies and which have been carried on blood-agar slants for nearly two years in general have given the same results as when determinations were made directly after the isolation of the organisms. The only exceptions which have been observed were found among type 4 organisms, especially when, through an oversight, they were not transferred to fresh medium after the stock cultures had become considerably dehydrated. Certain strains of this type have shown progressive increases in M L D, i. e., decreases in virulence. However, the changes in virulence were not great; even directly after isolation they never showed virulence greater than that represented by M L D $= 10^{-2}$ (0.01) c c.[15] We have found regularly that our measurements of virulence can be repeated with an accuracy within an order of magnitude of M L D (in c c.). Hence we consider that the differences observed for different types and recorded in our tables are significant.

We may refer again to our experimental findings which indicate the marked differences among the pneumococci of the several types with respect to their virulence for mice. So far as we are aware, these represent the first findings of this kind. Our tables present the data justifying the conclusion that there are clearly defined differences, of a quantitative nature, in the virulence of pneumococci of different types for white mice. Such differences in virulence must be taken into consideration in studies on the virulence of pneumococci. They may account for at least part of the confusion which is observed in such reports as those of Cotoni, Truche and Raphael,[16] in which data on the virulence of pneumococci are presented without regard to agglutination type.

That the sequence of decreasing virulence, 3, 1, 2, 4, is also the sequence for decreasing electrophoretic potential confirms our anticipations. It appears to us that electrophoretic potentials and virulence may now be numbered among the properties which show parallel differences among the different types of pneumococci.

CONCLUSIONS

From measurements on 76 strains of pneumococci isolated from cases of lobar pneumonia (19 type 1; 24 type 2; 7 type 3; and 26 type 4) it appears that the electrophoretic potentials are different for the several types.

The highest potentials, approximately 11 μ/sec, or 14 millivolts, are quite uniformly found on type 3 organisms.

The most probable sequence of decreasing potential is types 3, 1, 2, 4.

[15] These remarks apply only to measurements of virulence made by the technic described in this paper. Using other methods, entirely different results have been obtained. Correspondingly, the electrophoretic potentials were different from those recorded in our tables.

[16] The Pneumococcus and Pneumococcal Affections (Engl. ed.), 1924.

The potential on type 3 organisms is sharply marked off from the potentials on the others, generally being two or more times as high as those on organisms of the other types.

The potentials on types 1, 2 and 4 organisms are not sharply marked off, one group from the other. They average approximately 5-8 μ/sec for type 1; 3.5-6.5 μ/sec for type 2; and 3-6 for type 4.

Measurements of virulence of pneumococci for white mice by the methods detailed in this paper show distinct differences for the cultures of different types. The sequence of decreasing virulence is 3, 1, 2, 4. The minimum lethal doses (M L D) were found to be: type 3: 10^{-8} c c.; type 1: 10^{-7}-10^{-8} c c.; type 2: 10^{-4}-10^{-6}.; type 4: 10^{-2}-0.5 c c.

The sequence of decreasing electrophoretic potential is identical with the sequence for decreasing virulence. This finding is discussed, especially in the light of anticipations that this would be found, anticipations based on the commonly observed parallelisms (direct or inverse) between virulence, agglutinability and other characteristics of bacteria and on considerations of the rôle of the electrophoretic potential in the phenomenon of agglutination.

STUDIES ON RESPIRATORY DISEASES

XXII. SOME RELATIONS BETWEEN FATALITY IN LOBAR PNEUMONIA AND ELECTROPHORETIC POTENTIALS ON PNEUMOCOCCI

I. S. Falk, M. A. Jacobson and H. A. Gussin

From the Department of Hygiene and Bacteriology of the University of Chicago

In the preceding paper of this series [1] we discussed at some length measurements of electrophoretic potentials on pneumococci of the several types and of the virulence of these organisms for white mice. It is obviously impossible to correlate, by direct experimental methods, virulence for mice with virulence for men. It is possible, however, to obtain some indirect evidence on this point from comparable data on the fatal or nonfatal outcome in cases of lobar pneumonia from which are obtained the cultures whose virulence for white mice is determined. To such correlative data can be added the results of measurements on the electrophoretic potentials.

Without attempting a complete résumé of the literature which bears on the virulence of pneumococci for man and for laboratory animals, we may yet remark on a few pertinent findings by earlier investigators. Park and Williams [2] concluded that cultures obtained "from most pneumonias are more virulent for experimental animals than are those obtained from healthy individuals . . . ." Wadsworth [3] concluded from his researches that there is no experimental evidence that lobar pneumonia in man differs fundamentally from pneumococcus infection in laboratory animals. Dochez [4] came to the conclusion that "Strains of pneumococcus isolated from the blood of patients with lobar pneumonia were usually of high animal virulence. In a few instances where the organism isolated from the blood was of low virulence for animals, the patients recovered." Similarly, Avery, Chickering, Cole and Dochez [5] came to essentially the same conclusion. "Pneumococci isolated from the blood of pneumonia patients, as a rule, are of such virulence that 0.000,001 c c. of broth culture kills white mice in less than 36 hours. On the other hand, strains have been recovered from the same source which possess only moderate virulence, failing to kill white mice in much larger doses. The study of the virulence of pneumococcus isolated from the circulating blood during lobar pneumonia indicates that in general the intoxication is more severe and the prognosis graver, the greater the virulence of the infecting pneumococcus."

Received for publication, July 16, 1925.

1 Jour. Infect. Dis., 1925, 37, p. 481.
2 Jour. Exper. Med., 1905, 7, p. 403.
3 Ibid., 1912, 16, p. 78.
4 Ibid., 1912, 16, p. 680.
5 Monograph 7, Rockefeller Inst. for Med. Res., 1917.

On the other hand, Buerger[6] found that of pneumococcus strains isolated from the mouths of normal persons 79% were virulent to white mice; and that of those obtained from cases of pneumonia 77% were virulent. Truche, Cramer and Cotoni[7] expressed their scepticism that virulence for the mouse is a measure of virulence for man. In a more recent publication Cotoni, Truche and Raphael[8] present a compilation of the results of blood culture in pneumonia, with respect to the isolation of pneumococci, by some 20 investigators. Widely different results are listed, ranging from high to low proportions of successful isolations. No attempt is made, in this compilation, nor in many of the reports from which the data are drawn to refer the findings to the agglutinative type of pneumococci found. Nevertheless, Cotoni, Truche and Raphael come to the conclusion: "That pneumococci isolated from the blood are not more virulent than those obtained from other pathological material such as sputum or pus appears to be proved." There may be no inherent conflict, however, between this and the conclusions of Avery and his colleagues. It appears to us that until the results of more detailed studies on the pathologic anatomy of pneumococcus infection in the mouse become available, this animal may be taken as the indicator of the probable virulence of pneumococci for man.

We have shown[1] that there is a parallelism between the relative magnitude of the electrophoretic potentials and the virulence for white mice of pneumococci of the several types. The decreasing sequence for each of these properties is: types 3, 1, 2, 4. In the light of the preceding discussion it is significant to indicate that this is also the probable sequence of pneumococcus virulence for man, measuring the virulence of pneumococci of any one type by the fatality rate in a series of cases of lobar pneumonia. The most extensive study from which such data are available is that which was conducted by Cole and his colleagues. From a study of 720 cases of lobar pneumonia they report the following figures[9]:

Cases Associated with Pneumococci of Type	Mortality Rate in Percentage
3	44.3
1	35.6
2	29.5
4	13.2

The data have been purposely rearranged in the order of decreasing fatality rate in order that they may bring out more clearly the sequence. It is observed that the sequence (3, 1, 2, 4) is the same as that which we have reported for virulence toward mice and for electrophoretic potentials.

[6] Jour. Exper. Med., 1905, 7, p. 497.
[7] Ann. de l'Inst. Pasteur, 1911, 25, p. 480.
[8] The Pneumococcus and Pneumococcal Affections (Engl. ed.), 1924.
[9] Cole, R.: Nelson Loose-Leaf Med., 1922, 1, p. 248.

The cultures of pneumococci which became available in this laboratory for the studies reported here were being obtained in the course of an extensive investigation on the epidemiology of lobar pneumonia in Chicago, conducted by E. O. Jordan. As data were available on the fatal or nonfatal termination of each case, we thought it might be of some interest to determine whether there is any correlation between fatality and the magnitude of the electrophoretic potentials on the pneumococci isolated from the patient. We have therefore tabulated our data in the form presented in table 1, having calculated separately the average potentials on pneumococci of types 1, 2, 3 and 4 isolated from cases of lobar pneumonia which terminated fatally and nonfatally. Our earlier experimental findings, typified by the data in tables 8 and 9 of the preceding paper,[1] would suggest that strains isolated from fatal cases would be found to have relatively higher potentials than those isolated from nonfatal cases of lobar pneumonia caused by pneumococci of the same type.

TABLE 1

RELATIONS BETWEEN FATALITY OF LOBAR PNEUMONIA AND POTENTIALS ON PNEUMOCOCCI

Type	Electrophoretic Potential (μ/sec) on Pneumococci from	
	Fatal Cases	Nonfatal Cases
1	5.5	6.7
2, 2a	5.6	4.1
3	11.1	9.9
4	5.4	5.1

Examination of table 1 indicates that our anticipations are confirmed by the data for types 2, 3 and 4 and are contradicted by those for type 1.

Our data are based on measurements on seventy-six different strains of pneumococci. Hence, some of the averages are based on relatively small groups and must be interpreted with caution. Differences in the day of the disease on which the patients entered the hospital, the influences of complications to the pneumonias, age, sex, race and other secondary factors also render the strict interpretation of our data hazardous. The data are published here because of their possible significance in a theoretical analysis of virulence and because it is impossible to conduct further studies of this kind until a relatively large number of cases of lobar pneumonia occurring within a short interval of time again becomes available for investigations of this kind.

CONCLUSIONS

Earlier experiments have indicated that, using the technic described, the sequence of decreasing virulence of pneumococci for white mice is 3, 1, 2, 4, and that this is also the sequence for decreasing electrophoretic potential. As this is also the probable sequence of decreasing fatality rate in lobar pneumonia of man it was anticipated that strains of pneumococci isolated from fatal cases of pneumonia might show larger potentials than strains of the same type isolated from nonfatal cases. Our experimental findings reported here confirm this anticipation for pneumococci of types 2, 3 and 4 and contradict it for strains of type 1. If material becomes available for reinvestigation of these relations, it may prove possible to determine the value of potential measurements in the prognosis of lobar pneumonia.

STUDIES ON RESPIRATORY DISEASES

XXIII. ELECTROPHORETIC POTENTIAL AND VIRULENCE OF VARIANTS OF TYPE I PNEUMOCOCCI

I. S. FALK, M. A. JACOBSON AND H. A. GUSSIN

From the Department of Hygiene and Bacteriology of the University of Chicago

Numerous workers have demonstrated that when pathogenic bacteria are grown in vitro in the presence of homologous antiserum or in vivo in the peritoneal cavities of vaccinated animals, they commonly become more virulent for the specific host, show a lessened susceptibility to the bactericidal action of normal serum or specific antiserum and are found to have sustained a loss in agglutinability by specific or nonspecific agglutinating serum. Contrary to these usual findings, Friel[1] reported that pneumococci (Lister type "C"; Avery type 1) grown in the presence of antipneumococcus serum become more easily phagocytosed and that this alteration is persistent for a few subcultures in the progeny of the pneumococcus. He demonstrated the phenomenon with Friedländer's pneumobacterium, with a member of the Pasteurella group and later (Friel and Lister[2]) with B. pestis and Bact. coli communis, and named it "piantication." Contrary to the statement concerning this work given by Stryker[3] and apparently copied from her by other writers, Friel made no direct determinations of alterations in the virulence of "pianticated" bacteria, nor did he report any significant changes in their agglutinability. He assumed that increased phagocytability might be synonymous with reduced virulence. Stryker[3] has reported results of experiments which confirm those of Friel and, in addition, the findings that simultaneous with a loss in virulence for mice, increased phagocytability in the presence of normal serum and increased agglutinability there occurs a lessened tendency for capsule formation, a change in agglutinin absorption power and in antigenic capacities. She reports further that on subsequent cultivation of these modified strains of pneumococci in the absence of antiserum the modifications are persistent. Reversion to the characteristics of normal, untreated pneumococci occurs on passage through mice, the number of passages necessary for complete reversion being approximately proportional to the previous number of treatments in antiserum which the organism had received. Stryker has suggested a mechanism for these changes which is based on the concept of specific receptors.

Blake and Trask[4] have conducted studies along the same line and report that the

> Growth of pneumococcus Type I in homologous immune serum (1-20 dilutions in plain broth) results in marked loss of virulence accompanied by constant and distinct changes in agglutination reactions with respect both to the character of agglutination and the zone of optimum agglutination. These changes are not a gradual alteration of all members of a culture, but appear to be a comparatively rapid and complete change in individual organisms. At least two distinct variants have been derived from the parent culture which was a highly virulent

Received for publication, July 16, 1925.

[1] Publ. South Afr. Inst. Med. Res., Memoir 5, 1915.
[2] Ibid., Memoir 9, 1917.
[3] Jour. Exper. Med., 1916, 24, p. 49.
[4] Jour. Med. Res., 1923, 44, p. 100.

typical example of pneumococcus Type I. The descendants of these variants have maintained their peculiar cultural characteristics,* their characteristic agglutinability, and their virulence through many generations without reversion when carried on artificial media either by daily subculture or at monthly intervals. The original form is designated Type A and variant forms Type B and Type C. (Type A = smooth form, Type C = rough form of other authors.)

* A progressive reduction in colony size for A. B and C.

The agglutination characteristics of A, B, and C in Type I antipneumococcus serum are as follows:

	1:40	1:80	1:160	1:320	1:640	1:1280	1:2560	1:5120	1:10240	
Type A	±±	++	++	±	—	—	—	—	—	rapid coarse compact
Type B	±	+	+	++	++	±	—	—	—	intermediate
Type C	±	±	±	±	±	±	+	+	±	slow fine loose

Type A produces a large amount of specific soluble substance (Avery), Type B a moderate amount, Type C little if any. It is believed that the loss of the capacity to produce the soluble substance is the cause of the change in the agglutination reactions, both with respect to the character of the agglutination and the position of the zone of optimum agglutination.

The usual M.L.D. of A = 10^{-8} c c., of B = 10^{-2} c c. C is avirulent. Occasionally a mouse injected with 0.5 — 1.0 c c.* dies after 3 to 7 days. Under these circumstances only Type A organisms have been recovered from the peritoneal exudate and heart's blood.

* Of type C culture.

Type C organisms agglutinate in heterologous antipneumococcus serum, this agglutination being a P- anti P (Avery) agglutination. The extent to which this cross agglutination occurs probably depends upon the amount of Anti P in the sera used. . . .

Blake has also found that C provides a more effective antigen for the production of agglutinating antiserum than B, and B than A. We shall postpone to a later occasion a discussion whether these strains represent mutations from the original stock or merely separated variants preexistent in the parent culture.

The discovery that a strain of bacteria answering to the customary characteristics of a "pure culture" is not necessarily homogeneous is not new. The line along which heterogeneity is being extensively studied now, i. e., isolation of substrains which give different types of colonies on solid medium and which show marked differences in virulence for laboratory animals, takes its origin in relatively early observations which were not accorded sufficiently detailed study. To cite but a few of the more recent studies, such observations were reported by Teague and McWilliams [5] for Bact. typhosum, by Benians [6] for cultures of Bact. dysenteriae Shiga, by Arkwright [7] for Bact. dysenteriae Shiga, Bact. typhosum, Bact. paratyphosum B. and Bact. enteritidis, by Cowan [8] for streptococci and by Andrewes,[9] for organisms of the Salmonella

[5] Jour. Immunol., 1917, 2, p. 383.
[6] Jour. Path. & Bacteriol., 1920, 23, p. 171.
[7] Ibid., 1921, 24, p. 36. Arkwright and Goyle: Brit. Jour. Exper. Path., 1924, 5, p. 104.
[8] Brit. Jour. Exper. Path., 1922, 3, p. 187.
[9] Jour. Path. & Bacteriol., 1922, 25, p. 187.

group. The most extensive investigation pertinent to our researches has come from Griffith.[10] He reports that:

1. Virulent pneumococci become attenuated by growth in homologous immune serum.

2. The loss of virulence is associated with an alteration of the immunological characters. The attenuated pneumococcus does not stimulate the production of protective substances in the blood of inoculated rabbits.

3. There is a morphological distinction between the colonies of the virulent and the attenuated pneumococci. The virulent colonies are smooth and the attenuated rough in character, the distinction being similar to that between the R and S varieties of B. dysenteriae, etc., described by Arkwright.

4. The S pneumococcus produces in young broth cultures a specific soluble substance; the R pneumococcus does not.

5. The S form agglutinates with specific serum, producing a firm gelatinous precipitate; the R form produces loose clumps which are readily shaken up.

6. An R strain may revert in all respects to the S type, or may remain unchanged after many generations in subculture in plain blood broth. On the other hand, the morphological distinction between the R and the S forms may tend to disappear, while the immunological differences persist.

Griffith also reports that the S and R strains are equally bile soluble; that R colonies are not produced from S strains following growth in the presence of heterologous antiserum; that the R strains of pneumococci differ from the R strains of other organisms (Arkwright, etc.) in failing to show spontaneous agglutinability; and that an attempt to demonstrate the formation of an R from an S strain in the body of an immune mouse was unsuccessful.

It is significant to remark that in practically all essentials, Griffith's findings are in harmony with Stryker's and with Blake's. That the S strain of Griffith is a more effective antigen for the production of protective serum than the R strain and that the C strain of Blake provides a better agglutinogen than the A strain implies no necessary contradiction. It may merely serve to emphasize the oft cited conclusion from many researches concerning the questionable functional rôle of agglutinins in immunity.

De Kruif[11] has reported on a strain of the organism of rabbit septicemia, isolated from a typical culture, which gives a granular growth on solid medium,[12] is relatively avirulent and is spontaneously agglutinable in fluid cultures. He has suggested that the cause of the granular growth is the shifting of the zone of acid agglutination to the region around neutrality by the beef infusion and other ingredients of the culture medium. Northrop and De Kruif[13] later demonstrated — as such an explanation would demand — that the smooth growing, stable, virulent rabbit septicemia organisms (type D) bear a higher electrophoretic potential than the variant (type G).

The experiments reported here, part of a series of studies bearing in general on the nature of immune reactions, were designed to determine the extent of the parallel relations between electrophoretic potential and the virulence of variant strains of the pneumococcus. For such studies, the use of variant cultures of a single stock, occurring as they do among organisms which are, in a qualitative sense, essentially similar, provides that the differences in the characteristics studied are probably of a quantitative nature.

[10] Reports on Public Health and Med. Subjects, No. 18, Ministry of Health, London, 1923, p. 1.

[11] Jour. Gen. Physiol., 1922, 4, p. 395.

[12] This appears to be analogous to the rough (R) type of growth to which reference has been made.

[13] Jour. Gen. Physiol., 1922, 4, p. 655.

Professor F. G. Blake of the Yale School of Medicine provided us with cultures of the A, B and C strains of pneumococcus type I. Their origins and characteristics have already been described. We have carried them in stock for a year and a half on blood-agar slants, transferring them to fresh medium at weekly to biweekly intervals. Throughout this period they have retained their original characteristics. Measurements of electrophoretic potential and of virulence for white mice were conducted by the methods described in preceding papers.[14]

EXPERIMENTAL FINDINGS

Electrophoretic potentials.—Measurements of electrophoretic potential on the variants of type 1 pneumococcus were made on organisms cultivated in several different nutrient fluids and after the organisms had been washed free from the constituents of culture medium. The washings were made by sedimenting the bacteria in the centrifuge at about 3,000 r.p.m., resuspending them in water and in salt solution, and repeating the process from 2 to 10 times. Measurements of P_H were made colorimetrically. The results of typical experiments are given in tables 1-4.

TABLE 1

ELECTROPHORETIC POTENTIALS ON PNEUMOCOCCI TYPE 1, VARIETIES A, B AND C (BLAKE) *

Suspension in	Electrophoretic Potential in μ/sec			
	P_H	A	B	C
Dextrose broth	5.2	6.6	5.9	3.5
0.85% NaCl (4 washings)	6.6	7.7	7.8	11.6
Distilled water (2 washings)	6.2	...†	14.3	30.5

* Grown 24 hours in 0.25% dextrose broth, P_H = 7.8.
† Lost in manipulation.

TABLE 2

ELECTROPHORETIC POTENTIALS ON PNEUMOCOCCI TYPE 1, VARIETIES A, B AND C (BLAKE) *

Strain	Electrophoretic Potential in μ/sec				
	In Broth	In NaCl Solution after Washing			
		4 ×	6 ×	8 ×	10 ×
A	8.5	16.7	17.8	17.1	14.6
B	3.9	9.6	12.5	10.4	10.5
C	3.0	16.0	17.0	16.1	15.9

* Grown 24 hours in 0.25% dextrose broth, P_H = 7.8; suspensions in broth, P_H = 5.2-5.4; suspensions in 0.85% NaCl, P_H = 6-6.2.

[14] Jour. Infect. Dis., 1925, 37, p. 481.

TABLE 3

ELECTROPHORETIC POTENTIALS ON PNEUMOCOCCI TYPE 1, VARIETIES A, B AND C (BLAKE) *

Strain	Electrophoretic Potential in μ/sec								
	In Broth	In NaCl Solution after Washing				In Water after Washing			
		2 ×	4 ×	6 ×	8 ×	2 ×	4 ×	6 ×	8 ×
A...........	4.4	9.1	6.5	5.0	4.1	24.7	24.9	20.7	15.8
B...........	2.4	9.3	13.0	12.3	9.6	27.8	22.7	15.5	6.8
C...........	2.2	4.6	13.1	14.7	11.1	16.7	17.0	14.4	7.8

* Grown 40 hours in 0.25% dextrose broth, $P_H = 7.8$; suspensions in broth, $P_H = 5.2$; suspensions in 0.85% NaCl $P_H = 6$; suspensions in water, $P_H = 6.0\text{–}6.2$.

TABLE 4

ELECTROPHORETIC POTENTIALS ON PNEUMOCOCCI TYPE 1, VARIETIES A, B AND C (BLAKE) *

Strain	Dextrose Broth		Blake's Blood Broth	
	P_H	μ/sec	P_H	μ/sec
A..	5.6	7.1	6.6	7.0
B..	5.6	5.6	6.6	6.3
C..	5.6	3.8	6.6	5.8

* Grown 18 hours in dextrose and Blake's blood broths; 5% defibrinated sheep's blood to Blake's broth.

The findings exhibited in these tables have been duplicated many times. From the data in them it appears that:

1. Varieties A, B and C, grown in dextrose broth, in blood broth and in Blake's broth exhibit differences in electrophoretic potentials.
2. These differences, although inconstant in absolute value in various experiments, are always relatively the same.
3. The sequence of decreasing potential is A, B, C.
4. The potential is increased on washing the bacteria with water or salt solution.
5. Repeated washings may result in a subsequent fall in potential.
6. The sequence of potential values on washed organisms may be different from the sequence on organisms in the original culture medium.

B. Virulence.—Measurements of virulence of pneumococci are restricted in this discussion to the determinations of M L D for healthy white mice. The technic for these determinations have already been given in detail.[14] If cultures are tested directly after growth for 24 hours in dextrose broth, in Blake's broth or in blood broth, they may show variations within the following ranges:

Strain	M L D, C c.
A..	10^{-6} - 10^{-9}
B..	10^{-1} - 10^{-3}
C..	* - 10^{-3}

* No deaths.

When tested by the technic which we have reported gives more constant results we obtain, almost without exception, the findings illustrated by the experiment cited in table 5, typical of a large number of such tests which we have conducted.

TABLE 5

VIRULENCE OF PNEUMOCOCCI FOR WHITE MICE

Strain	M L D, C c.
A	10^{-8}
B	10^{-3}
C	—*

* No deaths.

Occasionally some of the mice which receive 0.5 c c. of an undiluted culture or of a 1 : 10 dilution of strain C will die. Our findings with respect to virulence completely confirm those of Blake which we have already discussed. The sequence of decreasing virulence is A, B, C.

COMMENT

In the preceding publications of this series we pointed out that an a priori analysis leads to the anticipation that if a culture is of relatively high virulence, is not easily phagocytosed, and is relatively inagglutinable, it will show a relatively high electrophoretic potential by comparison with other cultures of the same species. The parallelism of the virulence and the electrophoretic potential sequences for A, B, C varieties of pneumococci reported here confirm this anticipation.

In the first paper of this series we showed that washing cultures of pneumococci of types 1, 2, 3 and 4 result in increased electrophoretic velocities. The sequence of these velocities, however, remains the same for the several types. The data reported in tables 1-4 show that washing the variant strains with water or with salt solution increases the velocities and also changes their relative values. This finding implies that there is probably a fundamental difference in the constitution of the cells or of their secretions as between the variants and the typical varieties of pneumococci. Whether or not they can be related to differences in the exosmosis of salts of the nature reported by Guillemin and Larson [15] remains to be determined.

It would have been desirable, had it been possible, to determine whether changed relative potentials of washed pneumococci are simultaneous with changed relative virulence. Experiments undertaken to

[15] Ibid., 1922, 31, p. 349.

this end soon demonstrated that there are few viable organisms remaining in a suspension of washed cells. Hence these experiments were discontinued.

CONCLUSIONS

Two variant strains of pneumococci obtained by Dr. F. G. Blake from a type 1 culture grown in the presence of homologous antiserum retain their original characteristics when grown on blood agar.

We confirm the finding of early workers that these variant strains differ in virulence for white mice from the parent strain.

Our experiments demonstrate that the electrophoretic potentials on these strains parallel their virulence, the sequence for decreasing potential as well as for decreasing virulence being strains A, B, C.

We had previously demonstrated that washing pneumococci of types 1, 2, 3 and 4 with water or with salt solution results in changes in the absolute values of their electrophoretic potentials but not in the sequence of these values among the several types. The data reported in this paper show that sequence as well as the absolute magnitudes change when the pneumococcus variants are washed.

Our experiments suggest that electrophoretic potential is related in some fundamental manner to virulence, phagocytability, agglutinability, capsule formation and other characteristics of micro-organisms.

ADDENDUM

Winslow, Falk and Caulfield[16] have pointed out that the conversion to potential (in volts) of observed velocity of migration of a particle in an electrophoresis cell is conditioned by uncertainties which attach to the factors in the Helmholtz equation. These uncertainties are especially attendant on the values to be given to the coefficient of viscosity (η) and the dielectric constant (K) which enter in the following manner:

$$\text{P. D. (e. s. u.)} = \frac{4 \pi \eta v}{K X}$$

in which v is the observed velocity of migration in μ per second and X is the potential gradient in electrostatic units (e.s.u) in the cell. If for K we should use the dielectric constant for water, it is easily treated. If, however, for K the equivalent constant for the culture medium or for the film of fluid immediately contiguous to the micro-organism should be used, it cannot be evaluated at present. We have taken the

[16] Jour. Gen. Physiol., 1923, 6, p. 177.

precaution of measuring the relative viscosities of the cultures of pneumococci A, B and C in order to determine whether or not the velocities which are given in our tables and which are treated as linear functions of electrophoretic potentials are due to different alterations in viscosity produced by the different strains. Measurements with the Ostwald viscosimeter kindly made for us in this laboratory by R. W. Harrison showed the following values:

Strain	Viscosity of Culture Relative to Water ($\eta/\eta\omega$)
A	1.116
B	1.098
C	1.123

Hence it is obvious that the differences in electrophoretic velocities reported above are not due to differences in viscosity of the menstrua in which the bacteria are suspended.

STUDIES ON RESPIRATORY DISEASES

XXIV. ELECTROPHORETIC POTENTIAL, VIRULENCE AND SERUM AGGLUTINATION WITH SINGLE CELL CULTURES OF VARIANTS OF TYPE 1 PNEUMOCOCCI

I. S. FALK AND M. A. JACOBSON

From the Department of Hygiene and Bacteriology of the Univerity of Chicago

In a preceding publication [1] we reported on certain findings with two variant strains of pneumococci isolated from a type 1 culture by Blake and Trask of the Yale School of Medicine. They had obtained these strains from a culture grown in broth-containing homologous antiserum which showed marked loss of virulence accompanied by constant and distinct changes with respect to both the character of agglutination and the zone of optimum agglutination. We confirmed Blake and Trask's findings that culture A (original type 1 pneumococcus) kills white mice regularly following the intraperitoneal injection of 0.5 c c. containing 1×10^{-7}-1×10^{-8} c c. of culture; that "B" (the first derivative variant) is less virulent, being lethal to mice with an M L D of 1×10^{-3} c c.; and that "C" (the second derivative variant) is avirulent, usually failing to kill even when 0.5 c c. of an undiluted broth culture is injected into the peritoneal cavity of a mouse. Occasionally, injection of a large quantity of "C" will cause the death of a mouse. The peritoneal exudate and the heart blood then yield only "A" pneumococci.

We have also reported that these variant strains, kindly placed at our disposal by Dr. Blake, have retained their original chracteristics after a year's cultivation on blood agar. Our experiments demonstrated that the electrophoretic potentials on these strains parallel their virulence, the sequence for decreasing potential as well as for decreasing virulence being: A, B, C.

We have already reported confirmation of Blake and Trask's finding that the variant strains breed true to type. When grown in plain or sugar broths or on blood medium they do not revert to the original type. The only reversions which have been reported are those (C to A) which follow on a fatal infection in the mouse. The full significance of these experiments for genetic theory and the concepts of uniparental inheritance we propose to discuss in another place. Our purpose is to

Received for publication, August 11, 1925.

[1] Falk, I. S.; Jacobson, M. A., and Gussin, H. A.: Jour. Infect. Dis., 1925, 37, p. 499.

present here the results of experiments with single cell strains of A, B and C. These experiments were designed to cast some light on the problem which arises out of considerations of the various alternative conjectures which might be listed to account for the mechanism of serum action which results in the production of the variant strains. The solution of the problem demands experimental evidence on two scores: 1. Can variant strains of the B and C types be produced from a single cell strain of the A original culture? 2. What are the characteristics of single cell strains isolated from the B and C variant strains? The experiments reported here are designed to provide a tentative answer to the second of these questions.

HISTORY OF CULTURES

The cultures used in the experiments reported here were derived from the A, B and C strains of pneumococci placed at our disposal by Dr. F. G. Blake in February, 1924. Single cell isolations were made for us from broth cultures previously made from blood-agar cultures examined on blood-agar plates for their purity by Mr. A. F. Reith of this laboratory by the usual Barber micropipet method. The isolated single cells were inoculated into Blake's broth to which 5% defibrinated sheep blood had been added, and were incubated at 37 C. until turbidity was evident to the naked eye. Approximately half of the cultures failed to develop; in the other half growth was generally slow in the first 24 or 48 hours, but proceeded to a maximum between the 48th and 72nd hours. The cultures were streaked on blood-agar plates on several occasions and, with the exception noted on a subsequent page, were found to give only typical pneumococcus growth. These single cell subcultures were kept in stock in the icebox on sheep blood-agar slants, transferred at weekly to biweekly intervals.

As it is customary in bacteriologic literature to treat of single cell cultures as though the micropipet method for preparing them were entirely beyond criticism, it is pertinent to call attention to a possible source of error which is commonly overlooked. Mr. Reith informs us that occasionally when examining minute drops of culture under the microscope one is found in which two cocci or bacilli—as the case may be—are clearly discernible. Either because of its own motility or under the pressure of convection currents or movements in the fluid arising out of changes in the distribution of surface energies in the drop, one of the micro-organisms may be carried from the interior of the drop to the margin of contact with the glass. The micro-organism then behaves as though it were trapped in the interphase.[2] If the margin of the drop appears as a dark ring, the micro-organism may be lost from sight. When a drop which appears to contain only one cell is drawn into the micropipet and is later transferred to culture medium, the culture which is subsequently obtained may not always be truly a "single cell" strain. Care was taken in preparing the single cell strains which were used in our experiments to reduce to a minimum the probability that any one of our cultures is derived from more than one cell. Certain aspects of this problem in microisolation are being further examined in this laboratory.

Between December, 1924, and March, 1925, Mr. Reith prepared for us 15 single cell strains. The original cultures of Blake and Trask are designated: A orig.; B orig.; C orig. The single cell strains are: A1, A2, A3, A4, A5 and A6; B1, B2, B3, B4 and B5; C1, C2, C3 and C4. Each of these cultures has been examined for purity by microscopic and cultural methods on the occasion of each major experiment. Culture A1 was eliminated from the present series of experiments when it was found to be contaminated with a spore-forming bacillus. All medium used for the cultivation of stock cultures was examined for sterility after incubation for from 36 to 48 hours before use.

EXPERIMENTAL FINDINGS

Experiments on Electrophoretic Potential.—Measurements of electrophoretic potential were made by the method described before.[3] In table 1 we present the results of two experiments on the potentials of pneumococci in dextrose broth cultures and of pneumococci suspended in 0.85% NaCl solution after 4 washings with this salt solution. The findings presented here are entirely typical of those for six similar experiments which are omitted. At no point have differences been noted in the several experiments.

Even a cursory examination of table 1 will reveal that in dextrose broth cultures and in washed NaCl suspensions the electrophoretic potentials on organisms of the single cell strains agree very closely with the potentials on the cocci of the original strains. For the dextrose broth cultures the sequence of decreasing potential is A, B, C. In an earlier publication [1] we called attention to the curious experimental finding that if cultures of the usual type pneumococci (1, 2, 3 and 4)

[2] Mudd and Mudd give an analysis of phenomena of this type in Jour. Exper. Med., 1924, 40, pp. 633 and 647.

[3] Falk, I. S.; Gussin, H. A., and Jacobson, M. A.: Jour. Infect. Dis., 1925, 37, p. 481.

are rewashed in NaCl solution, the absolute magnitudes of their potentials are changed, but the sequence (3, 1, 2, 4) is unaltered; whereas, rewashing suspensions of the variant strains of pneumococci resulted in a change in the relative as well as in the absolute magnitudes of their potentials—the sequence is changed from A, B, C to A, C, B or C, A, B. Hence, it is significant to note in table 1 that repeated washing with NaCl solution resulted in an altered sequence for the single cell as well as for the original strains to C, A, B. We may therefore conclude that the electrophoretic potentials of single cell cultures are essentially the same as for the original parent strains from which they were derived.

TABLE 1

ELECTROPHORETIC POTENTIALS ON PNEUMOCOCCI OF THE ORIGINAL AND SINGLE CELL STRAINS

Strain	Electrophoretic Potential (μ/sec) in: Dextrose Broth (Final $P_H = 5$)	Electrophoretic Potential (μ/sec) in: 0.85% NaCl (After 4 Washings with 0.85% NaCl) (Final $P_H = 7$)
A orig.	8.1	9.4
A2	7.1	8.1
A3	7.9	7.1
A4	6.5	11.0
A5	7.1	9.4
A6	7.9	8.3
	average = 7.3	average = 8.8
B orig.	5.8	7.4
B1	5.9	6.8
B2	—*	6.8
B3	5.7	6.2
B4	5.9	8.1
B5	6.0	7.9
	average = 5.9	average = 7.2
C orig.	3.3	11.0
C1	4.3	12.6
C2	3.1	9.7
C3	3.2	9.4
C4	3.2	14.8
	average = 3.5	average = 11.6

* Contaminated culture.

Experiments on Virulence.—In the preceding papers of this series to which we have already referred we have discussed at length the parallel relations between virulence and electrophoretic potential. The term "virulence," as used here, applies to the lethality for white mice of pneumococcus cultures (or of their dilutions) prepared by the technic described in detail elsewhere.[3] The results of virulence measurements are expressed in terms of minimum lethal dose (M L D) in c c. In table 2 we present the findings from virulence experiment 10, one of several such experiments giving entirely similar results.

From the data in table 2 it is clearly evident that the virulence of variant strain B (M L D $= 1 \times 10^{-3}$) is less than that of the original type 1 strain (A) from which it was derived ($M\ L\ D = 1 \times 10^{-8}$) and that variant strain C is practically without virulence for white mice ($M\ L\ D = 0.5$ c c.). These results confirm the findings of Blake and Trask and of our earlier experiments.[1] It is also clear that the virulence of each of the single cell strains (A2-A6; B1-B5; C1-C4) is entirely similar to the virulence of the original parent strain from which it was derived.

The footnotes to table 2 call for a word of explanation. As we have indicated in our earlier paper on the variant strains of pneumococci,

TABLE 2

THE VIRULENCE OF THE ORIGINAL AND SINGLE CELL STRAINS OF PNEUMOCOCCI FOR WHITE MICE

Strain	M L D, C c.
A orig	1×10^{-8}
A2	10^{-8}
A3	10^{-8}
A4	10^{-8}
A5	10^{-8}
A6	10^{-8}
B orig	1×10^{-3}
B1	10^{-3}
B2	10^{-3}
B3	10^{-2}
B4	10^{-2}
B5	10^{-3}
C orig	—*
C1	—†
C2	—†
C3	—*
C4	—†
Controls (sterile broth)	—*

* No deaths.
†One mouse (of two) receiving 0.5 or 0.1 c c., dead after 48 hours.

Blake and Trask first reported—and we confirmed them—that an occasional mouse receiving a large dose of the C strain dies. From the peritoneal exudate or heart blood of such a mouse only type A organisms are recovered. In table 2 we note that in the experiment illustrated an occasional mouse receiving organisms of single cell cultures C1, C2 and C4 died. From its heart blood and peritoneal exudate we recovered type A organisms. Hence, in these respects, too, the single cell strains are indistinguishable from the parent strains.[4]

[4] We cannot entertain the objection which may be raised against the validity of such an experimental finding on the grounds that the pneumococci recovered from the dead mouse may not have been descended from the bacteria which had been injected into the living animal. Such an objection loses its force from the considerations that the findings cited are regular and that the spontaneous occurrence of pneumococci of the A type (Avery type 1) in mice dying from injections of other micro-organisms, from intercurrent infections, from traumatisms or other causes is of sufficient rarity (if it ever occurs) to be noteworthy.

Shortly after the isolation of our single cell strains, cultures of A2, A3, A4, B2 and C3 were sent to Dr. F. G. Blake. In a personal communication (April 20, 1925) he reports:

> Agglutination tests with your pure line strains A2, A3 and A4, B2 and C3, are the same as with our original A, B and C.
>
> Virulence tests with your A3, B2 and C3 have given the same results as with our A, B and C. Mice dying following injection with a large amount of C3 have yielded only A in cultures of peritoneal exudate and heart's blood.

Experiments on Serum Agglutination.—We have further undertaken a series of experiments to determine whether our single cell strains behave toward an agglutinating serum like the parent strains.

TABLE 3

SERUM AGGLUTINATION OF ORIGINAL AND SINGLE CELL STRAINS OF PNEUMOCOCCI

Strain	Final Serum Dilutions					Controls (No Serum) (Heated Serum)
	1:20	1:40	1:80	1:160	1:320	
A orig.	++++	+++	—	—	—	—
A2	++++	+++	—	—	—	—
A3	++++	+++	—	—	—	—
A4	++++	+++	—	—	—	—
A5	++++	+++	—	—	—	—
A6	++++	+++	—	—	—	—
B orig.	++++	++++	+++	+++	—	—
B1	++++	+++	+++	+++	—	—
B2	++++	+++	+++	+++	—	—
B3	++++	+++	+++	+++	—	—
B4	++++	+++	+++	+++	—	—
B5	++++	+++	+++	+++	—	—
C orig.	++++	++++	+++	+++	+++	—
C1	++++	++++	+++	+++	+++	—
C2	++++	++++	+++	+++	+++	—
C3	++++	++++	+++	+++	+++	—
C4	++++	++++	+++	+++	+++	—

— indicates no macroscopic agglutination; +, ++, +++, little, moderate and heavy agglutination; ++++, complete agglutination; supernatant fluid clear.

In table 3 we present the results of a typical experiment. The agglutination tests were made with the same cultures used for the virulence experiment illustrated in table 2. To 0.3 c c. of culture was added 0.3 c c. of 0.8% NaCl dilution of type 1 antipneumococcus agglutinating serum obtained from the N. Y. State Department of Health. The serum-culture mixtures were held in a water bath adjusted to 38 C. for one hour and in the icebox over night.

From table 3 it appears that the single cell strains behave like their respective parent strains with serial dilutions of agglutinating serum. It is significant to note that the sequence of increasing agglutinability of the strains (single cell and original) is: A, B, C.

SUMMARY AND CONCLUSIONS

Of a total of 15 single cell strains isolated from Blake and Trask's A, B and C cultures of pneumococci (A = type 1; B and C are variant strains obtained from A by growth in the presence of homologous antiserum) one (A1) showed evidences of contamination. Experiments with the remaining 14 (5 from A, 5 from B, 4 from C) and with the parent strains demonstrate that each of the single cell strains is indistinguishable from the parent strain from which it was derived with respect to electrophoretic potential, virulence for white mice and serum agglutination.

The parent strains (originally received from Dr. F. G. Blake Feb. 25, 1924) and the single cell strains (isolated between Dec. 27, 1924, and March 1, 1925) have been carried in stock on blood-agar slants through a large number of generations. At the time of this writing there have been no evidences of spontaneous changes in the parent strains (A orig., B orig., C orig.) or in the single cell strains. So far as concerns the characteristics studied, each breeds true.

It is not our intent to enter into a discussion of the significance of the data reported here for the concepts of genetics in forms showing uniparental inheritance until experiments now in progress have been completed. It is pertinent merely to reiterate the significance of the finding illustrated above that a single cell strain of the C variant reverts to A on passage through a mouse.

THE EFFECT OF HYDROGEN ION CONCENTRATION ON CERTAIN ANTIGENIC PROPERTIES OF CLOSTRIDIUM BOTULINUM *

I. S. FALK AND F. POWDERMAKER

From the Department of Hygiene and Bacteriology of the University of Chicago

From studies on anaphylaxis with pure proteins [1] it has become clear that certain properties of an antigen may be modified quantitatively by effecting reversible changes in such of its physicochemical properties as are functions of the P_H of the antigen solution. The indications are that it may prove possible to produce a more effective state of antibacterial or antitoxic immunity in an animal by immunization with physicochemically modified antigen or to produce such states when none can be produced by the usual methods. The experiments with Cl. botulinum were designed to provide some information on the specific antibody responses in rabbits inoculated with suspensions of Cl. botulinum (types A and B) adjusted to various hydrogen ion concentrations.

HISTORY OF CULTURES USED

Four cultures of Cl. botulinum were received from G. M. Dack of this department. They had been isolated by the single cell method and carried in beef heart medium. "Sall" is identical with "A55," a type A culture isolated by Starin and Dack [2] from canned corn which had been the cause of an outbreak of botulism in Colorado. Starin and Dack reported that "Sall" did not give the agglutination reaction with any potent type A antiserum tested against it, and that no effective agglutinating serum could be produced in animals into which it was introduced.

"DIA" is identical with culture "A1" in Mr. Dack's collection. It is a type A strain obtained by single cell isolation from culture 90 of Dr. K. Meyer. It was isolated from olives implicated in an outbreak of botulism in Greensburg, Pa. Starin and Dack report that it is agglutinated by homologous antiserum in dilution of 1:750 and is not agglutinated by type B antiserum. They also report that cultures of "Sall" possess higher toxicities than cultures of "DIA."

"126.7" is a type B organism, isolated by Dr. R. S. Graham of the University of Illinois from corn silage. Culture "126.7" was used only in the second series of our experiments.

"B64" is a type B organism of unknown origin. Starin and Dack report agglutinations of this organism with homologous antiserum in dilution of 1:1,500 and no agglutination with heterologous antiserum. Mr. Dack further informs us that in experiments which he has conducted antiserum produced against

Received for publication, July 16, 1925.

* This study was aided by a grant from the National Canners' Association.

[1] Falk and Caulfield: Jour. Immunol., 1923, 8, p. 239.

[2] Jour. Infect. Dis., 1923, 33, p. 169.

"126.7" or "B64" does not show cross-agglutinations with cultures of these organisms and that "126.7" is completely agglutinated by its hemologous antiserum in dilution of 1 to 375.

PREPARATION OF ANTIGENS

The cultures were carried in 0.5% beef heart infusion broth to which 2% Wolf's casein had been added. The P_H was 7.8. The organisms were transferred about once each month and slant cultures (incubated at 37 C.) were tested for the presence of aerobic contaminants. The antigen cultures were grown at 37 C. under sterile petrolatum in veal infusion medium to which 2% Wolf's casein digest[3] and 0.25% glucose had been added. The P_H was 7.8-8. The tubes or flasks of medium were held in boiling water for 15 minutes before being used for inoculations in order to remove dissolved oxygen. Agar slant controls were prepared from the original culture at each inoculation. At the close of the experimental work agar plates incubated at 37 C. in an atmosphere of hydrogen showed no evidences of anaerobic contaminants.

Young cultures were used throughout these experiments. Incubation of the cultures for from 24 to 48 hours was necessary before there was visible growth. Subsequently, maximum growth was obtained after from 4 to 6 hours' further incubation. Stained preparations showed only 1 or 2 spores to many hundreds of vegetative cells. The cultures were detoxified at 78 C. for 30 minutes. They were then centrifugalized and washed with sterile distilled water 6 times and held in the ice chest until used. The absence of toxin in the final suspensions was demonstrated by inoculations into mice. All of the suspensions except those of "Sall" were standardized by nephelometric comparisons with suspensions of preserved Bact. coli cells which had in turn been standardized against Cl. botulinum suspensions. The final suspensions of "Sall" clumped spontaneously in a "ropy" fashion so that turbidity readings were impossible. They were standardized instead by direct counts with the hemocytometer cell.

Each of the antigen suspensions was prepared at 3 different hydrogen ion concentrations, i. e., about P_H 2, 7.2 and 10. The suspensions at P_H 7.2 were unadjusted and represent the spontaneously acquired hydrogen ion concentration of washed Cl. botulinum cells in distilled water. The other acidities were obtained by appropriate additions of HCl or of NaOH. In the case of each adjusted suspension, the P_H adjustments were followed by thorough stirring of the suspensions and incubation at room temperature over night. In every case the P_H was tested the following day and found to be unchanged.

ANIMAL INOCULATIONS

The inoculations into rabbits were made intraperitoneally on 3 successive days. After a rest period of 3 days, inoculations were again made daily for 3 days. The last inoculations were given on the first day after a second rest period of 3 days. The following dosages were employed:

First inoculation	25,000,000 bacteria
Second inoculation	50,000,000 bacteria
Third inoculation	75,000,000 bacteria
Fourth to seventh inoculations	100,000,000 bacteria

Each of the antigens at each P_H was inoculated into 3 rabbits. In addition, one animal was given intraperitoneally 0.5 c c. N/5 HCl and another an equal amount of N/5 NaOH 15 minutes before inoculation with one of the antigens in

[3] Kahn, M. C.: J. Med. Res., 1922, 43, p. 155.

suspension at P_H 7.2. (A control of this kind was carried through for each of the antigens used.) The total number of animals used in this series was 33. It was found necessary to use both old and young animals. All were in good condition and had been under observation in the laboratory for some time. The largest and smallest animals were distributed through the various groups of triplicates so that the influence of the animal's size and age on antibody response could be evaluated. The inoculations appeared to result in only one death and a few transitory cases of diarrhea.

BLEEDINGS

A preliminary bleeding was made from the ear of one animal in each group of 3 on the seventh day after the last inoculation. In a few cases the final bleedings were made from the heart; in most they were made from the carotid artery 10 or 11 days after the last inoculation. The blood was caught in clean, sterile centrifuge tubes, held on ice over night, centrifugalized the next day and the separated serum stored on ice. No preservatives were added.

AGGLUTINATION TESTS

For the preparation of agglutination antigens, the cultures were grown and detoxified by the same methods used in the preparation of the antigens described above. The suspensions were filtered through paper and diluted to the proper turbidity with so-called "physiologic" salt solution (0.85% NaCl) of P_H 7.6. The final suspensions were at P_H 7.8-8. After suspension and serum had been mixed the tubes were incubated in a water bath adjusted to 48-50 C. for 2 hours and the agglutinations read after standing for 16-24 hours in the ice box. At each test each of the antigens was tested with normal rabbit serum and with salt solution.

RESULTS OF EXPERIMENTS

The first series of experiments resulted in the production of good agglutinating serum. No attempt was made in this series to determine the complement fixing capacities of each rabbit serum. In the second series, conducted during the late winter season to repeat the first, approximately one third of the animals died of intercurrent infections, and a few others showed considerable cachexia. Although complement-fixation as well agglutination tests were made with the second set, the results were irregular and inconclusive, apparently because no high titer serum was obtained. Hence we report here, in abridged statistical form, the results of the first series only.

The aim of the experiment was threefold, viz.: to determine the absolute agglutinating value of each serum produced, to determine the relative values of the acidulated and alkalinized by comparison with the untreated antigens, to determine the effect of acid and alkali treatment on the type A and type B specificities of the agglutinating responses. Hence we present in table 1 the results recalculated into relative terms which permit these evaluations. The maximum agglutinating dilutions have been expressed in percentages, taking as 100 the titer of each serum which was produced with antigens at $P_H = 7.2$. The average absolute values of the titers are presented in the last column of the table.

From inspection of table 1 on the agglutination of organisms by their homologous antiserum it appears that with organisms of type A ("DIA" and "Sall") more potent agglutinating serum was obtained in animals that received injections with acidulated or alkalinized than with neutral suspensions. With one exception (DIA/DIA-antigen

TABLE 1

THE INFLUENCE OF PH ON THE AGGLUTINOGENIC PROPERTIES OF CLOSTRIDIUM BOTULINUM *

Serum/Organism	Antigen at P_H = 2.0 %	Antigen at P_H = 7.2 %	Antigen at P_H = 12.0 %	Antigen + HCl %	Antigen + NaOH %	Absolute Titers (Av. for All P_H Antigens) 1:
Homologous Antigen and Serum						
DIA / DIA	104	100	198	204	42	870
B 64 / B 64	84	100	84	84	56	410
Sall / Sall	298	100	119	238	397	970
Heterologous Antigen and Serum						
DIA / Sall	36	100	105	32	129	830
Sall / DIA	32	100	54	35	21	570
DIA / B 64	45	100	37	49	30	300
Sall / B 64	0	100	147	0	194	150
B 64 / DIA	87	100	83	45	23	680
B 64 / Sall	100	100	7	198	88	410

* Each titer in the table is the average titer for 3 animals treated in a similar manner. "Per cent" titers calculated on the basis that the titer of the serum produced with $P_H = 7.2$ antigen equals 100.

+ NaOH) the separate injection of alkali and of neutral suspension resulted similarly in the production of more potent serum. Conversely, injections of type B suspensions (B64) which had been acidulated or alkalinized or which had been preceded by an injection (into the peritoneal cavity) of acid or alkali resulted in the production of less potent agglutinating serum than followed the injection of neutral ($P_H = 7.2$) suspensions of the same strain.

The data on the agglutinations of Cl. botulinum (types A and B) by heterologous serum show for the 24 combinations in which acidulated or alkalinized antigens were used: 18 in which the heterologous titration was reduced; 5 in which it was increased; 1 in which no change was effected.

If the data are collected in a somewhat different manner it becomes possible to evaluate the rôle of the bacteria used as antigens in the agglutination test in the determination of the titer. For table 2 the titers for a single strain are lumped, disregarding the P_H values of the antigens used in serum production. They are presented as absolute and as relative titers, taking for the latter the titers of the homologous serum and organisms as 100.

It appears from table 2 that: 1. The type A strains (DIA and Sall) are more easily agglutinated by their homologous than by their heterologous serum. 2. The DIA strain is more easily agglutinated by the type B serum than is the Sall strain. 3. The type B strain (B64) is less easily agglutinated than either of the type A strains.

TABLE 2

DIFFERENCES IN THE AGGLUTINABILITY OF CL. BOTULINUM OF TYPES A AND B BY HOMOLOGOUS AND HETEROLOGOUS ANTISERUM

Average Agglutination Titers

Organism	Serum DIA	Serum Sall	Serum B 64	All
DIA	870	570	680	710
Sall	830	970	410	740
B 64	300	150	410	280

Proportionate Agglutination Titers

Organism	Serum DIA, %	Serum Sall, %	Serum B 64, %	All, %
DIA	100	59	166	108
Sall	95	100	100	98
B 64	34	15	100	50

DISCUSSION

Starin and Dack have clearly enunciated the commonly accepted serologic specificities of the A and B types of Cl. botulinum. With the agglutination test and with the agglutinin absorption test they find no heterologous reactions between the two types. As our work was conducted with strains from their stock and are undoubtedly of the antitoxic types indicated in the text, we are somewhat at loss to account for our observations of the heterologous reactions noted in the table. At only one point does our technic of preparing antigen differ from theirs; that is in the use for antigen of 6 times washed bacteria in distilled water instead of salt solution. Although this appears to be a minor point in the eyes of many bacteriologists, in the light of the findings which are being reported from this laboratory on the effect of salt and other reagents on the electrophoretic potential on bacteria and the relation of this potential to the antigenic and other properties of bacteria, this divergence in technic assumes appreciable significance. This problem is being investigated further.

CONCLUSIONS

Using methods essentially like those of Starin and Dack, we have succeeded in producing in rabbits potent agglutinating serum for Cl. botulinum.

Such serum shows heterologous as well as homologous agglutinating potencies for strains of the antitoxic A and B types. (Since this paper was presented for publication, there has appeared the report by Schoenholz and Meyer,[4] which presents evidence of the same finding.)

The serological differences between the A and B types appear to be of a quantitative rather than qualitative nature.

The addition of acid (to $P_H = 2$) or of alkali (to $P_H = 10$) to the antigen suspensions or the separate injection into the peritoneal cavity of an equivalent quantity of acid or alkali effects the following changes: an increase in the agglutinating titer of an anti-A serum for type A organisms; a reduction in the titer of an anti-B serum for type B organisms; a reduction (in 18 of 24 cases) in the titer of an anti-A or an anti-B serum for the heterologous type of organism.

[4] Jour. Immunol., 1925, 10, p. 1.

DETOXICATION OF BACTERIAL VACCINES BY FORMALDEHYDE

W. B. Wherry and J. A. Bowen

From the Department of Bacteriology and Hygiene, University of Cincinnati

It seems highly probable from a study of the literature and from our own observations that the treatment of bacterial antigens with formaldehyde leads to their detoxication without effecting their antigenic value.

Costa, Boyer, and Placidi[1] successfully immunized rabbits against the bacillus of swine erysipelas by means of broth cultures killed with formaldehyde. According to them, the method was used as early as 1920 by Costa.

Durand[2] made experiments on the detoxication of the Shiga dysentery bacillus — this already having been accomplished by Ramon and Dumas[3]— and found that when the Shiga bacillus was incubated at 37 C. for 15 days with 0.5-1.0% of 40% formaldehyde it was detoxicated when compared with bacilli killed by heat or extracted with ether. The etherized and heated vaccines were of about the same toxicity for mice, a dose of 100 million killing on intraperitoneal injection, while it took from 300 to 900 million of the formaldehyde treated vaccine to kill. Experiments showed that the formaldehyde treated vaccine protected mice as well as the heated. Durand found it possible to inject 1,500,000,000 Shiga bacilli thus treated into man without reaction. while 500,000,000 of the heated ones gave a violent reaction. He was also able to detoxicate the gonococcus and reports good results from its use in gonorrheal ophthalmia.

Enlows[4] on immunizing rabbits against the Shiga bacillus found that it was fairly safe to inject 20,000,000 dead organisms subcutaneously or intramuscularly. However, the toxicity was variable, and sometimes heavy losses occurred. Inoculations were made on 3 successive days with a 7 to 10 day interval followed by 3 more doses, and the test dose given from 10 to 18 days later. Subcutaneous inoculations gave the greatest protection — 70%.

EXPERIMENTS

B. dysenteriae-Shiga.—We had already tried to detoxicate by thoroughly washing the heated bacilli in order to remove the neurotropic exotoxin of McCartney and Olitsky.[5] This was suggested by the work of Anderson on meningococci. While we were able to immunize some rabbits, we lost many, and did not succeed in producing agglutinating serum with a titer of over 1:200 or 1:300.

Received for publication, Aug. 3, 1925.

[1] Compt. rend Soc. de biol., 1925, 92, p. 1053.
[2] Ibid., p. 159.
[3] Paris méd., Dec. 6, 1924, p. 480.
[4] U. S. Pub. Health Reports, 1925, 40, p. 639.
[5] Jour. Exper. Med., 1923, 37, p. 767.

This year we tried Ramon's method in a manner different from that of Durand, as we were unacquainted with his work. The growth from a 24-hour agar slant culture of the Shiga bacillus was washed 3 times with 0.9% sodium chloride solution and suspended in 10 c c. of a 0.04 of 1% solution of formaldehyde. This was kept at 37 C. for 7 days and then washed twice with the salt solution and suspended in 10 c c. of 0.5% phenol. Cultures of the washed formaldehyde treated bacilli yielded no growth.

A control vaccine was prepared by heating a suspension of the bacilli at 60 C. for 45 minutes.

The results of intravenous innoculation in rabbits all weighing 2000$^+$ gm. were as follows:

No. 1 received 0.2 c c. of the heat killed vaccine. Paralysis on third day thereafter and death on fifth day.

No. 2 received 0.2 c c. of the formaldehyde killed vaccine every third day; total 1.2 c c. Four days after the last injection its serum showed a titer of 1:1280; no symptoms of intoxication.

No. 3 was treated like No. 2 but received 0.4 c c. doses; total 1.6 c c. Nine days after the last injection its serum titer was 1:2560; no intoxication.

No. 4 was treated like No. 2 but received 1.0 c c. doses; total 4.0 c c. Nine days after the last injection its serum titer was 1:8000$^+$; no intoxication.

Group agglutinins were present, for the serum of rabbit 4 gave complete agglutination of Shiga at 1:8000$^+$; Flexner at 1:160; Hiss Y at 1:80.

That rabbits are immunized against the living Shiga bacillus was shown as follows:

No. 5 received intravenous injections with 0.2 c c. of a suspension of living bacilli. Two days thereafter it developed a complete flaccid paralysis of the legs. This persisted for two days, when it was chloroformed. The entire intestinal tract was found to be intensely congested.

Rabbit 2 (immunized with formaldehyde killed vaccine) which received injections at the same time (9 days after last dose of vaccine) with an equivalent dose of the same suspension used in No. 5 remained perfectly well during a month's observation.

Rabbits 2, 3 and 4 were inoculated intravenously with 0.2 c c. of a suspension of living Shiga bacilli (40 days after the last dose of vaccine) as were 3 controls. One control paralyzed in 3 days died on the fourth day after injection. All of these, with an additional control, received injections again with 0.5 c c. of a suspension of living bacilli on the 8th day following the first injection of living bacilli. All rabbits apparently were normal for 24 hours following injection. On the second morning following, however, 1 of the control animals was found with all extremities paralyzed, and the other 2 were dead. At necropsy all were found with the rectum prolapsed, large gut distended with soft feces and gas, and the entire gut highly congested.

Treating the Shiga bacillus with 0.4% formaldehyde in 0.9% sodium chloride solution for 24 hours at 37 C. brought about detoxication. One agar slant culture thus treated was suspended in 5 c c. of 0.5% phenol. A 1,500 gm. rabbit received intravenously 3 doses of 1 c c. each, 3 days apart. There was no intoxication. The agglutination titer 7 days after the last injection was 1:5,000$^+$.

B. typhosus.—The growth from 3 agar slants was washed three times with 0.9% sodium chloride solution and suspended in this solution containing 0.04 of 1% formaldehyde. After incubation for 15 days at 37 C., the bacilli were washed 3 times with salt solution and suspended in 20 c c. of the solution containing 0.5% phenol. The formaldehyde treated washed suspension yielded no growth in aerobic and anaerobic cultures. Counts of fuchsin stained suspension showed that there were about 100 billion bacilli per c c.

Two men were given subcutaneous inoculations of 0.2 c c. at 3 day intervals. The first inoculation produced slight local congestion of the skin which subsided by the third day. The second injection was followed in 6 hours by slight malaise, aching of the muscles of the body, which had disappeared by the next morning. There was local tenderness and redness at the site of the inoculation, but this was almost negligible. The third inoculation was followed by local erythema and tenderness only like the first.

Suspensions of bacilli of about the same density (1.5 slants in 10 c c. salt solution) gave counts varying from 45 to 103 billion bacilli per c c. So the foregoing 0.2 c c. doses contained at least 9 billion bacilli.

SUMMARY

Incubation of B. dysenteriae-Shiga in solutions containing 0.04 of 1% formaldehyde for one week detoxicates the antigens. Large doses may be injected into rabbits without harm and potent agglutinating serum formed. Rabbits immunized in this way are resistant to doses of living bacilli which will kill controls. The results of preliminary experiments with typhoid bacilli indicate that treatment of the bacilli with formaldehye materially reduces their toxicity for human beings.

SEPARATION OF A SOLUBLE SPECIFIC SUBSTANCE FROM HEMOLYTIC STREPTOCOCCI

Edwin F. Hirsch

From the Henry Baird Favill Laboratory of St. Luke's Hospital, Chicago, Illinois. Aided by the Winfield Peck Memorial Fund

A soluble specifice substance has been extracted from many different bacteria. Nishimura [1] demonstrated the nuclein bases adenine, guanine xanthine and hypoxanthine in bacterial substance, and Galeotti,[2] by the Hammarsten method, isolated nucleoproteins. Since then the soluble substance obtained from various bacteria has been described generally as a nucleoprotein.

The first of these bacterial proteins was obtained from the cholera vibrio, the pest bacillus, and an organism resembling Bacillus ranicidus. In addition they have been obtained from the anthrax bacillus, M. melitensis, gonococcus, the bacillus of mytilus edulis, the pyocyaneus bacillus, the bacillus of Büffelseuche (Barbonne), the typhoid bacillus, the tubercle bacillus, the dysentery bacillus (Shiga-Kruse), from blastomyces, and from the pneumococcus.[3] Zinsser,[4] and Zinsser and Parker [5] have prepared residual antigens from typhoid bacilli, tubercle bacilli, pneumococci, influenza bacilli and Staphylococcus aureus. The substances so obtained are like the ones mentioned in that their solutions form precipitates with specific immune serums, and chemically they react much the same.

The presence of a soluble specific substance in broth cultures of bacteria has been known for many years, dating back to studies concerned with the demonstration of toxic substances in liquid medium filtrates and even in the tissues of an infected host. Thus Von Behring and Kitasato [6] demonstrated specific toxins in pleural exudates of diphtheric and tetanic animals. Although these experiments demonstrated simply specific toxin, the presence of specific bacterial substances dissolved in culture mediums and in tissues has been established by precipitin and complement-fixation tests. Fornet,[7] in 1906, detected substances precipitable with antityphoid serums in the blood and urine of typhoid patients. Ascoli [8] obtained specific precipitates in extracts of putrid spleen from animals with anthrax. Dochez and Avery [9] found a specific precipitable substance in filtrates of young broth cultures of pneumococci, and in the blood and urine of patients with pneumonia and of animals infected with

Received for publication, Aug. 8, 1925.

1 Arch. f. Hyg., 1893, 18, p. 318.
2 Ztschr. f. Phys. Chem., 1898, 25, p. 48.
3 Lustig, Kolle and Wassermann: Handb. d. path. Microorganismen, 1913, 2, p. 1362.
4 Jour. Exper. Med., 1921, 34, p. 495.
5 Jour. Exper. Med., 1923, 37, p. 275.
6 Deutsch. med. Wchnschr., 1890, 16, p. 1113.
7 München. med. Wchnschr., 1906, 53, p. 1862.
8 Zentralbl. f. Bakteriol., 1, O., 1911, 58, p. 62.
9 Jour. Exper. Med., 1917, 26, p. 477.

pneumococci. With their residue antigens Zinsser and Parker,[5] demonstrated complement fixation properties as well as precipitin reactions with homologous immune serums.

The methods used in the preparation of these bacterial extracts vary somewhat. Lustig[3] directed that the bacteria be treated with a 0.75-1% solution of NaOH. The mucoid solution is filtered and the filtrate poured into 2 or 3 liters of distilled water acidified with HCl or acetic acid. The white precipitate forming is washed with slightly acidified water, and then with distilled water until free from acid. The product may then be dried and reduced to a powder. Heating of this so-called nucleoprotein suspended in distilled water, according to Lustig, causes a partial coagulation of the substance. Zinsser and Parker prepared their residue antigens from bacteria grown on solid mediums, suspended in salt solution and centrifugalized. The bacteria were washed, dried over H_2SO_4 in a desiccator and ground with marbles. The pulverized bacteria were taken up in salt solution alkalinized to P_H 9.-9.4, and shaken for 4 hours, After centrifugation and filtering, 10% acetic acid is added drop by drop to the opalescent filtrate, until there is no further precipitation. The precipitate recovered by centrifugation is spoken of as a nucleo or phosphoprotein.

Heidelberger and Avery[10] prepared a soluble specific substance from pneumococci by dissolving the bacteria with bile and precipitating the dissolved substance with 10% acetic acid. The precipitate so obtained is recovered by centrifugation and is thoroughly washed 2 or 3 times in distilled water. Purification is accomplished by dissolving in alkalinized distilled water and reprecipitating with acetic acid. The final precipitate is washed quickly, twice with acetone and once with dry ether, and dried in a vacuum.

From 8-day broth cultures of pneumococci Heidelberger and Avery recovered by precipitation with alcohol and acetone a substance containing 0.2% N, which is essentially a polysaccharid, and which on hydrolysis yields 79% glucose. A precipitate formed with antipneumococcus serum in high dilutions (1 part in 17,000,000). They regard the specific substance identical with the carbohydrate and not simply adsorbed to it.

According to Lustig,[3] the dried nucleoprotein is a yellowish-white, granular mass which may be reduced to a white or grayish-white powder, insoluble in distilled water, and dilute acids, as well as such solvents as alcohol and ether. It is readily soluble in dilute alkali, less so in 10% sodium chloride. It is flocculated from an alkaline solution by neutralization or weak acidification, and also is precipitated from solution by the salts of the heavy metals, silver nitrate, alcohol, tannin, saturated ammonium sulphate, and magnesium sulphate. It reacts with the Millon and xanthoproteic tests.

The results of Pick[5] with extracts of the typhoid bacillus are not entirely in harmony with these observations. He obtained preparations precipitated by specific immune serums, but which failed to give a biuret test, and often no Millon reaction. The dissolved substance was not precipitated with tannic acid, picric acid, or uranium acetate. Zinsser and Parker obtained preparations from tubercle bacilli, pneumococci, staphylococci, influenza bacilli, typhoid bacilli, and meningococci, which likewise gave no biuret test, Hopkins-Cole, Millon, or sulphosalicylic acid reactions. Solutions of these preparations gave specific precipitin and complement-fixation tests. Heidelberger and Avery regard the soluble specific substance of the pneumococcus as essentially carbo-

[10] Ibid., 1923, 38, p. 73.

hydrate, although it contains 0.2% or less of nitrogen. They find this specific substance very stable. As regards the chemical difference between the soluble specific substances of pneumococcus types 2 and 3, they state that while both consist of about 75% polysaccharid and 25% unknown constituents, the type 2 substance after reduction is dextrorotatory, while the type 3 is laevorotatory; the former, if the salt of an acid, is the salt of a soluble acid, while the latter is the salt of an extremely strong acid, difficult to make soluble, so strong indeed that in highly dilute aqueous solutions it turns congo-red paper blue. An aqueous solution gave the Molisch reaction out to the limit of delicacy of the test. Fehling's solution was reduced only after hydrolysis, phosphorus was present only as a trace, sulphur and pentoses were absent. A 1% solution gave no biuret reaction, no precipitate with phosphotungstic acid, mercuric chloride, or neutral lead acetate. A heavy precipitate formed with basic lead acetate, and a slight turbidity with tannic acid. No color appeared with an iodine solution. By the usual method for isolating these socalled nucleoproteins from alkaline extracts of bacteria, Avery and Heidelberger obtained preparations which gave the usual qualitative color reactions characteristic of proteins of this nature. The nitrogen content of these was 16%, the phosphorus content 0.5%. The hydrolyzed protein give the purine reaction with Fehling's solution. The protein of pneumococcus as contrasted with the nonprotein soluble specific substance, these authors state, exhibits species specificity rather than the type specificity characteristic of the latter. There is general agreement among workers that all of these preparations react specifically by the formation of precipitates when mixed with immune serum and that they have a complement-fixing property. Zinsser and Parker, and Heidelberger and Avery were unable to stimulate antibodies in animals with their preparations. Lustig, however, reports specific immunity produced by the injection of such substances.

As streptococcus infections frequently are accompanied by severe and acute toxic symptoms, it is possible that some soluble toxin is formed that causes the clinical symptoms manifested by the patient. This has been demonstrated for the streptococcus of scarlet fever.[11] Streptococci, as is known generally, are resistant to the solvent action of ordinary reagents. The use of strong acid or alkaline solutions as solvents may so alter the substances dissolved as to render uncertain the results obtained by such methods. It seemed best, therefore, to choose a procedure which would subject the bacteria only to the action of mild reagents. The method developed is as follows:

Broth was prepared with fresh placenta tissue, 1 pound of the minced tissue per liter of water. To the filtered portion, 1% peptone and 0.8% sodium chloride were added. After heating to boiling, the reaction was adjusted to P_H 7.6, the mixture filtered and sterilized. To each 100 c c. by volume, approximately 20 c c. of sterile ascitic fluid was added. Containers of this medium were inoculated with a strain of Streptococcus hemolyticus, incubated at 37 C. for 48 hours, and the growth of bacteria recovered by centrifugation. The sediment so obtained was washed quickly in 0.9% salt solution. To the

[11] Dick, G. F., and Dick, G. H.: Jour. Am. Med. Assn., 1924, 82, p. 265.

bacteria N/10 NaOH was added enough to make a turbid suspension and the mixture transferred to a 250 c c. separatory funnel. Small quantities of ether added to this were thoroughly shaken into the mixture, and presently formed with the bacterial suspension a fairly stable emulsion. The emulsion so started was built up by adding small quantities of ether and shaking. When the amount of ether added exceeded that capable of remaining emulsified, the excess was removed, and the separatory funnel with its content stood upright for about 1 hour. At the end of this time two layers formed in the funnel—a lower, clear layer, and an upper, gummy layer. The clear lower layer was removed, and the gummy layer above, containing the emulsified ether, was broken up by rotating the separatory funnel. The ether, separating by this manipulation, was poured off or evaporated with a current of air. This left a turbid liquid which was filtered, the filtrate centrifugalized and the clear or slightly opalescent liquid electrodialyzed[12] against distilled water. When the reaction of the liquid came to the proper P_H by electrodialysis and adjustment with dilute acid or alkali there was a turbidity and, on standing, a copious flocculation of white particles. A reaction slightly acid or alkaline stabilized the particles, and there was no flocculation. However, the acid solution was more opalescent than the alkaline. The white flocculent precipitate was recovered by centrifugation, washed repeatedly in distilled water, used as such, or dried in a vacuum desiccator. Washing with distilled water usually results in a loss of some material, because the P_H of the distilled water used in washing does not coincide with the P_H (iso-electric) of flocculation. Finally the washed material may be reduced to a brown-white powder.

The material so obtained is soluble readily in alkaline solutions, and in this respect corresponds with extracts obtained from other bacteria. It is also soluble to a less extent in dilute acids (N/100). Increasing the acidity renders the solution more opalescent, and heating seems to change the solubility in acid solutions. The moist precipitate is slightly soluble in 0.9% sodium chloride solution, it is insoluble in 95% alcohol, acetone and ether. A solution of the precipitate in water containing a few drops of N/100 sodium hydroxide reacts with Millon's protein test, but not with the biuret test. There is no reduction of Haines' solution, no precipitation with 95% alcohol, or acetone. On heating alone and with dilute acetic acid there is a slight haze. One preparation not regarded as entirely pure contained about 10% nitrogen. A solution gave precipitin reactions with an antistreptococcus rabbit serum in dilutions as high as 8 parts in 100,000. This antistreptococcus immune serum has only a moderate titer. Solutions of many preparations made in that way gave precipitin reactions with antistreptococcus serums and with the serum of a rabbit receiving repeated injections with solutions of other similar preparations. There is no hemolysis when isotonic solutions of these preparations are mixed with red blood corpuscles.

[12] Locke, A. P., and Hirsch, E. F.: Jour. Infect. Dis., 1924, 35, p. 519.

SUMMARY

A soluble specific substance has been extracted from hemolytic streptococci. The chemical reactions of this substance resemble those of similar substances prepared from many bacteria by other investigators. Solutions of this substance give precipitin reactions in high dilution with antistreptococcus serums, and with the serum of rabbits injected with the substance.

INTRA-UTERINE INJECTION OF ACID-FAST BACILLI IN THE GUINEA-PIG

Yun Chan Sun, O. Ishii and Leo Loeb

From the Department of Pathology and Comparative Pathology, Washington University School of Medicine, St. Louis

The aim of this investigation was to provide a method that would allow us to follow the fate of micro-organisms in the animal under conditions which for certain purposes of research might be more advantageous than the usual methods of subcutaneous, intraperitoneal or intravenous injections. In the latter, the micro-organisms are distributed over a diffuse area in which their fate in many cases at least escapes control after a relatively short time. By confining them in a restricted and isolated area they should be more readily accessible to examination under variable experimental conditions. For this purpose it was necessary to select a cavity which could be isolated without serious consequences to the individual. The uterine cavity seemed to be the most suitable for this purpose, and we therefore injected the suspension of bacilli into the ligated segments of the uterus of the guinea-pig. In addition we hoped that by means of this method it might become possible to observe the mode of entrance of bacteria into the organism through intact mucous membranes. In the latter aim we did not succeed because of ulceration which occurs after injection of the micro-organisms used by us; but the former aim can be attained by this method.

Our method of procedure was as follows: We prepared a suspension of acid-fast bacilli in 0.85% NaCl solution; the strength of this suspension was approximately estimated by a comparison of its opacity with that of various dilutions of milk. We then exposed the uterus in the anesthetized guinea-pig and through application of 3 ligatures demarcated 2 segments in one of the uterine horns. The upper ligature was tied firmly and the uterus thus separated from the fallopian tube. A complete transverse incision was then made just below the lowest of the 3 ligatures, and the uterine horn was separated from the cervix. The opening of the uterus at the place of incision was surrounded by the plugs of cotton soaked in a solution of mercuric-chloride and through the opening about 0.1 or 0.2 c c. of the suspension was injected into the upper segment of the uterus. While the needle was retracted, the lower ligatures were tied firmly around the needle, in order to prevent the escape of the fluid from the uterine cavity. In the end we burnt the cut end of the uterus with a thermocauter in order to destroy any bacilli that might be adherent to the opening of the divided uterine horn when the needle was withdrawn. Following this the abdominal wound was closed.

Received for publication, Aug. 10, 1925.

Three strains of acid-fast bacilli were used by us, namely: (1) A culture of bovine tubercle bacilli obtained from Dr. V. A. Moore of Cornell University. This strain caused a progressive general tuberculosis in guinea-pigs. (2) A strain of acid-fast bacilli obtained from Dr. M. S. Fleisher of St. Louis University Medical School, and isolated from the lung in a case of human tuberculosis. It proved to be a relatively nonvirulent micro-organism. (3) A relatively nonvirulent strain of acid-fast bacilli obtained from the bacteriologic laboratory of Washington University. Altogether 113 guinea-pigs were used in these experiments; 47 of these received subcutaneous and 66 intra-uterine injections. In both the subcutaneous and the intra-auterine series, the virulent as well as the nonvirulent acid-fast bacilli were used. In a certain number of animals which had previously received subcutaneous or intra-uterine injections of the nonvirulent strains, subsequently a second injection was made with the virulent or nonvirulent bacilli in order to determine whether as the result of the first injection immunity had been produced.

A. RESULTS OF SUBCUTANEOUS INJECTION

1. Nonvirulent Cultures.

From 0.1 to 0.2 c c. of a suspension of the bacilli, which in the majority of cases corresponded in opacity approximately to a 1:20, but in some cases to a somewhat stronger or weaker, dilution of milk, was injected subcutaneously into guinea-pigs. A small nodule usually developed at the point of injection, which increased somewhat in size during the first 2 weeks and then began to retrogress. About 18 to 25 days after injection it had in most cases disappeared. In one series slight ulceration occurred at the site of injection, and healing was slightly delayed; but even in these cases healing occurred some time between 3 and 6 weeks. No general ill effects were noticed from these injections, and the internal organs were free from tuberculous infection.

2. Virulent Cultures.

After subcutaneous injection of the virulent bovine strain, a nodule developed subcutaneously; it increased in size within the first three weeks and then ulcerated. The ulcer usually persisted until the death of the animal. A smear of pus expressed from the nodule within the third week showed many tubercle bacilli within polymorphonuclear leukocytes, but some of the bacilli were probably outside of the leukocytes. Also smears from cheesy material showed the presence of many tubercle bacilli. About 7 to 8 weeks following inoculation tuberculous lesions were found in internal organs; the spleen and liver especially were affected; lesions in the lung were found less frequently and somewhat later than in the spleen. When the tuberculous infection became general, emaciation occurred, and the animals died. Guinea-pigs which had previously received subcutaneous injections or injections into the uterus with the nonvirulent, acid-fast bacilli, also developed general tuberculosis following subcutaneous injection of 0.05 c c. of the suspension of the virulent culture. No immunity was noticeable in these cases.

B. RESULTS OF INTRA-UTERINE INJECTION

1. Injection of Nonvirulent Strains of Acid-Fast Bacilli.

A large number of animals in this series that received injections gained weight during the period of observation; but some lost weight, and in a relatively small number of guinea-pigs some lesions were found outside the uterus. In one case consolidation was observed in the lung; in another animal pleurisy was noticed, and in a third a necrotic area was seen in the spleen. But these were exceptional findings. The most constant finding concerned the horn of the uterus into which injections had been made.

Changes in the Uterus.—Enlargement of the cavity was noticeable a few days following injection into the horn; the uterine wall was thickened. The swelling of the uterus increased as time went on, and in some cases the enlargement became extreme. Even as late as 5½ months after injection, the uterus was found markedly enlarged and tumor-like. Adhesions between the uterine wall and intestines were found in a number of cases. The cavity of the enlarged uterine horn contained either slightly turbid or purulent fluid. The fluid was usually decidedly purulent after the first three weeks. In some cases the content of the uterus was almost cheesy owing to the great preponderance of polymorphonuclear leukocytes and to the absorption of fluid. In control experiments in which a uterine segment was merely tied off by ligatures, without a preceding injection of acid-fast bacilli, a slight hemorrhage was found in the uterine cavity, which led to an enlargement. This was evidently due to hyperemia and hemorrhages which occurred during certain phases of the sexual cycle.

Study of Smears.—The content of the uterine cavity was studied in smears. Acid-fast bacilli were found in all animals except in two which were examined 3½ months after injection. The number of bacilli was especially large during the first few days. About 5 hours after injection the majority of them were found lying free in the cavity, although a large number of polymorphonuclear leukocytes were present. Following the fifth day by far the greater part of them had been taken up by leukocytes. After a few weeks only a small number of acid-fast bacilli were found free. Sometimes they were seen in bundles outside the cells, but it is possible that in this case the leukocytes, which had taken them up previously, had degenerated, and thus the bacilli were again set free. Up to 2 months many acid-fast bacilli were found in the uterine cavity, some of them enclosed in leukocytes, but others free. Besides the polymorphonuclear leukocytes, some large mononuclear cells were found, and some of these contained acid-fast granules, possibly the remnants of degenerating bacteria. Even as late as 5½ months after inoculation, clumps of acid-fast bacilli could be found in polymorphonuclear leukocytes. But as time progressed the number of bacilli detected in smears of the exudate decreased. How far we have to deal in this case with an absolute decrease in the number of the bacilli and how far the decrease is only apparent and due in reality to the increase in the number of leukocytes in the exudate which takes place is not yet certain; however, it is at least probable that an actual decrease of bacilli takes place.

Changes in the Uterine Wall.—During the first three weeks the dilatation of the uterus through the formation of exudate was slight; but it increased gradually. In the first few days we observed a loss of surface epithelium at various places which in some cases evidently was due to mechanical injury, while in other cases it resulted from hemorrhages in the mucosa breaking into the uterine lumen or to the formation of placentomata. Occasionally edema was found. Lymphocytes gradually increased in number, and the migration of polymorphonuclear leukocytes through the uterine wall into the lumen was pronounced. In addition to these pathologic alterations, the usual changes characteristic of the stages in the sexual cycle were noted.

In four animals in which the injection had been carried out at a stage of the sexual cycle in which the corpus luteum had sensitized the uterine mucosa, placentomata were found in the uterine horn into whch injections were made. This, however, is not a specific effect of the injection of the bacilli, as it follows any alteration of the surface of the mucosa, provided the latter is still sensitized and the lesion has not destroyed the mucosa. Acid-fast bacilli were found in the tissue of the uterine wall within the first few days following the injection. They usually occurred in places in which the epithelial covering had been lost and in which the connective tissue was edematous or showed predeciduomatous changes. They were also seen within a placentomatous area or in the lumen of glands. The bacilli were either free in the tissue, or they were enclosed in polymorphonuclear leukocytes or in tissue cells of an endothelial or decidual character.

Pressure effects on the uterine mucosa exerted by the exudate were slight at this period.

Between 3 and 8 weeks following injection, the dilatation of the uterus became more marked, and in consequence of the pressure exerted by the exudate the uterine wall became thinner. In several animals ulceration into the uterine lumen and the formation of abscesses in the uterine wall were observed, and in one case a necrotic area was found in the wall. Collections of polymorphonuclear leukocytes and lymphocytes in the tissue were noted commonly and leukocytes continued to migrate into the lumen of the uterus. At this period regenerative changes likewise became more prominent, leading to repair of the lesions and in particular to connective tissue proliferation around the lesions. The epithelium regenerated and covered the former ulcers.

Following the eighth week the dilatation became still more marked. Abscesses and necrotic areas were occasionally found in addition to leukocytic infiltration. Ulcers were still observed, and in one case the ulceration could be traced to the breaking through of an abscess into the uterine cavity. However, neither giant cells nor acid-fast bacilli could be demonstrated in the tissue.

2. Injection of Virulent Strains of Acid-Fast Bacilli.

After intrauterine injection of the virulent strain of tubercle bacilli, the guinea-pigs lost weight considerably. Tuberculous lesions outside of the uterus were found in all the animals examined 24 days after the injection or later. The distribution of these lesions was the same as in the series of animals receiving subcutaneous injections with the virulent strain; but in addition we observed that in several animals the abdominal wound did not heal during the period of observation and that an ulcer formed instead, an occurrence which we did not notice after intra-uterine injection of the nonvirulent acid-fast bacilli. In a few guinea-pigs adhesions between the uterus and the intestines were found at necropsy. The uterus was enlarged in guinea-pigs examined later than the ninth day following injection. The degree of enlargement was on the whole similar to that found in the first series. The uterine cavity contained purulent fluid.

A study of the smears of the exudate showed that the virulent bacilli behaved in the uterine cavity in a similar manner to the nonvirulent strain. They were usually found within polymorphonuclear leukocytes, but up to 30 days following injection some of them were also found lying outside of cells. Like the nonvirulent organisms, they persisted in the uterine cavity throughout the whole period of observation, and again a gradual decrease in the number of bacilli was noted. Placentomata were likewise found in this series in several cases. All except one had become necrotic at the time of examination.

Changes in the Uterine Wall.—The changes in the uterine wall differed in the two series of intra-uterine injections, although in the second series in which the virulent strain was used, the changes were in the beginning similar in character to those found in the first series; however, the lesions progressed more rapidly after injection of the virulent strain. In the first week we found hyperemia, edema, occasional hemorrhages in the mucosa and a migration of polymorphonuclear leukocytes into the lumen of the uterus. Gradually the collection of lymphocytes in the mucosa became more pronounced, and ulcers formed. Tubercle bacilli within leukocytes were found in the wall even in places in which the epithelium was still intact. They were also seen in epithelial and endothelial cells. No tuberculous lesions were found with the naked eye outside of the uterus during the first three weeks.

From 3 to 8 weeks following injection, ulceration into the lumen associated with edema and hemorrhages was noted in every case. Abscesses were common. In some cases pronounced follicle-like collections of lymphocytes were observed in the mucosa, but the typical lesion which predominated was the following formation: Surrounding a central area of necrosis was a layer of epithelioid cells, some of which had several nuclei; but typical giant cells were not seen. Here and there some collections of lymphocytes were found in the periphery of these nodules, and proliferating connective tissue tending to form a fibrous capsule around the lesions often extended deep into the muscular layers. These nodules were usually multiple, and if they were situated in the mucosa, the necrotic area broke through into the uterine cavity, and thus an ulcer developed. These lesions could be seen at any level in the uterine wall. They persisted, and thus in many cases the ulcers did not heal, in contradistinction to the ulcers of the first series which usually had a tendency to heal. Tubercle bacilli were commonly found in the areas surrounding the necrotic zone; again the bacilli in some cases were situated in endothelial cells.

Following the eighth week, the findings were on the whole the same as during the preceding period, only the lesions were more extensive, and the tuberculous processes became more extensive and general. In a number of cases the ovaries and the uterine horn into which no injections had been made were examined. Both were found to behave approximately in a normal manner as long as the general health of the guinea-pig was still good. But as soon as there was considerable loss of weight, a condition in the ovaries occurred which one of us [1] has previously described as an hypotypical state of the ovaries, which is characterized by the incomplete development of the ovarian follicles. This primary change in the ovaries resulted in corresponding changes in the sexual cycle.

COMMENT AND CONCLUSIONS

Our experiments lead to the following conclusions: 1. If we compare the subcutaneous and intra-uterine injection of the relatively nonvirulent acid-fast bacilli, we find that small nodules develop after subcutaneous injection, which usually disappear in the course of the next 2 to 4 weeks. As a rule, they leave no trace of their action as far as the gross examination of the animal is concerned, and thus no effect is produced which would be suitable for the long continued study of such organisms in the body. The condition is different after injection of these bacilli into ligated segments of the uterus of the guinea-pig. Here a lesion persisted throughout the whole time of observation, which extended over a period of more than 5 months. Thus a chronic lesion can readily be produced which remains visible to the naked eye. Within the exudate mainly consisting of polymorphonuclear leukocytes, the acid-fast bacilli persist and can be demonstrated, usually within the polymorphonuclear leukocytes. Their number gradually decreases, but whether this is an actual decrease in the number of bacilli or merely a relative decrease caused by the increase in the number of leukocytes is not certain. In our experiments a complete destruction of these microorganisms through the leukocytes had not yet been accomplished after a period extending over almost 6 months.

It is true that Prudden and Hodenpyl [2] and others, as Miller,[3] found after intraperitoneal or intravenous injection of virulent tubercle bacilli killed by heat, small lesions in the liver which could persist for a considerable period of time. These lesions, however, were very slight and irregular as to their situation and probably also as to their occurrence. After subcutaneous injection and even after intra-uterine injection of the nonvirulent acid-fast bacilli, we did not find outside the place of injection any lesion which we could definitely refer to the bacilli. In the large majority of cases no gross lesions were observed in any of the internal organs either on macroscopic or on microscopic

[1] Loeb, Leo: Zentralbl. f. Physiol., 1911, 25, p. 236; Virchows Arch. f. path. Anat., 1911, 206, p. 278; Biol. Bull., 1917, 32, p. 91.

[2] N. Y. Med. Jour., 1891, 53, p. 637.

[3] Jour. Path. & Bacteriol., 1905, 10, p. 1.

examination. If microscopic lesions existed at these places, they must have been difficult to detect.

2. While it is thus readily possible to produce chronic lesions in the uterus through injection of nonvirulent, acid-fast bacilli, the presence of those lesions and of the bacilli in the intra-uterine exudates did not lead to an immunity against a subsequent injection of either virulent tubercle bacilli or nonvirulent bacilli which were injected subcutaneously one or two months following the first inoculation. The lesions resulting from the second inoculation were not mitigated by the preceding inoculation of nonvirulent bacilli in our experiments in which relatively large doses of bacilli were injected.

3. If we compare the results of the subcutaneous and intra-uterine injections of virulent tubercle bacilli of bovine origin, we find also marked differences between the results of these two procedures, but the contrast between the subcutaneous and intra-uterine inoculations is in this case less marked than in the case of the nonvirulent strains. After inoculation of both types, we find (*a*) peristent local lesions and (*b*) generalized tuberculosis which establishes itself at about the same time in both cases. Notwithstanding these similarities, some important differences exist. In the case of the subcutaneous inoculation, the skin lesion soon ulcerates, and thus a lesion is produced which is open to secondary infection with other micro-organisms; the subcutaneous lesion as such remains relatively small. After intra-uterine injection we have a closed lesion, which while usually much more extensive than the subcutaneous lesion, provides a pure culture of tubercle bacilli within an exudate of leukocytes. This method of inoculation is much more suited to the study of changes in the infective activity of the bacilli induced through various experimental procedures than subcutaneous inoculation; but because of its strict localization, the intra-uterine method has also other advantages over intraperitoneal or intravenous injections, which latter lead to diffuse lesions and to caseation rather than to the production of an exudate such as is characteristic of intra-uterine injection.

Dobroklowski and Cornil[4] injected a suspension of tubercle bacilli into the vagina of guinea-pigs, and they thus obtained tuberculosis of the uterus, but in this case the bacilli were not enclosed in a uterine segment, and the lesions produced were not strictly comparable to these obtained in our experiments with virulent tubercle bacilli.

[4] Cited from Calmette, A.: L'Infection Bacillaire et La Tuberculose, 1922.

4. If we now inquire as to the factors which cause the difference in the behavior of the virulent and nonvirulent acid-fast bacilli in the uterus of the guinea-pig, we note first that both kinds of bacilli maintain themselves about equally well in the uterine cavity. Both are therefore approximately equally resistant toward the polymorphonuclear leukocytes and mononuclear cells which are found in the exudate. The difference between the two strains becomes noticeable if we examine the tissues. Within approximately the first week both kinds of bacilli may be found in the wall of the uterus, mainly within polymorphonuclear leukocytes, but also in other cells. Both cause certain pathologic changes in the wall of the uterus, namely, edema, hemorrhages, abscesses and ulceration, migration of leukocytes and lymphocytes; but with the virulent strain necrotic changes in the wall areas are prominent, while these are absent or slight with nonvirulent bacilli. After injection of the nonvirulent bacilli the tendency of the uterine ulcers is to heal, while after injection of the virulent bacilli healing of the ulcers is not observed. Further alterations associated with the extensive necroses following the injection of virulent tubercle bacilli are the production of epithelioid cells and far-reaching changes which are set up in other organs. Both the virulent and nonvirulent bacilli are taken up by leukocytes throughout the whole period of observation; but the virulent bacilli spread to other organs, while the nonvirulent bacilli do not spread. The extension of the pathologic processes depends therefore not so much on the long persistence of the bacilli in the exudate and their being carried away by the leukocytes, as on their power to cause necrotic changes in the tissues and the persistence of the bacilli around these necrotic areas.

In a few cases we observed that after intra-uterine injection of the tubercle bacilli the abdominal wounds did not tend to heal. It is possible that notwithstanding the precautions taken by us, an infection of the wound in the skin by tubercle bacilli did occur. However, it is probable that in the large majority of cases the injection of the bacilli was limited to the uterine cavity.

5. In both series the cyclic changes in ovary and uterus continue to take place as long as the general health of the guinea-pigs is not seriously affected. The less virulent acid-fast bacilli as well as the virulent tubercle bacilli do not exert any specific effect on these cyclic changes. Only when the weight of the animals decreases markedly do the hypotypical ovarian changes occur which we generally found

in underfed guinea-pigs; associated with these hypotypical ovarian changes occur changes in the uterus.

The surface injuries in the wall of the uterus caused by the injection of the bacilli may call forth the development of placentomata, provided the mechanical stimulus has been effective at a time when the uterine mucosa has been sensitized by the corpus luteum.

SUMMARY

To recapitulate the principal differences between our method of intra-uterine injection of nonvirulent, acid-fast bacilli or virulent tubercle bacilli, on the one hand, and the generally used subcutaneous, intraperitoneal or intravenous inoculation, on the other hand, we find that the former is followed by extensive, localized, well encapsulated lesions at the place of inoculation in which the bacilli persist noncontaminated in the exudate, while in the latter such persistent localized and encapsulated lesions are not found. Thus it is possible to produce notable localized chronic lesions with acid-fast bacilli which otherwise would call forth only transitory elusive changes. Intra-uterine as well as subcutaneous injection of virulent tubercle bacilli are followed equally by generalized tuberculosis. Notwithstanding the great difference in the general effects which follow intra-uterine injection of the virulent and nonvirulent acid-fast bacilli, both micro-organisms persist in the uterine cavity approximately equally well, and both are taken up by leukocytes; but with the nonvirulent bacilli the lesions remain localized, while with the virulent bacilli they extend to other organs. It may be suggested that this method might prove of interest in the study of processes of immunity as well as of certain other virulent micro-organisms the fate of which after subcutaneous, intraperitoneal or intravenous injection is difficult to establish.

NATURE OF THE TOXIC SUBSTANCES PRODUCED BY B. SUIPESTIFER

E. E. Ecker and M. L. Richardson

From the Department of Pathology, School of Medicine, Western Reserve University, Cleveland, Ohio

It has long been known that toxic substances occur in old cultures of organisms of the paratyphoid-enteritidis group. In from 8 to 14 day old cultures of B. suipestifer, these substances have been found by DeSchweinitz,[1] Voges,[2] Koske,[3] Joest,[4] Uhlenhuth, Hübener, Xylander and Bohtz.[5] However, little is known about the toxicity of culture filtrates of this organism obtained at the earlier period of maximal growth.

Ecker (1917),[6] Branham (1923),[7] Geiger (1924),[8] and Megrail and Smith (1925),[9] have demonstrated the presence of toxic substances in broth cultures of B. paratyphosus and of B. enteritidis within the first 24 hours of growth. Zinsser, Parker and Kuttner (1920) [10] observed similar substances in filtrates of liquid cultures, or filtrates of washings, of young cultures of typhoid, influenza bacilli and streptococci, grown on solid medium. According to these workers the products are probably nonspecific, appearing in cultures early, and with regularity. In general, they found the nature of the toxic effect, incubation time, etc., the same, regardless of the organism employed. Zinsser and his collaborators point out the difficulty of eliminating extractives, even in extremely young cultures. This fact complicates the study of the antigenic properties of the toxic substances. However, since our studies show considerable variability in the elaboration of toxic substances by different strains of paratyphosus, suipestifer, and proteus, it is apparent that the extractives, which must vary little or not at all, do not play an important part in the toxic properties of the cultures or filtrates. In fact, Geiger described a strain of B. paratyphosus A,

Received for publication, Aug. 10, 1925.

1 Philadelphia Med. News, 1890, 57, p. 237.
2 Centralbl. f. Bakteriol., I Abt., 1896, 20, p. 906.
3 Arb. a. d. k. Gsndhtsamte, 1904, 24, p. 305.
4 Schweinescuche und Schweinepest, 1906.
5 Ibid., 1908, 27, p. 425.
6 Jour. Infect. Dis., 1917, 21, p. 541.
7 Toxic Products of B. Enteritidis, University of Chicago, 1923.
8 Am. Jour. Pub. Health, 1924, 14, p. 578.
9 Ohio State Med. Jour., 1925, 21, p. 314.
10 Proc. Soc. Exper. Biol. & Med., 1920, 28, p. 49.

which he incubated at 37 C. for 6, 12, 24 and 48 hours in sugar-free broth, in beef heart broth, and in 1% dextrose broth, whose filtrates proved toxic only in 6 hour cultures in dextrose broth.

Further, it is important to decide, whether we are dealing with split products of the culture medium produced by growth of organisms, or with toxic products elaborated by them. According to Zinsser and his co-workers, the apparent nonspecificity of the filtrates, and the absence of antigenic activity, favor the idea that they are split products. According to the same writers, however, there are other facts not in accord with this idea, several of which will be mentioned subsequently. We believe that their apparent nonspecificity and their lack of antigenic activity are at present insufficient to support the idea that they are split products. As will be shown, we have definitely protected rabbits against the toxic substances of B. suipestifer by injection of antiserums from 10 to 15 minutes before the injection of the toxic filtrate. Another argument against the conception of split products is the occurrence of an incubation period of at least 40 to 75 minutes following intravenous administration of the toxic broth, also observed by Zinsser and his collaborators. This phenomenon alone differentiates them from the toxic amines. We have found that the toxicity of the filtrates varies in different species of animals and that the rabbit is most susceptible, the guinea-pig less so, and the mouse variable. The cat will also react, but to a lesser degree than the rabbit. In our earlier experiments (Ecker), the rabbit was therefore the animal chosen, and it is used predominantly in this work. As pointed out by one of us (Ecker), 24-hour culture filtrates of certain strains of B. paratyphosus B are fatal for rabbits, while filtrates of 3 and 6 day cultures may exhibit a diminished toxicity, which may again become more active in still older cultures. A maximal toxicity then may be obtained within the first 48 hours of growth.

Because of the rôle played by this group of bacteria in outbreaks of food-poisoning, and because of the slight knowledge we have concerning these substances, we considered it important to add further observations on their production in synthetic mediums, and particularly to investigate their antigenic power.

METHOD

Several strains of B. suipestifer were employed. One strain, no. 116, obtained from Dr. E. O. Jordan, has produced the most effective poison. The organisms were grown on lean veal infusion broth containing 0.5% NaCl and 2% Witte peptone, with a reaction of $P_H \pm 7$. They were also adapted to grow in the simplest possible synthetic medium, composed of asparagine 2, $MgSO_4$ 1, K_2HPO_4 1 and water 1,000 parts. The P_H varied between 6.8 and 7. The organisms were grown for various periods of time. Although the filtrates of 12-hour growth elicits definite symptoms, we have found the most marked reactions from filtrates of cultures of from 24 to 48-hour growth. Following aerobic growth, the cultures were passed through Berkefeld N candles. The filtrates were tested for sterility, but were used almost immediately after filtration because of possible deterioration. Most of the injections were intravenous, and a few which were intra-arterial were equally effective. Administration by stomach tube failed to produce apparent reaction. To test the antigenic effect of these products, rabbits were given repeated injections of synthetic medium filtrates in doses of from 3 to 6 c c. at the usual intervals. From 5 to 6 injections were given, and one week following the last injection, the animals were bled, and the fresh serum used in protection experiments. The average weight of the rabbits varied from 1 to 2 kilograms.

REACTION

The filtrate was injected into the ear vein in doses of from 2 to 5 c c., following which an incubation period varying from 40 to 75 minutes elapsed. Then followed rather rapidly a series of manifestations, principally dyspnea, general weakness particularly of the hind extremities, with flattening, commonly diarrhea, and finally either death, with or without convulsions, or gradual recovery. Recovery was frequently partial, with later reappearance of symptoms, and death after from 6 to 12 hours, or more. Control injections of sterile uninoculated medium were given in varying doses up to 10 c c. without apparent effects. Injections of filtrates placed in boiling water for from 3 to 5 minutes produced analogous reactions, but in general with more frequent or pronounced diarrhea. Filtrates from different strains showed considerable variation in their toxic properties. For instance, the filtrate of a 24-hour culture of a strain obtained from the New York City Board of Health caused considerable reaction without death, while filtrates from 2, 6 and 10 day cultures produced death. Table 1 demonstrates the results obtained with strain 416 (stock culture). Filtrates of 24, 48 hour and 4 day growth of 416 produced typical reactions with death, while 7 and 9 day culture filtrates gave only slight reactions (table 1).

A third strain (old stock strain) had an effect similar to that of 416. Marked reactions were obtained with ensuing death within 3 hours following intraveneous injection of 4 c c. filtrates, 24 and 48 hours and 4 days old. An 8-day filtrate caused dyspnea and weakness 50 minutes after injection. No other symptoms were observed, and the animal gradually recovered. A 12-day culture filtrate gave marked effects, with death during the night.

THE TOXICITY OF FILTRATES OF WASHINGS FROM ORGANISMS GROWN ON SOLID MEDIUM

Strain 116 (Jordan) was grown for 24 hours in Kolle flasks on ordinary plain agar. The organisms were then suspended in 0.85% NaCl, and the suspension passed through a Berkefeld N candle. Injection of 4 c c. of a filtrate of a 24-hour culture caused only slight dyspnea, and restlessness. Similar filtrates of a 48-hour culture caused marked reaction in 45 minutes, partial recovery in 3 hours and death in 48 hours. Death may have been due to pneumonia, which was demonstrated at necropsy. Injections of filtrates of 5 to 7 day cultures showed no reaction. Control injections prepared from sterile medium proved innocuous. Thus, it can be said that toxic substances may be obtained from washings of organisms grown on solid medium.

TABLE 1

EFFECT OF STERILE VEAL INFUSION BROTH CULTURE FILTRATES OF B. SUIPESTIFER 416 ON THE RABBIT. ALL INJECTIONS WERE INTRAVENOUS

Weight of Rabbits in Gm.	Age of Cultures	Hour of Injection	Results
2,000	24 hrs.	2:00 p. m.	3:00, weak, dyspnea; 5:00, partial recovery followed by marked weakness, diarrhea and dyspnea; death in 25 hours
2,000	48 hrs.	1:30 p. m.	2:30, general weakness, moderate dyspnea; remained sick; died in 23 hours
2,000	4 days	2:15 p. m.	3:20, general weakness; sick, moderate dyspnea; on side; died in 6 hours
2,000	7 days	11:00 a. m.	12:00, weak and dyspnea, but only slight; recovered
2,000	9 days	11:00 a. m.	12:00, slight dyspnea and weakness, otherwise no change

SYNTHETIC MEDIUM

Strain 116 was found to elaborate the most powerful poison in the synthetic medium described, and was therefore used in the majority of experiments of this group. Following 3 or 4 transplantations on this medium, luxuriant growth was obtained. Because of the considerable "lag" in this medium, optimal growth with the production of poison was advanced to 48-72 hours. More deaths occurred among animals that received injections with 48-hour old synthetic medium culture filtrates than with synthetic medium culture filtrate of cultures 72 hours old. Of 11 animals that received injections with 48 hour filtrates, 8 died in from 1 to 6 hours and 1 in 4 days; the remaining 2 showed a marked reaction, whereas of 23 animals receiving injections with 72-hour filtrates 12 died within the same period and 1 in 2 days. Of the rest, 7 had severe reaction with recovery. A strain received from Dr. Krumwiede, and which was isolated from tapioca pudding following a family outbreak of food poisoning, proved only mildly toxicogenic in broth. When grown in synthetic medium the filtrate was practically nontoxic. Animals that had received this filtrate and which received another injection with a synthetic medium filtrate of strain 116 on the next day, again reacted typically. It is difficult to explain the acute symptoms (6-9 hours following the ingestion of the pudding) in the case reported by Krumwiede,[11] on the basis of an infection alone. In the synthetic medium series, the symptoms observed were again, increasing dyspnea, weakness, diarrhea, but not as constant as in the case of broth culture filtrates, paresis of the posterior extremities, flattening, and death with or without convulsions.

Double or triple the doses of the uninoculated medium, used as a control failed to produce symptoms. The fact that the simple medium was hypotonic, led us to increase its salt content to isotonicity by the addition of NaCl, but no difference was found in the results.

Injection of as much as 30 c c. of the hypotonic medium into the vein of a rabbit did not tinge the serum of the animal.

We have also compared intra-arterial versus intravenous injection, but no difference has been noted.

Boiling of the toxic synthetic medium filtrate for 15 minutes left it poisonous, while autoclaving at 20 lbs. for 2 minutes greatly reduced its power. In one experiment, a 20-hour broth culture filtrate killed in 2 c c. doses within 90 minutes; 4 c c. of the same filtrate boiled for 5 minutes caused a severe reaction with death in 3 hours, while 2 c c. of the boiled filtrate gave a marked reaction, but no death resulted. A slight to moderate effect was obtained in cats following injection of 5 c c. of the synthetic medium filtrate.

PROTECTION EXPERIMENTS

As stated before, the serum of animals immunized with filtrates from synthetic medium was used in order to avoid, as much as possible, the by-products of the broth complex. In these experiments, however, we poisoned the animals with 20-hour broth culture filtrates to ensure maximal effects, and also to determine whether serums produced by the use of synthetic medium filtrates will protect against the broth cultures filtrates. Table 2 gives the results of such an experiment.

[11] Jour. Med. Res., 1922, 43, p. 53.

It appears from this table that severe reactions were obtained in animals which were given 2 and 3 c c. of a 20-hour broth culture filtrate. Both these animals succumbed in about 2 hours following the injection of the filtrate. A third animal, which received 1 c c. of the same filtrate, survived after a moderate reaction. A fourth animal, which received 5 c c. of broth, showed no reaction. Three animals, which received 4, 7.5 and 10 c c. of normal rabbit serum 10 minutes

TABLE 2

EFFECT OF IMMUNE SERUM ON STERILE VEAL INFUSION BROTH CULTURE FILTRATE OF B. SUIPESTIFER *

Rabbit's Weight in Gm.	Amount in C c. of Serum	Hour of Injec- tion	Toxic Broth in C c.	Hour of Injec- tion	Results
1,000	Immune 2.5	1:35 p. m.	2	1:46 p. m.	2:45 drowsy; quiet; slightly dyspneic; 3:30 normal
1,000	Immune 5.0	1:37 p. m.	2	1:50 p. m.	No reaction
1,000	Immune 7.5	1:40 p. m.	2	1:53 p. m.	No reaction
1,000	Immune 10.0	1:44 p. m.	2	1:55 p. m.	No reaction
1,000	Normal 10.0	2:10 p. m.	2	2:20 p. m.	3:00 urinates; defecates; weak hind legs; 3:06 moderate dyspnea; on side; sick; next day sick
2,000	Normal 7.5	2:14 p. m.	2	2:23 p. m.	3:00 restless, severe dyspnea; weak hind legs; 3:10 urinates; 3:12 severe diarrhea; died during night
1,500	Normal 4.0	2:15 p. m.	2	2:24 p. m.	3:05 sick; moderate dyspnea; 3:10 weak hind legs; 3:16 marked diarrhea; on side; died 48 hours
			Controls		
2,000	....	....	1	3:00 p. m.	3:45 sick; moderate dyspnea; slight diarrhea; next day normal
2,000	....	....	2	11:50 a. m.	1:20 severe dyspnea; oscillates; on side; 1:25 convulsions; urinates; 1:26 dead
1,250	....	....	3	12:45 p. m.	1:50 sick; convulsions, urinates; defecates; 155 convulsions; 2:00 dead
1,750	....	....	Nor. broth 5	3:00 p. m.	No reaction

* The serum was given prior to the poison. All injections were made intravenously. Age of culture 20 hours.

prior to the injection of the filtrate, reacted severely, but the two which received 4 and 7.5 c c., respectively, died in 48 and 24 hours. In a series of 4 animals receiving 2.5, 5, 7.5 and 10 c c. of the immune serum, only 1 receiving 2.5 c c. of the immune serum showed a transient dyspnea in 59 minutes following the injection of the filtrate, with no other apparent reaction. The 3 other animals which received the larger doses showed no symptoms. The serum therefore definitely protected.

Another factor in this experiment is the fact that the protected animals were of a smaller size than the control animals. Young animals have been very susceptible to the poison. In another series of animals, 1.5 c c. of a 20-hour broth culture filtrate caused severe reaction. Again normal serum failed to protect, while 5 c c. of the immune serum protected completely. A comparatively large dose of the immune serum was necessary to produce a maximal protection.

We have also attempted to determine whether or not the immune serums protect against the boiled filtrate (table 3).

TABLE 3

EFFECT OF IMMUNE SERUM ON BOILED TOXIC SUBSTANCE OF B. SUIPESTIFER *

Weight of Rabbits in Gm.	Amount of Serum Injected	Hour	Broth Filtrate 20 Hour Culture	Hour	Results
2,000	.....	....	Fresh 2 c c.	11:39 a. m.	12:18 moderate dyspnea; urinates; 12:20 marked dyspnea; 12:30 severe dyspnea; paresis of hind legs; 12:35 tremor; 12:50 dead
2,000	.....	....	Boiled 2 c c.	11:50 a. m.	12:40 moderate dyspnea; 1:00 marked diarrhea; dyspnea; survives
2,500	.....	....	Boiled 4 c c.	1:30 p. m.	2:10 urinates; 2:17 oscillates; severe diarrhea; 2:24 paresis of hind legs; marked dyspnea; 5:30 dead
875	Immune 5 c c.	2:50 p. m.	Boiled 4 c c.	3:03 p. m.	4:06 slight diarrhea; 4:45 slight dyspnea; survives
875	Immune 5 c c.	2:52 p. m.	Boiled 4 c c.	3:07 p. m.	4:30 slight diarrhea and dyspnea; survives
1,000	Normal 5 c c.	2:56 p. m.	Boiled 4 c c.	3.08 p. m.	4:05 moderate diarrhea; paresis of hind legs; moderate dyspnea; 4:10 on side, prostrated; died at night
875	Normal 5 c c.	2:55 p. m.	Boiled 4 c c.	3:05 p. m.	4:00 severe diarrhea; moderate dyspnea; paresis of hind legs; died ± 36 hrs.

* The filtrate was boiled for 5 minutes in boiling water.

From these results it is evident that the immune serum also protected against a lethal dose of the boiled filtrate, while normal serum failed to protect. The boiled filtrate caused a slight dyspnea and diarrhea in the protected animals.

Another phenomenon demonstrating tolerance is shown by the observation that following the second and third injections, animals react less and less to the poisonous filtrate.

PATHOLOGIC ANATOMY

Complete necropsies were made on all animals. The heart was often dilated, especially on the right side, and there was marked passive hyperemia of the veins of the mesentery and intestines. Passive hyperemia was apparent in the other abdominal viscera, especially the spleen and liver, but was not striking in the lungs. In animals that died shortly after the injections, peristalsis, much more active than that usually observed, persisted for a considerable period. Within the duodenum and upper jejunum the amount of mucus was distinctly in excess of the normal, and somewhat bile-tinged. Microscopic examination of the viscera added nothing new.

SUMMARY

Young cultures of B. suipestifer grown in 2% Witte peptone broth $P_H \pm 7$, on solid mediums, and in a simple synthetic medium, produce a poison of unknown nature, which upon intravenous injection into rabbits causes a characteristic series of acute changes after a definite incubation period of at least 40 minutes.

This substance appears to have some antigenic properties, but comparatively large doses of immune serum (5 c c.) are necessary to afford protection to rabbits. When the serum is given immediately (in from 10 to 15 minutes) prior to the dose of the poison itself, protection is afforded.

PRODUCTION OF TOXIC SUBSTANCES IN YOUNG CULTURES OF SINGLE CELL STRAINS OF B. PARATYPHOSUS B

E. E. ECKER AND EMERSON MEGRAIL

From the Departments of Pathology and of Bacteriology, School of Medicine, Western Reserve University, Cleveland, Ohio

It has been demonstrated by Ecker [1] and others, that young culture filtrates of B. paratyphosus of less than 24 hours' growth, contain soluble poisonous substances to which the rabbit, upon intravenous injection, is particularly sensitive. The toxicity of various culture filtrates of different strains is inconstant, and the purpose of the present study is to determine whether or not this phenomenon is exhibited by the components of a toxicogenic strain.

Two strains of B. paratyphosus B were used. Both of these have been employed by one of us (Ecker [1]). The filtrate of strain 180 caused considerable diarrhea in the rabbit, while the filtrate of strain 185 caused more severe symptoms, with convulsions and death. Five cells of each strain were isolated by a modified Barber single-cell pipet technic. The organisms were grown for 19 and 21 hours, respectively, in a 2% Witte peptone veal infusion broth containing 0.1% glucose and adjusted to P_H 7. The Berkefeld N. filtrates of the single cell strains, either fresh or boiled for 3 minutes on the water-bath, were injected intravenously into rabbits. As controls, the original strains, as well as uninoculated broth, were employed in the same manner. The results are presented in tables 1 and 2.

Examination of the tables shows that all the filtrates of the single cell strains, either fresh or boiled, in general produced the same train of symptoms as did the parent strains. In the boiled series the reactions were less severe. The filtrates of the single cell cultures of strain 185 showed the same severe toxicity as the original culture, and in the case of the filtrates of the single cell cultures of strain 180 diarrhea was as common as in the filtrate of the parent culture.

The original cultures showed the characteristics of B. paratyphosus B, as recently stated by Jordan.[2] Each blackened lead-acetate medium in 24 hours fermented, with gas production arabinose, xylose, dulcitol,

Received for publication, Aug. 10, 1925.

[1] Jour. Infect. Dis., 1917, 21, p. 541.
[2] Ibid., 1925, 36, p. 309.

and trehalose. Strains 185 fermented inosite, while strain 180 did not. Both strains reduced fuchsin after 3 days at 37 C.

The single cell strains showed no variation in the ordinary culture mediums, while in the differential sugar mediums only slight variations or delayed reactions were noted. One single cell strain 185-3 showed no visible gas production in arabinose (2 trials) in 30 days at 37 C. In

TABLE 1

RESULTS OF INTRAVENOUS INJECTION OF FRESH AND BOILED FILTRATES FROM SINGLE CELL CULTURES OF B. PARATYPHOSIS B, 180, 21 HOURS OLD

Rabbit's Weight in Gm.	No. of Culture	Amount Injected 3 C c.	Hour of Injection	Results
1,230	Original	Fresh	1:32 p. m.	2:07 diarrhea; 2:09 urinates; 2:15 on side, sick; 2:26 liquid stool, side, dyspnea; 2:50 sick; died in 4 days
1,320	Original	Boiled	1:45 p. m.	2:09 flattens, diarrhea; 2:16 paresis of hind legs, marked diarrhea; 2:50 sick; died in 6 days
1,630	Single 1	Fresh	1:20 p. m.	1:54 quiet; 2:06 paresis hind legs, flattens; 2:11 urinates; severe diarrhea; 2:13 on side, continued diarrhea; 2:20 rapid respiration; 12:50 apparently recovers; died in 14 days
1,630	Single 1	Boiled	1:40 p m.	2:25 marked diarrhea, flattens; 2:50 sick, on side, recovers
1,560	Single 2	Fresh	1:27 p. m.	2:04 flattens, rapid respiration; 2:10 respiration labored, falls on side; 2:38 paresis of hind legs; died in 14 days
1,690	Single 2	Boiled	1:43 p. m.	1:50 respiration rapid; 2:25 marked defecation; 2:30 diarrhea, sick, recovers
1,710	Single 3	Fresh	1:29 p. m.	1:38 respiration rapid; 2:08 flattens; 2:12 urinates; 2:15 paresis of hind legs; on side; 2:17 marked diarrhea; recovers
1,750	Single 3	Boiled	1:44 p. m.	1:50 respiration rapid; 2:27 sick, flattens, diarrhea, urinates; 2:50 sick, on side; recovers
2,750	Single 4	Fresh	1:15 p. m.	2:00 defecates; 2:03 flattens; 2:05 dyspnea; urinates; 2:10 paresis of hind legs; 2:10 on side; 2:30 very sick; recovers
2,680	Single 4	Boiled	1:19 p. m.	2:05 dyspnea; 2:10 defecates; 2:14 paresis of hind legs; flattens; 2:15 more defecation; urinates; rapid respiration; recovers
1,390	Single 5	Fresh	1:18 p. m.	1:55 flattens; defecates; 2:00 paresis of hind legs; urinates; marked dyspnea; 2:05 paresis of hind legs; on side; 2:08 more defecation; 2:30 very sick; recovers
1,580	Single 5	Boiled	1:21 p. m.	2:05 restless; 2:10 flattens; 2:12 paresis of hind legs; 2:15 more defecation; urinates; respiration rapid; recovers
1,500	Broth control	6 c c.	9:00 a. m.	No reaction

xylose the original 180 became alkaline in the open tube on the sixth day. The single cell strains of 180 became alkaline at about the same time, except one single cell 180-3 which remained acid continuously for 30 days. The other original 185 and its single cell forms remained acid for 14 days. In inosite all the pure-line strains showed the same reactions as the original cultures. In dulcitol both the original cultures showed acid and gas production for 3 days. After this time 180 became alkaline in the open tube, and 185 became alkaline throughout. Of the single cell strains, one of each, 180-2 and 185-2, showed fermentation for one day only. Single cell strain 180-3 produced acid and gas for 30 days, and single cell strain 185-3 for 12 days.

Variations of the same type were obtained in trehalose. Strain 185 and 4 of the single cell isolations did not show fermentation until the fifth day, while one, 185-4, showed it on the second day. These slight variations were not produced by the same single cell strain in the different carbohydrates.

TABLE 2

RESULTS OF INTRAVENOUS INJECTION OF FRESH AND BOILED FILTRATES FROM SINGLE CELL CULTURES OF B. PARATYPHOSUS B, 185, 19 HOURS OLD

Rabbit's Weight in Gm.	No. of Culture	Amount Injected 3 C c.	Hour of Injection	Results
1,630	Original	Fresh	1:20 p..m.	2:02 respiration rapid; 2:17 weak hind legs; 2:33 defecates; sick; died 4:00
1,890	Original	Boiled	1:30 p. m.	2:04 flattens; 2:09 weak hind legs; 2:22 diarrhea; 2:31 paresis hind legs; sick; died in 18 hours
2,190	Single 1	Fresh	1:24 p. m.	2:10 flattens, dyspnea; 2:12 paresis hind legs; 2:27 marked dyspnea; 2:30 convulsions; 3:40 dead
1,480	Single 1	Boiled	1:31 p. m.	2:30 weak hind legs; 2:37 slight diarrhea; 4:00 apparent recovery; died at night
1,810	Single 2	Fresh	1:25 p. m.	2:11 defecates; 2:20 more defecation; sick; died in 24 hours
1,930	Single 2	Boiled	1:33 p. m.	2:20 urinates; 3:00 paresis of hind legs; sick; died in 18.5 hours
2,010	Single 3	Fresh	1:27 p. m.	2:40 defecates; respiration rapid; 3:03 no paresis of hind legs; died in 18.5 hours
1,920	Single 3	Boiled	1:35 p. m.	2:37 rapid respiration; 3:07 paresis of hind legs; 3:25 defecates, sick; died in 48 hours
2,780	Single 4	Fresh	11:50 a. m.	12:45 rapid respiration; flattens; paresis of hind legs; 1:00 on side; semisolid diarrhea; recovered
2,500	Single 4	Boiled	11:57 a. m.	12:45 urinates; flattens; beginning paresis of hind legs; 1:00 on side; defecates; convulsions; diarrhea; marked dyspnea; 1:13 cries, convulsions; 1:15 dead
2,670	Single 5	Fresh	11:55 a. m.	12:45 dyspnea; sick; 1:03 marked dyspnea; paresis of hind legs; 1:15 on side; 1:25 convulsions, cries; 1:25 dead
2,540	Single 5	Boiled	11:59 a. m.	12:45 rapid respiration; excited; 12:50 convulsions; on side; died

SUMMARY AND CONCLUSIONS

Berkefeld N filtrates of 2% Witte peptone veal infusion broth cultures of 5 single cell strains from each of 2 cultures of B. paratyphosus B, 180 and 185, injected intravenously into rabbits proved to be as toxic as the filtrates of the parent cultures. Boiling of the filtrates for 3 minutes in a water-bath did not disclose a diminished toxicity, as compared with the boiled filtrates of the original cultures. No significant differences in cultural characteristics were noted between the single cell and parent strains.

ANTIBODY RESPONSE TO LARGE AND SMALL DOSES OF MULTIPLE AND OF SINGLE ANTIGENS, AND RESTIMULATION OF SPECIFIC ANTIBODY FORMATION BY HETEROLOGOUS ANTIGENS

Marion Corrigan

From the Albert Kuppenheimer Fund of the Michael Reese Hospital and the Nelson Morris Memorial Institute for Medical Research, Chicago

ANTIBODY RESPONSE TO LARGE AND SMALL DOSES OF MULTIPLE AND SINGLE ANTIGENS

Investigators have given much attention to the comparative effects of inoculations with multiple and with single bacterial antigens. Their interest has been focused on the response of the animal, to determining such questions in respect to antibodies as specificity, onset, persistency, susceptibility to restimulation, etc. Conclusions, however, differ as to the most effective method for inducing the highest titer.

Thus, to cite a few, Castellani[1] found that the simultaneous injection of multiple bacterial antigens was as productive of specific antibodies as the injection of a single antigen; that the immunity produced by multiple vaccines compared favorably with that produced by a single vaccine, except in the cases of B. typhosus and B. dysenteriae, in which the response to the multiple was inferior to the response to the single vaccine. Davison,[2] investigating the response of man and rabbits, decided that a mixed vaccine produced as high an immune titer for each of the constituent organisms as a single vaccine. Bull[3] produced in the same animal antitoxins of a fully competent strength against tetanus toxins and that of Bacterium perfringens. O'Brien[3] produced, simultaneously, antitoxins against toxins of tetanus, Bacterium perfringens, Vibrion septique and Bacterium edematicus. Reichel and Harkins[3] found that as good a response to each of 13 gm. negative, colon-like bacilli isolated from white scours in calves, could be obtained by injecting all the strains into a single animal as by injecting one strain. Polyvalent antigens containing pneumococci, streptococci and B. influenzae gave the same results as single antigens. Huntoon and Craig[3] state that there is no limit to the number of antigens that will elicit specific responses in an animal and that these responses approach quantitatively the response to a single antigen. G. H. Smith[4] produced specific ferments for Staphylococcus albus, streptococci, pneumococci, B. influenzae and Micrococcus catarrhalis by both single and multiple immuniza-

Received for publication, Aug. 14, 1925.

[1] Jour. Trop. Med., 1914, 17, p. 326.
[2] Arch. Int. Med., 1918, 21, p. 437.
[3] Cited by Huntoon and Craig: Jour. Immunol., 1921, 6, p, 235.
[4] Jour. Infect. Dis., 1915, 16, p. 313.

tion. On the other hand, Noble and Thomas [5] concluded that the degree of immunity (measured by lysis) was lower for animals inoculated with combined bacterial strains than for animals inoculated with a single strain.

Relative to dosage, Castellani,[1] Tsen,[6] Huntoon and Craig [3] concluded that there was no quantitative relationship between the antigen dose and the antibody response, and that the amount of agglutinin bore no relation to the amount of antigen given, whereas Friedberger [7] concluded that the antibody response corresponded quantitatively to the antigen injected. Smith and Brooks [8] stated further that the maximum agglutinating power of a serum was increased as the dose of vaccine was increased, while the date at which this maximum was reached was retarded. Vinaver and Frasey,[9] working with streptococci, contend that a horse vaccinated by a single injection of living, virulent streptococci, gave an immune serum superior to that obtained by fractional immunization.

Some of the divergent findings noted were believed to be worthy of reinvestigation in view of the almost universal use of multiple antigens of closely related bacterial species as practiced in the preventive immunization against typhoid and the paratyphoid fevers, and of the clinical use of mixed bacterial vaccines which often contain several species not closely related to each other. The points especially investigated were the antibody response to multiple as compared with single antigens, the multiple antigens consisting of closely related and of unrelated species; the relation of the height of antibody response to the dosage of antigen; and the restimulation of specific antibody formation to a previously injected antigen by introduced closely related and unrelated heterologous antigens. The agglutinin titer was used as a measure of antibody response.

TECHNIC

Half grown rabbits were used. The serums of the animals were tested for native antibodies against the contemplated antigen, after which testing, injections were made into a marginal ear vein of each rabbit. All bacterial antigens were prepared as follows: Eighteen hour broth or agar cultures of the organisms were washed 3 times with salt solution, resuspended in salt solution and heated at 56 C., for 30 minutes.

After receiving the first injection, the rabbits rested from 7 to 10 days, when the agglutinin titers of the serum were determined. In most cases immunization was continued by intravenous inoculations at 5 day intervals, each inoculation being preceded directly by a determination of the antibody titer of the animal's serum. When the animals received only one injection the titers of the serums were investigated at regular intervals.

Immunity was in all cases determined in terms of agglutinins. Dilutions of the unheated serum were made with salt solution. The diluted serum in each

5 Proc. Proc. Soc. Exper. Biol. & Med., 1919, 17, p. 10.

6 Jour. Med. Res., 1917, 37, p. 381.

7 Kolle and Wassermann: Handbuch d. path. Mikroorganismen, 1914, 4, p. 512.

8 Jour. Hyg., London, 1912, 12, p. 77.

9 Compt. rend. Soc. de biol., 1918, 82, p. 606.

tube measured 0.5 c c., to which was added 0.5 c c. of suspension of washed bacteria; the tubes were then incubated for 2 hours in a water-bath at 56 C., and readings were made after 12 hours in the ice-box.

Exper. 1.—Each of 5 rabbits was inoculated as follows: Rabbit 1 received 1 c c. of combined suspensions of B. typhosus, B. paratyphosus A, B. paratyphosus B; rabbit 2 received 3 c c. of the same suspensions; rabbit 3 received 1 c c. of suspension of B. typhosus; rabbit 4 received 1 c c. of suspension of B. paratyphosus A; rabbit 5 received 1 c c. of suspension of B. paratyphosus B.

The maximum agglutinins, appearing 12 days after injection, in the animal receiving the large dose of multiple antigen were B. typhosus 1:20,480, B. paratyphosus A 1:10,240, B. paratyphosus B. 1:5,120; in the animals receiving the single antigens B. typhosus 1:20,480, B. paratyphosus B. 1:20,480. The third animal inoculated with a single antigen, B. paratyphosus A, died accidentally. The maximum agglutinins in the animal receiving the small dose of multiple antigen differed in that they appeared later (30 days after injection) and in one case rose higher (B. paratyphosus B 1:1,310,720). Specific agglutinins for B. typhosus were 1: 5,120, for B. paratyphosus B. 1: 20,480.

Exper. 2.—In this set of tests the multiple antigen contained two unrelated bacterial strains, and the animals were immunized by 4 sucessive inoculations

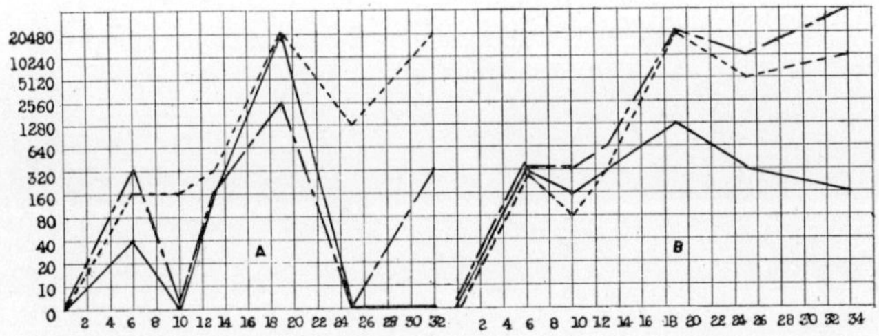

Chart 1.—The following system has been followed in all charts. The agglutinin titer is recorded on the ordinate. The period of time from the first bacterial injection to the last agglutinin determination is recorded on the abscissa. The solid line represents the specific agglutinin response to the small dose of multiple antigen. The alternating dot and dash line represents the response to the large dose of multiple antigen. The finely dotted line represents the response to the single antigen. In chart 1 streptococcus A and B. paratyphosus B are used as antigens; *A*, specific agglutinins for streptococcus A; *B*, specific agglutinins for B. paratyphosus B. Injections of antigen were given 10, 14, 20, and 22 days after the initial injection.

as follows: Rabbit 1 received, initially, 0.5 c c. of combined suspensions of endocarditis streptococcus A (Streptococcus mitis, Holman[10] classification) and B. paratyphosus B and subsequent injections of 1 c c. and of 2 c c. amounts; rabbit 2 received 0.25 c c. of the same suspension and subsequent injections of 0.5 c c. and of 1 c c. amounts; rabbit 3 received 0.25 c c. of suspension of B. paratyphosus B and subsequent injections of 0.5 c c. and of 1 c c. amounts; rabbit 4 received 0.25 c c. of suspension of endocarditis streptococcus A and subsequent injections of 0.5 c c. and of 1 c c. amounts (chart 1).

Maximum agglutinins for B. paratyphosus B, appearing 19 days after the first injection, in the animal receiving the single antigen and the animal receiving the large dose of multiple antigen were 1: 10,240; in the animal receiving the small dose of multiple antigen they were 1: 1,280. Maximum

[10] Jour. Med. Res., 1916, 34, p. 377.

agglutinins for streptococcus A, appearing 19 days after the first injection, were 1:20,480 in the animals receiving the single antigen and the small doses of multiple antigen. These agglutinins for the single antigen varied between 1:20,480 and 1:1,280 from the nineteenth to the thirty-first day, while these agglutinins for the small multiple antigen fell to zero. The maximum agglutinins for the large dose of multiple antigen were 1:1,280 on the nineteenth day, varying thereafter between 1:320 and 0.

Exper. 3.—An endocarditis streptococcus was again combined with a paratyphoid organism in the immunization of 4 rabbits. The method of immunizing was similar to that in exper. 2, rabbit 1 receiving the large dose of combined suspension of B. paratyphosus A and endocarditis streptococcus B (Streptococcus infrequens); rabbit 2, a small dose of the same suspension; rabbit 3, a suspension of B. paratyphosus A, and rabbit 4, a suspension of endocarditis streptococcus B.

Maximum agglutinins against B. paratyphosus A, appearing 26 days after the first injection, were 1:5,120 in the animals receiving the single, small and large multiple antigens. The contours of the agglutinin curves for the different antigens were similar. The maximum agglutinins against endocarditis strepto-

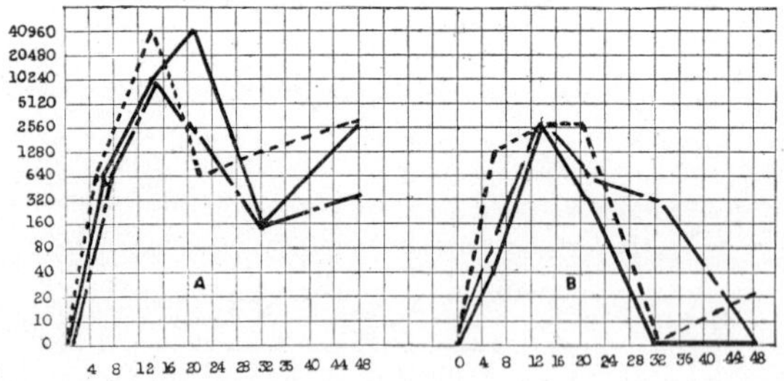

Chart 2.—Streptococcus A and Streptococcus B were used as antigens; *A*, specific agglutinins for streptococcus B; *B*, specific agglutinins for streptococcus A. Injections of antigen were given 7, 14 and 38 days after the initial injection.

coccus B were highest (1:5,120) in the animal receiving the single antigen. Here again the small dose of multiple antigen produced more agglutinins (1:5,120) than the large dose of multiple antigen (1:2,560).

Exper. 4.—In this experiment the strains of endocarditis streptococci employed in the preceding 2 experiments were used in combination for repeated intravenous inoculations. Rabbit 1 received large doses of suspensions of endocarditis streptococcus A and streptococcus B; rabbit 2 received small doses of the same; rabbit 3 received a suspension of streptococcus A, and rabbit 4 a suspension of endocarditis streptococcus B (chart 2).

Maximum agglutinins for streptococcus A, appearing 10 days after the first injection, were 1:2,560 in the animals receiving the single, the large and the small multiple antigens. The single antigen, however, elicited a more sustained agglutinin titer, 1:2,560 from the tenth to the twentieth day. Maximum agglutinins for streptococcus B in the animals receiving the single antigen (1:40,960 fourteen days after the first injection) and small dose of multiple antigen (1:40,960 twenty-one days after the first injection) were higher than the maximum agglutinins in the animal receiving the large dose of multiple antigen (1:10,240 fourteen days after the first injection).

Exper. 5.—The technic in this test differed from that used heretofore in that the supernatant broth of centrifuged cultures was used as an antigen in substitution for bacterial suspension, a method recommended by some immunologists. Three animals received successive inoculations as follows: Rabbit 1 received 1 c c. of the combined supernatant broths of streptococcus A and streptococcus B cultures; rabbit 2 received 1 c c. of the supernatant broth of streptococcus A culture; rabbit 3 received 1 c c. of the supernatant broth of streptococcus B culture.

Maximum agglutinins for streptococcus B were 1: 10,240 in the animals receiving the single and multiple antigens. Agglutinins for streptococcus A were higher in the animal receiving the single antigen (1: 1,280) than in the animal receiving the multiple antigen (1: 640). The single antigen elicited the more sustained response. The results of this test are comparable to those of the preceding tests in which bacterial suspensions were the antigenic factor.

Exper. 6.—The antigen used in this experiment contained 4 unrelated bacterial strains. Animals were immunized by 5 successive intravenous inoculations as follows:

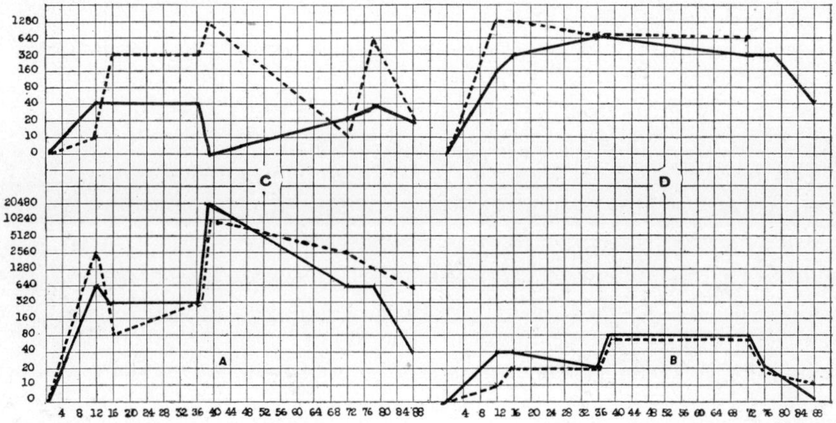

Chart 3.—B. typhosus, pneumococcus type 1, streptococcus A and B. dysenteriae (Hiss) were used as antigens; *A*, specific agglutinins for B. typhosus, *B*, specific agglutinins for pneumococcus type 1, *C*, specific agglutinins for streptococcus A; *D*, specific agglutinins for B. dysenteriae (Hiss). Injections of antigen were given 14, 17, 19 and 25 days after the initial injection.

Rabbit 1 received 0.5 c c. of combined suspensions of B. dysenteriae (Hiss), B. typhosus, pneumococcus type 1, and endocarditis streptococcus A; rabbit 2 received 0.5 c c. of a suspension of B. dysenteriae (Hiss); rabbit 3 received 0.5 c c. of a suspension of B. typhosus; rabbit 4 received 0.5 c c. of a suspension of streptococcus A; rabbit 5 received 0.5 c c. of a suspension of pneumococcus type 1 (chart 3).

Maximum agglutinins for B. dysenteriae (Hiss) 1: 640, B. typhosus 1: 10,240 and pneumococcus type 1 1: 80 were of equal titer in animals receiving the single and the animals receiving the combined antigen. The titer of agglutinins for streptococcus A was again highest in the animal inoculated with the single antigen, 1: 1,280. Maximum agglutinins for streptococcus A in the rabbit receiving the multiple antigen were 1: 40.

DISCUSSION

The initial antibody titer determined in from 7 to 10 days after the first bacterial injection ranged from 0 to 1:20,480, the titer in the majority of cases being, however, about 1:640. With but few exceptions (these usually involving streptococcic antigens), the large and small multiple and the single antigens elicited comparable immune responses.

The optimum antibody response to both single and multiple injections occurred approximately 3 weeks after the initial injection. The titers of the animals variously inoculated with multiple and with single antigens rose simultaneously, except when streptococci were used. In such cases the single antigen tended to give the highest antibody reaction, and the small multiple antigen surpassed the large multiple antigen in the stimulation of agglutinins.

As regards the persistence of agglutinin, it was found that the titers of animals inoculated with large doses of multiple bacillary antigens were sustained for the longest period of time. On the other hand, the response to streptococcic antigens was most persistent in the animals receiving injections with a single bacterial strain. Immunity from one injection was comparable in persistency to that produced by continuous injections.

In general it was noted that the response to the bacillary antigen was uninfluenced by volume or heterogeneity of inoculum, i. e., that the same agglutinin titer followed large and small, single and multiple injections of related and unrelated antigens. The results with streptococcic antigens were consistently superior in the animals immunized with single strains. Furthermore, small volumes of multiple streptococcic antigens were more effective than were large volumes.

In the use of bacillary vaccines small inoculations would appear to be as practical as large ones. In consideration of the high specific response to each constituent organism of mixed vaccine, it would seem advisable to employ such, in order that a wider but specific immunity may be induced. Thus the animal is not more taxed by being immunized with a triple vaccine than by being immunized with a typhoid vaccine alone, and in the first case is provided a relatively gratuitous protection against B. paratyphosus A and B. paratyphosus B. When it is desired to establish a high degree of immunity against members of the streptococcus group, strains of which are frequent components of therapeutic vaccines, it would seem that the best results may be obtainable from the use of single strains of streptococci.

RESTIMULATION OF SPECIFIC ANTIBODY FORMATION BY HETEROLOGOUS ANTIGENS

Davison[2] concluded that "an animal already immunized to one or more bacilli responds to subsequent inoculations of one or more different bacilli in two ways. First, it produces specific agglutinins, for the bacilli last injected, and second, it shows a temporary new increase in agglutinin titer for the bacilli injected first."

Dreyer and Walker[11] state that the injection of various heterologous antigens increased the production of specific agglutinins in an immunized animal, provided it retained some degree of acquired immunity; Dreyer, Gibson and Walker[12] found that paratyphoid B fever commonly causes a rise in the typhoid agglutinin of the serum of persons inoculated with typhoid. Rosher[13] concluded that an agglutinin titer was affected by subsequent injection of heterologous antigen only when this antigen bore a close relationship to the original antigen. Khanolkar[14] demonstrated that a previous injection of Gaertner's bacillus increased the capacity of an animal to respond to injection of B. enteriditis, whereas a previous injection with an unrelated organism had no effect on the immune response to B. enteriditis. In contrast to this last conclusion is the contention of Clark, Zellner and Stone[15] that nonspecific vaccination causes rabbits to respond when subsequently inoculated with B. typhosus, by building up a higher concentration of agglutinins against this unrelated antigen than normal rabbits under the same conditions. Thompson[16] found that animals inoculated with tuberculin, previous to receiving injections of sheep's red blood cells, respond to the latter by the production of 20 times the antibody content shown in the control animal. This antibody content was more persistent than that of the control animal which received no tuberculin. The highest antibody content was shown by the animal receiving the largest tuberculin injection. Hektoen[17] found that an injection of horse blood, 5 months after an injection of sheep blood and several weeks after the disappearance of sheep precipitins from the serum, resulted in the development of horse precipitins and sheep precipitins in about equal amounts. Harvey[18] states that the intravenous injection of a dose of antigen one tenth to one twentieth smaller than the original dose given 12 months previously, calls forth an agglutinin response in the inoculated pigeon, which is significantly greater than that elicited in the normal pigeon receiving the same dose. Herman[19] states that animals responding weakly to antigens (sheep corpuscles, and Streptococcus viridans) react vigorously to injections of heterologous antigens (given 5 days after the last injection) by an increased production of specific hemolysins and streptococcus agglutinins, whereas animals responding well to an antigen (B. typhosus) show no increase in B. typhosus agglutinins when

[11] Jour. Path. & Bacteriol., 1910, 14, p. 28.
[12] Lancet, 1916, 1, p. 466.
[13] Ibid., 1924, 2, p. 110.
[14] Jour. Path. & Bacteriol., 1924, 27, p. 181.
[15] Jour. Infect. Dis., 1922, 21, p. 25.
[16] Jour. Med. Res., 1922, 43, p. 37.
[17] Jour. Infect. Dis., 1917, 21, p. 279.
[18] Indian Jour. Med. Res., 1921-22, 9, p. 740.
[19] Jour. Infect. Dis., 1918, 23, p. 457.

injected with foreign proteins. Conradi and Bieling[20] noted an increase in typhoid agglutinins in typhoid immune animals following an injection of B. dysenteriae, B. coli or diphtheria bacillus. The rise was observed to follow quickly the new injection, and after reaching its height to fall rapidly; McIntosh and Kingsbury[21] were unable to increase the antibody content of the serum of animals immunized with B. typhosus and sheep's red blood cells by injecting arsphenamin and various lead salts "toward the end of the immunization curve."

TECHNIC

Two sets of experiments were made. In the first, immunized animals received reinjections once with bacterial antigens after their original antibody titer had fallen to zero. In the second set the animals received reinjections while retaining some immunity. The effect of restimulation was observed by determinations of the antibody titer for the organisms with which injections were first made and for the organisms with which subsequent injections were made.

Exper. 7.—In this experiment 4 immunized rabbits were used. When it was evident that these retained no agglutinins in the blood reinjections were made, 2 receiving organisms related to those previously injected and 2 receiving unrelated organisms. Thus, rabbit 1, originally immunized with B. paratyphosus A was inoculated once with 1 c c. of a suspension of B. typhosus. As the result of this inoculation there was a recurrence of B. paratyphosus A antibodies (0 to 1:160) in the serum. The response to B. typhosus (1:2,560) was comparable to that induced by the immunization of a normal rabbit. Into rabbit 2, originally immunized against streptococcus B, was injected 1 c c. of a suspension of streptococcus A. The injection of a related streptococcus caused practically no revival of antibodies against streptococcus B, the organism primarily used. The titer for streptococcus A was 1:5,120. Rabbit 3, originally immunized against streptococcus A, was inoculated with 1 c c. of a suspension of B. typhosus. The response to B. typhosus was 1:1,280, associated with a slight revival of streptococcus A antibodies (1:20). An injection of 1 c c. of streptococcus A into a rabbit formerly immunized against B. paratyphosus B caused a recovery of the B. paratyphosus B antibodies (1:160). The titer of the serum against streptococcus A was 1:5,120.

Exper. 8.—This differed from the preceding one in that the immunized animals received reinjections while retaining some agglutinins in the blood. Four rabbits were inoculated as previously. Rabbit 1, originally immunized against B. dysenteriae (Hiss), received 0.5 c c. of a suspension of B. paratyphosus A. An antibody titer of 1:1,280 was produced against B. paratyphosus A. The normal drop in Hiss antibody from 1:640 to 1:40 was not inhibited by the injection of the related organism. Rabbit 2, originally immunized against streptococcus A, was inoculated with 0.5 c c. of a suspension of endocarditis streptococcus C (Streptococcus nonhemolyticus 2). A rise in the titer from 1:20 to 1:20,480 of antibodies against streptococcus A occurred. Very little immune response was induced to streptococcus C (0 to 1:20). Inoculation with 0.5 c c. of a suspension of streptococcus C, of rabbit 3, originally immunized against B. typhosus, caused an increase in antibodies for B. typhosus from 1:640 to 1:2,560, followed by a marked decline in these, coincidental with a

[20] Deutsch. med. Wchnschr., 1916, 42, p. 1280.

[21] Brit. Jour. Exper. Path., 1924-5, 5, p. 18.

maximum rise in the titer of the antibodies for streptococcus C (from 1: 10 to 1: 5,120). Rabbit 4, originally inoculated with pneumococcus type 1, received an injection of 0.5 c c. of a suspension of B. typhosus. A delayed increase in pneumococcus antibodies occurred following this injection. The immune response to B. typhosus was 1: 10,240.

DISCUSSION

The reinjection of rabbits after the complete disappearance of agglutinins in the serum caused a slight recurrence of the original antibody. This recurrence was more notable in paratyphoid immunity than in streptococcus immunity; a fact indicating possibly, though the observations are too few to be conclusive, the ready susceptibility of the paratyphoid antibody to stimulation.

The response to restimulation did not seem to depend on the variety of bacteria injected. Thus an organism unrelated to that originally used in inducing immunity elicited as much response as a related organism. The fact that they had been previously immunized in no way affected the specific response of animals to reinjection.

The reinjection of animals retaining antibody resulted in many irregularities. Thus reinjection in two cases caused a decided rise in the titer of antibodies for the original antigen, in one case only a slight rise, while in another case reinjection in no manner interfered with the normal decrease of antibodies for the original antigen.

The rise in the titer of antibodies for the original antigen again seemed independent of the variety of bacteria injected. A rise occurred in one case in which an injection of streptococci was secondary to an injection of B. typhosus, and in another case in which an injection of a related organism followed an injection of streptococci.

SUMMARY

Polyvalent bacillary antigens in large or in small doses induced practically as high an agglutinin titer for each of their constituent organisms as did monovalent bacillary antigens. Polyvalent streptococcic antigens produced a lower titer than did monovalent streptococcic antigens. It was observed that small doses of polyvalent streptococcic antigen were more effective than large doses in the production of agglutinins.

The reinjection into formerly immunized animals retaining no antibodies in the blood caused a slight recurrence of antibodies for the original antigen accompanied by a normal production of antibodies for the bacteria used in the reinjection. The recurrence of antibodies seemed to be independent of the variety of bacteria subsequently injected.

The results of the reinjection into animals retaining antibodies in the blood varied. Reinjection in some cases caused a rise in the titer of the original antibodies, and on one occasion did not hinder the normal decrease of the original antibodies. Here again the reformation of the original antibodies did not depend on the variety of bacteria subsequently injected. The titer of the antibodies for the organism used in reinjection was comparable to that induced by injection into normal rabbits.

AN ATYPICAL WEIL-FELIX REACTION

RUTH GILBERT AND MARION COLEMAN

From the Division of Laboratories and Research, New York State Department of Health, Albany, Augustus Wadsworth, M.D., Director

Since the discovery by Weil and Felix,[1] in 1916, that certain strains of B. proteus are agglutinated in serum from cases of typhus fever, the so-called Weil-Felix reaction has been generally used in the diagnosis of this disease. Wolbach, Todd, and Palfrey indicate in their extensive monograph [2] that its value has been corroborated.

Tests with inactivated serums have led many observers to believe that this reaction may not be as specific as it has generally been considered. Hamburger and Bauch [3] reported that the agglutinins for B. proteus X 19 in the serums from two cases of typhus fever were appreciably diminished by heating at 50-55 C. for one-half hour. They were totally destroyed in one by heating at 56-60 C. for one-half hour and in the other by heating at 60-65 C. for one-half hour. They found that artificially produced agglutinins for the homologous culture were not affected by heating at 60 C. but were entirely destroyed by heating at 70-75 C. for one-half hour. Csepai [4] reports that the agglutinins in the serum from cases of typhus fever are destroyed by heating at 63 C., and Werner and Leoneanu [5] report the same reaction with a temperature of 65 C. Braun and Solomon [6] state that they have found the agglutinins produced artificially in rabbits to be unaffected by heating at 56 C., but that the agglutinins in serum from typhus fever cases are destroyed in one hour at this temperature. Prausnitz,[7] Schiff,[8] Buchner and Zorn [9] have all made observations similar to those reported by Braun and Solomon. Sonnenschein [10] describes two interesting cases of infection with B. proteus, the serum from which agglutinated B. proteus X 19 both before and after inactivation at 56 C. for 1 hour. On the other hand, Kathe [11]

Received for publication, Aug. 19, 1925.

1 Wien. klin. Wchnschr., 1916, 29, p. 33.
2 Etiology and Pathology of Typhus, 1922.
3 Deutsch. med. Wchnschr., 1917, 43, p. 1130.
4 Wien. klin. Wchnschr., 1917, 30, p. 1264.
5 München. med. Wchnschr., 1918, 65, p. 1377.
6 Centralbl. f. Bakteriol., I. O., 1918, 81, p. 20.
7 Ibid., 1920, 84, p. 103.
8 Ztschr. f. Immunitätsforsch. u. exper. Therap., 1920, 29, p. 11.
9 Ibid., 1921, 33, p. 115.
10 Wien. klin. Wchnschr., 1924, 37, p. 757; Deutsch. med. Wchnschr., 1924, 50, p. 102.
11 Ztschr. f. Hyg. u. Infectionskrankh., 1924, 103, p. 420.

has reported that in his experience with serums from 30 cases of typhus fever the agglutinins were not destroyed by heating at 56 C. They were slightly diminished in 15 instances but were increased in 10. By heating at 60 C. for 1 hour, the agglutinins in 2 of the serums were destroyed and in nearly all of the others were greatly diminished. After heating at 65 C. for 1 hour, the agglutinins in all of the serums except 4 were entirely destroyed. Maxey and Havens [12] report a Weil-Felix reaction in a series of cases in Alabama concerning the proper classification of which there was considerable doubt, but they do not mention the effect of inactivation of the serum from any of these cases.

Since in only a few instances a Weil-Felix reaction has been reported in cases other than typhus fever, the finding of relatively thermostabile agglutinins for B. proteus X 19 in a specimen of blood from a case in which a definite diagnosis could not be made appears to be worthy of note.

The specimen was sent to the laboratory by Dr. D. Edwards of East Hampton, N. Y. The patient, a married woman, about 30 years of age, was born in the eastern part of New York State, where she still lives. She had been only a short distance from home previous to her illness. On July 3, a tick was found on her back which was so firmly attached that when it was removed a minute portion of skin was pulled away with it. The first symptoms of illness were noted on July 10, but a physician was not consulted until the thirteenth. Complaint was made of headache, malaise, loss of appetite, rise in temperature, pain in the back and soreness in the muscles. Raised spots were noted on the back on the fourteenth; on the sixteenth, the rash appeared on the body and thighs; on the seventeenth, it had extended to include the palms of the hands and soles of the feet; on the eighteenth, the rash seen in some of the folds of the skin was hemorrhagic. It was noted to be fading on the twenty-sixth.

During the course of the disease headache, while present, was not intense. There was pain in the back and over the entire body. The patient was especially sensitive to touch. There was no confusion, but she was dull. It was necessary to speak sharply to make her hear. She always answered rationally, however, when she heard the question. The only pulmonary symptoms were small râles due to posture. The systolic murmur heard over the heart on the twenty-second was more marked at the base and rough in character. It diminished gradually in intensity as the disease progressed. The rash, appearing first on the back in the form of slightly elevated rose-colored spots, continued to develop for a week and was more marked at the height of the fever. It became maculopapular in 24 hours, gradually became darker, and was petechial within a week. The largest spots did not exceed a small pea in size. The tongue was slightly coated, but never became brown or dry, and was not enlarged. The first perceptible increase of pulse rate, which never became marked, was noted at the time the murmur was found. The patient did not seem so physically depressed as would have been expected during the periods when the temperature was high. The temperature varied from 106 to 101 F. from the fifth to the tenth day and then began to decline

[12] Am. Jour. Trop. Med., 1923, 3, p. 495.

by lysis. It became approximately normal after the twenty-eighth day of the illness.

A careful search for pediculi was made, but none could be found.

A number of physicians saw the patient, and several tentative diagnoses were made which included typhus fever, Brill's disease, tick-bite fever and Rocky Mountain spotted fever. Before the rash appeared, the attending physician considered the condition to be grippe. He found no definite enlargement of the spleen, gurgling nor other symptoms of typhoid. When the rash became maculopapular, he considered the condition to be spotted fever.

The serum on July 28 agglutinated B. proteus X 19 in a dilution of 1:1,600. It failed to agglutinate cultures of B. typhosus or paratyphosus A or B. In the routine complement fixation test, for syphilis, no fixation was obtained with the plain alcoholic antigen, but complete fixation (4+) was obtained with the cholesterinized antigen.

A portion of the serum was heated for 1 hour in the water-bath at approximately 56 C. As a control, serum from a typical case of typhus fever sent by Dr. Mooser, Mexico City, was heated at the same time. After inactivation the serum from the patient still agglutinated B. proteus X 19 in the same dilutions as before, while nearly all of the agglutinins had been removed from the control serum.

A series of tests was then made to compare the thermostability of the agglutinins in typhus fever serum and in artificially produced agglutinating serum. Portions of typhus serum and of immune rabbit serum were heated at 54, 56, and 58 C. for 1 hour in a water-bath. Agglutination tests showed that at some point between 54 and 56 C. the agglutinins for B. proteus X 19 in the specimen of typhus fever serum from Mexico City were destroyed, while the agglutinins in the immune rabbit serum remained unaffected by heating at 58 C. for 1 hour. Although all of the remaining serum from the patient had been heated to 56 C. for 30 minutes and an equal amount of glycerol added, it was demonstrated that the agglutinins in it resisted further heating for an hour at 58 C. So little of the serum remained after these tests had been made that further work to determine at what temperature the agglutinins were lost were made with a 1:100 dilution. The agglutinins were lost between 62 C. and 65 C., while those in the immune rabbit serum were still present after heating to 70 C. None was demonstrated, however, in serum heated at 75 C.

COMMENT

Although a definite diagnosis was not made, the clinical manifestations do not indicate typhus fever or Brill's disease. In a case of tick bite or relapsing fever there would undoubtedly have been a different temperature curve. Rocky Mountain spotted fever can probably be ruled out also, as it has been reported from a limited district only, and the agglutination of B. proteus X 19 in the serum would not be expected in this disease, since Kelly [13] found that serum from 9 cases did not agglutinate this culture. He states that: "While the series of tests is not large enough to warrant any definite conclusions, it suggests that the Weil-Felix reaction is negative in Rocky Mountain spotted fever and

[13] Jour. Infect. Dis., 1923, 32, p. 223.

may be of value in differentiating between this disease and typhus fever." The definite fixation with the cholesterinized antigen in the test for syphilis is suggestive, especially in view of the fact that two of the clinicians who saw the case thought that the rash might be due to syphilis. In this connection, a complication with an acute infectious process should be considered.

The high titer of the agglutinins for B. proteus X 19 and their relative thermostability might indicate the possibility of an infection by a microorganism of the proteus group.

SUMMARY

A case is described in which no definite diagnosis was made, the following diseases being, in turn, considered and rejected: grippe, typhoid, Brill's disease, tick-bite fever, Rocky Mountain spotted fever. Both before and after inactivation by heating at 62 C. the patient's serum agglutinated B. proteus X 19 in dilutions up to 1 : 1,600, whereas serum from cases known to be typhus fever lost the agglutinins for B. proteus X 19 at a point between 54 and 56 C. In immune rabbit serum the agglutinins were not destroyed until between 70 and 75 C. was reached. These results indicate the desirability of determining the relative thermolability of the agglutinins in serum from suspected cases of typhus fever.

CORRECTION

In the article by Ruth Tunnicliff, "Further Studies on a Diplococcus in Measles," which appeared on page 196 of the September issue, the second line from the end of the first paragraph, should read as follows: "marked reaction to the measles antigen, failed to react again after the."

GENERAL INDEX

A

PAGE

Abortion, infectious, rabbits in the study of - - - - - - 62
Acid, lactic, blood, in anaphylaxis - - - - - - - - 225
Acid, lactic, blood, in histamine shock - - - - - - - 229
Agglutination, serum, of pneumococcus - - - - - - - 507
Anaerobes from human saliva - - - - - - - - - - 87, 112
Anaphylaxis, canine, quantitative changes in blood sugar and lactic acid 225
Anemia, pernicious, fecal flora in - - - - - - - - - 161
Antibodies, isolation of - - - - - - - - - - - - 449
Antibodies, to sheep blood in experimental tuberculosis - - - - 82
Antibody response to different antigens - - - - - - - - 549
Antigen and antibody in precipitin reaction - - - - - - 321
Antigen, heterologous, restimulation of specific antibodies with - - - 549
Antigenic properties of tissue fibrinogen - - - - - - - - 49
Antigenic properties of certain glucoproteins - - - - - - 285
Antipneumococcus serum - - - - - - - - - - - 199, 309
Apfelbach, Carl W. Effect of diphtheria toxin on the myocardium of guinea-pigs - - - - - - - - - - - - - - 443
Arnold, Lloyd and Weiss, Emil. Isolation of bacteriophage free from bacterial protein - - - - - - - - - - - - - 411
Austin, Richard S. Extracts of normal tissue in experimental tuberculosis 256
Autoclave sterilization, temperatures attained - - - - - - 357

B

B. acidophilus cultures, effect of insulin - - - - - - - - 333
B. hofmanni, injections of, effect on diphtheria immunity - - - - 97
B. paratyphosus B., toxic substances in cultures of single cell strains of 546
B. subtilis, pathogenic, in chronic tuberculosis - - - - - - 340
B. suipestifer, toxic substances of - - - - - - - - - 538
B. tetani from human saliva - - - - - - - - - - 87
B. tuberculosis - - - - - - - - - - - - - 68, 465
B. welchii in pernicious anemia - - - - - - - - - - 161
B. welchii from human saliva - - - - - - - - - - 87
B. xerosis, effect on diphtheria immunity - - - - - - - - 97
Bacilli, acid-fast, intrauterine injections of - - - - - - 528
Bacilli, spore-free, gram-negative, aerobic, classification of - - - 232
Bacteria, nonglucose-fermenting, and insulin - - - - - - 329
Bacterial factors in pyorrhea alveolaris - - - - - - - 87, 112
Bacterial metabolism - - - - - - - - - - - 329, 333, 337
Bacterial proteins, bacteriophage free from - - - - - - 411
Bacterial vaccines, detoxications, by formaldehyde - - - - - 520
Bacteriophage - - - - - - - - - - - - - 35, 126, 411
Bacterium abortum - - - - - - - - - - - - - 62, 68

Bacterium enteritidis, toxic products of - - - - - - - - - 291
Bacterium, tuberculosis - - - - - - - - - - 68, 465
BAILEY, G. HOWARD. See ROSENAU, M. J. - - - - - - - - - 97
BECKWITH, T. D. and ROSE, E. J. Effect of medium on the rate of multiplication, virulence and heat susceptibility of hemolytic streptococci - 277
BENTON, ANNE, and LEIGHTON, ALAN. Actual temperature attained by mediums in autoclave sterilizations - - - - - - - 353
Blackhead, transmission of - - - - - - - - - - 265
Blood in histamine shock - - - - - - - - - - - 229
Blood, sheep, antibodies for, in experimental tuberculosis - - - - 82
Blood sugar in anaphylaxis, and histamine shock - - - - - 225, 229
Botulinum, Cl. antigenic properties and toxin production of - - - - 344
BOWEN, J. A. See WHERRY, W. B. - - - - - - - - - - 520
BRANHAM, SARA E. Toxic products of bacterium enteritidis and of related micro-organisms - - - - - - - - - - - - - 291

C

CALDWELL, MARY ESTILL. Viability of mycobacterium tuberculosis in a semi-acid environment - - - - - - - - - - - - - 465
CARPENTER, CHARLES M. See SCHOENFELD, ADALYN F. - - - - - 68
Carriers, pneumococcus, identification of - - - - - - - - 473
CHAMBERS, ELEANOR K., and THOMPSON, K. W. Quantitative changes in tissue glycogen, blood sugar, plasma inorganic phosphates and in blood lactic acid in canine histamine shock - - - - - - - - 229
Cholera vibrio, form and growth of - - - - - - - - - 75
Cl. botulinum, antigenic properties of, effect of hydrogen ion concentration on 514
Cl. botulinum in canned foods, toxin produced by - - - - - - 344
COLEMAN, MARION. See GILBERT, RUTH - - - - - - - - 559
COLLIER, JANE. See TYZZER, E. E. - - - - - - - - - - 265
CORPER, H. J. See HEKTOEN, LUDVIG - - - - - - - - - 82
CORRIGAN, MARION. Antibody response to large and small doses of single and multiple antigens and restimulation of specific antibody formation by a heterologous antigen - - - - - - - - - - 549
Cresol, mixtures with soaps, germicidal efficiency of - - - - - - 359
CROMWELL, H. W. Quantitative relations between antigen and antibody in the precipitin reaction - - - - - - - - - - - 321

D

Diphtheria immunity, production by B. hofmanni, B. xerosis, and avirulent bacilli - - - - - - - - - - - - - - - 97
Diphtheria toxin, effect on myocardium - - - - - - - 443
Diseases, respiratory - - - - - - - - 481, 495, 499, 507, 473
DOWNS, CORNELIA M. The antigenic properties of tissue fibrinogens - 49

E

ECKER, E. E., and MEGRAIL, EMERSON. Production of toxic substances in young cultures of single cell strains of B. paratyphosus B. - - - 546
ECKER, E. E., and RICHARDSON, M. L. Nature of toxic substances produced by B. suipestifer - - - - - - - - - - - - 538

Electrophoretic potential of pneumococci - - - - 481, 495, 499, 507
Enteritidis, bacterium, toxic products of - - - - - - - - - 291
Enteritidis and paratyphoid B. infections, relationship of, to hyperglycemia in rabbits - - - - - - - - - - - - - - 400

F

Falk, I. S.; Gussin, H. A., and Jacobson, M. A. Studies on respiratory diseases XXI. Electrophoretic potential and virulence of pneumococci, types 1, 2, 3, 4 - - - - - - - - - - - - - - 481
Falk, I. S.; Jacobson, M. A., and Gussin, H. A. Studies on respiratory diseases XXII. Electrophoretic potential and virulence of pneumococci, and electrophoretic potential of pneumococci - - - - - - 495
Falk, I. S.; Jacobson, M. A., and Gussin, H. A. Studies on respiratory diseases XXIII. Electrophoretic potential and virulence of variants of type 1 pneumococcus - - - - - - - - - - - 499
Falk, I. S., and Jacobson, M. A. Studies on respiratory diseases XXIV. Electrophoretic potential virulence and serum agglutination in single cell cultures of variants of type 1 pneumococcus - - - - - 507
Falk, J. S., and Powdermaker, F. The effect of hydrogen ion concentration on certain antigenic properties of Clostridium botulinum - - 514
Fecal flora in pernicious anemia - - - - - - - - - - 161
Felton, Lloyd D. The protective substance in antipneumococcic serum. I. Type 1 serum - - - - - - - - - - - - - - 199
Felton, Lloyd D. The protective substance in antipneumococcic serum. II. Effect of certain chemical manipulations on the stability of the protective substance in type 1 antipneumococcic serum - - - - - 309
Fibrinogen, tissue, antigenic properties of - - - - - - - - - 49
Foods, canned, toxin production by Cl. botulinum in - - - - - - 344
Formaldehyde, detoxication of bacterial vaccines by - - - - - 520

G

Gildow, E. M. See Warwick, B. L. - - - - - - - - - - 62
Gilbert, Ruth, and Coleman, Marion. An atypical Weil-Felix reaction 559
Glucoproteins, antigenic properties of - - - - - - - - - 285
Glycogen, tissue, in histamine shock - - - - - - - - - - 229
Goodner, Kenneth. Antigenic properties of certain glucoproteins - - 285
Gussin, H. A. See Falk, I. S., and Jacobson, M. A. - - - - 481, 495, 499
Guyer, M. F. Precipitin production through lens injury - - - - - 93

H

Hadley, F. B. See Warwick, B. L. - - - - - - - - - - 62
Hadley, Philip. Proliferative reaction to stimulate by the lytic principle (bacteriophage) and its significance - - - - - - - - - 35
Hagen, William A. The green coloration by certain streptococci on blood agar - - - - - - - - - - - - - - - - - 1
Hall, Ivan C. Bacterial factors in pyorrhea alveolaris. III. The Isolation of B. tetani, B. welchii and other nonsporulating anaerobes from human saliva - - - - - - - - - - - - - - - 87
Hall, Ivan C., and Howitt, Beatrice. Bacterial factors in pyorrhea alveolaris. IV. Micrococcus gazogenes, a minute gram-negative, nonsporulating anaerobe prevalent in human saliva - - - - - - - 112

Health, relationships of hard water to - - - - - - - - 13
HEKTOEN, LUDVIG, and CORPER, H. J. The formation of antibodies to sheep blood in experimental tuberculosis of rabbits - - - - - - 82
HENRICI, ARTHUR T. A statistical study of the form and growth of the cholera vibrio - - - - - - - - - - - - 75
D'HERELLE'S bacteriophage, observations on - - - - - - - - 126
Heterakis, transmission of blackhead in absence of - - - - - - 265
HIRSCH, EDWIN F. Separation of a soluble specific substance from hemolytic streptococci - - - - - - - - - - - - - 523
HIRSCH, EDWIN, F. See LOCKE, ARTHUR - - - - - - - - 449
Histamine shock, tissue changes in - - - - - - - - - 229
HOWITT, BEATRICE. See HALL, IVAN C. - - - - - - - - 112
Hydrogen ion concentration, effect on antigenic properties of Cl. botulinum 514
Hyperglycemia in rabbits in infection - - - - - - - 400

I

Immune properties, isolation of substances with - - - - - - - 449
Immunity, diphtheria, after injections of avirulent diphtheria bacilli - 97
Infections, enteritidis and paratyphoid B - - - - - - - - 400
Infection, mixed, with Bacterium abortum and Mycobacterium tuberculosis 68
Infection, tuberculosis, in vitro - - - - - - - - 418, 430
Influenza, pneumococcus carriers in - - - - - - - - - 473
Insulin, and bacterial metabolism - - - - - - - 329, 333, 337
ISCHII, O. See SUN, YUN CHAU, and LOEB, LEO - - - - - - - 528
ISHIKAWA, MITZUTERO. See KENDALL, A. I. - - - - - - 333, 337

J

JACOBSON, M. A. See FALK, I. S. - - - - - - 481, 495, 499, 507

K

KAHN, MORTON C. See MOENCH, L. MARY - - - - - - - - 161
KENDALL, A. I. Nonglucose-fermenting bacteria and insulin. Studies in bacterial metabolism LXXIII - - - - - - - - - - 329
KENDALL, A. I., and ISHIKAWA, MITZUTERO. Effect of insulin on cultures of B. bulgaricus and B. acidophilus. Studies in bacterial metabolism LXXIV - - - - - - - - - - - - - - - - 333
KENDALL, A. I. Effect of insulin in bacterial metabolism. Studies of bacterial metabolism LXXV - - - - - - - - - - - 337

L

Lactic acid, in anaphylaxis - - - - - - - - - - - 225
Lactic acid, in histamine shock - - - - - - - - - - - 229
LANG, F. J. On the reaction of lung tissue to tuberculosis infection in vitro 430
Lens injury, precipitin production through - - - - - - - 93
LEIGHTON, ALAN. See BENTON, ANNE - - - - - - - - - 353
Leukocytes, nongranular blood, in formation of tubercle - - - - 418
LOCKE, ARTHUR, and HIRSCH, EDWIN F. The isolation of substances with immune properties - - - - - - - - - - - - - 449
LOEB, LEO. See SUN YUN CHAU - - - - - - - - - 528

LONG, ESMOND R. Standardization of tuberculin. Assay on the basis of the spermatocyte reaction - - - - - - - - - - - 368
Lung tissue, reaction to tuberculosis in vitro - - - - - - - 430

M

MANNING, HELEN M. See MENTEN, MAUD L. - - - - - - - - 400
MARSHALL, MAX S. Observations on d'Herelles bacteriophage - - - 126
MAXIMOW, ALEXANDER A. Rôle of nongranular blood leukocytes in formation of tubercle - - - - - - - - - - - - - 418
MCCULLOUGH, MARGERY, and O'NEILL, FRANCIS I. Quantitative changes in blood sugar and lactic acid in canine anaphylaxis - - - - - - 225
Measles skin reaction - - - - - - - - - - - - - 193
MEGRAIL, EMERSON. See ECKER, E. E. - - - - - - - - - - 546
MENTEN, MAUD L., and MANNING, HELEN M. Relation of enteritidis-paratyphoid B. infections to hyperglycemia in rabbits - - - - - - 400
Metabolism, bacterial - - - - - - - - - - 329, 333, 337
Micrococcus gazogenes - - - - - - - - - - - - - 112
MOENCH, L. MARY; KAHN, M. C., and TORREY, JOHN C. Analysis of fecal flora in 33 cases of pernicious anemia, with particular reference to B. welchii - - - - - - - - - - - - - - - - 161
Mycobacterium tuberculosis - - - - - - - - - - - 68, 465
MYERS, JOHN T. Relationship of hard water to health. II. Effect of hard water on growth appearance and general well-being - - - - - 13
Myocardium of guinea-pigs, effect of diphtheria toxin on - - - - 443

O

O'NEILL, FRANCIS I. See MCCULLOUGH, MARGERY - - - - - - 225

P

Paratyphoid B., enteritidis, infection, relation to hyperglycemia - - - 400
PECKHAM, JANE F. Study of yeasts from human sources - - - - - 53
PERKINS, ROGER G. Classification of sporefree, gram-negative, nonsporulating aerobic rods, with special reference to fermentation and proteolysis - - - - - - - - - - - - - - - - 232
Phosphates, inorganic, in histamine shock - - - - - - - - 229
PINNER, MAX. See SWEANY, H. C. - - - - - - - - - - - 340
Pneumococcic serum against type I - - - - - - - - 199, 309, 507
Pneumococci, electrophoretic potential and virulence of - 481, 495, 499, 507
Pneumococcus carriers, identification of - - - - - - - - - 473
Pneumonia, lobar, relation of fatality of, to electrophoretic potential of pneumococci - - - - - - - - - - - - - - - 495
POWDERMAKER, F. See FALK, I. S. - - - - - - - - - - - 514
Precipitin, production from lens injury - - - - - - - - - 93
Precipitin reaction, quantitative relation of antibody and antigens in - 321
Proteins, bacterial, bacteriophage free from - - - - - - - 411
Protein, gluco-, antigenic properties of - - - - - - - - 285
Pyorrhea alveolaris, bacterial factors in - - - - - - - - 87, 112

R

Respiratory diseases - - - - - - - - - 473, 481, 495, 499, 507
RICHARDSON, M. L. See ECKER, E. E. - - - - - - - - - 538
ROSE, E. F. See BECKWITH, T. D. - - - - - - - - - - 277
ROSENAU, M. J., and BAILEY, G. HOWARD. Diphtheria immunity. Effect of repeated injections of avirulent diphtheria bacilli, B. hofmanni and B. xerosis in guinea-pigs - - - - - - - - - - - 97

S

Saliva, human, B. tetani, B. welchii and other anaerobes from - - 87, 112
SCHAFFER, J. M. See TILLEY, F. W. - - - - - - - - - - 359
SCHOENFELD, ADALYN F., and CARPENTER, CHARLES M. Mixed infection in guinea-pigs with bacterium abortum and mycobacterium tuberculosis 68
Serum agglutination of type 1 pneumococcus - - - - - - - - 507
Serum, antipneumococcic type 1 - - - - - - - 199, 309, 507
SHARP, WILLIAM B., and URBANTKE, ELSIE. Identification of fixed type pneumococcus carriers. A study of technical methods. Influenza studies XX - - - - - - - - - - - - - 473
Shock, histamine, tissue changes in - - - - - - - - - - 229
Skin reaction, a measles - - - - - - - - - - - - 193
SMITH, JOSEPH W., JR. Standardization of typhoid vaccine. Counting chamber method versus Wright's method - - - - - - - 385
Soaps, germicidal action of - - - - - - - - - - 181, 359
Spermatocyte reaction in standardization of tuberculosis - - - - - 368
Spore-free gram-negative rods, classification - - - - - - - 232
Sterilization, autoclave, actual temperatures in - - - - - - - 357
Streptococci, hemolytic, soluble specific substance from - - - - - 523
Streptococci, hemolytic, effect of medium on - - - - - - - 277
Streptococci, green coloration of, on blood agar - - - - - - 1
Subtilis bacillus, pathogenic, from chronic tuberculosis - - - - - 340
Sugar, blood, in anaphylaxis - - - - - - - - - - - 225
Sugar, blood, in histamine shock - - - - - - - - - - 229
SUN, YUN CHAU; ISCHII, O., and LOEB, LEO. Intrauterine injections of acid fast bacilli in the guinea-pig - - - - - - - - - - 528
SWEANY, H. C., and PINNER, MAX. A pathogenic subtilis bacillus from a patient with chronic tuberculosis - - - - - - - - - 340

T

TANNER, F. W. See THOMPSON, LUTHER - - - - - - - - - 344
Temperature, of medium, in autoclave sterilization - - - - - 353
THOMPSON, K. W. See CHAMBERS, ELEANOR K. - - - - - - - - 229
THOMPSON, LUTHER, and TANNER, F. W. Toxin production by Cl. botulinum in canned foods - - - - - - - - - - - - - 344
TILLEY, F. W., and SCHAFFER, J. M. Germicidal efficiency of coconut oil and linseed oil soaps and of their mixture with cresol - - - - - 359
Tissue fibrinogen, antigenic properties of - - - - - - - - - 49
Tissue glycogen, changes in histamine shock - - - - - - - 229
Tissue, normal, extracts of, in experimental tuberculosis - - - - - 256

Torrey, John C. See Moench, L. Mary - - - - - - - - 161
Toxin, diphtheria, effect on myocardium of - - - - - - - 443
Toxin, in canned foods, produced by Cl. botulinum - - - - - - 344
Tubercle, nongranular leukocyte in formation of - - - - - - 418
Tuberculin, spermatocyte reaction in standardization of - - - - 368
Tuberculosis, chronic, pathogenic subtilis bacillus in - - - - - - 340
Tuberculosis, experimental antibodies to sheep blood, in - - - - 82
Tuberculosis, experimental, extracts of normal organs in - - - - 256
Tuberculosis, infection in vitro, reaction of lung tissue to - - - - 430
Tuberculosis, mycobacterium - - - - - - - - - - 68, 465
Tunnicliff, Ruth. Further studies on a diplococcus on measles. A measles skin reaction - - - - - - - - - - - 193
Typhoid vaccine, standardization of - - - - - - - - - 385
Tyzzer, E. E., and Collier, Jane. Induced and natural transmission of blackhead in absence of Heterakis - - - - - - - 265

U

Urbantke, Elsie. See Sharp, William B. - - - - - - 473
Uterine, intra-injections of acid-fast bacilli - - - - - - - 528

V

Vaccines, bacterial, detoxication with formaldehyde - - - - - 520
Vaccine, typhoid, standardization of - - - - - - - - - 385
Vibrio, cholera, form and growth of - - - - - - - - - 75
Virulence of pneumococcus type 1 - - - - - - 481, 495, 499, 507
Virulence of hemolytic streptococci - - - - - - - - - 277

W

Walker, John C. The germicidal properties of soap - - - - - 181
Warwick, B. L.; Gildow, E. M., and Hadley, F. B. The use of rabbits in the study of infectious abortion - - - - - - - - - 62
Water, hard, relationship to health, well being - - - - - - - 13
Weil-Felix reaction, atypical - - - - - - - - - - 559
Weiss, Emil. See Arnold, Lloyd - - - - - - - - - - 411
Wherry, W. B., and Bowen, J. A. Detoxication of bacterial vaccines by formaldehyde - - - - - - - - - - - 520

X

Xerosis B. injections of, effect on diphtheria immunity - - - - 97

Y

Yeasts from human sources - - - - - - - - - - 53